CHILD SUPPORT:
THE LEGISLATION

AUSTRALIA
The Law Book Company
Brisbane · Sydney · Melbourne · Perth

CANADA
Carswell
Ottawa · Toronto . Calgary · Montreal · Vancouver

Agents

Steimatzky's Agency Ltd., Tel Aviv;
N.M. Tripathi (Private) Ltd., Bombay;
Eastern Law House (Private) Ltd., Calcutta;
M.P.P. House, Bangalore;
Universal Book Traders; Delhi;
Aditya Books, Delhi;
MacMillan Shuppan KK, Tokyo;
Pakistan Law House, Karachi, Lahore

CHILD SUPPORT: THE LEGISLATION

Commentary by

EDWARD JACOBS

*Barrister and Full-time Chairman in the
Independent Tribunal Service*

and

GILLIAN DOUGLAS

Senior Lecturer at Cardiff Law School

LONDON
SWEET & MAXWELL
1993

Published in 1993 by
Sweet & Maxwell Limited of
South Quay Plaza, 183 Marsh Wall,
London E14 9FT
Typeset by Tradespools Ltd., Frome, Somerset
Printed by Great Britain by
Clays Ltd., St. Ives plc

No natural forests were destroyed to make this product.
Only farmed timber was used and replanted.

A catalogue record for this book is
available from the British Library

ISBN 0 421 490101

The index was prepared by Elizabeth Ingham.

To J

For 3-4.3

PREFACE

This book is intended principally to provide guidance on the law and procedure of child support in so far as it concerns Chairmen and Members of Child Support Appeal Tribunals and those who appear before them. It sets out the full text of the legislation which will be applied by those tribunals and gives a commentary on the substantive issues that are within their jurisdiction. It also deals in detail with tribunal procedure, and the commentary to the Child Support Appeal Tribunals (Procedure) Regulations, although in no sense an official guide, will serve the function of a procedure guide until one is published by the Independent Tribunal Service.

There is a limited commentary on other aspects of child support law, including the important interface between the courts and the Child Support Agency and Appeal Tribunals. It is hoped that it will be possible to expand the commentary on these matters in subsequent editions.

It has been possible to incorporate changes into the text at galley proof stage in order to ensure that as far as possible the work represents the law as it will be in force when cases come before tribunals. Any changes in the law which were not available to us on April 30, 1993 will be covered in supplements to the work.

We wish to thank all those who have given of their time and help to improve the quality of this book. In particular we must thank Richard Smithson for his continuing help and support as well as his perceptive comments on procedural aspects. Barrie Stephens and Terry Lynch have selflessly tolerated interruptions to discuss points of law and procedure. Last but not least Jill Thomas has helped with, and relieved the monotony of, the otherwise lonely and tedious task of proof reading.

Child support law is ideally suited to the use of computer packages and we wish to thank Gareth Morgan for allowing us the use of copies of the Cradle Child Support Pocket Assessment System while we were preparing this book.

It must be emphasised that whatever the connection of the authors with the Independent Tribunal Service, the notes in this book represent their personal opinions. They are in no sense an official statement of ITS policy, still less of the view that will be taken by a tribunal. The function of a tribunal is to apply the law as it stands to the cases before it and our views on what the law is or should be will carry no more weight than those of the individual members of the tribunal or of those who argue cases before them.

Finally we invite constructive suggestions for improvement or for points to be dealt with in the notes. They may be addressed to either author and, although not acknowledged, will be gratefully received and carefully considered.

Edwards Jacobs
Full-time Chairman
ITS Regional Office
Oxford House
Hills Street
Cardiff CF1 2DR

Gillian Douglas
Senior Lecturer
Cardiff Law School
PO Box 427
Cardiff CF1 1XD

CONTENTS

Contents

TABLE OF ABBREVIATIONS

the Act	Child Support Act 1991
Amendment Regulations	Child Support (Miscellaneous Amendments) Regulations 1993
Arrears, Interest and Adjustment of Maintenance Assessments Regulations	Child Support (Arrears, Interest and Adjustment of Maintenance Assessments) Regulations 1992
Bonner	D. Bonner, R. White and I. Hooker, *Non-Means Tested Benefits – The Legislation*, Sweet & Maxwell
Collection and Enforcement Regulations	Child Support (Collection and Enforcement) Regulations 1992
Collection and Enforcement of Other Forms of Maintenance Regulations	Child Support (Collection and Enforcement of Other Forms of Maintenance) Regulations 1992
CSAT	Child Support Appeal Tribunal
Income Support Schedule	Schedule 2 to the Income Support (General) Regulations 1987
Information, Evidence and Disclosure Regulations	Child Support (Information, Evidence and Disclosure) Regulations 1992
Maintenance Assessment Procedure Regulations	Child Support (Maintenance Assessment Procedure) Regulations 1992
Maintenance Assessments and Special Cases Regulations	Child Support (Maintenance Assessments and Special Cases) Regulations 1992
Mesher	J. Mesher, *Income Related Benefits – The Legislation*, Sweet & Maxwell
Society security tribunals	Social Security Appeal Tribunals, Disability Appeal Tribunals and Medical Appeal Tribunals
Transitional Provisions Order	Child Support Act 1991 (Commencement No. 3 and Transitional Provisions) Order 1992

TABLE OF CASES

Table of Cases

TABLE OF STATUTES

Table of Statutes

TABLE OF STATUTORY INSTRUMENTS

TABLE OF SOCIAL SECURITY COMMISSIONER'S DECISIONS

Table of Social Security Commissioner's Decisions

INTRODUCTION AND OVERVIEW

A. INTRODUCTION

1. Background to the Act

The Child Support Act 1991 may be seen as representing the third plank in a programme of legislation promoted by the Government to stress the importance of parents' responsibilities to and for their children, especially when the parents' own relationship has broken down. The first was the Children Act 1989, which enacted a concept of "parental responsibility", meaning "all the rights, duties, powers, responsibilities and authority which by law a parent of a child has in relation to the child and his property." (section 3(1)). Parental responsibility can be shared between parents, and with third parties, but it can only be lost if a child is adopted. It, therefore, codifies the view, expressed by Margaret Thatcher in a famous phrase that, even if the relationship of the parents ends in breakdown and a marriage is terminated, "parenthood is for life." The second manifestation of this emphasis on parental responsibility can be seen in sections 56–58 of the Criminal Justice Act 1991, which extend the courts' powers to impose sanctions on those with parental responsibility for the delinquent behaviour of their children. Finally, the Child Support Act creates new machinery designed to ensure that, where parents have separated, absent parents continue to fulfil their parental responsibility, or in this case, liability, to provide financial support for their children.

The provenance of the Child Support Act is unusual in the field of family law. While most initiatives relating to the legal aspects of family relationships have emanated from, or have been referred to the Law Commission as part of its continuing programme of family law reform, the scheme upon which the Child Support Act is based emerged from a Government White Paper, *Children Come First*, Cm 1264 (1990). In the Foreword to that document, the Government stated that its proposals were "aimed at the ... objective of giving priority to the child's welfare if his family breaks up and clarifying and highlighting parental responsibility for securing that welfare." The impetus for the proposals was not the same, however, as that for the Children Act. Rather, the concern was over the apparently low levels of maintenance for children being ordered, and collected, when parental relationships broke down, and the consequential burden on the social security budget which had to meet the shortfall.

From the beginning of the 1980's, attention had been paid to the question of whether provision for the assessment and collection of child maintenance through private law mechanisms was satisfactory. Thus, the Matrimonial Causes Act 1973 was amended (by the Matrimonial and Family Proceedings Act 1984) to provide that, in deciding what financial provision orders should be made in the event of a divorce, the court should give first consideration to the welfare whilst a minor of any child of the family. Courts were circulated with information on current income support rates, and the National Foster Care Association's (NFCA) recommended rates for paying foster-parents, to provide some comparative information as to the real costs of raising children. Yet, despite this information, research carried out by the Government found that the "going rate" for maintenance for one child, of any age up to 18, was £18 per week in 1990, (White Paper, Volume 1, paragraph 1.5), while the NFCA recommended allowance was £34.02 per week for a child under the age of five. The Government found that maintenance awards represented only about 11 per cent. of total net incomes of absent parents on above average incomes. There were also wide variations in the amounts of maintenance being awarded. In one example of two fathers, each with one child and earning £150 per week net, one was ordered to pay £5 per week in maintenance, and the other £50 per week.

Research also indicated that maintenance awards were not being complied with or adequately enforced. In one survey of orders in a West London court, for example, 55 per cent. were in arrears, of which 57 per cent. involved sums in excess of £1,000 (Edwards, Gould and Halpern, "The Continuing Saga of Maintaining the Family after Divorce" [1990] Fam. Law 31). Where maintenance awards are low, there is little incentive to seek their enforcement, as is implicitly recognised by legislation, which provides that the leave of the court is required to enforce the payment of arrears of maintenance which became due more than 12 months before proceedings to enforce them are begun (section 32(1) of the Matrimonial Causes Act 1973, section 32(4) of the Domestic Proceedings and Magistrates' Courts Act 1978). There may appear to be even less incentive where the recipient is dependent upon social security benefits and will see none of the money.

Low levels of maintenance, and high proportions of orders in arrears were not new in the 1980's, and nor were they unique to the United Kingdom. Concern about the financial implications of marriage breakdown and the effect on children is a worldwide phenomenon (see Weitzman and MacLean (eds.) *Economic Consequences of Divorce: The International Perspective*, (Clarendon Press, 1992)), but the factor which appears to have influenced the UK Government to take action was the impact of these on the social security budget. The Government found that about 770,000 single parents, or around two-thirds of the total number of one-parent families, were dependent upon income support in 1989, compared with 330,000 such families in 1980 (White Paper, Volume 2, page i). Fewer than one quarter of these were receiving maintenance, while their benefits cost £3.2 billion in 1988–1989.

2. Encouraging and assisting parents with care to work

The first strand in the Government's strategy to tackle these problems was to introduce mechanisms intended to encourage lone parents to return to work, or to work more hours. In the White Paper, it was noted that only 40 per cent. of lone mothers were working, compared to 54 per cent. of married women with dependent children, yet three quarters of lone mothers receiving income support had expressed a wish to work (paragraph 1.5). The qualifying hours for entitlement to family credit were therefore reduced in April 1992 from 24 hours per week to 16 (see regulation 4(1) of the Family Credit (General) Regulations 1987 as amended), to enable more lone mothers to work on a part-time basis and thus combine child care with employment. As an incentive to parents to opt for more work and family credit, rather than work fewer hours in order to retain entitlement to income support, the Government also provided that the first £15 of maintenance received is disregarded in calculating the amount of family credit (and also Housing Benefit and Council Tax benefit), (see Schedule 2, paragraph 47 to the Family Credit (General) Regulations 1987 as amended) but not income support.

3. Small-scale reforms

The Government also enacted two other small-scale reforms to address these problems in the short term; amendments to the Social Security Act 1986, now contained in ss.107 and 108 of the Social Security Administration Act 1992 (discussed fully in the general note to those sections in *Mesher*) and the Maintenance Enforcement Act 1991: see N. Wikeley, *The Maintenance Enforcement Act 1991*, (Sweet & Maxwell Annotated Statutes). The former provides further public law mechanisms for enforcing the obligation of a liable relative to maintain his family when they are in receipt of income support. The latter aims to enhance the methods available to the courts to enforce private law maintenance orders, be they for the benefit of children or of spouses.

Under section 107 of the 1992 Act, where a parent is claiming income support for herself and her children, the Department of Social Security may seek recovery from the other parent of an amount to meet the claimant's income support personal allowance, in addition to allowances for his children, *even though the claimant is not (or has never been) the parent's spouse*. In other words, although the parent is not a liable relative in respect of the *claimant*, he can be required to contribute to her maintenance, even where she could not seek maintenance from him herself because they had never married. (If she ceases to claim income support, then although the order may be transferred to her by the Secretary of State under section 107(3), the element covering her allowance will not be included). The section therefore enables the Department to recover more of the actual costs of supporting the lone parent. Section 108 enables it to enforce a *private* maintenance order obtained by the claimant, even without her consent to such action being taken. The Department can therefore pursue the absent parent where a claimant is receiving income support and has no incentive or desire to do so herself.

The Maintenance Enforcement Act 1991 (which came into force on April 1, 1992 (Maintenance Enforcement Act 1991 (Commencement No. 2) Order 1992) and the substantive provisions of which apply only to England and Wales), empowers the courts to specify the method of payment of a maintenance order, including requiring the debtor to open a bank account from which payment may be made by standing order, unless there is a reasonable excuse for not doing so. It also enables a court to make an attachment of earnings order without having to wait for the order to fall into arrears.

Section 1 of the Act applies to any "qualifying periodical maintenance order" (an order which requires money to be paid periodically by one person—the debtor, who must be ordinarily resident in England and Wales—to another—the creditor—and which is a maintenance order within the meaning of Schedule 8 to the Administration of Justice Act 1970). Where the county court or High Court makes or has made such an order, it may, of its own motion, or on the application of an "interested party" (a debtor, creditor or applicant for a qualifying periodical maintenance order) order that payments be made by standing order, or any other method which requires the debtor to give his authority for payments of a specific amount to be made from his account to that of the creditor. Section 1(6) provides that where the court proposes to make such an order, and has given the debtor the opportunity of opening an account from which payments may be made, then if the court is satisfied that the debtor has failed, without reasonable excuse, to open such an account, the court may order the debtor to do so. These provisions are intended to prevent arrears building up by ensuring a regular and automatic means of payment of maintenance.

Alternatively, the court is given the power to make an attachment of earnings order under the Attachment of Earnings Act 1971, notwithstanding that, as was required hitherto, the debtor does not agree to the making of the order, or has not failed to make payments due to his wilful refusal or culpable neglect. Despite these changes, the utility of attachment of earnings orders still depends upon the debtor being in regular employment. There has been a decline in the making of such orders in the magistrates' courts since 1986, with 7,090 such orders made in that year, compared to 6,380 in 1991 (*Domestic Proceedings England and Wales 1991*, Home Office Statistical Bulletin 32/92).

Equivalent powers are given to the magistrates courts (and see the Magistrates Courts (Maintenance Enforcement Act 1991) (Miscellaneous Amendments) Rules 1992). Magistrates, in addition to their own jurisdiction to make periodical payments orders in favour of spouses and/or their children, by virtue of the Domestic

Proceedings and Magistrates' Courts Act 1978 and Schedule 1 to the Children Act 1989, also have jurisdiction to vary and enforce maintenance orders made by the county court or High Court and registered in the magistrates' court under Part I of the Maintenance Orders Act 1958. About 96,800 enforcement proceedings were decided by the magistrates in 1991, an increase of about 10,000 since 1986, but in 17 per cent. of these cases, the arrears were remitted, perhaps reflecting recognition of the difficulty many debtors may have in meeting their obligations.

Sections 2 to 8 of the 1991 Act amend the Magistrates' Courts Act 1980, Part II by inserting new sections 59, 59A, 59B, 60 and 76; the Domestic Proceedings and Magistrates' Courts Act 1978 by a new section 20ZA; and Schedule 1 to the Children Act 1989 by a new paragraph 6A. These provisions also enable the creditor who is receiving payments made to or through the justices' clerk to give the clerk authority to proceed in his own name for recovery of any arrears, rather than having to make an express request each time arrears accrue. Failure to comply with the order as to the correct method of payment is punishable, on complaint to a justice by the creditor, by order to pay a sum not exceeding £1,000, which is treated as a fine. Finally, a new section 94A is added to the Magistrates' Courts Act 1980, empowering the Secretary of State by order to provide that a magistrates' court, on hearing of a complaint for the enforcement, revocation, revival, variation or discharge of an English maintenance order, may order that interest at a prescribed rate be paid on so much of the sum due under the order as they may determine.

This Act can be viewed primarily as an interim measure, designed to improve the mechanisms for the collection and enforcement of private law maintenance until the Child Support Act is fully implemented, although it will continue to have a residual role where the Act is inapplicable (as to which, see discussion of the Act below), because only spousal maintenance has been ordered, for example. Research carried out for the Government in preparation for its White Paper found that in a sample of cases of arrears of maintenance recorded in magistrates' courts, there was a stoppage or reduction a year in two out of five cases (Volume 2, paragraph 5.1.3) with a median period of arrears of 15 weeks (paragraph 5.1.5). In cases where a specific reason for non-payment had been recorded, 52 per cent. were due to the absent parent's loss of income or job. In only five per cent. of cases was the absent parent recorded as having absconded (paragraph 5.4.2 and Table 32). These figures suggest that while arrears are common, there may be relatively little that can be done to recover them, if the main reason for their accrual is loss of income.

4. The significance of the Child Support Act

The Child Support Act is a much more fundamental attempt to alter the picture concerning parents' financial responsibility for children. The scheme it sets up appears to have been influenced in part by developments in the United States of America and Australia (see Weitzman and Maclean, *op. cit.* and Parker, "The Australian Child Support Scheme" [1990] Fam. Law 210) (even the name—"child support maintenance"—is clearly influenced by the United States; English law has always referred to maintenance or periodical payments, and Scottish law to aliment), and in part by the existing social security structure. The Act has two fundamental and radical features. First, there is the creation of new administrative machinery to assess, collect and enforce child support maintenance, through the Child Support Agency, at the same time taking away the powers of the civil courts to do so in most cases. When the Act is fully operational, the Agency is expected to have over 2,000,000 clients, and to make 3,000,000 assessments per year. Secondly, the Act provides a formula by which the amount of child support maintenance is to be calculated. The use of an Agency is intended to improve on the efficiency of the mechanisms for collecting maintenance from the absent parent, which, as indicated above, has not been impressive. The use of a formula is intended to prevent the kind of disparities in amounts being ordered by different courts which were illustrated in the example given above. The influence of the social security dimension is apparent in both of these features. The Agency and the methods of appeal to Child Support Appeal Tribunals and a Child Support Commissioner mirror the arrangements for the administration of social security benefits. The formula makes extensive use of benefit rates, and concepts used in social security legislation, in arriving at the amount of child support maintenance to be paid. Furthermore, liability under the Act extends only to the *parents* of a qualifying child. A private law obligation to maintain can be imposed, in England and Wales, on a spouse in respect of a "child of the family" (a child who has been "treated" by both parties to the marriage as a child of their family (section 52(1) of the Matrimonial Causes Act 1973, section 88(1) of the Domestic Proceedings and Magistrates' Courts Act 1987, section 105(1) of the Children Act 1989)). In Scotland, an obligation to aliment may be imposed on any person who has "accepted" a child as a "child of the family" (section 1(1)(d) of the Family Law (Scotland) Act 1985). The limitation of the Act to the parents of the child follows the social security scheme (see, for example, regulation 54 of the Income Support (General) Regulations 1987). It also reflects the Government's view that parents should accept financial responsibility for their "own" children, and not expect a stepparent or other carer, still less the State, to assume the burden. It is uncertain, however, whether the requirement imposed by the Act effectively to divide up the financial liabilities of parents who have children from different unions will add to the harmony of what are already complicated relationships in "blended" or "broken" families.

The greatest innovation introduced by the Act is the removal from the courts of the task of assessing, ordering and enforcing maintenance for children in most cases where they would currently do so. The Act applies where a parent of the child is an "absent parent" (section 3(2)), implying that the parents' marriage or relationship has broken down, or that they do not live together. Where there is a final termination of the relationship, most often, of course, by divorce, there will usually be a need to sort out not just the maintenance of the children, but any support for their carer (usually the mother) and also the disposition of any property the couple owned during their marriage or relationship. On a divorce, the courts have very extensive powers to allocate such property between the parties, irrespective of which spouse is the owner, or to order its settlement or disposal for the benefit of either spouse (see Matrimonial Causes Act 1973, Part II for England and Wales, and sections 8 to 14 of the Family Law (Scotland) Act 1985). Parties are encouraged by the legislation (see section 25A of the Matrimonial Causes Act 1973 for England and Wales, and section 9 of the Family Law (Scotland) Act 1985 for Scotland) to seek to arrive at a "clean break" settlement of their claims on each other, whereby the wife (usually) agrees to forego any periodical payments of maintenance in return for a larger share of the capital assets, in practice usually the matrimonial home. Although it is not permissible for a parent to escape liability to support his *children* through a clean break settlement of this type, under the old law, he might agree to the wife and children remaining in the matrimonial home as part of his obligation to support them, and offset this by the wife foregoing periodical payments, or perhaps by reducing the amount of money he paid in maintenance for the children. Such an option will become unattractive when the Child Support Act applies. This is because, first, as will be seen, the formula upon which the amount of maintenance is assessed requires that an element be included for the support of the *carer* where the child is under the age of 16. In effect, then, the absent parent is required to pay some maintenance for the former spouse or partner thus preventing a "clean break" from being achieved. Secondly, the formula does not cater for the situation where the absent parent makes a capital settlement in part recognition of his financial obligations to his children; the amount of maintenance they are deemed to require is fixed by reference to set rates (in fact, income support rates) and allowance is not made for capitalised payment in advance. It is expected, therefore, that clean break agreements will be less likely to be made in future where the spouses have children. Lawyers representing divorcing couples will have to find alternative methods of settling the parties' claims on each other, perhaps by greater use of attaching a charge to former matrimonial property, to be enforced if a claim is made under the Child Support Act (though query if this would be regarded as caught by section 9(4) which provides that any provision purporting to *restrict* the right of a person to apply for a maintenance assessment shall be void). Such mechanisms run counter to the spirit of the modern law of financial provision on divorce, and will do little to improve the quality of the relationship between the former spouses, who will have the prospect of a potential child support claim hanging over them until the children are grown-up. But of perhaps even greater immediate concern is the effect of the Act on clean break and other settlements made in the past, in the expectation that the husband could not be required to provide continuing support for the spouse under the private law. Although this could not prevent the Department of Social Security having recourse to the husband as a liable relative under section 106 (see the general note to that section in *Mesher* and *Hulley* v. *Thompson* [1981] 1 W.L.R. 159) and section 107 of the Social Security Administration Act, 1992, these provisions only relate to where income support is claimed. The Child Support Act formula will be used in assessing applications where no prescribed benefit is being received, and so a potentially much larger group of divorced absent parents will be at risk of being required to pay continuing support for the carer. It is unlikely that a court would regard a claim made by the carer under the Child Support Act as justifying the re-opening of a divorce settlement so that the husband could re-negotiate the package of capital arrangements previously arrived at (see *Barder* v. *Caluori* [1988] A.C. 440, which sets out the very limited circumstances in which a court should contemplate such a course of action).

The parties will continue to be able to make private maintenance agreements (section 9). However, the jurisdiction of the Agency to make an assessment cannot be ousted (section 9(3)), so that any agreement for a sum less than that arrived at by the formula would be at risk of being sidestepped by an application under the Act. Although the courts will retain their jurisdiction to make consent orders incorporating agreements for child maintenance (regulation 8(5) and the Child Maintenance (Written Agreements) Order 1993), it will not be possible for people on benefit to rely on an agreement for a lesser amount than that assessed by the formula. In future, the Agency is expected to be given the power to register, collect and enforce maintenance agreements so that consent orders for child maintenance will become unnecessary and irrelevant unless the parties have a particular desire to avoid the Agency.

The Child Support Act therefore appears to mark a significant turning-point in the direction of legal regulation of the family. Until the Act, the trend was towards what had been described as increasing "privatisation" of family law. The prevailing wisdom was that there should be less scrutiny by the court of the circumstances in which a marriage breakdown occurred, greater attention paid to the encouragement of agreements reached by the parents through negotiation in private, and trust of parents to put their children's interests first in arriving at settlements over the living arrangements after the divorce or relationship breakdown. The Child Support Act presents a rather different picture. It replaces the courts with an administrative body charged with responsibility for ensuring that adequate levels of maintenance are collected for child support; it restricts the possibility of parents reaching agreement on a figure other than that approved by the State through the formula (except in rare cases involving wealthy families who can afford to pay more than the formula assessment); it runs counter to the trend towards encouraging a couple to be financially independent of each other once their relationship has ended. It can therefore be characterised as the bold reassertion of the State's fundamental interest and superior role in the settlement of financial arrangements for children. It imposes a heavy burden on the staff of the Child Support Agency, and upon those who sit on the Child Support Appeal Tribunals to provide a service which will be sensitive to the needs of those who may be particularly vulnerable at a time of marriage or relationship breakdown. The courts have struggled to provide such a service in the past, and there have been many calls for the introduction of alternative methods of resolving family disputes, ranging from a Family Court made up of experts in child psychology and social workers, to compulsory mediation or conciliation procedures built in to the civil courts' procedures. The challenge for the new structure set up to cope with child support maintenance will be to determine whether it is capable of addressing these needs, and whether it can do so separately from the continuing role of the courts and legal process in tackling the other aspects of family breakdown.

B.   OUTLINE

This section outlines the basic structure of the Act and the regulations made under it. It provides a gateway into child support law for those unfamiliar with it by indicating the relevant section of the Act and in some cases relevant regulations; further guidance will be found in the general notes to those provisions. The outline is based on the (usually correct) assumption that a father has left his child in the care of the child's mother; "he" and "she" are used accordingly, although the roles of the parents may be reversed. In some cases reality is more complex and the structure of the Act has to be modified to reflect and deal with this fact. These cases are called "special cases" and are provided for under section 42 of the Act; some of these special cases are noted below.

For the phased introduction of the scheme and the relationship between the bodies charged with its administration and the courts, see the Child Support (Commencement No. 3 and Transitional Provisions) Order 1992 and sections 8, 10, 27, 30 and 45.

1.   The Child Support Agency

The Child Support Agency which is responsible for the administration of the Act is the first "Next Steps" agency to have been newly set up rather than hived off from the Civil Service. It is staffed by child support officers, headed by a Chief Child Support Officer whose duty is to advise them on their functions, to keep under review the operation of the Act, and to make annual reports to the Secretary of State (section 13).

2.   Who is covered by the Act?

Qualifying child

"Each parent of a qualifying child is responsible for maintaining him" under section 1(1) of the Act. A child is defined in section 55 as a person under the age of 16, or under the age of 19 and receiving full-time non-advanced education, who has not been married. Such a child is a "*qualifying child*" within section 3(1) if

"(*a*) one of his parents is, in relation to him, an absent parent; or

(*b*) both of his parents are, in relation to him, absent parents."

The Act fixes the amount of child support maintenance payable by the absent parent. If there is no absent parent, the child is not a qualifying child and the Act does not apply.

Absent parent

Section 54 defines a parent as "any person who is in law the mother or father of the child". This definition covers natural parents, parents by virtue of adoption and parents by virtue of the Human Fertilisation and Embryology Act 1990. A parent is an "*absent parent*" under section 3(2) if

"(*a*) the parent is not living in the same household with the child; and
  (*b*) the child has his home with a person who is, in relation to him, a person with care."

Where *both* parents are absent, this is a "special case" and both may be liable to pay child support (regulation 19 of the Maintenance Assessments and Special Cases Regulations.)

What if a person denies parentage?

A dispute may arise as to whether the absent parent is indeed the father of the qualifying child. Under section 26, if the alleged parent denies parentage, the child support officer may make a maintenance assessment provided the case falls within one of a number of categories where, in effect, a court will already have determined that he is to be regarded as the legal parent, for example an adoption order has been made, or a declaration or adjudgment given that he is the parent.

Where section 26 does not apply, the child support officer or the person with care (see below) may apply to the court (in the first instance, the magistrates' court: see section 45 below), for a declaration that he is, or is not, a parent of the child, under section 27 or 28.

Person with care

A person *with care* is defined as a person
"(*a*) with whom the child has his home;
  (*b*) who usually provides day to day care for the child (whether exclusively or in conjunction with any other person); and
  (*c*) [is a parent, guardian or person who has a residence order made under section 8 of the Children Act 1989 in his favour]."

More than one person may be a person with care in relation to the child under section 3(5). If both parents provide care, this is another "special case" and is covered by regulation 20 of the Maintenance Assessments and Special Cases Regulations. The significance of being a parent with care appears later.

3. Applying for a maintenance assessment

Either the person with care or an absent parent may apply to the Child Support Agency, under section 4(1), for a "maintenance assessment" to be made by a child support officer with respect to the qualifying child. In the case of Scotland, a child who has attained the age of 12 may also apply for an assessment under section 7(1). All the parties must be habitually resident in the United Kingdom for the Agency to have jurisdiction. They may also apply for the Agency to arrange for the collection and enforcement of the "child support maintenance" so assessed. An assessment fee and, where appropriate, a collection fee may be payable (section 47.)

The assessment mechanism is one which *may* be utilised by a person seeking maintenance for a child, but need not be, unless section 6 applies. This provides that if the person with care is the child's parent, and she is claiming income support, family credit or disability working allowance, she *shall* authorise the Agency, by completing a "maintenance application form" (MAF) under section 6(6), to recover child support maintenance from the absent parent. A MAF will be sent to all relevant benefit recipients at some point during the transitional period of the

Act's introduction, depending on the Agency's take on of work. The application is handled by a child support officer.

4. Obtaining information to make the assessment

Requirement to co-operate

A person applying under section 4, or who is under a duty to authorise action under section 6, must, so far as she reasonably can, supply information to the Agency to enable the absent parent to be traced (if necessary), and for the Agency to make the maintenance assessment. In the case of an application by a child under section 7 the duty rests on the absent parent and the person with care as well as the child. Concerns were expressed during the Bill's passage through Parliament that a parent dependent upon benefits, and therefore obliged to authorise action under section 6, might not wish to reveal the identity of the absent parent to the Agency, because she fears violence from him, or wishes to put a bad relationship behind her. According to the Department of Social Security, only one per cent. of lone parents decline to give the father's name because they fear violence. Seventy five per cent. of claimaints who have never married give the name, and of the twenty five per cent. who do not, half apparently say they do not know his identity.

Under sections 6(2) and 46(3), the requirements to give authorisation, or provide information, can be waived if the child support officer considers that there are reasonable grounds for believing that compliance would lead to a risk to the claimant, or any child living with her, suffering harm or undue distress as a result. In deciding this, the officer is required to consider the welfare of the child under section 2.

Reduced benefit direction

However, as a deterrent to claimants who might prefer to withhold information, section 46(5) provides that, where the child support officer considers that there are no reasonable grounds for non-compliance, he may give a "reduced benefit direction" whereby the amount of benefit otherwise payable will be reduced by 20 per cent. of the income support personal allowance for a single person aged at least 25, worth £8.80 per week in 1993–1994 (regulations 35 to 50 of the Maintenance Assessment Procedure Regulations.) The 20 per cent. reduction lasts for six months, and is then reduced to 10 per cent. for a further year. Thereafter, no reduction is made, unless the claimant has another child, and again refuses to co-operate without good reason. The claimant can appeal direct to the child support appeal tribunal (see below) against a reduced benefit direction. If the claimant ceases to receive benefit during the reduction period, the reduction is held over until she next claims.

Other sources of information

The absent parent will also be required to furnish information in order to discover his means and liabilities. Under section 14 of, and Schedule 2 to, the Act, and the Information, Evidence and Disclosure Regulations, absent parents and their current or recent employers are required to provide information. The Agency may also obtain information from the Inland Revenue in order to trace an absent parent or his employer, and from local authorities administering housing or council tax benefit, as to the income or housing costs of an absent parent or person with care. Section 15 provides that inspectors may be appointed to exercise powers of entry and enquiry with a view to obtaining information required under the Act. Such inspectors have power, under section 15(4), to enter, at all reasonable times, any premises other than those used solely as a dwelling-house and to question any person aged 18 or over on the premises. An occupier of the premises, an employer or employee working there, a person carrying on a trade, profession, vocation or business there, or an employee or agent of any of these, is required, under section 15(6), to furnish to the inspector all such information and documents as he may reasonably require.

Interim maintenance assessment

As a further incentive to candour, the officer may, under section 12, and after giving written notice of his intention where it is reasonably practicable to do so, make an *interim* maintenance assessment where it appears to him that he does not have sufficient information to form a final judgment. The amount of the interim assessment will depend upon whether it is the absent parent or that parent's partner who has, or can reasonably be expected to obtain, the information which is needed by the child support officer.

5.   Calculating the maintenance assessment

The formula for calculating the amount of child support maintenance which the absent parent must pay for the qualifying child is set out in Schedule 1 to the Act and in the Maintenance Assessment and Special Cases Regulations.

The maintenance requirement

The starting point is to calculate the child's maintenance requirement, defined as, "the minimum amount necessary for the maintenance of the qualifying child, or, where there is more than one qualifying child, all of them." The formula used is—

$MR = AG - CB$.

MR means the maintenance requirement. AG means the aggregate of the amount of income support which would be payable for the child, the adult income support allowance for a person over 25 for the child's carer if the child is aged under 16, plus family premium and, if the carer has no partner, the lone parent premium. CB is the child benefit payable for the child.

Assessable income

The next step is to calculate the contribution to this figure to be met by the absent parent. This is done first by working out his "assessable income". The formula for this is—

$A = N - E$

where A means the absent parent's assessable income, and N is the amount of that parent's net income after tax, National Insurance and half of pension contributions.

E means the absent parent's "*exempt income*". This represents a parent's "own essential expenses which must be met before maintenance is paid" (White Paper, Volume 1, paragraph 3.8). This is the sum of the income support personal allowance for an adult over 25, payable for the absent parent (but *not* including an allowance for a new partner), income support allowances for any of the absent parent's own children living with him in his new home (but *not* step-children) and any premiums payable for such children, plus *reasonable* housing costs. The absent parent's assessable income will therefore be his net income less his exempt income which will cover his basic expenses for himself and his own children.

A similar calculation is then carried out for the parent who is the person with care, using the formula—

$$C = M - F$$

where C is the assessable income of the person with care, M is defined as that person's net income, and F is their exempt income. These are calculated in the same way as N and E. (A non–parent with care is assessed as having nil assessable income.)

Where income support or other prescribed benefit (none has been prescribed at the time of writing) is paid to an absent parent or parent who is a person with care, they shall be taken to have *no* assessable income. However, the aim is that the absent parent should still make some contribution to his child's maintenance, and the "minimum amount" may be payable (see below).

Where the absent parent is not receiving benefit, but his assessable income is calculated as a negative amount because his exempt income exceeds his net income, it is taken to be nil, but again he may be liable to pay the minimum amount.

The absent parent's maintenance assessment

The child support officer must then calculate—

$$(A + C) \times P.$$

The two assessable incomes are added together, and multiplied by P, which is 0.5 or 50 per cent. If the result of this calculation is a sum equal to, or less than the child's maintenance requirement, then the absent parent must pay an amount equal to $A \times P$, *i.e.* half his assessable income.

What if the absent parent's assessable income exceeds the child's maintenance requirement?

It was considered in the White Paper that where the child's maintenance requirement could be met without exhausting the absent parent's assessable income, he should pay something over and above that amount, so that his children could share in his higher standard of living. The question was how much of his excess assessable income should be applied for this purpose. The Act provides for a proportion of 25 per cent. of the excess to be used to support the children, but to avoid unduly high amounts of maintenance being assessed, a complicated formula is used to set the maximum amount at the child's maintenance requirement *plus* three times the child's income support allowance and family premium per child.

Can the absent parent afford to pay?

There is one further stage to be completed. What if payment of child support maintenance from the absent parent's assessable income would leave him with a disposable income equivalent to, or below what he would be entitled to if claiming income support? "There is no point in alleviating one family's possible dependence on income support at the expense of creating such dependence for another family." (White Paper, Volume 1, paragraph 3.23). The amount of the assessment must therefore be adjusted

"with a view to securing so far as is reasonably practicable that payment by the absent parent of the amount ... so assessed will not reduce his disposable income below his protected income level."

Disposable income and protected income

Disposable income and protected income are calculated according to regulations 11 and 12 of the Maintenance Assessments and Special Cases Regulations. The absent parent is allowed, as "protected income", the amount of income support which would be payable to cover his own needs, those of his children living with him *and* any other dependents such as a new partner and step-children, his housing costs, council tax and an earnings disregard of £8 per week. Then, as an added incentive to keep him at work, if appropriate, an extra 10 per cent. of the amount by which his disposable income exceeds all these is allowed. In this way, the true financial obligations of the absent parent are taken into account, having been disregarded when assessing his exempt income earlier. The aim is to ensure that the child support maintenance to be paid leaves him with his protected level of income.

Minimum amount

As noted above, a person whose exempt income exceeds his net income, or who is in receipt of income support, is taken to have nil assessable income. Nonetheless, he may be required to pay the minimum amount. It is set at five per cent. of the adult income support allowance for a person over 25, currently £2.15 per week. Income support recipients will have this amount deducted from their benefit.

However, the minimimum amount will *not* be payable if any of a number of conditions is satisfied. These are set out in regulation 26 of, and Schedule 4 to, the Maintenance Assessments and Special Cases Regulations, and cover absent parents in receipt of benefits such as disability working allowance, and also, numerically more important, those who have a child living with them.

6. Duration and termination of assessments

Effective date

The assessment takes effect on the "effective date" which will usually be the date the maintenance enquiry form was sent (regulation 30 of the Maintenance Assessment Procedure Regulations).

The maintenance assessment can come to an end in two ways. First, it may *cease to have effect* on the occurrence of a certain event, for example when a fresh assessment is substituted, on the death of the absent parent or where the absent parent and person with care have been living together for a continuous period of six months. Secondly, it may be *cancelled* by the child support officer, for example where a person who applied for the assessment under section 4 asks for it to be cancelled, or the officer no longer has jurisdiction.

7. Review and appeal

Periodical reviews

A significant problem identified in the old law was the failure of maintenance awards to keep pace with inflation or to be uprated to meet changed circumstances. Section 16 of the Act and regulation 17 of the Maintenance Assessment Procedure Regulations provide for the maintenance assessment to be reviewed annually by a child support officer, in line with the annual adjustment of benefit rates and the fact that employees generally receive annual pay-rises.

Change of circumstances

By section 17, the absent parent or the person with care may themselves seek a review of a maintenance assessment, although only on the ground that by reason of a change of circumstances since the original assessment was made, the amount of child support maintenance payable would be significantly different if it were to be re-assessed. The kind of change of circumstances envisaged could include where the absent parent becomes unemployed, or acquires a new partner with whom he has a child, and therefore seeks a downward revision of his maintenance assessment. Equally, the person with care might seek an increased assessment if the absent parent has obtained a higher-paid job.

Under either section 16 or section 17, where a review is completed, the child support officer shall then make a fresh maintenance assessment, unless satisfied that the original assessment has ceased to have effect or should be brought to an end. In the case of a section 17 review however, this need not be done if the difference in amounts between the original assessment and that of the review is less than £10 or, where protected income level is relevant, £1 per week (Part VI of the Maintenance Assessment Procedure Regulations.)

Review at the child support officer's instigation

The child support officer may make a fresh maintenance assessment where he is satisfied that the one currently in force is defective by reason of having been made in ignorance of a material fact, based on a mistake as to a material fact, or being wrong in law; or that it would be appropriate to make a fresh assessment if application to do so were made under sections 17 or 18. In this way, mistakes in the assessment can be corrected without the parties being required to initiate a review.

Review as a form of appeal

A person who is aggrieved by a child support officer's decision may seek a review by another officer who was not involved in the original decision, under section 18. This second tier review may be done in respect of a decision to refuse an application for a maintenance assessment under section 4 or 7, or to refuse to carry out a review under section 17. It may also be done to challenge a maintenance assessment presently in force, or a cancellation or refusal of cancellation, of such an assessment. If the officer is satisfied that there are no reasonable grounds for supposing that the decision was made in ignorance of a material fact, was based on a mistake as to a material fact, or was wrong in law, he need not conduct a review.

Child support appeal tribunals

Where the applicant for the review under section 18 is aggrieved by the decision of the officer, either as to his review or his refusal to carry one out, then there is a right to appeal to a child support appeal tribunal under section 20. If the appeal is successful, the tribunal must remit the case to the Secretary of State to be dealt with by a child support officer, and may give such directions as it considers appropriate. Under section 24, a person aggrieved by a decision of the tribunal may appeal, on a question of law, to a Child Support Commissioner, with a further appeal on a question of law to the Court of Appeal under section 25. As noted above, appeals go to the court where they involve an issue of parentage (sections 20, 27 and 45.)

8. Collection and enforcement

One of the main purposes of the Act is to increase the amount of maintenance actually paid by the absent parent for his children. The Agency may carry out the collection and enforcement of assessments where this is requested by those applying for assessment under section 4 or 7, and it will automatically do so for assessments made under section 6. Child support maintenance is calculated weekly, but will be collected to coincide with pay days. Arrears and interest thereon may also be recovered by the Agency (section 41.)

The Agency may make "deduction from earnings" orders under section 31, to the liable person's employer. Such an order instructs him to make deductions from earnings and pay them to the Agency. For those who are unemployed and for whom a deduction from earnings order is therefore inappropriate, or for whom such an order has proved ineffective, further methods of enforcement may be used. Where a payment has been missed, the Agency may (having considered, *inter alia*, the welfare of the child) apply to a magistrates' court for a liability order against the liable person under section 33 which then allows for enforcement measures such as seizure of goods, or charging orders, to be sought under sections 35, 36 and 38. If maintenance is still not paid despite these measures and the court is of the opinion that there has been wilful refusal or culpable neglect on the part of the liable person, it may commit him to prison for a maximum of six weeks under section 40.

COMMISSIONERS' DECISIONS AND PRECEDENT

Apart from the legislation, the decisions of the Child Support Commissioners and the decisions of the same Commissioners in the often comparable social security jurisdiction will constitute the principal source of law which Child Support Appeal Tribunals will have to apply. Members and users of Child Support Appeal Tribunals will need to be familiar with how these decisions are cited and applied. This note explains how Commissioners' decisions are cited and reported, together with the binding system of precedent which governs when they must be followed.

Reported decisions

The system of citing reports of Commissioners' Decisions which was introduced in 1951 is as follows:

Reported Commissioners' decisions are cited in the following form: *R(IS) 4/91*. The R indicates that the decision is a reported one. The letters in brackets indicate the benefit which was involved in the appeal to the Commissioner. In this case IS stands for Income Support. Presumably Child Support cases will bear the letters CS. The numbers show that this was the fourth Income Support decision reported in 1991. Each benefit is numbered separately. There is, for example, an *R(SB) 4/91* as well as an *R(IS) 4/91*.

Where a decision is a decision of a tribunal of three Commissioners rather than a decision of a single Commissioner, the citation is sometimes followed by the words "Tribunal Decision" or (T). *R(IS) 4/91* was a tribunal decision.

Unreported decisions

Unreported decisions are cited in the following form: *CG 5/91*. The C indicates that the decision is a Commissioner's decision and the letters which follow it indicate the benefit involved. In this case the benefit is a claim for a death grant for funeral expenses. The numbers indicate that this was the fifth decision involving that type of benefit to be appealed to a Commissioner in 1991. Sometimes the initial C is followed by an (additional) S. This indicates that the case was a Scottish appeal. So CSB is an unreported Commissioner's decision on Supplementary Benefit, whilst CSSB is an unreported Commissioner's decision on Supplementary Benefit appealed from Scotland.

When a decision is reported it is given a new citation and number as explained above. So, for example, *R(IS) 4/91* was originally when unreported *CIS 203/89*.

Starred decisions

Any decision which is considered worth reporting is starred by the Commissioner who made it. It is then given an additional number: for example, *CG 5/91* was a starred decision which when starred was given the number *58/92*. The numbering of starred decisions is not dependent upon the benefit in question. The decisions are simply numbered consecutively as they are starred. When a decision is starred it is circulated amongst the Commissioners for comment before a decision is made by the Chief Commissioner whether or not to report it. Unreported decisions are never cited by their starred number, although that number does now appear on the face of the decision beside the star.

A decision may, therefore, in its life bear three different numbers.

Availability of decisions

A copy of all reported decisions is available at every Child Support Appeal Tribunal venue. Additionally, all chairmen are provided with a full set of reported decisions. Members and chairmen who wish to consult an unreported decision will find all starred decisions in the Regional Offices. Unstarred decisions which are not held by the Regional Office can be obtained by that office for the member or chairman.

Precedent

Precedent is the name given to the principle which determines which decisions a court or tribunal must follow. The principles governing Child Support Appeal Tribunals will be the same as those which apply to Social Security Appeal Tribunals. They must follow all relevant court decisions. The principles governing the relationship between tribunals themselves and between tribunals and the Commissioners are set out in *R(I) 12/75*:

1 A Child Support Appeal Tribunal is not bound by the decision of any other Child Support Appeal Tribunal.

2 A Child Support Appeal Tribunal is bound by all decisions of a single Commissioner or tribunal of Commissioners. This applies whether the decision is reported or unreported and whether or not it has been starred.

3 If there is a conflict between decisions of Commissioners a Child Support Appeal Tribunal should give more weight to a reported decision than to an unreported decision. It should follow a decision of a tribunal of Commissioners in preference to that of a single Commissioner. A single Commissioner is entitled to disregard a decision of a tribunal of Commissioners. However, this is not a practice which should be followed by Child Support Appeal Tribunals.

4 Where it is not possible to choose between decisions on the basis indicated in 3 above, the tribunal is entitled to follow the decision which it considers the better. There is no obligation to prefer an earlier decision or a later decision. The only governing factor is the quality of the decision itself.

5 The child support jurisdiction is separate from the social security jurisdiction. However, the Commissioners are the same and the law is in many respects the same or similar. There will often be a "sufficient practical relationship" between child support and social security provisions such that they should be interpreted uniformly and differences between them may be assumed to have some significance (see the approach of the Tribunal of Commissioners in the Common Appendix to *R(IS) 3/91* and *R(IS) 4/91*, paragraph 9.) In practice, therefore, tribunals will regard themselves as bound by relevant social security decisions just as they are by child support decisions in accordance with the above rules of precedent. This is of course subject to the important proviso that neither the wording nor the context of a particular provision requires a different interpretation in child support law. Care will therefore always be needed to ensure that decisions are not applied without consideration first being given to whether they are relevant.

Northern Ireland and Scotland

Northern Ireland has its own structure of tribunals and its own Commissioners separate from those who hear appeals in England, Wales and Scotland. The proper approach of a Child Support Appeal Tribunal in Great Britain to a decision of a Child Support Commissioner in Northern Ireland or a court decision in Northern Ireland relating to child support law may be found in *R(SB) 1/90*. If there is no decision of a Commissioner in Great Britain a decision of a Child Support Commissioner in Northern Ireland should be followed, provided that two conditions are met. First, the relevant statutory provision must be identically worded to the provision to be applied in Great Britain. Second, if the decision is a court decision or that of a tribunal of Commissioners it must be unanimous.

There are no separate Scottish Child Support Commissioners. Child Support Commissioners are appointed for Great Britain as a whole although some sit in Scotland. Those Commissioners do not confine themselves to cases arising in Scotland which will sometimes be dealt with in England and equally some cases from England will be dealt with in Scotland. Accordingly, no distinction is to be drawn between Commissioners' decisions from English and Welsh appeals on the one hand and Commissioners' decisions from Scottish appeals on the other (*R(U) 8/80*).

Child Support Act 1991

(1991 c.48)

ARRANGEMENT OF SECTIONS

The basic principles

An Act to make provision for the assessment, collection and enforcement of periodical maintenance payable by certain parents with respect to children of theirs who are not in their care; for the collection and enforcement of certain other kinds of maintenance; and for connected purposes. [25th July 1991.]

The basic principles

The duty to maintain

1.—(1) For the purposes of this Act, each parent of a qualifying child is responsible for maintaining him.

(2) For the purposes of this Act, an absent parent shall be taken to have met his responsibility to maintain any qualifying child of his by making periodical payments of maintenance with respect to the child of such amount, and at such intervals, as may be determined in accordance with the provisions of this Act.

(3) Where a maintenance assessment made under this Act requires the making of periodical payments, it shall be the duty of the absent parent with respect to whom the assessment was made to make those payments.

DEFINITIONS
"absent parent": see s.3(2).
"maintenance assessment": see s.54.
"parent": *ibid*.
"qualifying child": see s.3(1).

GENERAL NOTE

This section sets the framework of obligations around which the child support structure is built. Each parent of a qualifying child is responsible for maintaining that child. If a parent is an absent parent, a maintenance assessment may be made. It is the absent parent's duty to pay the sums fixed by that assessment. If payment is made as required, the obligation to maintain which is imposed by this section is discharged. In some cases the child support maintenance payable will be nil (see the general note to Sched. 1, para. 7). In such a case the absent parent is effectively absolved from paying child support maintenance for so long as the maintenance assessment remains in force.

The obligations imposed by this section only apply for the purposes of this Act. They do not affect the rights and obligations which apply outside the scope of the Act (see Part II of the Matrimonial Causes Act 1973, Part I of the Domestic Proceedings and Magistrates' Courts Act 1978, Part III of the Matrimonial and Family Proceedings Act 1984, Family Law (Scotland) Act 1985, Sched. 1 to the Children Act 1989 and ss.78(6) and 105 of the Social Security Administration Act 1992). The principal limitations on the scope of the duty are therefore as follows: (i) It does not apply unless one of the parents (as defined by s.54) is an absent parent as defined by s.3(2); (ii) It does not apply unless the child has a home with someone who qualifies as a person with care under s.3(3); (iii) It ceases to apply when the child ceases to be a child for the purposes of the Act under s.55; (iv) The Act does not affect cases where the court has jurisdiction under s.8; (v) Finally, the Act does not affect any consensual maintenance arrangements to which the parents may agree, except to the extent that the parties may not contract out of the Act (s.9).

Subs. (3)

Where there are two or more applications for a maintenance assessment in respect of the same absent parent but in relation to different qualifying children, the case is a special case by virtue of reg. 22 of the Maintenance Assessments and Special Cases Regulations. In such a case payment of each of the maintenance assessments satisfies the liability under this subsection of the absent parent or person treated as such (reg. 22(5)).

Welfare of children: the general principle

2. Where, in any case which falls to be dealt with under this Act, the Secretary of State or any child support officer is considering the exercise of any discretionary power conferred by this Act, he shall have regard to the welfare of any child likely to be affected by his decision.

DEFINITIONS
"child": see s.55.
"child support officer": see s.13.

GENERAL NOTE

The section applies to the Secretary of State and child support officers. It, therefore, applies to all the powers given to the Secretary of State by the Act, including the power to make delegated legislation. However, it does not apply to the rule-making powers which are given to the Lord Chancellor or the Lord Advocate. It applies to CSATs and to Commissioners when they are considering on appeal the decision which a child support officer should have made, but it does not apply when they are considering the exercise of powers of their own, such as the powers given to Commissioners by s.24(3). However, in cases to which this section does not apply, the welfare of any children likely to be affected will, on general principles, be a proper consideration in the exercise of any discretion.

The Secretary of State and child support officers must have regard to the welfare of any child likely to be affected by their decisions. It is only necessary that "regard" shall be had to the welfare of the child. This is less stringent than the requirement that the welfare of the child should be the "first" or "paramount" consideration, which applies in s.25(1) of the Matrimonial Causes Act 1973 and s.1(1) of the Children Act 1989 respectively. The children whose welfare must be considered are all those who are likely to be affected. Children other than the qualifying children may need to be considered. For example, if the absent parent has other children, their welfare must also be taken into account. One or both of the parents may also be a child within the meaning of the Act.

The welfare of children covers all the needs relating to their present condition and future development: physical, mental, emotional, educational and social (see especially the so-called "welfare checklist" in s.1(3) of the Children Act 1989, although it has no direct application to this Act). In an appropriate case the views of the child may be taken into account. A specific factor which should be taken into account is the possible prejudicial effect of delay on the welfare of a child. So important is this consideration that it is expressly made a general principle for the purpose of the Children Act 1989 by s.1(2) of that Act. In the child support context it will be of particular importance when a child support officer is considering whether or not to make an interim maintenance assessment under s.12.

In considering children's welfare, the emphasis will often be on the finances necessary and available to allow their needs to be met. These needs are not exclusively dependent upon money, but a minimum is necessary and among the most difficult decisions are likely to be those which involve assessing the impact of the distribution of limited resources on the welfare of the children affected.

This section only applies to discretionary powers conferred *by* this Act. It does not, therefore, apply to such powers conferred by regulations made under the Act, such as the power of a child support officer to cancel an interim maintenance assessment under regs. 8(6) and 9(1) of the Maintenance Assessment Procedure Regulations. This is to some extent underlined by the fact that elsewhere it has been felt necessary to make specific provision that the interests (rather than welfare) of a child are to be considered (reg. 24(2)(*c*) of the Maintenance Assessments and Special Cases Regulations). However, the welfare of any children likely to be affected will always be a factor which those exercising a power are entitled to take into consideration, regardless of whether or not there is specific provision to that effect.

In addition to the powers to make regulations the duty imposed by this section applies to the following sections of the Act: 4, 6, 12, 19, 29, 30, 31, 32, 35, 40 and 46. In practice it is likely to have little impact on the decisions made. It is, however, important for the authorities to show that regard has been had to the welfare of children affected.

The cases most likely to come to a tribunal which will require consideration of this section are under s.46 of the Act. If a tribunal is faced with a question which involves the exercise of a discretion by a child support officer, it will need first to identify any children who might be affected by the decision. If the tribunal decides that the welfare of one of those children is not likely to be affected, it should decide why that is so. The tribunal's record of decision should record the children whose interests were considered, its decision and the reasons for it. If the welfare of any child is likely to be affected, the tribunal should decide how it might be affected. Then it will need to weigh the competing interests of all the children affected. Finally, it will have to decide the impact which its conclusions on these matters should have on the exercise of the discretion. These matters should be included in the record of decision.

In any case which directly affects the welfare of a child there is power in exceptional cases to bar disclosure to a party in the case of information which might be damaging to the child (*Re B. (A minor) (Disclosure of Evidence)* [1993] 1 F.L.R. 191). Clearly, this can never be relied upon to prevent the disclosure of information to the Secretary of State or a child support officer.

Provisions like this section are inevitable in any legislation affecting children. However, the scope for the exercise of discretion is extremely limited in this Act. Where there is a discretion it may be supplemented by other specified criteria, as for example in s.46(3), although these do not displace the general duty created by this section. It may be that this section states one of the principles underlying the Act as a whole, but beyond that the recitation of the principle seems more to serve a ritual, political significance, than to provide a touchstone for the practical implementation of the Act. For procedural provisions relating to questions concerning the welfare of children in the context of reduced benefit directions, see reg. 42(2A) and (2B) of the Maintenance Assessment Procedure Regulations.

Meaning of certain terms used in this Act

3.—(1) A child is a "qualifying child" if—
(*a*) one of his parents is, in relation to him, an absent parent; or
(*b*) both of his parents are, in relation to him, absent parents.
(2) The parent of any child is an "absent parent", in relation to him, if—
(*a*) that parent is not living in the same household with the child; and
(*b*) the child has his home with a person who is, in relation to him, a person with care.
(3) A person is a "person with care", in relation to any child, if he is a person—
(*a*) with whom the child has his home

(*b*) who usually provides day to day care for the child (whether exclusively or in conjunction with any other person); and

(*c*) who does not fall within a prescribed category of person.

(4) The Secretary of State shall not, under subsection (3)(*c*), prescribe as a category—

(*a*) parents;

(*b*) guardians;

(*c*) persons in whose favour residence orders under section 8 of the Children Act 1989 are in force;

(*d*) in Scotland, persons having the right to custody of a child.

(5) For the purposes of this Act there may be more than one person with care in relation to the same qualifying child.

(6) Periodical payments which are required to be paid in accordance with a maintenance assessment are referred to in this Act as "child support maintenance".

(7) Expressions are defined in this section only for the purposes of this Act.

DEFINITIONS

"child": see s.55.

"maintenance assessment": see s.54.

"parent": *ibid.*

"prescribed": *ibid.*

GENERAL NOTE

Subs. (1)

To be a qualifying child, a person must satisfy two conditions. First, the person must be a child within the meaning of the Act. The basic definition in s.55 is elaborated on by Sched. 1 to the Maintenance Assessment Procedure Regulations. Second, one or both of the child's parents must be absent parents as defined in subs. (2).

Subs. (2)

If a person is to be an absent parent in relation to a child, three conditions must be satisfied. Two relate to the parent and one to the living arrangements of the child. First, the person must be a parent of the child as defined in s.54. Second, the person must not live in the same household with the child. Finally, the child's home must be with a person with care as defined in subs. (3).

General approach

The Act uses three different expressions: "household," "home" and "living [or residing] with." All three are used in this subsection. It is appropriate to make some general remarks on the proper use of the authorities and the application of the principles which they create to cases involving phrases such as these, *i.e.* cases where the application of the legal principles to the facts of a particular case turns on an individual analysis of the relevant factors of the case and their interrelation, and in which no single factor of itself is conclusive (*Simmons* v. *Pizzey* [1977] 2 All E.R. 432 at 441–442 *per* Lord Hailsham, L.C., and *R(G) 1/79*) and no definitive list of relevant factors is possible (*Crake* v. *Supplementary Benefits Commission* [1982] 1 All E.R. 498 at 502 *per* Woolf, J.). It will often be possible for different members of a tribunal to attribute different significance to an individual factor and, even when all the factors are considered as a whole, the result will often depend upon the individual member's impression, with the result that different members may quite properly come to different conclusions on the same facts.

These, and similar phrases which have been given the same meaning, occur in a variety of contexts and there are a number of decisions by courts and Commissioners interpreting them. Since there is a broad level of consistency in these phrases across the various contexts, the decisions will be helpful in interpreting these phrases in the context of child support law. Indeed, in *Santos* v. *Santos* [1972] 2 All E.R. 246 at 253 Sachs, L.J., was able to identify a prima facie meaning of "living apart" (the antithesis, it was said, of "living together") before going on to consider whether it was displaced by the particular statutory context of the Divorce Reform Act 1969. However, it is clear from the nature of the analysis which the courts undertake and the comments which the judges make from time to time (for example, Ormrod, L.J., in *Adeoso* v. *Adeoso* [1981] 1 All E.R. 107 at 109) that the context in which they are used may affect the precise scope given to the words and the nature and weight of the factors relevant to their application. In using decisions from other contexts, therefore, it is necessary to take account of the statutory context in which they were made as well as to have due regard to the language and statutory context of child support law.

Usually it will be immediately obvious how the principles apply to the living arrangements of those concerned, because the circumstances will be such that the result will be the same whichever concept is being applied. In such cases failure to reach the correct conclusion will be an error of law (*R.* v. *Birmingham Juvenile Court, ex p. N.* [1984] 2 All E.R. 688 at 690–691 *per* Arnold, P.). However, the arrangements which can be entered into are subject to infinite variation, and tribunals will on occasions need to determine with precision both the scope of each concept and its application to the individual facts of the particular case. It is particularly likely in such cases that the facts of the case will be open to alternative analyses. If this is so, the decision will be one of fact and degree, and there will be no error of law, provided that (i) the decision is based on the correct legal principles and (ii) it is one that could reasonably be made on the facts of the case (*ibid.* and *Simmons* v. *Pizzey, supra* at 441–442 *per* Lord Hailsham, L.C.).

Applying the law in cases such as this requires the exercise of a number of skills by CSAT members. They must be aware of the manifold variations in living arrangements which exist and analyse them in a way which both reflects the individual circumstances of the case concerned and produces a sensible result within the structure of the legislation. Care will need to be taken in making and recording findings of fact on all relevant matters, as well as in making and explaining the reasons for the tribunal's decision. Precedent must be used carefully: decisions must be followed in so far as they lay down general principles, but arguments based on the similarity of facts between two cases will always be misplaced, since minor differences can change the whole complexion of an arrangement. Reasons for decision which are framed by way of comparison with the facts in particular Commissioners' Decisions will lead to a successful appeal to a Commissioner, since it is not any single factor on its own which is decisive, but rather the combined effect of all relevant factors.

Household

The criteria to be taken into account in deciding which households exist are discussed in the general note to reg. 1 of the Maintenance Assessments and Special Cases Regulations. Although it will usually be obvious which households exist and who lives in which one, difficult cases will arise and attention will need to be paid to the relevant legal criteria. In the context of the definition of absent parent, the financial arrangements will be of central importance. The legal guidance on the factors to be taken into account in deciding whether a person is a member of a household is directed at the activities of adults. Where the circumstances do not provide an obvious answer, the approach to deciding the household in which a child lives should generally be as follows. First, consider the arrangements of the adults concerned and decide which households exist. Then, consider how the child fits into those arrangements by enquiring who bears the immediate financial responsibility for, and who fulfils the usual domestic responsibilities in respect of, that child. Findings of fact must be made on these matters. The relevant household will be the one with which the child has the closest connection. Deciding this will require the exercise of judicial judgment. It will involve identifying the significance of each of the relevant factors and attributing the appropriate weight to each. The reasons for decision should record that this judgment has been exercised and indicate why it was exercised in the way it was. Where a child has a sufficient degree of maturity and financial independence, it may be possible to apply the legal criteria for the existence of a household directly to the child, rather than approach the question in the way suggested here. In all cases, the decision should be based on objective facts, rather than on the perceptions of the persons concerned as to whether they live in the same or separate households, although in marginal cases these perceptions, including (depending on the child's age and maturity) those of the child concerned, may be an important consideration.

In the context of the Divorce Reform Act 1969, Wrangham, J., thought that it was not possible for persons to live in the same household without also living with each other (*Mouncer* v. *Mouncer* [1972] 1 All E.R. 289 at 291). However, as it is the purpose of child support law to require absent parents to contribute towards the cost of bringing up their children, it is possible that the position may be different and that there may be cases in which the arrangements within a family are such that one parent is a member of the same household as the child, but does not live in that household *with the child*. In such cases, attention will need to be given both to the question of which households exist and to the separate question of whether a particular member of a household may be described as living in it with the child. One type of case in which this distinction may need to be drawn is where one parent is working for substantial periods away from home, for example on an oil rig, or in another part of the country while the rest of the family stays in the family home until it is sold. Although the financial arrangements and emotional attachments may be such that the single household survives, the extent of the separation may result in it being inappropriate to regard the absent person as living in that household *with* the child. This analysis may also be appropriate where a relationship is coming to an end and the arrangements are moving in the direction of separate households. Those separate households may not yet have been completely established, but, in view of the steps being taken to separate the lives of the parties, it may nevertheless be appropriate to regard one of them as no longer living *with* the child in the surviving household, especially if responsibility for the child has for all practical purposes been abandoned by that parent. In practice, the evidence may not permit the distinctions suggested in this paragraph to be drawn and the making of the application for a maintenance assessment would be likely to lead to the household ceasing to exist.

It is possible that the child may be living with the absent parent, but not in the same household. If, for example, a father still lives in the family home, but has formed a separate household within it, the child may, depending on the circumstances, still be said to be living with both parents. Such circumstances will satisfy the definition in this subsection, since the child does not live in the same household as the father and the child's home is with the mother (albeit it is with the father as well) who can therefore qualify as a person with care.

The meaning of "home" and some of the other problems associated with the concept of living or residing with someone are discussed in the general note to subs. (3).

There are three special cases which affect this definition of "absent parent." The first special case is where both parents are absent parents. This is a special case by virtue of reg. 19 of the Maintenance Assessments and Special Cases Regulations. This case is relevant to the assessments which are made under s.11, the calculation of those assessments under Sched. 1, paras. 2 to 5 to the Act and the calculation of the maintenance requirement under Sched. 1, para. 1 to the Act. The second special case applies where two or more persons who do not live in the same household each provide day to day care for the same qualifying child and at least one of them is a parent of the child. This is a special case by virtue of reg. 20 of the Maintenance Assessments and Special Cases Regulations. In this case the regulation provides that in certain circumstances a parent who provides day to day care to some extent may *be treated as* an absent parent. That person may be required to pay child support maintenance, although only a proportion of the amount that would otherwise be payable. See the general note to reg. 20. It is important to distinguish cases where a person is an absent parent from those where the person *is treated as* an absent parent by virtue of reg. 20, since some provisions apply in one case but not in the other. The final relevant special case arises where one parent is an absent parent and the other is treated as one. This is a special case by virtue of reg. 21 of the Maintenance Assessments and Special Cases Regulations. In this case the parent who is treated as an absent parent is regarded as a parent with care for the purposes of the calculation of the amount of child support maintenance payable under Sched. 1.

Care must be taken not to analyse the concepts employed in this subsection in isolation and without regard to their interplay, particularly when one of the special cases applies. Take the following example: Parents have a daughter who is at boarding school. They pay the school fees, give her an allowance and pay for her travel and clothing. Accordingly, the household comprises both parents and the child, even while she is at school. The child's home is with the parents, but she lives at school during the term and with her parents during the holidays. During term-time the child is a member of the same household as her father, but does not live with him in it. Consequently, the first limb of the definition of absent parent is satisified. However, her home is with her mother (albeit with her father as well) and her mother would usually (together with the father) have day to day care of her daughter were she not at boarding school (reg. 27 of the Maintenance Assessments and Special Cases Regulations). Consequently, the mother is a person with care and second limb of the definition is satisfied. Thus the father appears to be an absent parent and the mother appears to be a person with care, although the same argument could reverse their roles. (The example being considered here is different from the case considered above where a parent is a member of a household, but lives separately from it for employment reasons. In that case the parent does not have day to day care of the child and so could not satisfy the definition of a person with care.)

It is clear that the philosophy underlying this legislation does not cover such a case, although it is within the wording of reg. 19 of the Maintenance Assessments and Special Cases Regulations, which creates a special case where both parents are absent parents. Two of the other special cases (regs. 20 and 24 of the Maintenance Assessments and Special Cases Regulations) come close to applying, but are drafted so as to apply only where the parents do not live in the same household. The solution to the apparent problem is to realise that the difficulty can only arise as a result of interpreting and applying the concepts employed in this subsection without regard to their inter-relationship in the context of the overall purpose and scheme of the Act. Although it is nowhere expressly stated, it is implicit within the structure of the Act and the regulations that (subject to the special cases) a person cannot be both an absent parent and a person with care with respect to the same qualifying child.

Subs. (3)

A number of matters turn on whether or not a person is a person with care, for example it determines who is entitled to apply for a maintenance assessment under s.4, whether s.5(1) applies and whether the

Secretary of State may require that he be authorised under s.6 to apply for a maintenance assessment. It is not essential that the person with care should be a parent of the child. Some provisions, however, only apply to a person with care who is also a parent, for example s.6. In some circumstances a parent who has part-time care of a child may be treated as an absent parent, although for some purposes that parent will still be treated as a person with care (see the discussion of regs. 20 and 21 of the Maintenance Assessments and Special Cases Regulations in the general note to subs. (2), above).

If a person is to be a person with care in respect of a child, three conditions must be satisfied. First, the child's home must be with the person. The tribunal's enquiry must concentrate on the nature and extent of the child's association with the person alleged to be the person with care, rather than on the child's association with particular premises. A child could still have a home with a person, although they have no fixed abode. (Compare the definition of "home" in reg. 1(2) of the Maintenance Assessments and Special Cases Regulations, which is concerned with the accommodation.) The financial arrangements are much less important here than when considering the meaning of household. The living and caring arrangements for the child will be an important consideration and in this context an enquiry should always be made as to who has parental responsibility for, or parental rights over, the child, whether, and if so, in whose favour, a residence order under s.8 of the Children Act 1989 has been made in respect of the child, and in whose favour any existing order for custody or care and control of the child was made. A home is a person's domestic base and a child's home, like anyone else's, is as much a matter of perception as it is a matter of observable fact. In the case of a child, the perception of the adults who have legal responsibility for the child will be central considerations. However, as the emphasis here is on reality of parental responsibility (rather than lawfulness, as in the case when considering habitual residence: see the general note to s.44), it will be the wishes of those persons who have actual, as opposed to legal, responsibility for the child that will be the relevant ones. Moreover, the perceptions of the child may deserve consideration, depending on the degree of maturity.

In view of the importance of perception in identifying a child's home, it is possible for a home to be with a particular person despite considerable absences. This is emphasised by reg. 27 of the Maintenance Assessments and Special Cases Regulations, which makes clear that a child's home may be with a person, although the child lives elsewhere for a substantial part of the year. This regulation provides for the special case where a child is at boarding school or in hospital. It operates only in relation to para. (*b*) of the definition of "person with care" and does not affect para. (*a*). Clearly, therefore, reg. 27 envisages that the fact that the child is separated from a person for lengthy periods does not of itself prevent that child's home being with that person. A child's home may be with a person despite the fact that they live in different households, for example, a child and a parent may maintain a separate household within a house which is shared with grandparents who share the care of the child. In such a case, the child does not live in the grandparents' household, but the arrangements may be such that the child's home is with them as well as with the mother.

The second limb of the definition of a person with care is that the person must provide day to day care for the child. This is not defined by the Act, but is defined by reg. 1(2) of the Maintenance Assessments and Special Cases Regulations. It covers persons who on average over the previous 12 months (or such other period as is more representative of the current arrangements for the care of the child) provided care for not less than two nights per week. The need to provide day to day care is modified if (a) the qualifying child is a boarder at a boarding school or an in-patient at a hospital and (b) as a result, the person who would otherwise be providing day to day care is not doing so. These circumstances constitute a special case by virtue of reg. 27 of the Maintenance Assessments and Special Cases Regulations. In this case, para. (*b*) of this subsection is modified so as to apply to the person who would usually be providing day to day care were the child not a boarder or in-patient. If a child is allowed to live with a parent under s.23(5) of the Children Act 1989, there is a special case by virtue of reg. 27A of the Maintenance Assessments and Special Cases Regulations and subs. 3(*b*) is modified to apply to that parent rather than to the person who usually provides day to day care.

The definition of day to day care in terms of overnight care can create problems when arrangments for day and night care are separated. A parent who works night shifts, for example, may have overall care of a child, except that the child is looked after by a nanny or sleeps with a neighbour while the parent is at work. In cases like this, the child is still in the parent's care, although that care is exercised through the agency of someone else. The situation becomes more difficult, however, if the person with whom the child spends the night is someone who is not acting on the parent's behalf. The child might, for example, be looked after at night by grandparents, who might wish to set up a claim as persons with care in competition to the parent. In this case, the child's home might be with the parent, but day to day care with the grandparents, with the result that there would be no person with care. The only way to avoid this would be to rely on the fact that the definition of day to day care in terms of overnight care only applies unless the context otherwise requires. Freed from the definition, it would be possible to have regard to the overall pattern of care for a child. However, it is not the case that the context of the legislation requires a different meaning; rather it is that the meaning produces inappropriate results when applied to particular sets of circumstances and those circumstances could arise in relation to any of the provisions in which the words are used. In other words, in order to avoid the inappropriate results, it would be necessary to disregard the definition completely.

Para. (*b*) expressly caters for the possibility that there may be joint persons with care, that is, that the care for a child may be provided only in conjunction with someone else. It may be difficult to decide in a particular case who is the person with care of a child, for example both a mother and the maternal grandparents may live with and care for a child. The child's home may be said to be with both mother and grandparents. It will then be necessary to inquire closely into the care arrangements to see who has day to day care of the child. Findings of fact will need to be made on this matter and if there is any dispute, the record of decision of the tribunal must explain why the decision was made. Where the living and caring arrangements do not permit a sensible choice to be made between the persons involved, the appropriate decision will be that there are persons with joint care.

The third condition which must be satisfied if a person is to be a person with care in respect of a child is that the person must not fall within one of the prescribed categories of person who may not be persons with care. These are set out in reg. 51 of the Maintenance Assessment Procedure Regulations and cover cases where the person with care is a local authority or a person with whom a child is placed or boarded by a local authority. In line with these exclusions, where a local authority has part-time care of a qualifying child, there is a special case by virtue of reg. 25 of the Maintenance Assessments and Special Cases Regulations and no child support maintenance is payable in respect of the proportion of the week that the child is in the care of the local authority.

Subs. (5)

There may be more than one person with care in respect of a child. This subsection covers two possibilities. The first is the possibility expressly catered for by subs. (3)(*b*), that there may be persons who jointly have care of a child on a day to day basis. The second possibility is that care is shared between different persons (as opposed to being provided jointly by them) so that each is a person with part-time care. (Depending on the circumstances, this may be a special case by virtue of reg. 24 of the Maintenance Assessments and Special Cases Regulations: see below.) Where there is more than one person with care, only those who have parental responsibility for, or parental rights over, the child may apply for a maintenance assessment (s.5(1)). Where there are applications for maintenance assessments from more than one such person, the one to be proceeded with is determined under reg. 4 of, and Sched. 2 to, the Maintenance Assessment Procedure Regulations.

Where there are persons with part-time care of a child who live in separate households but neither of whom is treated as an absent parent, the case is a special one by virtue of reg. 24 of the Maintenance Assessments and Special Cases Regulations and the child support maintenance payable may be apportioned between them by the Secretary of State. This applies regardless of whether all or any of the persons concerned have parental responsibility for the child. As the decision is made by the Secretary of State and not by a child support officer, it can never come before a CSAT.

Subs. (6)

From the point of view of the absent parent, payment of child support maintenance is an obligation which must be met. Other debts, such as hire purchase or court fines, do not have priority and are not taken into account when making a maintenance assessment. The absent parent must renegotiate other financial obligations with the creditors in order to ensure that all obligations may be met. From the point of view of the person with care, child support maintenance is income and may result in this person receiving less benefit than before or ceasing to be entitled to benefit altogether.

Child support maintenance

4.—(1) A person who is, in relation to any qualifying child or any qualifying children, either the person with care or the absent parent may apply to the Secretary of State for a maintenance assessment to be made under this Act with respect to that child, or any of those children.

(2) Where a maintenance assessment has been made in response to an application under this section the Secretary of State may, if the person with care or absent parent with respect to whom the assessment was made applies to him under this subsection, arrange for—

    (*a*)   the collection of the child support maintenance payable in accordance with the assessment;

(*b*) the enforcement of the obligation to pay child support maintenance in accordance with the assessment.

(3) Where an application under subsection (2) for the enforcement of the obligation mentioned in subsection (2)(*b*) authorises the Secretary of State to take steps to enforce that obligation whenever he considers it necessary to do so, the Secretary of State may act accordingly.

(4) A person who applies to the Secretary of State under this section shall, so far as that person reasonably can, comply with such regulations as may be made by the Secretary of State with a view to the Secretary of State or the child support officer being provided with the information which is required to enable—

(*a*) the absent parent to be traced (where that is necessary);

(*b*) the amount of child support maintenance payable by the absent parent to be assessed; and

(*c*) that amount to be recovered from the absent parent.

(5) Any person who has applied to the Secretary of State under this section may at any time request him to cease acting under this section.

(6) It shall be the duty of the Secretary of State to comply with any request made under subsection (5) (but subject to any regulations made under subsection (8)).

(7) The obligation to provide information which is imposed by subsection (4)—

(*a*) shall not apply in such circumstances as may be prescribed; and

(*b*) may, in such circumstances as may be prescribed, be waived by the Secretary of State.

(8) The Secretary of State may by regulations make such incidental, supplemental or transitional provision as he thinks appropriate with respect to cases in which he is requested to cease to act under this section.

(9) No application may be made under this section if there is in force with respect to the person with care and absent parent in question a maintenance assessment made in response to an application under section 6.

DEFINITIONS

"absent parent": see s.3(2).
"child support maintenance": see s.3(6).
"child support officer": see s.13.
"maintenance assessment": see s.54.
"person with care": see s.3(3).
"prescribed": see s.54.
"qualifying child": see s.3(1).

GENERAL NOTE

An application for a maintenance assessment may be made by (i) an absent parent, (ii) a person with care, (iii) the Secretary of State acting under the authority and on behalf of a parent with care and (iv) in Scotland a child who has attained the age of 12. Both (i) and (ii) are dealt with in this section, (iii) is dealt with in s.6 and (iv) is covered by s.7. The application of this section will be phased in between April 5, 1993 and April 6, 1997: see the general note to Part I of the Transitional Provisions Regulations.

Subs. (1)

Any absent parent and, subject to s.5(1), any person with care may apply for a maintenance assessment in respect of a child. This is subject to subs. (9). An absent parent may wish to apply in order to fix the extent of his responsibility under this Act (see s. 1(2)). Responsibility for the administration of child support law is split between the Secretary of State and a child support officer. In the case of applications for child support maintenance the application is made to the Secretary of State who must then refer it to a child support officer under s.11. Those matters which are for the Secretary of State are not subject to an appeal to a CSAT, although in an appropriate case action may be taken in court. However, some of the decisions of a child support officer are appealable to a CSAT.

Subs. (2)

A person with care or an absent parent may authorise (see subss. (2) and (3)) the Secretary of State to arrange for the collection of child support maintenance and the enforcement of the obligation to pay it. The obligation to pay which is referred to in para. (*b*) is the duty created by s.1(3). Matters relating to the collection and enforcement of child support maintenance are for the Secretary of State and are dealt with in ss.29 to 41.

Subs. (4)

A person who authorises the Secretary of State to arrange for collection and enforcement under subss. (2) and (3) is required to co-operate by providing the information specified in this subsection. The regulations are to be found in Part II of the Information Evidence and Disclosure Regulations. The duty to co-operate is a qualified one. This subsection provides that it only applies in so far as it is reasonably possible for that person to comply and it is further limited by the conditions set out in regs. 2(1) and 5. It may also be waived by the Secretary of State under subs. (7)(*b*), but only in prescribed circumstances. Wider duties concerning the provision of information are created under s.14(1) which are also contained in Part II of the Regulations. This subsection applies only to the supply of information, whereas s.14(1) applies to both information and evidence. For a discussion of the meaning of "information" in this section and for enforcement see the general note to s.14(1).

Subs. (8)

No regulations have been made under this subsection, although the circumstances in which the duty to disclose will arise are limited by reg. 2(1) to cases where either the information or evidence is in the possession of the person concerned or it can reasonably be expected to be acquired by that person.

Child support maintenance: supplemental provisions

5.—(1) Where—
(*a*) there is more than one person with care of a qualifying child; and
(*b*) one or more, but not all, of them have parental responsibility for (or, in Scotland, parental rights over) the child;
no application may be made for a maintenance assessment with respect to the child by any of those persons who do not have parental responsibility for (or, in Scotland, parental rights over) the child.

(2) Where more than one application for a maintenance assessment is made with respect to the child concerned, only one of them may be proceeded with.

(3) The Secretary of State may by regulations make provision as to which of two or more applications for a maintenance assessment with respect to the same child is to be proceeded with.

DEFINITIONS
"maintenance assessment": see s.54.
"parental responsibility": *ibid.*
"parental rights": *ibid.*
"person with care": see s.3(3).
"prescribed": see s.54.
"qualifying child": see s.3(1).

GENERAL NOTE
Subs. (1)

If there is more than one person with care, only those with parental responsibility for, or parental rights over, the qualifying child may apply for a maintenance assessment. However, if there is only one person with care, that person may apply for an assessment regardless of who has parental responsibility or rights.

Subss. (2) and (3)

Only one application for a maintenance assessment in respect of a child may be proceeded with. If more than one is made, the priority between any that cannot be eliminated under subs. (1) is determined under the provisions of reg. 4 of, and Sched. 2 to, the Maintenance Assessment Procedure Regulations. If an attempt is made to make an application for a maintenance assessment at a time when such an application may not be made by virtue of Part I of the Schedule to the Transitional Provisions Regulations, that application is ignored and is irrelevant to the question of priority of applications.

Applications by those receiving benefit

6.—(1) Where income support, family credit or any other benefit of a prescribed kind is claimed by or in respect of, or paid to or in respect of, the parent of a qualifying child she shall, if—

(*a*) she is a person with care of the child; and

(*b*) she is required to do so by the Secretary of State,

authorise the Secretary of State to take action under this Act to recover child support maintenance from the absent parent.

(2) The Secretary of State shall not require a person ("the parent") to give him the authorisation mentioned in subsection (1) if he considers that there are reasonable grounds for believing that—

(*a*) if the parent were to be required to give that authorisation; or

(*b*) if she were to give it,

there would be a risk of her, or of any child living with her, suffering harm or undue distress as a result.

(3) Subsection (2) shall not apply if the parent requests the Secretary of State to disregard it.

(4) The authorisation mentioned in subsection (1) shall extend to all children of the absent parent in relation to whom the parent first mentioned in subsection (1) is a person with care.

(5) That authorisation shall be given, without unreasonable delay, by completing and returning to the Secretary of State an application—

(*a*) for the making of a maintenance assessment with respect to the qualifying child or qualifying children; and

(*b*) for the Secretary of State to take action under this Act to recover, on her behalf, the amount of child support maintenance so assessed.

(6) Such an application shall be made on a form ("a maintenance application form") provided by the Secretary of State.

(7) A maintenance application form shall indicate in general terms the effect of completing and returning it.

(8) Subsection (1) has effect regardless of whether any of the benefits mentioned there is payable with respect to any qualifying child.

(9) A person who is under the duty imposed by subsection (1) shall, so far as she reasonably can, comply with such regulations as may be made by the Secretary of State with a view to the Secretary of State or the child support officer being provided with the information which is required to enable—

(*a*) the absent parent to be traced;

(*b*) the amount of child support maintenance payable by the absent parent to be assessed; and

(*c*) that amount to be recovered from the absent parent.

(10) The obligation to provide information which is imposed by subsection (9)—

(*a*) shall not apply in such circumstances as may be prescribed; and

(*b*) may, in such circumstances as may be prescribed, be waived by the Secretary of State.

(11) A person with care who has authorised the Secretary of State under subsection (1) but who subsequently ceases to fall within that subsection may request the Secretary of State to cease acting under this section.

(12) It shall be the duty of the Secretary of State to comply with any request made under subsection (11) (but subject to any regulations made under subsection (13)).

(13) The Secretary of State may by regulations make such incidental or transitional provision as he thinks appropriate with respect to cases in which he is requested under subsection (11) to cease to act under this section.

(14) The fact that a maintenance assessment is in force with respect to a person

with care shall not prevent the making of a new maintenance assessment with respect to her in response to an application under this section.

DEFINITIONS
"absent parent": see s.3(2).
"child": see s.55.
"child support maintenance": see s.3(6).
"child support officer": see s.13.
"family credit": see s.54.
"income support": *ibid.*
"maintenance assessment": *ibid.*
"parent": *ibid.*
"person with care": see s.3(3).
"prescribed": see s.54.
"qualifying child": see s.3(1).

GENERAL NOTE
The effect of Part I of the Transitional Provisions Regulations is that this section comes into operation on April 5, 1993.

Subs. (1)
This section allows the Secretary of State to require a parent who is a person with care to authorise him to recover child support maintenance in respect of a qualifying child. This applies even if a maintenance assessment is already in force (subs. (14)). Although it is not expressly stated in this section, it is clear from the side note and from the wording of the Maintenance Assessment Procedure Regulations (regs. 2(1) and 19(5)) that an application is made by the parent with care.

The consequence of failure to comply with the requirement to authorise the Secretary of State is that a child support officer may make a reduced benefit direction under s.46. It is irrelevant whether or not the identity of the absent parent is known to the Secretary of State. The person with care must authorise the Secretary of State to take action and it is the failure to do so that may trigger a reduced benefit direction. These powers are designed to prevent a parent who is covered by a payment of benefit from leaving financial responsibility for the child with the State rather than pursuing the absent parent for a maintenance assessment. Any application made is that of the parent with care, although it is made at the insistence of the Secretary of State. In this section, as in the whole of the Act, the absent parent is referred to as male and the person with care as female. This undoubtedly reflects the most likely case. However, the effect of s.6(*a*) of the Interpretation Act 1978 is that the gender of either parent is irrelevant.

Two conditions must be satisfied before the section can apply. First, certain benefits must have been claimed by or in respect of or be paid to or in respect of the person with care. The benefits are currently income support, family credit and (by virtue of reg. 34 of the Maintenance Assessment Procedure Regulations) disability working allowance. Other benefits may be added by regulations. It is not essential that the benefit should have been claimed by or paid to the parent. It is sufficient if it was claimed or paid in respect of that person. If, for example, Angela lives with her dependent daughter Beryl aged 15 who herself has a child, Charles, and Angela applies for income support, Angela's benefit will include an amount in respect of Beryl. As a result Beryl will fall within this subsection. The second condition which must be satisfied if this section is to apply is that the person with care must be a parent of the child. This section does not apply if the person with care is not a parent within the meaning of the Act.

Subs. (2)
This provides the exception where the Secretary of State may not require the parent with care to authorise recovery of child support maintenance on her behalf. The exception applies where there are reasonable grounds to believe that, if authorisation were given, there would be a risk of the parent, or any child living with the parent, suffering harm or undue distress. This is a narrow test, but it should be borne in mind that s.2 requires the welfare of any child likely to be affected to be taken into account. For a discussion of the provisions of this subsection, see the general note to the comparable provision in s.46 (3). If the exception applies, the Secretary of State may not require an authorisation, unless the parent concerned requests that the risk be disregarded (see subs. (3)).

The decision under this subsection is for the Secretary of State and so is not appealable. However, if he decides that there are no grounds, the same issue may have to be decided by a child support officer under s.46(3) and on appeal by a CSAT.

If the risk of harm or distress to the parent or any child living with the parent is only realised after the authorisation is given, or if fresh and more convincing evidence of the risk subsequently becomes available, the Secretary of State may reconsider his decision to require the authorisation.

Subs. (9)

The regulations are to be found in Part II of the Information Evidence and Disclosure Regulations. The consequence of failure to comply with these regulations is that a child support officer may make a reduced benefit direction under s.46. The qualified nature of this duty to co-operate is discussed in the general note to s.4(4). It may also be waived by the Secretary of State under subs. (10)(*b*), but only in prescribed circumstances. Wider duties concerning the provision of information are created under s.14 (1) which are also contained in Part II of the Regulations. This subsection applies only to the supply of information, whereas s.14(1) applies to both information and evidence. For a discussion of the meaning of "information" in this section and for enforcement see the general note to s.14(1).

Subs. (10)

No regulations have been made under this subsection, although the circumstances in which the duty to disclose will arise are limited by reg. 2(1) to cases where either the information or evidence is in the possession of the person concerned or it can reasonably be expected to be acquired by that person.

Subs. (13)

This subsection is narrower than similar provisions elsewhere in the Act in that it refers only to incidental and transitional provisions rather than to incidental, supplemental and transitional provisions: compare ss.4(8) and 7(9). However, any effect of this difference in wording is overriden by s.51(1) and (3). No regulations have been made under this subsection.

Right of child in Scotland to apply for assessment

7.—(1) A qualifying child who has attained the age of 12 years and who is habitually resident in Scotland may apply to the Secretary of State for a maintenance assessment to be made with respect to him if—

    (*a*) no such application has been made by a person who is, with respect to that child, a person with care or an absent parent; or

    (*b*) the Secretary of State has not been authorised under section 6 to take action under this Act to recover child support maintenance from the absent parent (other than in a case where he has waived any requirement that he should be so authorised).

(2) An application made under subsection (1) shall authorise the Secretary of State to make a maintenance assessment with respect to any other children of the absent parent who are qualifying children in the care of the same person as the child making the application.

(3) Where a maintenance assessment has been made in response to an application under this section the Secretary of State may, if the person with care, the absent parent with respect to whom the assessment was made or the child concerned applies to him under this subsection, arrange for—

    (*a*) the collection of the child support maintenance payable in accordance with the assessment;

    (*b*) the enforcement of the obligation to pay child support maintenance in accordance with the assessment.

(4) Where an application under subsection (3) for the enforcement of the obligation mentioned in subsection (3)(*b*) authorises the Secretary of State to take steps to enforce that obligation whenever he considers it necessary to do so, the Secretary of State may act accordingly.

(5) Where a child has asked the Secretary of State to proceed under this section, the person with care of the child, the absent parent and the child concerned shall, so far as they reasonably can, comply with such regulations as may be made by the Secretary of State with a view to the Secretary of State or the child support officer being provided with the information which is required to enable—

    (*a*) the absent parent to be traced (where that is necessary);

    (*b*) the amount of child support maintenance payable by the absent parent to be assessed; and

    (*c*) that amount to be recovered from the absent parent.

(6) The child who has made the application (but not the person having care of

him) may at any time request the Secretary of State to cease acting under this section.

(7) It shall be the duty of the Secretary of State to comply with any request made under subsection (6) (but subject to any regulations made under subsection (9)).

(8) The obligation to provide information which is imposed by subsection (5)—

(*a*) shall not apply in such circumstances as may be prescribed by the Secretary of State; and

(*b*) may, in such circumstances as may be so prescribed, be waived by the Secretary of State.

(9) The Secretary of State may by regulations make such incidental, supplemental or transitional provision as he thinks appropriate with respect to cases in which he is requested to cease to act under this section.

DEFINITIONS

"absent parent": see s.3(2).
"child": see s.55.
"child support maintenance": see s.3(6).
"maintenance assessment": see s.54.
"person with care": see s.3(3).
"prescribed": see s.54.
"qualifying child": see s.3(1).

GENERAL NOTE

This section applies only to Scotland (s.58(10)) and is a consequence of the different age of legal capacity in Scotland from England and Wales as a result of the limited effect of the Age of Legal Capacity (Scotland) Act 1991. It allows a child who has attained the age of 12 to apply for a maintenance assessment. Two conditions must be satisfied. First, no application must have been made by an absent parent or a person with care. Second, the Secretary of State must not have required that he be authorised under s.6 to apply for an assessment. An application by a child will authorise the Secretary of State to make an assessment in respect of all other qualifying children of the absent parent who are in the care of the person with care of the child who has applied under this section (subs. (2), although it is the child support officer, and not the Secretary of State, who *makes* an assessment).

After an application has been made the child may request the Secretary of State to cease acting under this section but the parent with care may not do so (subs. (6)). If requested by the child the Secretary of State must comply with the request, subject to any regulations made under subs. (9).

Except in these respects this section mirrors provisions in ss.4 and 6. Reference should be made to the general note to the equivalent provisions in those sections. The regulations referred to are to be found in the Information, Evidence and Disclosure Regulations. No regulations have been made under subss. (8) and (9), although the circumstances in which the duty to disclose will arise are limited by reg. 2(1) to cases where either the information or evidence is in the possession of the person concerned or it can reasonably be expected to be acquired by that person. Wider duties concerning the provision of information are created under s.14(1) which are also contained in Part II of the Regulations. This subsection applies only to the supply of information, whereas s.14(1) applies to both information and evidence. For a discussion of the meaning of "information" in this section and for enforcement see the general note to s.14(1).

The application of this section will be phased in between April 5, 1993 and April 6, 1997: see the general note to Part I of the Transitional Provisions Order.

Role of the courts with respect to maintenance for children

8.—(1) This subsection applies in any case where a child support officer would have jurisdiction to make a maintenance assessment with respect to a qualifying child and an absent parent of his on an application duly made by a person entitled to apply for such an assessment with respect to that child.

(2) Subsection (1) applies even though the circumstances of the case are such that a child support officer would not make an assessment if it were applied for.

(3) In any case where subsection (1) applies, no court shall exercise any power which it would otherwise have to make, vary or revive any maintenance order in relation to the child and absent parent concerned.

(4) Subsection (3) does not prevent a court from revoking a maintenance order.

(5) The Lord Chancellor or in relation to Scotland the Lord Advocate may by order provide that, in such circumstances as may be specified by the order, this section shall not prevent a court from exercising any power which it has to make a maintenance order in relation to a child if—

 (*a*) a written agreement (whether or not enforceable) provides for the making, or securing, by an absent parent of the child of periodical payments to or for the benefit of the child; and

 (*b*) the maintenance order which the court makes is, in all material respects, in the same terms as that agreement.

(6) This section shall not prevent a court from exercising any power which it has to make a maintenance order in relation to a child if—

 (*a*) a maintenance assessment is in force with respect to the child;

 (*b*) the amount of the child support maintenance payable in accordance with the assessment was determined by reference to the alternative formula mentioned in paragraph 4(3) of Schedule 1; and

 (*c*) the court is satisfied that the circumstances of the case make it appropriate for the absent parent to make or secure the making of periodical payments under a maintenance order in addition to the child support maintenance payable by him in accordance with the maintenance assessment.

(7) This section shall not prevent a court from exercising any power which it has to make a maintenance order in relation to a child if—

 (*a*) the child is, will be or (if the order were to be made) would be receiving instruction at an educational establishment or undergoing training for a trade, profession or vocation (whether or not while in gainful employment); and

 (*b*) the order is made solely for the purposes of requiring the person making or securing the making of periodical payments fixed by the order to meet some or all of the expenses incurred in connection with the provision of the instruction or training.

(8) This section shall not prevent a court from exercising any power which it has to make a maintenance order in relation to a child if—

 (*a*) a disability living allowance is paid to or in respect of him; or

 (*b*) no such allowance is paid but he is disabled,

and the order is made solely for the purpose of requiring the person making or securing the making of periodical payments fixed by the order to meet some or all of any expenses attributable to the child's disability.

(9) For the purposes of subsection (8), a child is disabled if he is blind, deaf or dumb or is substantially and permanently handicapped by illness, injury, mental disorder or congenital deformity or such other disability as may be prescribed.

(10) This section shall not prevent a court from exercising any power which it has to make a maintenance order in relation to a child if the order is made against a person with care of the child.

(11) In this Act "maintenance order", in relation to any child, means an order which requires the making or securing of periodical payments to or for the benefit of the child and which is made under—

 (*a*) Part II of the Matrimonial Causes Act 1973;

 (*b*) the Domestic Proceedings and Magistrates' Courts Act 1978;

 (*c*) Part III of the Matrimonial and Family Proceedings Act 1984;

 (*d*) the Family Law (Scotland) Act 1985;

 (*e*) Schedule 1 to the Children Act 1989; or

 (*f*) any other prescribed enactment,

and includes any order varying or reviving such an order.

DEFINITIONS
"absent parent": see s.3(2).
"child": see s.55.
"child benefit": see s.54.
"child support maintenance": see s.3(6).
"child support officer": see s.13.
"disability living allowance": see s.54.
"maintenance assessment": *ibid*.
"person with care": see s.3(3).
"prescribed": see s.54.
"qualifying child": see s.3(1).

GENERAL NOTE

Sections 8 to 10 provide for the relationship between maintenance assessments on the one hand and maintenance orders made by the courts and maintenance agreements on the other hand. Section 8 gives the child support scheme priority over the court system if a child support officer would have jurisdiction to make a maintenance assessment were an application to be made, regardless of whether or not an application has been made. In such a case the courts may not make, vary or revive a maintenance order, although they may revoke one. (See subss. (1) to (4).) However this is subject to the exceptions contained in subss. (6) to (8) and (10) and the Transitional Provisions Order.

Subs. (3)

Although the court loses it power to make, vary or revive a maintenance order, it retains the power to *enforce* such an order. This, however, will only apply to arrears which accrued prior to the child support officer assuming jurisdiction.

The Family Proceedings (Amendment) Rules 1993 amend the Family Proceedings Rules 1991 as amended [FPR] to deal with the situation where there is a dispute as to whether the court or the child support officer has jurisdiction.

By r.10.24, where an application is made for an order which in the opinion of the District Judge, considering the matter in the first instance without holding a hearing, is one which the court would be precluded from making by virtue of s.8 or s.9 (below), the proper officer (the chief clerk of the family proceedings department of the principal registry or the chief clerk of any other court or registry—FPR r.1.2) may send a notice (Form M34) to the applicant. Where the applicant has been sent such a notice, and informs the proper officer in writing, within 14 days of the date of the notice, that he wishes to persist with his application, the proper officer shall refer the matter back to the district judge for action. The district judge shall give such directions as he considers appropriate for the matter to be heard and determined by the court, and may provide for the hearing to be *ex parte*. The proper officer shall inform the applicant of the directions, and, in relation to the other parties, send them a copy of the application. If the hearing is to be *ex parte*, he shall give them brief information of the matter and inform them that they will be told of the result of the hearing in due course. If the hearing is *inter partes*, he shall inform them of the circumstances which led to the directions being given, and the directions.

Where the applicant does not inform the officer that he wishes to persist with his application, the application shall be treated as having been withdrawn.

If, after the hearing, the court determines that it would be prevented by s.8 or 9 of the Act from making the order applied for, it shall dismiss the application, giving reasons in writing, copies of which will be sent to the parties by the proper officer. The applicant could then appeal to a circuit judge under FPR r.8, or go to the child support officer for an assessment.

Rule 10.25 deals with "non-free-standing applications" for child maintenance. Where an application for such maintenance is contained in a petition or other document and a notice is sent under r.10.24(1), the document shall be treated as if it did not include the maintenance application. (If the court decides, under rr.10.24 that it *does* have jurisdiction to grant the application, it shall direct that the document be treated as if it contained the application.)

(Family proceedings forms and divorce petitions are amended by rr.7 to 16 and Scheds. 1 and 2 to require an applicant for child or spousal maintenance to provide the court with details of any child support assessment or proceedings, to enable the court to decide whether it has jurisdiction, and if so, what payments should be ordered.)

The Family Proceedings Courts (Child Support Act 1991) Rules 1993, rr. 6–12 make equivalent provision where applications are made to the family proceedings court.

Schedule 1 to the Maintenance Orders (Backdating) Order 1993 inserts s.31(11) into the Matrimonial Causes Act 1973, s.20(9A) into the Domestic Proceedings and Magistrates' Courts Act 1978, and Sched. 1, para. 6(9) into the Children Act 1989 to provide for backdating to the effective date or any later date where an application is made to vary or discharge an order which provided for periodical payments for children without apportioning the payments between them, and a maintenance assessment is made in respect of one or more, but not all of the children. This is to ensure that the absent parent is not obliged to continue paying the full amount under the order, in addition to the amount calculated under the maintenance assessment.

In the transitional phase of the introduction of child support law, the operation of this subsection is modified as provided for in para. 5 to the Schedule to the Transitional Provisions Order (as amended).

Subs. (5)

This subsection together with the Child Maintenance (Written Agreements) Order 1993 preserves the courts' power to make consent orders in respect of periodical payments to or for the benefit of a child, even though the child support officer has jurisdiction to carry out an assessment. It is assumed that the Order will in practice be used only in the short-term, as it is expected that the Secretary of State will exercise powers to register, collect and enforce maintenance agreements, obviating the need for the courts to do so. Parents in receipt of benefit will not be able to seek a consent order as a means of avoiding the jurisdiction of the child support officer because of the mandatory nature of s.6.

Subs. (7)

A court may make a maintenance order the sole purpose of which is to cover some or all of the payments for a child's instruction or training. The child must be receiving or going to receive some instruction.

Subs. (8)

A court may make a maintenance order the sole purpose of which is to meet some or all of the expenses attributable to a child's disability provided that either disability living allowance is payable to or in respect of the child or that the child is disabled as defined in subs. (9).

Subss. (6), (7) and (8)

Maintenance orders covered by these subsections are prescribed for the purposes of s.30 by reg. 2(*a*) of the Collection and Enforcement of Other Forms of Maintenance Regulations.

The Maintenance Orders (Backdating) Order 1993 adds s.29(7) and (8) to the Matrimonial Causes Act 1973, s.5(7) and (8) to the Domestic Proceedings and Magistrates' Courts Act 1978 and para. 7(7) and (8) to Sched. 1 to the Children Act 1989, to provide for where a maintenance assessment ceases to have effect or is cancelled under any provision of the Act, and an application for a periodical payments order in favour of the child is made. If the application for the order is made within six months of the date when the assessment ceased to have effect or, where the assessment was cancelled, the later of either the date it was cancelled or the date from which the cancellation first had effect, the order may begin from the date the assessment ceased to have effect, or the date with effect from which it was cancelled, or any later date. Again, the purpose is to remedy any shortfall in support which might otherwise occur between the ending of the assessment and the making of the order.

Schedule 1 to the Maintenance Orders (Backdating) Order 1993 allows maintenance orders to be backdated to the "earliest permitted date" which is the later of either (a) the date six months before the application was made, or (b) the effective date (see regs. 30 and 31 of the Maintenance Assessment Procedure Regulations) of a maintenance assessment made under the Child Support Act, (instead of to the date of the application to the court) provided that the application for the maintenance order is made within six months of the date of the assessment. The Order inserts s.29(5)(b) into the Matrimonial Causes Act 1973, s.5(5)(b) into the Domestic Proceedings and Magistrates' Courts Act 1978 and Sched. 1, para. 3(5)(b) into the Children Act 1989 to provide that where "top-up maintenance," etc. is awarded by a court, backdating can take place. This will protect the parent with care in the interim period between the making of the assessment (when an earlier order may have been superseded) and the application for the top-up.

Subs. (9)

This definition broadly follows that used in s.17(11) of the Children Act 1989 except that mental disorders must result in the child being substantially and permanently handicapped whereas under the 1989 Act any mental disorder is sufficient regardless of its effect. The extent to which the child must be blind or deaf is not specified. For the purpose of disability living allowance a person has to be 100 per cent. blind and 80 per cent. deaf: reg. 12(2) of the Social Security (Disability Living Allowance) Regulations 1991. In practice this is interpreted as meaning that vision is less than 6/60 using both eyes with glasses or that finger counting beyond one foot is not possible, and hearing is so limited that the person cannot hear a shout beyond one metre using both ears with aids out of doors. No regulations have been made under this subsection.

Subs. (10)

A court may make a maintenance order against a person with care.

Subs. (11)

The Affiliation Proceedings Act 1957 is prescribed for the purposes of this subsection by reg. 2 of the Maintenance Arrangements and Jurisdiction Regulations.

Agreements about maintenance

9.—(1) In this section "maintenance agreement" means any agreement for the making, or for securing the making, of periodical payments by way of maintenance, or in Scotland aliment, to or for the benefit of any child.

(2) Nothing in this Act shall be taken to prevent any person from entering into a maintenance agreement.

(3) The existence of a maintenance agreement shall not prevent any party to the agreement, or any other person, from applying for a maintenance assessment with respect to any child to or for whose benefit periodical payments are to be made or secured under the agreement.

(4) Where any agreement contains a provision which purports to restrict the right of any person to apply for a maintenance assessment, that provision shall be void.

(5) Where section 8 would prevent any court from making a maintenance order in relation to a child and an absent parent of his, no court shall exercise any power that it has to vary any agreement so as—

(*a*) to insert a provision requiring that absent parent to make or secure the making of periodical payments by way of maintenance, or in Scotland aliment, to or for the benefit of that child; or

(*b*) to increase the amount payable under such a provision.

DEFINITIONS

"absent parent": see s.3(2).

"child": see s.55.

"maintenance assessment": see s.54.

GENERAL NOTE

The Act does not prevent the making of a maintenance agreement, whether binding (contractually or otherwise) or not. However, a maintenance agreement cannot affect the operation of the Act. The provisions of such an agreement do not displace the child support scheme, nor can they provide that a person may not apply for a maintenance assessment. A maintenance agreement may still be useful, however. First, it may provide for the payment of a larger amount of maintenance than would be assessed under this Act. The Act does not affect the enforcement of such an arrangement. Second, even if the agreement does not provide for the payment of a larger sum than would be assessed under this Act, the parties may prefer to rely on the methods of enforcement available, in addition to or as a substitute for than the mechanisms provided under the Act. Section 8(5) and the Child Maintenance (Written Agreements) Order 1993 allow for provision to be made to permit the incorporation of an agreement into a court order.

Subs. (4)

The effect of this subsection is, in line with the policy decision of Ministers (and with the approach of the private law on maintenance, see *e.g.* s.23(4) of the Matrimonial Causes Act 1973 and s.3 of the Family Law (Scotland) Act 1985), to prevent clean breaks in respect of children. It refers to agreements in contrast to the other subsections which refer to *maintenance* agreements. It therefore catches all agreements which seek to restrict the right to apply for a maintenance assessment, regardless of whether they are maintenance agreements as defined by subs. (1) or not. This prevents the obvious avoidance measure of putting the restriction in a separate agreement, which would not be a maintenance agreement since it would provide for the avoidance of maintenance payments rather than for making or securing them. Agreements which, as part of an overall settlement on breakdown of a marriage or other relationship, make some provision conditional on no application for a maintenance assessment being made may, therefore, be caught by this provision. Whether or not these agreements expressly purport to restrict the right to apply for an assessment, such is their clear effect and purpose. However, only the provision itself is void. Other terms in the agreement remain valid, so the other parts of the overall settlement will still be effective. It is arguable, however, that an agreement incoporating a charge-back arrangement, whereby, for example, the husband transfers his interest in the matrimonial home to the wife, subject to a charge back for the aggregate of any sums payable by him under the Child Support Act, would not be regarded as an attempt to restrict the wife's right to apply under the Act but would simply enable the husband to avoid effectively paying her twice over.

Subs. (3) and (5)

In the transitional phases of the introduction of child support law, the operation of these subsections is modified as provided for in para. 5 of the Schedule to the Transitional Provisions Order (as amended).

Relationship between maintenance assessments and certain court orders and related matters

10.—(1) Where an order of a kind prescribed for the purposes of this subsection is in force with respect to any qualifying child with respect to whom a maintenance assessment is made, the order—

(*a*) shall, so far as it relates to the making or securing of periodical payments, cease to have effect to such extent as may be determined in accordance with regulations made by the Secretary of State; or

(*b*) where the regulations so provide, shall, so far as it so relates, have effect subject to such modifications as may be so determined.

(2) Where an agreement of a kind prescribed for the purposes of this subsection is in force with respect to any qualifying child with respect to whom a maintenance assessment is made, the agreement—

(*a*) shall, so far as it relates to the making or securing of periodical payments, be unenforceable to such extent as may be determined in accordance with regulations made by the Secretary of State; or

(*b*) where the regulations so provide, shall, so far as it so relates, have effect subject to such modifications as may be so determined.

(3) Any regulations under this section may, in particular, make such provision with respect to—

(*a*) any case where any person with respect to whom an order or agreement of a kind prescribed for the purposes of subsection (1) or (2) has effect applies to the prescribed court, before the end of the prescribed period, for the order or agreement to be varied in the light of the maintenance assessment and of the provisions of this Act;

(*b*) the recovery of any arrears under the order or agreement which fell due before the coming into force of the maintenance assessment,

as the Secretary of State considers appropriate and may provide that, in prescribed circumstances, an application to any court which is made with respect to an order of a prescribed kind relating to the making or securing of periodical payments to or for the benefit of a child shall be treated by the court as an application for the order to be revoked.

(4) The Secretary of State may by regulations make provision for—

(*a*) notification to be given by the child support officer concerned to the prescribed person in any case where that officer considers that the making of a maintenance assessment has affected, or is likely to affect, any order of a kind prescribed for the purposes of this subsection;

(*b*) notification to be given by the prescribed person to the Secretary of State in any case where a court makes an order which it considers has affected, or is likely to affect, a maintenance assessment.

(5) Rules may be made under section 144 of the Magistrates' Courts Act 1980 (rules of procedure) requiring any person who, in prescribed circumstances, makes an application to a magistrates' court for a maintenance order to furnish the court with a statement in a prescribed form, and signed by a child support officer, as to

whether or not, at the time when the statement is made, there is a maintenance assessment in force with respect to that person or the child concerned.

In this subsection—

"maintenance order" means an order of a prescribed kind for the making or securing of periodical payments to or for the benefit of a child; and

"prescribed" means prescribed by the rules.

DEFINITIONS

"child": see s.55.
"child support officer": see s.13.
"maintenance assessment": see s.54.
"prescribed": *ibid.*
"qualifying child": see s.3(1).

GENERAL NOTE

For the position in Scotland see the Child Support (Amendments to Primary Legislation) (Scotland) Order 1993 and Act of Sederunt (Child Support Act 1991) (Amendment of Ordinary Cause and Summary Cause Rules) 1993.

Subs. (1)

The maintenance orders to which this subsection applies are the same as those which fall within s.8(11) and regulations made thereunder (reg. 3(1) of the Maintenance Arrangements and Jurisdiction Regulations). These orders cease to have effect in accordance with reg. 3(2) to (6). In summary the orders cease to have effect in respect of any children with respect to whom a maintenance assessment has been made as from the effective date of the assessment. For this purpose the effective date is two days after the assessment is made. This is subject to some exceptions. These are: (i) where the order covers children in addition to those in respect of whom the maintenance assessment has been made without specifying separate amounts of maintenance for each child and (ii) where the order was made under s.8(7) or (8). In the case of Scotland when a maintenance order ceases to have effect and a child support officer subsequently loses jurisdiction to make a maintenance assessment with respect to a particular child covered by the order, the order revives so far as that child is concerned.

If a maintenance assessment is made while a maintenance order is in force in respect of the same child but is subsequently cancelled as having been made in error, and the maintenance order has ceased to have effect by virtue of reg. 3, the order is treated as having continued in force and any payments under the assessment are treated as if they were made under the order (reg. 8(1) of the Maintenance Arrangements and Jurisdiction Regulations as amended).

Subs. (2)

The agreements to which this subsection applies are maintenance agreements as defined by s.9(1) (reg. 4(1) of the Maintenance Arrangements and Jurisdiction Regulations). The extent of the enforceability of these agreements is covered by reg. 4(2) and (3). In summary the agreements become unenforceable in respect of any children with respect to whom a maintenance assessment has been made as from the effective date of the assessment. There is no special provision as to what constitutes the effective date, so the normal rules apply (see the general note to Sched. 1, para. 11). This is subject to an exception where the agreement covers children in addition to those in respect of whom the maintenance assessment has been made without specfying separate amounts of maintenance for each child. When a maintenance agreement becomes unenforceable and a child support officer subsequently loses jurisdiction to make a maintenance assessment with respect to a particular child covered by the agreement, the order becomes enforceable again so far as that child is concerned.

If a maintenance order is made while a maintenance assessment is in force in respect of the same child and subsequently revoked as having been made in error, the assessment is treated as not having been cancelled and any payments under the order are treated as if they were made under the assessment (reg. 8(2) of the Maintenance Arrangements and Jurisdiction Regulations).

Subs. (3)(a)

Schedule 1, para. 3 to the Maintenance Orders (Backdating) Order 1993 inserts s.31(12) into the Matrimonial Causes Act 1973 and s.20(9B) into the Domestic Proceedings and Magistrates' Courts Act 1978 to permit an order varying or discharging/revoking periodical payments in favour of a spouse to be backdated to the effective date (see regs. 30 and 31 of the Maintenance Assessment Procedure Regulations) of a maintenance assessment provided that the application for the maintenance order is made within six months of the date of the assessment. This is intended, *inter alia*, to cater for the situation where a previous order which contained provision for spousal maintenance and child maintenance is partly superseded by a maintenance assessment. The order might have provided a relatively small element for spousal maintenance, and a relatively large portion for child maintenance. A spouse might seek an upward variation of *her* maintenance where the assessment has produced an amount for the child smaller than that contained in the maintenance order, in order to ensure no overall loss of income for the family.

Subs. (4)

Regulation 5 of the Maintenance Arrangements and Jurisdiction Regulations provides for the child support officer to give notice of any maintenance assessment which is likely to affect a court order to the persons in respect of whom the maintenance assessment is in force and to the court itself. Regulation 6 provides for the court to give notice to the Secretary of State of any maintenance order which it makes and which is likely to affect a maintenance assessment. The way in which an order or assessment might be "affected" would appear to be that it should cease to have effect, or be cancelled. Where an *assessment* is made, reg. 3 will provide that the order, or part of it, will cease to have effect. A party to the order might seek a variation of the remaining part to take account of the assessment. Where an order is made, this will either be because the child support officer no longer has jurisdiction under s.44 or because it is an order which may continue to be made by virtue of s.8(6) to (8). Where the former is the case, the assessment should be cancelled under s.44 and reg. 7. See s.8 for further discussion of the provision made to avoid clashes of jurisdiction between the courts and the child support officer.

Subs. (5)

The Family Proceedings Courts (Child Support Act 1991) Rules 1993, rr. 8–12 provide for the appropriate statement to be made on revised Forms CHA13, CHA14, CHA15 and Forms 1, 2, 3 and 4.

Maintenance assessments

Maintenance assessments

11.—(1) Any application for a maintenance assessment made to the Secretary of State shall be referred by him to a child support officer whose duty it shall be to deal with the application in accordance with the provision made by or under this Act.

(2) The amount of child support maintenance to be fixed by any maintenance assessment shall be determined in accordance with the provisions of Part I of Schedule 1.

(3) Part II of Schedule 1 makes further provision with respect to maintenance assessments.

DEFINITIONS

"child support maintenance": see s.3(6).
"child support officer": see s.13.
"maintenance assessment": see s.54.

GENERAL NOTE

The application is made to the Secretary of State but the assessment is made by a child support officer (although see the wording of s.7(2)). An application must be referred to a child support officer. This reflects the arrangement in respect of claims in social security law.

When an assessment is made following an application under s.4 or 7, an assessment fee of £44 may become payable in respect of the assessment by the parent with care and the absent parent (regs. 2, 3(1) (*a*) and (2) and 4(1)(*a*) of the Child Support Fees Regulations). When an application is made under s.6, the assessment fee is payable by the absent parent (regs. 2, 3(1)(*b*) and (3) and 4(3)(*a*)). A collection fee of £34 will be payable in all cases under section 4, 6 or 7 of the Act and in any case in which the Secretary of State exercises his powers under s.4(2) or 7(3) (regs. 2, 3(2) and (3) and 4(3)(*b*)). Once a parent with care ceases to fall within s.6(1), the case is treated as if the application for a maintenance assessment had been made under s.4 with the consequence that a collection fee ceases to be automatically payable (reg. 3(4)).

Liability to pay fees is subject to the following exceptions: those on income support, family credit and disability working allowance; persons under 16 or under 19 but in full-time education which is not advanced education; persons whose assessable income is nil; and absent parents to whom the protected income provisions of Sched. 1 apply (reg. 3(5)). Where more than one assessment is in force in respect of a person, only one fee is payable (reg. 4(6)). Fees are a matter for the Secretary of State and not for a child support officer. Accordingly they can never be considered by a CSAT.

If both parents of a qualifying child are absent parents and an application for a maintenance assessment is made in relation to both parents, the case is a special case by virtue of reg. 19 of the Maintenance Assessments and Special Cases Regulations and a separate assessment must be made in relation to each absent parent (reg. 19(2)(*a*)).

Interim maintenance assessments

12.—(1) Where it appears to a child support officer who is required to make a maintenance assessment that he does not have sufficient information to enable him to make an assessment in accordance with the provision made by or under this Act, he may make an interim maintenance assessment.

(2) The Secretary of State may by regulations make provision as to interim maintenance assessments.

(3) The regulations may, in particular, make provision as to—

(*a*)   the procedure to be followed in making an interim maintenance assessment; and

(*b*)   the basis on which the amount of child support maintenance fixed by an interim assessment is to be calculated.

(4) Before making any interim assessment a child support officer shall, if it is reasonably practicable to do so, give written notice of his intention to make such an assessment to—

(*a*)   the absent parent concerned;

(*b*)   the person with care concerned; and

(*c*)   where the application for a maintenance assessment was made under section 7, the child concerned.

(5) Where a child support officer serves notice under subsection (4), he shall not make the proposed interim assessment before the end of such period as may be prescribed.

DEFINITIONS

"absent parent": see s.3(2).
"child support maintenance": see s.3(6).
"child support officer": see s.13.
"person with care": see s.3(3).
"prescribed": see s.54.

GENERAL NOTE

The regulations made under this section are contained in Part III of the Maintenance Assessment Procedure Regulations.

Subs. (1)

A child support officer may make an interim assessment if sufficient information is not available to make a maintenance assessment. In exercising the discretion conferred by this subsection, the child support officer must have regard to the welfare of any child likely to be affected by the decision (s.2). The possible prejudicial effect of delay in the making of a maintenance assessment will be of particular relevance here.

There are two categories of interim maintenance assessment, Category A and Category B. The amount of the interim assessment varies according to the classification of the assessment being made and the circumstances. The provisions of Part II of the Schedule to the Transitional Provisions Order do not apply to interim maintenance assessments (para. 7(2) of that Order).

The power to make an interim maintenance assessment is subject to reg. 19(3) and (4) of the Maintenance Assessments and Special Cases Regulations. This applies where both parents are absent parents and the application for a maintenance assessment is made in relation to both. In this case if information regarding the income of one absent parent is submitted and that of the other is not, an assessment must be made in respect of the parent whose income is known on the basis that the other parent's income is nil. A fresh assessment is then made when the necessary information becomes available. The effect of this is that an interim maintenance assessment cannot be made in relation to the parent whose income is known if the only thing standing in the way of a final assessment is lack of information about the other parent's income. However, an interim assessment may be made where some other information, such as information about the residence of one of the parties, is not available and of course an interim assessment can be made in relation to the other parent.

Subs. (2)

In addition to matters referred to elsewhere in this general note Part III of the Regulations deals with the following: (i) the effective date of the interim assessment (reg. 8(3)); (ii) the amount of child support maintenance payable after a maintenance assessment is finally made (reg. 8(4), (5), (8) and (10)); (iii) the cessation and cancellation of an interim assessment (regs. 8(6), (7) and (9) and 9(1) to (5)); (iv) reviews and appeals relating to interim assessments (regs. 8(11) and 9(6) to (8)).

Subs. (5)

The child support officer may not make an interim assessment until the end of the period of 14 days beginning with the day that notice was given or sent under subs. (4) (reg. 8(1)).

Child support officers

Child support officers

13.—(1) The Secretary of State shall appoint persons (to be known as child support officers) for the purpose of exercising functions—

(*a*)   conferred on them by this Act, or by any other enactment; or

(*b*)   assigned to them by the Secretary of State.

(2) A child support officer may be appointed to perform only such functions as may be specified in his instrument of appointment.

(3) The Secretary of State shall appoint a Chief Child Support Officer.

(4) It shall be the duty of the Chief Child Support Officer to—

(*a*)   advise child support officers on the discharge of their functions in relation to making, reviewing or cancelling maintenance assessments;

(*b*)   keep under review the operation of the provision made by or under this Act with respect to making, reviewing or cancelling maintenance assessments; and

(*c*)   report to the Secretary of State annually, in writing, on the matters with which the Chief Child Support Officer is concerned.

(5) The Secretary of State shall publish, in such manner as he considers appropriate, any report which he receives under subsection (4)(*c*).

(6) Any proceedings (other than for an offence) in respect of any act or omission of a child support officer which, apart from this subsection, would fall to be brought against a child support officer resident in Northern Ireland may instead be brought against the Chief Child Support Officer.

(7) For the purposes of any proceedings brought by virtue of subsection (6), the acts or omissions of the child support officer shall be treated as the acts or omissions of the Chief Child Support Officer.

DEFINITION
"maintenance assessment": see s.54.

GENERAL NOTE
Subs. (1)

A child support officer has a duty to act fairly and to obtain information necessary to deal with an application (*Duggan* v. *Chief Adjudication Officer, The Times,* December 19, 1988). Child support officers are modelled on adjudication officers in social security law. Adjudication officers have administrative duties only. They have no judicial or quasi-judicial function because there are no competing contentions on which the officer may adjudicate. The only duty is to decide on the validity of a claim. (See *R.* v. *Deputy Industrial Injuries Commissioner, exp. Moore* [1965] 1 Q.B. 456 at 486 *per* Diplock, L.J., and *R(SB) 11/89,* para. 7.) There are, however, important differences between the powers and duties of an adjudication officer and of a child support officer and they may result in the latter having a quasi-judicial function. So far as powers are concerned, the child support officer may, through the Secretary of State, have access to an inspector appointed under s.15 and to all the powers which that inspector has. An officer acting under s.18 has in all but name an appellate jurisdiction and has powers equivalent to those of a CSAT to correct and to set aside decisions under regs. 54 to 56 of the Maintenance Assessment Procedure Regulations. (Compare the position of an adjudication officer in these respects as set out in *CI 141/87*, para. 26(2).) So far as duties are concerned, the child support officer, although not holding a hearing, will often be faced with competing claims and allegations from the absent parent, the person with care and, in Scotland, the child. This is particularly so when the officer is conducting a review under s.18.

A child support officer has power to decide whether or not delegated legislation is within the power conferred by the Act (*Chief Adjudication Officer* v. *Foster* [1993] 1 All E.R. 705). In the context of the social security jurisdiction the House of Lords in *Foster* said that an adjudication officer would be expected to refer such a question to a social security tribunal. No power of referral exists in the child support jurisdiction.

Subs. (4)

The chief child support officer issues a child support officer's guide which is used by child support officers in the performance of their duties. CSATs (and child support officers for that matter) must apply the law. If there is any conflict between the law and the guide, the law must prevail. The guide has no special status when it comes to interpreting the law. It represents nothing more than one view of the proper interpretation of the relevant provision. When cited to a CSAT it is merely an argument which must be assessed and accepted or rejected by the CSAT like any other argument on the law.

Information

Information required by Secretary of State

14.—(1) The Secretary of State may make regulations requiring any information or evidence needed for the determination of any application under this Act, or any question arising in connection with such an application, or needed in connection with the collection or enforcement of child support or other maintenance under this Act, to be furnished—

(*a*) by such persons as may be determined in accordance with regulations made by the Secretary of State; and

(*b*) in accordance with the regulations.

(2) Where the Secretary of State has in his possession any information acquired by him in connection with his functions under any of the benefit Acts, he may—

(*a*) make use of that information for purposes of this Act; or

(*b*) disclose it to the Department of Health and Social Services for Northern Ireland for purposes of any enactment corresponding to this Act and having effect with respect to Northern Ireland.

(3) The Secretary of State may by regulations make provision authorising the disclosure by him or by child support officers, in such circumstances as may be prescribed, of such information held by them for purposes of this Act as may be prescribed.

(4) The provisions of Schedule 2 (which relate to information which is held for purposes other than those of this Act but which is required by the Secretary of State) shall have effect.

DEFINITIONS

"benefit Acts": see s.54.

"child support officer": see s.13

"prescribed": see s.54.

GENERAL NOTE

Subs. (1)

For the application of this subsection to the Crown see s.57(1). This subsection contains the general enabling power under which the Secretary of State may obtain the information or evidence necessary for the implementation of the Act. It applies to both information and to evidence, and therefore covers cases where information has been supplied but the evidence is lacking to prove it. The regulations made under this subsection are contained in Part II of the Information, Evidence and Disclosure Regulations. They create wider duties than those created under ss.4(4), 6(9) and 7(5). These subsections each limit the duty to cases where the person can reasonably comply. There is no equivalent to this limitation in this subsection. However, the duty created by reg. 2(1) limits the duty to supply information or evidence to cases where the information or evidence is in a person's possession or it is reasonable to expect a person to acquire it. Thus the Act emphasises the reasonableness of compliance with the duty to *supply*, whereas the regulation emphasises the reasonableness of *acquiring* the information or evidence. However, it is difficult to see any practical significance in this difference.

In normal use "information" suggests facts. However, the word here must be interpreted in the context of the stage at which and the purpose for which this section (and ss.4, 6, 7, 15 and 57(1) which also refer to "information") operates. This section operates at the preliminary stage of gathering the material which will be placed before either the Secretary of State or a child support officer for a decision to be made. It will be for the Secretary of State or the officer to decide what of the material available constitutes a fact on which reliance should be placed in making a decision. So factual information is what is obtained after evidence has been gathered and assessed. It is this information which is "required" or "needed" for the purposes specified in ss.4(4), 6(9), 7(5), 14(1) and 15(1). However, those subsections refer to "information" as something which the Secretary of State can require the person concerned to provide. It cannot therefore refer to the end product of a process of evaluation of evidence. The word must be used in a more legalistic sense of an assertion on a matter of relevant fact. "Evidence" means a document or further details which helps to test the accuracy of the assertion of relevant fact. The distinction between "information" and "evidence" is often artificial and difficult to draw in practice. Thus the production of a wage slip will be both information and evidence, as will a statement like "I know he earns £200 a week because I saw his accounts". Moreover, at the decision making stage before the Secretary of State, a child support officer or a CSAT any assertion of relevant fact is itself evidence of the truth of the fact asserted (see the general note to reg. 11 of the Tribunal Procedure Regulations). There is no discernible purpose behind the differences of wording in these sections and the best interpretation is that the various provisions are co-extensive.

Information supplied to the Secretary of State is not subject to absolute privilege and so statements made therein may give rise to an action for libel (*Purdew* v. *Seress-Smith, The Times*, September 9, 1992).

There is no single provision dealing with enforcement of the obligation to provide information or evidence. However, a variety of means exist by which pressure may be brought to bear to try to ensure that necessary information or evidence is obtained: (i) An interim maintenance assessment may be made under s.12 if the child support officer has insufficient information to enable an assessment to be made in accordance with the provision made by or under the Act. This will principally be directed against an absent parent, although if that parent's income is such that a maintenance assessment higher than the value of the interim assessment would be made, making such an assessment may work in that parent's favour; (ii) An inspector may be appointed under s.15 and that may lead to an offence being committed under s.15(9). This may be directed against any person under a duty to supply information; (iii) A reduced benefit direction may be made under s.46. This will be directed against the parent with care; (iv) In some circumstances where information about income or capital is already known to the child support officer and confirmation or more up-to-date information cannot be obtained, it may be appropriate to infer that there has been an intentional deprivation of that income or capital so that Sched. 1, para. 27 to the Maintenance Assessments and Special Cases Regulations applies. Alternatively the circumstances may justify an inference that there has been a failure to secure income or capital within that paragraph; (v) Failure by one person to provide information or evidence may be remedied by obtaining it from another source under the wide powers given in the Information, Evidence and Disclosure Regulations; (vi) A person who fails to maintain a person whom he is liable to maintain may commit an offence under s.105 of the Social Security Administration Act 1992, but note that the duty to maintain created by s.1(1) of the Child Support Act cannot be used as a basis for that offence since it only applies for the purpose of this Act; (vii) It may also be possible to obtain an order under s.106 of the Social Security Administration Act 1992 for the recovery of benefit from a person liable to maintain another who receives income support. Once again the duty created by s.1(1) of this Act cannot be used for this purpose.

Subs. (3)

The regulations made under this subsection are contained in Part III of the Information, Evidence and Disclosure Regulations. The unauthorised disclosure of information may be an offence under s.50.

Powers of inspectors

15.—(1) Where, in a particular case, the Secretary of State considers it appropriate to do so for the purpose of acquiring information which he or any child support officer requires for purposes of this Act, he may appoint a person to act as an inspector under this section.

(2) Every inspector shall be furnished with a certificate of his appointment.

(3) Without prejudice to his being appointed to act in relation to any other case, or being appointed to act for a further period in relation to the case in question, an inspector's appointment shall cease at the end of such period as may be specified.

(4) An inspector shall have power—

(*a*) to enter at all reasonable times—

    (i) any specified premises, other than premises used solely as a dwelling-house; and

    (ii) any premises which are not specified but which are used by any specified person for the purpose of carrying on any trade, profession, vocation or business; and

(*b*) to make such examination and enquiry there as he considers appropriate.

(5) An inspector exercising his powers may question any person aged 18 or over whom he finds on the premises.

(6) If required to do so by an inspector exercising his powers, any person who is or has been—

(*a*) an occupier of the premises in question;

(*b*) an employer or an employee working at or from those premises;

(*c*) carrying on at or from those premises any trade, profession, vocation or business;

(*d*) an employee or agent of any person mentioned in paragraphs (*a*) to (*c*),

shall furnish to the inspector all such information and documents as the inspector may reasonably require.

(7) No person shall be required under this section to answer any question or to give any evidence tending to incriminate himself or, in the case of a person who is married, his or her spouse.

(8) On applying for admission to any premises in the exercise of his powers, an inspector shall, if so required, produce his certificate.

(9) If any person—

(*a*) intentionally delays or obstructs any inspector exercising his powers; or

(*b*) without reasonable excuse, refuses or neglects to answer any question or furnish any information or to produce any document when required to do so under this section,

he shall be guilty of an offence and liable on summary conviction to a fine not exceeding level 3 on the standard scale.

(10) In this section—

"certificate" means a certificate of appointment issued under this section;

"inspector" means an inspector appointed under this section;

"powers" means powers conferred by this section; and

"specified" means specified in the certificate in question.

DEFINITION

"child support officer": see s.13.

GENERAL NOTE

For the application of this section to the Crown see s.57(2) and (3). An inspector appointed under this section may enter Crown premises in order to exercise any powers conferred by this section provided that the Queen is not in residence (reg. 7 of the Information, Evidence and Disclosure Regulations).

An inspector may only be appointed to acquire "information". However, the confusion noted in the general note to s.14 is apparent here also. Subsection (7) grants exemption from the giving of self-incriminating "evidence", while the offence created by subs. (9) applies to the failure to produce documents as well as to the failure to give information, so that the documents must be required as evidence rather than for the information they contain.

Subs. (4)(a)(i)

The limitation to this sub-paragraph only applies to premises which are used *solely* as a dwelling-house. Depending on the circumstances it may not apply in cases where the person is running a business from home. Where there is living accommodation which is separate from the work place, for example a flat over a shop, the inspector will be able to enter the shop but not the flat. However where a business is run from the study or a kitchen table, the inspector may enter the whole premises.

Reviews and appeals

Periodical reviews

16.—(1) The Secretary of State shall make such arrangements as he considers necessary to secure that, where any maintenance assessment has been in force for a prescribed period, the amount of child support maintenance fixed by that assessment ("the original assessment") is reviewed by a child support officer under this section as soon as is reasonably practicable after the end of that prescribed period.

(2) Before conducting any review under this section, the child support officer concerned shall give, to such persons as may be prescribed, such notice of the proposed review as may be prescribed.

(3) A review shall be conducted under this section as if a fresh application for a maintenance assessment had been made by the person in whose favour the original assessment was made.

(4) On completing any review under this section, the child support officer concerned shall make a fresh maintenance assessment, unless he is satisfied that the original assessment has ceased to have effect or should be brought to an end.

(5) Where a fresh maintenance assessment is made under subsection (4), it shall take effect—

    (*a*) on the day immediately after the end of the prescribed period mentioned in subsection (1); or

    (*b*) in such circumstances as may be prescribed, on such later date as may be determined in accordance with regulations made by the Secretary of State.

(6) The Secretary of State may by regulations prescribe circumstances (for example, where the maintenance assessment is about to terminate) in which a child support officer may decide not to conduct a review under this section.

DEFINITIONS

"child support maintenance": see s.3(6).

"child support officer": see s.13.

"maintenance assessment": see s.54.

"prescribed": *ibid.*

GENERAL NOTE

The Act provides for review in a number of ways. A review may arise automatically (this section). It may also be instigated by one of the parties concerned either on the ground that a decision was wrong (s.18) or on the ground that there has been a change of circumstances since the decision which justifies it being changed (s.17). Alternatively, a review may be instigated by a child support officer (s.19). Reviews of reduced benefit directions made under s.46 are covered by reg. 42 of the Maintenance Assessment Procedure Regulations and reviews of decisions relating to contribution to maintenance by deduction from benefit are covered by Sched. 4 to the Maintenance Assessments and Special Cases Regulations. Reviews have been the subject of some difficult decisions in social security law. Fortunately much of the learning from that jurisdiction is inapplicable in view of the drafting in child support law. However, the drafting in this context gives rise to its own difficult questions and it is not always clear to what extent the principles from social security law are applicable in the child support context.

This section provides for regular reviews of all maintenance assessments, interim or otherwise. It must be read in conjunction with regs. 17 and 18 of the Maintenance Assessment Procedure Regulations.

Subs. (1)

A periodic review is to be conducted after a maintenance assessment, or a fresh maintenance assessment following a review under s.17, has been in force for a period of 52 weeks (regs. 17(1) and (2) and 18(2)). Special provision is made for the case where a review is conducted under s.17 and the notice of that review is given or sent not earlier than eight weeks prior to a periodic review, but no assessment is made following that review as a result of the operation of reg. 20, 21 or 22 (which deal with minimum permissible adjustment to maintenance as a result of a review under s.17). In this case the review is treated as if it were made under s.16 and the fresh assessment made is the one that would have been made had it not been for the operation of reg. 20, 21 or 22 (reg. 18(1)). Since the fresh assessment is treated as if it were made following a s.16 review, it will come into force in accordance with subs. (5)(*a*).

In determining the period of time within which it is reasonably practicable for the review to be carried out, it is permissible to take into account matters independent of the individual assessment, such as the number of assessments awaiting review and the number of child support officers available to deal with the work load (*R.* v. *Secretary of State for Social Services, ex p. CPAG* [1989] 1 All E.R. 1047 at 1054 *per* Woolf, L.J.).

Subs. (2)

A child support officer must give 14 days' notice of the proposed review to the relevant persons as defined in reg. 1(2) (reg. 17(4)). The officer shall request all relevant persons, subject to the exceptions in reg. 17(6) and (7), to provide such information or evidence as to their current circumstances as may be specified (reg. 17(5)).

Subs. (5)(b)

No regulations have been made under this paragraph.

Subs. (6)

A child support officer may decide not to conduct a review if any fresh maintenance assessment made following the review would cease to have effect within 28 days of its effective date (reg. 17(3)).

Reviews on change of circumstances

17.—(1) Where a maintenance assessment is in force—

(*a*) the absent parent or person with care with respect to whom it was made; or

(*b*) where the application for the assessment was made under section 7, either of them or the child concerned,

may apply to the Secretary of State for the amount of child support maintenance fixed by that assessment ("the original assessment") to be reviewed under this section.

(2) An application under this section may be made only on the ground that, by reason of a change of circumstance since the original assessment was made, the amount of child support maintenance payable by the absent parent would be significantly different if it were to be fixed by a maintenance assessment made by reference to the circumstances of the case as at the date of the application.

(3) The child support officer to whom an application under this section has been referred shall not proceed unless, on the information before him, he considers that it is likely that he will be required by subsection (6) to make a fresh maintenance assessment if he conducts the review applied for.

(4) Before conducting any review under this section, the child support officer concerned shall give to such persons as may be prescribed, such notice of the proposed review as may be prescribed.

(5) A review shall be conducted under this section as if a fresh application for a maintenance assessment had been made by the person in whose favour the original assessment was made.

(6) On completing any review under this section, the child support officer concerned shall make a fresh maintenance assessment, unless—

(*a*) he is satisfied that the original assessment has ceased to have effect or should be brought to an end; or

(*b*) the difference between the amount of child support maintenance fixed by the original assessment and the amount that would be fixed if a fresh assessment were to be made as a result of the review is less than such amount as may be prescribed.

DEFINITIONS
"absent parent": see s.3(2).
"child": see s.55.
"child support maintenance": see s.3(6).
"child support officer": see s.13.
"maintenance assessment": see s.54.
"person with care": see s.3(3).
"prescribed": see s.54.

GENERAL NOTE
This section provides for reviews where there has been a change of circumstances since a maintenance assessment was made. It must be read in conjunction with regs. 19 to 23 of the Maintenance Assessment Procedure Regulations. It does not apply to Category A interim maintenance assessments (reg. 8(11)). It only applies where there is a maintenance assessment in force. Where this is not the case, but a change of circumstances occurs which would justify the making of an assessment, the proper course is to apply for a maintenance assessment under s.4, 6 or 7. A child support officer dealing with a review under this section has no power to correct any errors in the assessment which may be identified in the course of the review. These must be dealt with separately, by a review under either s.18 or 19.

Subs. (1)
In accordance with the usual division of responsibility between the Secretary of State and the child support officer, the application is made to the former who then refers it to the latter. An application for a review under this section of a maintenance assessment which is in force and which was made following an application under s.6 is deemed to be made if the parent with care under that assessment authorises the Secretary of State to take action against the same absent parent in respect of an additional child (reg. 19(5)).

The burden of proof is on the applicant for the review to show on the balance of probabilities that there has been a relevant change of circumstances. If the child support officer is satisfied that there has been such a change, a fresh assessment will be made unless the case falls within subs. (6).

Subs. (2)
The effect of this paragraph is unclear. It specifies the ground on which an application for review may be sought, namely that as a result of a change of circumstances, the maintenance payable would be significantly different if assessed at the date of the application for the review. The requirement that the maintenance would be "significantly different" causes problems. Unlike subs. (3), this is not expressly tied to subs. (6), although in practice the words are likely to be interpreted by reference to that subsection. The emphasis on the application for review and the ground of the application, rather than on the circumstances in which a fresh assessment may be made following the review, suggests that the subsection goes to jurisdiction and that an application for a review which is not based on this ground will not be valid and so will not be referred by the Secretary of State to a child support officer. This interpretation is not satisfactory for a number of reasons. It will often be difficult or impossible to decide whether a change of circumstances will produce a significant difference in the child support maintenance payable until the review has begun. At best it allows the Secretary of State to filter out clear cases in which a fresh assessment would not be made, which is an unsatisfactory basis for a provision which goes to jurisdiction. Moreover, it has the effect that this subsection overlaps with subs. (3) which provides that a child support officer shall not proceed with a review unless it appears likely that a fresh assessment will be made. The better view is that, despite the emphasis on the application, the subsection is providing the basis on which a fresh assessment may be made, provided that the condition in subs. (6) is met.

A party who applies for a review should indicate whether the application is made under s.17 or 18. However, a technicality should not be used to defeat a meritorious application for review, so that if it is possible to see from the application that it properly refers to a particular basis, it should be dealt with under that head (*CSSB 465/89*, para. 9).

At the risk of stating the obvious, it is essential that circumstances should have changed from the actual position at the time when the assessment currently in force was made. It is not enough that the circumstances are different from the position which the child support officer who made the current assessment believed them to be. Such a case does not involve a change of circumstances. At best it involves a mistake or ignorance of material fact and must be dealt with under s.18 or 19.

A change of law may amount to a change of circumstances (*R(G) 1/80*, para. 12 and *R(A) 4/81*, para. 8). In order to amount to a change of circumstances, a change in the law must render the assessment inaccurate (*R(I) 56/54*, para. 28 and *R(A) 2/81*, para. 15). This will be the case, for example, where the change of law is retrospective (*R(G) 3/58*, para. 10).

After a change of circumstances has been through the adjudication process, it ceases to be a change of circumstance and cannot be relied upon again (Common Appendix to *CSSB 281/89*, *CSSB 297/89*, *CSSB 298/89*, *CSSB 308/89* and *CSSB 433/89*, para. 40).

Subs. (3)

This subsection provides that the child support officer shall not proceed, unless it is likely that a fresh assessment will be required under subs. (6). Thus, the officer must refuse to proceed, if it is likely that there has been no change of circumstance or that the difference in amount between the original and fresh assessments would be less than the prescribed minimum. The wording of this subsection (it says simply "proceed" rather than "proceed with the review") and its position before subs. (4) (which requires notice before a review can be conducted) show that it can apply as soon as an application has been received so as to prevent any further action by the officer as well as at any subsequent stage. This provision can save the time and cost both of collecting the information and evidence necessary for a review and of undertaking calculations, but it also allows the officer to make a judgment on the likely outcome of a case before all the relevant details have been collected and to do so on the basis of the likely, rather than the certain, outcome of the review. However, a disappointed applicant may seek a review of the refusal to proceed under s.18.

Subs. (4)

14 days' notice must be given (reg. 19(1)).

Subs. (5)

The officer shall request all relevant persons to provide such information or evidence as to their current circumstances as may be specified (reg. 19(2)). This duty is subject to the exceptions in reg. 19(3), (4) and (4A) (*ibid*).

Subs. (6)

If the effect of the change of circumstances is that the assessment has ceased to have effect or should be brought to an end, that will be the effect. If the effect of the change of circumstances is that the amount of maintenance payable should be different, a fresh assessment will be made unless the amount of the difference is less than the prescribed minimum. The minimum is fixed in absolute terms; there is no sliding scale according to the amount of maintenance payable under the original assessment.

The prescribed amount is determined by regs. 20 to 22. The amount is £1 per week if the protected income provisions of Sched. 1, para. 6 apply or if the children in respect of whom the fresh assessment would be made are not identical with those in respect of whom the original assessment was made (reg. 20(2) and (3)). In all other cases, it is £10 per week (reg. 20(1)).

Specific provision is made for the application of reg. 20 to two of the special cases. If the case is a special case by virtue of reg. 22 of the Maintenance Assessments and Special Cases Regulations (multiple applications in respect of the same absent parent) and there is a change in the circumstances of the absent parent, the provisions of reg. 20 apply to the aggregate amount of the fresh assessments (reg. 21(2)). If there has been a change in the circumstances of a person with care and not of the absent parent, the provisions of reg. 20 apply to each fresh assessment (reg. 21(3)). If the case is a special case by virtue of reg. 23 of the Maintenance Assessments and Special Cases Regulations (person with care of children of more than one absent parent), the provisions of reg. 20 apply to each assessment (reg. 22(2)).

Reviews of decisions of child support officers

18.—(1) Where—

(*a*) an application for a maintenance assessment is refused; or

(*b*) an application, under section 17, for the review of a maintenance assessment which is in force is refused,

the person who made that application may apply to the Secretary of State for the refusal to be reviewed.

(2) Where a maintenance assessment is in force—

(*a*) the absent parent or person with care with respect to whom it was made; or

(*b*) where the application for the assessment was made under section 7, either of them or the child concerned, may apply to the Secretary of State for the assessment to be reviewed.

(3) Where a maintenance assessment is cancelled the appropriate person may apply to the Secretary of State for the cancellation to be reviewed.

(4) Where an application for the cancellation of a maintenance assessment is refused, the appropriate person may apply to the Secretary of State for the refusal to be reviewed.

(5) An application under this section shall give the applicant's reasons (in writing) for making it.

(6) The Secretary of State shall refer to a child support officer any application under this section which is duly made; and the child support officer shall conduct the review applied for unless in his opinion there are no reasonable grounds for supposing that the refusal, assessment or cancellation in question—

(*a*) was made in ignorance of a material fact;

(*b*) was based on a mistake as to a material fact;

(*c*) was wrong in law.

(7) The Secretary of State shall arrange for a review under this section to be conducted by a child support officer who played no part in taking the decision which is to be reviewed.

(8) Before conducting any review under this section, the child support officer concerned shall give to such persons as may be prescribed, such notice of the proposed review as may be prescribed.

(9) If a child support officer conducting a review under this section is satisfied that a maintenance assessment or (as the case may be) a fresh maintenance assessment should be made, he shall proceed accordingly.

(10) In making a maintenance assessment by virtue of subsection (9), a child support officer shall, if he is aware of any material change of circumstance since the decision being reviewed was taken, take account of that change of circumstance in making the assessment.

(11) The Secretary of State may make regulations—

(*a*) as to the manner in which applications under this section are to be made;

(*b*) as to the procedure to be followed with respect to such applications; and

(*c*) with respect to reviews conducted under this section.

(12) In this section "appropriate person" means—

(*a*) the absent parent or person with care with respect to whom the maintenance assessment in question was, or remains, in force; or

(*b*) where the application for that assessment was made under section 7, either of those persons or the child concerned.

DEFINITIONS

"absent parent": see s.3(2).

"child": see s.55.

"child support officer": see s.13.

"maintenance assessment": see s.54.

"person with care": see s.3(3).

"prescribed": see s.54.

GENERAL NOTE

Structure

This section creates a structure which is complex and not entirely clear. The procedure is set in motion by an application (subss. (1) to (5)). This application is made to the Secretary of State, who must refer it to a child support officer who played no part in taking the decision of which a review is sought (subss. (6) and (7)). The officer must decide whether to conduct a review. This requires a decision to be made on whether or not there are reasonable grounds to believe that one of the heads specified in subs. (6) is satisfied. If there are grounds to justify conducting a review, notice of a proposed review will be given and the officer will in due course make a decision (subss. (8) to (10)).

Extensions of section 18

The provisions of this section are extended to cover the following cases:

Regulation 12 of the Arrears, Interest and Adjustment of Maintenance Assessments Regulations extends this section to cover decisions by a child support officer on adjustments of the amount payable under a maintenance assessment and calculations of arrears or interest on arrears. However, the power given by subs. (10) to a child support officer is not extended to such reviews (reg. 12(1)).

Generally an absent parent may not apply for a review of an interim maintenance assessment (reg. 8(11) of the Maintenance Assessment Procedure Regulations). However, an absent parent may apply for a review of a refusal by a child support officer to cancel an interim maintenance assessment following an application under reg. 9(1) of the Maintenance Assessment Procedure Regulations. Subsections (5) to (8) of this section apply to such reviews and subs. (6) is modified to reflect this (reg. 9(6) to (8)).

The provisions of subs. (2) apply to a maintenance assessment which has been, but is no longer, in force (reg. 29(1) of the Maintenance Assessment Procedure Regulations).

By virtue of reg. 52(4) of the Maintenance Assessment Procedure Regulations, this section applies to permit reviews of decisions by a child support officer on whether a maintenance assessment has ceased to have effect. Subsections (5) to (9) and (11) apply to such reviews, and subss. (6) and (9) are modified to reflect this (reg. 52(5)).

Subsections (5) to (7) apply in modified form to reviews of decisions relating to contribution to maintenance by deduction from benefit (Sched. 4, paras. 6 and 7 of the Maintenance Assessments and Special Cases Regulations).

Subs. (5)

For a discussion of the meaning of "reasons" see the general notes to regs. 3(10) and 8(1) of the Tribunal Procedure Regulations.

Subs. (6)

The general rule is that applications for review under this section will only be valid and referred to a child support officer, if they are made within 28 days of notification of the decision to which the application relates (regs. 24(1) and 29(2)), unless there has been unavoidable delay (regs. 24(2) and 29(3)). The only exception to this rule is that it does not apply to applications for review made under subs. (2), although it does apply to applications made under that subsection as extended by reg. 29(1). If more than one application for review of the same decision is referred to a child support officer, only one review is carried out (reg. 26).

This subsection provides an initial hurdle which must be overcome if the review is to be conducted. It is clear from the wording of this subsection that the decision must be, and can only be, taken before the officer embarks on a review. In contrast to s.17(3), the officer's only power is to decide not to conduct the review; there is no power to decide not to proceed with it once it has begun. The question for the child support officer is whether there are reasonable grounds to believe that the decision was based on incorrect facts or was wrong in law. As with s.17(3), this is a time- and cost-saving provision which allows a child support officer to make an initial judgment on the likely outcome of a review. The judgment will be made on the basis of the reasons supplied under subs. (5), but without inviting representations, and so without the information which might emerge from those representations. However, a disappointed applicant may appeal to a CSAT under s.20(1)(*b*).

If the officer considers that the hurdle created by this subsection is overcome and proceeds to conduct the review, it is not possible for the decision to be challenged before a CSAT or a Commissioner. A number of factors support this interpretation: (i) The words "in his opinion" show that this is a subjective decision which is not to be challenged except in so far as there is an express power so to do. The only express power is contained in s.20(1)(*b*) and it is limited to cases where the application to review is refused. Section 20(1) could easily have been worded to allow an appeal against any decision taken by a child support officer under s.18. However, it does not do so and the wording used can only apply to refusals under this subsection and to decisions made once a review has been conducted; (ii) The time- and cost-saving nature of the decision suggests that it is not appropriate to re-open it once the review has been conducted; (iii) Moreover, the decision under this subsection is one taken on limited information, namely, the application for a review. It would be inappropriate to allow it to be reconsidered with the benefit of hindsight in the light of the information which has emerged in the course of the review. In short this subsection contains an initial procedural hurdle and not a requirement which goes to the jurisdiction of the child support officer, a CSAT or a Commissioner.

The burden of proof is on the person who alleges the decision under review was wrong (*R(I) 1/71*, paras. 9 and 16). If the child support officer is carrying out a single review following two or more applications for a review of the same decision (see above), the burden is on each applicant to establish the alleged error which each has identified. An alternative way of looking at this is to say that there is a presumption that the decision being reviewed is not erroneous.

Paragraphs (*a*) and (*b*) only apply to a "material fact." The meaning of these words has been discussed in social security law. In that context it is essential that there should be a proven fact and not merely an assertion. However, it is not essential that the fact should be sufficient to show that the decision under review was wrong. The appropriate test was discussed in *Saker* v. *Secretary of State for Social Services* which is reported with *R(I) 1/88*. The test was formulated in two different ways. Lloyd, L.J., said that a fact was material if it was a fact to which the officer or tribunal would have wished to direct its mind regardless of whether or not it would have affected the decision made. Nicholls, L.J., said that the test would *generally* be satisfied if the fact would have called for serious consideration and might have affected the decision. Since Staughton, L.J., was able to agree with both judgments, it is likely that there is little or no practical difference between the two formulations.

This meaning requires some adjustment in the child support context. First, in view of the fact that this subsection operates before a review is conducted, it is not essential that the matter in question should be a proven fact. It is sufficient that there should be reasonable grounds that it might be proven. Second, *Saker* permits a review to be undertaken, even if the fact in question would not justify the revision of the decision under review. Whereas the process of review and revision in social security law is conducted on the basis of the request for the review and of any enquiries the adjudication officer chooses to make, in this context it is conducted on the more formal basis of representations invited from relevant persons. It is appropriate, therefore, that reviews should not be conducted on the basis of an alleged fact which would have been considered, but which would not have affected the decision. In short, the structure of a s.18 review, with its time-saving provision and formal representations, is opposed to the leniency with which *Saker* interpeted the words "material fact."

After a review on the basis of ignorance of a material fact has been through the adjudication process, there can no longer be said to be ignorance of that fact and it cannot be relied upon again (Common Appendix to *CSSB 281/89*, *CSSB 297/89*, *CSSB 298/89*, *CSSB 308/89* and *CSSB 433/89*, para. 40). However, this is not the position in the case of a mistake as to fact.

Paragraph (*c*) can present problems where the decision in question turns on the interpretation of facts on which different child support officers could reach different conclusions, such as whether a person was habitually resident in the United Kingdom, or whether persons were living in the same household. The fact that the officer acting under s.18 would have reached a different conclusion from the other officer is not sufficient to make the earlier decision wrong in law for the purposes of this paragraph. However, if the earlier officer's decision was one that no officer, properly advised and acting reasonably, could have reached on the evidence, then the earlier decision will be wrong in law (*Crake* v. *Supplementary Benefits Commission* [1982] 1 All E.R. 498 at 501 *per* Woolf, J.). These problems are, of course, avoided if the case falls within para. (*a*) or (*b*).

Subs. (8)

14 days' notice of a proposed review must be given to relevant persons and representations, in writing or in person, must be invited from them (reg. 25).

Subs. (9)

The officer must make an assessment, or a fresh asssessment, if satisfied that one should be made. This duty is not expressly tied to the heads in subs. (6). There would be no problem in tying the duty in this subsection to proof of an error of law, but to tie it to proof of ignorance of, or mistake as to, a material fact would not be possible, if the *Saker* interpretation is accepted, since, according to that case, a material fact is not necessarily one which affected the decision being reviewed (see the general note to subs. (6)). Since this subsection is not tied to subs. (6), it is possible that a child support officer might be satisfied that a fresh assessment should be made in a case other than one where the original assessment was affected by ignorance of, or mistake as to, material fact or by an error of law (or a change of circumstances, which is covered by s.17). The most likely case in which this could arise is where two officers, looking at the same facts and properly advised, could each reasonably reach different conclusions. Examples of when this might occur have been given in the general note to subs. (6). Other examples might arise where the child support officer has a discretion which could reasonably be exercised in different ways. If the view of the officer acting under this section can be substituted for that of the officer who made the decision under review, the result is that an assessment, or a fresh assessment, may be made on a basis which of itself would not have overcome the hurdle imposed by subs. (6).

This interpretation of this subsection is in line with the above analysis of subs. (6). It means that once a case has overcome the hurdle in subs. (6), the child support officer is entitled to make a fresh decision on the whole of the circumstances of the case. However, it could be argued that an equally rational interpretation would be that the section is written so as to prevent decisions being changed simply because different officers take different but equally reasonable views of the same facts. There are three possible responses to this argument. The first is that in practice as a matter of comity or courtesy one child support officer's view would not readily be substituted for that of a fellow officer in the circumstances being considered. The second possible answer is that it is far from easy to distinguish, in the type of case being considered here, between a case which involves an error of law and one which does not, so it would often be possible to justify making a maintenance assessment, or a fresh assessment, on the ground that the original decision involved an error of law. The final and best response is that the argument is based on a confusion between the concept of a review in social security law and the very different review process in child support law. In the latter context the procedure is more akin to an appeal (see the appeal-like procedures laid down in reg. 25 of the Maintenance Assessment Procedure Regulations) and it is appropriate that the child support officer should have the power to conduct a complete reconsideration of the case (subject to overcoming the initial filter of subs. (6)) and reach a fresh decision as the officer considers appropriate, just as a CSAT or Commissioner would do.

If the fresh assessment is being considered in a review of a refusal of an application to review under s.17, the same limitations as to minimum alteration apply as apply to reviews made under that section (reg. 27).

Subs. (10)

A change of circumstances is not one of the heads in subs. (6) which justifies a child support officer conducting a review. However, if such a change is identified in the course of a review, it may be taken into account in the making of the fresh assessment. This convenient procedure prevents the need for either a separate application and review under s.17 or action by the officer under s.19. It is not clear whether the fact that there has been a material change of circumstance is by itself sufficient to justify a fresh assessment under subs. (9). The wording suggests that the change of circumstance is to be taken into account at the stage of the making of the fresh assessment, but it is silent as to whether or not it may be taken into account at the earlier stage of deciding whether an assessment should be made. If a change of circumstance is the only matter which would justify a fresh assessment, the need for further action under s.17 or 19 would be avoided if the decision could be made under s.18. This could be justified as allowing the child support officer to make a fresh decision on the whole of the case as it appears at the time of the s.18 decision. However, the better view is that there are two reasons which show that a fresh assessment under this section may not be solely made on the basis of a change of circumstances. The first is that a fresh assessment under this section would result in a right to appeal to a CSAT under s.20 (1) which would not arise if the decision were made under s.17 or 19, thereby avoiding the two tier review structure prior to an appeal on this issue. The second reason is that acting under this section in such circumstances would avoid the prescribed minimum alteration laid down by s.17(6)(*b*). This is in contrast to the position where a review is conducted under s.19, or under this section following an application under subs. (1)(*b*), in which cases the assessment is subject to those limitations (see the general notes to s.19 and subs. (9)).

Reviews at instigation of child support officers

19.—(1) Where a child support officer is not conducting a review under section 16, 17 or 18 but is nevertheless satisfied that a maintenance assessment which is in force is defective by reason of—

   (*a*) having been made in ignorance of a material fact;
   (*b*) having been based on a mistake as to a material fact; or
   (*c*) being wrong in law,

he may make a fresh maintenance assessment on the assumption that the person in whose favour the original assessment was made has made a fresh application for a maintenance assessment.

   (2) Where a child support officer is not conducting such a review but is nevertheless satisfied that if an application were to be made under section 17 or 18 it would be appropriate to make a fresh maintenance assessment, he may do so.

   (3) Before making a fresh maintenance assessment under this section, a child

support officer shall give to such persons as may be prescribed such notice of his proposal to make a fresh assessment as may be prescribed.

DEFINITIONS
"child support officer": see s.13.
"maintenance assessment": see s.54.
"prescribed": *ibid.*

GENERAL NOTE
This section allows for the making of a fresh assessment on the initiative of a child support officer. It is a useful measure which allows an officer to act in clear cases where a fresh maintenance assessment is appropriate without requiring an application for a review to be made to the Secretary of State. Any officer may act. This section is not limited, as s.18 is, to action by an officer other than the one who took the earlier decision. Although this section allows an officer to act in circumstances which would justify a fresh assessment being made on a review under s.18, the officer does not act under that section. Accordingly, s.20(1) does not apply, with the effect that no appeal lies against a decision under this section. (See, however, the wording of reg. 10(4)(c) of the Maintenance Assessment Procedure Regulations, which appears to equate reviews conducted under s.19 which could have been conducted under s.18 with those conducted under s.18, requiring the same notice of the provisions of s.20 to be given in each case.) If a party wishes to appeal, an application must be made for a review under s.18 in order to generate a decision which is subject to appeal to a CSAT.

If the fresh assessment which is made under this section could have been made under s.17 or 18(1)(*b*), the same limitations as to minimum alteration apply as apply to reviews made under that section (regs. 23, 27 and 28 of the Maintenance Assessment Procedure Regulations).

The provisions of s.19 are extended by reg. 12(5) and (6) of the Arrears, Interest and Adjustment of Maintenance Assessments Regulations to cover decisions by a child support officer on adjustments of the amount payable under a maintenance assessment and calculations of arrears or interest on arrears.

Subs. (1)
This subsection allows a fresh maintenance assessment to be made on a child support officer's own initiative provided that (i) the officer is not at the time conducting a review under s.16, 17 or 18 and (ii) there is an assessment in force which (iii) is defective on one of three specified grounds. The subsection creates a more stringent test than that laid down in s.18(6). There, it is only necessary for the child support officer to be satisfied that there are reasonable grounds for believing that a decision may be wrong. Here it is necessary for the officer to be satisfied that it is defective. This means that "material fact" cannot bear the meaning here which was given to those words in a social security context in *Saker* v. *Secretary of State for Social Services* which is reported with *R(I) 1/88* (see the general note to s.18(6)). Instead it must mean a fact which would have affected the decision made. Moreover, this subsection only applies to maintenance assessments, whereas s.18(6) applies to refusals and cancellations as well as to assessments.

Subs. (2)
This subsection also allows a fresh maintenance assessment to be made on a child support officer's own initiative, provided (i) that the officer is not at the time conducting a review under ss.16, 17 or 18, but (ii) that it would be appropriate to make a *fresh* assessment, if an application were made under either of those sections. This power only allows the making of a fresh assessment and so can only be used where there is an existing assessment. It can, therefore, be used to make a fresh assessment where a child support officer becomes aware of a change of circumstances. It can also be used, if an officer becomes aware that an application for a fresh assessment under s.17 was incorrectly refused, since that is something which could be done under s.18. However, it cannot be used to overturn a refusal to make a maintenance assessment, nor can it be used to cancel an assessment or to revoke a cancellation. In so far as the current maintenance assessment was defective when it was made, this subsection overlaps with subs. (1).

Subs. (3)
This subsection has not been brought into force.

Appeals

20.—(1) Any person who is aggrieved by the decision of a child support officer—

(*a*)   on a review under section 18;

(*b*)   to refuse an application for such a review,

may appeal to a child support appeal tribunal against that decision.

(2) Except with leave of the chairman of a child support appeal tribunal, no appeal under this section shall be brought after the end of the period of 28 days beginning with the date on which notification was given of the decision in question.

(3) Where an appeal under this section is allowed, the tribunal shall remit the case to the Secretary of State, who shall arrange for it to be dealt with by a child support officer.

(4) The tribunal may, in remitting any case under this section, give such directions as it considers appropriate.

DEFINITIONS

"child support appeal tribunal": see s.54.

"child support officer": see s.13.

GENERAL NOTE

If a person purports to appeal before a child support officer makes a decision under s.18, there is technically no appeal. A fresh appeal must be made when a decision has been made. However, a chairman may decide to treat the first "appeal" as inchoate until the s.18 decision is given, as the Commissioner did in *CIS 8/90*, para. 7, rather than require a fresh appeal. See the general note to s.45 below for discussion of appeals concerning parentage which are to be heard by a court rather than by a CSAT.

Subs. (1)

A right of appeal to a CSAT arises against a decision made under s.18 of the Act. The provisions of that section are extended as noted in the general note to that section. This section also applies (in whole or in part) to appeals against reviews under reg. 42 of the Maintenance Assessment Procedure Regulations following a reduced benefit direction (reg. 42(10)) and to appeals against reviews or refusals to review decisions relating to contribution to maintenance by deduction from benefit under Sched. 5, para. 6 to the Maintenance Assessments and Special Cases Regulations (Sched. 5, para. 8 to those Regulations). A right of appeal also arises under s.46(7).

If the appeal is against the refusal to review, the CSAT will have to decide whether there were grounds for review. If it decides that there were, the case must be referred to the Secretary of State who must arrange for a child support officer to carry out the review. The CSAT cannot carry out the review itself, since it has no power to deal with questions first arising on an appeal (see the general note to s.21). For further discussion of the significance of the wording of this subsection, see the general note to s.18(6).

Any "person aggrieved" by a decision of a child support officer may appeal to a CSAT. This phrase occurs in a variety of statutory contexts. It is possible to distill from the authorities some general principles which will govern its interpretation in this context, but it is less easy to anticipate how they will be applied in practice by the full-time chairman based at the Central Office in Salford Quays. A person aggrieved is one who has a close connection with the decision of the child support officer, whose interests are immediately affected by it, and who feels that this effect is adverse. The difficulty lies in deciding how close that connection must be and the nature of the interest that must be affected. Attempts at prediction are likely to miss the mark, but two possible areas of difficulty may be tentatively suggested. One is where the decision has a consequential financial effect, for example, a partner of the absent parent may feel that the decision takes inadequate account of her children, or a spouse who is not the person with care may feel that her own maintenance will be less as a result of the decision. The other possible area of difficulty is where the person seeking to appeal has an emotional rather than a financial interest, for example, where a grandparent feels that the decision makes inadequate provision for the children.

The requirement that the person seeking to appeal should be aggrieved determines who may appeal, but it does not limit the grounds on which an appeal may be based. An appeal lies to a CSAT as of right; it is not necessary to obtain leave and it is likely that minimal grounds will be accepted as sufficient (see the general note to reg. 3(10) of the Tribunal Procedure Regulations). Thus, "aggrieved" will not be used to impose any test of the strength of the grounds of appeal, or of the importance of the decision for the person concerned. It will not, therefore, be interpreted so as to bring in any requirement that the decision should be burdensome or oppressive to the person concerned.

The majority of appeals will not raise difficult questions of interpretation. They will be made by persons who are clearly persons aggrieved: the absent parent, the person with care and, in the case of Scotland, a child who has attained the age of 12. It is clear from basic principles that a child support officer may not appeal to a CSAT. Such an officer has no interest in a decision other than to ensure that the law has been correctly applied, and cannot, therefore, be aggrieved. This view is supported by a comparison with the wording of s.24(1), which expressly includes a child support officer, and by common sense, which shows that child support officers would not appeal against each other's decisions, still less against their own decisions under s.18.

Subs. (2)

The time for lodging an appeal may be extended for special reasons (reg. 3 of the Tribunal Procedure Regulations).

Subs. (3)

An appeal which succeeds, whether in whole or in part, must be remitted to the Secretary of State who must refer it to a child support officer for implementation. In such cases, the decision of the CSAT should, in addition to stating the substantive decision of the tribunal, expressly refer the case to the Secretary of State.

Subs. (4)

This power to give directions is conferred on the tribunal as a whole and not on the chairman. In this respect it is in contrast to the power to give directions under reg. 5 of the Tribunal Procedure Regulations. See also reg. 13(4) of the Tribunal Procedure Regulations.

Child support appeal tribunals

21.—(1) There shall be tribunals to be known as child support appeal tribunals which shall, subject to any order made under section 45, hear and determine appeals under section 20.

(2) The Secretary of State may make such regulations with respect to proceedings before child support appeal tribunals as he considers appropriate.

(3) The regulations may in particular make provision—

(*a*) as to procedure;

(*b*) for the striking out of appeals for want of prosecution;

(*c*) as to the persons entitled to appear and be heard on behalf of any of the parties;

(*d*) requiring persons to attend and give evidence or to produce documents;

(*e*) about evidence;

(*f*) for authorising the administration of oaths;

(*g*) as to confidentiality;

(*h*) for notification of the result of an appeal to be given to such persons as may be prescribed.

(4) Schedule 3 shall have effect with respect to child support appeal tribunals.

DEFINITION

"prescribed": see s.54.

GENERAL NOTE

Subs. (1)

A CSAT's jurisdiction is determined by reference to s.20, which in turn refers to s.18, which is extended as noted in the general note to that section. A right of appeal to a CSAT also arises under s.46 (7) and reg. 42(9) of the Maintenance Assessment Procedure Regulations.

A CSAT has a statutory, appellate jurisdiction. Since the jurisdiction is statutory it cannot be extended by consent (*R(SB) 15/87*, paras. 10–11). This becomes significant if a procedural pre-requisite to the tribunal's jurisdiction has not been complied with. The question then arises whether the need for compliance may be waived, if the party for whose benefit or protection the step exists is prepared to waive the need for compliance. Waiver is possible, but only in cases where there is no public interest in insisting on strict compliance (*ibid*).

Since the jurisdiction is only appellate, a CSAT has no original jurisdiction (*R(SB) 42/83*, para. 8). This is significant in view of an important omission from the powers of a CSAT, which is the result of the lack of any appropriate enabling provision in the Act. CSATs, unlike SSATs, DATs and the Child Support Commissioners, have no power to deal with questions which first arise before them, but which could have been dealt with by a child support officer, if they had arisen earlier. A CSAT will, therefore, need to be careful not to deal with questions which have not already been considered by a child support officer. If it does deal with such a question, it will be acting without jurisdiction.

What constitutes a question has been given little consideration in the social security context. Since those tribunals have power to deal with questions whether they first arise before them or not, it is not relevant to consider whether something amounts to a question or not. However, since a CSAT does not have jurisdiction to consider questions first arising, it becomes important to consider what does and does not constitute a question for these purposes. No attempt at an exhaustive definition will be made here. Sometimes a matter may be labelled as a question (reg. 52(1) of the Maintenance Assessment Procedure Regulations). Sometimes something is clearly a question, although it is not labelled as such, for example, whether a person is habitually resident in the United Kingdom or the level of an absent parent's assessable income. Other things are clearly not questions. Matters of evidence are not questions, for example, a rent book which is produced for the first time before the tribunal as proof that a parent was resident in the jurisdiction. Matters of evidence may properly be dealt with by the tribunal. Arguments are not the same as questions. A party may, therefore, argue that a child is habitually resident in the jurisdiction because the parent with care is habitually resident here. This is a proper matter for decision by the tribunal. Drawing these distinctions is easy when there is only a single relevant concept in the legislation, as is the case with habitual residence. It is more complex when the legislation introduces a number of subconcepts. The calculation of income, for example, has a number of component parts. The amount of a self-employed earner's earnings is clearly a question. Whether the earner's records, produced for the first time before the CSAT, constitute proof of income is certainly a matter of evidence for the CSAT. However, it is far from clear whether the issue of whether some period other than the 52 weeks preceeding the application should be used to assess income is of itself a question, or merely an argument which is relevant to the more general question of the earner's earnings.

It will not be necessary for a tribunal to decide whether or not an issue constitutes a question, if the issue has arisen before the child support officer and so has not first arisen before the CSAT. Accordingly, it is necessary to consider when a question arises. Certainly a question does not arise until it has become relevant, and once it has arisen, it is not necessary that the child support officer should have made a decision on it. Unfortunately these matters are also not free from difficulty. Take as an example the issue of whether some period other than 52 weeks should be used for determining earnings. This will always have arisen in the sense that the child support officer should have considered it as a possibility, if only to pass over it on the basis that there is no reason to believe that the conditions for applying that provision are satisfied. However, if the application of the provision does amount to a question, can it be said that it arose for decision by a child support officer, unless and until there were grounds to suggest that it might be an appropriate case in which to apply that provision?

The consequence of this lack of jurisdiction is that questions which do first arise before a CSAT must be referred to the Secretary of State so that it may be referred to a child support officer for decision. The position if one of the parties is dissatisfied with the officer's decision is unclear. The Act was not drafted with references such as these in mind. Strictly following the procedures allowed for in the Act produces this result: if a maintenance assessment is in force, the officer will act under s.19 of the Act. If there is no maintenance assessment in force, the officer will act as on an application for a maintenance assessment. In either case the decision will not be subject to appeal to a CSAT until it has been through the s.18 review procedure, since the right of appeal is tied to a decision under that section. A more practical procedure would be to adjourn the hearing of the appeal until the child support officer has made a decision on the question, and then to proceed with the appeal on the basis of the decision on that question. This has the beneficial effect of avoiding delays and the making of fresh appeals, but raises difficult questions of the extent to which the original decision appealed against can survive the decision on the question. In practice, these problems may be more theoretical than real. The tribunal's decision will not necessarily be a nullity, even if it acts outside its jurisdiction, since it may be that the requirements of a fresh appeal against any new decision will in the circumstances have been impliedly waived by the parties (*R(SB) 15/87*, paras. 9–11).

Delegated legislation may only be made within the scope of the power conferred by the Act. The scope of the enabling statutory power is relevant both to the interpretation and to the validity of delegated legislation which purports to be made under it. If the language is susceptible to different meanings, one of which is within the scope of the enabling power and one of which is outside it, the provision will be given the meaning which renders it valid. There are, however, problems with this approach: (i) It may not be easy to identify the relevant enabling power. Regulations may be made under stated sections and "all other powers enabling in that behalf" and the omission of a power to make a particular type of provision from one enabling section does not prevent that power falling within another (perhaps more generally worded) enabling section (*R. v. Secretary of State for Social Security, ex p. Rouse, The Times,*

February 1, 1993); (ii) The power may be worded very broadly (for example, s.51(1)). If a provision in delegated legislation cannot be interpreted in a way which renders it valid, it is said to be *ultra vires* and is invalid and unenforceable. A CSAT has power both to interpret delegated legislation and to decide whether it is *ultra vires* on the ground that the provision in question is illegal, *i.e.* that it is outside the scope of the enabling power (*Chief Adjudication Officer* v. *Foster* [1993] 1 All E.R. 705). Whether delegated legislation is open to challenge on the grounds that it was made in a way which was affected by some procedurally impropriety or that its content is irrational, and, if so, whether CSATs and Child Support Commissioners have power to review legislation on either ground, is undecided. For a fuller statement of the nature of and grounds for judicial review see the introductory general note to the Tribunal Procedure Regulations.

It should be obvious, but history shows that it bears repeating, that it is the duty of members of CSATs to apply the law as it is and not as they would wish it to be (*R(U) 7/81*, para. 8).

Subs. (2)
The relevant regulations are the Tribunal Procedure Regulations.

Child Support Commissioners

22.—(1) Her Majesty may from time to time appoint a Chief Child Support Commissioner and such number of other Child Support Commissioners as she may think fit.

(2) The Chief Child Support Commissioner and the other Child Support Commissioners shall be appointed from among persons who—

(*a*) have a 10 year general qualification; or

(*b*) are advocates or solicitors in Scotland of 10 years' standing.

(3) The Lord Chancellor, after consulting the Lord Advocate, may make such regulations with respect to proceedings before Child Support Commissioners as he considers appropriate.

(4) The regulations—

(*a*) may, in particular, make any provision of a kind mentioned in section 21(3); and

(*b*) shall provide that any hearing before a Child Support Commissioner shall be in public except in so far as the Commissioner for special reasons directs otherwise.

(5) Schedule 4 shall have effect with respect to Child Support Commissioners.

DEFINITION
"general qualification": see s.54.

GENERAL NOTE
Subs. (3)
The regulations are contained in the Child Support Commissioners (Procedure) Regulations.

Subs. (4)(b)
This is the reverse of the position in a CSAT where the hearing is in private unless the chairman otherwise directs (reg. 11(7) of the Tribunal Procedure Regulations). This reflects the fact that before a CSAT the issues are likely to be mainly of concern to the parties, but that when a case comes to a Commissioner there will be a wider interest as the appeal may decide matters which are relevant to other cases. It is, however, strange that the Act provides that regulations shall make the provision rather than simply enacting the provision directly.

Child Support Commissioners for Northern Ireland

23.—(1) Her Majesty may from time to time appoint a Chief Child Support Commissioner for Northern Ireland and such number of other Child Support Commissioners for Northern Ireland as she may think fit.

(2) The Chief Child Support Commissioner for Northern Ireland and the other

Child Support Commissioners for Northern Ireland shall be appointed from among persons who are barristers or solicitors of not less than 10 years' standing.

(3) Schedule 4 shall have effect with respect to Child Support Commissioners for Northern Ireland, subject to the modifications set out in paragraph 8.

(4) Subject to any Order made after the passing of this Act by virtue of subsection (1)(a) of section 3 of the Northern Ireland Constitution Act 1973, the matters to which this subsection applies shall not be transferred matters for the purposes of that Act but shall for the purposes of subsection (2) of that section be treated as specified in Schedule 3 to that Act.

(5) Subsection (4) applies to all matters relating to Child Support Commissioners, including procedure and appeals, other than those specified in paragraph 9 of Schedule 2 to the Northern Ireland Constitution Act 1973.

Appeal to Child Support Commissioner

24.—(1) Any person who is aggrieved by a decision of a child support appeal tribunal, and any child support officer, may appeal to a Child Support Commissioner on a question of law.

(2) Where, on an appeal under this section, a Child Support Commissioner holds that the decision appealed against was wrong in law he shall set it aside.

(3) Where a decision is set aside under subsection (2), the Child Support Commissioner may—

(a) if he can do so without making fresh or further findings of fact, give the decision which he considers should have been given by the child support appeal tribunal;

(b) if he considers it expedient, make such findings and give such decision as he considers appropriate in the light of those findings; or

(c) refer the case, with directions for its determination, to a child support officer or, if he considers it appropriate, to a child support appeal tribunal.

(4) Any reference under subsection (3) to a child support officer shall, subject to any direction of the Child Support Commissioner, be to a child support officer who has taken no part in the decision originally appealed against.

(5) On a reference under subsection (3) to a child support appeal tribunal, the tribunal shall, subject to any direction of the Child Support Commissioner, consist of persons who were not members of the tribunal which gave the decision which has been appealed against.

(6) No appeal lies under this section without the leave—

(a) of the person who was the chairman of the child support appeal tribunal when the decision appealed against was given or of such other chairman of a child support appeal tribunal as may be determined in accordance with regulations made by the Lord Chancellor; or

(b) subject to and in accordance with regulations so made, of a Child Support Commissioner.

(7) The Lord Chancellor may by regulations make provision as to the manner in which, and the time within which, appeals under this section are to be brought and applications for leave under this section are to be made.

(8) Where a question which would otherwise fall to be determined by a child support officer first arises in the course of an appeal to a Child Support Commissioner, he may, if he thinks fit, determine it even though it has not been considered by a child support officer.

(9) Before making any regulations under subsection (6) or (7), the Lord Chancellor shall consult the Lord Advocate.

DEFINITIONS
"child support appeal tribunal": see s.54.
"child support officer": see s.13.

GENERAL NOTE
Subs. (1)

An appeal lies to a Commissioner from a decision of a CSAT. It may lie at the instance of either a party aggrieved or a child support officer. The meaning of "person aggrieved" is discussed in the general note to s.20(1). A child support officer has no personal interest in a decision, but may appeal on behalf of one of the parties, or in order to obtain an authoritative decision on a particular point from a Commissioner. The decision appealed must be a final one (which includes one that is subject to liberty to restore). There can be no appeal against an interlocutory decision of the tribunal, such as a decision to adjourn (*CA 126/89*, paras. 9–11 and *CIS 64/91*). The decision appealed must be that of the tribunal. There can be no appeal against a decision or ruling of a chairman (*CSB 103/84*, paras. 12–13 and *CSB 1182/89*, para. 8 and the decisions cited therein). However, if a hearing follows an interlocutory decision or a chairman's ruling and the CSAT makes a decision, that decision may be subject to an appeal on the ground that the interlocutory decision or the chairman's ruling adversely affected the party's case or the presentation of it, or that the ruling occasioned a breach of the rules of natural justice (*CSB 103/84*, para. 14). (For other possible action, see the general note to reg. 12(1) of the Tribunal Procedure Regulations.)

Before seeking leave to appeal it is worth considering whether an application to set aside the decision under reg. 15 of the Tribunal Procedure Regulations would be more appropriate. Such an application will be heard much more quickly than an appeal and does not affect the party's right to seek leave to appeal.

Question of law

An appeal lies to a Commissioner on a question of law. There can be no appeal, if a question of law cannot be identified (*R.* v. *The Social Security Commissioner and the Social Security Appeal Tribunal, ex p. Pattni* [1993] Fam. Law 213. A chairman should approach an application for leave to appeal in two stages. The first question to ask is whether the notice of appeal raises a question of law. A decision will raise a question of law: (i) if it contains a false proposition *ex facie*; (ii) if it is supported by no evidence; (iii) if the facts are such that no one acting judicially and properly instructed as to the relevant law could have come to that decision; (iv) if there has been a breach of the rules of natural justice; (v) if there has been a breach of reg. 13(2)(*b*) of the Tribunal Procedure Regulations, which requires the decision to contain a statement of reasons for the decision and of the findings on questions of fact material to the decision (*R(SB) 11/83*, para. 13). The fact that a decision was based on a provision in delegated legislation which the minister had no power to make will always constitute an error of law (*Chief Adjudication Officer* v. *Foster* [1993] 1 All E.R. 705). It is ground (v) which provides the basis for most successful appeals. For the problems in identifying a question of law, as opposed to fact, where different tribunals properly directed and acting reasonably could come to different conclusions, see the general note to s.18(6)(*c*).

If the notice of appeal raises a question of law, the chairman should then ask whether the question is an arguable one. There must be material in the case indicating that a sensible argument could be made that an error has occurred (*R(SB) 1/81*, para. 4). If the case is an arguable one, leave to appeal should be given. The chairman is not required to decide whether or not the appeal will succeed. That is a matter for the Commissioner. Moreover, the granting of leave does not amount to an admission by the chairman that the decision is wrong. This is emphasised by the wording of the subsection which refers to a question, rather than to an error, of law. In order to obtain leave to appeal, the appellant must show that the case raises a question of law, and in order to succeed in the appeal, he or she must show that there has been an error of law.

A chairman should as a general rule avoid commenting on an application for leave to appeal and merely grant or refuse the application. It is always inappropriate to attempt to justify the tribunal's decision, and it is quite wrong to try to supplement the reasoning of the tribunal. However, in two cases some comment is justified. The first case is where the chairman grants leave for a reason which is different from that advanced by the claimant in the application for leave to appeal. This will alert the Commissioner to the basis upon which leave has been given. The second case is where there is an allegation of impropriety in the conduct of the tribunal. A record of the chairman's recollection of events given relatively close to the events in question is useful, especially if the matters were not recorded in the notes of proceedings. Applications for leave to appeal which raise allegations of misconduct should be lodged as soon as possible after the hearing (*R(I) 11/63*, para. 20).

Subs. (3)

This subsection gives Commissioners powers to make findings of fact, to give a final decision and to refer the case back to a CSAT or to a child support officer. It is to be hoped that they will use these powers whenever possible to ensure that a final decision is made at as early a date as possible, especially in view of the possibility of a delay being prejudicial to the welfare of a child (see the general note to s.2).

In particular, these powers allow Commissioners to give their own decisions in cases where the decision of the CSAT was clearly the correct one to reach, but it has to be set aside on appeal because of some technical defect.

Subs. (4)

The decision originally appealed against will be the decision made under s.18 or s.46. This subsection refers to the child support officer who made that decision, and not to the officer who made the decision which was reviewed.

Subss. (6) and (7)

The regulations are contained in Part II of the Child Support Commissioners (Procedure) Regulations.

Subs. (8)

This procedural provision gives a Commissioner the discretion to deal with questions which might have been dealt with by a child support officer but have not been. It saves the need to refer the matter back to the Secretary of State for reference to a child support officer for decision. This is especially valuable in child support law where there is a two tier review process before a case can come to a CSAT. It is, therefore, a convenient provision and is to be interpreted liberally (*R(I) 4/75*, para. 12). It is unfortunate that no equivalent power has been conferred on CSATs.

The Commissioner should consider the application of this subsection in two stages. The first issue to decide is whether the question falls within the subsection. If the question does fall within the subsection, the next issue is whether, and if so in what manner, the discretion should be exercised.

The scope of the subsection

The subsection only applies to questions which would otherwise fall to be determined by a child support officer. It cannot be used for questions which are for the Secretary of State or for the courts. It can be used to cure the Commissioner's lack of jurisdiction, for example, where there has been no decision on a s.18 review, the Commissioner can give a decision. It can also be used where there are questions which are relevant to the decision which the Commissioner will have to make, but which have not been dealt with by a child support officer. It is, therefore, an appropriate way to correct errors made by a child support officer (*R(F) 1/72*). This is subject to the requirement, discussed below, that the question should first arise in the course of the appeal.

This subsection can, therefore, operate in two ways. It can operate to give a Commissioner power to make decisions which there would otherwise have been power to make, provided the matter had come to the Commissioner via a child support officer's decision. It can also operate to give a Commissioner power to make decisions which there would otherwise have been no power to take, for example, to review a child support officer's decision.

Only questions first arising in the course of the appeal are covered. This is ambiguous. It could mean that the question must first be identified in the course of the appeal, or it could mean that the question only arises because of the course taken by the appeal. The Commissioners have given it the first meaning.

The question must first arise in the course of *the appeal*. This is wider than "the course of *the hearing*" (*CS 101/86*, para. 5). The question might, therefore, arise at an interlocutory stage or during an adjournment, as well as during the hearing itself.

The question must *first* arise in the course of the appeal and not before. So if the question has arisen and a decision has been given in respect of it whether by a child support officer or by a CSAT, it does not fall within this subsection (*CS 104/87*, para. 2).

The discretion

The subsection gives a discretion to deal with a case. It must be exercised judicially. The Commissioner will consider (i) the wishes of the parties and (ii) whether a decision on the question is essential to the disposal of the case, but (iii) the paramount consideration will be the requirements of natural justice. It does not override the need for all parties to have a proper chance to prepare for, and to present evidence and argument on every matter in issue in, the appeal. The Commissioner will need to consider whether the parties have had an adequate chance to deal with the question. An important factor will be whether there has been notice of the question, either in the written submission of the child support officer or in the grounds stated in the notice of appeal or in some other document which has been sent to all the parties (*R(I) 4/75*, para. 12). If the parties have not had a proper chance to deal with the question, the Commissioner may decide to adjourn to allow time for this. Alternatively, the Commissioner may decide to exercise the discretion against dealing with the question.

Appeal from Child Support Commissioner on question of law

25.—(1) An appeal on a question of law shall lie to the appropriate court from any decision of a Child Support Commissioner.

(2) No such appeal may be brought except—

   (*a*) with leave of the Child Support Commissioner who gave the decision or, where regulations made by the Lord Chancellor so provide, of a Child Support Commissioner selected in accordance with the regulations; or

   (*b*) if the Child Support Commissioner refuses leave, with the leave of the appropriate court.

(3) An application for leave to appeal under this section against a decision of a Child Support Commissioner ("the appeal decision") may only be made by:—

   (*a*) a person who was a party to the proceedings in which the original decision, or appeal decision, was given;

   (*b*) the Secretary of State; or

   (*c*) any other person who is authorised to do so by regulations made by the Lord Chancellor.

(4) In this section—

"appropriate court" means the Court of Appeal unless in a particular case the Child Support Commissioner to whom the application for leave is made directs that, having regard to the circumstances of the case, and in particular the convenience of the persons who may be parties to the appeal, the appropriate court is the Court of Session; and

"original decision" means the decision to which the appeal decision in question relates.

(5) The Lord Chancellor may by regulations make provision with respect to—

   (*a*) the manner in which and the time within which applications must be made to a Child Support Commissioner for leave under this section; and

   (*b*) the procedure for dealing with such applications.

(6) Before making any regulations under subsection (2), (3) or (5), the Lord Chancellor shall consult the Lord Advocate.

GENERAL NOTE
Subs. (1)
The meaning of "question of law" is discussed in the general note to s.24(1).

Subss. (2), (3) and (5)
The provisions are contained in reg. 25 of the Child Support Commissioners (Procedure) Regulations.

Subs. (4)
The Family Proceedings (Amendment) Rules 1993 amend the Family Proceedings Rules 1991 (as amended) to insert r.3.23 which applies to any appeal to the Court of Appeal.

Where leave is granted by the Commissioner, the notice of appeal must be served within six weeks from the date on which notice of the grant was given in writing to the appellant. Where leave is granted by the Court of Appeal upon an application made within six weeks of the date on which notice of the Commissioner's refusal of leave was given in writing to the appellant, the notice of appeal must be served before the end of the six week period, or within seven days after the date on which leave is granted. This provision is based on the procedure applicable to social security appeals contained in RSC, Ord. 59, r. 21.

Disputes about parentage

26.—(1) Where a person who is alleged to be a parent of the child with respect to whom an application for a maintenance assessment has been made ("the alleged parent") denies that he is one of the child's parents, the child support officer concerned shall not make a maintenance assessment on the assumption that the alleged parent is one of the child's parents unless the case falls within one of those set out in subsection (2).

(2) The Cases are—

CASE A

Where the alleged parent is a parent of the child in question by virtue of having adopted him.

CASE B

Where the alleged parent is a parent of the child in question by virtue of an order under section 30 of the Human Fertilisation and Embryology Act 1990 (parental orders in favour of gamete donors).

CASE C

Where—

(a) either—
  (i) a declaration that the alleged parent is a parent of the child in question (or a declaration which has that effect) is in force under section 56 of the Family Law Act 1986 (declarations of parentage); or
  (ii) a declarator by a court in Scotland that the alleged parent is a parent of the child in question (or a declarator which has that effect) is in force; and
(b) the child has not subsequently been adopted.

CASE D

Where—

(a) a declaration to the effect that the alleged parent is one of the parents of the child in question has been made under section 27; and
(b) the child has not subsequently been adopted.

CASE E

Where—

(a) the child is habitually resident in Scotland;
(b) the child support officer is satisfied that one or other of the presumptions set out in section 5(1) of the Law Reform (Parent and Child) (Scotland) Act 1986 applies; and
(c) the child has not subsequently been adopted.

CASE F

Where—

(a) the alleged parent has been found, or adjudged, to be the father of the child in question—
  (i) in proceedings before any court in England and Wales which are relevant proceedings for the purposes of section 12 of the Civil Evidence Act 1968; or
  (ii) in affiliation proceedings before any court in the United Kingdom, (whether or not he offered any defence to the allegation of paternity) and that finding or adjudication still subsists; and
(b) the child has not subsequently been adopted.

(3) In this section—

"adopted" means adopted within the meaning of Part IV of the Adoption Act 1976 or, in relation to Scotland, Part IV of the Adoption (Scotland) Act 1978; and

"affiliation proceedings", in relation to Scotland, means any action of affiliation and aliment.

DEFINITIONS
"child": see s.55.
"child support officer": see s.13.
"maintenance assessment": see s.54.
"parent": *ibid.*

GENERAL NOTE
This section allows child support officers, CSATs and Child Support Commissioners to make decisions on parentage in specified, clear-cut cases only. More contentious cases are within the jurisdiction of the court which has the appropriate powers to handle them. Section 27 gives the Secretary of State (but not a CSAT) power to apply to a court for a declaration as to parentage. If such an issue arises before a CSAT, it must decide that it has no jurisdiction and refer the matter to the Secretary of State who will decide whether to apply for a declaration.

Reference to court for declaration of parentage

27.—(1) Where—
(a) a child support officer is considering whether to make a maintenance assessment with respect to a person who is alleged to be a parent of the child, or one of the children, in question ("the alleged parent");
(b) the alleged parent denies that he is one of the child's parents; and
(c) the child support officer is not satisfied that the case falls within one of those set out in section 26(2),
the Secretary of State or the person with care may apply to the court for a declaration as to whether or not the alleged parent is one of the child's parents.

(2) If, on hearing any application under subsection (1), the court is satisfied that the alleged parent is, or is not, a parent of the child in question it shall make a declaration to that effect.

(3) A declaration under this section shall have effect only for the purposes of this Act.

(4) In this section "court" means, subject to any provision made under Schedule 11 to the Children Act 1989 (jurisdiction of courts with respect to certain proceedings relating to children) the High Court, a county court or a magistrates' court.

(5) [Amends the Civil Evidence Act 1968, s.12(5).]

(6) This section does not apply to Scotland.

DEFINITIONS
"child": see s.55.
"child support officer": see s.13.
"maintenance assessment": see s.54.
"parent": *ibid.*
"person with care": see s.3(3).

GENERAL NOTE
This section provides for a court to have the power to make a declaration of parentage where the alleged parent denies that he is a parent. A court can direct that scientific tests take place to determine parentage, under ss.20–25 of the Family Law Reform Act 1969 as amended. Note that the declaration has effect only for the purposes of the Child Support Act, although no doubt it will have practical significance for other proceedings concerning the alleged parent and the child.

See the general note to s.45 below for a discussion of the jurisdiction of the courts in respect of proceedings for a declaration.

Power of Secretary of State to initiate or defend actions of declarator: Scotland

28.—(1) Where—

(*a*) a child support officer is considering whether to make a maintenance assessment with respect to a person who is alleged to be a parent of the child, or one of the children, in question ("the alleged parent");

(*b*) the alleged parent denies that he is a parent of the child in question; and

(*c*) the child support officer is not satisfied that the case falls within one of those set out in section 26(2),

the Secretary of State may bring an action for declarator of parentage under section 7 of the Law Reform (Parent and Child) (Scotland) Act 1986.

(2) The Secretary of State may defend an action for declarator of non-parentage or illegitimacy brought by a person named as the alleged parent in an application for a maintenance assessment.

(3) This section applies to Scotland only.

DEFINITIONS
  "child": see s.55.
  "child support officer": see s.13.
  "maintenance assessment": see s.54.
  "parent": *ibid.*

Collection and enforcement

Collection of child support maintenance

29.—(1) The Secretary of State may arrange for the collection of any child support maintenance payable in accordance with a maintenance assessment where—

(*a*) the assessment is made by virtue of section 6; or

(*b*) an application has been made to the Secretary of State under section 4(2) or 7(3) for him to arrange for its collection.

(2) Where a maintenance assessment is made under this Act, payments of child support maintenance under the assessment shall be made in accordance with regulations made by the Secretary of State.

(3) The regulations may, in particular, make provision—

(*a*) for payments of child support maintenance to be made—

  (i) to the person caring for the child or children in question;

  (ii) to, or through, the Secretary of State; or

  (iii) to, or through, such other person as the Secretary of State may, from time to time, specify;

(*b*) as to the method by which payments of child support maintenance are to be made;

(*c*) as to the intervals at which such payments are to be made;

(*d*) as to the method and timing of the transmission of payments which are made, to or through the Secretary of State or any other person, in accordance with the regulations;

(*e*) empowering the Secretary of State to direct any person liable to make payments in accordance with the assessment—

  (i) to make them by standing order or by any other method which requires one person to give his authority for payments to be made from an account of his to an account of another's on specific dates during the period for which the authority is in force and without the need for any further authority from him;

  (ii) to open an account from which payments under the assessment may be made in accordance with the method of payment which that person is obliged to adopt;

(f) providing for the making of representations with respect to matters with which the regulations are concerned.

DEFINITIONS

"child": see s.3(6).

"child support maintenance": *ibid.*

"maintenance assessment": see s.54.

GENERAL NOTE

Subs. (1)

The Secretary of State may arrange for the collection of child support maintenance in two different cases. First, if he has required the person with care to authorise its recovery, his power to arrange collection is automatic under s.6(6)(*b*) and no further application is necessary. Second, where an application for child support maintenance has been made under s.4(1) or 7(1), an application to the Secretary of State may be made under s.4(2) or 7(3). It is possible for parties to have sought a maintenance assessment under these sections, but to make their own private arrangements for collection of the child support maintenance so assessed. In such a case, either party may subsequently apply to use the collection service at a later date.

When an assessment is made following an application under s.4, 6 or 7 a collection fee of £34 may become payable, in respect of the assessment, by the parent with care and the absent parent. See the Child Support Fees Regulations and the general note to section 11.

If collection of child support maintenance is arranged under this section in respect of a qualifying child whose parent with care is a spouse or former spouse to whom periodical payments under a maintenance order are payable, that order is prescribed for the purposes of s.30 by reg. 2(*b*) of the Collection and Enforcement of Other Forms of Maintenance Regulations.

Subs. (2)

This subsection applies to payment of child support maintenance generally and not just to cases where collection is being arranged by the Secretary of State under subs. (1). The regulations are contained in Part II of the Collection and Enforcement Regulations. They deal with the person to whom payment should be made (reg. 2), the method, interval and method of transmission of payment and representations about these matters (regs. 3 to 6), and notice to the liable person concerning payment (reg. 7). All decisions under the regulations are for the Secretary of State and so are not appealable to a CSAT.

Subs. (3)

Payments may be required to be made by the "liable person" (see reg. 2(2) and s.31 of the Act): (i) direct to the person caring for the child or children in question, or, where an application was made by a child under s.7, to that child; (ii) to or through the Secretary of State; or (iii) to or through such other person as is specified by the Secretary of State. The liable person and the person entitled to receive the payments will be provided with an opportunity to make representations as to the method of payment, and these will be taken into account when determining how the maintenance is to be paid. The aim is to arrange the most secure approach to payment.

The method of payment will vary according to the particular circumstances in the case. Payment direct by the liable person to the person caring for the child or children may be required to be made by standing order or equivalent, such as direct debit, cheque or postal order, or cash. Although para. (*e*)(ii) provides for the Regulations to give the Secretary of State the power to direct the liable person to open an account from which payments can be made, reg. 3(2) more realistically empowers the Secretary of State to direct the liable person to take all reasonable steps to open an account. There may be situations where a bank or similar institution is not prepared to take a liable person on as a customer, in which case one of the other methods will have to be specified. These provisions may be compared with those under the Maintenance Enforcement Act 1991, where courts are given similar powers to collect maintenance. Under section 1(6) of that Act, the court must first give the debtor an opportunity to open an account, and may, if satisfied that the debtor has failed, without reasonable excuse, to do so, then order him or her to comply. Under s.29 and the regulations, the Secretary of State may require the liable person to take reasonable steps to comply without first offering an opportunity to him or her to do so voluntarily.

The date and intervals of payment will be specified by the Secretary of State, and timed to coincide with the liable person's receipt of salary or wages, with due allowance made for clearance of cheques, etc. Where the payments are made to or through the Secretary of State rather than to the person caring for the child or children, payments may be made to the recipient at different times or intervals from when they are received by the Secretary of State. For example, the liable person may make payments monthly, but the person caring for the child or children may be paid by the Secretary of State fortnightly.

A notice will be sent to the liable person under reg. 7 as to the requirements about payment, as soon as is reasonably practicable after the making of the maintenance assessment and after any change in the requirements referred to in any previous such notice.

Collection and enforcement of other forms of maintenance

30.—(1) Where the Secretary of State is arranging for the collection of any payments under section 29 or subsection (2), he may also arrange for the collection of any periodical payments, or secured periodical payments, of a prescribed kind which are payable to or for the benefit of any person who falls within a prescribed category.

(2) The Secretary of State may arrange for the collection of any periodical payments or secured periodical payments of a prescribed kind which are payable for the benefit of a child even though he is not arranging for the collection of child support maintenance with respect to that child.

(3) Where—

   (a)   the Secretary of State is arranging, under this Act, for the collection of different payments ("the payments") from the same absent parent;

   (b)   an amount is collected by the Secretary of State from the absent parent which is less than the total amount due in respect of the payments; and

   (c)   the absent parent has not stipulated how that amount is to be allocated by the Secretary of State as between the payments,

the Secretary of State may allocate that amount as he sees fit.

(4) In relation to England and Wales, the Secretary of State may by regulations make provision for sections 29 and 31 to 40 to apply, with such modifications (if any) as he considers necessary or expedient, for the purpose of enabling him to enforce any obligation to pay any amount which he is authorised to collect under this section.

(5) In relation to Scotland, the Secretary of State may by regulations make provision for the purpose of enabling him to enforce any obligation to pay any amount which he is authorised to collect under this section—

   (a)   empowering him to bring any proceedings or take any other steps (other than diligence against earnings) which could have been brought or taken by or on behalf of the person to whom the periodical payments are payable;

   (b)   applying sections 29, 31 and 32 with such modifications (if any) as he considers necessary or expedient.

DEFINITIONS

  "absent parent": see s.3(2)

  "child": see s.55.

  "child support maintenance": see s.3(6).

  "prescribed": see s.54.

GENERAL NOTE

The payments and categories of persons covered by this section are prescribed by reg. 2 of the Collection and Enforcement of Other Forms of Maintenance Regulations. In the case of England and Wales, reg. 3 applies the provisions of ss.29(2) and (3) and 31 to 40 to payments covered by this section. In the case of Scotland, reg. 4 provides that the Secretary of State may bring any proceedings or take any other steps other than diligence against earnings which could have been taken by or on behalf of the person to whom the payments are payable, and applies the provisions of ss.29(2) and (3), 31 and 32 to those payments.

This section empowers the Secretary of State to collect periodical payments ordered by a court, when arranging for the collection of child support maintenance under the Act. Periodical payments are not defined, but the Regulations (see below) provide that secured periodical payments are included. The periodical payments may be to or for the benefit of the person with care who is a spouse or former spouse, and not just for children. It is expected that the Secretary of State will start collection of top-up maintenance from April 11, 1994 and other forms of maintenance, including spousal maintenance, from April 8, 1996.

Subs. (1)

Arrangements for the collection of other forms of maintenance are provided for by the Collection and Enforcement of Other Forms of Maintenance Regulations. These prescribe the following periodical payments and persons as covered by section 30(1):

(i) Payments under a maintenance order (note, not a maintenance agreement) made in relation to a child in accordance with s.8(6) (top-up maintenance); s.8(7) (maintenance to cover the costs of education or training); or s.8(8) (periodical payments to meet expenses attributable to disability);

(ii) Periodical payments under a maintenance order (not a maintenance agreement in England and Wales, but, in Scotland, registered minutes of agreement are included) payable to or for the benefit of a spouse or former spouse, who is the person with care of a child who is a qualifying child in respect of whom a child maintenance assessment is in force for which collection has been arranged under s.29;

(iii) Periodical payments under a maintenance order (not an agreement) payable to or for the benefit of a former child of the family of the person against whom the order is made, and who has his home with the person with care.

A child of the family is defined for England and Wales by s.52(1) of the Matrimonial Causes Act 1973, as amended by Sched. 12, para. 33 to the Children Act 1989, as:

"in relation to the parties to a marriage . . .

(a) a child of both of those parties; and

(b) any other child, not being a child who is placed with those parties as foster parents by a local authority or voluntary organisation, who has been treated by both of those parties as a child of their family."

Whether a child has been treated as a child of the family is a question of fact judged objectively (*Teeling* v. *Teeling* [1984] F.L.R. 808). The fact that the husband mistakenly believes the child is his does not prevent the child being a child of the family, if the husband treats the child as such (*W.(R.J.)* v. *W.(S.J.)* [1972] Fam. Law 152).

For Scotland, the same phrase is defined differently, by referring to a child who has been "*accepted*" as a child of the family (s.1(1)(*d*) of the Family Law (Scotland) Act 1985). It is arguable that a husband has not accepted a child as a child of his family, if he did not know that the child was not his (see the previous position in English law, when acceptance was the criterion: *P.* v. *P.* [1969] 1 W.L.R. 898).

The aim of this third category is to provide a collection mechanism for all the children having their home with the person with care, and to avoid the situation where only one or some children are benefiting from the collection service because they are the subjects of a maintenance assessment, while another or others are dependent upon the court machinery for enforcement.

Subs. (2)

This provides that periodical payments for the benefit of a child may be collected even though the Secretary of State is not collecting child support maintenance with respect to that child. This subsection has not been brought into force.

Subs. (3)

This provision gives the Secretary of State a discretion to apportion payments between different families to whom the absent parent is liable, as he sees fit. If the absent parent has stipulated how an amount is to be allocated, this would appear to be binding, but it is arguable that it would not be permitted where the absent parent chose to give priority to children whose carer is not a parent in receipt of benefit under s.6, or to a former spouse rather than the children.

Subs. (4)

The aim of the section is to enable the Secretary of State to use the same methods of collection and enforcement regardless of the origin of the payments. Hence, reg. 3 of the Regulations provides that, in relation to England and Wales, ss.29(2) and (3) and 31 to 40 of the Act and any regulations made under those sections, apply for the purpose of enabling the Secretary of State to enforce any obligation to pay the prescribed forms of maintenance, as modified to provide that references to child support maintenance shall be read as references to periodical payments and references to maintenance assessments as maintenance orders.

Subs. (5)

Regulation 4 of the Regulations provides that, in relation to Scotland, the Secretary of State may bring any proceedings and take any other steps (other than diligence against earnings) which could have been brought or taken by or on behalf of the person to whom the periodical payments are payable. Sections 29(2) and (3), 31 and 32 of the Act and any regulations made under those sections, apply as modified to read as if referring to periodical payments and maintenance orders.

These regulations do not apply to any periodical payments which fall due before the date specified by notice in writing to the absent parent that the Secretary of State is arranging for payments to be collected, and that date shall not be earlier than the date the notice is given (reg. 5).

Deduction from earnings orders

31.—(1) This section applies where any person ("the liable person") is liable to make payments of child support maintenance.

(2) The Secretary of State may make an order ("a deduction from earnings order") against a liable person to secure the payment of any amount due under the maintenance assessment in question.

(3) A deduction from earnings order may be made so as to secure the payment of—

(*a*) arrears of child support maintenance payable under the assessment;

(*b*) amounts of child support maintenance which will become due under the assessment; or

(*c*) both such arrears and such future amounts.

(4) A deduction from earnings order—

(*a*) shall be expressed to be directed at a person ("the employer") who has the liable person in his employment; and

(*b*) shall have effect from such date as may be specified in the order.

(5) A deduction from earnings order shall operate as an instruction to the employer to—

(*a*) make deductions from the liable person's earnings; and

(*b*) pay the amounts deducted to the Secretary of State.

(6) The Secretary of State shall serve a copy of any deduction from earnings order which he makes under this section on—

(*a*) the person who appears to the Secretary of State to have the liable person in question in his employment; and

(*b*) the liable person.

(7) Where—

(*a*) a deduction from earnings order has been made; and

(*b*) a copy of the order has been served on the liable person's employer,

it shall be the duty of that employer to comply with the order; but he shall not be under any liability for non-compliance before the end of the period of 7 days beginning with the date on which the copy was served on him.

(8) In this section and in section 32 "earnings" has such meaning as may be prescribed.

DEFINITIONS

"child support maintenance": see s.3(6).

"prescribed": see s.54.

GENERAL NOTE

The enforcement of a liability to pay child support maintenance is a matter for the Secretary of State and not for the person with care or a child support officer. Consequently enforcement can never come before a CSAT. In securing the enforcement of a liability to pay, the Secretary of State must first consider whether or not a deduction from earnings order under this section is appropriate. If it is appropriate, one must be made and further action can only be taken if it proves ineffective (s.33(1)(*b*)(ii)). If it is inappropriate, any default in payment of child support maintenance allows the Secretary of State to proceed to the next step, which is to apply for a liability order from a magistrates' court or sheriff under s.33. This opens the way for steps to be taken to recover the maintenance. In England and Wales, these steps are distress and sale, garnishee proceedings and a charging order (ss.35 and 36). If these steps are unsuccessful, a warrant for commitment to prison may be issued under s.40. In Scotland, the relevant steps are poinding and sale, arrestment and action of furthcoming or sale (s.38).

A deduction from earnings order operates as an instruction to the liable person's employer to deduct amounts from his or her earnings and pay these to the Secretary of State. It is similar to attachment of earnings in England and Wales (earnings arrestment in Scotland). As with attachment of earnings orders, as amended by the Maintenance Enforcement Act 1991 ss.1(4)(*b*) and 2(3)(*d*), an order can be made before the liable person has fallen into arrears. Nonetheless, such an order is intended to be used only when other methods have failed or appear likely to fail. The Secretary of State will first have tried to deal with arrears by means of agreement with the liable person or by trying a new method of payment (see s.41 below). The limitations of the deduction from earnings order are that it can only be used where the liable person is employed and that it is not appropriate if the person changes jobs frequently. Regulations providing for the detailed arrangements are made under section 32.

Where a deduction from earnings order is made in Great Britain and the liable person works for an employer in Northern Ireland, or *vice versa*, the deduction from earnings order will have effect in the territory in which the liable person is working, as if made under the provision for that territory. Any appeal in connection with the order shall be made under the provision for the territory in which the liable person is resident (Sched. 1, paras. 10 and 12 to the Child Support (Northern Ireland Reciprocal Arrangements) Regulations 1993).

For arrangements concerning deductions from the pay of servicemen and merchant seamen, see the Child Support Act 1991 (Consequential Amendments) Order 1993.

Subs. (1)
The "liable person" will be the absent parent.

Subs. (2)
A deduction from earnings order is made by the Secretary of State. This should make it possible for one to be made more quickly and easily than an attachment of earnings or earnings arrestment order, which has to be made by a court. Giving a public authority, rather than a court, the power to make such an order is not new. It also exists in relation to collection of the community charge, and council tax. A deduction from earnings order may be made against someone in the employment of the Crown, but in such a case the operation of s.32(8) is modified (s.57(4)).

Subs. (8)
"Earnings" is defined in reg. 8 of the Collection and Enforcement Regulations.

Regulations about deduction from earnings orders

32.—(1) The Secretary of State may by regulations make provision with respect to deduction from earnings orders.

(2) The regulations may, in particular, make provision—

(*a*) as to the circumstances in which one person is to be treated as employed by another;

(*b*) requiring any deduction from earnings under an order to be made in the prescribed manner;

(*c*) requiring an order to specify the amount or amounts to which the order relates and the amount or amounts which are to be deducted from the liable person's earnings in order to meet his liabilities under the maintenance assessment in question;

(*d*) requiring the intervals between deductions to be made under an order to be specified in the order;

(*e*) as to the payment of sums deducted under an order to the Secretary of State;

(*f*) allowing the person who deducts and pays any amount under an order to deduct from the liable person's earnings a prescribed sum towards his administrative costs;

(*g*) with respect to the notification to be given to the liable person of amounts deducted, and amounts paid, under the order;

(*h*) requiring any person on whom a copy of an order is served to notify the Secretary of State in the prescribed manner and within a prescribed period if he does not have the liable person in his employment or if the liable person ceases to be in his employment;

(*i*) as to the operation of an order where the liable person is in the employment of the Crown;

(*j*) for the variation of orders;

(*k*) similar to that made by section 31(7), in relation to any variation of an order;

(*l*) for an order to lapse when the employer concerned ceases to have the liable person in his employment;

(*m*) as to the revival of an order in such circumstances as may be prescribed;

(*n*) allowing or requiring an order to be discharged;

(*o*) as to the giving of notice by the Secretary of State to the employer concerned that an order has lapsed or has ceased to have effect.

(3) The regulations may include provision that while a deduction from earnings order is in force—

(*a*) the liable person shall from time to time notify the Secretary of State, in the prescribed manner and within a prescribed period, of each occasion on which he leaves any employment or becomes employed, or re-employed, and shall include in such a notification a statement of his earnings and expected earnings from the employment concerned and of such other matters as may be prescribed;

(*b*) any person who becomes the liable person's employer and knows that the order is in force shall notify the Secretary of State, in the prescribed manner and within a prescribed period, that he is the liable person's employer, and shall include in such a notification a statement of the liable person's earnings and expected earnings from the employment concerned and of such other matters as may be prescribed.

(4) The regulations may include provision with respect to the priority as between a deduction from earnings order and—

(*a*) any other deduction from earnings order;

(*b*) any order under any other enactment relating to England and Wales which provides for deductions from the liable person's earnings;

(*c*) any diligence against earnings.

(5) The regulations may include a provision that a liable person may appeal to a magistrates' court (or in Scotland to the sheriff) if he is aggrieved by the making of a deduction from earnings order against him, or by the terms of any such order, or there is a dispute as to whether payments constitute earnings or as to any other prescribed matter relating to the order.

(6) On an appeal under subsection (5) the court or (as the case may be) the sheriff shall not question the maintenance assessment by reference to which the deduction from earnings order was made.

(7) Regulations made by virtue of subsection (5) may include provision as to the powers of a magistrates' court, or in Scotland of the sheriff, in relation to an appeal (which may include provision as to the quashing of a deduction from earnings order or the variation of the terms of such an order).

(8) If any person fails to comply with the requirements of a deduction from earnings order, or with any regulation under this section which is designated for the purposes of this subsection, he shall be guilty of an offence.

(9) In subsection (8) "designated" means designated by the regulations.

(10) It shall be a defence for a person charged with an offence under subsection (8) to prove that he took all reasonable steps to comply with the requirements in question.

(11) Any person guilty of an offence under subsection (8) shall be liable on summary conviction to a fine not exceeding level two on the standard scale.

DEFINITIONS
   "earnings": see s.31(8).
   "liable person": see s.31(1).
   "maintenance assessment": see s.54.
   "prescribed": *ibid.*

GENERAL NOTE
   The regulations made under this section are contained in Part III of the Collection and Enforcement Regulations.
   They apply, as modified, to other forms of maintenance prescribed for the purposes of s.30 by the Collection and Enforcement of Other Forms of Maintenance Regulations (see above). The scheme set out is based closely on that which applies to the Attachment of Earnings Act 1971. However, the time limits for compliance by the liable person and the employer are more restrictive in relation to deduction from earnings orders (a seven-day requirement is used, compared with 10 days or a "specified period" in the Attachment of Earnings Act 1971). Whereas a court has power to order the debtor to attend to give employment details, the Secretary of State has no such power, although see below for powers to require these details to be supplied.

Subs. (2)
   Regulation 8(2) provides that a relationship of employer and employee is treated as subsisting where one person, as principal and not as servant or agent, pays to the other any sum defined as earnings. Earnings are defined in paras. (3) and (4) of this regulation. They are any sums payable by way of wages or salary (including fees, bonus, commission, overtime pay or other emoluments); sums payable by way of pension (including an annuity in respect of past service); and statutory sick pay. They do not include sums payable by any public department of the Government of Northern Ireland or a territory outside the UK; pay or allowances to members of Her Majesty's forces; pension, allowances or benefit payable under any enactment relating to social security; pension or allowances payable in respect of disablement or disability; guaranteed minimum pension within the meaning of the Social Security Pensions Act 1975. Regulation 9 provides that a deduction from earnings order shall specify certain items of information, including the name and address of the liable person, the normal deduction rate, protected earnings rate, and address to which the deducted amounts must be sent.
   As with the Attachment of Earnings Act 1971, a deduction from earnings order is made up of a normal deduction rate and a protected earnings rate. The former specifies the amount to be deducted from earnings by the employer at each pay-day (which amount could include payment of interest as well as arrears, as provided for by the Arrears, Interest and Adjustment of Maintenance Assessments Regulations, see s.41 below); the latter specifies that the liable person's earnings must not fall below his or her exempt income, as calculated for the current maintenance assessment. The employer may pay the amounts deducted to the Secretary of State by cheque, automated credit transfer, or other method specified by the Secretary of State.
   In order to enable the Secretary of State to direct a deduction from earnings order to the employer, reg. 15 requires the liable person, within seven days of being given written notice, to provide details of his or her employer's name and address, the amount of earnings, place and nature of work and any works or pay number. If the liable person leaves employment or becomes employed or re-employed, he or she must notify the Secretary of State in writing within seven days. Regulations 2(2) and 3 of the Information, Evidence and Disclosure Regulations also make provision for the liable person and/or a current or recent employer to provide information to enable the Secretary of State to discover the liable person's gross earnings and deductions from those earnings.
   Regulation 23 provides for the case where the liable person is in the employment of the Crown.

Subs. (7)
   Regulation 22 provides that a liable person may appeal against a deduction from earnings order to a magistrates' court in England and Wales, or the sheriff in Scotland, having jurisdiction in the area in which he or she resides. The grounds for such an appeal are: (a) that the order is defective; or (b) that the payments in question do not constitute earnings.

Subs. (8)
   The requirements for which failure to comply (in the absence of a defence under subs. (10)) will amount to an offence are: (i) the requirements on the liable person to supply details of his or her employment under reg. 15; (ii) the requirements on the employer to notify the Secretary of State when the liable person is not, or has ceased to be in his or her employment, or when a person in relation to whom a deduction from earnings order is in force is one of his or her employees, under reg. 16; (iii) the requirement on the employer to comply with any variation of a deduction from earnings order under reg. 19.

If a deduction from an earnings order is made under s.31 against someone in the employment of the Crown, this section only applies to failures to comply with regulations made under this section (s. 57(4)).

Liability orders

33.—(1) This section applies where—
   (*a*)   a person who is liable to make payments of child support maintenance ("the liable person") fails to make one or more of those payments; and
   (*b*)   it appears to the Secretary of State that—
      (i)   it is inappropriate to make a deduction from earnings order against him (because, for example, he is not employed); or
      (ii)   although such an order has been made against him, it has proved ineffective as a means of securing that payments are made in accordance with the maintenance assessment in question.

(2) The Secretary of State may apply to a magistrates' court or, in Scotland, to the sheriff for an order ("a liability order") against the liable person.

(3) Where the Secretary of State applies for a liability order, the magistrates' court or (as the case may be) sheriff shall make the order if satisfied that the payments in question have become payable by the liable person and have not been paid.

(4) On an application under subsection (2), the court or (as the case may be) the sheriff shall not question the maintenance assessment under which the payments of child support maintenance fell to be made.

DEFINITIONS
   "child support maintenance": see s.3(6).
   "maintenance assessment": see s.54.

GENERAL NOTE
   A liability order may be made if there has been any default in the payment of child support maintenance, but only if a deduction from an earnings order is inappropriate or has proved ineffective. Its effect is to permit other steps to be taken for enforcement.
   Where payments have not been made or made regularly, the Secretary of State may decide to seek a liability order from the Magistrates' Court, in England and Wales, or the sheriff in Scotland. In determining whether to do so, the Secretary of State must have regard to the welfare of any child likely to be affected (s.2). Unlike a deduction from an earnings order, a liability order can only be made when payments have fallen into arrears, and it is therefore to be seen as a method of enforcement rather than collection. The liability order does not of itself operate to enforce the maintenance assessment, but enables the Secretary of State to use other enforcement measures to do so. It operates in the same way as liability orders used to enforce the community charge or council tax. The enforcement measures which can be used are distress and sale of the liable person's goods, garnishee proceedings or charging order in England and Wales (ss.35 and 36); enforcement by diligence in Scotland (s.38); and commitment to prison in both jurisdictions (s.40). There is provision for enforcement of liability orders throughout the United Kingdom in s.39. Not all the mechanisms available to courts to enforce their orders have been included for the benefit of the Secretary of State. There is no provision for oral examination of the liable person as governed by reg. 7 of the Family Proceedings Rules 1991, which enables rigorous cross-examination of a respondent to take place as a means of discovering exactly what his income, assets and liabilities are, on pain of being in contempt of court. Nor can a judgment summons be sought, which enables the court to examine the respondent on oath as to his means, and to make such order as it considers appropriate as to the payment of arrears. The judgment summons has become popular as a means of enforcing financial orders made on divorce (see *Woodley* v. *Woodley* [1993] Fam. Law 24 and the commentary thereto), but presumably it has been omitted from the Secretary of State's possible armoury because control vests with the court, not the applicant for the summons. The possibility of instituting bankruptcy proceedings has also been omitted, no doubt because this would not be appropriate to seeking to ensure that the liable person pays, and continues to pay his or her maintenance assessment. Access to the High Court for enforcement is also not available, perhaps because of the cost.
   Where an application is to be made for a liability order against a liable person who is resident in Northern Ireland, it shall be made under the provision for that territory, even though the liability arose, or the maintenance assessment was made, under the provisions for Great Britain, and *vice versa*. Any

appeal in connection with the liability order, or action as a consequence of the order, shall be made under the provision for the territory in which the liable person is resident (Sched. 1, paras. 11 and 12 to the Child Support (Northern Ireland Reciprocal Arrangements) Regulations 1993).

Subs. (1)

This subsection sets out the criteria which must be satisfied before the Secretary of State can seek a liability order. The liable person must have failed to make one or more payments of child support maintenance, and it must appear that a deduction from earnings order is inappropriate or has proved ineffective. A deduction from earnings order will be inappropriate where the liable person is unemployed, and unlikely to be appropriate where he or she is self-employed. It might also be inappropriate where it would prove embarrassing to the liable person for his or her employer to discover that child support maintenance had been assessed. Regulations 2(2) and 3 of the Information, Evidence and Disclosure Regulations, which make provision for the liable person and/or a current or recent employer to provide information to enable the Secretary of State to discover the liable person's gross earnings and deductions from those earnings, may be relevant to enable the Secretary of State to decide whether to seek the liability order.

Subs. (2)

The application for a liability order is made by way of complaint to the magistrates' court having jurisdiction in the area in which the liable person resides (reg. 28(1) of the Collection and Enforcement Regulations). The application may not be instituted more than six years after the day on which the payment in question became due. For Scotland, see Act of Sederunt (Child Support Rules) 1993.

Subs. (3)

The only questions for the Magistrates' Court or sheriff are whether the payments have become payable by the liable person and have not been paid. The court may not, for example, question the desirability of the Secretary of State choosing to seek a liability order in the light of the welfare of any child likely to be affected, or the appropriateness of the enforcement mechanisms which result from obtaining the liability order. A liable person wishing to challenge the Secretary of State's decision to seek the order must go by way of judicial review.

Subs. (4)

The Magistrates' Court or sheriff may not question the maintenance assessment. This is in line with the exclusive jurisdiction of the Secretary of State and CSATs over assessments. If the maintenance assessment is to be challenged, the liable person would have to utilise the usual procedures for review in ss.17 or 18 (see above).

Regulations about liability orders

34.—(1) The Secretary of State may make regulations in relation to England and Wales—

   (*a*) prescribing the procedure to be followed in dealing with an application by the Secretary of State for a liability order;

   (*b*) prescribing the form and contents of a liability order; and

   (*c*) providing that where a magistrates' court has made a liability order, the person against whom it is made shall, during such time as the amount in respect of which the order was made remains wholly or partly unpaid, be under a duty to supply relevant information to the Secretary of State.

(2) In subsection (1) "relevant information" means any information of a prescribed description which is in the possession of the liable person and which the Secretary of State has asked him to supply.

DEFINITIONS

   "liability order": see s.33(2).

   "prescribed": see s.54.

GENERAL NOTE

   This section provides for regulations concerning England and Wales. Section 37 below covers Scotland. The relevant regulations are contained in Part IV of, and Sched. 1 to, the Collection and Enforcement Regulations. They apply, as modified, to other forms of maintenance prescribed for the purposes of s.30 by the Collection and Enforcement of Other Forms of Maintenance Regulations (see above).

Subs. (1)

Part IV of the Regulations provides for the Secretary of State to give the liable person at least seven days' notice of intention to apply for a liability order. The notice must set out the amount of child support maintenance which is claimed to be owing and not paid, and the amount of any interest on arrears payable (see s.41 below). The application may not be made more than six years after the day on which payment of the amount in question became due (see s.41 below for comparison with the courts' approach to payments in arrears). Schedule 1 to the Regulations sets out the form prescribed for the liability order. Regulation 29 provides for the enforcement of liability orders made in different parts of the United Kingdom.

Subs. (2)

This subsection has not been brought into force.

Enforcement of liability orders by distress

35.—(1) Where a liability order has been made against a person ("the liable person"), the Secretary of State may levy the appropriate amount by distress and sale of the liable person's goods.

(2) In subsection (1), "the appropriate amount" means the aggregate of—

(*a*) the amount in respect of which the order was made, to the extent that it remains unpaid; and

(*b*) an amount, determined in such manner as may be prescribed, in respect of the charges connected with the distress.

(3) The Secretary of State may, in exercising his powers under subsection (1) against the liable person's goods, seize—

(*a*) any of the liable person's goods except—

(i) such tools, books, vehicles and other items of equipment as are necessary to him for use personally by him in his employment, business or vocation;

(ii) such clothing, bedding, furniture, household equipment and provisions as are necessary for satisfying his basic domestic needs; and

(*b*) any money, banknotes, bills of exchange, promissory notes, bonds, specialties or securities for money belonging to the liable person.

(4) For the purposes of subsection (3), the liable person's domestic needs shall be taken to include those of any member of his family with whom he resides.

(5) No person levying a distress under this section shall be taken to be a trespasser—

(*a*) on that account; or

(*b*) from the beginning, on account of any subsequent irregularity in levying the distress.

(6) A person sustaining special damage by reason of any irregularity in levying a distress under this section may recover full satisfaction for the damage (and no more) by proceedings in trespass or otherwise.

(7) The Secretary of State may make regulations supplementing the provisions of this section.

(8) The regulations may, in particular—

(*a*) provide that a distress under this section may be levied anywhere in England and Wales;

(*b*) provide that such a distress shall not be deemed unlawful on account of any defect or want of form in the liability order;

(*c*) provide for an appeal to a magistrates' court by any person aggrieved by the levying of, or an attempt to levy, a distress under this section;

(*d*) make provision as to the powers of the court on an appeal (which may include provision as to the discharge of goods distrained or the payment of compensation in respect of goods distrained and sold).

DEFINITIONS
"liability order": see s.33(2).
"prescribed": see s.54.

GENERAL NOTE
This section does not extend to Scotland (s. 58(9)).

Where the Secretary of State decides to levy distress as the appropriate means of enforcement, the liability order will operate effectively as if it were a warrant of distress issued by the magistrates, authorising the Secretary of State to levy distress within the terms of this section and of regs. 30 to 32 of the Collection and Enforcement Regulations.

Subs. (1)

By reg. 30, the person levying distress on behalf of the Secretary of State must carry written authorisation, which must be shown to the liable person if requested. Copies of regs. 30 and 31 of, and Sched. 2 to, the Regulations, a memorandum setting out the appropriate amount (see below), a memorandum setting out details of any arrangement entered into regarding the taking into possession of goods distrained and a notice setting out the liable person's rights of appeal under reg. 31 must be handed to the liable person or left at the premises where the distress is levied.

Subs. (2)

The amount to be raised by distress and sale is the amount of child support maintenance unpaid, which may include interest on the arrears (see s.41 below). The provisions dealing with charges in relation to distress are reg. 32 of, and Sched. 2 to, the Collection and Enforcement Regulations.

Subs. (3)

Under subs. (3)(*b*) cash belonging to the liable person may not be seized, contrary to the position under reg. 54(2) of the Magistrates' Courts Rules 1981.

Subs. (7)

The regulations are contained in Part IV of the Collection and Enforcement Regulations.

Subs. (8)

Regulation 31(1) provides that a person aggrieved by the levy of, or attempt to levy, distress may appeal by way of complaint to the magistrates' court having jurisdiction in the area in which that person resides. The right is not limited to the liable person; it would appear that a member of that person's family, or a person disputing ownership of the goods seized, could appeal. However, the only ground for allowing the appeal is that the levy or attempted levy was irregular, i.e. that it was procedurally defective. For example, in *Evans* v. *South Ribble Borough Council* [1992] 2 All E.R. 695, it was held that a bailiff, unable to gain lawful entry, had not levied effective distress by posting a written notice of distress through the letterbox. Whereas the courts tend to use the *threat*, rather than the actual carrying-out of a levy, as the means of inducing a debtor to pay up, postponing the issue of the warrant upon conditions as to the amounts and times of payment, a magistrates' court would be unable to adopt this approach in hearing an appeal under reg. 31. It may be that the Secretary of State will adopt a similar stance having obtained his liability order.

Enforcement in county courts

36.—(1) Where a liability order has been made against a person, the amount in respect of which the order was made, to the extent that it remains unpaid, shall, if a county court so orders, be recoverable by means of garnishee proceedings or a charging order, as if it were payable under a county court order.

(2) In subsection (1) "charging order" has the same meaning as in section 1 of the Charging Orders Act 1979.

DEFINITION
"liability order": see s.33(2).

GENERAL NOTE
The section gives jurisdiction only to the county courts, not the High Court.

Garnishee proceedings are used to obtain arrears from the liable person, by diverting money owed to him or her by a third party or held by a third party on behalf of the liable person. The usual example will be where the liable person has a bank account with a credit balance, which is a debt owed to that person by the bank. The effect of a garnishee order is to require the third party to pay the money to the creditor. The procedures governing the making of garnishee orders are contained in the County Court Rules 1981, Ord. 30.

Charging orders secure payment of arrears from funds or property belonging to the liable person. They are governed by the Charging Orders Act 1979 and the County Court Rules 1981, Ord. 31. Section 1(1) of that Act defines a charging order as one "imposing on any such property of the debtor as may be specified in the order a charge for securing the payment of any money due or to become due under the judgment or order." By s.2, a charge may be imposed only on a beneficial interest held by the debtor in land, securities consisting of government stock, stock of any body (other than a building society) incorporated within England and Wales, stock of any body incorporated outside England and Wales, but registered in England and Wales, or funds in court. The charge may be imposed, for example, upon a matrimonial home which is jointly owned by the debtor and a new spouse or partner, in respect of the debtor's beneficial interest in that home. The charging order may be enforced by an application for an order for sale. Difficulties may arise in deciding whether a charging order should take priority over the interest of the new spouse or partner. In *Harman* v. *Glencross* [1986] 2 F.L.R 241, the Court of Appeal held that where no proceedings have been instituted by the new spouse against the debtor before the charging order nisi is made, it should normally be made absolute, and the spouse seek protection of his or her rights in the property (including, in particular, the right to occupy) under s.30 of the Law of Property Act 1925. Even where the spouse has begun divorce proceedings against the debtor before the order nisi, it would require exceptional circumstances before the court would transfer the debtor's interest in the property to the spouse, thereby defeating the creditor. However, the Court noted that the creditor was an individual rather than a "faceless corporation" (*per* Balcombe, L.J., at p. 251). Section 1(5) of the Charging Orders Act requires the court to consider all the circumstances of the case in deciding whether to make the order; the Court considered that the competing interests of the spouse and the creditor should be weighed. Since the spouse is likely to suffer more hardship than the Secretary of State, it is arguable that a charging order might be refused where such hardship could be demonstrated.

Regulations about liability orders: Scotland

37.—(1) Section 34(1) does not apply to Scotland.

(2) In Scotland, the Secretary of State may make regulations providing that where the sheriff has made a liability order, the person against whom it is made shall, during such time as the amount in respect of which the order was made remains wholly or partly unpaid, be under a duty to supply relevant information to the Secretary of State.

(3) In this section "relevant information" has the same meaning as in section 34(2).

DEFINITION
"liability order": see s.33(2).

GENERAL NOTE
Subss. (2) and (3)
These subsections have not been brought into force.

Enforcement of liability orders by diligence: Scotland

38.—(1) In Scotland, where a liability order has been made against a person, the order shall be warrant anywhere in Scotland—

(*a*) for the Secretary of State to charge the person to pay the appropriate amount and to recover that amount by a poinding and sale under Part II of the Debtors (Scotland) Act 1987 and, in connection therewith, for the opening of shut and lockfast places;

(*b*) for an arrestment (other than an arrestment of the person's earnings in the hands of his employers) and action of furthcoming or sale,

and shall be apt to found a Bill of Inhibition or an action of adjudication at the instance of the Secretary of State.

(2) In subsection (1) the "appropriate amount" means the amount in respect of which the order was made, to the extent that it remains unpaid.

DEFINITION
"liability order": see s.33(2).

Liability orders: enforcement throughout United Kingdom

39.—(1) The Secretary of State may by regulations provide for—
(*a*) any liability order made by a court in England and Wales; or
(*b*) any corresponding order made by a court in Northern Ireland,
to be enforced in Scotland as if it had been made by the sheriff.

(2) The power conferred on the Court of Session by section 32 of the Sheriff Courts (Scotland) Act 1971 (power of Court of Session to regulate civil procedure in the sheriff court) shall extend to making provision for the registration in the sheriff court for enforcement of any such order as is referred to in subsection (1).

(3) The Secretary of State may by regulations make provision for, or in connection with, the enforcement in England and Wales of—
(*a*) any liability order made by the sheriff in Scotland; or
(*b*) any corresponding order made by a court in Northern Ireland,
as if it had been made by a magistrates' court in England and Wales.

(4) Regulations under subsection (3) may, in particular, make provision for the registration of any such order as is referred to in that subsection in connection with its enforcement in England and Wales.

DEFINITION
"liability order": see s.33(2).

GENERAL NOTE

This section provides for the enforcement of liability orders throughout the United Kingdom. It obviates the need for the Secretary of State to seek fresh orders should the liable person move to another part of the United Kingdom. For the position concerning orders made, or to be enforced, in Northern Ireland, see Sched. 1 para. 12 to the Child Support (Northern Ireland Reciprocal Arrangements) Regulations 1993 (provisions for the territory in which the liable person is resident to govern the action to be taken).

Subs. (1)

The provisions dealing with enforcement in Scotland are regs. 26 and 29(2) of the Collection and Enforcement Regulations.

Subs. (3)

The provision dealing with enforcement in England and Wales is reg. 29(3) and (4) of the Collection and Enforcement Regulations.

Subss. (3) and (4)

Before a liability order made in Scotland or Northern Ireland can be enforced in England and Wales, it must be registered in accordance with the provisions of Part II of the Maintenance Orders Act 1950. Regulation 29(4) provides that a Scottish liability order shall be treated as if it were a decree for payment of aliment within s.16(2)(*b*) of that Act, and that a liability order made in Northern Ireland shall be treated as if it were an order for alimony, maintenance or other payments within s.16(2)(*c*). Section 17 of the 1950 Act sets out the procedure for registration. It requires the application for registration to be made to the court which made the original order, which then sends a certified copy of the order to the appropriate court in England and Wales, which will be the magistrates' court for the area in which the liable person appears to be. The order will then be enforced as if it had been made by a magistrates' court in England and Wales.

Commitment to prison

40.—(1) Where the Secretary of State has sought—
  (*a*) to levy an amount by distress under this Act; or
  (*b*) to recover an amount by virtue of section 36,
and that amount, or any portion of it, remains unpaid he may apply to a magistrates' court for the issue of a warrant committing the liable person to prison.

(2) On any such application the court shall (in the presence of the liable person) inquire as to—
  (*a*) the liable person's means; and
  (*b*) whether there has been wilful refusal or culpable neglect on his part.

(3) If, but only if, the court is of the opinion that there has been wilful refusal or culpable neglect on the part of the liable person it may—
  (*a*) issue a warrant of commitment against him; or
  (*b*) fix a term of imprisonment and postpone the issue of the warrant until such time and on such conditions (if any) as it thinks just.

(4) Any such warrant—
  (*a*) shall be made in respect of an amount equal to the aggregate of—
    (i) the amount mentioned in section 35(1) or so much of it as remains outstanding; and
    (ii) an amount (determined in accordance with regulations made by the Secretary of State) in respect of the costs of commitment; and
  (*b*) shall state that amount.

(5) No warrant may be issued under this section against a person who is under the age of 18.

(6) A warrant issued under this section shall order the liable person—
  (*a*) to be imprisoned for a specified period; but
  (*b*) to be released (unless he is in custody for some other reason) on payment of the amount stated in the warrant.

(7) The maximum period of imprisonment which may be imposed by virtue of subsection (6) shall be calculated in accordance with Schedule 4 to the Magistrates' Courts Act 1980 (maximum periods of imprisonment in default of payment) but shall not exceed six weeks.

(8) The Secretary of State may by regulations make provision for the period of imprisonment specified in any warrant issued under this section to be reduced where there is part payment of the amount in respect of which the warrant was issued.

(9) A warrant issued under this section may be directed to such person or persons as the court issuing it thinks fit.

(10) Section 80 of the Magistrates' Courts Act 1980 (application of money found on defaulter) shall apply in relation to a warrant issued under this section against a liable person as it applies in relation to the enforcement of a sum mentioned in subsection (1) of that section.

(11) The Secretary of State may by regulations make provision—
  (*a*) as to the form of any warrant issued under this section;
  (*b*) allowing an application under this section to be renewed where no warrant is issued or term of imprisonment is fixed;
  (*c*) that a statement in writing to the effect that wages of any amount have been

paid to the liable person during any period, purporting to be signed by or on behalf of his employer, shall be evidence of the facts stated;

(*d*) that, for the purposes of enabling an inquiry to be made as to the liable person's conduct and means, a justice of the peace may issue a summons to him to appear before a magistrates' court and (if he does not obey) may issue a warrant for his arrest;

(*e*) that for the purpose of enabling such an inquiry, a justice of the peace may issue a warrant for the liable person's arrest without issuing a summons;

(*f*) as to the execution of a warrant for arrest.

(12) Subsections (1) to (11) do not apply to Scotland.

(13) For the avoidance of doubt, it is declared that a sum payable under a liability order is a sum decerned for aliment for the purposes of the Debtors (Scotland) Act 1880 and the Civil Imprisonment (Scotland) Act 1882.

(14) Where a liability order has been made, the Secretary of State (and he alone) shall be regarded as, and may exercise all the powers of, the creditor for the purposes of section 4 (imprisonment for failure to obey decree for alimentary debt) of the Civil Imprisonment (Scotland) Act 1882.

DEFINITIONS
"liability order": see s.33(2).
"liable person": see s.33(1)(*a*).

GENERAL NOTE
The ultimate sanction for the Secretary of State will be to seek to have the liable person committed to prison for non-payment. Apart from the community charge and council tax, the only civil debt for which imprisonment remains a sanction is maintenance. The sanction is intended for those who will not, rather than those who cannot, pay. It has been said that such a sanction is

"a power of extreme severity. Indeed, it might be argued that the existence of such a power in a society which long ago closed the Marshalsea prison and abandoned imprisonment as a remedy for the enforcement of debts, is anomalous. Certainly, Parliament has made it plain that the power is to be exercised sparingly and only as a last resort."

(Waite, J., in *R.* v. *Luton Magistrates' Court, ex p. Sullivan* [1992] 2 F.L.R. 196 at 201.)

Subsections (1) to (11) do not apply to Scotland (subs. (12)); subss. (13) and (14) provide that the Civil Imprisonment (Scotland) Act 1882 applies to commitment in Scotland for non-payment of child support maintenance.

The court has a discretion whether to commit, or suspend commitment of, the liable person to prison, and must take account of his or her means. It, therefore, has an opportunity to re-assess the financial assumptions about the absent parent upon which the Secretary of State has worked in arriving at the maintenance assessment. No doubt, if the court considered that a warrant of commitment should not be made, the Secretary of State would consider reviewing his assessment.

Subs. (1)
The Secretary of State must have tried distress or enforcement through the county court first, emphasising that commitment is intended as a last resort. Regulations 33 and 34 of the Collection and Enforcement Regulations deal with the application and the warrant.

Subs. (2)
The liable person must be present at the hearing. To ensure his or her presence, reg. 33(1) empowers a justice of the peace having jurisdiction for the area in which the liable person resides to issue a summons for him or her to appear before a Magistrates' court and, if this is not obeyed, or as an alternative, to issue a warrant for the liable person's arrest.

The court must find wilful refusal or culpable neglect on the part of the liable person (*Bernstein* v. *O'Neill* [1989] 2 F.L.R. 1). In *R.* v. *Luton Magistrates' Court, ex p. Sullivan* [1992] 2 F.L.R. 196, the Divisional Court held, in relation to non-payment of maintenance under the private law, that the liable person's conduct must amount to deliberate defiance or reckless disregard; default by way of improvidence or dilatoriness was insufficient. Justices must be scrupulous in allowing the liable person the opportunity to make his or her case, and this will generally require that at least an opportunity be afforded for the liable person to obtain legal advice. Regrettably, the duty solicitor scheme operating at magistrates' courts does not extend to those facing commitment for non-payment; the result may be that where the liable person is brought to court and claims not to have been aware of the hearing, and hence not to have sought advice, the hearing should be adjourned to enable this to be done. The liable person should be allowed the assistance of a friend at any hearing if this is requested (*R.* v. *Wolverhampton Stipendiary Magistrate, ex p. Mould, The Times*, November 16, 1992).

Subs. (3)

It is common to postpone issue of the warrant on condition that the liable person makes regular payments of maintenance as they fall due and pays towards clearing the arrears. A liable person who breaches the condition may be committed to prison in his or her absence, provided that notice of the hearing was given (*R.* v. *Northampton Magistrates' Court, ex p. Newell, The Times*, September 18, 1992). The warrant must be in the form specified in Sched. 3 to the Collection and Enforcement Regulations.

Subs. (4).

Regulation 34(2) provides that the amount in respect of costs shall be such amount as in the view of the court is equal to the costs reasonably incurred by the Secretary of State in respect of the costs of commitment.

Subs. (7).

Schedule 4 to the Magistrates' Courts Act 1980 provides a sliding scale relating the length of imprisonment to the amount of arrears.

Subs. (8)

The provision dealing with part-payment is reg. 34(5) and (6) of the Collection and Enforcement Regulations.

Subs. (11).

The provisions dealing with these matters are regs. 33 and 34 of, and Sched. 3 to, the Collection and Enforcement Regulations.

Arrears of child support maintenance

41.—(1) This section applies where—
  (*a*) the Secretary of State is authorised under section 4, 6 or 7 to recover child support maintenance payable by an absent parent in accordance with a maintenance assessment; and
  (*b*) the absent parent has failed to make one or more payments of child support maintenance due from him in accordance with that assessment.
  (2) Where the Secretary of State recovers any such arrears he may, in such circumstances as may be prescribed and to such extent as may be prescribed, retain them if he is satisfied that the amount of any benefit paid to the person with care of the child or children in question would have been less had the absent parent not been in arrears with his payments of child support maintenance.
  (3) In such circumstances as may be prescribed, the absent parent shall be liable to make such payments of interest with respect to the arrears of child support maintenance as may be prescribed.
  (4) The Secretary of State may by regulations make provision—
  (*a*) as to the rate of interest payable by virtue of subsection (3);
  (*b*) as to the time at which, and person to whom, any such interest shall be payable;
  (*c*) as to the circumstances in which, in a case where the Secretary of State has been acting under section 6, any such interest may be retained by him;
  (*d*) for the Secretary of State, in a case where he has been acting under section 6 and in such circumstances as may be prescribed, to waive any such interest (or part of any such interest).
  (5) The provisions of this Act with respect to—
  (*a*) the collection of child support maintenance;
  (*b*) the enforcement of any obligation to pay child support maintenance,

shall apply equally to interest payable by virtue of this section.

(6) Any sums retained by the Secretary of State by virtue of this section shall be paid by him into the Consolidated Fund.

DEFINITIONS

"absent parent": see s.3(2).
"child": see s.55.
"child support maintenance": see s.3(6).
"maintenance assessment": see s.54.
"person with care": see s.3(3).
"prescribed": see s.54.

GENERAL NOTE

This section authorises the Secretary of State to recover arrears of child support maintenance. One of the failings of the private maintenance system was the requirement (until s.59A of the Maintenance Enforcement Act 1991) that the payee had to take action to recover arrears, rather than to have an automatic system of pursuing these through the court's own action. Where either the person with care (or in Scotland, the qualifying child) has applied for the Secretary of State to collect the child support maintenance, or s.6 applies, it is for the Secretary of State to take action to recover arrears. The Arrears, Interest and Adjustment of Maintenance Assessments Regulations provide the detailed arrangements for the recovery of arrears. Where a payment falls into arrears, the Secretary of State will seek to make an arrangement with the liable person to pay off the arrears, the incentive for agreeing to the arrangement being to avoid interest otherwise being charged on them. Where arrears are not successfully recovered, they will fall to be collected, along with the continuing liability to make payments, through other enforcement measures detailed in ss.31 to 40 above. There is no provision for a review of a decision as to arrears, or appeal to a CSAT. However, reg. 15 provides that an application may be made under reg. 55 of the Maintenance Assessment Procedure Regulations for the decision to be set aside. If this failed, the absent parent would have to seek a review of the assessment itself under ss.17 or 18, and reg. 10 provides for how arrears are to be taken into account in adjusting the amount of child support maintenance payable. Regulation 12 provides for a review under s.18 of the Act to be possible in respect of such an adjustment.

Subs. (1)

The Secretary of State should take prompt action to recover arrears, so that large amounts of money owed do not build up. The court system experienced long delays in enforcing arrears, due, in part at least, to the requirement noted above that the payee take action to recover them. It was accordingly provided that no arrears more than 12 months old could be enforced without the leave of the court (s.32 of the Matrimonial Causes Act 1973; s.32(4) of the Domestic Proceedings and Magistrates' Courts Act 1978). Such a situation should not arise under this Act. Arrears of child support maintenance are a private debt owed by the absent parent to the person with care. Consequently, the Secretary of State has no power to remit any arrears, although he has power to refrain from enforcing payment, which in practice may amount to the same thing.

The Secretary of State may enter into a written agreement with the absent parent, called an "arrears agreement", setting out the amounts and dates of payments of arrears to be made (reg. 5(1)). If, within 28 days of the "due date" (specified in accordance with reg. 4 of the Collection and Enforcement Regulations), the absent parent clears all arrears or enters into an arrears agreement and adheres to its terms, there shall be no liability to pay interest on the arrears (reg. 5(3)). If the agreement is entered into after 28 days, interest accrues until the date of the agreement but not thereafter (reg. 5(4)).

Subs. (2)

Regulation 8 of the Arrears, Interest and Adjustment of Maintenance Assessments Regulations provides that where the person with care is paid income support, the Secretary of State may retain the amount of arrears equal to the difference between the amount of income support actually paid to that person, and the amount which would have been paid if the arrears had not accrued.

Subs. (3)

Interest is payable only where the Secretary of State has served an arrears notice in respect of the arrears. The notice must itemise the amounts of child support maintenance due and unpaid; set out the provisions as to arrears and interest contained in the Regulations; and request the absent parent to pay all outstanding arrears (reg. 2(3)).

Interest is not payable in respect of any period terminating earlier than 14 days before the date the arrears notice is served on the absent parent (reg. 3(2)). Where the absent parent did not know, and could not reasonably have been expected to know, of the existence of the arrears, or they have arisen solely because of an operational or administrative error on the part of the Secretary of State or a child support officer, the absent parent will not be liable to pay interest. It will be for the absent parent to prove that this regulation is applicable. Where a fresh maintenance assessment is made with retrospective effect after a review or appeal to a CSAT, interest is payable in respect of the retrospective period, but is calculated by reference to the fresh assessment and before any adjustment is made under reg. 10 (reg. 3(4) and (5)).

Subs. (4)

Provision to charge interest upon maintenance arrears was included in the changes made to the enforcement of private maintenance obligations by s.8 of the Maintenance Enforcement Act 1991 (inserting s.94A into the Magistrates' Courts Act 1980). As regards child support, reg. 6(1) sets the rate of interest payable at one per cent. above median base rate. Interest is only payable on arrears, and not upon the interest already due (reg. 6(2)).

Under reg. 7, the interest is payable to the person with care, unless the assessment was made under s.6 of the Act and income support is or has been paid to the parent with care. In such a case, the interest may be retained by the Secretary of State unless he considers that, had full payment been made, the parent with care would not have been entitled to income support. If that is the position, that parent will receive the interest. Interest is apportioned where child support maintenance is payable to more than one person. Parents with care receiving family credit or disability working allowance will be entitled to receive the interest.

Special cases

Special cases

42.—(1) The Secretary of State may by regulations provide that in prescribed circumstances a case is to be treated as a special case for the purposes of this Act.

(2) Those regulations may, for example, provide for the following to be special cases—

(*a*)　each parent of a child is an absent parent in relation to the child;

(*b*)　there is more than one person who is a person with care in relation to the same child;

(*c*)　there is more than one qualifying child in relation to the same absent parent but the person who is the person with care in relation to one of those children is not the person who is the person with care in relation to all of them;

(*d*)　a person is an absent parent in relation to more than one child and the other parent of each of those children is not the same person;

(*e*)　the person with care has care of more than one qualifying child and there is more than one absent parent in relation to those children;

(*f*)　a qualifying child has his home in two or more separate households.

(3) The Secretary of State may by regulations make provision with respect to special cases.

(4) Regulations made under subsection (3) may, in particular—

(*a*)　modify any provision made by or under this Act, in its application to any special case or any special case falling within a prescribed category;

(*b*)　make new provision for any such case; or

(*c*)　provide for any prescribed provision made by or under this Act not to apply to any such case.

DEFINITIONS

　"absent parent": see s.3(2).

　"child": see s.55.

　"parent": see s.54.

　"person with care": see s.3(3).

　"prescribed": see s.54.

　"qualifying child": see s.3(1)

GENERAL NOTE
Subs. (1)

The basic structure of the Act presupposes the typical case of a child who has two parents, one of whom has left the household. However, there are a number of ways in which reality may vary from this model. These are represented by the special cases which adjust the provisions of the Act to cater for these variations. The regulations made under this section are contained in Part III of the Maintenance Assessments and Special Cases Regulations.

Subs. (3)

The regulations made under this section are contained in Part III of the Maintenance Assessments and Special Cases Regulations and regs. 21 and 22 of the Maintenance Assessment Procedure Regulations.

The special cases under this section and their significance are in summary as follows. For a detailed discussion reference should be made to the general notes to the relevant regulations and to the general notes to the provisions affected.

Special case	Significance
Both parents are absent parents (reg. 19).	If the person with care is a body corporate or unincorporate, the lone parent premium is not payable. If an application is made in relation to both absent parents, separate assessments are made for each absent parent taking into account the assessable income of the other absent parent. If both absent parents have applied for a maintenance assessment under s.4, the Secretary of State is bound by the duty in s.4(6), unless and until both absent parents request under s.4(5) that he cease to act (reg. 52(8) of the Maintenance Assessment Procedure Regulations).
A parent with part-time care of the child (reg. 20).	The parent may be treated as an absent parent and be required to pay a proportion of the child support maintenance that would be paid by a wholly absent parent.
Other persons with part-time care (reg. 24).	The Secretary of State may apportion child support maintenance between the persons who have part-time care.
One parent is absent and the other is treated as absent (reg. 21).	References to persons with care in the maintenance assessment provisions of Sched. 1 to the Act are treated as references to the person who is treated as an absent parent.
Multiple applications in respect of the same absent parent (reg. 22).	The assessable income of the absent parent is scaled down in each application by reference to the maintenance requirements. Special provision is also made regarding the minimum amount prescribed under s.16(6)(*b*) (regs. 21 and 23 of the Maintenance Assessment Procedure Regulations).
Person with care of children of more than one absent parent (reg. 23).	The calculation of some elements of the maintenance requirements is scaled down by reference to the number of absent parents. Special provision is also made regarding the minimum amount prescribed under s.16(6)(*b*) (regs. 22 and 23 of the Maintenance Assessment Procedure Regulations) and the prescribed minimum amount under Sched. 1, para. 7 to the Act (reg. 22(4)).
Child in care of local authority (reg. 25).	No child support maintenance is payable in respect of the nights for which the local authority provides care.
Cases where child support is not payable (reg. 26).	Self-explanatory.
Child is boarder or in-patient (reg. 27).	Person who would otherwise be providing day to day care is treated as the person with care.
Child allowed by local authority to live with parent (reg. 27A).	Section 3(3)(*b*) applies to the parent with whom the child is allowed to live rather than to the person who usually provides day to day care.

Contribution to maintenance by deduction from benefit

43.—(1) This section applies where—

(*a*) by virtue of paragraph 5(4) of Schedule 1, an absent parent is taken for the purposes of that Schedule to have no assessable income; and

(*b*) such conditions as may be prescribed for the purposes of this section are satisfied.

(2) The power of the Secretary of State to make regulations under [¹section 5 of the Social Security Administration Act 1992 by virtue of subsection (1)(*t*),] (deductions from benefits) may be exercised in relation to cases to which this section applies with a view to securing that—

(*a*) payments of prescribed amounts are made with respect to qualifying children in place of payments of child support maintenance; and

(*b*) arrears of child support maintenance are recovered.

AMENDMENT

1. Sched. 2, para. 113 to the Social Security Consequential Provisions Act 1992 (July 1, 1992).

DEFINITIONS

"absent parent": see s.3(2).
"assessable income": see Sched. 1, para. 5.
"child support maintenance": see s.3(6).
"prescribed": see s.54.
"qualifying child": see s.3(1).

GENERAL NOTE
Subs. (1)(b)
   The provision containing these conditions is reg. 28(1) of the Maintenance Assessments and Special Cases Regulations. See also Sched. 4 to those Regulations.

Jurisdiction

Jurisdiction

44.—(1) A child support officer shall have jurisdiction to make a maintenance assessment with respect to a person who is—

(*a*) a person with care;

(*b*) an absent parent; or

(*c*) a qualifying child,

only if that person is habitually resident in the United Kingdom.

(2) Where the person with care is not an individual, subsection (1) shall have effect as if paragraph (*a*) were omitted.

(3) The Secretary of State may by regulations make provision for the cancellation of any maintenance assessment where—

(*a*) the person with care, absent parent or qualifying child with respect to whom it was made ceases to be habitually resident in the United Kingdom;

(*b*) in a case falling within subsection (2), the absent parent or qualifying child with respect to whom it was made ceases to be habitually resident in the United Kingdom; or

(*c*) in such circumstances as may be prescribed, a maintenance order of a prescribed kind is made with respect to any qualifying child with respect to whom the maintenance assessment was made.

DEFINITIONS
"absent parent": see s.3(2).
"child support officer": see s.13.

"maintenance assessment": see s.54.
"maintenance order": see s.8(11).
"person with care": see s.3(3).
"prescribed": see s.54.
"qualifying child": see s.3(1).

GENERAL NOTE
Subs. (1)

Habitual residence means the same as ordinary residence (*V.* v. *B.* [1991] 1 F.L.R. 266 and *Kapur* v. *Kapur* [1984] F.L.R. 928), although there is an argument that a person may be ordinarily resident, but not habitually resident, in two jurisdictions at the same time. It is difficult to distill a principle from some of the briefly reported cases (e.g. *Rellis* v. *Hart* [1992] G.W.D. para. 1456). The leading authority is the House of Lords decision in *Shah* v. *Barnet London Borough Council* [1983] 1 All E.R. 226 and in particular the speech of Lord Scarman at 234–236. From this and other authorities the following propositions emerge:

(i)   The words are not a term of art and are to be given their ordinary and natural meaning unless it can be shown that the statutory framework or the legal context in which the words are used requires a different meaning (*Shah*). There is nothing in the present framework or context to displace this meaning.

(ii)   The normal meaning of habitual residence is "a man's abode in a particular place or country which he has adopted voluntarily and for settled purposes as part of the regular order of his life for the time being, whether of short or long duration" (*Shah*). Residence is therefore something different from presence (*CA 35/92*, paras. 5 and 14). Accordingly, a person may be habitually resident within the jurisdiction while working abroad. This important point has been missed in the draft of the Child Support Officer's Guide available at the time of writing which cites cases on absence and presence in the section dealing with habitual residence. Residence must also be distinguished from the English concept of domicile (*R(U) 8/88*, Appendix 1, para. 6).

(iii)   This basic definition of habitual residence is subject to the exception that the person's presence in a particular jurisdiction must be lawful (*Shah*). Thus it may be relevant to know whether an immigrant is lawfully within the country or whether a child has been abducted. The habitual residence of children is discussed below.

(iv)   For the most part the definition concentrates on observable facts, but there will seldom be direct evidence of a person's intention. The proper approach to dealing with conflicts of affidavit evidence on intention was explained by the Court of Appeal in *Re F. (A Minor) (Child Abduction)* [1992] 1 F.L.R. 548. In the context of summary proceedings for the return of a child to a country in which it was alleged that he had been habitually resident before being abducted, the court held that where there is irreconcilable affidavit evidence and no oral testimony available, the judge should look to see if there is independent extraneous evidence in support of one side, although that evidence would have to be compelling before it could be preferred to the sworn testimony of a deponent. Usually, however, the person's intention will have to be inferred from all the circumstances of the case, in which case the primary facts will have to be included in the findings of fact and the drawing of the inference explained in the tribunal's reasons for decision.

(v)   The person's intention will be relevant in two respects. First, the residence must be voluntary. Involuntary residence such as a result, for example, of kidnapping or imprisonment would negative the will to be there (*Shah*). However, this may not be a universal requirement. In *Re MacKenzie* [1940] 4 All E.R. 310 a lady came on a visit to this country which she intended to be temporary. She became insane while here and spent the next 54 years in an asylum. Morton, J., discussed *I.R.C.* v. *Lysaght* [1928] A.C. 234, (one of the decisions relied on by the House of Lords in *Shah*), but distinguished it, holding that it did not decide that involuntary residence had to be wholly disregarded for ascertaining a person's habitual residence. In view of the very great degree of continuity in the case he held that the lady was habitually resident in this country despite her lack of choice. Where someone is looking after an adult who lacks the capacity to form an intention, the residence and wishes of the former will be relevant to the habitual residence of the latter: see the discussion of the habitual residence of children in (xi) below.

(vi)   The second way in which intention is relevant is that there must be a settled purpose. There need be no intention to remain permanently or even indefinitely. A short and definite period will be sufficient. In *CA 35/92*, for example, a lady was held to be ordinarily resident in Malta when she went there for health reasons with the intention of returning within 18 months. All that is required is that there should be sufficient continuity that can properly be described as settled. Education can be a sufficient purpose (*Kapur* v. *Kapur*), as would health (*CA 35/92*).

(vii)   Lack of evidence of the actual places within a jurisdiction where a person has stayed is not fatal to a decision that a person has been habitually resident there, although it is a factor to be taken into account (*Re Brauch, ex p. Britannic Securities and Investments Ltd.* [1978] 1 All E.R. 1004).

(viii)   In order to acquire habitual residence it is necessary to show not only a settled purpose but also that the person has spent an appreciable period of time in the jurisdiction (*Re J. (A Minor) (Abduction: Custody Rights)* [1990] 2 A.C. 562). What constitutes a sufficient period is a decision to be reached in the light of the circumstances of the individual case. Ultimately, however, it is the quality rather than the duration of the residence that is important (*Cruse* v. *Chittum* [1974] 2 All E.R. 940). This suggests that in appropriate circumstances habitual residence could be acquired in a single day. However, it is unclear how quickly habitual residence can be acquired. The proposition attributed to *Re J.* above appears inconsistent with *Lewis* v. *Lewis* [1956] 1 All E.R. 375, in which it was held that the boarding of a ship to resume a former home in this country would be sufficient to establish habitual residence here. This case is a clear authority for the proposition that habitual residence can be acquired in a single day if the person concerned has had an habitual residence in one place, moved to another, and then abandoned that other place to return to the former home. However, the authority on which this decision was based, *MacRae* v. *MacRae* [1949] 2 All E.R. 34, is suspect in suggesting, contrary to the view of the House of Lords in *Re J.*, that habitual residence may be acquired as easily as it is lost. The fact of resumption of a former home may be sufficient to distinguish *Re J.*, although it must be admitted that the case of *R.* v. *Lancashire County Council, ex p. Huddleston* [1986] 2 All E.R. 941, which is discussed below, is inconsistent with this argument. Moreover, in *Re M. (Minors) (Residence), The Times*, November 6, 1992 a mother with parental responsibility for children allowed them to go to live in Scotland (a separate jurisdiction) and then decided on their returning to stay with her for a holiday that they should remain with her in England. Balcombe, L.J., thought that the children did not thereby immediately become habitually resident in England, whereas Hoffmann, L.J., thought they did. However, since the issue was not essential to the court's decision, these views are *obiter*. In view of the state of the authorities, the question of whether habitual residence can be acquired in a single day must be considered to be as yet undecided.

(ix)   Since habitual residence depends upon there being a settled purpose, a person will cease to be habitually resident once such a settled purpose ceases to exist. Habitual residence can therefore be lost on a single day (*Re J.*). Since it may not be so easily acquired, it is possible that a person may have no place of habitual residence: see the discussion in (viii) above.

(x)   Absences from a place are not sufficient to lose habitual residence if they are purely temporary (*Shah* and *Lewis*). It will be necessary for the tribunal to establish the number and duration of any absences, as well as the reasons for them, in order to decide whether on balance they are sufficient to displace a person's habitual residence. However, lengthy absences will result in loss of habitual residence even if there is an intention ultimately to return. In *Huddleston* a family had left England for Hong Kong when their daughter was five-years-old, intending ultimately to return. However, they remained abroad for 13 years as a result of the father's employment which required him to be exclusively abroad. When the daughter returned, it was held that she was not ordinarily resident in the United Kingdom.

(xi)   Usually the habitual residence of children will be determined by that of the persons with whom they live lawfully (*Re J.*). If the child lives with only one parent by agreement, it will that parent's residence which is significant. However, this will not be the case if the child has been abducted, unless the dispossessed parent has acquiesced. Acquiescence is the informed consent by a person to something which would otherwise amount to an infringement of that person's rights. Where the person has not expressly acquiesced, acquiescence may be inferred. The approach to be taken in deciding whether or not to infer that a person has acquiesced was explained by Balcombe, L.J., in *Re A. (Minors) (Abduction: Acquiescence)* [1992] 2 F.L.R. 14 at 22:

"acquiescence can be inferred from inactivity and silence on the part of the parent from whose custody, joint or single, the child has been wrongfully removed. In such a case . . . the court would have to look at all the circumstances of the case, and in particular, the reasons for the inactivity on the part of the wronged parent and the length of the period over which the inactivity persisted, in order to decide whether it was legitimate to infer acquiescence on his or her part."

It has been said that implied acquiescence will occur certainly after six months and in appropriate cases after as little as three months (*Re P. (G.E.)* [1964] 3 All E.R. 977 at 982 *per* Lord Denning, M.R.), although the authority is an old one and the proposition may be stated too starkly. In some cases children will be of sufficient age and maturity to form a settled purpose separate from that of the persons with whom they live. This of itself will not affect the children's habitual residence, unless the circumstances permit a separate habitual residence to exist. This might occur, for example, where a child is at a school or college abroad during term-time and returns home only for the vacations. In cases where children are of an age likely to be capable of forming their own settled purpose, an inquiry and findings of fact will be necessary as to their maturity to decide on such a purpose and on their freedom to act on it.

The important factor in the case of children is with whom they lawfully reside. In deciding this, any existing order for custody or care and control will be an important consideration as in *Re P. (G.E.)*. As cases in which the concept of custody is still relevant become fewer, as a result of the Children Act 1989, the emphasis will be on who has parental responsibility and on the effect of any residence order made under s.8 of that Act. In *Re M. (Minors) (Residence)*, *The Times*, November 6, 1992, for example, a decision by an unmarried mother, who lived in England and who had sole parental responsibility for children who were then living with their grandparents in Scotland, that they should henceforth live with her, was sufficient to end their habitual residence in Scotland.

Re M. shows that it is not necessarily the place where the parent who has habitual residence (or custody) lives that matters, but the place where the parent allows the children to live; so the children's habitual residence was initially in Scotland until permission to live there was withdrawn by the mother. This is in contrast to *R. v. Redbridge London Borough Council, ex p. East Sussex County Council*, *The Times*, December 31, 1992. Mentally handicapped twins had originally lived with their parents in Redbridge. When the parents returned to Nigeria, the twins remained at school in Redbridge with the fees paid by the parents. It was held that the twins ceased to be habitually resident in this country when their parents left. The decision may have been influenced by the earlier decision of *R. v. Waltham Forest London Borough Council, ex p. Vale*, *The Times*, February 25, 1985, or it may be that a special consideration applies where there is a mental handicap. In either case it is difficult to see why any different principle from that applicable in other childhood cases should apply. (The habitual residence of adults who lack capacity is touched on in (v) above.)

(xii)   Whether or not habitual residence has been established is a question of fact to be decided in all the circumstances of the case (*Shah* and *Re J.*). The tribunal will therefore need to make findings of fact on all of the factors considered above that are relevant to the appeal and to indicate in the reasons for decision that the correct test has been applied. It will be dangerous and an error of law to make decisions based on the similarity of the facts to those in other reported decisions, since each case depends on its own combination of facts. Commmissioners' Decisions do, however, provide some indication of the range of factors which a CSAT might wish to investigate in deciding on habitual residence (see the factors taken into account in *R(U) 8/88* and the decisions cited therein).

Subs. (3)

Where a person with care, an absent parent or a qualifying child ceases to be habitually resident in the United Kingdom, a child support officer is under a duty to cancel a maintenance assessment in force with effect from the date on which the person ceased to be habitually resident in the jurisdiction (reg. 7 of the Maintenance Arrangements and Jurisdiction Regulations).

Where a person with care believes that an assessment has ceased to have effect or should be cancelled, that person is under a duty to notify the Secretary of State of this belief and the reasons for it and to provide the Secretary of State with such information as he reasonably requires to allow a determination to be made on whether the assessment has ceased to have effect or should be cancelled (reg. 6 of the Information, Evidence and Disclosure Regulations).

The Maintenance Orders (Backdating) Order 1993 amends s.29 of the Matrimonial Causes Act 1973, s.5 of the Domestic Proceedings and Magistrates' Courts Act 1978 and Sched. 1, para. 3 to the Children Act 1989 to provide that where a maintenance assessment is cancelled or has ceased to have effect because the Secretary of State no longer has jurisdiction under the Act, and an application is made within six months for maintenance to replace the assessment, the order made can be backdated to the date of the cancellation or ceasing to have effect, to ensure minimal or no loss of income for the child.

Jurisdiction of courts in certain proceedings under this Act

45.—(1) The Lord Chancellor or, in relation to Scotland, the Lord Advocate may by order make such provision as he considers necessary to secure that appeals, or such class of appeals as may be specified in the order—

(*a*)   shall be made to a court instead of being made to a child support appeal tribunal; or

(*b*)   shall be so made in such circumstances as may be so specified.

(2) In subsection (1), "court" means—

(*a*)   in relation to England and Wales and subject to any provision made under Schedule 11 to the Children Act 1989 (jurisdiction of courts with respect to certain proceedings relating to children) the High Court, a county court or a magistrates' court; and

(*b*)   in relation to Scotland, the Court of Session or the sheriff.

(3) Schedule 11 to the Act of 1989 shall be amended in accordance with subsections (4) and (5).

(4) [Adds Schedule 11, Part I, paragraph 1(2A) to the Children Act 1989.]

(5) [Amends Schedule 11, Part I, paragraphs 1(3), 2(3) to the Children Act 1989.]

(6) Where the effect of any order under subsection (1) is that there are no longer any appeals which fall to be dealt with by child support appeal tribunals, the Lord Chancellor after consultation with the Lord Advocate may by order provide for the abolition of those tribunals.

(7) Any order under subsection (1) or (6) may make—

(*a*)   such modifications of any provision of this Act or of any other enactment; and

(*b*)   such transitional provision,

as the Minister making the order considers appropriate in consequence of any provision made by the order.

DEFINITION

"child support appeal tribunal": see s. 54.

GENERAL NOTE

Subs. (1)

The Child Support Appeals (Jurisdiction of Courts) Order 1993 provides that appeals under s.20 are to go to a court rather than to a CSAT where the question involved is whether a particular person is a parent of the child. This will enable the court to order scientific tests to determine parentage by virtue of powers available under ss.20–25 of the Matrimonial Causes Act 1973 as amended.

Schedule 2 to the Maintenance Orders (Backdating) Order 1993 amends s.65(1) of the Magistrates' Courts Act 1980 to provide that appeals under s.20, or references for a declaration of parentage, brought to the magistrates by virtue of s.27, are family proceedings.

Subss. (3) to (5)

The Children (Allocation of Proceedings) (Amendment) Order 1993 provides that child support cases heard by courts in accordance with ss.20, 27 and 45 will be commenced in the Magistrates' Courts and may be transferred to another Magistrates' Court or up to the county court or High Court in line with the same criteria as apply in the Children (Allocation of Proceedings) Order 1991.

The High Court (Distribution of Business) Order 1993 provides that any proceedings under the Child Support Act which are heard in the High Court are to be assigned to the Family Division.

The Family Proceedings (Amendment) Rules 1993 amend the Family Proceedings Rules 1991 (as amended) to cater for where a child support case has been transferred up from the magistrates' court. New rr. 3.21 and 3.22 are inserted to provide that r. 4.6 shall apply to an application under s.27 of the Child Support Act for a declaration of parentage, and to an appeal under s.20. The new rules allow the court to give such directions as it thinks proper with regard to the conduct of the proceedings. In particular, the court may direct that the proceedings shall proceed as if they had been commenced by originating summons or originating application and that any document served or other thing done while the proceedings were pending in another court, including a magistrates' court, shall be treated for such purposes as may be specified in the direction as if provided for by the rules of court applicable in the court to which the proceedings have been transferred.

An application under s.27 (but not an appeal under s.20) may be heard and determined by a district judge (r. 3.21(4)).

The Children (Admissibility of Hearsay Evidence) Order 1993 supersedes and revokes the 1991

Order (S.I. 1991 No. 1115), and extends to civil proceedings under the Child Support Act in the Magistrates' Courts the power to admit evidence notwithstanding that it is hearsay.

Miscellaneous and supplemental

Failure to comply with obligations imposed by section 6

46.—(1) This section applies where any person ("the parent")—
(*a*) fails to comply with a requirement imposed on her by the Secretary of State under section 6(1); or
(*b*) fails to comply with any regulation made under section 6(9).
(2) A child support officer may serve written notice on the parent requiring her, before the end of the specified period, either to comply or to give him her reasons for failing to do so.
(3) When the specified period has expired, the child support officer shall consider whether, having regard to any reasons given by the parent, there are reasonable grounds for believing that, if she were to be required to comply, there would be a risk of her or of any children living with her suffering harm or undue distress as a result of complying.
(4) If the child support officer considers that there are such reasonable grounds, he shall—
(*a*) take no further action under this section in relation to the failure in question; and
(*b*) notify the parent, in writing, accordingly.
(5) If the child support officer considers that there are no such reasonable grounds, he may give a reduced benefit direction with respect to the parent.
(6) Where the child support officer gives a reduced benefit direction he shall send a copy of it to the parent.
(7) Any person who is aggrieved by a decision of a child support officer to give a reduced benefit direction may appeal to a child support appeal tribunal against that decision.
(8) Sections 20(2) to (4) and 21 shall apply in relation to appeals under subsection (7) as they apply in relation to appeals under section 20.
(9) A reduced benefit direction shall take effect on such date as may be specified in the direction.
(10) Reasons given in response to a notice under subsection (2) may be given either in writing or orally.
(11) In this section—
"comply" means to comply with the requirement or with the regulation in question; and "complied" and "complying" shall be construed accordingly;
"reduced benefit direction" means a direction, binding on the adjudication officer, that the amount payable by way of any relevant benefit to, or in respect of, the parent concerned be reduced by such amount, and for such period, as may be prescribed;
"relevant benefit" means income support, family credit or any other benefit of a kind prescribed for the purposes of section 6; and
"specified", in relation to any notice served under this section, means specified in the notice; and the period to be specified shall be determined in accordance with regulations made by the Secretary of State.

DEFINITIONS
"adjudication officer": see s.54.
"child support officer": see s.13
"family credit": see s.54.
"income support": *ibid.*
"prescribed": *ibid.*

GENERAL NOTE

This section provides for the consequences of a parent with care's failure to comply with a requirement imposed by the Secretary of State under s.6. The regulations made under this section are contained in Part IX of the Maintenance Assessment Procedure Regulations. They deal with the maximum duration, amount, notice, review, suspension, cancellation and termination of a reduced benefit direction.

Subs. (2)

The Secretary of State must give the parent with care six weeks' notice of intention to refer the case to a child support officer (reg. 35(1) and (2)). The child support officer must then give the parent 14 days in which to comply or to supply reasons for failing to do so (reg. 35(3)). In other words, the parent with care has a six weeks cooling off period and then a further two weeks to reconsider.

Subs. (3)

No reduced benefit direction may be made, if there are reasonable grounds to believe that there would be a risk of the parent or any child living with the parent suffering harm or undue distress. The test here is the same as that under s.6(2), although here the decision is made by a child support officer rather than by the Secretary of State and so is appealable under subs. (7). The child who suffers harm or distress need not be the child of the absent parent. The emphasis is on the suffering of harm or distress. How it comes about is not relevant. Consequently, it will be sufficient if the person with care suffers undue distress as a result of believing, however unreasonably, that the giving of the authorisation might lead to violence on the part of the absent parent. The harm which may be suffered may be physical or mental. Any physical harm will suffice as will any mental effect which amounts to harm. However, if the mental effect does not amount to harm, it must be undue. This test is narrower than, but additional to, that which applies under s.2 where the "welfare" of a child has to be taken into account.

The bar to a reduced benefit direction only applies, if the risk of harm or distress would arise as a result of complying. If the risk would exist regardless of compliance and is not increased thereby, the bar does not apply and a direction may still be given, although these matters may not easily be susceptible to proof.

Statements made in the course of conciliation which indicate that the maker is likely to cause serious harm to the well-being of a child are admissible (*Re D. (Minors) (Conciliation: Privilege)* [1993] 1 FLR 932), as may be evidence given in wardship proceedings (*Re M. (Wardship: Disclosure of Documents)*, *The Independent*, August 26, 1992.

Subs. (5)

The child support officer has a discretion, even if reasonable grounds do not exist under subs. (3). The provisions of subss. (3), (4) and (5) do not displace the duty in s.2. The welfare of any children affected must still be considered, if the terms of subs. (3) are not satisfied. If the officer exercises the discretion to make a reduced benefit direction, the amount and period of any reduction in benefit as a result of the direction is determined under reg. 36. There can only be one direction in force in relation to a parent at one time (reg. 36(8)).

Subs. (7)

The meaning of "person aggrieved" is discussed in the general note to s.20(1). There is no need to go through a second tier review under s.18 before appealing, as reduced benefit directions will have been through two levels of consideration, once by the Secretary of State under s.6 and once under this section.

Fees

47.—(1) The Secretary of State may by regulations provide for the payment, by the absent parent or the person with care (or by both), of such fees as may be prescribed in cases where the Secretary of State takes any action under section 4 or 6.

(2) The Secretary of State may by regulations provide for the payment, by the absent parent, the person with care or the child concerned (or by any or all of them), of such fees as may be prescribed in cases where the Secretary of State takes any action under section 7.

(3) Regulations made under this section—

(a) may require any information which is needed for the purpose of determining the amount of any such fee to be furnished, in accordance with the regulations, by such person as may be prescribed;

(b)   shall provide that no such fees shall be payable by any person to or in respect of whom income support, family credit or any other benefit of a prescribed kind is paid; and

(c)   may, in particular, make provision with respect to the recovery by the Secretary of State of any fees payable under the regulations.

DEFINITIONS
"absent parent": see s.3(2).
"child": see s.55.
"family credit": see s.54.
"income support": *ibid.*
"person with care": see s.3(3).
"prescribed": see s.54.

GENERAL NOTE
The regulations made under this section are the Child Support Fees Regulations. The effect of the regulations is noted in the commentary to ss.11 and 29.

Right of audience

48.—(1) Any person authorised by the Secretary of State for the purposes of this section shall have, in relation to any proceedings under this Act before a magistrates' court, a right of audience and the right to conduct litigation.

(2) In this section "right of audience" and "right to conduct litigation" have the same meaning as in section 119 of the Courts and Legal Services Act 1990.

GENERAL NOTE
This section does not extend to Scotland (s. 58(9)).

Right of audience: Scotland

49. In relation to any proceedings before the sheriff under any provision of this Act, the power conferred on the Court of Session by section 32 of the Sheriff Courts (Scotland) Act 1971 (power of Court of Session to regulate civil procedure in sheriff court) shall extend to the making of rules permitting a party to such proceedings, in such circumstances as may be specified in the rules, to be represented by a person who is neither an advocate nor a solicitor.

GENERAL NOTE
This section applies to Scotland only (s. 58(10)).

Unauthorised disclosure of information

50.—(1) Any person who is, or has been, employed in employment to which this section applies is guilty of an offence if, without lawful authority, he discloses any information which—

(a)   was acquired by him in the course of that employment; and

(b)   relates to a particular person.

(2) It is not an offence under this section—

(a)   to disclose information in the form of a summary or collection of information so framed as not to enable information relating to any particular person to be ascertained from it; or

(b)   to disclose information which has previously been disclosed to the public with lawful authority.

(3) It is a defence for a person charged with an offence under this section to prove that at the time of the alleged offence—

(a)   he believed that he was making the disclosure in question with lawful authority and had no reasonable cause to believe otherwise; or

(b) he believed that the information in question had previously been disclosed to the public with lawful authority and had no reasonable cause to believe otherwise.

(4) A person guilty of an offence under this section shall be liable—

(a) on conviction on indictment, to imprisonment for a term not exceeding two years or a fine or both; or

(b) on summary conviction, to imprisonment for a term not exceeding six months or a fine not exceeding the statutory maximum or both.

(5) This section applies to employment as—

(a) the Chief Child Support Officer;

(b) any other child support officer;

(c) any clerk to, or other officer of, a child support appeal tribunal;

(d) any member of the staff of such a tribunal;

(e) a civil servant in connection with the carrying out of any functions under this Act,

and to employment of any other kind which is prescribed for the purposes of this section.

(6) For the purposes of this section a disclosure is to be regarded as made with lawful authority if, and only if, it is made—

(a) by a civil servant in accordance with his official duty; or

(b) by any other person either—

(i) for the purposes of the function in the exercise of which he holds the information and without contravening any restriction duly imposed by the responsible person; or

(ii) to, or in accordance with an authorisation duly given by, the responsible person;

(c) in accordance with any enactment or order of a court;

(d) for the purpose of instituting, or otherwise for the purposes of, any proceedings before a court or before any tribunal or other body or person mentioned in this Act; or

(e) with the consent of the appropriate person.

(7) "The responsible person" means—

(a) the Lord Chancellor;

(b) the Secretary of State;

(c) any person authorised by the Lord Chancellor, or Secretary of State, for the purposes of this subsection; or

(d) any other prescribed person, or person falling within a prescribed category.

(8) "The appropriate person" means the person to whom the information in question relates, except that if the affairs of that person are being dealt with—

(a) under a power of attorney;

(b) by a receiver appointed under section 99 of the Mental Health Act 1983;

(c) by a Scottish mental health custodian, that is to say—

(i) a curator bonis, tutor or judicial factor; or

(ii) the managers of a hospital acting on behalf of that person under section 94 of the Mental Health (Scotland) Act 1984; or(b)

(d) by a mental health appointee, that is to say—

(i) a person directed or authorised as mentioned in sub-paragraph (a) of rule 41(1) of the Court of Protection Rules 1984; or

(ii) a receiver ad interim appointed under sub-paragraph (b) of that rule;

the appropriate person is the attorney, receiver, custodian or appointee (as the case may be) or, in a case falling within paragraph (a), the person to whom the information relates.

DEFINITIONS

"Chief Child Support Officer": see s.13.

"child support appeal tribunal": see s.54.

"child support officer": see s.13.
"prescribed": see s.54.

GENERAL NOTE
Subs. (5)
   The other kinds of employment prescribed for the purposes of this subsection are contained in reg. 11 of the Information, Evidence and Disclosure Regulations.

Supplementary powers to make regulations

51.—(1) The Secretary of State may by regulations make such incidental, supplemental and transitional provision as he considers appropriate in connection with any provision made by or under the Act.
   (2) The regulations may, in particular, make provision—
   (*a*)   as to the procedure to be followed with respect to—
         (i)   the making of applications for maintenance assessments;
        (ii)   the making, cancellation or refusal to make maintenance assessments;
       (iii)   reviews under sections 16 to 19;
   (*b*)   extending the categories of case to which section 18 or 19 applies;
   (*c*)   as to the date on which an application for a maintenance assessment is to be treated as having been made;
   (*d*)   for attributing payments made under maintenance assessments to the payment of arrears;
   (*e*)   for the adjustment, for the purpose of taking account of the retrospective effect of a maintenance assessment, of amounts payable under the assessment;
   (*f*)   for the adjustment, for the purpose of taking account of over-payments or under-payments of child support maintenance, of amounts payable under a maintenance assessment;
   (*g*)   as to the evidence which is to be required in connection with such matters as may be prescribed;
   (*h*)   as to the circumstances in which any official record or certificate is to be conclusive (or in Scotland, sufficient) evidence;
   (*i*)   with respect to the giving of notices or other documents;
   (*j*)   for the rounding up or down of any amounts calculated, estimated or otherwise arrived at in applying any provision made by or under this Act.
   (3) No power to make regulations conferred by any other provision of this Act shall be taken to limit the powers given to the Secretary of State by this section.

DEFINITIONS
   "child support maintenance": see s.3(6).
   "maintenance assessment": see s.54.
   "prescribed": *ibid.*

GENERAL NOTE
   The regulations dealing with the adjustment of the amount payable under a maintenance assessment are contained in the Arrears, Interest and Adjustment of Maintenance Assessments Regulations.

Regulations and orders

52.—(1) Any power conferred on the Lord Chancellor, the Lord Advocate or the Secretary of State by this Act to make regulations or orders (other than a deduction from earnings order) shall be exercisable by statutory instrument.
   (2) No statutory instrument containing (whether alone or with other provisions) regulations made under section 4(7), 5(3), 6(1), (9) or (10), 7(8), 12(2), 41(2), (3)

or (4), 42, 43(1), 46 or 47 or under Part I of Schedule 1, or an order made under section 45(1) or (6), shall be made unless a draft of the instrument has been laid before Parliament and approved by a resolution of each House of Parliament.

(3) Any other statutory instrument made under this Act (except an order made under section 58(2)) shall be subject to annulment in pursuance of a resolution of either House of Parliament.

(4) Any power of a kind mentioned in subsection (1) may be exercised—

(*a*) in relation to all cases to which it extends, in relation to those cases but subject to specified exceptions or in relation to any specified cases or classes of case;

(*b*) so as to make, as respects the cases in relation to which it is exercised—

  (i) the full provision to which it extends or any lesser provision (whether by way of exception or otherwise);

  (ii) the same provision for all cases, different provision for different cases or classes of case or different provision as respects the same case or class of case but for different purposes of this Act;

  (iii) provision which is either unconditional or is subject to any specified condition;

(*c*) so to provide for a person to exercise a discretion in dealing with any matter.

Financial provisions

53. Any expenses of the Lord Chancellor or the Secretary of State under this Act shall be payable out of money provided by Parliament.

Interpretation

54. In this Act—

"absent parent", has the meaning given in section 3(2);

"adjudication officer" has the same meaning as in the benefit Acts;

"assessable income" has the meaning given in paragraph 5 of Schedule 1;

"benefit Acts" means the [¹Social Security Contributions and Benefits Act 1992 and the Social Security Administration Act 1992];

"Chief Adjudication Officer" has the same meaning as the benefit Acts;

"Chief Child Support Officer" has the meaning given in section 13;

"child benefit" has the same meaning as in the Child Benefit Act 1975;

"child support appeal tribunal" means a tribunal appointed under section 21;

"child support maintenance" has the meaning given in section 3(6);

"child support officer" has the meaning given in section 13;

"deduction from earnings order" has the meaning given in section 31(2);

"disability living allowance" has the same meaning as in the [²benefit Acts];

"family credit" has the same meaning as in the benefit Acts;

"general qualification" shall be construed in accordance with section 71 of the Courts and Legal Services Act 1990 (qualification for judicial appointments);

"income support" has the same meaning as in the benefit Acts;

"interim maintenance assessment" has the meaning given in section 12;

"liability order" has the meaning given in section 33(2);

"maintenance agreement" has the meaning given in section 9(1);

"maintenance assessment" means an assessment of maintenance made under this Act and, except in prescribed circumstances, includes an interim maintenance assessment;

"maintenance order" has the meaning given in section 8(11);

"maintenance requirement" means the amount calculated in accordance with paragraph 1 of Schedule 1;

"parent", in relation to any child, means any person who is in law the mother or father of the child;

"parental responsibility" has the same meaning as in the Children Act 1989;

"parental rights" has the same meaning as in the Law Reform (Parent and Child) (Scotland) Act 1986;

"person with care" has the meaning given in section 3(3);

"prescribed" means prescribed by regulations made by the Secretary of State;

"qualifying child" has the meaning given in section 3(1).

AMENDMENTS
1.   Sched. 2, para. 114(*a*) to the Social Security Consequential Provisions Act 1992 (July 1, 1992).
2.   Sched. 2, para. 114(*b*) to the Social Security Consequential Provisions Act 1992 (July 1, 1992).

GENERAL NOTE
"parent."
   A parent is someone who is in law the mother or father of a child. Step-parents, foster parents and persons who treat a child as their own are not within the definition.

"parental responsibility."
   This is defined by s.3 of the Children Act 1989 as all the rights, duties, powers, responsibility and authority which by law a parent of a child has in relation to the child and the child's property including those of a guardian of the child's estate.

"maintenance assessment."
   Generally a reference to a maintenance assessment includes a reference to an interim maintenance assessment. For the cases in which this is not so, see reg. 8(2), (11) and (12) of the Maintenance Assessment Procedure Regulations.

Meaning of "child"

55.—(1) For the purposes of this Act a person is a child if—
   (*a*)   he is under the age of 16;
   (*b*)   he is under the age of 19 and receiving full-time education (which is not advanced education)—
      (i)   by attendance at a recognised educational establishment; or
      (ii)   elsewhere, if the education is recognised by the Secretary of State; or
   (*c*)   he does not fall within paragraph (*a*) or (*b*) but—
      (i)   he is under the age of 18, and
      (ii)   prescribed conditions are satisfied with respect to him.
   (2) A person is not a child for the purposes of this Act if he—
   (*a*)   is or has been married;
   (*b*)   has celebrated a marriage which is void; or
   (*c*)   has celebrated a marriage in respect of which a decree of nullity has been granted.
   (3) In this section—
"advanced education" means education of a prescribed description; and
"recognised educational establishment" means an establishment recognised by the Secretary of State for the purposes of this section as being, or as comparable to, a university, college or school.
   (4) Where a person has reached the age of 16, the Secretary of State may recognise education provided for him otherwise than at a recognised educational establishment only if the Secretary of State is satisfied that education was being so provided for him immediately before he reached the age of 16.
   (5) The Secretary of State may provide that in prescribed circumstances education is or is not to be treated for the purposes of this section as being full-time.
   (6) In determining whether a person falls within subsection (1)(*b*), no account shall be taken of such interruptions in his education as may be prescribed.
   (7) The Secretary of State may by regulations provide that a person who ceases

to fall within subsection (1) shall be treated as continuing to fall within that subsection for a prescribed period.

(8) No person shall be treated as continuing to fall within subsection (1) by virtue of regulations made under subsection (7) after the end of the week in which he reaches the age of 19.

DEFINITION
  "prescribed": see s.54.

GENERAL NOTE
  This section must be read in conjunction with Sched. 1 to the Maintenance Assessment Procedure Regulations. References to paragraphs in this note are to paragraphs in that Schedule.
  A child is a person who comes comes under one of the four heads established by this section. The definition is modelled on the definition which is used for child benefit, although not without exception. There are many Commissioners' decisions on provisions similar to those used here, but as the wording of those provisions has varied considerably from time to time great care is required in applying those decisions to the present wording. The heads all require a decision on when a person attained a particular age. A person attains an age on the beginning of the relevant anniversary of the date of his birth (s.9(1) of the Family Law Reform Act 1969 and s.6(1) of the Age of Legal Capacity (Scotland) Act 1991).
  There is a general exception in subs. (2) for persons who are married or who have been either married or through a ceremony of marriage. For the circumstances in which a marriage will be void or voidable see ss.11 and 12 of the Matrimonial Causes Act 1973.

1. Persons under the age of 16
  Every person under the age of 16 is a child (s.55(1)(*a*)). This applies whether or not the person is in education.

2. Persons under the age of 19 who are in education
  For a person to be a child under this head, the following conditions must be satisfied (s.55(1)(*b*)).
  (i) The person must be under the age of 19.
  (ii) The person must be receiving full-time education. This condition may be established in two ways. The first way is to bring the case within para. 3. This paragraph does not provide an exhaustive definition of full-time education, but deems a person to be in full-time education if certain facts are established. These are that the person (a) attends (b) a course of education (c) at a recognised educational establishment and (d) that the hours spent on receiving instruction or tuition, undertaking supervised study, examination or practical work or taking part in any exercise, experiment or project for which provision is made in the curriculum of the course, exceed 12 per week. The time spent on meal breaks and unsupervised study is disregarded. Study is supervised if the person is in the presence or close proximity of a teacher or tutor who may preserve order, enhance diligence and give appropriate assistance (*CF 9/91*, para. 13). In view of requirement (c), this way of proving full-time education is of no use to someone who is not in a recognised educational establishment. A CSAT will need to make findings of fact on all these matters. In the case of (c) the relevant facts will be the name of the establishment attended and whether or not the Secretary of State has recognised it as an educational establishment (s.55(3)).
  The second way is to prove as a matter of fact in all the circumstances of the case that the person is undergoing full-time education (*R(F) 2/85*, paras. 13 and 17(2)). These words are to be given their natural and ordinary meaning (*R(F) 4/62*, para. 5). In that case a course which involved attendance for 13 hours and 45 minutes a week did not constitute "full-time instruction". Attendance solely for the purpose of taking examinations was not sufficient in *R(F) 2/85*, since the person had left school and returned solely to sit for examinations. This must be distinguished from the normal case of someone who continues at school but whose time is free before and between examinations for revision. In such a case it is within the usual meaning of the words in this context to say that the person is receiving full-time education.
  (iii) The education must not be advanced education. This is defined by para. 2. The precise terms of the definition are not repeated here. Put shortly, advanced education means education above A-level standard.
  (iv) Finally, either the educational establishment attended or the education itself must be recognised by the Secretary of State. Where a person who has reached 16 is receiving education which is not provided at a recognised educational establishment, it can only be recognised by the Secretary of State if the person was receiving such education immediately before reaching 16 (s.55(4)). This provision differs from the similar provision in s.142(2) of the Social Security Contributions and Benefits Act 1992.
  Certain interruptions are ignored for the purpose of this head (s.55(6)) and these are set out in para. 4.

A period of up to six months of any interruption is ignored to the extent to which it is attributable to a reasonable cause. School holidays (provided the person intends to return to education afterwards), illness and delays associated with moving house or school are obvious examples of delays with reasonable causes. The six month period may be extended where the interruption or its continuance is attributable to the illness or disability of mind or body of the person concerned. The extension may be for such period as is reasonable in the circumstances. The illness or disability need not have been the original cause of the interruption; it is sufficient if it merely prolongs an interruption. The tribunal will need to find facts as to the duration of the interruption and the reasons for it. The reasons for decision will need to record that the tribunal gave its mind to the question of the reasonableness of the cause and, where appropriate, the extension of the six month period.

However, any interruption for whatever cause is not ignored in two cases (para. 4(2)). The first case is where the interruption is, or is likely to be, immediately followed by a period during which youth training with an allowance is provided. The second case is where it is, or is likely to be, immediately followed by a period during which the person receives education by virtue of the person's employment or office.

3. Persons under the age of 18 and available for work or training

This head applies to persons under the age of 18 in respect of whom prescribed conditions are met (s.55(1)(c)). These conditions are set out in para. 1 as follows: (i) The person must be registered for work, or for youth training with certain bodies. Youth training is defined in para. 6; (ii) The person is not engaged in remunerative work. This means work of not less than 24 hours a week for which payment is made or which is done in the expectation of payment (para. 6). Temporary work is disregarded if it is due to end before the so-called "extension period" expires; if there is evidence that the person is working, the tribunal in the exercise of its inquisitorial function will need to enquire whether that work is temporary, and if so when it is likely to end; (iii) The extension period has not expired; (iv) Immediately before the extension period began the person was a child under one of the other three heads. The definition of the extension period is in para. 1(2). "Week" is defined in para. 6 as a period of seven days beginning with a Monday. The period begins on the first day of the week in which a person ceased to be a child under any head other than this one (i.e. other than 3). When it ends depends on when the person ceased to come within head 1 or 4. This is called the cessation date in the table below.

Cessation dates (inclusive)	Period ends
January 4, 1993 to April 18, 1993	April 4, 1993
April 19, 1993 to September 5, 1993	July 18, 1993
September 6, 1993 to January 2, 1994	January 2, 1994
January 3, 1994 to April 10, 1994	April 3, 1994
April 11, 1994 to September 4, 1994	July 10, 1994
September 5, 1994 to January 1, 1995	January 1, 1995

The definition of the extension period and the terminal date which applies under head 4 below is based on the assumption that there are three school or college terms which end on more or less similar dates each year. As greater variation in practice arises, so the basis for these definitions will be undermined. Moreover, there is one instance where the extension period will end before it begins. The definition of the extension period makes sense for all persons who have at some time in their lives been in full-time non-advanced education. However, it does not make sense in those rare but real cases where a child has never been in such education. Take as an example a person who becomes 16 on September 1, 1994 and who has never been in such education. For this person the extension period begins on September 1, 1994 but ends on July 10, 1994. In effect there is no extension period.

This head does not apply to a person who is engaged in training under youth training or who is entitled to income support (para. 1(3)). A person is not entitled to income support unless a claim has been made or is treated as having been made (s.1(1) of the Social Security Administration Act 1992).

4. Persons under the age of 19 who have left education

A person who leaves full-time, non-advanced education may still be treated as a child for a period (s.55(7) and para. 5). The period begins when the person leaves education or attains the age of 16, whichever is later. It ends at the end of the week which includes the terminal date. A week is a period of seven days beginning with a Monday (para. 6). The terminal date is defined in para. 5(3). It is the first of the following Mondays which occurs after the person's full-time education ceases: January 4, 1993, April 19, 1993, September 6, 1993, January 3, 1994, April 11, 1994 and September 5, 1994.

If the person attains the age of 19 on or before the day on which this period would expire, he or she ceases to be a child at the end of the week which includes the last Monday before the person attained the age of 19 (para. 5(1)). If a person ceases full-time education before reaching the upper limit of compulsory school age, the terminal date is that which next follows the date on which the person would have attained that age (para. 5(2)).

The provisions of para. 5 do not apply to a person who is engaged in remunerative work as defined in para. 6 unless the work is temporary and due to cease before the terminal date (para. 5(5)). If there is evidence that the person is working, the tribunal in the exercise of its inquisitorial function will need to enquire whether that work is temporary and, if so, when it is likely to end.

Special provision is made for someone who takes examinations after leaving full-time education (para. 5(6) to (8)). Such a person remains a child for a period after leaving education. The following matters must be established: (i) The person must have been in full-time education which is not advanced education. The meaning of these phrases has been discussed above; (ii) The person must have been entered as a candidate for an examination; (iii) The entry must have been made while the person was receiving the education; (iv) The examination must be an external one. Therefore, an internal college or school examination will not bring the case within this provision; (v) The entry to the examination must have been in connection with the education. If these conditions are satisfied, it is necessary to decide for what period the person is treated as a child after leaving full-time non-advanced education. The period begins with the date when the person ceases to receive such education or when the person attains the age of 16 if that is later. The period ends with the first terminal date after the examinations or with the expiry of the week (Monday to Sunday) which includes the last Monday before the person's 19th birthday, whichever is earlier.

Corresponding provision for and co-ordination with Northern Ireland

56.—(1) An Order in Council made under paragraph 1(1)(*b*) of Schedule 1 to the Northern Ireland Act 1974 which contains a statement that it is made only for purposes corresponding to those of the provisions of this Act, other than provisions which relate to the appointment of Child Support Commissioners for Northern Ireland—

    (*a*) shall not be subject to sub-paragraphs (4) and (5) of paragraph 1 of that Schedule (affirmative resolution of both Houses of Parliament); but

    (*b*) shall be subject to annulment in pursuance of a resolution of either House of Parliament.

(2) The Secretary of State may make arrangements with the Department of Health and Social Services for Northern Ireland with a view to securing, to the extent allowed for in the arrangements, that—

    (*a*) the provision made by or under this Act ("the provision made for Great Britain"); and

    (*b*) the provision made by or under any corresponding enactment having effect with respect to Northern Ireland ("the provision made for Northern Ireland"),

provide for a single system within the United Kingdom.

(3) The Secretary of State may make regulations for giving effect to any such arrangements.

(4) The regulations may, in particular—

    (*a*) adapt legislation (including subordinate legislation) for the time being in force in Great Britain so as to secure its reciprocal operation with the provision made for Northern Ireland; and

    (*b*) make provision to secure that acts, omissions and events which have any effect for the purposes of the provision made for Northern Ireland have a corresponding effect for the purposes of the provision made for Great Britain.

Application to Crown

57.—(1) The power of the Secretary of State to make regulations under section 14 requiring prescribed persons to furnish information may be exercised so as to require information to be furnished by persons employed in the service of the Crown or otherwise in the discharge of Crown functions.

(2) In such circumstances, and subject to such conditions, as may be prescribed, an inspector appointed under section 15 may enter any Crown premises for the purpose of exercising any powers conferred on him by that section.

(3) Where such an inspector duly enters any Crown premises for those purposes, section 15 shall apply in relation to persons employed in the service of the Crown or otherwise in the discharge of Crown functions as it applies in relation to other persons.

(4) Where a liable person is in the employment of the Crown, a deduction from earnings order may be made under section 31 in relation to that person; but in such a case subsection (8) of section 32 shall apply only in relation to the failure of that person to comply with any requirement imposed on him by regulations made under section 32.

DEFINITIONS
"deduction from earnings order": see s.31(2).
"liable person": see s.31(1)(*a*).
"prescribed": see s.54.

GENERAL NOTE
Subs. (1)
This subsection refers generally to s.14. However, since it relates to the Secretary of State's powers to "require" disclosure it only applies to s.14(1) and not to s.14(3) which allows him to "authorise" disclosure. For a discussion of the meaning of "information" in this section see the commentary to s.14(1).

Short title, commencement and extent, etc.

58.—(1) This Act may be cited as the Child Support Act 1991.

(2) Section 56(1) and subsections (1) to (11) and (14) of this section shall come into force on the passing of this Act but otherwise this Act shall come into force on such date as may be appointed by order made by the Lord Chancellor, the Secretary of State or Lord Advocate, or by any of them acting jointly.

(3) Different dates may be appointed for different provisions of this Act and for different purposes (including, in particular, for different cases or categories of case).

(4) An order under subsection (2) may make such supplemental, incidental or transitional provision as appears to the person making the order to be necessary or expedient in connection with the provisions brought into force by the order, including such adaptations or modifications of—

(*a*)   the provisions so brought into force;
(*b*)   any provisions of this Act then in force; or
(*c*)   any provision of any other enactment,
as appear to him to be necessary or expedient.

(5) Different provision may be made by virtue of subsection (4) with respect to different periods.

(6) Any provision made by virtue of subsection (4) may, in particular, include provision for—

(*a*)   the enforcement of a maintenance assessment (including the collection of sums payable under the assessment) as if the assessment were a court order of a prescribed kind;
(*b*)   the registration of maintenance assessments with the appropriate court in connection with any provision of a kind mentioned in paragraph (*a*);

    (*c*) the variation, on application made to a court, of the provisions of a mainten-
ance assessment relating to the method of making payments fixed by the
assessment or the intervals at which such payments are to be made;

    (*d*) a maintenance assessment, or an order of a prescribed kind relating to one
or more children, to be deemed, in prescribed circumstances, to have been
validly made for all purposes or for such purposes as may be prescribed.

In paragraph (*c*) "court" includes a single justice.

(7) The Lord Chancellor, the Secretary of State or the Lord Advocate may by
order make such amendments or repeals in, or such modifications of, such enactments as may be specified in the order, as appear to him to be necessary or expedient in consequence of any provision made by or under this Act (including any
provision made by virtue of subsection (4)).

(8) This Act shall, in its application to the Isles of Scilly, have effect subject to
such exceptions, adaptations and modifications as the Secretary of State may by
order prescribe.

(9) Sections 27, 35 and 48 and paragraph 7 of Schedule 5 do not extend to
Scotland.

(10) Sections 7, 28 and 49 extend only to Scotland.

(11) With the exception of sections 23 and 56(1), subsections (1) to (3) of this
section and Schedules 2 and 4, and (in so far as it amends any enactment extending
to Northern Ireland) Schedule 5, this Act does not extend to Northern Ireland.

(12) Until Schedule 1 to the Disability Living Allowance and Disability Working Allowance Act 1991 comes into force, paragraph 1(1) of Schedule 3 shall have
effect with the omission of the words "and disability appeal tribunals" and the
insertion, after "social security appeal tribunals", of the word "and".

(13) The consequential amendments set out in Schedule 5 shall have effect.

(14) [Amends the Children Act 1989, Schedule 1, paragraph 2(6).]

DEFINITIONS
  "child": see s.55.
  "maintenance assessment": see s.54.
  "prescribed": *ibid.*

GENERAL NOTE
Subs. (12)
  It has not been necessary to bring this subsection into force.

SCHEDULE 1   **Section 11**

MAINTENANCE ASSESSMENTS

PART I

CALCULATION OF CHILD SUPPORT MAINTENANCE

The maintenance requirement

1.—(1) In this Schedule "the maintenance requirement" means the amount, calculated in
accordance with the formula set out in sub-paragraph (2), which is to be taken as the minimum amount necessary for the maintenance of the qualifying child or, where there is more
than one qualifying child, all of them.

  (2) The formula is—

$$MR = AG - CB$$

where—

MR is the amount of the maintenance requirement;

AG is the aggregate of the amounts to be taken into account under sub-paragraph (3); and

CB is the amount payable by way of child benefit (or which would be so payable if the person with care of the qualifying child were an individual) or, where there is more than one qualifying child, the aggregate of the amounts so payable with respect to each of them.

(3) The amounts to be taken into account for the purpose of calculating AG are—

    (*a*) such amount or amounts (if any), with respect to each qualifying child, as may be prescribed;

    (*b*) such amount or amounts (if any), with respect to the person with care of the qualifying child or qualifying children, as may be prescribed; and

    (*c*) such further amount or amounts (if any) as may be prescribed.

(4) For the purposes of calculating CB it shall be assumed that child benefit is payable with respect to any qualifying child at the basic rate.

(5) In sub-paragraph (4) "basic rate" has the meaning for the time being prescribed.

The general rule

2.—(1) In order to determine the amount of any maintenance assessment, first calculate—

$$(A + C) \times P$$

where—

A is the absent parent's assessable income;

C is the assessable income of the other parent, where that parent is the person with care, and otherwise has such value (if any) as may be prescribed; and

P is such number greater than zero but less than 1 as may be prescribed.

(2) Where the result of the calculation made under sub-paragraph (1) is an amount which is equal to, or less than, the amount of the maintenance requirement for the qualifying child or qualifying children, the amount of maintenance payable by the absent parent for that child or those children shall be an amount equal to—

$$A \times P$$

where A and P have the same values as in the calculation made under sub-paragraph (1).

(3) Where the result of the calculation made under sub-paragraph (1) is an amount which exceeds the amount of the maintenance requirement for the qualifying child or qualifying children, the amount of maintenance payable by the absent parent for that child or those children shall consist of—

    (*a*) a basic element calculated in accordance with the provisions of paragraph 3; and

    (*b*) an additional element calculated in accordance with the provisions of paragraph 4.

The basic element

3.—(1) The basic element shall be calculated by applying the formula—

$$BE = A \times G \times P$$

where—

BE is the amount of the basic element;

A and P have the same values as in the calculation made under paragraph 2(1); and

G has the value determined under sub-paragraph (2).

(2) The value of G shall be determined by applying the formula—

$$G = \frac{MR}{(A + C) \times P}$$

where—

MR is the amount of the maintenance requirement for the qualifying child or qualifying children; and

A, C and P have the same values as in the calculation made under paragraph 2(1).

The additional element

4.—(1) Subject to sub-paragraph (2), the additional element shall be calculated by applying the formula—

$$AE = (1 - G) \times A \times R$$

where—

AE is the amount of the additional element;

A has the same value as in the calculation made under paragraph 2(1);

G has the value determined under paragraph 3(2); and

R is such number greater than zero but less than 1 as may be prescribed.

(2) Where applying the alternative formula set out in sub-paragraph (3) would result in a lower amount for the additional element, that formula shall be applied in place of the formula set out in sub-paragraph (1).

(3) The alternative formula is—

$$AE = Z \times Q \times \left(\frac{A}{A + C}\right)$$

where—

A and C have the same values as in the calculation made under paragraph 2(1);

Z is such number as may be prescribed; and

Q is the aggregate of—
  (*a*) any amount taken into account by virtue of paragraph 1(3)(*a*) in calculating the maintenance requirement; and
  (*b*) any amount which is both taken into account by virtue of paragraph 1(3)(*c*) in making that calculation and is an amount prescribed for the purposes of this paragraph.

Assessable income

5.—(1) The assessable income of an absent parent shall be calculated by applying the formula—

$$A = N - E$$

where—

A is the amount of that parent's assessable income;

N is the amount of that parent's net income, calculated or estimated in accordance with regulations made by the Secretary of State for the purposes of this sub-paragraph; and

E is the amount of that parent's exempt income, calculated or estimated in accordance with regulations made by the Secretary of State for those purposes.

(2) The assessable income of a parent who is a person with care of the qualifying child or children shall be calculated by applying the formula—

$$C = M - F$$

where—

C is the amount of that parent's assessable income;

M is the amount of that parent's net income, calculated or estimated in accordance with regulations made by the Secretary of State for the purposes of this sub-paragraph; and

F is the amount of that parent's exempt income, calculated or estimated in accordance with regulations made by the Secretary of State for those purposes.

(3) Where the preceding provisions of this paragraph would otherwise result in a person's assessable income being taken to be a negative amount his assessable income shall be taken to be nil.

(4) Where income support or any other benefit of a prescribed kind is paid to or in respect of a parent who is an absent parent or a person with care that parent shall, for the purposes of this Schedule, be taken to have no assessable income.

Protected income

6.—(1) This paragraph applies where—

(a) one or more maintenance assessments have been made with respect to an absent parent; and

(b) payment by him of the amount, or the aggregate of the amounts, so assessed would otherwise reduce his disposable income below his protected income level.

(2) The amount of the assessment, or (as the case may be) of each assessment, shall be adjusted in accordance with such provisions as may be prescribed with a view to securing so far as is reasonably practicable that payment by the absent parent of the amount, or (as the case may be) aggregate of the amounts, so assessed will not reduce his disposable income below his protected income level.

(3) Regulations made under sub-paragraph (2) shall secure that, where the prescribed minimum amount fixed by regulations made under paragraph 7 applies, no maintenance assessment is adjusted so as to provide for the amount payable by an absent parent in accordance with that assessment to be less than that amount.

(4) The amount which is to be taken for the purposes of this paragraph as an absent parent's disposable income shall be calculated, or estimated, in accordance with regulations made by the Secretary of State.

(5) Regulations made under sub-paragraph (4) may, in particular, provide that, in such circumstances and to such extent as may be prescribed—

(a) income of any child who is living in the same household with the absent parent; and

(b) where the absent parent is living together in the same household with another adult of the opposite sex (regardless of whether or not they are married), income of that other adult,

is to be treated as the absent parent's income for the purposes of calculating his disposable income.

(6) In this paragraph the "protected income level" of a particular absent parent means an amount of income calculated, by reference to the circumstances of that parent, in accordance with regulations made by the Secretary of State.

The minimum amount of child support maintenance

7.—(1) The Secretary of State may prescribe a minimum amount for the purposes of this paragraph.

(2) Where the amount of child support maintenance which would be fixed by a maintenance assessment but for this paragraph is nil, or less than the prescribed minimum amount, the amount to be fixed by the assessment shall be the prescribed minimum amount.

(3) In any case to which section 43 applies, and in such other cases (if any) as may be prescribed, sub-paragraph (2) shall not apply.

Housing costs

8. Where regulations under this Schedule require a child support officer to take account of the housing costs of any person in calculating, or estimating, his assessable income or disposable income, those regulations may make provision—
- (*a*) as to the costs which are to be treated as housing costs for the purpose of the regulations;
- (*b*) for the apportionment of housing costs; and
- (*c*) for the amount of housing costs to be taken into account for prescribed purposes not to exceed such amount (if any) as may be prescribed by, or determined in accordance with, the regulations.

Regulations about income and capital

9. The Secretary of State may by regulations provide that, in such circumstances and to such extent as may be prescribed—
- (*a*) income of a child shall be treated as income of a parent of his;
- (*b*) where the child support officer concerned is satisfied that a person has intentionally deprived himself of a source of income with a view to reducing the amount of his assessable income, his net income shall be taken to include income from that source of an amount estimated by the child support officer;
- (*c*) a person is to be treated as possessing capital or income which he does not possess;
- (*d*) capital or income which a person does possess is to be disregarded;
- (*e*) income is to be treated as capital;
- (*f*) capital is to be treated as income.

References to qualifying children

10. References in this Part of this Schedule to "qualifying children" are to those qualifying children with respect to whom the maintenance assessment falls to be made.

PART II

GENERAL PROVISIONS ABOUT MAINTENANCE ASSESSMENTS

Effective date of assessment

11.—(1) A maintenance assessment shall take effect on such date as may be determined in accordance with regulations made by the Secretary of State.

(2) That date may be earlier than the date on which the assessment is made.

Form of assessment

12. Every maintenance assessment shall be made in such form and contain such information as the Secretary of State may direct.

Assessments where amount of child support is nil

13. A child support officer shall not decline to make a maintenance assessment only on the ground that the amount of the assessment is nil.

Consolidated applications and assessments

14. The Secretary of State may by regulations provide—

(*a*) for two or more applications for maintenance assessments to be treated, in prescribed circumstances, as a single application; and

(*b*) for the replacement, in prescribed circumstances, of a maintenance assessment made on the application of one person by a later maintenance assessment made on the application of that or any other person.

Separate assessments for different periods

15. Where a child support officer is satisfied that the circumstances of a case require different amounts of child support maintenance to be assessed in respect of different periods, he may make separate maintenance assessments each expressed to have effect in relation to a different specified period.

Termination of assessments

16.—(1) A maintenance assessment shall cease to have effect—

(*a*) on the death of the absent parent, or of the person with care, with respect to whom it was made;

(*b*) on there no longer being any qualifying child with respect to whom it would have effect;

(*c*) on the absent parent with respect to whom it was made ceasing to be a parent of—

   (i) the qualifying child with respect to whom it was made; or

   (ii) where it was made with respect to more than one qualifying child, all of the qualifying children with respect to whom it was made;

(*d*) where the absent parent and the person with care with respect to whom it was made have been living together for a continuous period of six months;

(*e*) where a new maintenance assessment is made with respect to any qualifying child with respect to whom the assessment in question was in force immediately before the making of the new assessment.

(2) A maintenance assessment made in response to an application under section 4 or 7 shall be cancelled by a child support officer if the person on whose application the assessment was made asks him to do so.

(3) A maintenance assessment made in response to an application under section 6 shall be cancelled by a child support officer if—

(*a*) the person on whose application the assessment was made ("the applicant") asks him to do so; and

(*b*) he is satisfied that the applicant has ceased to fall within subsection (1) of that section.

(4) Where a child support officer is satisfied that the person with care with respect to whom a maintenance assessment was made has ceased to be a person with care in relation to the qualifying child, or any of the qualifying children, with respect to whom the assessment was made, he may cancel the assessment with effect from the date on which, in his opinion, the change of circumstances took place.

(5) Where—

(*a*) at any time a maintenance assessment is in force but a child support officer would no longer have jurisdiction to make it if it were to be applied for at that time; and

(*b*) the assessment has not been cancelled, or has not ceased to have effect, under or by virtue of any other provision made by or under this Act,

it shall be taken to have continuing effect unless cancelled by a child support officer in accordance with such prescribed provision (including provision as to the effective date of cancellation) as the Secretary of State considers it appropriate to make.

(6) Where both the absent parent and the person with care with respect to whom a maintenance assessment was made request a child support officer to cancel the assessment, he may do so if he is satisfied that they are living together.

(7) Any cancellation of a maintenance assessment under sub-paragraph (5) or (6) shall have effect from such date as may be determined by the child support officer.

(8) Where a child support officer cancels a maintenance assessment, he shall immediately notify the absent parent and person with care, so far as that is reasonably practicable.

(9) Any notice under sub-paragraph (8) shall specify the date with effect from which the cancellation took effect.

(10) A person with care with respect to whom a maintenance assessment is in force shall provide the Secretary of State with such information, in such circumstances, as may be prescribed, with a view to assisting the Secretary of State or a child support officer in determining whether the assessment has ceased to have effect, or should be cancelled.

(11) The Secretary of State may by regulations make such supplemental, incidental or transitional provision as he thinks necessary or expedient in consequence of the provisions of this paragraph.

DEFINITIONS
"absent parent": see s.3(2).
"child": see s.55.
"child benefit": see s.54.
"child support officer": see s.13.
"income support": see s.54.
"maintenance assessment": see s.54.
"parent": see s.54.
"person with care": see s.3(3).
"prescribed": see s.54.
"qualifying child": see s.3(1).

GENERAL NOTE
Overview of Part I
Part I of this Schedule contains the core provisions which deal with the calculation of maintenance assessments. It must be read in conjunction with the Maintenance Assessments and Special Cases Regulations. The calculations which must be made are expressed as formulae; this makes it easy to state the calculation which must be made, but not necessarily easy to understand why the calculation is relevant or what its effect will be. It is helpful to have an overview of the structure and terminology in order better to understand the details. The following paragraphs provide this overview.

There are broadly two types of calculation which have to be made in order to calculate a maintenance assessment. One is based on the actual financial circumstances of the person concerned. The other is based on figures from income support law (supplemented sometimes by an element based on the party's actual financial circumstances) which are to be found in the Income Support Schedule. These figures are used for the purpose of the calculation only. It is not necessary that any party should be in receipt of, or entitled to, income support. As the income support figures increase each year in the annual uprating of benefits, so the figures used for child support purposes will increase, although they will only be fed into an existing maintenance assessment when it is reviewed.

The underlying philosophy of child support law is that parents should bear the cost of bringing up their children. Parents who are looking after their children have to meet or contribute to the cost. Parents who are absent must pay child support maintenance to the person with care of the child. The extent to which the parents contribute or pay child support maintenance depends upon the respective levels of their income, after taking account of notional expenses. The "cost" is not the real cost of bringing up a child but a notional figure fixed by law. It is with the fixing of this figure that the calculation of a maintenance assessment begins.

The first step to take when calculating a maintenance assessment is to determine the *maintenance requirement* for the child (para. 1). This is based on income support figures minus child benefit. It represents the minimum desirable level of maintenance for the child, although in practice the amount payable may be more or less, depending on the income of the absent parent and of any parent with care of the child.

The second step is to calculate the *assessable income* of the absent parent, and of the person with care if that person is also a parent of the child (para. 5). This should be approached in two stages. Begin by calculating the *net income* of the parent. This calculation is largely based on the parent's financial circumstances. However, some income is *attributed* to the parent, and income from certain sources is disregarded (more on this in a moment). Next, the parent's *exempt income* must be calculated. This is largely based on income support figures supplemented by an element of the parent's financial circumstances. The exempt income is deducted from the net income to fix the assessable income. It is important to distinguish between the exempt income and the income disregarded in determining the net income. The former is a figure largely derived from income support figures, while the latter is actual income from specified sources. They must not be confused, as the net income figure (which excludes disregarded income but not exempt income) is used for another purpose (see below).

Now that the assessable income of the parents has been calculated, it is possible to move to the third step and calculate the prima facie amount of child support maintenance payable. As a minimum, the parents are expected to put up to one half of their assessable incomes towards meeting the maintenance requirement for their child (para. 2). They contribute in proportion to their respective incomes. If their joint assessable incomes exceed the maintenance requirement, a greater contribution to the cost of the child's upbringing is expected. If this is the case, any maintenance payable by an absent parent will be made up of two elements, a *basic element* and an *additional element*. The basic element is a percentage of half of the absent parent's assessable income (para. 3). It will either be equal to the maintenance requirement or, if the person with care is a parent who has income as well as the absent parent, it will be the same percentage of the maintenance requirement as the absent parent's income represents of the parents' joint incomes. The additional element reflects the fact that there are extra resources for the parents to devote to the child. It is a percentage of one-quarter of the absent parent's assessable income and is subject to a ceiling (para. 4).

The figure produced by these formulae is not necessarily the amount of child support maintenance that will be paid. The Schedule contains two longstops which provide a measure of protection for the child and the absent parent. The protection for the child is found in para. 7, which provides that in most cases there is a minimum amount of child support maintenance which must be paid, regardless both of the results of the calculations in the third step and of the respective incomes of the absent parent and the person with care. This is known as the *prescribed minimum amount* and is fixed at a percentage of an income support figure. The protection for the absent parent is found in para. 6 which provides that as far as possible the amount of child support maintenance payable should not reduce the parent's *disposable income* below the *protected income level*. The calculation of disposable income takes account of the income of the absent parent and of any (heterosexual, but not homosexual) partner as well as of any children living with them. It is calculated in very much the same way as the net income (hence the importance of distinguishing between disregarded income and exempt income). The protected income level is fixed by reference to income support figures supplemented by some elements of the family's actual financial circumstances. If there is a conflict between these two protections, the protection for the child has priority and the prescribed minimum amount is payable, even if the result is to reduce the absent parent's disposable income below the protected income level.

The result of these calculations is that most absent parents will retain between 70 and 85 per cent. of their assessable income, with the remainder being used for child support maintenance.

Special Cases

Where the case is a special case within Part III of the Maintenance Assessments and Special Cases Regulations, the provisions of this Schedule may be modified. Modifications which are relevant to a particular paragraph of this Schedule are noted either in the general note to that paragraph or in the general note to the relevant regulation thereunder. The modifications which are of general application are as follows:

Where both parents of a qualifying child are absent parents and an application is made in relation to them both, separate assessments must be made in respect of each (reg. 19(2)(*a*) of the Maintenance Assessments and Special Cases Regulations).

Where one parent is an absent parent and the other is *treated as* an absent parent under reg. 20 of the Maintenance Assessments and Special Cases Regulations, references in this Schedule to a parent who is a person with care should be read as references to the person who is treated as an absent parent under reg. 20 (reg. 21).

Where two or more persons who do not live in the same household each provide day to day care for the same qualifying child and none of those persons is a parent who is treated as an absent parent under reg. 20 of the Maintenance Assessments and Special Cases Regulations, the case is a special one by virtue of reg. 24 of those Regulations. The person whose application is being dealt with is entitled to receive the whole of the child support maintenance payable, subject to the Secretary of State's right to apportion the payment in proportion to the provision of care (reg. 24(2)). As this is a decision which relates to payment rather than calculation, it is a matter for the Secretary of State and not a child support officer. Consequently, no appeal lies to a CSAT.

Where a local authority and a person each provide day to day care for a qualifying child, the case is a

109

special case by virtue of reg. 25 of the Maintenance Assessments and Special Cases Regulations. If this case applies, the child support maintenance is calculated in accordance with this Schedule. It is then divided by seven in order to find a daily amount. The daily amount is paid for each night in respect of which the person other than the local authority provides day to day care. Maintenance is not payable in respect of any night for which the local authority provides day to day care. See reg. 25(2).

Para. 1

This paragraph provides for the calculation of the maintenance requirement for a qualifying child. The maintenance requirement is not necessarily the amount of maintenance which will become payable. That figure may be either more or less than the requirement. The significance of the maintenance requirement is that it provides a figure which is the minimum desirable maintenance payment, although it will not always be attained. For the significance of the maintenance requirement in other calculations see para. 2(2) and (3). It is also used to fix the amount of a Category A interim maintenance assessment (see the general notes to s.12 of the Act and the regulations made thereunder).

The maintenance requirement is the total of certain amounts derived from income support law (AG in the formula) less the amount of child benefit in respect of the child (CB in the formula).

AG is prescribed by reg. 3 of the Maintenance Assessments and Special Cases Regulations. It is the total of the following amounts fixed by reference to the Income Support Schedule. The appropriate amounts are those applicable on the effective date (reg. 3(2)).

- (*a*) The personal allowance for a child of the age of each qualifying child. The age is that of the child on the effective date.
- (*b*) If the child is aged less than 16, the personal allowance for a single claimant aged not less than 25. The age of the child is determined at the effective date. Although the personal allowance is that of an adult aged not less than 25, the age of the person with care is irrelevant and will apply even if that person is aged less than 25.
- (*c*) The family premium.
- (*d*) If the person with care has no partner, the lone parent premium. This does not apply if both parents are absent parents and the person with care is a body of persons corporate or unincorporate (reg. 19 of the Maintenance Assessments and Special Cases Regulations).

The amounts under (*b*), (*c*), and (*d*) need to be modified if the case is a special case by virtue of reg. 23 of the Maintenance Assessments and Special Cases Regulations. See the general note to reg. 3.

CB is prescribed by reg. 4 of the Maintenance Assessments and Special Cases Regulations. It is the rate of child benefit applicable to the child in question at the effective date. The rate is fixed by the Child Benefit and Social Security (Fixing and Adjustment of Rates) Regulations 1976.

Para. 2

The first step in applying this paragraph is to decide whose assessable incomes are to be taken into account for the purpose of this paragraph. If the person with care is not a parent of the child, only the assessable income of the absent parent is taken into account under this paragraph. This is the effect of reg. 5(*a*) of the Maintenance Assessments and Special Cases Regulations. If the person with care is a parent of the child, the joint assessable incomes of the absent parent and the person with care are taken into account. There is a special case if both parents are absent parents. In this case if the application has been made in respect of both absent parents, the joint assessable incomes of both parents are considered (reg. 19(2)(*b*) of the Maintenance Assessments and Special Cases Regulations). However, if there is information about the income of one parent but not about the other's, the maintenance assessment in relation to the first parent is calculated on the basis that the income of the other parent is nil and a fresh assessment is made when the information about the other parent's income becomes available (reg. 19(3) and (4)). These special provisions do not apply if the application for a maintenance assessment has been made in respect of only one parent. In this case that parent's assessable income is the only relevant income for the purposes of this paragraph.

The second step is to determine the assessable income of each relevant parent under para. 5 of this Schedule. This income is usually applied directly in the formula. However, in two special cases only a proportion is fed into the formula. Since this may be relevant to the calculation under both this and some subsequent paragraphs, the third step is to decide if either of these special cases applies and if so, its effect. The first special case arises where two or more applications for maintenance assessments have been made in respect of the same person who is, or who is treated as, an absent parent but those applications relate to different children (reg. 22 of the Maintenance Assessments and Special Cases Regulations). In this case the proportion of the absent parent's assessable income that is taken into account is determined by the formula in reg. 22(2). The amount of assessable income taken into account in this case is the same proportion as the maintenance requirement for the application being considered represents of the total of the maintenance requirements for all the applications in question. The second special case is where the person with care is the person with care of two or more qualifying children and there are different persons who are, or who are treated as, absent parents in relation to at least two of those children (reg. 23(4)). In this case, if the person with care is the parent of any of the children, the proportion of the parent with care's assessable income which is taken into account is determined by the formula in reg. 22(2). In other words, the amount of assessable income taken into account in this case is the same proportion as the maintenance requirement for the application being considered represents of the total of the maintenance requirements for all the applications made by the person with care.

The amount of the assessable income which is taken into account for the purposes of this paragraph may therefore be 100 per cent. or, if one of the special cases applies, less. In either case it will be referred to as "the relevant income." The relevant incomes fixed under this paragraph will also be used in paras. 3 and 4.

When the relevant incomes to be used in the formula have been assessed, the fourth step is to multiply those incomes by P. P is prescribed by reg. 5(*b*) of the Maintenance Assessments and Special Cases Regulations. It is 0.5. Thus the result of the calculation will be half of the total of the relevant incomes.

The fifth step is to compare this figure with the maintenance requirement fixed under para. 1. If it is equal to or less than the maintenance requirement, the maintenance payable by the absent parent for that child is half of the absent parent's relevant income (para. 2(2)). The effect is that the maintenance payable is half of the absent parent's relevant income regardless of the person with care's relevant income. It is the person with care who must bear the consequences of the shortfall. This is all subject to paras. 6 and 7 (see below).

If the figure produced by the formula is more than the maintenance requirement, it is necessary to make further calculations in order to decide the maintenance payable. The amount payable will consist of two elements: a basic element and an additional element (para. 2(3)). The calculation of the basic element is governed by para. 3 and the calculation of the additional element is governed by para. 4. The essence of these calculations is that half of the absent parent's relevant income is used in calculating the basic element, a quarter is used in calculating the additional element and the remaining quarter is not used at all.

Para. 3

This paragraph provides for the fixing of the basic element of maintenance which is payable. It only applies if the calculation under para. 2(1) results in a figure which is higher than the maintenance requirement. The relevant formula is set out in para. 3(1). At first sight the formula may appear complicated. However its effect is simple. If the person with care is either not a parent of the child or is a parent but has no relevant income, the basic element is equal to the maintenance requirement. In any other case the basic element is the same percentage of the maintenance requirement as the absent parent's relevant income represents of the joint relevant incomes of the parents. It is only in this latter case that it is necessary to work through the formula.

The formula starts with the absent parent's relevant income. It then takes half (i.e. the value of P) of this and further reduces it by the value of G. The formula for calculating G is in para. 3(2). It is found by dividing the result of the calculation made under para. 2(1) (half of the relevant incomes) into the maintenance requirement fixed under para. 1. The figure produced when the formula has been applied is equal to that proportion of the maintenance requirement which is equivalent to the absent parent's share of the joint relevant incomes. The effect is that as the absent parent's relevant income rises in relation to the parent with care's relevant income, so the percentage represented by G goes up and the higher the amount of the maintenance requirement which is payable as the basic element. The proportion of the maintenance requirement which the parent with care is expected to bear correspondingly reduces.

With the maintenance requirement covered, the calculation goes on to fix an additional amount. This reflects the fact that the absent parent alone or in conjunction with the parent with care can afford to contribute more than the maintenance requirement towards the child's maintenance.

Para. 4

This paragraph provides for two different formulae which may be used for setting the additional element of maintenance which is payable. They only apply if the calculation under para. 2(1) results in a figure which is higher than the maintenance requirement. The so-called "alternative formula" in para. 4(3) sets the ceiling on the amount of additional element which an absent parent will be expected to pay. The other formula, which is set out in para. 4(1), will be used if it produces a lower figure than the alternative formula (para. 4(2)).

Sub-para. 4(1)

The formula in para. 4(1) fixes a percentage of the absent parent's relevant income. It starts with the absent parent's relevant income. It then takes a quarter (i.e. the value of R set by reg. 6(1) of the Maintenance Assessments and Special Cases Regulations) of this and further reduces it. The percentage of the quarter share of the absent parent's relevant income which is, subject to the overall ceiling, to form the additional element is found by deducting the figure for G (which was fixed under para. 3(2)) from 1. The quickest way to work this out is to deduct half of the basic element from one-quarter of the absent parent's relevant income. The effect is that as the absent parent's relevant income rises in relation to the parent with care's, so the basic element and the absent parent's total maintenance payment rise, while the additional element decreases.

Sub-para. 4(3)

The alternative formula sets the maximum amount of additional element which will be payable. The formula for the additional element which is used in para. 4(1) fixes the additional element as a percentage of the absent parent's relevant income. However, the alternative formula in para. 4(3) sets the ceiling on the amount of additional element by reference to figues from income support law, although relevant incomes do have a part to play.

The alternative formula is fixed as follows. Start with the relevant income support personal allowance figures for the children. They were used in the calculation of the maintenance requirement under para. 1. Then add to these an amount equal to the income support family premium for *each* child (reg. 6(2)(*b*) of the Maintenance Assessments and Special Cases Regulations). The total is Q. Next multiply this by Z which is 3 (reg. 6(2)(*a*) of the Maintenance Assessments and Special Cases Regulations). The final step is only necessary if the person with care is a parent of the child and has relevant income. This step fixes a proportion of the Q×Z calculation. This proportion is equal to the percentage which the absent parent's relevant income represents of the total relevant incomes. It is found by dividing the latter into the former.

Assuming that no special case applies, the overall effect of this calculation is as follows: If the person with care is the other parent of the child, the higher the absent parent's relevant income in relation to the parent with care's relevant income, the higher the percentage of the Q×3 calculation that is taken into account and therefore the higher the maximum amount of additional element payable. If the person with care is not the other parent of the child, the ceiling on the additional amount is simply Q multiplied by 3.

Para. 5

The assessable income of the absent parent and of any parent with care is determined by reference to regs. 7 to 10 of, and Scheds. 1 and 2 to, the Maintenance Assessments and Special Cases Regulations. Reference should be made to the general notes to those regulations and Schedules.

Where the assessable income of an absent parent or a parent with care is nil, that person does not have to pay an assessment or a collection fee (reg. 3(5)(*c*) of the Child Support Fees Regulations). This does not affect any fee payable by the other parent (reg. 3(6)(*b*) of these Regulations).

Para. 6

The absent parent's protected income level must be calculated in accordance with reg. 11 of the Maintenance Assessments and Special Cases Regulations. It is the total of the following amounts fixed by reference to the Income Support Schedule. The appropriate amounts are those applicable on the effective date (reg. 11(5)). The effective date is determined under para. 11. In summary the amounts to be added together are as follows. Any Income Support premiums are only taken into account if the conditions of entitlement would be satisfied.

(i)   Appropriate Income Support premium for the absent parent according to whether or not there is a partner.
(ii)   Housing costs.
(iii)   The Income Support lone parent premium but only if the conditions for the disability premium are not satisfied.
(iv)   The Income Support disability premium.
(v)   The Income Support severe disability premium and/or the carer premium.
(vi)   The Income Support family premium.
(vii)   The relevant Income Support personal allowances for each child who is a member of the absent parent's family and the disabled child premium for each relevant child.
(viii) Any other Income Support premium, the conditions for which would be satisfied by the absent parent or his family if that parent were a claimant.
(ix)   Fees payable for living in accommodation provided under the National Assistance Act 1948 or the National Health Service Act 1977 or in a nursing or residential care home.
(x)   Council tax payable by the absent parent or that parent's partner for their home less any council tax benefit.
(xi)   £8.
(xii)   If the total of the income of the absent parent, of any partner of the absent parent and of any child who is a member of the absent parent's family exceeds the total of (i) to (xi), ten per cent. of the

excess. For this purpose the income of the absent parent and of any partner is calculated as follows: Take their net income as calculated under reg. 7. Add to this the basic rate of child benefit and any maintenance payable in respect of any member of the family. Then deduct any maintenance payments by the absent parent or the partner under a maintenance order where a maintenance assessment could not be made.

Where these provisions apply to an absent parent, that person does not have to pay an assessment or a collection fee (reg. 3(5)(*d*) of the Child Support Fees Regulations). This does not affect any fee payable by the parent with care (reg. 3(6)(*b*) of these Regulations).

Where there are two or more applications for a maintenance assessment in respect of the same person who is, or who is treated as, an absent parent but those applications relate to different qualifying children, the case is a special case by virtue of reg. 22 of the Maintenance Assessments and Special Cases Regulations. In this case if the total of the assessments made would reduce the disposable income of that absent parent below the protected income level, the total is reduced by the minimum necessary to prevent this occurring. However, the total must not be reduced below the minimum amount of child support maintenance under para. 7 below. The individual assessments are reduced in the same proportion as they bear to each other (see reg. 22(3)).

If there is a person who is treated as an absent parent under reg. 20 of the Maintenance Assessments and Special Cases Regulations, the provisions of this paragraph are only applied after the application of the effect of the formula in reg. 20(4) has been calculated (reg. 20(6)).

Para. (7)

In most cases an absent parent will be required to pay a minimum amount of child support maintenance even if the maintenance assessment as calculated under this Schedule would otherwise be lower. The minimum amount is fixed by reg. 13 of the Maintenance Assessments and Special Cases Regulations. It is five per cent. of the income support personal allowance for a single claimant aged not less than 25. If the figure is not a multiple of five, it is rounded up to the next higher multiple of five pence.

In some cases the minimum amount does not apply and the child support maintenance is fixed at nil. This is the position in those cases which are special cases by virtue of reg. 26 of the Maintenance Assessments and Special Cases Regulations. In order to come within this regulation, the circumstances must be such that the minimum amount fixed under this paragraph would otherwise be payable and one of certain additional factors applies. These factors are in summary:

(i)   the absent parent's income includes one or more of the items listed in Schedule 4 to the Maintenance Assessments and Special Cases Regulations;
(ii) the absent parent is a member of a family of which at least one member is a child or young person;
(iii) the absent parent is a child;
(iv) the absent parent is a prisoner;
(v)   the absent parent's net income is less than the minimum amount of child support maintenance.

Where there are two or more applications for a maintenance assessment in respect of the same person who is, or who is treated as, an absent parent but those applications relate to different qualifying children, the case is a special case by virtue of reg. 22 of the Maintenance Assessments and Special Cases Regulations. In this case the minimum amount of child support maintenance is payable and is apportioned between the individual assessments in the same ratio as the maintenance requirements bear to each other (reg. 22(4)).

If there is a person who is treated as an absent parent under reg. 20 of the Maintenance Assessments and Special Cases Regulations, the provisions of this paragraph are only applied after the application of the effect of the formula in reg. 20(4) has been calculated (reg. 20(6)).

Para. 11

The basic rules determining the effective date are contained in regs. 30 and 31 of the Maintenance Assessment Procedure Regulations.

For the purpose of reg. 3(5) of the Maintenance Arrangements and Jurisdiction Regulations the effective date of an assessment is two days after the assessment is made.

Where multiple applications for maintenance assessments are treated as a single application, the effective date is determined by reference to the earlier or earliest application (reg. 4(3) of the Maintenance Assessment Procedure Regulations).

Where reg. 8(3) of the Maintenance Procedure Regulations applies, the effective date of an interim maintenance assessment is in the third week following the giving of notice by a child support officer of an intention to make such an assessment under s.12 of the Act on the same day of the week as that on which a maintenance enquiry form was given or sent to the absent parent, or would have been given or sent but for deliberate avoidance of receipt of the form by the absent parent.

Para. (16)

Where a person with care believes that an assessment has ceased to have effect or should be cancelled, that person is under a duty to notify the Secretary of State of this belief and the reasons for it, and to provide the Secretary of State with such information as he reasonably requires to allow a determination to be made as to whether the assessment has ceased to have effect or should be cancelled (reg. 6 of the Information, Evidence and Disclosure Regulations).

SCHEDULE 2   **Section 14(4)**

PROVISION OF INFORMATION TO SECRETARY OF STATE

Inland Revenue records

1.—(1) This paragraph applies where the Secretary of State or the Department of Health and Social Services for Northern Ireland requires information for the purpose of tracing—
- (*a*) the current address of an absent parent; or
- (*b*) the current employer of an absent parent.

(2) In such a case, no obligation as to secrecy imposed by statute or otherwise on a person employed in relation to the Inland Revenue shall prevent any information obtained or held in connection with the assessment or collection of income tax from being disclosed to—
- (*a*) the Secretary of State;
- (*b*) the Department of Health and Social Services for Northern Ireland; or
- (*c*) an officer of either of them authorised to receive such information in connection with the operation of this Act or of any corresponding Northern Ireland legislation.

(3) This paragraph extends only to disclosure by or under the authority of the Commissioners of Inland Revenue.

(4) Information which is the subject of disclosure to any person by virtue of this paragraph shall not be further disclosed to any person except where the further disclosure is made—
- (*a*) to a person to whom disclosure could be made by virtue of sub-paragraph (2); or
- (*b*) for the purposes of any proceedings (civil or criminal) in connection with the operation of this Act or of any corresponding Northern Ireland legislation.

Local authority records

2.—(1) This paragraph applies where—
- (*a*) the Secretary of State requires relevant information in connection with the discharge by him, or by any child support officer, of functions under this Act; or
- (*b*) the Department of Health and Social Services for Northern Ireland requires relevant information in connection with the discharge of any functions under any corresponding Northern Ireland legislation.

(2) The Secretary of State may give a direction to the appropriate authority requiring them to give him such relevant information in connection with any housing benefit or community charge benefit to which an absent parent or person with care is entitled as the Secretary of State considers necessary in connection with his determination of—
- (*a*) that person's income of any kind;
- (*b*) the amount of housing costs to be taken into account in determining that person's income of any kind; or
- (*c*) the amount of that person's protected income.

(3) The Secretary of State may give a similar direction for the purposes of enabling the Department of Health and Social Services for Northern Ireland to obtain such information for the purposes of any corresponding Northern Ireland legislation.

(4) In this paragraph—
"appropriate authority" means—
- (*a*) in relation to housing benefit, the housing or local authority concerned; and

(*b*) in relation to community charge benefit, the charging authority or, in Scotland, the levying authority; and

"relevant information" means information of such a description as may be prescribed.

DEFINITIONS

"absent parent": see s.3(2).
"child support officer": see s.13.
"person with care": see s.3(3).
"prescribed": see s.54.

GENERAL NOTE

From a date to be appointed "council tax benefit" will be substituted for "community charge benefit" and "bill authority" will be substituted for "charging authority" (Sched. 13, para. 94 to the Local Government Finance Act 1992).

Para. 2(4)

"Relevant information" is defined by reg. 4 of the Information, Evidence and Disclosure Regulations.

SCHEDULE 3   Section 21(4)

CHILD SUPPORT APPEAL TRIBUNALS

The President

1.—(1) The person appointed [¹ . . . . . .] as President of the social security appeal tribunals, medical appeal tribunals and disability appeal tribunals shall, by virtue of that appointment, also be President of the child support appeal tribunals.

(2) It shall be the duty of the President to arrange such meetings of the chairmen and members of child support appeal tribunals, and such training for them, as he considers appropriate.

(3) The President may, with the consent of the Secretary of State as to numbers, remuneration and other terms and conditions of service, appoint such officers and staff as he thinks fit for the child support appeal tribunals and their full-time chairmen.

Membership of child support appeal tribunals

2.—(1) A child support appeal tribunal shall consist of a chairman and two other persons.

(2) The chairman and the other members of the tribunal must not all be of the same sex.

(3) Sub-paragraph (2) shall not apply to any proceedings before a child support appeal tribunal if the chairman of the tribunal rules that it is not reasonably practicable to comply with that sub-paragraph in those proceedings.

The chairmen

3.—(1) The chairman of a child support appeal tribunal shall be nominated by the President.

(2) The President may nominate himself or a person drawn—

(*a*) from the appropriate panel appointed by the Lord Chancellor, or (as the case may be) the Lord President of the Court of Session, under section 7 of the Tribunals and Inquiries Act 1971;

(*b*) from among those appointed under paragraph 4; or

(*c*) from among those appointed [² . . . . . .] to act as full-time chairmen of social security appeal tribunals.

(3) Subject to any regulations made by the Lord Chancellor, no person shall be nominated as a chairman of a child support appeal tribunal by virtue of sub-paragraph (2)(*a*) unless he

has a 5 year general qualification or is an advocate or solicitor in Scotland of 5 years' standing.

4.—(1) The Lord Chancellor may appoint regional and other full-time chairmen for child support appeal tribunals.

(2) A person is qualified to be appointed as a full-time chairman if he has a 7 year general qualification or is an advocate or solicitor in Scotland of 7 years' standing.

(3) A person appointed to act as a full-time chairman shall hold and vacate office in accordance with the terms of his appointment, except that he must vacate his office at the end of the completed year of service in which he reaches the age of 72 unless his appointment is continued under sub-paragraph (4).

(4) Where the Lord Chancellor considers it desirable in the public interest to retain a full-time chairman in office after the end of the completed year of service in which he reaches the age of 72, he may from time to time authorise the continuance of that person in office until any date not later than that on which that person reaches the age of 75.

(5) A person appointed as a full-time chairman may be removed from office by the Lord Chancellor, on the ground of misbehaviour or incapacity.

(6) Section 75 of the Courts and Legal Services Act 1990 (judges etc. barred from legal practice) shall apply to any person appointed as a full-time chairman under this Schedule as it applies to any person holding as a full-time appointment any of the offices listed in Schedule 11 to that Act.

(7) The Secretary of State may pay, or make such payments towards the provision of, such remuneration, pensions, allowances or gratuities to or in respect of persons appointed as full-time chairmen under this paragraph as, with the consent of the Treasury, he may determine.

Other members of child support appeal tribunals

5.—(1) The members of a child support appeal tribunal other than the chairman shall be drawn from the appropriate panel constituted under this paragraph.

(2) The panels shall be constituted by the President for the whole of Great Britain, and shall—

(*a*)   act for such areas; and

(*b*)   be composed of such persons,

as the President thinks fit.

(3) The panel for an area shall be composed of persons appearing to the President to have knowledge or experience of conditions in the area and to be representative of persons living or working in the area.

(4) Before appointing members of a panel, the President shall take into consideration any recommendations from such organisations or persons as he considers appropriate.

(5) The members of the panels shall hold office for such period as the President may direct.

(6) The President may at any time terminate the appointment of any member of a panel.

Clerks of tribunals

6.—(1) Each child support appeal tribunal shall be serviced by a clerk appointed by the President.

(2) The duty of summoning members of a panel to serve on a child support appeal tribunal shall be performed by the clerk to the tribunal.

Expenses of tribunal members and others

7.—(1) The Secretary of State may pay—

(*a*)   to any member of a child support appeal tribunal, such remuneration and travelling and other allowances as the Secretary of State may determine with the consent of the Treasury;

(b) to any person required to attend at any proceedings before a child support appeal tribunal, such travelling and other allowances as may be so determined; and

(c) such other expenses in connection with the work of any child support appeal tribunal as may be so determined.

(2) In sub-paragraph (1), references to travelling and other allowances include references to compensation for loss of remunerative time.

(3) No compensation for loss of remunerative time shall be paid to any person under this paragraph in respect of any time during which he is in receipt of other remuneration so paid.

Consultation with Lord Advocate

8. Before exercising any of his powers under paragraph 3(3) or 4(1), (4) or (5), the Lord Chancellor shall consult the Lord Advocate.

AMENDMENTS
1. Sched. 1 to the Social Security Consequential Provisions Act 1992 (July 1, 1992).
2. Sched. 1 to the Social Security Consequential Provisions Act 1992 (July 1, 1992).

DEFINITIONS
"child support appeal tribunal": see s.54.
"general qualification": see s.54.

GENERAL NOTE
Para. 2(1)
There is no provision for an appeal to be heard by an incomplete tribunal. It is, therefore, especially important that if a member is unable to attend, the clerk should be notified as soon as possible to allow a replacement to be arranged. As this rule differs from that which applies in a SSAT, chairmen will need to be on guard against applying the wrong rule. They will also need to consider its potential effect if an appeal is adjourned part-heard. In a SSAT if this is done and one of the members is unable to attend, the adjourned hearing may proceed with the chairman and only one member. This is not possible in a CSAT and is a reason for avoiding adjournments part-heard if at all possible.

Para. 2(2) and (3)
The combined effect of these two sub-paragraphs is that the tribunal must comprise at least one member of each sex unless the chairman rules that it would not be reasonably practicable to comply with the rule in those proceedings. It is for the chairman who is listed to hear the appeal to make the ruling. Regulation 1(3) of the Tribunal Procedure Regulations does not apply to this Schedule, so a full-time chairman may only act if listed as the chairman. There is no appeal against a ruling since this is a decision for a chairman, not for a CSAT. The ruling should be made as early as possible so as to cause the minimum inconvenience to the parties whose hearing is postponed. If a session is listed with a tribunal consisting of three members of the same sex or if a subsequent substitution produces this result, the clerk should supply the chairman with the information necessary to judge whether or not it was reasonably practicable to comply with the rule in those proceedings. This information will include the steps taken to comply with the rule and the reasons why a member of the opposite sex could not be summoned. It is to be hoped that in practice the only such cases which occur will be those where a member has to be substituted after listing. It is undesirable from the point of view of the convenience of the parties if a case is initially listed with three members of the same sex and then postponed. Chairmen should check the constitution of their tribunals as soon as they receive the appeal papers to see if any ruling is required under this provision.

The relevant factors which may be taken into account are very limited. The only factors which the chairman is entitled to take into account are those relevant to the practicability of having a mixture of sexes on the tribunal. No account should be taken of the wishes of the parties involved, as is the current practice in SSATs, even if this leads to the postponement of a hearing which all the parties wish to proceed. No account should be taken of the nature of the hearing, so that it is irrelevant that it will deal only with procedural matters and that the merits of the case will not be considered.

"Proceedings" is often used in a general sense to cover all the steps in an appeal, as for example in reg. 5 of the Tribunal Procedure Regulations. In this context a narrower meaning is required. In deciding what constitutes "proceedings" the importance of continuity must be considered. If a case is adjourned and the next hearing is a complete rehearing of the case, each hearing will constitute fresh proceedings and a ruling on the membership of the tribunal for the first hearing will not cover the second. However, if a case is listed before the same members following the adjournment of an appeal part-heard or on a reference back to the tribunal to resolve a dispute in the working out of the tribunal's decision, the two hearings constitute a single proceeding for the purpose of this provision. If the position were otherwise, the need to test reasonable practicability for each hearing would require that appeals be completely reheard in these cases. Adjourning part-heard is not a practice to be encouraged in view of the difficulties of picking up a case after the passage of time and the problems of fixing a date convenient for all members. However, in some cases an adjournment of a part-heard case is unavoidable and it is preferable that it should be taken by the same tribunal rather than being completely reheard.

Para. (5)

This paragraph contains the only conditions for appointment of members of CSATs. The person's nationality is, therefore, irrelevant, provided the person fulfills the requirements of sub-para. (3).

SCHEDULE 4   **Section 22(5)**

CHILD SUPPORT COMMISSIONERS

Tenure of office

1.—(1) Every Child Support Commissioner shall vacate his office at the end of the completed year of service in which he reaches the age of 72.

(2) Where the Lord Chancellor considers it desirable in the public interest to retain a Child Support Commissioner in office after the end of the completed year of service in which he reaches the age of 72, he may from time to time authorise the continuance of that Commissioner in office until any date not later than that on which he reaches the age of 75.

(3) A Child Support Commissioner may be removed from office by the Lord Chancellor on the ground of misbehaviour or incapacity.

Commissioners' remuneration and their pensions

2.—(1) The Lord Chancellor may pay, or make such payments towards the provision of such remuneration, pensions, allowances or gratuities to or in respect of persons appointed as Child Support Commissioners as, with the consent of the Treasury, he may determine.

(2) The Lord Chancellor shall pay to a Child Support Commissioner such expenses incurred in connection with his work as such a Commissioner as may be determined by the Treasury.

Commissioners barred from legal practice

3. Section 75 of the Courts and Legal Services Act 1990 (judges etc. barred from legal practice) shall apply to any person appointed as a Child Support Commissioner as it applies to any person holding as a full-time appointment any of the offices listed in Schedule 11 to that Act.

Deputy Child Support Commissioners

4.—(1) The Lord Chancellor may appoint persons to act as Child Support Commissioners (but to be known as deputy Child Support Commissioners) in order to facilitate the disposal of the business of Child Support Commissioners.

(2) A deputy Child Support Commissioner shall be appointed—

(a) from among persons who have a 10 year general qualification or are advocates or solicitors in Scotland of 10 years' standing; and

(b) for such period or on such occasions as the Lord Chancellor thinks fit.

(3) Paragraph 2 applies to deputy Child Support Commissioners as if the reference to pensions were omitted and paragraph 3 does not apply to them.

Tribunals of Commissioners

5.—(1) If it appears to the Chief Child Support Commissioner (or, in the case of his inability to act, to such other of the Child Support Commissioners as he may have nominated to act for the purpose) that an appeal falling to be heard by one of the Child Support Commissioners involves a question of law of special difficulty, he may direct that the appeal be dealt with by a tribunal consisting of any three of the Child Support Commissioners.

(2) If the decision of such a tribunal is not unanimous, the decision of the majority shall be the decision of the tribunal.

Finality of decisions

6.—(1) Subject to section 25, the decision of any Child Support Commissioner shall be final.

(2) Sub-paragraph (1) shall not be taken to make any finding of fact or other determination embodied in, or necessary to, a decision, or on which it is based, conclusive for the purposes of any further decision.

Consultation with Lord Advocate

7. Before exercising any of his powers under paragraph 1(2) or (3), or 4(1) or (2)(*b*), the Lord Chancellor shall consult the Lord Advocate.

Northern Ireland

8. In its application to Northern Ireland this Schedule shall have effect as if—

(*a*)   for any reference to a Child Support Commissioner (however expressed) there were substituted a corresponding reference to a Child Support Commissioner for Northern Ireland;

(*b*)   in paragraph 2(1), the word "pensions" were omitted;

(*c*)   for paragraph 3, there were substituted—

"**3.** A Child Support Commissioner for Northern Ireland, so long as he holds office as such, shall not practise as a barrister or act for any remuneration to himself as arbitrator or referee or be directly or indirectly concerned in any matter as a conveyancer, notary public or solicitor.";

(*d*)   in paragraph 4—

(i)   for paragraph (*a*) of sub-paragraph (2) there were substituted—

"(a) from among persons who are barristers or solicitors of not less than 10 years' standing; and";

(ii)   for sub-paragraph (3) there were substituted—

"(3) Paragraph 2 applies to deputy Child Support Commissioners for Northern Ireland, but paragraph 3 does not apply to them."; and

(*e*)   paragraphs 5 to 7 were omitted.

DEFINITION
"general qualification": see s.54.

GENERAL NOTE
Para. 5(1)
Tribunals of Commissioners still occasionally sit. However, they are used infrequently in view of the possibility of an appeal from a Commissioner under s.25 of the Act. It is a pity that greater use is not made of them. If a Commissioner who was minded to give a decision which disagreed with that in another decision were to request that a Tribunal of Commissioners hear the appeal, CSATs would not be faced with so many conflicting decisions.

The Child Support (Information, Evidence and Disclosure) Regulations 1992

(S.I. 1992 No. 1812)

Made by the Secretary of State for Social Security under sections 4(4), 6(9), 7(5), 14(1) and (3), 50(5), 51, 54 and 57 of, and paragraphs 16(10) of Schedule 1 to and 2(4) of Schedule 2 to, the Child Support Act 1991 and all other powers enabling him in that behalf.

PART I

GENERAL

Citation, commencement and interpretation

1.—(1) These Regulations may be cited as the Child Support (Information, Evidence and Disclosure) Regulations 1992 and shall come into force on 5th April 1993.

(2) In these Regulations, unless the context otherwise requires—

"the Act" means the Child Support Act 1991;

"appropriate authority" means—
- (a)   in relation to housing benefit, the housing or local authority concerned; and
- (b)   in relation to council tax benefit, the billing authority or, in Scotland, the levying authority;

"local authority" means, in relation to England and Wales, the council of a county, a metropolitan district, a London Borough or the Common Council of the City of London and, in relation to Scotland, a regional council or an islands council;

"Maintenance Assessments and Special Cases Regulations" means the Child Support (Maintenance Assessments and Special Cases) Regulations 1992;

"Maintenance Assessment Procedure Regulations" means the Child Support (Maintenance Assessment Procedure) Regulations 1992;

"parent with care" means a person who, in respect of the same child or children, is both a parent and a person with care;

"related proceedings" means proceedings in which a relevant court order was or is being sought;

"relevant court order" means—
- (a)   an order as to periodical or capital provision or as to variation of property rights made under an enactment specified in paragraphs (a) to (e) of section 8(11) of the Act or prescribed under section 8(11)(f) of the Act in relation to a qualifying child or a relevant person; or
- (b)   an order under Part II of the Children Act 1989 (Orders With Respect To Children In Family Proceedings) in relation to a qualifying child or, in Scotland, an order under section 3 of the Law Reform (Parent and Child) (Scotland) Act 1986 or a decree of declarator under section 7 of that Act in relation to a qualifying child;

"relevant person" means—
- (a)   a person with care;
- (b)   an absent parent;
- (c)   a parent who is treated as an absent parent under regulation 20 of the Maintenance Assessments and Special Cases Regulations;
- (d)   where the application for an assessment is made by a child under section 7 of the Act, that child,

in respect of whom a maintenance assessment has been applied for or is or has been in force.

(3) In these Regulations, unless the context otherwise requires, a reference—
- (a)   to a numbered regulation is to the regulation in these Regulations bearing that number,
- (b)   in a regulation to a numbered paragraph is to the paragraph in that regulation bearing that number;
- (c)   in a paragraph to a lettered or numbered sub-paragraph is to the sub-paragraph in that paragraph bearing that letter or number.

PART II

FURNISHING OF INFORMATION OR EVIDENCE

Persons under a duty to furnish information or evidence

2.—(1) Where an application for a maintenance assessment has been made under the Act, a person falling within a category listed in paragraph (2) shall, subject to the restrictions specified in that paragraph, furnish such information or evidence as is required by the Secretary of State and which is needed to enable a determination to be made in relation to one or more of the matters listed in regulation 3(1), and the person concerned has that information or evidence in his possession or can reasonable be expected to acquire that information or evidence.

(2) The persons who may be required to furnish information or evidence, and the matter or matters with respect to which such information or evidence may be required, are as follows—

(a) the relevant persons, with respect to the matters listed in regulation 3(1);

(b) a person who is alleged to be a parent of a child with respect to whom an application for a maintenance assessment has been made who denies that he is one of that child's parents, with respect to the matters listed in sub-paragraphs (b) and (d) of regulation 3(1);

(c) the current or recent employer of the absent parent or the parent with care in relation to whom an application for a maintenance assessment has been made, with respect to the matters listed in sub-paragraphs (d), (e), (f), (h) and (j) of regulation 3(1);

(d) the local authority in whose area a person falling within a category listed in sub-paragraphs (a) and (b) above resides or has resided, with respect to the matter listed in sub-paragraph (a) of regulation 3(1);

(e) a person specified in paragraph (3) below, in any case where, in relation to the qualifying child or qualifying children or the absent parent—

(i) there is or has been a relevant court order; or

(ii) there have been, or are pending, related proceedings before a court,

with respect to the matters listed in sub-paragraphs (g), (h) and (k) or regulation 3(1).

(3) The persons who may be required to furnish information or evidence in relation to a relevant court order or related proceedings under the provisions of paragraph (2)(e) are:—

(a) in England and Wales—

(i) in relation to the High Court, the senior district judge of the principal registry of the Family Division or, where proceedings were instituted in a district registry, the district judge;

(ii) in relation to a county court, the proper officer of that court within the meaning of Order 1, Rule 3 of the County Court Rules 1981;

(iii) in relation to a magistrates' court, the clerk to the justices of that court;

(b) in Scotland—

(i) in relation to the Court of Session, the Deputy Principal Clerk of Session;

(ii) in relation to a sheriff court, the sheriff clerk.

DEFINITIONS

"the Act": see reg. 1(2).

"local authority": *ibid.*

"parent with care": *ibid.*

"related proceedings": *ibid.*

"relevant court order": *ibid.*

"relevant person": *ibid.*

GENERAL NOTE

Para. (2)

The Family Proceedings (Amendment) Rules 1993 amend the Family Proceedings Rules 1991 (as amended) by inserting r. 10.21A to provide that nothing in rr. 10.20 or 10.21 of those Rules (which limit the circumstances in which inspection, etc. of documents in court and disclosure of addresses can be required) shall prevent a person required to furnish information or evidence from doing so.

Purposes for which information or evidence may be required

3.—(1) The Secretary of State may require information or evidence under the provisions of regulation 2 only if that information or evidence is needed to enable—

(*a*)   a decision to be made as to whether, in relation to an application for a maintenance assessment, there exists a qualifying child, an absent parent and a person with care;

(*b*)   a decision to be made as to whether a child support officer has jurisdiction to make a maintenance assessment under section 44 of the Act;

(*c*)   a decision to be made, where more than one application has been made, as to which application is to be proceeded with;

(*d*)   an absent parent to be identified;

(*e*)   an absent parent to be traced;

(*f*)   the amount of child support maintenance payable by an absent parent to be assessed;

(*g*)   the amount payable under a relevant court order to be ascertained;

(*h*)   the amounts specified in sub-paragraphs (*f*) and (*g*) to be recovered from an absent parent;

(*i*)   the amount of interest payable with respect to arrears of child support maintenance to be determined;

(*j*)   the amount specified in sub-paragraph (*i*) to be recovered from an absent parent;

(*k*)   any related proceedings to be identified.

(2) The information or evidence to be furnished in accordance with regulation 2 may in particular include information and evidence as to—

(*a*)   the habitual residence of the person with care, the absent parent and any child in respect of whom an application for a maintenance assessment has been made;

(*b*)   the name and address of the person with care and of the absent parent, their marital status, and the relationship of the person with care to any child in respect of whom the application for a maintenance assessment has been made;

(*c*)   the name, address and date of birth of any such chld, that child's marital status, and any education that child is undergoing;

(*d*)   the persons who have parental responsibility for (or, in Scotland, parental rights over) any qualifying child where there is more than one person with care;

(*e*)   the time spent by a qualifying child in respect of whom an application for a maintenance assessment has been made with each person with care, where there is more than one such person;

(*f*)   the matters relevant for determining, in a case falling within section 26 of the Act (disputes about parentage), whether that case falls within one of the Cases set out in subsection (2) of that section, and if it does not, the matters relevant for determining the parentage of a child whose parentage is in dispute;

(*g*)   the name and address of any current or recent employer of an absent parent or a parent with care, and the gross earnings and the deductions from those earnings deriving from each employment;

(*h*)   the address from which an absent parent or parent with care who is self-employed carries on his trade or business, the trading name, and the gross receipts and expenses and other outgoings of the trade or business;

(*i*)   any other income of an absent parent and a parent with care;

(*j*)   any income, other than earnings, of a qualifying child;

(*k*)   amounts payable and paid under a relevant court order or a maintenance agreement;

(*l*)   the persons living in the same household as the absent parent or living in the same household as the parent with care, their relationship to the absent parent or the parent with care, as the case may be, and to each other, and, in the case of the children of any such party, the dates of birth of those children;

(*m*) the matters set out in sub-paragraphs (*g*) and (*h*) in relation to the persons specified in sub-paragraph (*l*) other than any children living in the same household as the absent parent or the parent with care, as the case may be;

(*n*) income other than earnings of the persons living in the same household as the absent parent or the parent with care;

(*o*) benefits related to disability that the absent parent, parent with care and other persons living in the same household as the absent parent or the parent with care are entitled to or would be entitled to if certain conditions were satisfied;

(*p*) the housing costs to be taken into account for the purposes of determining assessable or disposable income;

(*q*) the identifying details of any bank, building society or similar account held in the name of the absent parent or the person with care, and statements relating to any such account;

(*r*) the matters relevant for determining whether—
  (i) a maintenance assessment has ceased to have effect or should be cancelled under the provisions of paragraph 16 of Schedule 1 to the Act;
  (ii) a person is a child within the meaning of section 55 of the Act.

DEFINITIONS
"parent with care": see reg. 1(2).
"related proceedings": *ibid.*

GENERAL NOTE
See the general note to reg. 2.

Information from an appropriate authority in connection with housing benefit or council tax benefit

4. For the purposes of paragraph 2 of Schedule 2 to the Act, "relevant information" means—

(*a*) information as to the amount of housing costs of an absent parent or person with care which are treated as eligible rent for housing benefit purposes, and the entitlement to housing benefit at the date the Secretary of State gives a direction under paragraph 2(2) of that Schedule;

(*b*) information as to the amount of council tax payable by an absent parent or person with care, and as to the entitlement to council tax benefit at the date the Secretary of State gives a direction under paragraph 2(2) of that Schedule.

DEFINITION
"the Act": see reg. 1(2).

Time within which information or evidence is to be furnished

5. Subject to the provisions of regulations 2(5), 6(1), 17(5) and 19(2) of the Maintenance Assessment Procedure Regulations, any information or evidence furnished in accordance with regulations 2 and 3 shall be furnished as soon as is reasonably practicable in the particular circumstances of the case.

DEFINITION
"Maintenance Assessment Procedure Regulations": see reg. 1(2).

Continuing duty of persons with care

6. Where a person with care with respect to whom a maintenance assessment has been made believes that, by virtue of section 44 or 55 of, or paragraph 16 of Schedule 1 to, the Act, the assessment has ceased to have effect or should be cancelled, she shall, as soon as is reasonably practicable, inform the Secretary of State of that belief, and of the reasons for it, and shall provide such other information as the Secretary of State may reasonably require, with a view to assisting the Secretary of State or a child support officer in determining whether the assessment has ceased to have effect, or should be cancelled.

DEFINITION
"the Act": see reg. 1(2).

Powers of inspectors in relation to Crown residences

7. Subject to Her Majesty not being in residence, an inspector appointed under section 15 of the Act may enter any Crown premises for the purpose of exercising any powers conferred on him by that section.

DEFINITION
"the Act": see reg. 1(2).

PART III

DISCLOSURE OF INFORMATION

Disclosure of information to a court or tribunal

8. The Secretary of State or a child suypport officer may disclose any information held by them for the purposes of the Act to—
   (*a*) a court;
   (*b*) any tribunal or other body or person mentioned in the Act;
   (*c*) any tribunal established under the benefit Acts,
where such disclosure is made for the purposes of any proceedings before any of those bodies relating to this Act or the benefit Acts.

DEFINITION
"the Act": see reg. 1(2).

GENERAL NOTE
Para. 8(b)
   The reference to "person" here is qualified by the later reference to "proceedings before any of those bodies". Thus, this paragraph permits disclosure to a person but only for the purpose of proceedings before one of the bodies covered. It would, for example, cover disclosure to the Secretary of State or an adjudication officer for the purposes of proceedings before a Social Security Appeal Tribunal.

Disclosure of information to an appropriate authority for use in the exercise of housing benefit or council tax benefit functions

9. The Secretary of State or a child support officer may disclose information held by him for the purposes of the Act to, and as required by, an appropriate authority for use in the exercise of its functions relating to housing benefit or council tax benefit.

DEFINITIONS
"the Act": see reg. 1(2).
"appropriate authority": *ibid.*

Disclosure of information to the Secretary of State

10. A child support officer may disclose any information held by him for the purposes of the Act to, and as required by, the Secretary of State for use in connection with the functions of the Secretary of State under any of the benefit Acts.

DEFINITION
"the Act": see reg. 1(2).

Employment to which section 50 of the Act applies

11. For the purposes of section 50 of the Act (unauthorised disclosure of information) the following kinds of employment are prescribed in addition to those specified in paragraphs (*a*) to (*e*) of section 50(5)—
  (*a*) the Comptroller and Auditor General;
  (*b*) the Parliamentary Commissioner for Administration;
  (*c*) the Health Service Commissioner for England;
  (*d*) the Health Service Commissioner for Wales;
  (*e*) the Health Service Commissioner for Scotland;
  (*f*) any member of the staff of the National Audit Office;
  (*g*) any other person who carries out the administrative work of that Office, or who provides, or is employed in the provision of, services to it;
  (*h*) any officer of any of the Commissioners referred to in paragraphs (*b*) to (*e*) above; and
  (*i*) any person who provides, or is employed in the provision of, services to the Department of Social Security.

DEFINITION
"the Act": see reg. 1(2).

The Child Support (Maintenance Assessment Procedure) Regulations 1992

(S.I. 1992 No. 1813)

Made by the Secretary of State for Social Secretary under sections 3(3), 5(3), 6(1), 12, 16, 17, 18, 42(3), 46(11), 51, 52(4), 54 and 55 of, and paragraphs 11, 14 and 16 of Schedule 1 to, the Child Support Act 1991 and all other powers enabling him in that behalf.

ARRANGEMENT OF REGULATIONS

PART I

General

PART II

Applications for a maintenance assessment

PART III

Interim maintenance assessments

PART IV

Notifications following certain decisions by child support officers

PART V

Periodical reviews

PART I

GENERAL

Citation, commencement and interpretation

1.—(1) These Regulations may be cited as the Child Support (Maintenance Assessment Procedure) Regulations 1992 and shall come into force on 5th April 1993.

(2) In these Regulations, unless the context otherwise requires—

"the Act" means the Child Support Act 1991;

"applicable amount" is to be construed in accordance with Part IV of the Income Support Regulations;

"applicable amounts Schedule" means Schedule 2 to the Income Support Regulations;

"award period" means a period in respect of which an award of family credit or disability working allowance is made;

"balance of the reduction period" means, in relation to a direction that is or has been in force, the portion of the period specified in a direction in respect of which no reduction of relevant benefit has been made;

"benefit week" in relation to income support, has the same meaning as in the Income Support Regulations, and, in relation to family credit and disability working allowance, is to be construed in accordance with the Social Security (Claims and Payments) Regulations 1987;

"direction" means reduced benefit direction;

"disability working allowance" has the same meaning as in the Social Security Contributions and Benefits Act 1992;

"day to day care" has the same meaning as in the Maintenance Assessments and Special Cases Regulations;

"effective application" means any application that complies with the provisions of regulation 2;

"effective date" means the date on which a maintenance assessment takes effect for the purposes of the Act;

131

"Income Support Regulations" means the Income Support (General) Regulations 1987;

"Information, Evidence and Disclosure Regulations" means the Child Support (Information, Evidence and Disclosure) Regulations 1992;

"Maintenance Assessments and Special Cases Regulations" means the Child Support (Maintenance Assessments and Special Cases) Regulations 1992;

"maintenance period" has the meaning prescribed in regulation 33;

"obligation imposed by section 6 of the Act" is to be construed in accordance with section 46(1) of the Act;

"parent with care" means a person who, in respect of the same child or children, is both a parent and a person with care;

"the parent concerned" means the parent with respect to whom a direction is given;

"protected income level" has the same meaning as in paragraph 6(6) of Schedule 1 to the Act;

"relevant benefit" means income support, family credit or disability working allowance;

"relevant person" means—

(a) a person with care;

(b) an absent parent;

(c) a parent who is treated as an absent parent under regulation 20 of the Maintenance Assessments and Special Cases Regulations;

(d) where the application for an assessment is made by a child under section 7 of the Act, that child,

in respect of whom a maintenance assessment has been applied for or is or has been in force.

(3) In these Regulations, references to a direction as being "in operation", "suspended", or "in force" shall be construed as follows—

a direction is "in operation" if, by virtue of that direction, relevant benefit is currently being reduced;

a direction is "suspended" if either—

(a) after that direction has been given, relevant benefit ceases to be payable, or becomes payable at one of the rates indicated in regulation 40(3); or

(b) at the time that the direction is given, relevant benefit is payable at one of the rates indicated in regulation 40(3),

and these Regulations provide for relevant benefit payable from a later date to be reduced by virtue of the same direction;

a direction is "in force" if it is either in operation or is suspended, and cognate terms shall be construed accordingly.

(4) The provisions of Schedule 1 shall have effect to supplement the meaning of "child" in section 55 of the Act.

(5) The provisions of these Regulations shall have general application to cases prescribed in regulations 19 to 26 of the Maintenance Assessments and Special Cases Regulations as cases to be treated as special cases for the purposes of the Act, and the terms "absent parent" and "person with care" shall be construed accordingly.

(6) Except where express provision is made to the contrary, where, by any provision of the Act or of these Regulations—

(a) any document is given or sent to the Secretary of State, that documents shall, subject to paragraph (7), be treated as having been so given or sent on the day it is received by the Secretary of State; and

(b) any document is given or sent to any person, that document shall, if sent by post to that person's last known or notified address, and subject to paragraph (8), be treated as having been given or sent on the second day after the day of posting, excluding any Sunday or any day which is a bank holiday in England, Wales, Scotland or Northern Ireland under the Banking and Financial Dealings Act 1971.

(7) Except where the provisions of regulation 8(6), 24(2), 29(3) or 31(6)(*a*) apply, the Secretary of State may treat a document given or sent to him as given or sent on such day, earlier than the day it was received by him, as he may determine, if he is satisfied that there was unavoidable delay in his receiving the document in question.

(8) Where, by any provision of the Act or of these Regulations, and in relation to a particular application, notice or notification—

(*a*)   more than one document is required to be given or sent to a person, and more than one such document is sent by post to that person but not all the documents are posted on the same day; or

(*b*)   documents are required to be given or sent to more than one person, and not all such documents are posted on the same day,

all those documents shall be treated as having been posted on the later or, as the case may be, the latest day of posting.

(9) In these Regulations, unless the context otherwise requires, a reference—

(*a*)   to a numbered Part is to the Part of these Regulations bearing that number;

(*b*)   to a numbered Schedule is to the Schedule to these Regulations bearing that number;

(*c*)   to a numbered regulation is to the regulation in these Regulations bearing that number;

(*d*)   in a regulation or Schedule to a numbered paragraph is to the paragraph in that regulation or Schedule bearing that number;

(*e*)   in a paragraph to a lettered or numbered sub-paragraph is to the sub-paragraph in that paragraph bearing that letter or number.

PART II

APPLICATIONS FOR A MAINTENANCE ASSESSMENT

Applications under section 4, 6 or 7 of the Act

2.—(1) Any person who applies for a maintenance assessment under section 4 or 7 of the Act shall do so on a form (a "maintenance application form") provided by the Secretary of State.

(2) Maintenance application forms provided by the Secretary of State under section 6 of the Act or under paragraph (1) shall be supplied without charge by such persons as the Secretary of State appoints or authorises for that purpose.

(3) A completed maintenance application form shall be given or sent to the Secretary of State.

(4) Subject to paragraph (5), an application for a maintenance assessment under the Act shall be an effective application if it is made on a maintenance application form and that form has been completed in accordance with the Secretary of State's instructions.

(5) Where an application is not effective under the provisions of paragraph (4), the Secretary of State may—

(*a*)   give or send the maintenance application form to the person who made the application, together, if he thinks appropriate, with a fresh maintenance application form, and request that the application be re-submitted so as to comply with the provisions of that paragraph; or

(*b*)   request the person who made the application to provide such additional information or evidence as the Secretary of State specifies, and if a completed application form or, as the case may be, the additional information or evidence requested is received by the Secretary of State within 14 days of the date of his request, he shall treat the application as made on the date on which the earlier or earliest application would have been treated as made had it been effective under the provisions of paragraph (4).

(6) Subject to paragraph (7), a person who has made an effective application may amend his application by notice in writing to the Secretary of State at any time before a maintenance assessment is made.

(7) No amendment under paragraph (6) shall relate to any change of circumstances arising after the effective date of a maintenance assessment resulting from an effective application.

Applications on the termination of a maintenance assessment

3.—(1) Where a maintenance assessment has been in force with respect to a person with care and a qualifying child and that person is replaced by another person with care, an application for a maintenance assessment with respect to that person with care and that qualifying child may for the purposes of regulation 30(2)(*b*)(ii) and subject to paragraph (3) be treated as having been received on a date earlier than that on which it was received.

(2) Where a maintenance assessment has been made in response to an application by a child under section 7 of the Act and either—

(*a*) a child support officer cancels that assessment following a request from that child; or

(*b*) that child ceases to be a child for the purposes of the Act,

any application for a maintenance assessment with respect to any other children who were qualifying children with respect to the earlier maintenance assessment may for the purposes of regulation 30(2)(*b*)(ii) and subject to paragraph (3) be treated as having been received on a date earlier than that on which it was received.

(3) No application for a maintenance assessment shall be treated as having been received under paragraph (1) or (2) on a date—

(*a*) more than 8 weeks earlier than the date on which the application was received; or

(*b*) on or before the first day of the maintenance period in which the earlier maintenance assessment ceased to have effect.

Multiple applications

4.—(1) The provisions of Schedule 2 shall apply in cases where there is more than one application for a maintenance assessment.

(2) The provisions of paragraphs 1, 2 and 3 of Schedule 2 relating to the treatment of two or more applications as a single application, shall apply where no request is received by the Secretary of State to cease acting in relation to all but one of the applications.

(3) Where, under the provisions of paragraph 1, 2 or 3 of Schedule 2, two or

more applications are to be treated as a single application, that application shall be treated as an application for a maintenance assessment to be made with respect to all of the qualifying children mentioned in the applications, and the effective date of that assessment shall be determined by reference to the earlier or earliest application.

DEFINITION
"effective date": see reg. 1(2).

Notice to other persons of an application for a maintenance assessment

5.—(1) [[1] Subject to paragraph (2A), where] an effective application for a maintenance assessment has been made the Secretary of State shall as soon as is reasonably practicable give notice in writing of that application to the relevant persons other than the applicant.

(2) The Secretary of State shall [[2] subject to paragraph (2A),] give or send to any person to whom notice has been given under paragraph (1) a form (a "maintenance enquiry form") and a written request that the form be completed and returned to him for the purpose of enabling the application for the maintenance assessment to be proceeded with.

[[3](2A) The provisions of paragraphs (1) and (2) shall not apply where the Secretary of State is satisfied that an application for a maintenance assessment can be dealt with in the absence of a completed and returned maintenance enquiry form.]

(3) Where the person to whom notice is being given under paragraph (1) is an absent parent, that notice shall specify the effective date of the maintenance assessment if one is to be made, and set out in general terms the provisions relating to interim maintenance assessments.

AMENDMENTS
1. Reg. 2(2) of the Amendment Regulations (April 5, 1993).
2. Reg. 2(3) of the Amendment Regulations (April 5, 1993).
3. Reg. 2(4) of the Amendment Regulations (April 5, 1993).

DEFINITIONS
"absent parent": see reg. 1(5).
"effective date": see reg. 1(2).
"relevant person": *ibid.*

Response to notification of an application for a maintenance assessment

6.—(1) Any person who has received a maintenance enquiry form given or sent under regulation 5(2) shall complete that form in accordance with the Secretary of State's instructions and return it to the Secretary of State within 14 days of its having been given or sent.

(2) Subject to paragraph (3), a person who has returned a completed maintenance enquiry form may amend the information he has provided on that form at any time before a maintenance assessment is made by notifying the Secretary of State in writing of the amendments.

(3) No amendment under paragraph (2) shall relate to any change of circumstances arising after the effective date of any maintenance assessment made in response to the application in relation to which the maintenance enquiry form was given or sent.

DEFINITION
"effective date": see reg. 1(2).

Death of a qualifying child

7.—(1) Where the child support officer concerned is informed of the death of a qualifying child with respect to whom an application for a maintenance assessment has been made, he shall—

(*a*) proceed with the application as if it had not been made with respect to that child if he has not yet made an assessment;

(*b*) treat any assessment already made by him as not having been made if the relevant persons have not been notified of it and proceed with the application as if it had not been made with respect to that child.

(2) Where all of the qualifying children with respect to whom an application for a maintenance assessment has been made have died, and either the assessment has not been made or the relevant persons have not been notified of it, the child support officer shall treat the application as not having been made.

DEFINITION
"relevant person": see reg. 1(2).

PART III

INTERIM MAINTENANCE ASSESSMENTS

Amount and duration of an interim maintenance assessment

8.—(1) Where a child support officer serves notice under section 12(4) of the Act of his intention to make an interim maintenance assessment, he shall not make the interim assessment before the end of a period of 14 days commencing with the date that notice was given or sent.

[¹(1A) There shall be two categories of interim maintenance assessment, Category A interim maintenance assessments and Category B interim maintenance assessments.

(1B) An interim maintenance assessment made by a child support officer shall be—

(*a*) a Category A interim maintenance assessment, where the information that is required by him as to the income of the absent parent to enable him to make an assessment in accordance with the provisions of Part I of Schedule 1 to the Act has not been provided by that absent parent, and that parent has that information in his possession or can reasonably be expected to acquire it;

(*b*) a Category B interim maintenance assessment, where the information that is required by him as to the income of the partner or other member of the family of the absent parent or parent with care to enable him to make an assessment in accordance with the provisions of Part I of Schedule 1 to the Act has not been provided by that partner or other member of the family, and that partner or other member of the family has that information in his possession or can reasonably be expected to acquire it.]

(2) The amount of child support maintenance fixed by [²a Category A] interim maintenance assessment shall be 1.5 multiplied by the amount of the maintenance requirement in respect of the qualifying child or qualifying children concerned calculated in accordance with the provisions of paragraph 1 of Schedule 1 to the Act,

and paragraphs 2 to 9 of that Schedule shall not apply to [³Category A] interim maintenance assessments.

[⁴(2A) The amount of child support maintenance fixed by a Category B interim maintenance assessment shall be determined in accordance with paragraphs (2B) and (2C).

(2B) Where a child support officer is unable to determine the exempt income—

    (*a*)   of an absent parent under regulation 9 of the Maintenance Assessments and Special Cases Regulations because he is unable to determine whether regulations 9(2) of those Regulations applies;

    (*b*)   of a parent with care under regulaiton 10 of those Regulations because he is unable to determine whether regulation 9(2) of the Regulations, as modified by and applied by regulation 10 of those Regulations applies,

the amount of the Category B interim maintenance assessment shall be the maintenance assessment calculated in accordance with Part I of Schedule 1 to the Act on the assumption that—

    (i)   in a case falling with sub-paragraph (*a*), regulation 9(2) of those Regulations does apply;

    (ii)   in a case falling with sub-paragraph (*b*), regulation 9(2) of those Regulations as modified by and applied by regulation 10 of those Regulations does apply.

(2C) Where the disposable income of an absent parent would, without taking account of the income of any member of his family, bring him within the provisions of paragraph 6 of Schedule 1 to the Act (protected income), and a child support officer is unable to ascertain the disposable income of the other members of his family, the amount of the Category B interim maintenance assessment shall be the maintenance assessment calculated in accordance with Part I of Schedule 1 to the Act on the assumption that the provisions of paragraph 6 of Schedule 1 to the Act do not apply to the absent parent.]

(3) Where the provisions of regulation 30(2)(*a*) or (4) apply, the effective date of an interim maintenance assessment shall be such date, being not earlier than the first and not later than the seventh day following the expiry of the period of 14 days specified in paragraph (1), as falls on the same day of the week as the date specified in regulation 30(2)(*a*).

(4) Where a maintenance assessment is made after an interim maintenance assessment has been in force, child support maintenance calculated in accordance with Part I of Schedule 1 to the Act shall be payable in respect of the period preceding that during which the interim maintenance assessment was in force.

(5) The child support maintenance payable under the provisions of paragraph (4) shall be payable in respect of the period between the effective date of the assessment (or, where separate assessments are made for different periods under paragraph 15 of Schedule 1 to the Act, the effective date of the assessment in respect of the earliest such period) and the effective date of the interim maintenance assessment.

(6) Where a child support officer is satisfied that there was unavoidable delay by the absent parent in completing and returning a maintenance enquiry form under the provisions of regulation 6(1), or in providing information or evidence that is required by the Secretary of State for the determination of an application for a maintenance assessment, he may cancel an interim maintenance assessment which is in force.

(7) An interim maintenance assessment shall not be cancelled under paragraph (6) with effect from a date earlier than that on which the provisions of regulation 6(1) could have been complied with.

(8) Subject to paragraphs (6), (7) and (10), the child support maintenance payable in respect of any period in respect of which an interim maintenance assessment is in force shall not be adjusted following the making of a maintenance assessment.

(9) An interim maintenance assessment shall cease to have effect on the first day

of the maintenance period during which the Secretary of State receives the information which enables a child support officer to make the maintenance assessment or assessments in relation to the same absent parent, person with care, and qualifying child or qualifying children, calculated in accordance with Part I of Schedule 1 to the Act.

(10) Where a maintenance assessment calculated in accordance with Part I of Schedule 1 to the Act is made following an interim maintenance assessment and the amount of child support maintenance payable under that assessment in respect of the period during which the interim maintenance assessment was in force is higher than the amount fixed by the interim maintenance assessment determined in accordance with paragraph (2), the amount of child support maintenance payable in respect of that period shall be that fixed by the maintenance assessment calculated in accordance with Part I of Schedule 1 to the Act.

(11) Subject to regulation 9(6), for the purposes of sections 17 and 18 of the Act a maintenance assessment shall not include [⁵a Category A] interim maintenance assessment.

(12) The provisions of regulations 29, 31, 32, 33(5) and 55 shall not apply to [⁶Category A] interim maintenance assessments.

[⁷(13) In this regulation "family" and "partner" have the same meaning as in the Maintenance Assessments and Special Cases Regulations.]

AMENDMENTS
1. Reg. 3(2) of the Amendment Regulations (April 5, 1993).
2. Reg. 3(3)(*a*) of the Amendment Regulations (April 5, 1993).
3. Reg. 3(3)(*b*) of the Amendment Regulations (April 5, 1993).
4. Reg. 3(4) of the Amendment Regulations (April 5, 1993).
5. Reg. 3(5) of the Amendment Regulations (April 5, 1993).
6. Reg. 3(6) of the Amendment Regulations (April 5, 1993).
7. Reg. 3(7) of the Amendment Regulations (April 5, 1993).

DEFINITIONS
"absent parent": see reg. 1(5).
"the Act": see reg. 1(2).
"effective date": *ibid*.
"Maintenance Assessments and Special Cases Regulations": *ibid*.
"maintenance period": *ibid*.
"person with care": see reg 1(5).

GENERAL NOTE
Effective date
The effective date of a maintenance assessment is set by reference to para. (3) and reg. 30. This paragraph applies where there is no maintenance assessment in force and a maintenance enquiry form has been given or sent to the absent parent or would have been given or sent if the absent parent had not deliberately avoided receipt of the form. In such a case the effective date is in the third week following the giving of notice of intention to make an interim maintenance assessment. In other cases the effective date is fixed as provided by reg. 30.

Child support maintenance payable when assessment is made under Sched. 1
When a child support officer is able to make a maintenance assessment under Sched. 1 to the Act, three periods need to be considered. (i) The period between the effective date of that assessment and the effective date of the interim maintenance assessment. In respect of this period child support maintenance is payable at the rate set by the assessment under Sched. 1 (paras. (4) and (5)). (ii) The period during which the interim assessment was in force. The child support maintenance payable in respect of this period is only adjusted in two circumstances (para. (8)). First where the completion and return of the maintenance enquiry form by the absent parent has been unavoidably delayed the interim assessment may be cancelled with effect from the date on which the form could have been completed and returned (paras. (6) and (7)). This cancellation may be retrospective. Second it is increased in line with the final maintenance assessment when that assessment is higher than the amount fixed by the interim assessment (para. (10)). As a general rule therefore if an interim assessment exceeds the final assessment the excess is not recoverable by the abent parent as a penalty for delaying the making of the assessment.

(iii) The period following the termination of the interim assessment. In respect of this period the sum fixed by the assessment under Sched. 1 is payable.

Termination of the interim assessment

There is no limit on the maximum duration of an interim maintenance assessment. It may continue indefinitely subject to periodical reviews under s.16 of the Act. It may come to an end in the following ways. (i) It may be cancelled under para. (6) where the completion and return of the maintenance enquiry form by the absent parent has been unavoidably delayed. The child support officer has a discretion to cancel the interim assessment in these circumstances but not a duty to do so. In exercising this discretion regard should be had to the welfare of any child likely to be affected, although s.2 of the Act does not apply to powers contained in regulations. This will include the children living with or supported by the absent parent as well as the qualifying children. The assessment may only be cancelled with effect from the date on which the form could have been completed and returned (para. (7)). (ii) An absent parent may apply in writing at any time for an assessment to be cancelled under reg. 9(1). Here too the child support officer should have regard to the welfare of any children likely to be affected. (iii) An interim assessment automatically ceases to have effect on the day the Secretary of State receives information which enables a child support officer to make an assessment under the provisions of Sched. 1, regardless of the source of that information (para. (9)).

Para. (11)

Subject to the provision made by reg. 9(6) and (7) with regard to reviews under s.18 of the Act, ss.17 and 18 do not apply to interim maintenance assessments. However, the wording of s.19(1) is capable of being applied to interim maintenance assessments. Section 19(2) cannot apply to cases which could fall within s.17 but it is capable of applying to cases where s.18 as modified by reg. 9(7) is applicable.

Cancellation of an interim maintenance assessment

9.—(1) An absent parent with respect to whom [[1]a Category A interim maintenance assessment] is in force may apply to a child support officer for that interim assessment to be cancelled.

(2) Any application made under paragraph (1) shall be in writing, and shall include a statement of the grounds for the application.

(3) A child support officer who receives an application under the provisions of paragraph (1), shall—

    (*a*) decide whether the interim maintenance assessment is to be cancelled and, if so, the date with effect from which it is to be cancelled;

    (*b*) in any case where he does cancel an interim maintenance assessment, decide whether it is appropriate for a maintenance assessment to be made in accordance with the provisions of Part I of Schedule 1 to the Act;

    (*c*) in any case where he has decided that it is appropriate for a maintenance assessment to be made in accordance with the provisions of Part I of Schedule 1 to the Act, make that assessment.

(4) Where a child support officer has made a decision under paragraph (3), he shall immediately notify the applicant, so far as that is reasonably practicable, and shall give the reasons for his decision in writing.

(5) A notification under paragraph (4) shall include information as to the provisions of sections 18 and 20 of the Act and regulation 24(1) and, where an assessment is made in accordance with the provisions of Part I of Schedule 1 to the Act, the provisions of sections 16 and 17 of the Act.

(6) Where a child support officer has made a decision following an application under paragraph (1), the absent parent may apply to the Secretary of State for a review of that decision and, subject to the modification set out in paragraph (7), the provisions of section 18(5) to (8) of the Act shall apply to such a review.

(7) The modification referred to in paragraph (6) is that section 18(6) of the Act shall have effect as if for "the refusal, assessment or cancellation in question" there is substituted "the decision following an application under regulation 9(1) of the Child Support (Maintenance Assessment Procedure) Regulations 1992".

(8) Regulations 10, 11 [[2]24] and 25 shall apply to reviews under paragraph (6).

AMENDMENTS
1. Reg. 4(2) of the Amendment Regulations (April 5, 1993).
2. Reg. 4(3) of the Amendment Regulations (April 5, 1993).

DEFINITIONS
"absent parent": see reg. 1(5).
"the Act": see reg. 1(2).

GENERAL NOTE
Para. (2)
For a discussion of the meaning of "grounds" see the general note to reg. 3(10) of the Tribunal Procedure Regulations.

Para. (3)
This paragraph confers an almost unlimited discretion on a child support officer to cancel a Category A interim assessment on written application by the absent parent. It is subject to reg. 8(9) and regard should be had to the welfare of any children likely to be affected. For other ways in which an interim assessment may terminate see the general note to reg. 8.

PART IV

NOTIFICATIONS FOLLOWING CERTAIN DECISIONS BY CHILD SUPPORT OFFICERS

Notification of a new or a fresh maintenance assessment

10.—(1) Where a child support officer makes a new or a fresh maintenance assessment following—
   (*a*) an application under section 4, 6 or 7 of the Act; or
   (*b*) a review under section 16, 17, 18 or 19 of the Act,
he shall immediately notify the relevant persons, so far as that is reasonably practicable, of the amount of the child support maintenance under that assessment.

(2) A notification under paragraph (1) shall set out, in relation to the maintenance assessment in question—
   (*a*) the maintenance requirement;
   (*b*) the effective date of the assessment;
   (*c*) the absent parent's assessable income and, where relevant, his protected income level;
   (*d*) the assessable income of a parent with care;
   (*e*) details as to the minimum amount of child support maintenance payable by virtue of regulations made under paragraph 7 of Schedule 1 to the Act; and
   (*f*) details as to apportionment where a case is to be treated as a special case for the purposes of the Act under section 42 of the Act.

(3) Except where a person gives written permission to the Secretary of State that the information, in relation to him, mentioned in sub-paragraphs (*a*) and (*b*) below may be conveyed to other persons, any document given or sent under the provisions of paragraph (1) or (2) shall not contain—
   (*a*) the address of any person other than the recipient of the document in question (other than the address of the office of the child support officer concerned) or any other information the use of which could reasonably be expected to lead to any such person being located;
   (*b*) any other information the use of which could reasonably be expected to lead to any person, other than a qualifying child or a relevant person, being identified.

(4) A notification under paragraph (1) shall include information as to the following provisions—

(a) where a new maintenance assessment is made following an application under the Act or a fresh maintenance assessment is made following a review under section 16 of the Act, sections 16, 17 and 18 of the Act;

(b) where a fresh maintenance assessment is made following a review under section 17 of the Act, or following a review under section 19 of the Act where the child support officer conducting such a review is satisfied that if an application were to be made under section 17 of the Act it would be appropriate to make a fresh maintenance assessment, sections 16 and 18 of the Act;

(c) where a fresh maintenance assessment is made following a review under section 18 of the Act, or following a review under section 19 of the Act where the child support officer conducting such a review is satisfied that if an application were to be made under section 18 of the Act, it would be appropriate to make a fresh maintenance assessment, sections 16, 17 and 20 of the Act.

DEFINITIONS
"absent parent": see reg. 1(5).
"the Act": see reg. 1(2).
"effective date": *ibid.*
"parent with care": *ibid.*
"protected income level": *ibid.*
"relevant person": *ibid.*

GENERAL NOTE
This regulation applies to reviews under reg. 9(6) (reg. 9(8)).

Reg. 10(2)
If the case falls within Part II of the Schedule to the Transitional Provisions Order, the notification must include the total amount covered by para. 7(1)(a) of that Schedule (para. 10 to that Schedule).

Notification of a refusal to conduct a review

11.—(1) Where a child support officer refuses an application for a review under section 17 of the Act on the grounds set out in section 17(3) of the Act, or an application for a review under section 18 of the Act on the grounds set out in section 18(6) of the Act, he shall immediately notify the applicant, so far as that is reasonably practicable, and shall give the reasons for his refusal in writing.

(2) A notification under paragraph (1) shall include information as to the following provisions—

(a) where the refusal is on the grounds set out in section 17(3) of the Act, sections 16 and 18 of the Act and regulations 24(1) and 31(7);

(b) where the refusal is on the grounds set out in section 18(6) of the Act, sections 16, 17 and 20 of the Act.

DEFINITION
"the Act": see reg. 1(2).

GENERAL NOTE
This regulation applies to reviews under reg. 9(6) (reg. 9(8)).

Notification of a refusal to make a new or a fresh maintenance assessment

12.—(1) Where a child support officer refuses an application for maintenance assessment under the Act, or refuses to make a fresh assessment following a review under [¹section 17 of the Act or to make an assessment or a fresh assessment following a review under section] 18 of the Act, he shall immediately notify the following persons, so far as that is reasonably practicable—

    (*a*) where an application for a maintenance assessment under section 4 or 6 of the Act is refused, the applicant;

    (*b*) where an application for a maintenance assessment under section 7 of the Act is refused, the applicant child and the other relevant persons who have been notified of the application;

    (*c*) where there is a refusal to make a fresh assessment following a review under section 17 or 18 of the Act, the relevant persons[²;]

[²(*d*) where there is a refusal to make an assessment following a review under section 18 of the Act, the applicant,]

and shall give the reasons for his refusal in writing.

(2) A notification under paragraph (1) shall include information as to the following provisions—

    (*a*) where an application for a maintenance assessment under the Act is refused, section 18 of the Act and regulation 24(1);

    (*b*) where there is a refusal to make a fresh assessment following a review under section 17 of the Act, sections 16 and 18 of the Act and regulation 24(1):

    (*c*) where there is a refusal to make a fresh assessment following a review under section 18 of the Act, sections 16, 17 and 20 of the Act[³;]

[³(*d*) where there is a refusal to make an assessment following a review under section 18 of the Act, section 20 of the Act.]

AMENDMENTS
1. Reg. 5(2)(*a*) of the Amendment Regulations (April 5, 1993).
2. Reg. 5(2)(*b*) of the Amendment Regulations (April 5, 1993).
3. Reg. 5(3) of the Amendment Regulations (April 5, 1993).

DEFINITIONS
"the Act": see reg. 1(2).
"relevant person": *ibid*.

Notification of a refusal to cancel a maintenance assessment

13.—(1) Where a child support officer refuses a request under paragraph 16 of Schedule 1 to the Act for a maintenance assessment to be cancelled, or refuses to cancel a maintenance assessment following a review under section 18 of the Act, he shall immediately notify the following persons, so far as that is reasonably practicable—

    (*a*) where a request for a cancellation under paragraph 16 of Schedule 1 to the Act is refused, the applicant, or, as the case may be, the applicants;

    (*b*) where the cancellation of a maintenance assessment following a review under section 18 of the Act is refused, the relevant persons,

and shall give the reasons for his refusal in writing.

(2) A notification under paragraph (1) shall include information as to the following provisions—

    (*a*) where a request for a cancellation under paragraph 16 of Schedule 1 to the Act is refused, sections 16 and 18 of the Act and regulation 24(1);

    (*b*) where the cancellation of a maintenance assessment following a review under section 18 of the Act is refused, sections 16, 17 and 20 of the Act.

DEFINITIONS
"the Act": see reg. 1(2).
"relevant person": *ibid*.

Notification of a cancellation of a maintenance assessment

14.—(1) Where a child support officer cancels a maintenance assessment, he shall immediately notify the relevant persons, so far as that is reasonably practicable, and shall give the reasons for the cancellation in writing.

(2) A notification under paragraph (1) shall include information as to the provisions of section 18 of the Act and regulations 24(1) and 31(8).

DEFINITIONS
  "the Act": see reg. 1(2).
  "relevant person": *ibid.*

Notification of a refusal to reinstate a cancelled maintenance assessment

15.—(1) Where a child support officer, following a review under section 18(3) of the Act, refuses to reinstate a maintenance assessment that has been cancelled, he shall immediately notify the relevant persons, so far as that is reasonably practicable, and shall give the reasons for his refusal in writing.

(2) A notification under paragraph (1) shall include information as to the provisions of section 20 of the Act.

DEFINITIONS
  "the Act": see reg. 1(2).
  "relevant person": *ibid.*

Notification when an applicant under section 7 of the Act ceases to be a child

16. Where a maintenance assessment has been made in response to an application by a child under section 7 of the Act and that child ceases to be a child for the purposes of the Act, a child support officer shall immediately notify, so far as that is reasonably practicable—

(*a*) the other qualifying children [[1]who have attained the age of 12 years] and the absent parent with respect to whom that maintenance assessment was made; and

(*b*) the person with care.

AMENDMENT
  1.   Reg. 6 of the Amendment Regulations (April 5, 1993).

DEFINITIONS
  "absent parent": see reg. 1(5).
  "the Act": see reg. 1(2).
  "person with care": see reg 1(5).

PART V

PERIODICAL REVIEWS

Intervals between periodical reviews and notice of a periodical review

17.—[[1](1) Subject to regulation 18(1), where a maintenance assessment in force is—

(*a*) an assessment that has not been previously reviewed;

(*b*) a fresh assessment following an earlier review under section 16 of the Act; or

    (*c*)   a fresh assessment following a review under section 17 of the Act,
that assessment shall be reviewed by a child support officer under section 16 of the Act after it has been in force for a period of 52 weeks.

(2) Where a maintenance assessment in force is a fresh maintenance assessment following a review under section 18 or 19 of the Act, that assessment shall be reviewed by a child support officer under section 16 of the Act after it has been in force for a period of 52 weeks less the period between the effective date of the previous assessment falling within paragraph (1) above and the effective date of the fresh assessment following the review under section 18 or 19 of the Act.]

(3) A child support officer may decide not to conduct a review under paragraph (1) if a fresh maintenance assessment following such a review would cease to have effect within 28 days of the effective date of that fresh assessment.

(4) Before a child support officer conducts a review under section 16 of the Act, he shall give 14 days' notice of the proposed review to the relevant persons.

(5) Subject to paragraphs (6) and (7), a child support officer shall request every person to whom he is giving notice under paragraph (4) to provide, within 14 days, and in accordance with the provisions of regulations 2 and 3 of the Information, Evidence and Disclosure Regulations such information or evidence as to his current circumstances as may be specified.

(6) The provisions of paragraph (5) shall not apply in relation to any person to whom or in respect of whom income support is payable or to a person with care where income support is payable to or in respect of the absent parent.

(7) The provisions of paragraph (5) shall not apply in relation to a relevant person where—

    (*a*)   [²the case is one] prescribed in regulation 22 or 23 of the Maintenance Assessments and Special Cases Regulations as a case to be treated as a special case for the purposes of the Act;

    (*b*)   there has been a review under section 16 or 17 of the Act in relation to another maintenance assessment in force relating to that person;

    (*c*)   the child support officer concerned has notified that person of the assessments following that review not earlier than 13 weeks prior to the date a review under section 16 of the Act is due under paragraph (1); and

    (*d*)   the child support officer has no reason to believe that there has been a change in that person's circumstances.

AMENDMENTS
1.   Reg. 7(2) of the Amendment Regulations (April 5, 1993).
2.   Reg. 7(3) of the Amendment Regulations (April 5, 1993).

DEFINITIONS
    "absent parent": see reg. 1(5).
    "the Act": see reg. 1(2).
    "effective date": *ibid.*
    "Information, Evidence and Disclosure Regulations": *ibid.*
    "person with care": see reg. 1(5).
    "relevant person": see reg. 1(2).

Review under section 17 of the Act treated as a review under section 16 of the Act

18.—(1) Where, under provisions of regulation 19(1), a child support officer gives notice of a review under section 17 of the Act, that notice is given or sent not earlier than 8 weeks prior to the next review, under the provisions of regulation 17(1), of the maintenance assessment in force, and the review under section 17 of the Act does not result in a fresh maintenance assessment by virtue of the provisions of regulation 20, 21 or 22, that review shall be treated as a review under section 16 of the Act, and the fresh assessment that would have been made but for the provisions of regulation 20, 21 or 22, as the case may be, shall be the assessment following that review.

(2) Where there is a fresh assessment under the provisions of paragraph (1), the next review under the provisions of regulation 17(1) shall be of that fresh assessment.

DEFINITION
   "the Act": see reg. 1(2).

PART VI

REVIEWS ON A CHANGE OF CIRCUMSTANCES

Conduct of a review on a change of circumstances

19.—(1) Where a child support officer proposes to conduct a review under section 17 of the Act, he shall give 14 days' notice of the proposed review to the relevant persons.

(2) Subject to [¹paragraphs (3), (4) and (4A)], a child support officer proposing to conduct a review under section 17 of the Act shall request every person to whom he is giving notice under paragraph (1) to provide within 14 days, and in accordance with the provisions of regulations 2 and 3 of the Information, Evidence and Disclosure Regulations, such information or evidence as to his current circumstances as may be specified.

(3) The provisions of paragraph (2) shall not apply in relation to any person to whom or in respect of whom income support is payable.

(4) Where an application for a review under section 17 of the Act is made at the time that a review under section 16 of the Act is being conducted, the child support officer concerned may proceed with the review under section 17 of the Act notwithstanding that he has not complied with the provisions of paragraph (2) if in his opinion such compliance is not required in the particular circumstances of the case.

[²(4A) The provisions of paragraph (2) shall not apply in relation to a relevant person where—
   (a)   the case is one prescribed in regulation 22 or 23 of the Maintenance Assessments and Special Cases Regulations as a case to be treated as a special case for the purposes of the Act;
   (b)   there has been a review under section 16 or 17 of the Act in relation to another maintenance assessment in force relating to that person;
   (c)   the child support officer concerned has notified that person of the assessments following that review not earlier than 13 weeks prior to the date the child support officer gives notice under paragraph (1); and
   (d)   the child support officer has no reason to believe that there has been a change in that person's circumstances.]

(5) Where maintenance assessment is in force with respect to a parent with care and an absent parent in response to an application by the parent with care under section 6 of the Act, and the parent with care authorises the Secretary of State to take action under the Act to recover child support maintenance from that absent parent in relation to an additional child of whom she is a parent with care and he is an absent parent, that authorisation shall be treated by the Secretary of State as an application for review under section 17 of the Act.

AMENDMENTS
   1.   Reg. 8(2) of the Amendment Regulations (April 5, 1993).
   2.   Reg. 8(3) of the Amendment Regulations (April 5, 1993.)

DEFINITIONS

"absent parent": see reg. 1(5).
"the Act": see reg. 1(2).
"Information, Evidence and Disclosure Regulations": *ibid.*
"Maintenance Assessments and Special Cases Regulations": *ibid.*
"parent with care": *ibid.*
"relevant person": *ibid.*

Fresh assessments following a review on a change of circumstances

20.—(1) Subject to [¹paragraphs (2) to (4)] and regulations 21 and 22, a child support officer who has completed a review under section 17 of the Act shall not make a fresh assessment if the difference between the amount of child support maintenance fixed by the assessment currently in force and the amount that would be fixed if a fresh assessment were to be made as a result of the review is less than £10.00 per week.

(2) Where a child support officer who has completed a review under section 17 of the Act determines that, were a fresh assessment to be made as a result of the review, the circumstances of the absent parent are such that the provisions of paragraph 6 of Schedule 1 to the Act would apply to that assessment, he shall not make a fresh assessment if the difference between the amount of child support maintenance fixed by the original assessment and the amount that would be fixed if a fresh assessment were to be made as a result of the review is less than £1.00 per week.

(3) Where a child support officer who has completed a review under section 17 of the Act determines that, were a fresh assessment to be made as a result of the review, the children in respect of whom that assessment would be made are not identical with the children in respect of whom the original assessment was made, he shall not make a fresh assessment if the difference between the amount of child support maintenance fixed by the original assessment and the amount that would be fixed if a fresh assessment were to be made as a result of the review is less than £1.00 per week.

[²(4) Where a child support officer on completing a review under section 17 of the Act determines that—

(*a*) the absent parent is, by virtue of paragraph 5(4) of Schedule 1 to the Act, to be taken for the purposes of that Schedule to have no assessable income; or

(*b*) the case falls within paragraph 7(2) of Schedule 1 to the Act,

he shall make a fresh maintenance assessment.]

AMENDMENTS

1. Reg. 9(2) of the Amendment Regulations (April 5, 1993).
2. Reg. 9(3) of the Amendment Regulations (April 5, 1993).

DEFINITIONS

"absent parent": see reg. 1(5).
"the Act": see reg. 1(2).

Fresh assessments following a review on a change of circumstances: special case prescribed by regulation 22 of the Maintenance Assessments and Special Cases Regulations

21.—(1) The provisions of paragraphs (2) and (3) shall apply on a review under section 17 of the Act where a case is to be treated as a special case for the purposes of the Act by virtue of regulation 22 of the Maintenance Assessments and Special Cases Regulations.

(2) Where there is a change in the circumstances of the absent parent (whether or not there is also a change in the circumstances of one or more of the persons with care), a child support officer shall not make fresh assessments if the difference be-

tween the aggregate amount of child support maintenance fixed by the assessments currently in force and the aggregate amount that would be fixed if fresh assessments were to be made as a result of the review is less than £10.00 per week or, where the circumstances of the absent parent are such that the provisions of paragraph 6 of Schedule 1 to the Act would apply to those fresh assessments, that difference is less than £1.00 per week.

(3) Where there is a change in the circumstances of one or more of the persons with care but not in that of the absent parent, the provisions of regulation 20 shall apply in relation to each fresh assessment.

DEFINITIONS
"absent parent": see reg. 1(5).
"the Act": see reg. 1(2).
"Maintenance Assessments and Special Cases Regulations": *ibid.*
"person with care": see reg 1(5).

Fresh assessments following a review on a change of circumstances: special case prescribed by regulation 23 of the Maintenance Assessments and Special Cases Regulations

22.—(1) The provisions of paragraph (2) shall apply on a review under section 17 of the Act where a case is to be treated as a special case for the purposes of the Act by virtue of regulation 23 of the Maintenance Assessments and Special Cases Regulations.

(2) Where there is a change in the circumstances of the person with care or in the circumstances of one or more of the absent parents, the provisions of regulation 20 shall apply to each fresh assessment.

DEFINITIONS
"absent parent": see reg. 1(5).
"the Act": see reg. 1(2).
"Maintenance Assessments and Special Cases Regulations": *ibid.*
"person with care": see reg 1(5).

Reviews conducted under section 19 of the Act as if a review under section 17 of the Act had been applied for

23. The provisions of regulations 20, 21 and 22 shall apply to a review under section 19 of the Act which has been conducted as if an application for a review under section 17 of the Act had been made.

DEFINITION
"the Act": see reg. 1(2).

PART VII

REVIEWS OF A DECISION BY A CHILD SUPPORT OFFICER

Time limits for an application for a review of a decision by a child support officer

24.—(1) Subject to paragraph (2), the Secretary of State shall not refer any application for a review under section 18(1), (3) or (4) of the Act or under section 18 of the Act as extended by regulation 9(6) to a child support officer unless that application is received by the Secretary of State within 28 days of the date of notification to the applicant of the decision whose review he seeks.

(2) Where the Secretary of State receives an application for a review under section 18(1), (3) or (4) of the Act or under section 18 of the Act as extended by regulation 9(6) more than 28 days after the date of notification to the applicant of the decision whose review he seeks, the Secretary of State may refer that application to a child support officer is he is satisfied that there was unavoidable delay in making the application.

[¹(3) Where—

    (*a*) a child support officer refuses an application for a maintenance assessment on the grounds of lack of jurisdiction;

    (*b*) the applicant makes no application at that stage for that refusal to be reviewed under section 18(1)(*a*) of the Act but applies to a court for a maintenance order in relation to the children concerned;

    (*c*) the court refuses to make a maintenance order on the grounds of lack of jurisdiction; and

    (*d*) the applicant then makes an application for the refusal mentioned in sub-paragraph (*a*) to be reviewed under section 18(1)(*a*) of the Act,

the date the applicant is notified of the court's decision shall, for the purposes of paragraphs (1) and (2), be treated as the date of the notification to the applicant of the decision whose review he seeks.]

AMENDMENT

   1.   Reg. 10(2) of the Amendment Regulations (April 5, 1993).

DEFINITION

   "the Act": see reg. 1(2).

GENERAL NOTE

This regulation applies to reviews under reg. 9(6) (reg. 9(8)).

Notice of a review of a decision by a child support officer

   25.—(1) Where on an application for a review under section 18 of the Act a child support officer proposes to conduct such a review, he shall give 14 days' notice of the proposed review to the relevant persons.

(2) A child support officer proposing to conduct a review under section 18 of the Act shall—

    (*a*) send to the relevant persons the applicant's reasons for making the application for the review;

    (*b*) where a maintenance assessment is in force, send to the relevant persons the information that was included, under the provisions of regulation 10(2), in the notification of that assessment made under the provisions of regulation 10(1);

    (*c*) invite representations, either in person or in writing, from the relevant persons on any matter relating to the review and set out the provisions of paragraphs (3) to (6) in relation to such representations.

(3) Subject to paragraph (4), where the child support officer conducting the review does not within 14 days of the date on which notice of the review was given receive a request from a relevant person to make representations in person, or receives such a request and arranges for an appointment for such representations to be made but that appointment is not kept, he may complete the review in the absence of such representations from that person.

(4) Where the child support officer conducting the review is satisfied that there was good reason for failure to keep an appointment, he shall provide for a further opportunity for the making of representations by the relevant person concerned before he completes the review.

(5) Where the child support officer conducting the review does not receive written representations from a relevant person within 14 days of the date on which notice of the review was given, he may complete the review in the absence of written representations from that person.

(6) Except where a person gives written permission to the Secretary of State that the information, in relation to him, mentioned in sub-paragraphs (*a*) and (*b*) below may be conveyed to other persons, any document given or sent under the provisions of paragraph (1) or (2) shall not contain—

(*a*)   the address of any person other than the recipient of the document in question (other than the address of the office of the child support officer concerned) or any other information the use of which could reasonably be expected to lead to any such person being located;

(*b*)   any other information the use of which could reasonably be expected to lead to any person other than a qualifying child or relevant person being identified.

DEFINITIONS
  "the Act": see reg. 1(2).
  "relevant person": *ibid.*

GENERAL NOTE
  This regulation applies to reviews under reg. 9(6) (reg. 9(8)).

Procedure on a review of a decision by a child support officer

26.—(1) Where the Secretary of State has referred more than one application for a review to a child support officer under section 18 of the Act in relation to the same decision and that child support officer proposes to conduct a review but has not given notice under regulation 25(1), he shall give notice to the relevant persons under regulation 25(1) and shall conduct one review taking account of all the representations made and all the evidence before him.

(2) Where the child support officer conducting a review under section 18 of the Act has given notice under regulation 25(1) and has a further application referred to him by the Secretary of State in relation to the same decision before he has completed his review, he shall notify the person who has made that further application that he is already conducting a review of that decision and that he will take into account the information contained in that application.

DEFINITIONS
  "the Act": see reg. 1(2).
  "relevant person": *ibid.*

[¹Review under section 18 of the Act where parentage is an issue

26A. Where an applicant for a review under section 18 of the Act gives as one, but not the only, reason for making the application that—

(*a*)   the decision of which he seeks the review has been made on the basis that a particular person (whether the applicant or some other person) either is, or is not, a parent of a child in question; and

(*b*)   the decision should not have been made on that basis,

the Secretary of State shall treat the application as two applications, one relating solely to the issue of parentage and the other relating to all other matters giving rise to the application, and shall proceed accordingly.]

AMENDMENT
1. Reg. 11 of the Amendment Regulations (April 5, 1993).

DEFINITION
"the Act": see reg. 1(2).

Review following an application under section18(1)(*b*) of the Act

27. Where a child support officer has completed a review following an application for a review under section 18(1)(*b*) of the Act, regulations 20 to 22 shall apply in relation to any fresh assessment following that review.

DEFINITION
"the Act": see reg. 1(2).

Reviews conducted under section 19 of theAct as if a review under section 18(1)(*b*) of the Act had been applied for

28. The provisions of regulation 27 shall apply to a review under section 19 of the Act which has been conducted as if an application for a review under section 18(1)(*b*) of the Act had been made.

DEFINITION
"the Act": see reg. 1(2).

Extension of provisions of section 18(2) of the Act

29.—(1) The provisions of section 18(2) of the Act shall apply where a maintenance assessment has been in force but is no longer in force if the condition specified in paragraph (2) is satisfied.

(2) The condition mentioned in paragraph (1) is that, subject to paragraph (3), the application for a review under section 18(2) of the Act as extended by this regulation is received by the Secretary of State within 28 days of the date of notification to the applicant of the maintenance assessment whose review he seeks.

(3) Where the Secretary of State receives such an application more than 28 days after the date of notification to the applicant of the maintenance assessment whose review he seeks, the Secretary of State may refer that application to a child support officer if he is satisfied that there was unavoidable delay.

DEFINITION
"the Act": see reg. 1(2).

GENERAL NOTE
This regulation does not apply to Category A interim maintenance assessments (reg. 8(12)).

PART VIII

COMMENCEMENT AND TERMINATION OF MAINTENANCE ASSESSMENTS AND MAINTENANCE PERIODS

Effective dates of new maintenance assessments

30.—(1) Subject to relation 8(3), the effective date of a new maintenance assessment following an application under section 4, 6 or 7 of the Act shall be the date determined in accordance with paragraphs (2) to (4).

(2) Where no maintenance assessment is in force with respect to the person with care and absent parent, the effective date of a new assessment shall be—

(*a*)   the date a maintenance enquiry form is given or sent to an absent parent in a case where the application for a maintenance assessment is made by a person with care or by a child under section 7 of the Act; or

(*b*)   the date an effective maintenance application form is received by the Secretary of State in a case where the application for a maintenance assessment—

(i)   is made by an absent parent; or

(ii)   is an application in relation to which the provisions of regulation 3 have been applied.

(3) The provisions of regulation 1(6)(*b*) shall not apply to paragraph (2)(*a*).

(4) Where a child support officer is satisfied that an absent parent has deliberately avoided receipt of a maintenance enquiry form, he may determine the date on which the form would have given or sent but for such avoidance, and that date shall be the relevant date for the purposes of paragraph (2)(*a*).

DEFINITIONS
"absent parent": see reg. 1(5).
"the Act": see reg. 1(2).
"effective date": *ibid*.
"person with care": see reg 1(5).

Effective dates of maintenance assessments following a review under sections 16 to 19 of the Act

31.—(1) Where a fresh maintenance assessment is made following a review under section 16 of the Act, the effective date of that assessment shall be 52 weeks after the effective date of the previous assessment.

(2) Subject to paragraph (4), where an application is made under section 17 of the Act for a review of a maintenance assessment in force, and a fresh maintenance assessment is made in accordance with the provisions of regulation 20, 21 or 22, the effective date of that assessment shall be the first day of the maintenance period in which the application is received.

(3) Where a case falls within regulation 18(1), the effective date of the fresh assessment shall be the first day of the maintenance period in which the assessment is made.

(4) Where an application is made under section 17 of the Act for a review of a maintenance assessment in force following the death of a qualifying child and a fresh maintenance assessment is made in accordance with the provisions of regulation 20, 21 or 22, the effective date of that assessment shall be the first day of the maintenance period during the course of which that child died.

(5) Where, following a review under section 18(1)(*a*) of the Act, a maintenance assessment is made following a refusal to make a maintenance assessment, the effective date of that assessment shall be the effective date of the assessment that would have been made if the application for a maintenance assessment had not been refused.

(6) Subject to paragraphs (7), (10) and (11), where an application is made under section 18(2) of the Act for a review of a maintenance assessment in force, the effective date of a fresh assessment (if one is made) following such a review shall be—

(*a*)   where the application is received by the Secretary of State within 28 days of the date of notification of that assessment, or on a later date but the Secretary of State is satisfied that there was unavoidable delay, the effective date as determined on the review;

(*b*) subject to sub-paragraph (*a*), where the application is received by the Secretary of State later than 28 days after the date of notification of that assessment, the first day of the maintenance period in which the application is received.

(7) Where an application is made under section 18(1)(*b*) of the Act for a review of a refusal of an application under section 17 of the Act for the review of a maintenance assessment which is in force, the effective date of a fresh maintenance assessment (if one is made) shall be the date determined under paragraph (2).

(8) Where, following a review under section 18(3) of the Act, a cancelled maintenance assessment is reinstated, the effective date of the reinstated assessment shall be the date on which the cancelled assessment ceased to have effect.

(9) Where there has been a misrepresentation or failure to disclose a material fact on the part of the person with care or absent parent in connection with an application for a maintenance assessment under the Act, or a review under section 16 or 17 of the Act, and that misrepresentation or failure has resulted in an incorrect assessment or a series of incorrect assessments, the effective date of a fresh assessment (or of a fresh assessment in relation to the earliest relevant period) following discovery of the misrepresentation or failure shall be the effective date of the incorrect assessment or the first incorrect assessment, as the case may be.

(10) Where a fresh maintenance assessment is made on a review under section 18 or 19 of the Act by reason of an assessment having been made in ignorance of a material fact or having been based on a mistake as to a material fact and that ignorance or mistake, as the case may be, is attributable to an operational or administrative error on the part of the Secretary of State or of a child support officer, the effective date of that fresh assessment shall be the effective date of the assessment that has been reviewed.

(11) Subject to paragraphs (9), (10), (12), (13) and (14), where a fresh maintenance assessment is made under section 19 of the Act, the effective date of the assessment shall be the first day of the maintenance period in which the assessment is made.

(12) Where a fresh maintenance assessment is made under section 19 of the Act following the death of a qualifying child, the effective date of that assessment shall be the first day of the maintenance period during which that child died.

(13) Where a child support officer on a review under section 18 or 19 of the Act is satisfied that a maintenance assessment which is or has been in force is defective by reason of a mistake as to the effective date of that assessment, the effective date of a fresh assessment shall be that determined in accordance with regulation 30 or in accordance with paragraphs (1) to (12), as the case may be.

(14) Where a child support officer on a review under section 19 of the Act is satisfied that if an application were to be made under section 18 of the Act it would be appropriate to make a fresh maintenance assessment, and does so, the effective date of that fresh assessment shall be determined in accordance with paragraphs (5) to (8).

Definitions
 "absent parent": see reg. 1(5).
 "the Act": see reg. 1(2).
 "effective date": *ibid.*
 "person with care": see reg 1(5).

General Note
 This regulation does not apply to Category A interim maintenance assessments (reg. 8(12)).

Para. (9)
 A misrepresentation is a positive and deliberate statement (*R(SB) 9/85*, para. 7). It may be made wholly innocently, so belief in the truth of what is said is irrelevant. It is important to pay careful attention to the following: (i) the precise terms of the statement made; (ii) the precise terms of any declaration

signed; (iii) any qualifications to the statements or declarations (*R(SB) 9/85*, para. 7); and (iv) any accompanying conduct which qualifies the contents of the form (*R(SB) 18/85*, para. 10).

There can be no failure to disclose unless there has been a breach of a legal or moral duty to disclose (*R(SB) 21/82*, para. 4(2)). Usually the duty will be a legal one and will be based on the Information, Evidence and Disclosure Regulations. Normally disclosure will be made after the event to which it relates has occurred, but it may be effectively made in advance (*CSIS 25/89*, para. 3 and *CSB 727/89*). If disclosure is made to the appropriate office, it is effective and no continuing duty of disclosure will arise. However, if disclosure is made to another office and the person should have realised that it had not been passed on, a further duty arises and further disclosure must be made. On disclosure generally see *R(SB) 15/87*.

Cancellation of a maintenance assessment

32. Where a child support officer cancels a maintenance assessment under paragraph 16(2) or (3) of Schedule 1 to the Act, the assessment shall cease to have effect from the date of receipt of the request for the cancellation of the assessment or from such later date as the child support officer may determine.

DEFINITION
    "the Act": see reg. 1(2).

GENERAL NOTE
    This regulation does not apply to Category A interim maintenance assessments (reg. 8(12)).

[¹Cancellation of maintenance assessments made under section 7 of the Act where the child is no longer habitually resident in Scotland]

32A.—(1) Where a maintenance assessment made in response to an application by a child under section 7 of the Act is in force and that child ceases to be habitually resident in Scotland, a child support officer shall cancel that assessment.

(2) In any case where paragraph (1) applies, the assessment shall cease to have effect from the date that the child support officer determines is the date on which the child concerned ceased to be habitually resident in Scotland.]

AMENDMENT
    1.   Reg. 12 of the Amendment Regulations (April 5, 1993).

DEFINITION
    "the Act": see reg. 1(2).

Maintenance periods

33.—(1) The child support maintenance payable under a maintenance assessment shall be calculated at a weekly rate and be in respect of successive maintenance periods, each such period being a period of 7 days.

(2) Subject to paragraph (6), the first maintenance period shall commence on the effective date of the first maintenance assessment, and each succeeding maintenance period shall commence on the day immediately following the last day of the preceding maintenance period.

(3) The maintenance periods in relation to a fresh maintenance assessment following a review under section 16, 17, 18 or 19 of the Act shall coincide with the maintenance periods in relation to the earlier assessment, had it continued in force, and the first maintenance period in relation to a fresh assessment shall commence on the day following the last day of the last maintenance period in relation to the earlier assessment.

(4) The amount of child support maintenance payable in respect of a maintenance period which includes the effective date of a fresh maintenance assessment shall be the amount of maintenance payable under that fresh assessment.

(5) The amount of child support maintenance payable in respect of a mainten-ance period during the course of which a cancelled maintenance assessment ceases to have effect shall be the amount of maintenance payable under that assessment.

(6) Where a case is to be treated as a special cases for the purposes of the Act by virtue of regulation 22 of the Maintenance Assessments and Special Cases Regu-lations (multiple applications relating to an absent parent) and an application is made by a person with care in relation to an absent parent where there is already a maintenance assessment in force in relation to that absent parent and a different person with care, the maintenance periods in relation to an assessment made in res-ponse to that application shall coincide with the maintenance periods in relation to the earlier maintenance assessment, and the first such period shall commence not later than 7 days after the date of notification to the relevant persons of the later maintenance assessment.

DEFINITIONS
  "absent parent": see reg. 1(5).
  "the Act": see reg. 1(2).
  "effective date": *ibid.*
  "maintenance period": *ibid.*
  "person with care": see reg. 1(5).
  "relevant person": see reg. 1(2).

GENERAL NOTE
Para. (5)
  This paragraph does not apply to Category A interim maintenance assessments (reg. 8(12)).

PART IX

REDUCED BENEFIT DIRECTIONS

Prescription of disability working allowance for the purposes of section 6 of the Act

34. Disability working allowance shall be a benefit of a prescribed kind for the purposes of section 6 of the Act.

DEFINITIONS
  "the Act": see reg. 1(2).
  "disability working allowance": *ibid.*

Periods for compliance with obligations imposed by section 6 of the Act

35.—(1) Where the Secretary of State considers that a parent has failed to comply with an obligation imposed by section 6 of the Act he shall serve written notice on that parent that, unless she complies with that obligation, he intends to refer the case to a child support officer for the child support officer to take action under section 46 of the Act if the child support officer considers such action to be appropriate.

(2) The Secretary of State shall not refer a case to a child support officer prior to the expiry of a period of 6 weeks from the date he serves notice under paragraph (1) on the parent in question, and the notice shall contain a statement to that effect.

(3) Where the Secretary of State refers a case to a child support officer and the child support officer serves written notice on a parent under section 46(2) of the Act, the period to be specified in that notice shall be 14 days.

  "the Act": see reg. 1(2).
  "obligation imposed by section 6 of the Act": *ibid.*

Amount of and period of reduction of relevant benefit under a reduced benefit direction

36.—(1) The reduction in the amount payable by way of a relevant benefit to, or in respect of, the parent concerned and the period of such reduction by virtue of a direction shall be determined in accordance with paragraphs (2) to (9).

(2) Subject to paragraph (6) and regulations 37, 38(7) and 40, there shall be a reduction for a period of 26 weeks from the day specified in the direction under the provisions of section 46(9) of the Act in respect of each such week equal to

$0.2 \times B$

where B is an amount equal to the weekly amount, in relation to the week in question, specified in column (2) of paragraph 1(1)(*e*) of the applicable amounts Schedule.

(3) Subject to paragraph (6) and regulations 37, 38(7) and 40, at the end of the period specified in paragraph (2) there shall be a reduction from the day immediately succeeding the last day of that period for a period of 52 weeks of an amount in respect of each sum equal to

$0.1 \times B$

where B has the same meaning as in paragraph (2).

(4) Subject to paragraph (5), a direction shall come into operation on the first day of the second benefit week following the review, carried out by the adjudication officer in consequence of the direction, of the relevant benefit that is payable.

(5) Where the relevant benefit is income support and the provisions of regulation 26(2) of the Social Security (Claims and Payments) Regulations 1987 (deferment of payment of different amount of income support) apply, a direction shall come into operation on such later date as may be determined by the Secretary of State in accordance with those provisions.

(6) Where the benefit payable is income support and there is a change in the benefit week whilst a direction is in operation, the periods of the reductions specified in paragraphs (2) and (3) shall be—
  (*a*) where the reduction is that specified in paragraph (2), a period greater than 25 weeks but less than 26 weeks;
  (*b*) where the reduction is that specified in paragraph (3), a period greater than 51 weeks but less than 52 weeks,
and ending on the last day of the last benefit week falling entirely within the period of 26 weeks specified in paragraph (2), or the period of 52 weeks specified in paragraph (3), as the case may be.

(7) Where the weekly amount specified in column (2) of paragraph (1)(1)(*e*) of the applicable amounts Schedule changes on a day when a direction is in operation, the amount of the reduction of the relevant benefit shall be changed—
  (*a*) where the benefit is income support, from the first day of the first benefit week to commence for the parent concerned on or after the day that weekly amount changes;
  (*b*) where the benefit is family credit or disability working allowance, from the first day of the next award period of that benefit for the parent concerned commencing on or after the day that weekly amount changes.

(8) Only one direction in relation to a parent shall be in force at any one time.

(9) Where a direction has been in operation for the aggregate of the periods specified in paragraphs (2) and (3) ("the full period"), no further direction shall be given with respect to the same parent on account of that parent's failure to comply

with the obligations imposed by section 6 of the Act in relation to any child in relation to whom the direction that has been in operation for the full period was given.

DEFINITIONS
   "the Act": see reg. 1(2).
   "applicable amounts Schedule": *ibid.*
   "benefit week": *ibid.*
   "direction": *ibid.*
   "disability working allowance": *ibid.*
   "in force": see reg. 1(3).
   "in operation": *ibid.*
   "parent concerned": see reg. 1(2).
   "relevant benefit": *ibid.*

GENERAL NOTE
Para. (2)
   The relevant benefit is reduced for 26 weeks by 20 per cent. of the income support personal allowance for a single person aged 25 or more. For the amount of the allowance and the calculation of the deduction, see regs. 37 and 50 and the Income Support Schedule.

Para. (3)
   After the initial six month deduction, the relevant benefit is reduced by 10 per cent. of the income support personal allowance for a single person aged 25 or more for a further 52 weeks. For the amount of the allowance and the calculation of the deduction, see regs. 37 and 50 and the Income Support Schedule.

Para. (8)
   This principle is worked out in the context of directions relating to additional children by reg. 47.

Para. (9)
   Once the maximum period of 78 weeks has expired, no further reduction may be imposed on the parent with care in relation to any failure to comply with s.6 of the Act in respect of any child covered by the direction. However, this is subject to reg. 38(7).

Modification of reduction under a reduced benefit direction to preserve minimum entitlement to relevant benefit

37. Where in respect of any benefit week the amount of the relevant benefit that would be payable after it has been reduced following a direction would, but for this regulation, be nil or less than the minimum amount of that benefit that is payable as determined—

   (*a*)   in the case of income support, by regulation 26(4) of the Social Security (Claims and Payments) Regulations 1987;
   (*b*)   in the case of family credit and disability working allowance, by regulation 27(2) of those Regulations,
the amount of that reduction shall be decreased to such extent as to raise the amount of that benefit to the minimum amount that is payable.

DEFINITIONS
   "benefit week": see reg. 1(2).
   "direction": *ibid.*
   "disability working allowance": *ibid.*
   "relevant benefit": *ibid.*

GENERAL NOTE
   The amount of the reduction of a benefit payment under the direction must, if necessary, be reduced so as to preserve the minimum amount of that benefit which is payable.

Suspension of a reduced benefit direction when relevant benefit ceases to be payable

38.—(1) Where relevant benefit ceases to be payable to, or in respect of, the parent concerned at a time when a direction is in operation, that direction shall, subject to paragraph (2), be suspended for a period of 52 weeks from the date the relevant benefit has ceased to be payable.

(2) Where a direction has been suspended for a period of 52 weeks and no relevant benefit is payable at the end of that period, it shall cease to be in force.

(3) Where a direction is suspended and relevant benefit again becomes payable to or in respect of the parent concerned, the amount payable by way of that benefit shall, subject to regulations 40, 41 and 42, be reduced in accordance with that direction for the balance of the reduction period.

(4) The amount or, as the case may be, amounts of the reduction to be made during the balance of the reduction period shall be determined in accordance with regulation 36(2) and (3).

(5) No reduction in the amount of benefit under paragraph (3) shall be made before the expiry of a period of 14 days from service of the notice specified in paragraph (6), and the provisions of regulation 36(4) shall apply as to the date when the direction again comes into operation.

(6) Where relevant benefit again becomes payable to or in respect of a parent with respect to whom a direction is suspended she shall be notified in writing by a child support officer that the amount of relevant benefit paid to or in respect of her will again be reduced, in accordance with the provisions of paragraph (3), if she continues to fail to comply with the obligations imposed by section 6 of the Act.

(7) Where a direction has ceased to be in force by virtue of the provisions of paragraph (2), a further direction in respect of the same parent given on account of that parent's failure to comply with the obligations imposed by section 6 of the Act in relation to one or more of the same qualifying children shall, unless it also ceases to be in force by virtue of the provisions of paragraph (2), be in operation for the balance of the reduction period relating to the direction that has ceased to be in force, and the provisions of paragraph (4) shall apply to it.

DEFINITIONS

"the Act": see reg. 1(2).
"balance of the reduction period": *ibid.*
"direction": *ibid.*
"in force": see reg. 1(3).
"in operation": *ibid.*
"obligation imposed by section 6 of the Act": see reg. 1(2).
"parent concerned": *ibid.*
"relevant benefit": *ibid.*
"suspended": see reg. 1(3).

GENERAL NOTE

If the parent with care ceases to receive any benefit to which the direction relates, the direction is suspended for a maximum of 52 weeks. If, at the end of that time, no relevant benefit is still in payment, the direction then ceases to be in force, although a further direction may be issued for the balance of the reduction period. If relevant benefit becomes payable within the 52 weeks, the direction comes into operation for the balance of the reduction period, although not until the parent has been given 14 days' notice.

Para. (7)

This power to issue a further direction for the balance of the reduction period is subject to regs. 36(8) and 47(3).

Reduced benefit direction where family credit or disability working allowance is payable and income support becomes payable

39.—(1) Where a direction is in operation in respect of a parent to whom or in respect of whom family credit or disability working allowance is payable, and income support becomes payable to or in respect of that parent, income support shall become a relevant benefit for the purposes of that direction, and the amount payable by way of income support shall be reduced in accordance with that direction for the balance of the reduction period.

(2) The amount or, as the case may be, the amounts of the reduction to be made during the balance of the reduction period shall be determined in accordance with regulation 36(2) and (3).

DEFINITIONS
    "balance of the reduction period": see reg. 1(2).
    "direction": *ibid.*
    "disability working allowance": *ibid.*
    "in operation": see reg. 1(3).
    "relevant benefit": see reg. 1(2).

GENERAL NOTE
    A reduced benefit direction may be transferred or extended from family credit or disability working allowance to income support, but not from income support to one of those benefits.

Suspension of a reduced benefit direction when a modified applicable amount is payable

40.—(1) Where a direction is given or is in operation at a time when income support is payable to or in respect of the parent concerned but her applicable amount falls to be calculated under the provisions mentioned in paragraph (3), that direction shall be suspended for so long as the applicable amount falls to be calculated under the provisions mentioned in that paragraph, or 52 weeks, whichever period is the shorter.

(2) Where a case falls within paragraph (1) and a direction has been suspended for a period of 52 weeks, it shall cease to be in force.

(3) The provisions of paragraph (1) shall apply where the applicable amount in relation to the parent concerned falls to be calculated under—

    (*a*) regulation 19 of and Schedule 4 to the Income Support Regulations (applicable amounts for persons in residential care and nursing homes);

    (*b*) regulation 21 of and paragraphs 1 to 3 of Schedule 7 to the Income Support Regulations (patients);

    (*c*) regulation 21 of and paragraphs 10B, 10C [[1] ...] and 13 of Schedule 7 to the Income Support Regulations (persons in residential accommodation).

AMENDMENT
    1. Reg. 13 of the Amendment Regulations (April 5, 1993).

DEFINITIONS
    "applicable amount": see reg. 1(2).
    "direction": *ibid.*
    "in force": see reg. 1(3).
    "in operation": *ibid.*
    "Income Support Regulations": see reg. 1(2).
    "parent concerned": *ibid.*
    "suspended": see reg. 1(3).

GENERAL NOTE

A direction is suspended for so long as income support is paid to or in respect of a parent who is a patient or who is in a residential care or nursing home or in residential accommodation, up to a maximum of 52 weeks, after which it ceases to be in force.

Termination of a reduced benefit direction following compliance with obligations imposed by section 6 of the Act

41.—(1) Where a parent with care with respect to whom a direction is in force complies with the obligations imposed by section 6 of the Act, that direction shall cease to be in force on the date determined in accordance with paragraph (2) or (3), as the case may be.

(2) Where the direction is in operation, it shall cease to be in force on the last day of the benefit week during the course of which the parent concerned complied with the obligations imposed by section 6 of the Act.

(3) Where the direction is suspended, it shall cease to be in force on the date on which the parent concerned complied with the obligations imposed by section 6 of the Act.

DEFINITIONS

"benefit week": see reg. 1(2).
"direction": *ibid.*
"in force": see reg. 1(3).
"in operation": *ibid.*
"obligation imposed by section 6 of the Act": see reg. 1(2).
"parent concerned": *ibid.*
"parent with care": *ibid.*

GENERAL NOTE

The parent with care who is in breach of s.6 of the Act and is subject to a reduced benefit direction as a result has a continuing power to remedy the breach by supplying the required information. The direction ceases to have effect in accordance with paras. (2) and (3) when the breach is remedied. Notification of the termination, specifying the date of and reasons for the termination, must be served on the adjudication officer by a child support officer and a copy must be sent to the parent concerned (reg. 49). Compliance brings a direction to an end, but benefit deducted while the direction is in force is not reimbursed to the parent with care.

Review of a reduced benefit direction

42.—(1) Where a parent with care with respect to whom a direction is in force [¹or some other person] gives the Secretary of State reasons—

(a) additional to any reasons given by [²the parent with care] in response to the notice served on her under section 46(2) of the Act for having failed to comply with the obligations imposed by section 6 of the Act; or

(b) as to why [³the parent with care] should no longer be required to comply with the obligations imposed by section 6 of the Act,

the Secretary of State shall refer the matter to a child support officer who shall conduct a review of that direction ("a review") to determine whether the direction is to continue or is to cease to be in force.

(2) Where a parent with care with respect to whom a direction is in force [⁴or some other person] gives a child support officer reasons of the kind mentioned in paragraph (1), a child support officer shall conduct a review to determine whether the direction is to continue or is to cease to be in force.

[⁵(2A) Where a direction is in force and the Secretary of State becomes aware that a question arises as to whether the welfare of a child is likely to be affected by the direction continuing to be in force, he shall refer the matter to a child support officer who shall conduct a review to determine whether the direction is to continue or is to cease to be in force.

(2B) Where a direction is in force and a child support officer becomes aware that a question arises as to whether the welfare of a child is likely to be affected by the direction continuing to be in force, a child support officer shall conduct a review to determine whether the direction is to continue or is to cease to be in force.]

(3) A review shall not be carried out by the child support officer who gave the direction with respect to the parent concerned.

(4) Where the child support officer who is conducting a review considers that the parent concerned is no longer to be required to comply with the obligations imposed by section 6 of the Act, the direction shall cease to be in force on the date determined in accordance with paragraph (5) or (6), as the case may be.

(5) Where the direction is in operation, it shall cease to be in force on the last day of the benefit week during the course of which [⁶the reasons specified in paragraph (1) were given].

(6) Where the direction is suspended, it shall cease to be in force on the date on which [⁶the reasons specified in paragraph (1) were given].

[⁷ . . .]

(8) A child support officer shall on completing a review immediately notify the parent concerned of his decision, so far as that is reasonably practicable, and shall give the reasons for his decision in writing.

[⁸(9) A parent with care who is aggrieved by a decision of a child support officer following a review may appeal to a child support appeal tribunal against that decision.

(10) Sections 20(2) to (4) and 21 of the Act shall apply in relation to appeals under paragraph (9) as they apply in relation to appeals under section 20 of the Act.

(11) A notification under paragraph (8) shall include information as to the provisions of paragraphs (9) and (10).]

AMENDMENTS
1. Reg. 14(2)(*a*) of the Amendment Regulations (April 5, 1993).
2. Reg. 14(2)(*b*) of the Amendment Regulations (April 5, 1993).
3. Reg. 14(2)(*c*) of the Amendment Regulations (April 5, 1993).
4. Reg. 14(3) of the Amendment Regulations (April 5, 1993).
5. Reg. 14(4) of the Amendment Regulations (April 5, 1993).
6. Reg. 14(5) of the Amendment Regulations (April 5, 1993).
7. Reg. 14(6) of the Amendment Regulations (April 5, 1993).
8. Reg. 14(7) of the Amendment Regulations (April 5, 1993).

DEFINITIONS
"the Act": see reg. 1(2).
"direction": *ibid.*
"in force": see reg. 1(3).
"in operation": *ibid.*
"obligation imposed by section 6 of the Act": see reg. 1(2).
"parent concerned": *ibid.*
"parent with care": *ibid.*
"suspended": see reg. 1(3).

GENERAL NOTE
Para. (1)
This regulation provides the only power of review in the case of reduced benefit directions. The wording of ss. 16 to 19 of the Act does not cover such cases. The review undertaken is one which is instigated in the circumstances set out in this paragraph and is not available on request by the person with care. It is not equivalent to a second tier review under s. 18 of the Act which is not an essential preliminary to a right of appeal to a CSAT, either under para. (9) below or under s.46(7) of the Act. The child support officer cannot refuse to conduct the review when the question is referred by the Secretary of State, but the decision on review may be that the reduced benefit direction should continue. For further discussion of the scope of this paragraph and of the right to appeal under para. (9), see the general notes to regs. 46 and 48.

Para. (3)
The review must be carried out by a different officer from the one who gave the direction. In this respect the paragraph mirrors the approach of s.18(7) of the Act.

Para. (4)
Notification of the termination, specifying the date of and reasons for the termination, must be served on the adjudication officer by a child support officer and a copy must be sent to the parent concerned (reg. 49). This is in addition to the notification of the officer's decisions and reasons under para. (8).

Para. (9)
This creates a right of appeal against the decision on the review in addition to the right of appeal which exists under s.46(7) of the Act.

Termination of a reduced benefit direction where a maintenance assessment is made following an application by a child under section 7 of the Act

43. Where a qualifying child of a parent with respect to whom a direction is in force applies for a maintenance assessment to be made with respect to him under section 7 of the Act, and an assessment is made in response to that application in respect of all of the qualifying children in relation to whom the parent concerned failed to comply with the obligations imposed by section 6 of the Act, that direction shall cease to be in force from the date determined in accordance with regulation 45.

DEFINITIONS
"the Act": see reg. 1(2).
"direction": *ibid.*
"in force": see reg. 1(3).
"obligation imposed by section 6 of the Act": see reg. 1(2).
"parent concerned": *ibid.*

GENERAL NOTE
Where a maintenance assessment is made following an application by a qualifying child under s.7, the consequences of the parent with care's refusal to supply the information under reg. 6 will have been circumvented and the direction will cease to be in force in accordance with reg. 45. If the direction is allowed to continue in force as a result of an error by the Secretary of State or a child support officer, the error may be corrected under reg. 46. Notification of the termination, specifying the date of and reasons for the termination, must be served on the adjudication officer by a child support officer and a copy must be sent to the parent concerned (reg. 49).

Termination of a reduced benefit direction where a maintenance assessment is made following an application by an absent parent under section 4 of the Act

44. Where—
(a) an absent parent applies for a maintenance assessment to be made under section 4 of the Act with respect to all of his qualifying children in relation to whom the other parent of those children is a person with care;
(b) a direction is in force with respect to that other parent following her failure to comply with the obligations imposed by section 6 of the Act in relation to those qualifying children; and
(c) an assessment is made in response to that application by the absent parent for a maintenance assessment,
that direction shall cease to be in force on the date determined in accordance with regulation 45.

DEFINITIONS
"absent parent": see reg. 1(5).
"the Act": see reg. 1(2).

"direction": *ibid.*
"in force": see reg. 1(3).
"obligation imposed by section 6 of the Act": see reg. 1(2)
"person with care": see reg 1(5).

GENERAL NOTE

Where a maintenance assessment is made following an application by the absent parent under s.4, the consequences of the parent with care's refusal to supply the information under reg. 6 will have been circumvented and the direction will cease to be in force in accordance with reg. 45. If the direction is allowed to continue in force as a result of an error by the Secretary of State or a child support officer, the error may be corrected under reg. 46. Notification of the termination, specifying the date of and reasons for the termination, must be served on the adjudication officer by a child support officer and a copy must be sent to the parent concerned (reg. 49).

Date from which a reduced benefit direction ceases to be in force following a termination under regulation 43 or 44

45.—(1) The date a direction ceases to be in force under the provisions of regulation 43 or 44 shall be determined in accordance with paragraphs (2) and (3).

(2) Where the direction is in operation, it shall cease to be in force on the last day of the benefit week during the course of which the Secretary of State is supplied with the information that enables a child support officer to make the assessment.

(3) Where the direction is suspended, it shall cease to be in force on the date on which the Secretary of State is supplied with the information that enables a child support officer to make the assessment.

DEFINITIONS
"benefit week": see reg. 1(2).
"direction": *ibid.*
"in force": see reg. 1(3).
"in operation": *ibid.*
"suspended": *ibid.*

Cancellation of a reduced benefit direction in cases of error

46. Where a child support officer is satisfied that a direction was given as a result of an error on the part of the Secretary of State or a child support officer, or though not given as a result of such an error has not subsequently ceased to be in force as a result of such an error, the child support officer shall cancel the direction and it shall be treated as not having been given, or as having ceased to be in force on the date it would have ceased to be in force if that error had not been made, as the case may be.

DEFINITIONS
"direction": see reg. 1(2).
"in force": see reg. 1(3).

GENERAL NOTE

The effect of this regulation may not be immediately obvious on first reading. It requires a child support officer to cancel a reduced benefit direction in two cases where there has been an error. The error may have been one of fact or one of law or an administrative one, including a failure to give the required notice of a cancellation under this regulation to the adjudication officer under reg. 49. The first case is where the direction was made as a result of an error on the part of the Secretary of State or a child support officer. In this case, the direction is treated as never having been made. The second case is where the direction should have ceased to be in force but did not, as a result of an error by the Secretary of State or a child support officer. In this case, the direction is treated as having ceased to be in force from the date when it would have ceased had it not been for the error. The second case only applies where the direction should have "ceased to be in force." This language is in contrast to the wording used in regs. 38, 40 and 48 which deal with suspension of a direction. (This point is reinforced by the wording of reg. 49(1).) Any error in giving effect to a suspension under reg. 38 or 40 is likely to be made by an adjudication officer (as to which see below), but an error could be made under reg. 48 by the Secretary of State or a child support officer. Such a case is not covered by this regulation.

Only errors of the Secretary of State or a child support officer are within this regulation. Errors of an adjudication officer or of the Secretary of State in his social security jurisdiction are not covered. If an adjudication officer fails to give effect to the termination of a direction, that cannot be corrected by a child support officer and must be dealt with by an adjudication officer.

The correction of the error is a matter for a child support officer, even if the error was that of the Secretary of State. This power is additional to the powers of a child support officer to correct accidental errors in decisions or reasons for decisions under reg. 54 and to set aside decisions under reg. 55. If a child support officer fails to cancel a direction despite an error, the parent cannot appeal to a CSAT under s.46(7) of the Act as the right to appeal in that section only applies to the *giving* of a reduced benefit direction. The parent may be able to seek a review under reg. 42 and then appeal under reg. 42(9). The power to review envisages matters which affect the duty to comply with s.6 of the Act, rather than the penalty imposed as a result of the failure. However, the wording of reg. 42(1)(b) is wide enough to cover cases where the obligation to comply is still being imposed through the reduced benefit direction. If this right of appeal to a CSAT cannot be used, the parent will have to apply for judicial review.

Where a child support officer acts to cancel a reduced benefit direction, notification of the termination, specifying the date of and reasons for the termination, must be served on the adjudication officer by a child support officer and a copy must be sent to the parent concerned (reg. 49).

Reduced benefit directions where there is an additional qualifying child

47.—(1) Where a direction is in operation or would be in operation but for the provisions of regulation 40 and a child support officer gives a further direction with respect to the same parent on account of that parent failing to comply with the obligations imposed by section 6 of the Act in relation to an additional qualifying child of whom she is a person with care, the earlier direction shall cease to be in force on the last day of the benefit week preceding the benefit week on the first day of which, in accordance with the provisions of regulation 36(4), the further direction comes into operation, or would come into operation but for the provisions of regulation 40.

(2) Where a further direction comes into operation in a case falling within paragraph (1), the provisions of regulation 36 shall apply to it.

(3) Where a direction has ceased to be in force by virtue of regulation 38(2) and a child support officer gives a direction with respect to the same parent on account of that parent's failure to comply with the obligations imposed by section 6 of the Act in relation to an additional qualifying child, no further direction shall be given with respect to that parent on account of her failure to comply with the obligations imposed by section 6 of the Act in relation to one or more children in relation to whom the direction that has ceased to be in force by virtue of regulation 38(2) was given.

(4) Where a case falls within paragraph (1) or (3) and the further direction, but for the provisions of this paragraph would cease to be in force by virtue of the provisions of regulation 41 or 42, but the earlier direction would not have ceased to be in force by virtue of the provisions of those regulations, the later direction shall continue in force for a period ("the extended period") calculated in accordance with the provisions of paragraph (5) and the reduction of relevant benefit shall be determined in accordance with paragraphs (6) and (7).

(5) The extended period for the purposes of paragraph (4) shall be

$(78-F-S)$ weeks

where—
F is the number of weeks for which the earlier direction was in operation; and
S is the number of weeks for which the later direction has been in operation.

(6) Where the extended period calculated in accordance with paragraph (5) is greater than 52 weeks, there shall be a reduction of relevant benefit in respect of the number of weeks in excess of 52 determined in accordance with regulation 36(2),

and a reduction of relevant benefit in respect of the remaining 52 weeks determined in accordance with regulation 36(3).

(7) Where the extended period calculated in accordance with paragraph (5) is equal to or less than 52 weeks, there shall be a reduction of relevant benefit in respect of that period determined in accordance with regulation 36(3).

(8) In this regulation "an additional qualifying child" means a qualifying child of whom the parent concerned is a person with care and who was either not such a qualifying child at the time the earlier direction was given or had not been born at the time the earlier direction was given.

DEFINITIONS
"benefit week": see reg. 1(2).
"direction": *ibid.*
"in force": see reg. 1(3).
"in operation": *ibid.*
"obligation imposed by section 6 of the Act": see reg. 1(2).
"parent concerned": *ibid.*
"person with care": see reg. 1(5).
"relevant benefit": see reg. 1(2).

GENERAL NOTE
This regulation works out the principle established by reg. 36(8), that there may only be one direction in force at any one time, in the context of directions in respect of additional children, as defined by para. (8). Any direction which is in operation, or which is suspended under reg. 40, ceases to be in force when the new direction is made (para. (1)), and no further direction may be issued under reg. 38(7) (para. (3)). If, however, the new direction would otherwise cease to be in force by virtue of reg. 41 or 42, it will continue in force for the balance of the reduction period outstanding on the earlier direction when that ceased to be in force under this regulation (paras. (4) to (7)).

Notification of the termination, specifying the date of and reasons for the termination, must be served on the adjudication officer by a child support officer and a copy must be sent to the parent concerned (reg. 49).

Suspension and termination of a reduced benefit direction where the sole qualifying child ceases to be a child or where the parent concerned ceases to be a person with care

48.—(1) Where, whilst a direction is in operation—
(a) there is, in relation to that direction, only one qualifying child, and that child ceases to be a child within the meaning of the Act; or
(b) the parent concerned ceases to be a person with care,
the direction shall be suspended from the last day of the benefit week during the course of which the child ceases to be a child within the meaning of the Act, or the parent concerned ceases to be a person with care, as the case may be.

(2) Where, under the provisions of paragraph (1), a direction has been suspended for a period of 52 weeks and no relevant benefit is payable at that time, it shall cease to be in force.

(3) If during the period specified in paragraph (1) the former child again becomes a child within the meaning of the Act or the parent concerned again becomes a person with care and relevant benefit is payable to or in respect of that parent, a reduction in the amount of that benefit shall be made in accordance with the provisions of paragraphs (3) to (7) of regulation 38.

DEFINITIONS
"the Act": see reg. 1(2).
"direction": *ibid.*
"in operation": see reg. 1(3).
"parent concerned": see reg. 1(2).
"person with care": see reg. 1(5).
"relevant benefit": see reg. 1(2).

"suspended": see reg. 1(3).

GENERAL NOTE
Para. (1)

If a suspension under reg. 48 is not put into effect, the error should be picked up through the termination of a maintenance assessment procedures, but it is conceivable that the decision on that point might not be carried through to the reduced benefit direction. Regulation 46 does not cover errors relating to the suspension of a reduced benefit direction (see the general note to that regulation), so other means must be found to do so if drawing the matter to the attention of the Secretary of State or a child support officer does not result in a correction. If reg. 48 applies because the only child covered by the direction ceases to be a qualifying child, the parent could seek a review under reg. 42 and make use of the right to appeal given by reg. 42(9).

Notification of the termination or suspension, specifying the date of and reasons for the it, must be served on the adjudication officer by a child support officer and a copy must be sent to the parent concerned (reg. 49).

Para. (3)

A child might cease to be a qualifying child and become one again as a result of a change in educational arrangements (see the general note to s.55 of the Act).

Notice of termination of a reduced benefit direction

49.—(1) Where a direction ceases to be in force under the provisions of regulations 41 to 44 or 46 to 48, or is suspended under the provisions of regulation 48, a child support officer shall serve notice of such termination or suspension, as the case may be, on the adjudication officer and shall specify the date on which the direction ceases to be in force or is suspended, as the case may be.

(2) Any notice served under paragraph (1) shall set out the reasons why the direction has ceased to be in force or has been suspended.

(3) The parent concerned shall be served with a copy of any notice served under paragraph (1).

DEFINITIONS
"direction": see reg. 1(2).
"in force": see reg. 1(3).
"parent concerned": see reg. 1(2).
"suspended": see reg. 1(3).

Rounding provisions

50. Where any calculation made under this Part of these Regulations results in a fraction of a penny, that fraction shall be treated as a penny if it exceeds one half, and shall otherwise be disregarded.

PART X

MISCELLANEOUS PROVISIONS

Persons who are not persons with care

51.—(1) For the purposes of the Act the following categories of person shall not be persons with care—
   (*a*) a local authority;
   (*b*) a person with whom a child who is looked after by a local authority is placed by that authority under the provisions of the Children Act 1989,

[¹except where that person is a parent of such a child and the local authority allow the child to live with that parent under section 23(5) of that Act;]

(c)   in Scotland, a person with whom a child is boarded out by a local authority under the provisions of section 21 of the Social Work (Scotland) Act 1968.

(2) In paragraph (1) above—

"local authority" means, in relation to England and Wales, the council of a county, a metropolitan district, a London Borough or the Common Council of the City of London and, in relation to Scotland, a regional council or an islands council;

"a child who is looked after by a local authority" has the same meaning as in section 22 of the Children Act 1989.

AMENDMENT

1.   Reg. 15 of the Amendment Regulations (April 5, 1993).

DEFINITIONS

"the Act": see reg. 1(2).
"person with care": see reg. 1(5).

GENERAL NOTE

Section 22 of the Children Act 1989 defines "a child who is looked after by a local authority" as a child who is in the local authority's care and for whom the authority provides accommodation for a continuous period of more than 24 hours in the exercise of any functions (in particular those under the Children Act itself) which stand referred to their social services committee under the Local Authority Social Services Act 1970.

In line with this provision, where a local authority has part-time care of a qualifying child the case is a special one by virtue of reg. 25 of the Maintenance Assessments and Special Cases Regulations and no child support maintenance is payable for the proportion of the week that the child is in the care of the local authority.

Terminations of maintenance assessments

52.—(1) Where the Secretary of State is satisfied that a question arises as to whether a maintenance assessment has ceased to have effect under the provisions of paragraph 16(1)(a) to (d) of Schedule 1 to the Act, he shall refer that question (a "termination question") to a child support officer.

(2) Where a child support officer has made a decision on a termination question (a "termination decision") he shall immediately notify the following persons of his decision, so far as that is reasonably practicable—

(a)   in a case falling within paragraph 16(1)(a) of Schedule 1 to the Act, the surviving relevant persons;

(b)   in a case falling within paragraph 16(1)(b), (c) or (d) of Schedule 1 to the Act, the relevant persons.

(3) Any notification under paragraph (2) shall give the reasons for the termination decision made, include information as to the provisions of section 18 of the Act, and explain the provisions of paragraph (4).

(4) The persons specified in paragraph (2) may apply to the Secretary of State for a review of a termination decision as if it were a case falling within section 18 of the Act and, subject to the modifications set out in paragraph (5), section 18(5) to (9) and (11) of the Act shall apply to such a review.

(5) The modifications referred to in paragraph (4) are—

(a)   section 18(6) of the Act shall have effect as if for "the refusal, assessment or cancellation" there is substituted "the termination decision";

(b)   section 18(9) of the Act shall have effect as if for "a maintenance assessment or (as the case may be) a fresh maintenance assessment" there is substituted "a different termination decision."

(6) The provisions of regulation 24 as to time limits for an application for a

review of a decision by a child support officer shall apply to reviews under paragraph (4).

(7) Where a child support officer has completed a review of a termination decision he shall immediately notify the persons specified in paragraph (2), so far as that is reasonably practicable, of the review decision, give the reasons for that decision in writing, and notify them of the provisions of section 20 of the Act.

(8) Where a case falls within regulation 19 of the Maintenance Assessments and Special Cases Regulations and both absent parents have made an application for a maintenance assessment under section 4 of the Act, the Secretary of State shall be under the duty imposed by section 4(6) of the Act only if both absent parents have, under section 4(5) of the Act, requested the Secretary of State to cease acting under section 4 of the Act.

DEFINITIONS
   "absent parent": see reg. 1(5).
   "the Act": see reg. 1(2).
   "relevant person": *ibid.*

Authorisation of representative

53.—(1) A person may authorise a representative, whether or not legally qualified, to receive notices and other documents on his behalf and to act on his behalf in relation to the making of applications and the supply of information under any provision of the Act or these Regulations.

(2) Where a person has authorised a representative for the purposes of paragraph (1) who is not legally qualified, he shall confirm that authorisation in writing to the Secretary of State.

DEFINITION
   "the Act": see reg. 1(2).

Correction of accidental errors in decisions

54.—(1) Subject to regulation 56, accidental errors in any decision or record of a decision may at any time be corrected by a child support officer and a correction made to, or to the record of, a decision shall be deemed to be part of the decision or of that record.

(2) A child support officer who has made a correction under the provisions of paragraph (1) shall immediately notify the persons who were notified of the decision that has been corrected, so far as that is reasonably practicable.

GENERAL NOTE
   For a discussion of the similar provision in the Tribunal Procedure Regulations, see the general note to reg. 14 of those Regulations.

Setting aside of decisions on certain grounds

55.—(1) Subject to paragraph (7) and regulation 56, on an application made by a relevant person, a decision may be set aside by a child support officer on the grounds that the interests of justice so require, and in particular that a relevant document in relation to that decision was not sent to, or was not received at an appropriate time by the person making the application or his representative or was sent but not received at an appropriate time by the child support officer who gave the decision.

(2) Any application made under paragraph (1) shall be in writing, shall include a

statement of the grounds for the application, and shall be made by giving or sending it to the Secretary of State within 28 days of the date of notification of the decision in question.

(3) Where an application to set aside a decision is being considered by a child support officer under paragraph (1), he shall notify the relevant persons other than the applicant of the application and they shall be given 14 days to make representations as to that application.

(4) The provisions of regulation 25(6) shall apply to notifications under paragraph (5).

(5) A child support officer who has made a determination on an application to set aside a decision shall immediately notify the relevant persons, so far as that is reasonably procticable, and shall give the reasons for his determination in writing.

(6) For the purposes of determining an application to set aside a decision under this regulation, there shall be disregarded regulation 1(6)(b) and any provision in any enactment or instrument to the effect that any notice or other document required or authorised to be given or sent to any person shall be deemed to have been given or sent if it was sent by post to that person's last known or notified address.

(7) The provisions of paragraphs (1) to (6) shall not apply to any document given or sent under any provision of Part IX.

DEFINITION
"relevant person": see reg. 1(2).

GENERAL NOTE
For a discussion of the similar provision in the Tribunal Procedure Regulations, see the general notes to regs. 2, 3 and 15 of those Regulations. This regulation does not apply to Category A interim maintenance assessments (reg. 8(12)).

Provisions common to regulations 54 and 55

56.—(1) In determining whether the time limits specified in regulation 17, 19, 24 or 25 have been complied with, there shall be disregarded any day falling before the day on which notification is given of a correction made to, or to the record of, a decision made under regulation 54 or on which notification is given that a decision shall not be set aside following an application made under regulation 55, as the case may be.

(2) The power to correct errors under regulation 54 or to set aside decisions under regulation 55 shall not be taken to limit any other powers to correct errors or set aside decisions that are exercisable apart from these Regulations.

GENERAL NOTE
This regulation makes equivalent provision in the context of these regulations to that made by reg. 16 of the Tribunal Procedure Regulations.

[¹Action by the Secretary of State on receipt of an application under section 17 or 18 of the Act where a question as to the entitlement to benefit arises

57.—(1) Where an application for a review under section 17 or 18 of the Act has been made to the Secretary of State and he is of the opinion that the application gives rise to a question as to the entitlement to benefit of any person, he may disclose the information contained in that application to an adjudication officer or, in the case of housing benefit or council tax benefit, to an appropriate authority.

(2) Where the Secretary of State discloses information under paragraph (1), he need not refer the application to a child support officer earlier than the expiration of a period of 28 days beginning with the date prescribed in paragraph (3).

(3) The date prescribed for the purposes of paragraph (2) is the second day after

the date the Secretary of State receives the application for a review under section 17 or 18 of the Act, excluding any Saturday, Sunday, or any day which is a bank holiday in England, Wales, Scotland or Northern Ireland under the Banking and Financial Dealings Act 1971.

(4) In this regulation—

(*a*) "benefit" is to be construed in accordance with the benefit Acts;

(*b*) "appropriate authority" means—

    (i) in relation to housing benefit, the housing or local authority concerned; and

    (ii) in relation to council tax benefit, the billing authority or, in Scotland, the levying authority.]

AMENDMENT

1. Reg. 16 of the Amendment Regulations (April 5, 1993).

DEFINITION

"the Act": see reg. 1(2).

SCHEDULE 1   **Regulation 1(4)**

MEANING OF "CHILD" FOR THE PURPOSES OF THE ACT

Persons of 16 or 17 years of age who are not in full-time non-advanced education

1.—(1) Subject to sub-paragraph (3), the conditions which must be satisfied for a person to be a child within section 55(1)(*c*) of the Act are—

(*a*) the person is registered for work or for training under youth training with—

    (i) the Department of Employment;

    (ii) the Ministry of Defence;

    (iii) in England and Wales, a local education authority within the meaning of the Education Acts 1944 to 1992;

    (iv) in Scotland, an education authority within the meaning of section 135(1) of the Education (Scotland) Act 1980 (interpretation); or

    (v) for the purposes of applying Council Regulation (EEC) No. 1408/71, any corresponding body in another Member State;

(*b*) the person is not engaged in remunerative work, other than work of a temporary nature that is due to cease before the end of the extension period which applies in the case of that person;

(*c*) the extension period which applies in the case of that person has not expired; and

(*d*) immediately before the extension period begins, the person is a child for the purposes of the Act without regard to this paragraph.

(2) For the purposes of paragraphs (*b*), (*c*) and (*d*) of sub-paragraph (1), the extension period—

(*a*) begins on the first day of the week in which the person would no longer be a child for the purposes of the Act but for this paragraph; and

(*b*) where a person ceases to fall within section 55(1)(*a*) of the Act or within paragraph 5—

    (i) on or after the first Monday in September, but before the first Monday in January of the following year, ends on the last day of the week which falls immediately before the week which includes the first Monday in January in that year;

    (ii) on or after the first Monday in January but before the Monday following Easter Monday in that year, ends on the last day of the week which falls 12 weeks after the week which includes the first Monday in January in that year;

    (iii) at any other time of the year, ends on the last day of the week which falls 12 weeks after the week which includes the Monday following Easter Monday in that year.

(3) A person shall not be a child for the purposes of the Act under this paragraph if—

(*a*) he is engaged in training under youth training; or

    (*b*) he is entitled to income support.

Meaning of "advanced education" for the purposes of section 55 of the Act

2. For the purposes of section 55 of the Act "advanced education" means education of the following description—

    (*a*) a course in preparation for a degree, a Diploma of Higher Education, a higher national diploma, a higher national diploma or higher national certificate of the Business and [¹Technology] Education Council or the Scottish Vocational Education Council or a teaching qualification; or

    (*b*) any other course which is of a standard above that of an ordinary national diploma, a national diploma or national certificate of the Business and [¹Technology] Education Council or the Scottish Vocational Education Council, the advanced level of the General Certificate of Education, a Scottish certificate of education (higher level) or a Scottish certificate of sixth year studies.

Circumstances in which education is to be treated as full-time education

3. For the purposes of section 55 of the Act education shall be treated as being full-time if it is received by a person attending a course of education at a recognised educational establishment and the time spent receiving instruction or tuition, undertaking supervised study, examination or practical work or taking part in any exercise, experiment or project for which provision is made in the curriculum of the course, exceeds 12 hours per week, so however that in calculating the time spent in pursuit of the course, no account shall be taken of time occupied by meal breaks or spent on unsupervised study, whether undertaken on or off the premises of the educational establishment.

Interruption of full-time education

4.—(1) Subject to sub-paragraph (2), in determining whether a person falls within section 55(1)(*b*) of the Act no account shall be taken of a period (whether beginning before or after the person concerned attains age 16) of up to 6 months of any interruption to the extent to which it is accepted that the interruption is attributable to a cause which is reasonable in the particular circumstances of the case; and where the interruption or its continuance is attributable to the illness or disability of mind or body of the person concerned, the period of 6 months may be extended for such further period as a child support officer considers reasonable in the particular circumstances of the case.

(2) The provisions of sub-paragraph (1) shall not apply to any period of interruption of a person's full-time education which is likely to be followed immediately or which is followed immediately by a period during which—

    (*a*) provision is made for the training of that person, and for an allowance to be payable to that person, under youth training; or

    (*b*) he is receiving education by virtue of his employment or of any office held by him.

Circumstances in which a person who has ceased to receive full-time education is to be treated as continuing to fall within section 55(1) of the Act

5.—(1) Subject to sub-paragraphs (2) and (5), a person who has ceased to receive full-time education (which is not advanced education) shall, if—

    (*a*) he is under the age of 16 when he so ceases, from the date on which he attains that age; or

    (*b*) he is 16 or over when he so ceases, from the date on which he so ceases,

be treated as continuing to fall within section 55(1) of the Act up to and including the week including the terminal date or if he attains the age of 19 on or before that date up to and including the week including the last Monday before he attains that age.

(2) In the case of a person specified in sub-paragraph (1)(*a*) or (*b*) who had not attained the upper limit of compulsory school age when he ceased to receive full-time education, the terminal date in his case shall be that specified in paragraph (*a*), (*b*) or (*c*) of sub-paragraph (3), whichever next follows the date on which he would have attained that age.

(3) In this paragraph the "terminal date" means—

(*a*) the first Monday in January; or

(*b*) the Monday following Easter Monday; or

(*c*) the first Monday in September,

whichever first occurs after the date on which the person's said education ceased.

(4) In this paragraph "compulsory school age" means—

(*a*) in England and Wales, compulsory school age as determined in accordance with section 9 of the Education Act 1962;

(*b*) in Scotland, school age as determined in accordance with sections 31 and 33 of the Education (Scotland) Act 1980.

(5) A person shall not be treated as continuing to fall within section 55(1) of the Act under this paragraph if he is engaged in remunerative work, other than work of a temporary nature that is due to cease before the terminal date.

(6) Subject to sub-paragraphs (5) and (8), a person whose name was entered as a candidate for any external examination in connection with full-time education (which is not advanced education), which he was receiving at that time, shall so long as his name continued to be so entered before ceasing to receive such education be treated as continuing to fall within section 55(1) of the Act for any week in the period specified in sub-paragraph (7).

(7) Subject to sub-paragraph (8), the period specified for the purposes of sub-paragraph (6) is the period beginning with the date when that person ceased to receive such education ending with—

(*a*) whichever of the dates in sub-paragraph (3) first occurs after the conclusion of the examination (or the last of them, if there are more than one); or

(*b*) the expiry of the week which includes the last Monday before his 19th birthday, whichever is the earlier.

(8) The period specified in sub-paragraph (7) shall, in the case of a person who has not attained the age of 16 when he so ceased, begin with the date on which he attained that age.

Interpretation

6. In this Schedule—

"Education Acts 1944 to 1992" has the meaning prescribed in section 94(2) of the Further and Higher Education Act 1992;

"remunerative work" means work of not less than 24 hours a week—

(*a*) in respect of which payment is made; or

(*b*) which is done in expectation of payment;

"week" means a period of 7 days beginning with a Monday;

"youth training" means—

(*a*) arrangements made under section 2 of the Employment and Training Act 1973 (functions of the Secretary of State) or section 2 of the Enterprise and New Towns (Scotland) Act 1990;

(*b*) arrangements made by the Secretary of State for persons enlisted in Her Majesty's forces for any special term of service specified in regulations made under section 2 of the Armed Forces Act 1966 (power of Defence Council to make regulations as to engagement of persons in regular forces); or

(*c*) for the purposes of the application of Council Regulation (EEC) No. 1408/71, any corresponding provisions operated in another Member State,

for purposes which include the training of persons who, at the beginning of their training, are under the age of 18.

AMENDMENT

1. Reg. 17 of the Amendment Regulations (April 5, 1993).

DEFINITION

"the Act": see reg. 1(2).

GENERAL NOTE

These provisions are discussed in the general note to s.55 of the Act.

MULTIPLE APPLICATIONS

No maintenance assessment in force: more than one application for a maintenance assessment by the same person under section 4 or 6 or under sections 4 and 6 of the Act

1.—(1) Where a person makes an effective application for a maintenance assessment under section 4 or 6 of the Act and, before that assessment is made, makes a subsequent effective application under that section with respect to the same absent parent or person with care, as the case may be, those applications shall be treated as a single application.

(2) Where a parent with care makes an effective application for a maintenance assessment—

(a) under section 4 of the Act; or

(b) under section 6 of the Act,

and, before that assessment is made, makes a subsequent effective application—

(c) in a case falling within paragraph (a), under section 6 of the Act; or

(d) in a case falling within paragraph (b), under section 4 of the Act,

with respect to the same absent parent, those applications shall, if the parent with care does not cease to fall within section 6(1) of the Act, be treated as a single application under section 6 of the Act, and shall otherwise be treated as a single application under section 4 of the Act.

No maintenance assessment in force: more than one application by a child under section 7 of the Act

2. Where a child makes an effective application for a maintenance assessment under section 7 of the Act and, before that assessment is made, makes a subsequent effective application under that section with respect to the same person with care and absent parent, both applications shall be treated as a single application for a maintenance assessment.

No maintenance assessment in force: applications by different persons for a maintenance assessment

3.—(1) Where the Secretary of State receives more than one effective application for a maintenance assessment with respect to the same person with care and absent parent, he shall refer each such application to a child support officer and, if no maintenance assessment has been made in relation to any of the applications, the child support officer shall determine which application he shall proceed with in accordance with sub-paragraphs (2) to (11).

(2) Where there is an application by a person with care under section 4 or 6 of the Act and an application by an absent parent under section 4 of the Act, the child support officer shall proceed with the application of the person with care.

(3) Where there is an application for a maintenance assessment by a qualifying child under section 7 of the Act and a subsequent application is made with respect to that child by a person who is, with respect to that child, a person with care or an absent parent, the child support officer shall proceed with the application of that person with care or absent parent, as the case may be.

(4) Where, in a case falling within sub-paragraph (3), there is more than one subsequent application, the child support officer shall apply the provisions of sub-paragraph (2), (8), (9) or (11), as is appropriate in the circumstances of the case, to determine which application he shall proceed with.

(5) Where there is an application for a maintenance assessment by more than one qualifying child under section 7 of the Act in relation to the same person with care and absent parent, the child support officer shall proceed with the application of the elder or, as the case may be, eldest of the qualifying children.

(6) Where a case is to be treated as a special case for the purposes of the Act under regulation 19 of the Maintenance Assessments and Special Cases Regulations (both parents are absent) and an effective application is received from each absent parent, the child support officer shall proceed with both applications, treating them as a single application for a maintenance assessment.

(7) Where, under the provisions of regulation 20 of the Maintenance Assessments and Special Cases Regulations (persons treated as absent parents), two persons are to be treated as absent parents and an effective application is received from each such person, the child support officer shall proceed with both applications, treating them as a single application for a maintenance assessment.

(8) Where there is an application under section 6 of the Act by a parent with care and an application under section 4 of the Act by another person with care who has parental responsibility for (or, in Scotland, parental rights over) the qualifying child or qualifying children with respect to whom the application under section 6 of the Act was made, the child support officer shall proceed with the application under section 6 of the Act by the parent with care.

(9) Where—
    (*a*) more than one person with care makes an application for a maintenance assessment under section 4 of the Act in respect of the same qualifying child or qualifying children (whether or not any of those applications is also in respect of other qualifying children);
    (*b*) each such person has parental responsibility for (or, in Scotland, parental rights over) that child or children; and
    (*c*) under the provisions of regulation 20 of the Maintenance Assessments and Special Cases Regulations one of those persons is to be treated as an absent parent,
the child support officer shall proceed with the application of the person who does not fall to be treated as an absent parent under the provisions of regulation 20 of those Regulations.

(10) Where, in a case falling within sub-paragraph (9), there is more than one person who does not fall to be treated as an absent parent under the provisions of regulation 20 of those Regulations, the child support officer shall apply the provisions of paragraph (11) to determine which application he shall proceed with.

(11) Where—
    (*a*) more than one person with care makes an application for a maintenance assessment under section 4 of the Act in respect of the same qualifying child or qualifying children (whether or not any of those applications is also in respect of other qualifying children); and
    (*b*) either—
        (i) none of those persons has parental responsibility for (or, in Scotland, parental rights over) that child or children; or
        (ii) the case falls within sub-paragraph (9)(*b*) but the child support officer has not been able to determine which application he is to proceed with under the provisions of sub-paragraph (9),
the child support officer shall proceed with the application of the principal provider of day to day care, as determined in accordance with sub-paragraph (12).

(12) Where—
    (*a*) the applications are in respect of one qualifying child, the application of that person with care with whom the child spends the greater or, as the case may be, the greatest proportion of his time;
    (*b*) the applications are in respect of more than one qualifying child, the application of that person with care with whom the children spend the greater or, as the case may be, the greatest proportion of their time, taking account of the time each qualifying child spends with each of the persons with care in question;
    (*c*) the child support officer cannot determine which application he is to proceed with under paragraph (*a*) or (*b*), and child benefit is paid in respect of the qualifying child or qualifying children to one but not any other of the applicants, the application of the applicant to whom child benefit is paid;

(*d*) the child support officer cannot determine which application he is to proceed with under paragraph (*a*), (*b*) or (*c*), the application of that applicant who in the opinion of the child support officer is the principal provider of day to day care for the child or children in question.

(13) Subject to sub-paragraph (14), where, in any case falling within sub-paragraphs (2) to (11), the applications are not in respect of identical qualifying children, the application that the child support officer is to proceed with as determined by those paragraphs shall be treated as an application with respect to all of the qualifying children with respect to whom the applications were made.

(14) Where the child support officer is satisfied that the same person with care does not provide the principal day to day care for all of the qualifying children with respect to whom an assessment would but for the provisions of this paragraph be made under sub-paragraph (13), he shall make separate assessments in relation to each person with care providing such principal day to day care.

Maintenance assessment in force: subsequent application for a maintenance assessment with respect to the same persons

4. Where a maintenance assessment is in force and a subsequent application is made under the same section of the Act for an assessment with respect to the same person with care, absent parent, and qualifying child or qualifying children as those with respect to whom the assessment in force has been made, that application shall not be proceeded with unless the Secretary of State treats that application as an application for a review under section 17 of the Act.

Maintenance assessment in force: subsequent application for a maintenance assessment under section 6 of the Act

5. Where a maintenance assessment is in force following an application under section 4 or 7 of the Act and the person with care makes an application under section 6 of the Act, any maintenance assessment made in response to that application shall replace the assessment currently in force.

Maintenance assessment in force: subsequent application for a maintenance assessment in respect of additional children

6.—(1) Where a maintenance assessment made in response to an application by an absent parent under section 4 of the Act is in force and that assessment is not in respect of all of his children who are in the care of the person with care with respect to whom that assessment has been made, an assessment made in response to an application by that person with care under section 4 of the Act with respect to—

(*a*) the children in respect of whom the assessment currently in force was made; and

(*b*) the additional child, or as the case may be, one or more of the additional children in that person's care who are children of that absent parent,

shall replace the assessment currently in force.

(2) Where—

(*a*) a maintenance assessment made in response to an application by an absent parent or a person with care under section 4 of the Act is in force;

(*b*) that assessment is not in respect of all of the children of the absent parent who are in the care of the person with respect to whom that assessment has been made; and

(*c*) the absent parent makes a subsequent application in respect of an additional qualifying child or additional qualifying children of his in the care of the same person,

that application shall be treated as an application for a maintenance assessment in respect of all of the qualifying children concerned, and the assessment made shall replace the assessment currently in force.

(3) Where a maintenance assessment made in response to an application by a child under section 7 of the Act is in force and the person with care of that child makes an application for a maintenance assessment under section 4 of the Act in respect of [¹one or more children of the absent parent who are in her care, that application shall be treated as an application for a

maintenance assessment with respect to all the children of the absent parent who are in her care, and] that assessment shall replace the assessment currently in force.

AMENDMENT
   1.   Reg. 18 of the Amendment Regulations (April 5, 1993).

DEFINITIONS
   "absent parent": see reg. 1(5).
   "the Act": see reg. 1(2).
   "day to day care": *ibid.*
   "effective application": *ibid.*
   "parent with care": *ibid.*
   "person with care": see reg. 1(5).

GENERAL NOTE
   If an attempt is made to make an application for a maintenance assessment at a time when such an application may not be made by virtue of Part I of the Schedule to the Transitional Provisions Order, that application is ignored and is irrelevant to the question of priority of applications.

The Child Support (Maintenance Assessments and Special Cases) Regulations 1992

(S.I. 1992 No. 1815)

Made by the Secretary of State for Social Security under sections 42, 43, 51, 52(4) and 54 of, and paragraphs 1, 2 and 4 to 9 of Schedule 1 to, the Child Support Act 1991 and all other powers enabling him in that behalf.

ARRANGEMENT OF REGULATIONS

PART I

General

PART 1

GENERAL

Citation, commencement and interpretation

1.—(1) These Regulations may be cited as the Child Support (Maintenance Assessments and Special Cases) Regulations 1992 and shall come into force on 5th April 1993.

(2) In these Regulations unless the context otherwise requires—

"the Act" means the Child Support Act 1991;

"claimant" means a claimant for income support;

"Contributions and Benefits Act" means the Social Security Contributions and Benefits Act 1992;

"council tax benefit" has the same meaning as in the Local Government Finance Act 1992;

[[1]"couple" means a married or unmarried couple;]

"course of advanced education" means—

(a) a full-time course leading to a postgraduate degree or comparable qualification, a first degree or comparable qualification, a Diploma of Higher Education, a higher national diploma, a higher national diploma or higher national certificate of the Business and [[2]Technology] Education Council or the Scottish Vocational Education Council or a teaching qualification; or

(b) any other full-time course which is a course of a standard above that of an ordinary national diploma, a national diploma or national certificate of the Business and [[2]Technology] Education Council or the Scottish Vocational Education Council, the advanced level of the General Certificate of Education, a Scottish certificate of education (higher level) or a Scottish certificate of sixth year studies;

"covenant income" means the gross income payable to a student under a Deed of Covenant by a parent;

"day" includes any part of a day;

"day to day care" means care of not less than 2 nights per week on average during—

(a) the 12 month period ending with the relevant week; or

(b) such other period, ending with the relevant week, as in the opinion of the child support officer is more representative of the current arrangements for the care of the child in question;

and for the purposes of this definition, where a child is a boarder at a boarding school or is an in-patient in a hospital, the person who, but for those circumstances, would otherwise provide day to day care of the child, shall be treated as providing day to day care during the periods in question.

"disability working allowance" has the same meaning as in section 129 of the Contributions and Benefits Act;

"earnings" has the meaning assigned to it by paragraph 1 or 3, as the case may be, of Schedule 1;

"effective date" means the date on which a maintenance assessment takes effect for the purposes of the Act;

"eligible housing costs" shall be construed in accordance with Schedule 3;

"employed earner" has the same meaning as in section 2(1)(*a*) of the Contributions and Benefits Act;

"family" means—

(*a*) a married or unmarried couple (including the members of a polygamous marriage) and any child or children living with them for whom at least one member of that couple has day to day care;

(*b*) where a person who is not a member of a married or unmarried couple has day to day care of a child, that person and any such child or children;

and for the purposes of this definition a person shall not be treated as having day to day care of a child who is a member of that person's household where the child in question is being looked after by a local authority within the meaning of section 22 of the Children Act 1989 or, in Scotland, where the child is boarded out with that person by a local authority under the provisions of section 21 of the Social Work (Scotland) Act 1968;

"grant" means any kind of educational grant or award and includes any scholarship, exhibition, allowance or bursary but does not include a payment made under section 100 of the Education Act 1944 or section 73 of the Education (Scotland) Act 1980;

"grant contribution" means any amount which a Minister of the Crown or an education authority treats as properly payable by another person when assessing the amount of a student's grant and by which that amount is, as a consequence, reduced;

"home" means—

(*a*) the dwelling in which a person and any family of his normally live; or

(*b*) if he or they normally live in more than one home, the principal home of that person and any family of his,

and for the purpose of determining the principal home in which a person normally lives no regard shall be had to residence in a residential care home or a nursing home during a period which does not exceed 52 weeks or, where it appears to the child support officer that the person will return to his principal home after that period has expired, such longer period as that officer considers reasonable to allow for the return of that person to that home;

"housing benefit" has the same meaning as in section 130 of the Contributions and Benefits Act;

"Housing Benefit Regulations" means the Housing Benefit (General) Regulations 1987;

"Income Support Regulations" means the Income Support (General) Regulations 1987;

[³"Independent Living (1993) Fund" means the charitable trust of that name established by a deed made between the Secretary of State for Social Security of the one part and Robin Glover Wendt and John Fletcher Shepherd of the other part;

"Independent Living (Extension) Fund" means the charitable trust of that name established by a deed made between the Secretary of State for Social Security of the one part and Robin Glover Wendt and John Fletcher Shepherd of the other part;]

"Maintenance Assessment Procedure Regulations" means the Child Support (Maintenance Assessment Procedure) Regulations 1992;

"married couple" means a man and a woman who are married to each other and are members of the same household;

"non-dependant" means a person who is a non-dependant for the purposes of either—

(*a*) regulation 3 of the Income Support Regulations; or

(*b*) regulation 3 of the Housing Benefit Regulations,
or who would be a non-dependant for those purposes if another member of the household in which he is living were entitled to income support or housing benefit as the case may be;

"nursing home" has the same meaning as in regulation 19(3) of the Income Support Regulations;

"occupational pension scheme" has the same meaning as in section 66(1) of the Social Security Pensions Act 1975;

"ordinary clothing or footwear" means clothing or footwear for normal daily use, but does not include school uniforms, or clothing or footwear used solely for sporting activities;

"parent with care" means a person who, in respect of the same child or children, is both a parent and a person with care;

"partner" means—
(*a*) in relation to a member of a married or unmarried couple who are living together, the other member of that couple;
(*b*) in relation to a member of a polygamous marriage, any other member of that marriage with whom he lives;

"patient" means a person (other than a person who is serving a sentence of imprisonment or detention in a young offender institution within the meaning of the Criminal Justice Act 1982 as amended by the Criminal Justice Act 1988) who is regarded as receiving free in-patient treatment within the meaning of the Social Security (Hospital In-Patients) Regulations 1975;

"person" does not include a local authority;

"personal pension scheme" has the same meaning as in section 84(1) of the Social Security Act 1986 and, in the case of a self-employed earner, includes a scheme approved by the Inland Revenue under Chapter IV of Part XIV of the Income and Corporation Taxes Act 1988;

"polygamous marriage" means any marriage during the subsistence of which a party to it is married to more than one person and in respect of which any ceremony of marriage took place under the law of a country which at the time of that ceremony permitted polygamy;

"prisoner" means a person who is detained in custody pending trial or sentence upon conviction or under a sentence imposed by a court other than a person whose detention is under the Mental Health Act 1983 or the Mental Health (Scotland) Act 1984;

"relevant child" means a child of an absent parent or a parent with care who is a member of the same family as that parent;

"relevant Schedule" means Schedule 2 to the Income Support Regulations (income support applicable amounts);

[⁴"relevant week" means—
(*a*) in relation to an application for child support maintenance—
  (i) in the case of the person making the application, the period of 7 days immediately preceding the date on which the appropriate maintenance assessment application form (being an effective application within the meaning of regulation 2(4) of the Maintenance Assessment Procedure Regulations) is submitted to the Secretary of State;
  (ii) in the case of a person to whom a maintenance assessment enquiry form is given or sent as the result of such application, the period of 7 days immediately preceding the date on which that form is given to him or, as the case may be, the date on which it is treated as having been sent to him under regulation 1(6)(*b*) of the Maintenance Assessment Procedure Regulations;
(*b*) in relation to a review of a maintenance assessment under section 16 or 17 of the Act, the period of 7 days immediately preceding the date on which a request is made for information or evidence under regulation 17(5) or, as

the case may be, regulation 19(2) of the Maintenance Assessment Procedure Regulations;]

"residential care home" has the same meaning as in regulation 19(3) of the Income Support Regulations;

"retirement annuity contract" means an annuity contract for the time being approved by the Board of Inland Revenue as having for its main object the provision of a life annuity in old age or the provision of an annuity for a partner or dependant and in respect of which relief from income tax may be given on any premium;

"self-employed earner" has the same meaning as in section 2(1)(*b*) of the Contributions and Benefits Act;

"student" means a person, other than a person in receipt of a training allowance, who is aged less than 19 and attending a full-time course of advanced education or who is aged 19 or over and attending a full-time course of study at an educational establishment; and for the purposes of this definition—

(*a*) a person who has started on such a course shall be treated as attending it throughout any period of term or vacation within it, until the last day of the course or such earlier date as he abandons it or is dismissed from it;

(*b*) a person on a sandwich course (within the meaning of paragraph 1(1) of Schedule 5 to the Education (Mandatory Awards) Regulations 1988) shall be treated as attending a full-time course of advanced education or, as the case may be, of study;

"student loan" means a loan which is made to a student pursuant to arrangements made under section 1 of the Education (Student Loans) Act 1990;

[⁵ ...]

"training allowance" has the same meaning as in regulation 2 of the Income Support Regulations;

"unmarried couple" means a man and a woman who are not married to each other but are living together as husband and wife;

"weekly council tax" means the annual amount of the council tax in question payable in respect of the year in which the effective date falls, divided by 52;

"year" means a period of 52 weeks;

"youth training" means—

(*a*) arrangements made under section 2 of the Employment and Training Act 1973 or section 2 of the Enterprise and New Towns (Scotland) Act 1990;

(*b*) arrangements made by the Secretary of State for persons enlisted in Her Majesty's forces for any special term of service specified in regulations made under section 2 of the Armed Forces Act 1966 (power of Defence Council to make regulations as to engagement of persons in regular forces);

for purposes which include the training of persons who, at the beginning of their training, are under the age of 18.

[⁶(2A) Where any provision of these Regulations requires the income of a person to be estimated and that or any other provision of these Regulations requires that the amount of such estimated income is to be taken into account for any purpose after deducting from it a sum in respect of income tax or of primary Class 1 contributions under the Contributions and Benefits Act or of contributions paid by that person towards an occupational or personal pension scheme, then—

(*a*) the amount to be deducted in respect of income tax shall be calculated by applying to that income the rates of income tax applicable at the effective date less only the personal relief to which that person is entitled under Chapter 1 of Part VII of the Income and Corporations Taxes Act 1988 (personal relief); but if the period in respect of which that income is to be estimated is less than a year, the amount of the personal relief deductible under this sub-paragraph shall be calculated on a pro rata basis;

(*b*) the amount to be deducted in respect of Class 1 contributions under the Contributions and Benefits Act shall be calculated by applying to that income the appropriate primary percentage applicable in the relevant week; and

(c) the amount to be deducted in respect of contributions paid by that person towards an occupational or personal pension scheme shall be one-half of the sums so paid.]

(3) In these Regulations, unless the context otherwise requires, a reference—

(a) to a numbered Part is to the Part of these Regulations bearing that number;

(b) to a numbered Schedule is to the Schedule to these Regulations bearing that number;

(c) to a numbered regulation is to the regulation in these Regulations bearing that number;

(d) in a regulation or Schedule to a numbered paragraph is to the paragraph in that regulation or Schedule bearing that number;

(e) in a paragraph to a lettered or numbered sub-paragraph is to the sub-paragraph in that paragraph bearing that letter or number.

(4) The regulations in Part II and the provisions of the Schedules to these Regulations are subject to the regulations relating to special cases in Part III.

AMENDMENTS

1. Reg. 19(2)(b) of the Amendment Regulations (April 5, 1993).
2. Reg. 19(2)(a) of the Amendment Regulations (April 5, 1993).
3. Reg. 19(2)(c) of the Amendment Regulations (April 5, 1993).
4. Reg. 19(2)(d) of the Amendment Regulations (April 5, 1993).
5. Reg. 19(2)(e) of the Amendment Regulations (April 5, 1993).
6. Reg. 19(3) of the Amendment Regulations (April 5, 1993).

GENERAL NOTE

"day to day care"

For the problems produced by the concentration in this definition on overnight care see the general note to s.3(3) of the Act.

"partner"

A person's partner is defined as the other member of a couple or another member of a polygamous marriage who is living with the person. A couple may be married or unmarried. Each is defined in reg. 1(2). In the case of a married couple they must be of the opposite sex and be members of the same household. In the case of an unmarried couple they must be of the opposite sex and be living together as husband and wife. There is no reference to the need for an unmarried couple to be living in the same household. There may be exceptional cases in which a couple are not members of the same household, and there will be many cases in which a couple live together in the same household but not as husband and wife. Tribunals should, therefore, be alert to the possibility of an unusual case arising. Homosexuals are not recognised as a couple for the purposes of these definitions. Gender is fixed at birth, so a man who has changed sex and now lives with another man is not living with a partner for the purpose of this definition.

There is no single model of what constitutes a household or of what amounts to living together as husband and wife. There are nowadays a great variety of arrangements. Some allow couples a great deal of individual freedom within a relationship, while others which exist between unattached individuals are very similar to those which are often associated with couples. The proper approach to cases such as this is discussed in the general note to s.3 of the Act.

Household

A household is an abstract concept (*Santos* v. *Santos* [1972] 2 All E.R. 236 at 255 *per* Sachs, L.J.). It can survive changes of membership, as *R.* v. *Birmingham Juvenile Court, ex p. N.* [1984] 2 All E.R. 688 shows. The legal test concentrates on the arrangements of the persons concerned rather than the accommodation (*R.* v. *Birmingham Juvenile Court supra* at 691 *per* Arnold, P.). It is not possible to be a member of more than one household at a time (*R(SB) 8/85*).

Whether or not a couple are living in the same household is determined by an analysis of the objective facts of their living arrangements. Findings of fact are needed on the following: (i) The nature of the accommodation; (ii) The living arrangements within it, including the distribution of domestic duties and the way they spend their leisure time; (iii) The financial arrangements between the parties; (iv) It will also frequently be useful to investigate how and why the couple came to make the living arrangements which they did. The fact that an arrangement was entered into as a result of a shortage of funds, or in an emergency or in order to secure accommodation, for example, may point towards the couple operating separate households within shared accommodation. On the other hand shift work may explain arrangements which at first sight suggest that the two people are living separate lives; (v) The relationship between the couple will also be relevant. If a couple have a close relationship but keep their financial arrangements separate, their relationship may point nonetheless to there being a single household.

Particular care is needed in applying the criteria to arrangements which are just beginning or which are coming to an end (see the comments of Woolf, J., in *Crake* v. *Supplementary Benefits Commission* [1982] 1 All E.R. 498 at 502). A couple may be unwilling to mingle their lives inextricably at first. Alternatively, a developing relationship against a constant background of living arrangements may indicate that a single household has gradually been formed. At the other end of a relationship, it may prove difficult to separate lives which have been shared for a number of years, perhaps decades. In such cases small, perhaps unilateral, alterations in a couple's arrangements will indicate that separate households have been established. Although a household is an abstract concept and the legal test is not primarily concerned with the accommodation, there are limits to the possibilities of establishing separate households in cramped accommodation and in *Adeoso* v. *Adeoso* [1981] 1 All E.R. 107 at 110 Ormrod, L.J., said that it was not possible to form separate households in a two room flat.

Absences from the shared accommodation do not necessarily indicate that a couple are no longer living together (*Re M.* [1964] 2 All E.R. 1017 at 1024 *per* Buckley, J., and *Santos supra* at 251–3 *per* Sachs, L.J., and *R(SB) 30/83*), nor do they indicate that there is no longer a single household. It is necessary to consider the frequency and duration of the separations as well as the reasons for them.

Living as husband and wife

Financial arrangements within marriage are very varied, and equal if not greater variation is to be expected among unmarried couples. It has already been said, but bears emphasising, that tribunals must be alert both to the range of possible arrangements and to the need to investigate the reason for the arrangements. Arrangements which have an arms' length or even commercial appearance may have an explanation.

The fact that a couple are living in the same household is an important, perhaps essential, finding before they can be held to be living as husband and wife. However, of itself this is not sufficient to justify such a conclusion. It is necessary to investigate how and why they share a common household (*Crake* v. *Supplementary Benefits Commission* [1982] 1 All E.R. 498 at 502 *per* Woolf, J.). A number of matters have come to be considered as relevant factors in determining whether a couple are living as husband and wife, and a CSAT should investigate each.

Stability during the course of a relationship is an important indicator. Instability while not decisive against the couple living as husband and wife, would be an indicator in this direction. However stability need not and does not by itself show that a couple are living in this relationship.

How the couple are known to and seen by others is a factor to be considered. If the impression is one that has been created or encouraged by the parties (for example, by using the same surname as in *R(G) 1/74*), it will be a pointer towards the couple living as husband and wife. However, although how others view the couple is a relevant consideration (*Adeoso* v. *Adeoso* [1981] 1 All E.R. 107 at 109 *per* Ormrod, L.J.), the tribunal will need to be cautious for two reasons. First, this is less likely to be important when a relationship is first formed; according to Woolf J., in *Crake supra* at 502, *Adeoso* is to be interpreted as a case concerned with the termination rather than the inception of a relationship. Second, others may not have been motivated in forming their views by the full range of factors which a tribunal is required to take into account. The fact that a couple have retained separate identities is not so easy to interpret, since many married couples strive to retain their separate identity and do not use the same surname.

The fact that a couple have children whom they are bringing up together is a strong indication of their commitment to each other, the stability of their relationship and of how they are seen by others.

The sexual arrangements between the parties need to be investigated sensitively by the tribunal and the significance of the answers needs to be assessed carefully. It is possible, although unusual, for a married couple not to have a sexual relationship, so its absence may be a strong factor against a couple living together as husband and wife, although the age of the couple may be a factor as well as the possibility of impotence. However, the presence of a sexual relationship is by no means a decisive factor in favour of a couple living as husband and wife. It is an error of law not to investigate this aspect of a relationship, but it is an error of judgment to do so insensitively.

As with the decision whether there is a separate household so here it may be particularly difficult to analyse a relationship which is just beginning or just coming to an end. Obviously stability cannot be established at once and the parties' intentions or declared intentions will be relevant. Similarly the fact that a relationship has been stable in the past does not indicate that it has remained so.

PART II

CALCULATION OR ESTIMATION OF CHILD SUPPORT MAINTENANCE

Calculation or estimation of amounts

2.—(1) Where any amount falls to be taken into account for the purposes of these Regulations, it shall be calculated or estimated as a weekly amount and, except where the context otherwise requires, any reference to such an amount shall be construed accordingly.

(2) Subject to regulation 13(2), where any calculation made under these Regulations results in a fraction of a penny that fraction shall be treated as a penny if it is either one half or exceeds one half, otherwise it shall be disregarded.

(3) A child support officer shall calculate the amounts to be taken into account for the purposes of these Regulations by reference, as the case may be, to the dates, weeks, months or other periods specified herein provided that if he becomes aware of a material change of circumstances occurring after such date, week, month or other period but before the effective date, he shall take that change of circumstances into account.

DEFINITION
"effective date": see reg. 1(2).

Calculation of AG

3.—(1) The amounts to be taken into account for the purposes of calculating AG in the formula set out in paragraph 1(2) of Schedule 1 to the Act are—

(*a*) with respect to each qualifying child, an amount equal to the amount specified in column (2) of paragraph 2 of the relevant Schedule for a person of the same age (income support personal allowance for child or young person);

(*b*) with respect to a person with care of a qualifying child aged less than 16, an amount equal to the amount specified in column (2) of paragraph 1(1)(*e*) of the relevant Schedule (income support personal allowance for a single claimant aged not less than 25);

(*c*) an amount equal to the amount specified in paragraph 3 of the relevant Schedule (income support family premium);

(*d*) where the person with care of the qualifying child or children has no partner, an amount equal to the amount specified in paragraph 15(1) of the relevant Schedule (income support lone parent premium).

(2) The amounts referred to in paragraph (1) shall be the amounts applicable at the effective date.

DEFINITIONS
"the Act": see reg. 1(2).
"effective date": *ibid.*
"partner": *ibid.*
"relevant Schedule": *ibid.*

GENERAL NOTE
This regulation fixes the value of AG for the purposes of Sched. 1, para. 1 to the Act.

Para. (1)
It is important to remember that the purpose of taking these amounts into account is to fix the maintenance requirement for the child. Although some of the figures are the personal allowances or premiums which reflect the circumstances of the person with care, it is no part of this calculation to fix any maintenance for a spouse or former spouse who has care of the child. It is for the courts rather than the

child support officer or a CSAT to fix maintenance for spouses and former spouses. The use of these figures will not affect the figure fixed by the courts, although the courts will no doubt consider the likely outcome of any maintenance assessment when deciding upon a spouse's periodical payments. The fact that maintenance may have been fixed at a lower rate by a court will not affect the calculation of a child's maintenance requirement, but see the Maintenance Orders (Backdating) Order 1993 for the circumstances where spousal maintenance might be increased in the light of a maintenance assessment.

Sub-paras. (1)(b) to (d)

The amounts under these sub-paragraphs need to be modified where the person with care is the person with care of two or more children, and in respect of at least two of those children there are different persons who are or who are treated as absent parents. This is a special case by virtue of reg. 23. In this case the amounts are divided by the number of persons who are or who are treated as absent parents. For this purpose if both parents of a child are or are treated as absent parents, they count as one (reg. 23(2) and (3)).

Sub-para. (1)(d)

The lone parent premium is not included in a case where the person with care is a body of persons corporate or unincorporate and both parents are absent parents (reg. 19(2)(*c*)).

Para. (2)

The effective date is determined under Sched. 1, para. 11 to the Act and regs. 30 and 31 of the Maintenance Assessment Procedure Regulations.

Basic rate of child benefit

4. For the purposes of paragraph 1(4) of Schedule 1 to the Act "basic rate" means the rate of child benefit which is specified in regulation 2(1) of the Child Benefit and Social Security (Fixing and Adjustment of Rates) Regulations 1976 (rates of child benefit) applicable to the child in question at the effective date.

DEFINITIONS
"the Act": see reg. 1(2).
"effective date": *ibid.*

GENERAL NOTE

This regulation fixes the value of CB for the purposes of Sched. 1, para. 1 to the Act. It does so by reference to the Child Benefit and Social Security (Fixing and Adjustment of Rates) Regulations 1976. Accordingly the value of CB will differ according to whether or not the child in question is the only, elder or eldest child for whom the person with care is responsible. Only child benefit is deducted. The child benefit increase, which is sometimes known as one parent benefit, is not deducted.

The general rule

5. For the purposes of paragraph 2(1) of Schedule 1 to the Act—
 (*a*) the value of C, otherwise than in a case where the other parent is the person with care, is nil; and
 (*b*) the value of P is 0.5.

DEFINITION
"the Act": see reg. 1(2).

GENERAL NOTE

This regulation fixes the value of C and P under Sched. 1, para. 2 to the Act for the purpose of determining the amount of any maintenance assessment. The value of P is also used in the calculation of the basic element under Sched. 1, para. 3 in cases where the figure calculated under para. 2 exceeds the maintenance requirement.

The additional element

6.—(1) For the purposes of the formula in paragraph 4(1) of Schedule 1 to the Act, the value of R is 0.25.

(2) For the purposes of the alternative formula in paragraph 4(3) of Schedule 1 to the Act—

(*a*) the value of Z is 3;

(*b*) the amount for the purposes of paragraph (*b*) of the definition of Q is the same as the amount specified in regulation 3(1)(*c*) (income support family premium) in respect of each qualifying child.

DEFINITION

"the Act": see reg. 1(2).

GENERAL NOTE

Para. (1)

This paragraph fixes the share of the absent parent's assessable income which is used for the calculation of the additional element of child support maintenance in all cases except where the ceiling set by Sched. 1, para. 4(3) to the Act applies.

Para. (2)

This paragraph fixes the value of Z and prescribes one of the values to be taken into account in fixing the value of Q for the purpose of calculating the ceiling to the additional element of child support maintenance under Sched. 1, para. 4(3) to the Act.

Net income: calculation or estimation of N

7.—(1) Subject to the following provisions of this regulation, for the purposes of the formula in paragraph 5(1) of Schedule 1 to the Act, the amount of N (net income of absent parent) shall be the aggregate of the following amounts—

(*a*) the amount, determined in accordance with Part I of Schedule 1, of any earnings of the absent parent;

(*b*) the amount, determined in accordance with Part II of Schedule 1, of any benefit payments under the Contributions and Benefits Act paid to or in respect of the absent parent;

(*c*) the amount, determined in accordance with Part III of Schedule 1, of any other income of the absent parent;

(*d*) the amount, determined in accordance with Part IV of Schedule 1, of any income of a relevant child which is treated as the income of the absent parent;

(*e*) any amount, determined in accordance with Part V of Schedule 1, which is treated as the income of the absent parent.

(2) Any amounts referred to in Schedule 2 shall be disregarded.

(3) Where an absent parent's income consists—

(*a*) only of a youth training allowance; or

(*b*) in the case of a student, only of grant, an amount paid in respect of grant contribution or student loan or any combination thereof; or

(*c*) only of prisoner's pay,

then for the purposes of determining N such income shall be disregarded.

(4) Where a parent and any other person are beneficially entitled to any income but the shares of their respective entitlements are not ascertainable the child support officer shall estimate their respective entitlements having regard to such information as is available but where sufficient information on which to base an estimate is not available the parent and that other person shall be treated as entitled to that income in equal shares.

(5) Where any income normally received at regular intervals has not been re-

ceived it shall, if it is due to be paid and there are reasonable grounds for believing it will be received, be treated as if it had been received.

DEFINITIONS
"the Act": see reg. 1(2).
"Contributions and Benefits Act": *ibid.*
"earnings": *ibid.*
"effective date": *ibid.*
"grant": *ibid.*
"grant contribution": *ibid.*
"person": *ibid.*
"prisoner": *ibid.*
"student": *ibid.*
"student loan": *ibid.*
"training allowance": *ibid.*

GENERAL NOTE
This regulation provides for the calculation of an absent parent's net income for the purposes of Sched. 1, para. 5(1) to the Act. The net income of a parent who is a person with care for the purpose of para. 5(2) is calculated on the same basis (reg. 8).

Para. (1)
The calculation of net income takes account of the actual and deemed income of the parent, calculated in accordance with this regulation and Scheds. 1 and 2 to these Regulations. It covers the earnings, benefits and other income of the parent together with amounts which are treated as income of that parent. The calculation is, therefore, based on real figures rather than on the amounts fixed by reference to the Income Support Schedule.

Para. (2)
In addition to the items referred to in Sched. 2, the items referred to in para. (3) are disregarded, if they are the parent's only income.

Para. (4)
This paragraph applies where a parent is beneficially entitled to income together with someone else. It only applies to determine the respective share of entitlement of each party to income. It does not allow an estimate to be made of what that income is. Still less does it allow an estimate to be made of income when there is no question of shared entitlement. It will, therefore, be of no help where a parent is in business alone or with another but either has no accounts or refuses to produce them. The order in which to consider the application of this paragraph is as follows: (i) Is there evidence of the respective shares of the income? This may take the form of an express agreement or it may be implicit in, for example, the past practice of the parties. If there is such evidence, no problem arises; (ii) If there is no such evidence, it may be possible to reach a decision by the application of a presumption, for example that the property producing the income is held in proportion to the contribution of each party to its purchase price or that partners share equally in the profits of a business; (iii) If the parent's share of the income cannot be calculated in either of the ways so far considered, is there any evidence which will allow it to be estimated? An estimate is a conclusion which is reached by a rougher and readier method than a calculation. Uncertainty is inherent in this approach and there will be less confidence in its accuracy than in the result of a calculation. However, an estimate is more than a guess and must be based on sufficient evidence to allow a reasonably accurate figure to be reached. Whether or not sufficient evidence exists is a question of degree; (iv) Only if there is no basis for either a calculation or an estimate will the equal shares presumption in this paragraph be applied.

Para. (5)
This is likely to represent a problem for a child support officer rather than for a CSAT. By the time a case progresses to a tribunal, or even to a review under s.18 of the Act, it will have become clear whether or not the income has been received. Strictly, the test is whether reasonable grounds exist for believing that it will be received and not whether the passage of time shows that it has or has not been received. However the paragraph is silent as to the time at which the existence of reasonable grounds should be tested. An appeal before a CSAT is by way of a complete rehearing and the tribunal may take account of evidence which has become available since the child support officer's decision was made, so the practical approach may well be taken that regard should be had to the true position once it has become clear.

187

Net income: calculation or estimation of M

8. For the purposes of paragraph 5(2) of Schedule 1 to the Act, the amount of M (net income of the parent with care) shall be calculated in the same way as N is calculated under regulation 7 but as if references to the absent parent were references to the parent with care.

DEFINITIONS
"the Act": see reg. 1(2).
"parent with care": *ibid.*

GENERAL NOTE
See the general note to reg. 7.

Exempt income: calculation or estimation of E

9.—(1) For the purposes of paragraph 5(1) of Schedule 1 to the Act, the amount of E (exempt income of absent parent) shall, subject to paragraphs (3) and (4), be the aggregate of the following amounts—

   (a)   an amount equal to the amount specified in column (2) of paragraph 1(1)(e) of the relevant Schedule (income support personal allowance for a single claimant aged not less than 25);

   (b)   an amount in respect of housing costs determined in accordance with regulations 14 to 18;

   (c)   where—

      (i) the absent parent is the parent of a relevant child; and

     (ii) if he were a claimant, the condition in paragraph 8 of the relevant Schedule (income support lone parent premium) would be satisfied but the conditions referred to in sub-paragraph (1)(d) would not be satisfied;

an amount equal to the amount specified in column (2) of paragraph 15(1) of that Schedule (income support lone parent premium);

   (d)   where, if the parent were a claimant aged less than 60, the conditions in paragraph 11 of the relevant Schedule (income support disability premium) would be satisfied in respect of him, an amount equal to the amount specified in column (2) of paragraph 15(4)(a) of that Schedule (income support disability premium);

   (e)   where—

      (i) if the parent were a claimant, the conditions in paragraph 13 of the relevant Schedule (income support severe disability premium) would be satisfied, an amount equal to the amount specified in column (2) of paragraph 15(5)(a) of that Schedule (except that no such amount shall be taken into account in the case of an absent parent in respect of whom an invalid care allowance under section 70 of the Contributions and Benefits Act is payable to some other person);

     (ii) if the parent were a claimant, the conditions in paragraph 14ZA of the relevant Schedule (income support carer premium) would be satisfied in respect of him, an amount equal to the amount specified in column (2) of paragraph 15(7) of that Schedule;

   (f)   where, if the parent were a claimant, the conditions in paragraph 3 of the relevant Schedule (income support family premium) would be satisfied in respect of a relevant child of that parent, the amount specified in that paragraph or, where those conditions would be satisfied only by virtue of the case being one to which paragraph (2) applies, half that amount;

   (g)   in respect of each relevant child—

      (i) an amount equal to the amount of the personal allowance for that child, specified in column (2) of paragraph 2 of the relevant Schedule (income support personal allowance) or, where paragraph (2) applies, half that amount;

    (ii) if the conditions set out in paragraph 14(*b*) and (*c*) of the relevant Schedule (income support disabled child premium) are satisfied in respect of that child, an amount equal to the amount specified in column (2) of paragraph 15(6) of the relevant Schedule or, where paragraph (2) applies, half that amount;

  (*h*) where the absent parent in question or his partner is living in—

    (i) accommodation provided under Part III of the National Assistance Act 1948;

    (ii) accommodation provided under paragraphs 1 and 2 of Schedule 8 to the National Health Service Act 1977; or

    (iii) a nursing home or residential care home;

the amount of the fees paid in respect of the occupation of that accommodation or, as the case may be, that home.

(2) This paragraph applies where—

  (*a*) the absent parent has a partner;

  (*b*) the absent parent and the partner are parents of the same relevant child; and

  (*c*) the income of the partner, calculated under regulation 7(1) [[1](but excluding the amount mentioned in sub-paragraph (*d*) of that regulation)] as if that partner were an absent parent to whom that regulation applied, exceeds the aggregate of—

    (i) the amount specified in column 2 of paragraph 1(1)(*e*) of the relevant Schedule (income support personal allowance for a single claimant aged not less than 25);

    (ii) half the amount of the personal allowance for that child specified in column (2) of paragraph 2 of the relevant Schedule (income support personal allowance);

    (iii) half the amount of any income support disabled child premium specified in column (2) of paragraph 15(6) of that Schedule in respect of that child;

    (iv) half the amount of any income support family premium specified in paragraph 3 of the Schedule except where such premium is payable irrespective of that child; and

    (v) the amount by which the housing costs of the absent parent, calculated in accordance with these Regulations, have been reduced by an apportionment under regulation 17.

(3) Where an absent parent does not have day to day care of any relevant child for 7 nights each week but does have day to day care of one or more such children for fewer than 7 nights each week, any amounts to be taken into account under sub-paragraphs (1)(*c*) and (*f*) shall be reduced so that they bear the same proportion to the amounts referred to in those sub-paragraphs as the average number of nights each week in respect of which such care is provided has to 7.

(4) Where an absent parent has day to day care of a relevant child for fewer than 7 nights each week, any amounts to be taken into account under sub-paragraph (1) (*g*) in respect of such a child shall be reduced so that they bear the same proportion to the amounts referred to in that sub-paragraph as the average number of nights each week in respect of which such care is provided has to 7.

(5) The amounts referred to in paragraph (1) are the amounts applicable at the effective date.

AMENDMENT

  1. Reg. 20 of the Amendment Regulations (April 5, 1993).

DEFINITIONS

  "the Act": see reg. 1(2).

  "claimant": *ibid*.

"Contributions and Benefits Act": *ibid.*
"day to day care": *ibid.*
"effective date": *ibid.*
"nursing home": *ibid.*
"partner": *ibid.*
"relevant child": *ibid.*
"relevant Schedule": *ibid.*
"residential care home": *ibid.*

GENERAL NOTE
Paras. (3) and (4)
For other ways in which the shared financial costs of bringing up children may be taken into account, see regs. 11(3) and (4), 24 and 25 and the general notes thereto.

Exempt income: calculation or estimation of F

10. For the purposes of paragraph 5(2) of Schedule 1 to the Act, the amount of F (exempt income of parent with care) shall be calculated in the same way as E is calculated under regulation 9 but as if references to the absent parent were references to the parent with care [¹except that paragraphs (3) and (4) of that regulation shall apply only in a case where the parent with care shares day to day care of the child mentioned in those paragraphs with one or more other persons.]

AMENDMENT
1.   Reg. 21 of the Amendment Regulations (April 5, 1993).

DEFINITIONS
"the Act": see reg. 1(2).
"day to day care": *ibid.*
"parent with care": *ibid.*

Protected income

11.—(1) For the purposes of paragraph 6 of Schedule 1 to the Act the protected income level of an absent parent shall, subject to paragraphs (3) and (4), be the aggregate of the following amounts—
 (*a*) where—
   (i) absent parent does not have a partner, an amount equal to the amount specified in column (2) of paragraph 1(1)(*e*) of the relevant Schedule (income support personal allowance for a single claimant aged not less than 25 years);
   (ii) the absent parent has a partner, an amount equal to the amount specified in column (2) of paragraph 1(3)(*c*) of the relevant Schedule (income support personal allowance for a couple where both members are aged not less than 18 years);
   (iii) the absent parent is a member of a polygamous marriage, an amount in respect of himself and one of his partners, equal to the amount specified in sub-paragraph (ii) and, in respect of each of his other partners, an amount equal to the difference between the amounts specified in sub-paragraph (ii) and sub-paragraph (i);
 (*b*) an amount in respect of housing costs determined in accordance with regulations 14, 15, 16 and 18, or, in a case where the absent parent is a non-dependant member of a household who is treated as having no housing costs by regulation 15(10)(*a*), the non-dependant amount which would be calculated in respect of him under regulation 15(5);
 (*c*) where, if the absent parent were a claimant, the condition in paragraph 8 of the relevant Schedule (income support lone parent premium) would be

satisfied but the condition set out in paragraph 11 of that Schedule (income support disability premium) would not be satisfied, an amount equal to the amount specified in column (2) of paragraph 15(1) of that Schedule (income support lone parent premium);

(*d*) where, if the parent were a claimant, the conditions in paragraph 11 of the relevant Schedule (income support disability premium) would be satisfied, an amount equal to the amount specified in column (2) of paragraph 15(4) of that Schedule (income support disability premium);

(*e*) where, if the parent were a claimant, the conditions in paragraph 13 or 14ZA of the relevant Schedule (income support severe disability and carer premiums) would be satisfied in respect of either or both premiums, an amount equal to the amount or amounts specified in column (2) of paragraph 15(5) or, as the case may be, (7) of that Schedule in respect of that or those premiums (income support premiums);

(*f*) where, if the parent were a claimant, the conditions in paragraph 3 of the relevant Schedule (income support family premium) would be satisfied, the amount specified in that paragraph;

(*g*) in respect of each child who is a member of the family of the absent parent—

  (i) an amount equal to the amount of the personal allowance for that child, specified in column (2) of paragraph 2 of the relevant Schedule (income support personal allowance);

  (ii) if the conditions set out in paragraphs 14(*b*) and (*c*) of the relevant Schedule (income support disabled child premium) are satisfied in respect of that child, an amount equal to the amount specified in column (2) of paragraph 15(6) of the relevant Schedule;

(*h*) where, if the parent were a claimant, the conditions specified in Part III of the relevant Schedule would be satisfied by the absent parent in question or any member of his family in relation to any premium not otherwise included in this regulation, an amount equal to the amount specified in Part IV of that Schedule (income support premiums) in respect of that premium;

(*i*) where the absent parent in question or his partner is living in—

  (i) accommodation provided under Part III of the National Assistance Act 1948;

  (ii) accommodation provided under paragraphs 1 and 2 of Schedule 8 to the National Health Service Act 1977; or

  (iii) a nursing home or residential care home,

the amount of the fees paid in respect of the occupation of that accommodation or, as the case may be, that home;

(*j*) the amount of council tax which the absent parent in question or his partner is liable to pay in respect of the home for which housing costs are included under sub-paragraph (*b*) less any council tax benefit;

(*k*) an amount of £8.00;

(*l*) where the income of—

  (i) the absent parent in question;

  (ii) any partner of his; and

  (iii) any child or children for whom an amount is included under sub-paragraph (*g*)(i);

exceeds the sum of the amounts to which reference is made in sub-paragraphs (*a*) to (*k*), 10 per centum of the excess.

(2) For the purposes of sub-paragraph (*l*) of paragraph (1) "income" shall be calculated—

(*a*) in respect of the absent parent in question or any partner of his, in the same manner as N (net income of absent parent) is calculated under regulation 7 except—

  (i) there shall be taken into account the basic rate of any child benefit and any maintenance which in either case is in payment in respect of any member of the family of the absent parent;

    (ii) there shall be deducted the amount of any maintenance under a maintenance order which the absent parent or his partner is paying in respect of a child in circumstances where an application for a maintenance assessment could not be made in accordance with the Act in respect of that child; and

  (b) in respect of any child in that family, as being the total of that child's income but only to the extent that such income does not exceed the amount included under sub-paragraph (g) of paragraph (1) (income support personal allowance for a child and income support disabled child premium) reduced, as the case may be, under paragraph (4).

(3) Where an absent parent does not have day to day care of any child (whether or not a relevant child) for 7 nights each week but does have day to day care of one or more such children for fewer than 7 nights each week, any amounts to be taken into account under sub-paragraphs (c) and (f) of paragraph (1) (income support lone parent premium and income support family premium) shall be reduced so that they bear the same proportion to the amounts referred to in those sub-paragraphs as the average number of nights each week in respect of which such care is provided has to 7.

(4) Where an absent parent has day to day care of a child (whether or not a relevant child) for fewer than 7 nights each week any amounts in relation to that child to be taken into account under sub-paragraph (g) of paragraph (1) (income support personal allowance for child and income support disabled child premium) shall be reduced so that they bear the same proportion to the amounts referred to in that sub-paragraph as the average number of nights in respect of which such care is provided has to 7.

(5) The amounts referred to in paragraph (1) shall be the amounts applicable at the effective date.

DEFINITIONS
  "the Act": see reg. 1(2).
  "claimant": *ibid.*
  "council tax benefit": *ibid.*
  "couple": *ibid.*
  "effective date": *ibid.*
  "family": *ibid.*
  "non-dependant": *ibid.*
  "nursing home": *ibid.*
  "partner": *ibid.*
  "polygamous marriage": *ibid.*
  "relevant Schedule": *ibid.*
  "residential care home": *ibid.*

GENERAL NOTE
Para. (1)
  This paragraph provides a definitive statement of the elements which together constitute protected income. No other items are included, regardless of their importance or of any obligation (legal or otherwise) to make the payments. Contributions towards a student's education costs, and the costs of keeping in touch with the parent's children, for example, are not taken into account.

Sub-para. (1)(b)
  The circumstances of the whole family are considered when determining protected income, so there is no apportionment of housing costs.

Sub-para. (1)(l)
  The effect of including this ten per cent. in protected income is to prevent any increase in income being clawed back in maintenance, thereby providing a disincentive to increase income.

For other ways in which the shared financial costs of bringing up children may be taken into account, see regs. 9(3) and (4), 24 and 25 and the general notes thereto.

Disposable income

12.—(1) For the purposes of paragraph 6(4) of Schedule 1 to the Act (protected income), the disposable income of an absent parent shall be the aggregate of his income and any income of any member of his family calculated in like manner as under regulation 11(2).

(2) Subject to paragraph (3), where a maintenance assessment has been made with respect to the absent parent and payment of the amount of that assessment would reduce his disposable income below his protected income level the amount of the assessment shall be reduced by the minimum amount necessary to prevent his disposable income being reduced below his protected income level.

(3) Where the prescribed minimum amount fixed by regulations under paragraph 7 of Schedule 1 to the Act is applicable (such amount being specified in regulation 13) the amount payable under the assessment shall not be reduced to less than the prescribed minimum amount.

DEFINITIONS
"the Act": see reg. 1(2).
"family": *ibid.*

The minimum amount

13.—(1) Subject to regulation 26, for the purposes of paragraph 7(1) of Schedule 1 to the Act the minimum amount shall be for 5 per centum of the amount specified in paragraph 1(1)(*e*) of the relevant Schedule (income support personal allowance for single claimant aged not less than 25).

(2) Where an amount calculated under paragraph (1) results in a sum other than a multiple of 5 pence, it shall be treated as the sum which is the next higher multiple of 5 pence.

DEFINITION
"the Act": see reg. 1(2).

Eligible housing costs

14. Schedule 3 shall have effect for the purpose of determining the costs which are eligible to be taken into account as housing costs for the purposes of these Regulations.

Amount of housing costs

15.—(1) Subject to the provisions of this regulation and regulations 16 to 18, a parent's housing costs shall be the aggregate of the eligible housing costs payable in respect of his home.

(2) Where a local authority has determined that a parent is entitled to housing benefit, the amount of his housing costs shall, subject to paragraphs (4) to (9), be the weekly amount treated as rent under regulations 10 and 69 of the Housing Benefit Regulations (rent and calculation of weekly amounts) less the amount of housing benefit.

(3) Where a parent has eligible housing costs and another person who is not a member of his family is also liable to make payments in respect of the home, the amount of the parent's housing costs shall be his share of those costs.

(4) Where one or more non-dependants are members of the parent's household,

there shall be deducted from the amount of any housing costs determined under the preceding paragraphs of this regulation any non-dependant amount or amounts determined in accordance with the provisions of paragraphs (5) to (9).

(5) The non-dependant amount shall be an amount equal to the amount which would be calculated under [¹paragraphs (1), (2) and (9) of regulation 63] of the Housing Benefit Regulations (non-dependant deductions) for the non-dependant in question if he were a non-dependant in respect of whom a calculation were to be made under [²those paragraphs (disregarding any other provision of that regulation)].

(6) For the purposes of paragraph (5)—

    (*a*)   in the case of a couple or, as the case may be, the members of a polygamous marriage—

        (i) regard shall be had to their joint weekly income; and

       (ii) only one deduction shall be made at whichever is the higher rate.

(7) Where a person is a non-dependant in respect of more than one joint occupier of a dwelling (except where the joint occupiers are a couple or members of a polygamous marriage), the deduction in respect of that non-dependant shall be apportioned between the joint occupiers having regard to the number of joint occupiers and the proportion of the housing costs in respect of the home payable by each of them.

(8) No deduction shall be made in respect of any non-dependants occupying the home of the parent, if the parent or any partner of his is—

    (*a*)   blind or treated as blind by virtue of paragraph 12 of the relevant Schedule (income support additional condition for the higher pensioner and disability premiums); or

    (*b*)   receiving in respect of himself either—

        (i) attendance allowance under section 64 of the Contributions and Benefits Act; or

       (ii) the care component of disability living allowance.

(9) No deduction shall be made in respect of a non-dependant—

    (*a*)   if, although he resides with the parent, it appears to the child support officer that his home is normally elsewhere; or

    (*b*)   if he is in receipt of a training allowance paid in connection with a Youth Training Programme established under section 2 of the Employment and Training Act 1973 or section 2 of the Enterprise and New Towns (Scotland) Act 1990; or

    (*c*)   if he is a student; or

    (*d*)   if he is aged under 25 and in receipt of income support; or

    (*e*)   if he is not residing with the parent because he is a prisoner or because he has been a patient for a period, or two or more periods separated by not more than 28 days, exceeding 6 weeks.

(10) A parent shall be treated as having no housing costs where—

    (*a*)   he is a non-dependant member of a household and is not responsible for meeting housing costs except to another member, or other members, of that household; or

    (*b*)   but for this paragraph, his housing costs would be less than nil.

AMENDMENT

    1.   Regulation 22 of the Amendment Regulations (April 5, 1993).

    2.   Regulation 22 of the Amendment Regulations (April 5, 1993).

DEFINITIONS

    "Contributions and Benefits Act": see reg. 1(2).

    "couple": *ibid.*

    "eligible housing costs": *ibid.*

    "family": *ibid.*

    "home": *ibid.*

"housing benefit": *ibid.*
"Housing Benefit Regulations": *ibid.*
"Income Support Regulations": *ibid.*
"non-dependant": *ibid.*
"partner": *ibid.*
"patient": *ibid.*
"polygamous marriage": *ibid.*
"prisoner": *ibid.*
"student": *ibid.*
"training allowance": *ibid.*

Weekly amount of housing costs

16. Where a parent pays housing costs—
(*a*) on a weekly basis, the amount of such housing costs shall be the weekly rate payable at the effective date;
(*b*) on a monthly basis, the amount of such housing costs shall be the monthly rate payable at the effective date, multiplied by 12 and divided by 52;
(*c*) on any other basis, the amount of such housing costs shall be the rate payable at the effective date, multiplied by the number of payment periods, or the nearest whole number of payment periods (any fraction of one half being rounded up), falling within a period of 365 days and divided by 52.

DEFINITION
  "effective date": see reg. 1(2).

Apportionment of housing costs: exempt income

17. For the purposes of calculating or estimating exempt income the amount of the housing costs of a parent shall be—
(*a*) where the parent does not have a partner, the whole amount of the housing costs;
(*b*) where the parent has a partner, the proportion of the amount of the housing costs calculated by multiplying those costs by—

$$\frac{0.75 + (A \times 0.2)}{1.00 + (B \times 0.2)}$$

where—
A is the number of relevant children (if any);
B is the number of children in that parent's family (if any);
(*c*) where the parent is a member of a polygamous marriage the proportion of the amount of the housing costs calculated by multiplying those costs by—

$$\frac{0.75 + (A \times 0.2)}{1.00 + (X \times 0.25) + (B \times 0.2)}$$

where—
A and B have the same meanings as in sub-paragraph (*b*); and
X is the number which is one less than the number of partners.

DEFINITIONS
  "partner": see reg. 1(2).
  "polygamous marriage": *ibid.*
  "relevant child": *ibid.*

Excessive housing costs

18.—1 Subject to paragraph (2), the amount of the housing costs of an absent parent which are to be taken into account—

(a) under regulation 9(1)(b) shall not exceed the greater of £80.00 or half the amount of N as calculated or estimated under regulation 7;

(b) under regulation 11(1)(b) shall not exceed the greater of £80.00 or half of the amount calculated in accordance with regulation 11(2).

(2) The restriction imposed by paragraph (1) shall not apply where—

(a) the absent parent in question—

   (i) has been awarded housing benefit (or is awaiting the outcome of a claim to that benefit);

  (ii) has the day to day care of any child; or

 (iii) is a person to whom a disability premium under paragraph 11 of the relevant Schedule applies in respect of himself or his partner or would so apply if he were entitled to income support and were aged less than 60;

(b) the absent parent in question, following a divorce from, or the breakdown of his relationship with, his former partner, remains in the home he occupied with his former partner;

(c) the absent parent in question has paid the housing costs under the mortgage, charge or agreement in question for a period in excess of 52 weeks before the date of the first application for child support maintenance in relation to a qualifying child of his and there has been no increase in those costs other than an increase in the interest payable under the mortgage or charge or, as the case may be, in the amount payable under the agreement under which the home is held;

(d) the housing costs in respect of the home in question would not exceed the amount set out in paragraph (1) but for an increase in the interest payable under a mortgage or charge secured on that home or, as the case may be, in the amount payable under any agreement under which it is held; or

(e) the absent parent is responsible for making payments in respect of housing costs which are higher than they would be otherwise by virtue of the unavailability of his share of the equity of the property formerly occupied with his partner and which remains occupied by that former partner.

DEFINITIONS

"day to day care": see reg. 1(2).
"home": *ibid.*
"housing benefit": *ibid.*
"partner": *ibid.*
"relevant Schedule": *ibid.*

PART III

SPECIAL CASES

Both parents are absent

19.—(1) Subject to regulation 27, where the circumstances of a case are that each parent of a qualifying child is an absent parent in relation to that child (neither being a person who is treated as an absent parent by regulation 20(2)) that case shall be treated as a special case for the purposes of the Act.

(2) For the purposes of this case—

(a) where the application is made in relation to both absent parents, separate assessments shall be made under Schedule 1 to the Act in respect of each so as to determine the amount of child support maintenance payable by each absent parent;

(b) subject to paragraph (3), where the application is made in relation to both absent parents, the value of C in each case shall be the assessable income of the other absent parent and where the application is made in relation to only one the value of C in the case of the other shall be nil;

(c) where the person with care is a body of persons corporate or unincorporate, the value of AG shall not include any amount mentioned in regulation 3(1) (d) (income support lone parent premium).

(3) Where, for the purposes of paragraph (2)(b), information regarding the income of the other absent parent has not been submitted to the Secretary of State or to a child support officer within the period specified in regulation 6(1) of the Maintenance Assessment Procedure Regulations then until such information is acquired the value of C shall be nil.

(4) When the information referred to in paragraph (3) is acquired the child support officer shall make a fresh assessment which shall have effect from the effective date in relation to that other absent parent.

DEFINITIONS
"the Act": see reg. 1(2).
"effective date": *ibid.*
"Maintenance Assessment Procedure Regulations": *ibid.*
"person": *ibid.*

GENERAL NOTE
This special case applies where both parents of a qualifying child are absent parents. It does not apply when a child has only one parent and that parent is an absent parent. For a discussion reference should be made to the general notes to reg. 3 above and to ss.11 and 12 of, and Sched. 1 to, the Act.

Persons treated as absent parents

20.—(1) Where the circumstances of a case are that—

(a) two or more persons who do not live in the same household each provide day to day care for the same qualifying child; and

(b) at least one of those persons is a parent of that child,

that case shall be treated as a special case for the purposes of the Act.

(2) For the purposes of this case a parent who provides day to day care for a child of his in the following circumstances is to be treated as an absent parent for the purposes of the Act and these Regulations—

(a) a parent who provides such care to a lesser extent that the other parent, person or persons who provide such care for the child in question;

(b) where the persons mentioned in paragraph (1)(a) include both parents and the circumstances are such that care is provided to the same extent by both but each provides care to a greater or equal extent than any other person who provides such care for that child—

(i) the parent who is not in receipt of child benefit for the child in question; or

(ii) if neither parent is in receipt of child benefit for that child, the parent who, in the opinion of the child support officer, will not be the principal provider of day to day care for that child.

(3) Subject to paragraphs (5) and (6), where a parent is treated as an absent parent under paragraph (2) child support maintenance shall be payable by that

parent in respect of the child in question and the amount of the child support maintenance so payable shall be calculated in accordance with the formula set out in paragraph (4).

(4) The formula for the purposes of paragraph (3) is—

$$T = X - \left\{ (X+Y) \times \frac{J}{7 \times L} \right\}$$

where—

T is the amount of child support maintenance payable;

X is the amount of child support maintenance which would be payable by the parent who is treated as an absent parent, assessed under Schedule 1 to the Act as if paragraphs 6 and 7 of that Schedule did not apply, and, where the other parent is an absent parent, as if the value of C was the assessable income of the other parent;

Y is—

  (i) the amount of child support maintenance assessed under Schedule 1 to the Act payable by the other parent if he is an absent parent or which would be payable if he were an absent parent, and for the purposes of such calculation the value of C shall be the assessable income of the parent treated as an absent parent under sub-paragraph (2); or,

  (ii) if there is no such other parent, shall be nil;

J is the total of the weekly average number of nights for which day to day care is provided by the person who is treated as the absent parent in respect of each child included in the maintenance assessment and shall be calculated to 2 decimal places;

L is the number of children who are included in the maintenance assessment in question.

(5) Where the value of T calculated under the provisions of paragraph (4) is less than zero, no child support maintenance shall be payable.

(6) The liability to pay any amount calculated under paragraph (4) shall be subject to the provision made for protected income and minimum payments under paragraphs 6 and 7 of Schedule 1 to the Act.

DEFINITIONS
"the Act": see reg. 1(2).
"day to day care": *ibid.*
"person": *ibid.*

GENERAL NOTE
The typical case to which this special case will apply is where care of a child is split between the child's parents, although it is not so limited. For additional discussion to that below reference should be made to the general note to s.3 of the Act.

Para. (1)
If neither parent is concerned in the day to day care of the child, reg. 24 applies.

Para. (2)
In deciding whether someone provides day to day care and if so for how many nights, reg. 27 is ignored. This can produce the result that a person is a person with care under s.3(3) of the Act but is treated as an absent parent under this regulation. If, for example, a child lives with one parent at weekends and is a boarder at school during the week but stays with the other parent on weekdays in the school holidays, that other parent may be a person with care for the purposes of s.3 by virtue of reg. 27, but will be treated as an absent parent under this regulation.

Para. (4)
Put crudely the effect of the formula is as follows: If the person who is treated as an absent parent is the only parent of the child, that person pays the proportion of the assessment in respect of each child which represents the number of nights on average each week that the child spends in someone else's care. If there is also another parent of the child, the formula takes account of the assessment which would be made in respect of that parent on the assumption that that parent was an absent parent. (In such

a case reg. 21 will apply.) In this case, the formula takes an amount equal to the proportion of the joint assessments for the parents which represents the number of nights on average per week which the child spends in the care of the person who is treated as an absent parent and deducts that figure from the assessment for that person. If the result in either case is less than zero, no child support maintenance is payable. The effect of the protected income level and minimum amount of child support maintenance (Sched. 1, paras. 6 and 7 to the Act) is disregarded until these calculations have been made (para. (6).)

One parent is absent and the other is treated as absent

21.—(1) Where the circumstances of a case are that one parent is an absent parent and the other parent is treated as an absent parent by regulation 20(2), that case shall be treated as a special case for the purposes of the Act.

(2) For the purpose of assessing the child support maintenance payable by an absent parent where this case applies, each reference in Schedule 1 to the Act to a parent who is a person with care shall be treated as a reference to a person who is treated as an absent parent by regulation 20(2).

DEFINITION
   "the Act": see reg. 1(2).

GENERAL NOTE
   For a discussion reference should be made to the general note to s.3 of, and Sched. 1 to, the Act.

Multiple applications relating to an absent parent

22.—(1) Where the circumstances of a case are that—
(a) two or more applications for a maintenance assessment have been made which relate to the same absent parent (or to a person who is treated as an absent parent by regulation 20(2)); and
(b) those applications relate to different children,
that case shall be treated as a special case for the purposes of the Act.

(2) For the purposes of assessing the amount of child support maintenance payable in respect of each application where paragraph (1) applies, for references to the assessable income of an absent parent in the Act and in these Regulations there shall be substituted references to the amount calculated by the formula—

$$A \times \frac{B}{D}$$

where—
A is the assessable income of the absent parent;
B is the maintenance requirement calculated in respect of the application in question;
D is the sum of the maintenance requirements as calculated for the purposes of each application relating to the absent parent in question.

(3) When more than one maintenance assessment has been made with respect to the absent parent and payment by him of the aggregate of the amounts of those assessments would reduce his disposable income below his protected income - level, the aggregate amount of those assessments shall be reduced (each being reduced by reference to the same proportion as those assessments bear to each other) by the minimum amount necessary to prevent his disposable income being reduced below his protected income level provided that the aggregate amount payable under those assessments shall not be reduced to less than the minimum amount prescribed in regulation 13(1).

[¹(4) Where the aggregate of the child support maintenance payable by the absent parent is less than the minimum amount prescribed in regulation 13(1), the child support maintenance payable shall be—

    (i) that prescribed minimum amount apportioned between the two or more applications in the same ratio as the maintenance requirements in question bear to each other; or

    (ii) where, because of the application of regulation 2(2), such an apportionment produces an aggregate amount which is different from that prescribed amount, that different amount.]

(5) Payment of each of the maintenance assessments calculated under this regulation shall satisfy the liability of the absent parent (or a person treated as such) to pay child support maintenance.

AMENDMENT
    1.   Regulation 23 of the Amendment Regulations (April 5, 1993).

DEFINITION
    "the Act": see reg. 1(2).

GENERAL NOTE
    For a discussion reference should be made to the general note to Sched. 1 to the Act.
    Where this special case applies, special provision is made regarding the minimum amount prescribed under s.16(6)(*b*) of the Act (regs. 21 and 23 of the Maintenance Assessment Procedure Regulations).

Person caring for children of more than one absent parent

23.—(1) Where the circumstances of a case are that—

  (*a*) a person is a person with care in relation to two or more qualifying children; and

  (*b*) in relation to at least two of those children there are different persons who are absent parents or persons treated as absent parents by regulation 20(2);

that case shall be treated as a special case for the purposes of the Act.

(2) In calculating the maintenance requirements for the purposes of this case, for any amount which (but for this paragraph) would have been included under regulation 3(1)(*b*), (*c*) or (*d*) (amounts included in the calculation of AG) there shall be substituted an amount calculated by dividing the amount which would have been so included by the relevant number.

(3) In paragraph (2) "the relevant number" means the number equal to the total number of persons who, in relation to those children, are either absent parents or persons treated as absent parents by regulation 20(2) except that where in respect of the same child both parents are persons who are either absent parents or persons who are treated as absent parents under that regulation, they shall count as one person.

(4) Where the circumstances of a case fall within this regulation and the person with care is the parent of any of the children, for C in paragraph 2(1) of Schedule 1 to the Act (the assessable income of that person) there shall be substituted the amount which would be calculated under regulation 22(2) if the references therein to an absent parent were references to a parent with care.

DEFINITIONS
    "the Act": see reg. 1(2).
    "person": *ibid.*

GENERAL NOTE
    For a discussion reference should be made to the general notes to reg. 3 above and to Sched. 1 to the Act.
    Where this special case applies, special provision is made regarding the minimum amount prescribed under s.16(6)(*b*) of the Act (regs. 22 and 23 of the Maintenance Assessment Procedure Regulations).

Persons with part-time care—not including a person treated as an absent parent

24.—(1) Where the circumstances of a case are that—

(*a*) two or more persons who do not live in the same household each provide day to day care for the same qualifying child; and

(*b*) those persons do not include any parent who is treated as an absent parent of that child by regulation 20(2),

that case shall be treated as a special case for the purposes of the Act.

(2) For the purposes of this case—

(*a*) the person whose application for a maintenance assessment is being proceeded with shall, subject to paragraph (*b*), be entitled to receive all the child support maintenance payable under the Act in respect of the child in question;

(*b*) on request being made to the Secretary of State by—

(i) that person; or

(ii) any other person who is providing day to day care for the child and who intends to continue to provide that care,

the Secretary of State may make arrangements for the payment of any child support maintenance payable under the Act to the persons who provide such care in the same ratio as that in which it appears to the Secretary of State, that each is to provide such care for the child in question;

(*c*) before making an arrangement under sub-paragraph (*b*), the Secretary of State shall consider all of the circumstances of the case and in particular the interests of the child, the present arrangements for the day to day care of the child in question and any representations or proposals made by the persons who provide such care for that child.

DEFINITIONS

"the Act": see reg. 1(2).
"day to day care": *ibid.*
"person": *ibid.*

GENERAL NOTE

This special case applies where the care of a child is split between persons none of whom is treated as an absent parent under reg. 20. It allows the Secretary of State to apportion the child support maintenance between the persons concerned. For further discussion to that below reference should be made to the general notes to s.3 of, and Sched. 1 to, the Act.

A person with part-time care within the scope of this regulation does not automatically become a person with care for the purposes of the definition in s.3(3) of the Act. It is still necessary for all aspects of that definition to be satisfied before a person becomes a person with care. This regulation does not therefore override the need for the child's home to be with a person before that person becomes a person with care. It, therefore, allows the Secretary of State to apportion the child support maintenance in favour of a person who is not a person with care and who as a result could not apply for a maintenance assessment.

Para. (1)

If a parent is concerned in the day to day care of the child, reg. 20 applies.

Para. (2)(b)

The Secretary of State, if he apportions the child support maintenance, must do so in the same ratio that each person provides care for the child. This is a different formulation from that employed in reg. 25 and may allow apportionment on some basis other than the number of nights for which care is provided by each person. The Secretary of State may, for example, wish to take account of the fact that one person bears a greater burden of the cost of bringing up the child than the other, such as assuming responsibility for the cost of clothing.

Para (2)(c)

The specific provision that the interests of a child are to be considered underlines the point made in the commentary to s.2 of the Act that the duty created by that section to have regard to the welfare of any children likely to be affected applies only to powers created by the Act and not to powers created by regulations. There are in any case two differences between the requirement here and the duty in s.2. First, the requirement here is to consider the interests, rather than the welfare, of the child. Second, the duty here relates only to the qualifying child in question, rather than to any child likely to be affected.

Care provided in part by a local authority

25.—(1) Where the circumstances of a case are that a local authority and a person each provide day to day care for the same qualifying child, that case shall be treated as a special case for the purposes of the Act.

(2) In a case where this regulation applies—

  (*a*) child support maintenance shall be calculated in respect of that child as if this regulation did not apply;

  (*b*) the amount so calculated shall be divided by 7 so as to produce a daily amount;

  (*c*) in respect of each night for which day to day care for that child is provided by a person other than the local suthority, the daily amount relating to that period shall be payable by the absent parent (or, as the case may be, by the person treated as an absent parent under regulation 20(2));

  (*d*) child support maintenance shall not be payable in respect of any night for which the local authority provides day to day care for that qualifying child.

DEFINITIONS

  "the Act": see reg. 1(2).
  "day to day care": *ibid.*
  "person": *ibid.*

GENERAL NOTE

No child support maintenance is payable for the proportion of the week which a child spends in the care of a local authority. This is in line with reg. 51 of the Maintenance Assessment Procedure Regulations which provides that for the purposes of s.3(3)(*c*) of the Act local authorities and persons with whom a child is placed or boarded by a local authority may not be persons with care. For further discussion reference should be made to the general notes to s.3 of and Sched. 1 to the Act and to reg. 51 of the Maintenance Assessment Procedure Regulations.

Para. (2)

This rigid formula does not permit the degree of flexibility attainable under the different wording used in reg. 24. It does not, therefore, allow any regard to be had to the fact that one party providing the care bears a greater financial burden out of proportion to the number of nights for which care is provided, for example, by providing the child's clothing.

Cases where child support maintenance is not to be payable

26.—(1) Where the circumstances of a case are that—

  (*a*) but for this regulation the minimum amount prescribed in regulation 13(1) would apply; and

  (*b*) any of the following conditions are satisfied—

    (i) the income of the absent parent includes one or more of the payments or awards specified in Schedule 4 or would include such a payment but for a provision preventing the receipt of that payment by reason of it overlapping with some other benefit payment or would, in the case of the payments referred to in paragraph (*a*)(i) or (iv) of that Schedule, include such a payment if the relevant contribution conditions for entitlement had been satisfied;

    (ii) an amount to which regulation 11(1)(*f*) applies (protected income: income support family premium) is taken into account in calculating or estimating the protected income of the absent parent;

    (iii) the absent parent is a child within the meaning of section 55 of the Act;

    (iv) the absent parent is a prisoner; or

    (v) the absent parent is a person in respect of whom N (as calculated or esti-
mated under regulation 7(1)) is less than the minimum amount prescribed by regulation 13(1),

the case shall be treated as a special case for the purposes of the Act.

(2) For the purposes of this case—

  (*a*) the requirement in paragraph 7(2) of Schedule 1 to the Act (minimum
amount of child support maintenance fixed by an assessment to be the prescribed minimum amount) shall not apply;

  (*b*) the amount of the child support maintenance to be fixed by the assessment
shall be nil.

DEFINITIONS
  "the Act": see reg. 1(2).
  "person": *ibid*.
  "prisoner": *ibid*.

GENERAL NOTE
  For a discussion reference should be made to the general note to Sched. 1 to the Act.

Child who is a boarder or an in-patient

  27.—(1) Where the circumstances of a case are that—

  (*a*) a qualifying child is a boarder at a boarding school or is an in-patient in a
hospital; and

  (*b*) by reason of those circumstances, the person who would otherwise provide
day to day care is not doing so,

that case shall be treated as a special case for the purposes of the Act.

  (2) For the purposes of this case, section 3(3)(*b*) of the Act shall be modified so
[¹that] for the reference to the person who usually provides day to day care for the
child there shall be substituted a reference to the person who would usually be providing such care for that child but for the circumstances specified in paragraph (1).

AMENDMENT
  1. Regulation 24 of the Amendment Regulations (April 5, 1993).

DEFINITIONS
  "the Act": see reg. 1(2).
  "day to day care": *ibid*.
  "person": *ibid*.

GENERAL NOTE
  This special case provides that a person is not prevented from being a person with care of a child
solely on account of the fact that the child is at boarding school or in hospital. It applies for the purpose
of the definition of "person with care" in s.3(3) of the Act, but has no application for the purpose of reg.
20 above. For further discussion reference should be made to the general notes to reg. 20 and to s.3 of
the Act.

[¹Child who is allowed to live with his parent under section 23(5) of the Children Act 1989

  27A.—(1) Where the circumstances of a case are that a qualifying child who is
in the care of a local authority in England and Wales is allowed by the authority to
live with a parent of his under section 23(5) of the Children Act 1989, that case
shall be treated as a special case for the purposes of the Act.

  (2) For the purposes of this case, section 3(3)(*b*) of the Act shall be modified so
that for the reference to the person who usually provides day to day care for the

child there shall be substituted a reference to the parent of a child whom the local authority allow the child to live with under section 23(5) of the Children Act 1989.]

AMENDMENT
   1.   Regulation 25 of the Amendment Regulations (April 5, 1993).

DEFINITIONS
   "the Act": see reg. 1(2).
   "day to day care": *ibid.*

Amount payable where absent parent is in receipt of income support or other prescribed benefit

28.—(1) Where the condition specified in section 43(1)(*a*) of the Act is satisfied in relation to an absent parent (assessable income to be nil where income support or other prescribed benefit is paid), the prescribed conditions for the purposes of section 43(1)(*b*) of the Act are that—

   (*a*)   the absent parent is aged 18 or over;
   (*b*)   he does not satisfy the conditions in paragraph 3 of the relevant Schedule (income support family premium) [¹and does not have day to day care of any child (whether or not a relevant child)]; and
   (*c*)   [²his income does not include] one or more of the payments or awards specified in Schedule 4 (other than by reason of a provision preventing receipt of overlapping benefits or by reason of a failure to satisfy the relevant contribution conditions).

(2) For the purposes of section 43(2)(*a*) of the Act, the prescribed amount shall be equal to the minimum amount prescribed in regulation 13(1) for the purposes of paragraph 7(1) of Schedule 1 to the Act.

[³(3) Subject to paragraph (4), where—

   (*a*)   an absent parent is liable under section 43 of the Act and this regulation to make payments in place of payments of child support maintenance with respect to two or more qualifying children in relation to whom there is more than one parent with care; or
   (*b*)   that absent parent and his partner (within the meaning of regulation 2(1) of the Social Security (Claims and Payments) Regulations 1987) are both liable to make such payments,

the prescribed amount mentioned in paragraph (2) shall be apportioned between the persons with care in the same ratio as the maintenance requirements of the qualifying child or children in relation to each of those persons with care bear to each other.]

[⁴(4) If, in making the apportionment required by paragraph (3), the effect of the application of regulation 2(2) would be such that the aggregate amount payable would be different from the amount prescribed in paragraph (2) the Secretary of State shall adjust the apportionment so as to eliminate that difference; and that adjustment shall be varied from time to time so as to secure that, taking one week with another and so far as is practicable, each person with care receives the amount which she would have received if no adjustment had been made under this paragraph.

(5) The provisions of Schedule 5 shall have effect in relation to cases to which section 43 of the Act and this regulation apply.]

AMENDMENTS
   1.   Regulation 26(1)(*a*) of the Amendment Regulations (April 5, 1993).
   2.   Regulation 26(1)(*b*) of the Amendment Regulations (April 5, 1993).
   3.   Regulation 2(2) of the Child Support (Maintenance Assessments and Special Cases) Amendment Regulations 1993 (April 26, 1993).
   4.   Regulation 26(2) of the Amendment Regulations (April 5, 1993).

DEFINITIONS
"the Act": see reg. 1(2).
"day to day care": *ibid.*
"relevant Schedule": *ibid.*

GENERAL NOTE
This regulation is not expressly described as a special case. However, it is in the Part of the Regulations headed "Special Cases" and it is made under s.43 of the Act which together with s.42 is headed "Special Cases."

SCHEDULE 1

CALCULATION OF N AND M

PART 1

EARNINGS

Chapter 1

Earnings of an employed earner

1.—(1) Subject to sub-paragraphs (2) and (3), "earnings" means in the case of employment as an employed earner, any remuneration or profit derived from that employment and includes—

(a) any bonus, commission, royalty or fee;

(b) any holiday pay except any payable more than 4 weeks after termination of the employment;

(c) any payment by way of a retainer;

(d) any payment made by the parent's employer in respect of any expenses not wholly, exclusively and necessarily incurred in the performance of the duties of the employment;

(e) any award of compensation made under section 68(2) or 71(2)(a) of the Employment Protection (Consolidation) Act 1978 (remedies and compensation for unfair dismissal);

(f) any such sum as is referred to in section 112 of the Contributions and Benefits Act (certain sums to be earnings for social security purposes);

(g) any statutory sick pay under Part I of the Social Security and Housing Benefits Act 1982 or statutory maternity pay under Part V of the Social Security Act 1986;

(h) any payment in lieu of notice and any compensation in respect of the absence or inadequacy of any such notice but only insofar as such payment or compensation represents loss of income;

(i) any payment relating to a period of less than a year which is made in respect of the performance of duties as—

(i) an auxiliary coastguard in respect of coast rescue activities;

(ii) a part-time fireman in a fire brigade maintained in pursuance of the Fire Services Acts 1947 to 1959;

(iii) a person engaged part-time in the manning or launching of a lifeboat;

(iv) a member of any territorial or reserve force prescribed in Part I of Schedule 3 to the Social Security (Contributions) Regulations 1979;

(j) any payment made by a local authority to a member of that authority in respect of the performance of his duties as a member, other than any expenses wholly, exclusively and necessarily incurred in the performance of those duties.

205

(2) Earnings shall not include—

(*a*)   any payment in respect of expenses wholly, exclusively and necessarily incurred in the performance of the duties of the employment;

(*b*)   any occupational pension;

(*c*)   any payment where—

   (i) the employment in respect of which it was made has ceased; and

   (ii) a period of the same length as the period by reference to which it was calculated has expired since that cessation but prior to the effective date;

(*d*)   any advance of earnings or any loan made by an employer to an employee;

(*e*)   any amount received from an employer during a period when the employee has withdrawn his services by reason of a trade dispute;

(*f*)   any payment in kind;

(*g*)   where, in any week or other period which falls within the period by reference to which earnings are calculated, earnings are received both in respect of a previous employment and in respect of a subsequent employment, the earnings in respect of the previous employment.

(3) The earnings to be taken into account for the purposes of calculating N and M shall be gross earnings less—

(*a*)   any amount deducted from those earnings by way of—

   (i) income tax;

   (ii) primary Class 1 contributions under the Contributions and Benefits Act; and

(*b*)   one half of any sums paid by the parent towards an occupational or personal pension scheme.

2.—(1) Subject to sub-paragraphs (2) to (4)—

(*a*)   where a person is paid weekly, the amount of those earnings shall be determined by aggregating the amounts received in the 5 weeks ending with the relevant week and dividing by 5;

(*b*)   where a person is paid monthly, the amount of those earnings shall be determined by aggregating the amounts received in the 2 months ending with the relevant week, multiplying the aggregate by 6 and dividing by 52;

(*c*)   where a person is paid by reference to some other period, the amount of those earnings shall be determined by aggregating the amounts received in the 3 months ending with the relevant week, multiplying the aggregate by 4 and dividing by 52.

(2) Where a person's earnings include a bonus or commission which is paid during the period of 52 weeks ending with the relevant week and is paid separately from, or, in relation to a longer period than, the other earnings with which it is paid, the amount of that bonus or commission shall be determined by aggregating such payments received in the 52 weeks ending with the relevant week and dividing by 52.

(3) Subject to sub-paragraph (4), the amount of any earnings of a student shall be determined by aggregating the amount received in the year ending with the relevant week and dividing by 52 or, where the person in question has been a student for less than a year, by aggregating the amount received in the period starting with his becoming a student and ending with the relevant week and dividing by the number of complete weeks in that period.

(4) Where a calculation would, but for this sub-paragraph, produce an amount which, in the opinion of the child support officer, does not accurately reflect the normal amount of the earnings of the person in question, such earnings, or any part of them, shall be calculated by reference to such other period as may, in the particular case, enable the normal weekly earnings of that person to be determined more accurately and for this purpose the child support officer shall have regard to—

(*a*)   the earnings received, or due to be received, from any employment in which the person in question is engaged, has been engaged or is due to be engaged;

(*b*)   the duration and pattern, or the expected duration and pattern, of any employment of that person.

Chapter 2

Earnings of a self-employed earner

3.—(1) Subject to sub-paragraphs (2) and (3) and to paragraph 4, "earnings" in the case of employment as a self-employed earner means the gross receipts of the employment including, where an allowance in the form of periodic payments is paid under section 2 of the Employment and Training Act 1973 or section 2 of the Enterprise and New Towns (Scotland) Act 1990 in respect of the relevant week for the purpose of assisting him in carrying on his business, the total of those payments made during the period by reference to which his earnings are determined under paragraph 5.

(2) Earnings shall not include—

(a) any allowance paid under either of those sections in respect of any part of the period by reference to which his earnings are determined under paragraph 5 if no part of that allowance is paid in respect of the relevant week;

(b) any income consisting of payments received for the provision of board and lodging accommodation unless such payments form the largest element of the recipient's income.

(3) [¹Subject to sub-paragraph (7),] there shall be deducted from the gross receipts referred to in sub-paragraph (1)—

(a) [²except in a case to which paragraph 4 applies,] any expenses which are reasonably incurred and are wholly and exclusively defrayed for the purposes of the earner's business in the period by reference to which his earnings are determined under paragraph 5(1) or, where paragraph 5(2) applies, any such expenses relevant to the period there mentioned (whether or not defrayed in that period);

(b) [²except in a case to which paragraph 4 applies,] any value added tax paid in the period by reference to which earnings are determined in excess of value added tax received in that period;

(c) any amount in respect of income tax determined in accordance with sub-paragraph (5);

(d) any amount in respect of National Insurance contributions determined in accordance with sub-paragraph (6);

(e) one half of any premium paid in respect of a retirement annuity contract or a personal pension-scheme.

(4) For the purposes of sub-paragraph (3)(a)—

(a) such expenses include—

   (i) repayment of capital on any loan used for the replacement, in the course of business, of equipment or machinery, or the repair of an existing business asset except to the extent that any sum is payable under an insurance policy for its repair;

   (ii) any income expended in the repair of an existing business asset except to the extent that any sum is payable under an insurance policy for its repair;

   (iii) any payment of interest on a loan taken out for the purposes of the business;

(b) such expenses do not include—

   (i) repayment of capital on any other loan taken out for the purposes of the business;

   (ii) any capital expenditure;

   (iii) the depreciation of any capital asset;

   (iv) any sum employed, or intended to be employed, in the setting up or expansion of the business;

   (v) any loss incurred before the beginning of that period by reference to which earnings are determined;

   (vi) any expenses incurred in providing business entertainment;

   (vii) any loss incurred in any other employment in which he is engaged as a self employed earner.

(5) For the purposes of sub-paragraph (3)(c), the amount of income tax to be allowed against earnings shall be calculated [³on the basis of chargeable earnings and] as if those earnings, less any personal allowance applicable to the earner under Chapter 1 of Part VII of

the Income and Corporation Taxes Act 1988 (Personal Relief) (or where the earnings are determined over a period of less than a year, a proportionate part of such relief), were assessable to income tax at the rates of tax applicable at the effective date.

(6) For the purposes of sub-paragraph (3)(*d*), the amount to be deducted in respect of National Insurance contributions shall be the total of—

    (*a*) the amount of Class 2 contributions (if any) payable under section 11(1) or, as the case may be, (4) of the Contributions and Benefits Act; and

    (*b*) the amount of Class 4 contributions (if any) payable under section 15(2) of that Act, at the rates applicable [⁴to the chargeable earnings] at the effective date.

[⁵(7) In the case of self-employed earner whose employment is carried on in partnership or is that of a share fisherman within the meaning of the Social Security (Mariners' Benefits) Regulations 1975, sub-paragraph (3) shall have effect as though it requires a deduction from the earner's gross receipts of an amount calculated by—

    (*a*) deducting from the gross receipts of the partnership or fishing boat the sums mentioned in heads (*a*) and (*b*) of that sub-paragraph; and

    (*b*) deducting from the earner's share of the balance after such deductions the sums mentioned in heads (*c*) to (*e*) of that sub-paragraph.

(8) In sub-paragraphs (5) and (6) "chargeable earnings" means the gross receipts of the employment less any deductions mentioned in sub-paragraph (3)(*a*) and (*b*).]

4. In a case where a person is self-employed as a childminder the amount of earnings referable to that employment shall be one-third of the gross receipts.

5.—(1) Subject to sub-paragraphs (2) and (3)—

    (*a*) where a person has been a self-employed earner for 52 weeks or more including the relevant week, the amount of his earnings shall be determined by reference to the average of the earnings which he has received in the 52 weeks ending with the relevant week;

    (*b*) where the person has been a self-employed earner for a period of less than 52 weeks including the relevant week, the amount of his earnings shall be determined by reference to the average of the earnings which he has received during that period.

(2) Where a person who is a self-employed earner provides in respect of the employment a profit and loss account and, where appropriate, a trading account or a balance sheet or both, and the profit and loss account is in respect of a period at least 6 months but not exceeding 15 months and that period terminates within the 12 months immediately preceding the effective date, the amount of his earnings shall be determined by reference to the average of the earnings over the period to which the profit and loss account relates and such earnings shall include receipts relevant to that period (whether or not received in that period).

(3) Where a calculation would, but for this sub-paragraph, produce an amount which, in the opinion of the child support officer, does not accurately reflect the normal amount of the earnings of the person in question, such earnings, or any part of them, shall be calculated by reference to such other period as may, in the particular case, enable the normal weekly earnings of that person to be determined more accurately and for this purpose the child support officer shall have regard to—

    (*a*) the earnings received, or due to be received, from any employment in which the person in question is engaged, or has been engaged or is due to be engaged;

    (*b*) the duration and pattern, or the expected duration and pattern, of any employment of that person.

(4) In sub-paragraph (2)—

    (*a*) "balance sheet" means a statement of the financial position of the employment disclosing its assets, liabilities and capital at the end of the period in question;

    (*b*) "profit and loss account" means a financial statement showing net profit or loss of the employment for the period in question; and

    (*c*) "trading account" means a financial statement showing the revenue from sales, the cost of those sales and the gross profit arising during the period in question.

PART II

BENEFIT PAYMENTS

6.—(1) The benefit payments to be taken into account in calculating or estimating N and M shall be determined in accordance with this Part.

(2) "Benefit payments" means any benefit payments under the Contributions and Benefits Act except amounts to be disregarded by virtue of Schedule 2.

(3) The amount of any benefit payment to be taken into account shall be determined by reference to the rate of that benefit applicable at the effective date.

7.—(1) Where a benefit payment under the Contributions and Benefits Act includes an adult or child dependency increase—

(*a*) if that benefit is payable to a parent, the income of that parent shall be calculated or estimated as if it did not include that amount;

(*b*) if that benefit is payable to some other person but includes an amount in respect of the parent, the income of the parent shall be calculated or estimated as if it included that amount.

(2) Subject to sub-paragraph (3), payments to a person by way of family credit shall be treated as the income of the parent who has qualified for them by his engagement in, and normal engagement in, remunerative work.

(3) Subject to sub-paragraphs (4) and (5), where family credit is payable and the amount which is payable has been calculated by reference either to the weekly earnings of the absent parent and another person or the parent with care and another person—

(*a*) if during the period which is used to calculate his earnings under paragraph 2 or, as the case may be, paragraph 5, the weekly earnings of that parent exceed those of the other person, the amount payable by way of family credit shall be treated as the income of that parent;

(*b*) if during that period the normal weekly earnings of that parent equal those of the other person, half of the amount payable by way of family credit shall be treated as the income of that parent; and

(*c*) if during that period the normal weekly earnings of that parent are less than those of that other person, the amount payable by way of family credit shall not be treated as the income of that parent.

(4) Where—

(*a*) family credit (calculated, as the case may be, by reference to the weekly earnings of the absent parent and another person or the parent with care and another person) is in payment; and

(*b*) not later than the effective date either or both the persons by reference to whose engagement and normal engagement in remunerative work that payment has been calculated has ceased to be so employed,

half of the amount payable by way of family credit shall be treated as the income of the parent in question.

(5) Where—

(*a*) family credit is in payment; and

(*b*) not later than the effective date the person or, if more than one, each of the persons by reference to whose engagement, and normal engagement, in remunerative work that payment has been calculated is no longer the partner of the person to whom that payment is made,

the payment in question shall only be treated as the income of the parent in question where he is in receipt of it.

PART III

OTHER INCOME

8. The amount of the other income to be taken into account in calculating or estimating N and M shall be the aggregate of the following amounts determined in accordance with this Part.

9. Any periodic payment of pension or other benefit under an occupational or personal pension scheme or a retirement annuity contract or other such scheme for the provision of income in retirement.

10. Any payment received on account of the provision of board and lodging which does not come within Part I of this Schedule.

11. Subject to regulation 7(3)(*b*) and paragraph 12, any payment to a student of—

(*a*) a grant;

(*b*) an amount in respect of grant contribution;

(*c*) covenant income except to the extent that it has been taken into account under sub-paragraph (*b*);

(*d*) a student loan.

12. The income of a student shall not include any payment—

(*a*) intended to meet tuition fees or examination fees;

(*b*) intended to meet additional expenditure incurred by a disabled student in respect of his attendance on a course;

(*c*) intended to meet additional expenditure connected with term time residential study away from the student's educational establishment;

(*d*) on account of the student maintaining a home at a place other than at which he resides during his course;

(*e*) intended to meet the cost of books, and equipment (other than special equipment) or, if not so intended, an amount equal to the amount allowed under regulation 38(2)(*f*) of the Family Credit (General) Regulations 1987 towards such costs;

(*f*) intended to meet travel expenses incurred as a result of his attendance on the course.

13. Any interest, dividend or other income derived from capital.

14. Any maintenance payments in respect of a parent.

15. Any other payments or other amounts received on a periodical basis which are not otherwise taken into account under Part I, II, IV or V of this Schedule.

16.—(1) Subject to sub-paragraphs (2) to (6) the amount of any income to which this Part applies shall be calculated or estimated—

(*a*) where it has been received in respect of the whole of the period of 26 weeks which ends at the end of the relevant week, by dividing such income received in that period by 26;

(*b*) where it has been received in respect of part of the period of 26 weeks which ends at the end of the relevant week, by dividing such income received in that period by the number of complete weeks in respect of which such income is received and for this purpose income shall be treated as received in respect of a week if it is received in respect of any day in the week in question.

(2) The amount of maintenance payments made in respect of a parent—

(*a*) where they are payable weekly and have been paid at the same amount in respect of each week in the period of 13 weeks which ends at the end of the relevant week, shall be the amount equal to one of those payments;

(*b*) in any other case, shall be the amount calculated by aggregating the total amount of those payments received in the period of 13 weeks which ends at the end of the relevant week and dividing by the number of weeks in that period in respect of which maintenance was due.

(3) In the case of a student—

(*a*) the amount of any grant and any amount paid in respect of grant contribution shall be calculated by apportioning it equally between the weeks in respect of which it is payable;

(b) the amount of any covenant income shall be calculated by dividing the amount payable in respect of a year by 52 (or, where such amount is payable in respect of a lesser period, by the number of complete weeks in that period) and, subject to sub-paragraph (4), deducting £5.00;

(c) the amount of any student loan shall be calculated by apportioning the loan equally between the weeks in respect of which it is payable and, subject to sub-paragraph (4), deducting £10.00.

(4) For the purposes of sub-paragraph (3)—

(a)   not more than £5.00 shall be deducted under sub-paragraph (3)(b);

(b)   not more than £10.00 in total shall be deducted under sub-paragraphs (3)(b) and (c).

(5) Where in respect of the period of 52 weeks which ends at the end of the relevant week a person is in receipt of interest, dividend or other income which has been produced by his capital, the amount of that income shall be calculated by dividing the aggregate of the income so received by 52.

(6) Where a calculation would, but for this sub-paragraph, produce an amount which, in the opinion of the child support officer, does not accurately reflect the normal amount of the other income of the person in question, such income, or any part of it, shall be calculated by reference to such other period as may, in the particular case, enable the other income of that person to be determined more accurately and for this purpose the child support officer shall have regard to the nature and pattern of receipt of such income.

PART IV

INCOME OF CHILD TREATED AS INCOME OF PARENT

17. The amount of any income of a child which is to be treated as the income of the parent in calculating or estimating N and M shall be the aggregate of the amounts determined in accordance with this Part.

18. Where a child has income which falls within the following paragraphs of this Part and that child is a member of the family of his parent (whether that child is a qualifying child in relation to that parent or not), the relevant income of that child shall be treated as that of his parent.

19. Where child support maintenance is being assessed for the support of only one qualifying child, the relevant income of that child shall be treated as that of the parent with care.

20. Where child support maintenance is being assessed to support more than one qualifying child, the relevant income of each of those children shall be treated as that of the parent with care to the extent that it does not exceed the aggregate of—

(a)   the amount determined under—

    (i)   regulation 3(1)(a) (calculation of AG) in relation to the child in question; and

    (ii)   the total of any other amounts determined under regulation 3(1)(b) to (d) which are applicable in the case in question divided by the number of children for whom child support maintenance is being calculated,

less the basic rate of child benefit (within the meaning of regulation 4) for the child in question; and

(b)   three times the total of the amounts calculated under regulation 3(1)(a) (income support personal allowance for child or young person) in respect of that child and regulation 3(1)(c) (income support family premium).

21. Where child support maintenance is not being assessed for the support of the child whose income is being calculated or estimated, the relevant income of that child shall be treated as that of his parent to the extent that it does not exceed the amount determined under regulation 9(1)(g).

22. Where a benefit under the Contributions and Benefits Act includes an adult or child dependency increase in respect of a relevant child, the relevant income of that child shall be calculated or estimated as if it included that amount.

23. For the purposes of this Part, "the relevant income of a child" does not include—

(*a*) any earnings of the child in question;

(*b*) payments by an absent parent in respect of the child for whom maintenance is being assessed;

(*c*) where the class of persons who are capable of benefiting from a discretionary trust include the child in question, payments from that trust except in so far as they are made to provide for food, ordinary clothing and footwear, gas, electricity or fuel charges or housing costs; or

(*d*) any interest payable on arrears of child support maintenance for that child.

24. The amount of the income of a child which is treated as the income of the parent shall be determined in the same way as if such income were the income of the parent.

PART V

AMOUNTS TREATED AS THE INCOME OF A PARENT

25. The amounts which fall to be treated as income of the parent in calculating or estimating N and M shall include amounts to be determined in accordance with this Part.

26. Where a child support officer is satisfied—

(*a*) that a person has performed a service either—

(i) without receiving any remuneration in respect of it; or

(ii) for remuneration which is less than that normally paid for that service;

(*b*) that the service in question was for the benefit of—

(i) another person who is not a member of the same family as the person in question; or

(ii) a body which is neither a charity nor a voluntary organisation;

(*c*) that the service in question was performed for a person who, or as the case may be, a body which was able to pay remuneration at the normal rate for the service in question;

(*d*) that the principal purpose of the person undertaking the service without receiving any or adequate remuneration is to reduce his assessable income for the purposes of the Act; and

(*e*) that any remuneration foregone would have fallen to be taken into account as earnings,

the value of the remuneration foregone shall be estimated by a child support officer and an amount equal to the value so estimated shall be treated as income of the person who performed those services.

27. Subject to paragraphs 28 to 30, where the child support officer is satisfied that, otherwise than in the circumstances set out in paragraph 26, a person has intentionally deprived himself of—

(*a*) any income or capital which would otherwise be a source of income;

(*b*) any income or capital which it would be reasonable to expect would be secured by him,

with a view to reducing the amount of his assessable income, his net income shall include the amount estimated by a child support officer as representing the income which that person would have had if he had not deprived himself of or failed to secure that income, or as the case may be, that capital.

28. No amount shall be treated as income by virtue of paragraph 27 in relation to—

(*a*) one parent benefit;

(*b*) if the parent is a person to, or in respect of, whom income support is payable, unemployment benefit;

(*c*) a payment from a discretionary trust or a trust derived from a payment made in consequence of a personal injury.

29. Where an amount is included in the income of a person under paragraph 27 in respect of income which would become available to him on application, the amount included under that paragraph shall be included from the date on which it could be expected to be acquired.

30. Where a child support officer determines under paragraph 27 that a person has deprived himself of capital which would otherwise be a source of income, the amount of that capital shall be reduced at intervals of 52 weeks, starting with the week which falls 52 weeks after the first week in respect of which income from it is included in the calculation of the assessment in question, by an amount equal to the amount which the child support officer estimates would represent the income from that source in the immediately preceding period of 52 weeks.

31. Where a payment is made on behalf of a parent or a relevant child in respect of food, ordinary clothing or footwear, gas, electricity or fuel charges, housing costs or council tax, an amount equal to the amount which the child support officer estimates represents the value of that payment shall be treated as the income of the parent in question except to the extent that such amount is—

(*a*) disregarded under paragraph 38 of Schedule 2;

(*b*) a payment of school fees paid by or on behalf of someone other than the absent parent.

32. Where paragraph 26 applies the amount to be treated as the income of the parent shall be determined as if it were earnings from employment as an employed earner and in a case to which paragraph 27 or 31 applies the amount shall be determined as if it were other income to which Part III of this Schedule applies.

AMENDMENTS
1.   Regulation 27(1)(*a*) of the Amendment Regulations (April 5, 1993).
2.   Regulation 27(1)(*b*) of the Amendment Regulations (April 5, 1993).
3.   Regulation 27(2) of the Amendment Regulations (April 5, 1993).
4.   Regulation 27(3) of the Amendment Regulations (April 5, 1993).
5.   Regulation 27(4) of the Amendment Regulations (April 5, 1993).

DEFINITIONS
"Contributions and Benefits Act": see reg. 1(2).
"covenant income": *ibid.*
"earnings": *ibid.*
"effective date": *ibid.*
"employed earner": *ibid.*
"family": *ibid.*
"grant": *ibid.*
"grant contribution": *ibid.*
"occupational pension scheme": *ibid.*
"parent with care": *ibid.*
"partner": *ibid.*
"person": *ibid.*
"personal pension scheme": *ibid.*
"retirement annuity contract": *ibid.*
"self-employed earner": *ibid.*
"student": *ibid.*
"student loan": *ibid.*
"year": *ibid.*

GENERAL NOTE
Para. 1(1)
This sub-paragraph defines the types of payment which count as earnings, subject to the exclusions in sub-para. (2). The definition is in two parts. The basic definition is that earnings are any remuneration or profit derived from the employment. The words "derived from" are wide and mean "having their origin in" (*R(SB) 21/86*, para. 12). They cover all payments whether by an employer or by a third party, such as a tip. This basic definition is expanded to include the matters set out in heads (*a*) to (*j*). These heads either cover payments which are not already covered by the basic definition or avoid argument on matters that might otherwise give rise to doubt.

Para. 1(1)(b)

Holiday pay becomes payable on the day on which it first becomes due to be paid (*R(SB) 11/85*, para. 16(1)). This may or may not coincide with the actual date of payment (*ibid.*). The date is determined by the contract of employment. Where evidence of the express terms of the contract is not available or the contract is silent on the point, it may be possible to infer that the date of actual payment is the date when it became due (*R(RS) 33/83*, para. 21(3)). This may, however, not always be possible, for example, where the practice shows no consistency.

Para. 1(1)(d)

The way to approach questions under this head is in two stages. First, identify the expense. Then, decide why it was incurred. However, difficult questions can arise.

Suppose that the evidence proves that a parent who would not otherwise have a car has to have one for the purpose of employment and uses it for both personal and business use. The car has to be taxed and insured. The expense is easy to identify; it is the payment of the tax and the insurance premium. The difficulty arises because in order to decide why the expense was incurred it is necessary to decide when it was incurred. If the expense was incurred at a single moment when the tax or insurance became due, it is possible to say that the sole reason why the expense was incurred was for the performance of the duties of the employment, since were it not for the employment the expense would not have been incurred. However, if the expense is seen as being incurred each time the car is used or throughout the time covered by the tax or insurance, it is no longer possible to say that it is incurred solely for the performance of the duties, because it is also put to personal use.

Para. 1(2)(a)

See the note to para. 1(1)(*d*).

Para. 1(2)(c)

If for example four weeks accrued holiday pay is received after a parent leaves the employment it is disregarded provided that there is a gap of at least four weeks between the leaving of the employment and the effective date of the maintenance assessment.

Para. 1(2)(d)

This covers, for example, loans to buy season tickets and advances of monthly salary to tide the employee over the first month of employment. Advance of earnings must mean payments of earnings before the date on which the employee is contractually entitled to them. The sums advanced must be treated as received when they were due to be received. However, producing this obvious and sensible result from the Schedule is not easy. It is difficult to avoid the conclusion that the simplest possibility of an express provision dealing with this eventuality has been overlooked. The problem could be avoided by disregarding the period covered by the advance in calculating income in reliance on the power conferred by para. 2(4). Another approach would be to treat the sums as being "remuneration or profit derived from the employment" under sub-para. (1) on the date they were due. This is supported by the wording which refers to "advance of earnings" which suggests sums which would otherwise fall within sub-para. (1) and that the payment is only disregarded for the period of the advance. If the advances are regular it might be possible to infer that the contractual basis of payment has been changed and the practice taken as evidence of the terms of the new agreement. Attempts to make use of other paragraphs in this Schedule either (para. 15) put the paragraph in direct conflict with para. 1(2)(*d*) or (paras. 26 and 27) flounder on the fact that the income has been received, albeit in advance.

Para. 1(2)(g)

This express provision avoids the need to make use of para. 2(4) to produce a more accurate reflection of the parent's normal income.

Para. 2(4)

This provision is of most assistance when special circumstances existed during the prima facie period prescribed by para. 2(1), for example the period might cover the Christmas season when sales assistants earn overtime that is not available most of the year. However it has other uses and tribunal members will derive hours of harmless amusement from attempting to determine the normal earnings of an employment, such as that of a university canteen assistant, in respect of which there is no consistent normality. The purist approach is to look at the matter at the time the decision is being made and to rely on reviews under s.17 of the Act to deal with changes thereafter. This ensures a fair calculation for the parent concerned, although it is time consuming and tedious and there is an inevitable lag between the change of circumstances and the making of a fresh assessment. An alternative approach is to take the total annual income and divide it by 52 in the sure and certain hope that over the course of a year things may average out. This brings the advantages of certainty and continuity at the expense of possible financial difficulties at certain periods of the year for a parent on low income. There is some support for this latter approach in the express provision for student income in para. 2(3).

Para. 3(1)

There has been uncertainty in the context of the comparable provision in family credit law as to the treatment of loans made either before the start of the business to allow it to be set up or during its course in order to keep it going or to expand. It is now clear as a result of the consent order made by the Court of Appeal on August 21, 1992 in *Kostanczux* v. *Chief Adjudication Officer* (on appeal from *CFC 4/91*) that "capital receipts not generated by a [parent's] business do not form part of the gross receipts of employment." Interesting as the theoretical status of a consent order of the Court of Appeal may be, the position in practice is clear. *CFC 4/91* should not be followed and CSATs should adopt the wording of the order, for which in any event there is authority in *CFC 24/89*. Consequently, business loans do not constitute earnings.

Para. 3(3)(a)

This paragraph differs from para. 1(1)(*d*) and (2)(*a*) in that it is sufficient that expenses are reasonably incurred rather than necessarily incurred. This is a matter of judgment for the CSAT and the basis of its decision on reasonableness will have to be explained in the reasons for decision. The expenses must also be wholly and exclusively defrayed for the purposes of the business and this is a matter of fact. Where expenditure has been put to both business and personal use, such as a telephone bill, it may be apportioned and any apportionment which has been accepted by the Inland Revenue for tax purposes may be relied upon by the CSAT if there is no evidence to the contrary (*CFC 25/89*).

Para. 5(3)

This provision is more likely to be used than the equivalent in para. 2(4) as the income of the self-employed is more likely to fluctuate. The sensible approach is to view the income over a sufficiently long period to allow fluctuations to be evened out as far as possible. There is support for this in sub-para. (2) which allows reliance on accounts for a period of between six and 15 months.

Para. 7

Sub-paras. (2) to (5) apply to family credit but not to disability working allowance. Sub-paragraph (2) attributes family credit to the partner who is in remunerative work rather than to the claimant. This is very strange.

Para. 26

Tribunals will in particular need to pay careful attention to the following points:

(i) The precise nature of the service needs to be identified. Until this has been done it is impossible to decide the normal rate for the service. Merely identifying a job by a title such as shop assistant will often be insufficient since there will be a range of work and of remuneration associated with such broad descriptions.

(ii) Evidence will be needed of the normal rate for the services identified. This will need to be examined to ensure that it relates to work of the same description as that performed by the person. Again reliance on job titles may mislead.

(iii) The paragraph pre-supposes that the services are such that there is a normal rate for them. This gives rise to a number of problems. The first is that there will often not be a rate for a particular job but a range of payments. Actual payment will depend on a number of factors. The service performed will be one, but others will include the locality where the work is undertaken, the state of the job market at the time, the employee's qualifications and experience and the ability of the employer to pay. The emphasis in this paragraph is on remuneration that has been foregone and that will require all factors relevant to the level of that remuneration to be considered. Second, it may well be that quite apart from the matters just considered there is a range of payments for the work with some employers paying better than others. If the payment falls outside that range there will be no difficulty in applying sub-paragraph (*a*) (ii), although the possible application of sub-paragraph (*c*) will then have to be considered. Otherwise an estimate will have to be made of the payment which the employer in question was likely to make. A third problem is that the services may be unique; for example a person may be assisting in the running of a business by performing a combination of duties which do not correspond to any single job in the job market. In such a case the CSAT must undertake a more hypothetical exercise and attribute an appropriate income to the work. The alternative approach would be to hold that if there is no equivalent job with which to compare the work in question, the paragraph does not apply and no earnings are attributed to the person in respect of it. This approach cannot be right; it amounts to saying that the more unique and therefore in a sense the more valuable the work to an employer, the less likely it is that earnings will be attributed in respect of it.

(iv) It is essential to establish that the principal purpose of undertaking the service without appropriate remuneration is to reduce the person's assessable income. This is a subjective test. Often the only direct evidence of purpose will be the person's own assertion. If this is not accepted, it will be necessary to infer what that purpose was. Before a CSAT can decide that a person acted in order to reduce assessable income it will have to find that the person was aware at least in general terms of the significance of the level of income for child support purposes. In considering why a person acted in a particular way any change in that person's activities or in the payment for those activities will need to be identified and investigated. Any inference will have to be justified in the CSAT's reasons for decision (*R(SB) 40/85*, para. 9).

Income which falls within this paragraph is treated as earnings from employment as an employed earner (para. 32).

Para. 27

This paragraph is the companion to para. 26. It deals with disposals of and failures to obtain income or income-earning capital whereas para. 26 deals with services. Paragraph 27 is unhappily worded. At one point it refers to the intentional deprivation of something a person has never had. The wording used later in the paragraph is better in referring to deprivation or failure to secure.

Sub-para. (*a*) applies where a person has had income or capital but no longer has it. It only deals with deprivation of income or capital. It does not deal with the use to which it is put. So it does not allow income to be taken into account which is used to fund a large mortgage or high personal pension contributions. It is for the person to prove that the income or capital has been disposed of (*R(SB) 38/85*, para. 18). If this cannot be proved the person must be taken as still in possession of the income or capital. No question of applying this paragraph then arises and the person will be unable to claim any benefit that might otherwise be derived from para. 30. If deprivation is proved, it is necessary to investigate whether it was done intentionally with a view to reducing assessable income. The test is a subjective one, although the reasonableness of a person's action will be a relevant factor in assessing any evidence by that person on the reasons for so acting. Usually the CSAT will have to infer the purpose for the deprivation (see the general note to para. 26 on inferences of intention). A person is deprived of capital even if it is replaced by something else (*R(SB) 40/85*, para. 8). So a person who spends money on the purchase of an item of equal value is still deprived of that money. However, the fact that something is acquired in exchange will be relevant to the question whether the deprivation was effected with a view to reducing the assessable income. Since there is no discretion in this paragraph, it is only through this reasoning that the expenditure of capital on the purchase of non-income producing assets can escape this paragraph. If an income producing resource is disposed of and replaced by a lower income producing resource it will be possible to apply this paragraph to the difference.

Sub-para. (*b*) applies where a person has never had the income or capital in question but has failed to secure it in circumstances in which it would be reasonable to expect that it would be secured. Whether securing the income or capital was to be expected is an objective consideration, but it is still necessary to establish an intention to deprive with a view to reducing assessable income. The application of this paragraph will give rise to difficult decisions for CSATs. Some cases of failure to secure income will be relatively straightforward: the person may have failed to cash a cheque (*CSB 598/89*, para. 11), to claim a benefit (subject to para. 28) or to put money in an account bearing as high a rate of interest as possible. In other cases detailed consideration of evidence will be needed before a CSAT can decide whether it was reasonable to expect the income to be secured. For example, a dividend may not have been declared by a company in which a person has an interest. It is obvious that a dividend should have been declared if that person had such control over the company as to be able to determine or influence the dividend provided that it would be appropriate to declare a dividend given the financial position and the plans of the company. Evidence on each of these matters will need to be considered. Yet other cases will present difficult decisions on how far a person can be expected to act in securing income: for example, the chances of a person securing a particular job or type of job. Decisions on failure to secure capital will almost always be difficult. Capital here must mean capital which produces income. A person with sufficient cash may be expected to subscribe to a rights issue, but a CSAT cannot be expected to decide which shares a stock market investor could reasonably be expected to purchase. Moreover, the concern with this paragraph is with income which will be derived from the capital that should have been secured. There will, however, often be a risk attached to capital investment and this will need to be taken into account in deciding whether or not it was reasonable to expect a particular investment to be secured. In practice it is unlikely that a CSAT will be willing to second-guess investment decisions even with the benefit of hindsight except in blatant cases.

In contrast to para. 26, it is only necessary to establish that the deprivation or failure to secure was "with a view to" reducing assessable income. It is not necessary to show that this was its principal purpose. It may therefore be possible to catch cases under this paragraph which fail to satisfy the principal purpose test for paragraph 26.

Income which falls within this paragraph is treated as other income to which Part III of this Schedule applies (para. 32).

Para. 28(c)

Personal injury in the form of a disease also covers injuries suffered as a result of the disease such as an amputation necessary as a result of contracting meninigitis and septicaemia (*R(SB) 2/89*, para. 15). The key factor is the nature of the injury and not the particular loss for which the income from the trust is compensation. It would therefore cover financial loss as a result of an injury (such as loss of earnings) as much as the loss of amenity or the pain and suffering associated with the injury.

SCHEDULE 2

AMOUNTS TO BE DISREGARDED WHEN CALCULATING OR ESTIMATING N AND M

1. The amounts referred to in this Schedule are to be disregarded when calculating or estimating N and M (parent's net income).

2. An amount in respect of income tax applicable to the income in question where not otherwise allowed for under these Regulations.

3. Where a payment is made in a currency other than sterling, an amount equal to any banking charge or commission payable in converting that payment to sterling.

4. Any amount payable in a country outside the United Kingdom where there is a prohibition against the transfer to the United Kingdom of that amount.

5. Any compensation for personal injury and any payments from a trust fund set up for that purpose.

6. Any advance of earnings or any loan made by an employer to an employee.

7. Any payment by way of, or any reduction or discharge of liability resulting from entitlement to, housing benefit or council tax benefit.

8. Any disability living allowance, mobility supplement or any payment intended to compensate for the non-payment of any such allowance or supplement.

9. Any payment which is—

(*a*)   an attendance allowance under section 64 of the Contributions and Benefits Act;

(*b*)   an increase of disablement pension under section 104 or 105 of that Act (increases where constant attendance needed or for exceptionally severe disablement);

(*c*)   a payment made under regulations made in exercise of the power conferred by Schedule 8 to that Act (payments for pre-1948 cases);

(*d*)   an increase of an allowance payable in respect of constant attendance under that Schedule;

(*e*)   payable by virtue of articles 14, 15, 16, 43 or 44 of the Personal Injuries (Civilians) Scheme 1983 (S.I. 1983 No. 686) (allowances for constant attendance and exceptionally severe disablement and severe disablement occupational allowance) or any analogous payment; or

(*f*)   a payment based on the need for attendance which is paid as part of a war disablement pension.

10. Any payment under section 148 of the Contributions and Benefits Act (pensioners' Christmas bonus).

11. Any social fund payment within the meaning of Part VIII of the Contributions and Benefits Act.

12. Any payment made by the Secretary of State to compensate for the loss (in whole or part) of entitlement to housing benefit.

13. Any payment made by the Secretary of State to compensate for loss of housing supplement under regulation 19 of the Supplementary Benefit (Requirements) Regulations 1983.

14. Any payment made by the Secretary of State to compensate a person who was entitled to supplementary benefit in respect of a period ending immediately before 11th April 1988 but who did not become entitled to income support in respect of a period beginning with that day.

15. Any concessionary payment made to compensate for the non-payment of income support, disability living allowance, or any payment to which paragraph 9 applies.

16. Any payments of child benefit to the extent that they do not exceed the basic rate of that benefit as defined in regulation 4.

17. Any payment made under regulations 9 to 11 or 13 of the Welfare Food Regulations 1988 (payments made in place of milk tokens or the supply of vitamins).

18. Subject to paragraph 20 and to the extent that it does not exceed £10.00—

   (*a*) war disablement pension or war widow's pension or a payment made to compensate for non-payment of such a pension;

   (*b*) a pension paid by the government of a country outside Great Britain and which either—

      (i) is analogous to a war disablement pension; or

      (ii) is analogous to a war widow's pension.

19.—(1) Except where sub-paragraph (2) applies and subject to sub-paragraph (3) and paragraphs 20, 38 and 47, £10.00 of any charitable or voluntary payment made, or due to be made, at regular intervals.

(2) Subject to sub-paragraph (3) and paragraphs 38 and 47, any charitable or voluntary payment made or due to be made at regular intervals which is intended and used for an item other than food, ordinary clothing or footwear, gas, electricity or fuel charges, housing costs of any member of the family or the payment of council tax.

(3) Sub-paragraphs (1) and (2) shall not apply to a payment which is made by a person for the maintenance of any member of his family or of his former partner or of his children.

(4) For the purposes of sub-paragraph (1) where a number of charitable or voluntary payments fall to be taken into account they shall be treated as though they were one such payment.

20.—(1) Where, but for this paragraph, more than £10.00 would be disregarded under paragraphs 18 and 19(1) in respect of the same week, only £10.00 in aggregate shall be disregarded and where an amount falls to be deducted from the income of a student under paragraph 16(3)(*b*) or (*c*) of Schedule 1, that amount shall count as part of the £10.00 disregard allowed under this paragraph.

(2) Where any payment which is due to be paid in one week is paid in another week, sub-paragraph (1) and paragraphs 18 and 19(1) shall have effect as if that payment were received in the week in which it was due.

21. In the case of a person participating in arrangements for training made under section 2 of the Employment and Training Act 1973 or section 2 of the Enterprise and New Towns (Scotland) Act 1990 (functions in relation to training for employment etc.) or attending a course at an employment rehabilitation centre established under section 2 of the 1973 Act—

   (*a*) any travelling expenses reimbursed to the person;

   (*b*) any living away from home allowance under section 2(2)(*d*) of the 1973 Act or section 2(4)(*c*) of the 1990 Act;

   (*c*) any training premium,

but this paragraph, except in so far as it relates to a payment mentioned in sub-paragraph (*a*), (*b*) or (*c*), does not apply to any part of any allowance under section 2(2)(*d*) of the 1973 Act or section 2(4)(*c*) of the 1990 Act.

22. Where a parent occupies a dwelling as his home and that dwelling is also occupied by a person, other than a non-dependant or a person who is provided with board and lodging accommodation, and that person is contractually liable to make payments in respect of his occupation of the dwelling to the parent, the amount or, as the case may be, the amounts specified in paragraph 19 of Schedule 2 to the Family Credit (General) Regulations 1987 which apply in his case, or, if he is not in receipt of family credit, the amounts which would have applied if he had been in receipt of that benefit.

23. Where a parent, who is not a self-employed earner, is in receipt of rent or any other money in respect of the use and occupation of property other than his home, that rent or other payment to the extent of any sums which that parent is liable to pay by way of—

[¹(a) payments which are to be taken into account as eligible housing costs under sub-paragraphs (b), (c), (d) and (t) of paragraph 1 of Schedule 3 (eligible housing costs for the purposes of determining exempt income and protected income) and paragraph 3 of that Schedule (exempt income: additional provisions relating to housing costs);]

(b)   council tax payable in respect of that property;

(c)   water and sewerage charges in respect of that property.

24. Where a parent provides board and lodging accommodation in his home otherwise than as a self-employed earner—

(a)   £20.00 of any payment for that accommodation made by the person to whom that accommodation is provided; and

(b)   where any such payment exceeds £20.00, 50 per centum of the excess.

25. Any payment made to a person in respect of an adopted child who is a member of his family that is made in accordance with any regulations made under section 57A or pursuant to section 57A(6) of the Adoption Act 1976 (permitted allowances) or, as the case may be, section 51 of the Adoption (Scotland) Act 1978 (schemes for the payment of allowances to adopters)—

(a)   where the child is not a child in respect of whom child support maintenance is being assessed, to the extent that it exceeds [²the aggregate of the amounts to be taken into account in the calculation of E under regulation 9(1)(g)], reduced, as the case may be, under regulation 9(4);

(b)   in any other case, to the extent that it does not exceed the amount of the income of a child which is treated as that of his parent by virtue of Part IV.

26. Where a local authority makes a payment in respect of the accommodation and maintenance of a child in pursuance of paragraph 15 of Schedule 1 to the Children Act 1989 (local authority contribution to child's maintenance) to the extent that it exceeds the amount referred to in [³regulation 9(1)(g)] (reduced, as the case may be, under regulation 9(4)).

27. Any payment received under a policy of insurance taken out to insure against the risk of being unable to maintain repayments on a loan taken out to acquire an interest in, or to meet the cost of repairs or improvements to, the parent's home and used to meet such repayments, to the extent that the payment received under that policy does not in any period exceed the total of—

(a)   any interest payable on that loan;

(b)   any capital repayable on that loan; and

(c)   any premiums payable on that policy.

28. In the calculation of the income of the parent with care, any maintenance payments made by the absent parent in respect of his qualifying child.

29. Any payment made by a local authority to a person who is caring for a child under section 23(2)(a) of the Children Act 1989 (provision of accommodation and maintenance by a local authority for children whom the authority is looking after), or, as the case may be, section 21 of the Social Work (Scotland) Act 1968 or by a voluntary organisation under section 59(1)(a) of the Children Act 1989 (provision of accommodation by voluntary organisations) or by a care authority under regulation 9 of the Boarding Out and Fostering of Children (Scotland) Regulations 1985 (provision of accommodation and maintenance for children in care).

30. Any payment made by a health authority, local authority or voluntary organisation in respect of a person who is not normally a member of the household but is temporarily in the care of a member of it.

31. Any payment made by a local authority under section 17 or 24 of the Children Act 1989 or, as the case may be, section 12, 24 or 26 of the Social work (Scotland) Act 1968 (local authorities' duty to promote welfare of children and powers to grant financial assistance to persons looked after, or in, or formerly in, their care).

32. Any resettlement benefit which is paid to the parent by virtue of regulation 3 of the

Social Security (Hospital In-Patients) Amendment (No. 2) Regulations 1987 (transitional provisions).

33.—(1) Any payment or repayment made—

(*a*) as respects England and Wales, under regulation 3, 5 or 8 of the National Health Service (Travelling Expenses and Remission of Charges) Regulations 1988 (travelling expenses and health service supplies);

(*b*) as respects Scotland, under regulation 3, 5 or 8 of the National Health Service (Travelling Expenses and Remission of Charges) (Scotland) Regulations 1988 (travelling expenses and health service supplies).

(2) Any payment or repayment made by the Secretary of State for Health, the Secretary of State for Scotland or the Secretary of State for Wales which is analogous to a payment or repayment mentioned in sub-paragraph (1).

34. Any payment made (other than a training allowance), whether by the Secretary of State or any other person, under the Disabled Persons Employment Act 1944 or in accordance with arrangements made under section 2 of the Employment and Training Act 1973 to assist disabled persons to obtain or retain employment despite their disability.

35. Any contribution to the expenses of maintaining a household which is made by a non-dependant member of that household.

36. Any sum in respect of a course of study attended by a child payable by virtue of regulations made under section 81 of the Education Act 1944 (assistance by means of scholarship or otherwise), or by virtue of section 2(1) of the Education Act 1962 (awards for courses of further education) or section 49 of the Education (Scotland) Act 1980 (power to assist persons to take advantage of educational facilities).

37. Where a person receives income under an annuity purchased with a loan which satisfies the following conditions—

(*a*) that loan was made as part of a scheme under which not less than 90 per centum of the proceeds of the loan were applied to the purchase by the person to whom it was made of an annuity ending with his life or with the life of the survivor of two or more persons (in this paragraph referred to as "the annuitants") who include the person to whom the loan was made;

(*b*) that the interest on the loan is payable by the person to whom it was made or by one of the annuitants;

(*c*) that at the time the loan was made the person to whom it was made or each of the annuitants had attained the age of 65;

(*d*) that the loan was secured on a dwelling in Great Britain and the person to whom the loan was made or one of the annuitants owns an estate or interest in that dwelling; and

(*e*) that the person to whom the loan was made or one of the annuitants occupies the dwelling on which it was secured as his home at the time the interest is paid,

the amount, calculated on a weekly basis equal to—

(i) where, or insofar as, section 26 of the Finance Act 1982 (deduction of tax from certain loan interest) applies to the payments of interest on the loan, the interest which is payable after the deduction of a sum equal to income tax on such payments at the basic rate for the year of assessment in which the payment of interest becomes due;

(ii) in any other case the interest which is payable on the loan without deduction of such a sum.

38. Any payment of the description specified in paragraph 39 of Schedule 9 to the Income Support Regulations (disregard of payments made under certain trusts and disregard of certain other payments) and any income derived from the investment of such payments.

39. Any payment made to a juror or witness in respect of attendance at court other than compensation for loss of earnings or for loss of a benefit payable under the Contributions and Benefits Act.

40. Any special war widows' payment made under—

(*a*) the Naval and Marine Pay and Pensions (Special War Widows Payment) Order 1990 made under section 3 of the Naval and Marine Pay and Pensions Act 1865;

(*b*) the Royal Warrant dated 19th February 1990 amending the Schedule to the Army Pensions Warrant 1977 (Army Code No. 13045);

(*c*) the Queen's Order dated 26th February 1990 made under section 2 of the Air Force (Constitution) Act 1917;

(*d*) the Home Guard War Widows Special Payments Regulations 1990 made under section 151 of the Reserve Forces Act 1980;

(*e*) the Orders dated 19th February 1990 amending Orders made on 12th December 1980 concerning the Ulster Defence Regiment made in each case under section 140 of the Reserve Forces Act 1980 (Army Code No. 60589),

and any analogous payment by the Secretary of State for Defence to any person who is not a person entitled under the provisions mentioned in sub-paragraphs (*a*) to (*e*).

41. Any payment to a person as holder of the Victoria Cross or the George Cross or any analogous payment.

42. Any payment made either by the Secretary of State for the Home Department or by the Secretary of State for Scotland under a scheme established to assist relatives and other persons to visit persons in custody.

43. Any amount by way of a refund of income tax deducted from profits or emoluments chargeable to income tax under Schedule D or Schedule E.

44. Maintenance payments (whether paid under the Act or otherwise) insofar as they are not treated as income under Part III or IV.

45. Where following a divorce or separation—

(*a*) capital is divided between the parent and the person who was his partner before the divorce or separation; and

(*b*) that capital is intended to be used to acquire a new home for that parent or to acquire furnishings for a home of his,

income derived from the investment of that capital for one year following the date on which that capital became available to the parent.

[⁴**46.** Except in the case of a self-employed earner, payments in kind.]

47. Any payment made by the Joseph Rowntree Memorial Trust from money provided to it by the Secretary of State for Health for the purpose of maintaining a family fund for the benefit of severely handicapped children.

48. Any payment of expenses to a person who is—

(*a*) engaged by a charitable or voluntary body; or

(*b*) a volunteer,

if he otherwise derives no remuneration or profit from the body or person paying those expenses.

[⁵**48A.** Any guardian's allowance under Part III of the Contributions and Benefits Act.

48B. Any payment in respect of duties mentioned in paragraph 1(1)(*i*) of Chapter 1 of Part I of Schedule 1 relating to a period of one year or more.]

49. In this Schedule—

"concessionary payment" means a payment made under arrangements made by the Secretary of State with the consent of the Treasury which is charged either to the National Insurance Fund or to a Departmental Expenditure Vote to which payments of benefit under the Contributions and Benefits Act are charged;

"health authority" means a health authority established under the National Health Service Act 1977 or the National Health Service (Scotland) Act 1978;

"mobility supplement" has the same meaning as in regulation 2(1) of the Income Support Regulations;

"war disablement pension" and "war widow" have the same meanings as in section 150 (2) of the Contributions and Benefits Act.

AMENDMENTS

1. Regulation 28 of the Amendment Regulations (April 5, 1993).
2. Regulation 29 of the Amendment Regulations (April 5, 1993).
3. Regulation 30 of the Amendment Regulations (April 5, 1993).
4. Regulation 31 of the Amendment Regulations (April 5, 1993).

5. Regulation 32 of the Amendment Regulations (April 5, 1993).

DEFINITIONS
"Contributions and Benefits Act": see reg. 1(2).
"council tax benefit": *ibid.*
"earnings": *ibid.*
"family": *ibid.*
"home": *ibid.*
"housing benefit": *ibid.*
"non-dependant": *ibid.*
"ordinary clothing or footwear": *ibid.*
"parent with care": *ibid.*
"partner": *ibid.*
"person": *ibid.*
"self-employed earner": *ibid.*
"student": *ibid.*
"training allowance": *ibid.*

GENERAL NOTE
Para. (19)
Whether a payment is voluntary is judged by looking at the payer and not the payee. Consequently a payment by British Coal to a miner's widow in lieu of concessionary coal is not a voluntary payment (*R.* v. *Doncaster Metropolitan Borough Council, ex p. Boulton, The Times*, December 31, 1992).

SCHEDULE 3

ELIGIBLE HOUSING COSTS

Eligible housing costs for the purposes of determining exempt income and protected income

1. Subject to the following provisions of this Schedule, the following payments in respect of the provision of a home shall be eligible to be taken into account as housing costs for the purposes of these Regulations—

(a) payments of, or by way of, rent;

(b) mortgage interest payments;

(c) interest payments under a hire purchase agreement to buy a home;

(d) interest payments on loans for repairs and improvements to the home[1], including interest on a loan for any service charge imposed to meet the cost of such repairs and improvements;]

(e) payments by way of ground rent or in Scotland, payments by way of feu duty;

(f) payments under a co-ownership scheme;

(g) payments in respect of, or in consequence of, the use and occupation of the home;

(h) where the home is a tent, payments in respect of the tent and the site on which it stands;

(i) payments in respect of a licence or permission to occupy the home (whether or not board is provided);

(j) payments by way of mesne profits or, in Scotland, violent profits;

(k) payments of, or by way of, service charges, the payment of which is a condition on which the right to occupy the home depends;

(l) payments under or relating to a tenancy or licence of a Crown tenant;

(m) mooring charges payable for a houseboat;

(n) where the home is a caravan or a mobile home, payments in respect of the site on which it stands;

(o) any contribution payable by a parent resident in an almshouse provided by a housing association which is either a charity of which particulars are entered in the register of charities established under section 4 of the Charities Act 1960 (register of charities) or an exempt charity within the meaning of that Act, which is a contribution towards the cost of maintaining that association's almshouses and essential services in them;

(*p*) payments under a rental purchase agreement, that is to say an agreement for the purchase of a home under which the whole or part of the purchase price is to be paid in more than one instalment and the completion of the purchase is deferred until the whole or a specified part of the purchase price has been paid;

(*q*) where, in Scotland, the home is situated on or pertains to a croft within the meaning of section 3(1) of the Crofters (Scotland) Act 1955, the payment in respect of the croft land;

(*r*) where the home is provided by an employer (whether under a condition or term in a contract of service or otherwise), payments to that employer in respect of the home, including payments made by the employer deducting the payment in question from the remuneration of the parent in question;

[² ...]

(*t*) payments in respect of a loan taken out to pay off another loan but only to the extent that it was incurred for that purpose and only to the extent to which the interest on that other loan would have been met under this paragraph.

Loans for repairs and improvements to the home

2. For the purposes of paragraph 1(*d*) "repairs and improvements" means major repairs necessary to maintain the fabric of the home and any of the following measures undertaken with a view to improving its fitness for occupation—

(*a*) installation of a fixed bath, shower, wash basin or lavatory, and necessary associated plumbing;

(*b*) damp proofing measures;

(*c*) provision of improvement of ventilation and natural lighting;

(*d*) provision of electric lighting and sockets;

(*e*) provision or improvement of drainage facilities;

(*f*) improvement of the structural condition of the home;

(*g*) improvements to the facilities for the storing, preparation and cooking of food;

(*h*) provision of heating, including central heating;

(*i*) provision of storage facilities for fuel and refuse;

(*j*) improvements to the insulation of the home;

(*k*) other improvements which the child support officer considers reasonable in the circumstances.

Exempt income: additional provisions relating to eligible housing costs

3.—(1) The additional provisions made by this paragraph shall have effect only for the purposes of calculating or estimating exempt income.

(2) Subject to sub-paragraph (6), where the home of an absent parent or, as the case may be, a parent with care, is subject to a mortgage or charge and that parent makes periodical payments to reduce the capital secured by that mortgage or charge of an amount provided for in accordance with the terms thereof, the amount of those payments shall be eligible to be taken into account as the housing costs of that parent.

(3) Subject to sub-paragraph (6), where the home of an absent parent or, as the case may be, a parent with care, is held under an agreement and certain payments made under that agreement are included as housing costs by virtue of paragraph 1 of this Schedule, the weekly amount of any other payments which are made in accordance with that agreement by the parent in order either—

(*a*) to reduce his liability under that agreement; or

(*b*) to acquire the home to which it relates,

shall also be eligible to be taken into account as housing costs.

(4) Where a policy of insurance has been obtained and retained for the purpose of discharging a mortgage or charge on the home of the parent in question, the amount of the premiums paid under that policy shall be eligible to be taken into account as a housing cost.

(5) Where a policy of insurance has been obtained and retained for the purposes of discharging a mortgage or charge on the home of the parent in question and also for the purpose of accruing profits on the maturity of the policy, the part of the premiums paid under that policy which are necessarily incurred for the purpose of discharging the mortgage or charge shall be eligible to be taken into account as a housing cost; and, where that part cannot be ascertained, 0.0277 per centum of the amount secured by the mortgage or charge shall be deemed to be the part which is eligible to be taken into account as a housing cost.

(6) For the purposes of sub-paragraphs (2) and (3), housing costs shall not include—

(*a*) any payment of arrears or payments in excess of those which are required to be made under or in respect of a mortgage, charge or agreement to which either of those sub-paragraphs relate;

(*b*) payments under any second or subsequent mortgage on the home to the extent that they are attributable to arrears or would otherwise not be eligible to be taken into account as housing costs;

(*c*) premiums payable in respect of any policy of insurance against loss caused by the destruction of or damage to any building or land.

Conditions relating to eligible housing costs

4.—(1) Subject to the following provisions of this paragraph the housing costs referred to in this Schedule shall be included as housing costs only where—

(*a*) they are incurred in relation to the parent's home;

(*b*) the parent or, if he is one of a family, he or a member of his family, is responsible for those costs; and

(*c*) the liability to meet those costs is to a person other than a member of the same household.

(2) For the purposes of sub-paragraph (1)(*b*) a parent shall be treated as responsible for housing costs where—

(*a*) because the person liable to meet those costs is not doing so, he has to meet those costs in order to continue to live in the home and either he was formerly the partner of the person liable, or he is some other person whom it is reasonable to treat as liable to meet those costs; or

(*b*) he pays a share of those costs in a case where—

 (i) he is living in a household with other persons;

 (ii) those other persons include persons who are not close relatives of his or his partner;

 (iii) a person who is not such a close relative is responsible for those costs under the preceding provisions of this paragraph or has an equivalent responsibility for housing expenditure; and

 (iv) it is reasonable in the circumstances to treat him as sharing that responsibility.

Accommodation also used for other purposes

5. Where amounts are payable in respect of accommodation which consists partly of residential accommodation and partly of other accommodation, only such proportion thereof as is attributable to residential accommodation shall be eligible to be taken into account as housing costs.

Ineligible service and fuel charges

6. Housing costs shall not include—

(*a*) where the costs are inclusive of ineligible service charges within the meaning of paragraph 1 of Schedule 1 to the Housing Benefit (General) Regulations 1987 (ineligible service charges), the amounts attributable to those ineligible service charges or, where that amount is not separated from or separately identified within the housing costs to be met under this paragraph, such part of the payments made in respect of those housing costs which are fairly attributable to the provision of those ineligible services having regard to the costs of comparable services;

(*b*) where the costs are inclusive of any of the items mentioned in paragraph 5(2) of Schedule 1 to the Housing Benefit (General) Regulations 1987 (payment in respect of fuel charges), the deductions prescribed in that paragraph unless the parent provides evidence on which the actual or approximate amount of the service charge for fuel may be estimated, in which case the estimated amount; and

(c) charges for water, sewerage or allied environmental services and where the amount of such charges is not separately identified, such part of the charges in question as is attributable to those services.

Interpretation

7. In this Schedule except where the context otherwise requires—

"close relative" means a parent, parent-in-law, son, son-in-law, daughter, daughter-in-law, step-parent, step-son, step-daughter, brother, sister, or the spouse of any of the preceding persons or, if that person is one of an unmarried couple, the other member of that couple;

"co-ownership scheme" means a scheme under which the dwelling is let by a housing association and the tenant, or his personal representative, will, under the terms of the tenancy agreement or of the agreement under which he became a member of the association, be entitled, on his ceasing to be a member and subject to any conditions stated in either agreement, to a sum calculated by reference directly or indirectly to the value of the dwelling.

"housing association" has the meaning assigned to it by section 1(1) of the Housing Association Act 1985.

AMENDMENTS
1. Regulation 33(*a*) of the Amendment Regulations (April 5, 1993).
2. Regulation 33(*b*) of the Amendment Regulations (April 5, 1993).

DEFINITIONS
"family": see reg. 1(2).
"home": *ibid.*
"parent with care": *ibid.*
"partner": *ibid.*
"person": *ibid.*

GENERAL NOTE
The provisions of this Schedule are based on Sched. 3 to the Income Support (General) Regulations.

Para. 1

This paragraph lays down the eligible housing costs for all purposes except the calculation of exempt income where the provisions are supplemented by para. 3. Where repayment of a loan or credit is concerned, only interest payments are included and not capital payments. Housing costs are not defined. They bear their normal meaning of costs associated with the provision of housing for an individual or a family (Common Appendix to *R(IS) 3/91* and *R(IS) 4/91*, para. 10). This is subject to para. 4 below. As a result of the Amendment Regulations, payments analogous to those listed are not within the scope of the paragraph.

Sub-para. (d)

If this head is to be satisfied there must be a loan. It is not sufficient that a debt, for example to cover private street works, is deferred and paid in instalments with interest (*R(SB) 3/87*, para. 7). Repairs and improvements are defined in para. 2.

Sub-para. (g)

This is a broad provision the extent of which is uncertain. It does not cover capital repayments or premiums on insurance policies since these are the subject of specific provision in para. 3 which would be unnecessary if these items fell under this sub-paragraph. Payments in respect of road charges and interest paid on them are charges in respect of a home (*R(SB) 3/87*, para. 8).

Sub-para. (k)

Service charges are not defined. Their meaning was discussed by the Tribunal of Commissioners whose decision appears in the Common Appendix to *R(IS) 3/91* and *R(IS) 4/91*, paras. 11 and 15. The words are to be interpreted liberally and mean charges made for services provided in connection with housing. They must be charges which involve the determination and arrangement of a service, which would otherwise be for the occupier to decide on and arrange, in a manner binding on the occupier and which cannot be withdrawn from at leisure. They must bind all those with the same interest in the property or they must run with the land so as to bind successors in occupancy. The service charges which are covered are limited by para. 6.

Para. 2

This paragraph defines repairs and improvements for the purposes of para. 1(*d*). Repair covers both the remedying of defects and steps taken to prevent these, such as the painting of a house to preserve the woodwork (*CSB 420/85*, paras. 11–12). However, where the alleged repair is of the preventive kind, evidence and findings of fact will be needed on whether the work may properly be considered to have been undertaken as a repair or only for cosmetic reasons (*ibid.* at para. 12). It would, for example, if the painting of a house were being considered, be necessary to inquire into the state of the paint work at the time and whether the change was merely to change the colour.

Repairs must be "*necessary* to maintain the fabric of the home", a strict test. They must also be "major." Whether a repair is or is not major is a question of fact (*CSB 265/87*, para. 10). It is a comparative term whose meaning is bound to be somewhat fluid and imprecise, but it will always be relevant to take into account the cost as well as the nature of and the time taken for the work (*ibid.* at paras. 10 and 12). Chimney-sweeping cannot be a repair (*ibid.* at para. 7).

Improvements need not be major but they must fall within one of the categories listed and they must be undertaken with a view to improving the fitness of the home for occupation. The test is a subjective one; the reasonableness of the improvements is not a factor except under (*k*) but this will be a relevant consideration in assessing the credibility of the evidence on this issue. Moreover the work must be undertaken with a view not just to improving the home but to improving its fitness for occupation. The paragraph assumes that there should be a minimum standard of accommodation and allows the cost of bring the home up to that standard to be taken into account as eligible housing costs. So the test is whether the work is carried out with a view to bringing the home up to a standard above the minimum in a particular respect. This provision is not a licence to install a replacement or additional bathroom or further electric sockets where the current provision is adequate. Care is also needed with self-build homes to ensure that this paragraph is not used to cover the costs of completion rather than of the improvement of a home.

Sub-para. (a)

Unlike its social security counterpart, this sub-paragraph does not cover sinks.

Sub-para. (k)

The improvements must be made with a view to improving the home's fitness for occupation. This is wider than fitness for habitation and would cover access to the premises (*R(SB) 3/87*, para.10).

Para. 3

The terms of this paragraph are useful not only in their own right but also for the light they shed on the scope of some of the sub-paragraphs in paragraph 1. It makes special provision for the purposes of calculating exempt income by extending the eligible housing costs under para. 1 to include capital repayments and endowment policy premiums in so far as they cover the capital repayments. Where the policy is designed to produce a profit as well as to cover the capital, for example in a with profits endowment or a pension mortgage, the part of the premiums necessarily incurred for the purpose of discharging a mortgage or charge should be identifiable by expert evidence. Where this is not possible or the evidence is not available, 0.0277 per cent. of the sum secured is used as the eligible housing cost. This figure is sufficient to ensure that the debt would be covered assuming an annual rate of return of eight per cent. over 25 years. Payments of arrears or voluntary additional payments of capital are not covered, nor is the cost of insurance against loss of or damage to the building or land.

Para. 4(1)

This sub-paragraph lays down three conditions all of which must be satisfied in order for the housing costs to be eligible for child support purposes. First, the costs must be incurred in relation to the parent's own home; costs which are met, for example, in respect of the home of a relative or a divorced spouse are not covered. Second, the parent or a member of the parent's family must be responsible for them. It is clear from para. 4(1)(*c*) and (2) that what matters is legal responsibility rather than a voluntary assumption of payment. However, in two cases persons are treated as responsible for costs which they are not legally liable to meet: see sub-para. (2). What matters is legal liability and not whether the person liable is paying the costs. It will not be unusual for example for spouses or partners to be jointly and severally liable on a mortgage but for the payments to be met by only one of them. Third, the liability must be to someone who is not a member of the same household. This goes some way to prevent collusion between members of a household. It may be possible for parties to arrange their affairs so that there are separate households, and tribunals will need to be astute to distinguish genuine arrangements which do result in separate households, even if those arrangements are made in order to fall within sub-para. (1), and shams.

Para. 4(2)

This sub-paragraph provides for two cases in which persons who are paying housing costs for which they are not liable are treated as if they were responsible for those costs. The first is where the person who is liable is not paying and the parent is making payments in order to continue to live in the home. It must be necessary for the parent to meet the costs in order to continue to live in the home. Failure must therefore put the home at risk. So failure to pay a loan which is not secured on the home will not be sufficient. In practice even if the loan is secured on the home eviction for non-payment is a difficult and lengthy process. However tribunals are likely to regard all cases in which the risk of eviction may arise in the event of non-payment as falling within this head. The typical case covered will be where the parent has been deserted by a former partner who is liable for housing costs but is refusing to pay them. If this is the case then the parent is treated as responsible for the costs. The parent may also be treated as responsible in other cases, for example if a grandparent was meeting the costs. In these other cases however it must be reasonable to treat the parent as liable; no issue of reasonableness arises if the person liable was a former partner. The second case covered is where the parent is sharing housing costs with others who also live in the accommodation of whom at least one who is not a close relative is liable or treated as liable for those costs, provided that it is reasonable to treat the parent as sharing the responsibility for the costs. The wording speaks of others in the plural, but by virtue of s.6(*c*) of the Interpretation Act 1978 this will include the singular. Findings of fact on each element of each case will be necessary and decisions on reasonableness will need to be justified in the reasons for decision.

Para. 5

This allows costs to be apportioned in cases where premises are used for a dual purpose. However it only covers cases where there is separate accommodation which is put to each use, such as where living accommodation is connected to retail premises or where a business is run from a distinct and separate part of accommodation. It does not cover cases where a business is run from a part of a person's home which is also used for other purposes, such as a business run from a desk in the corner of the living room.

Para. 6

Para. 1 of the Schedule reads as follows.

"1. The following service charges shall not be eligible to be met by housing benefit—

(*a*) charges in respect of day-to-day living expenses including, in particular, all provision of—

    (i) subject to paragraph 1A meals (including the preparation of meals or provision of unprepared food);

    (ii) laundry (other than the provision of premises or equipment to enable a person to do his own laundry);

    (iii) leisure items such as either sports facilities (except a children's play area), or television rental and licence fees (except radio relay charges, charges made in respect of the conveyance and the installation and maintenance of equipment for such conveyance of a television broadcasting service which is not a domestic satellite service, or charges made in respect of the conveyance and the installation and maintenance of equipment for such conveyance of a television programme service where in respect of the claimant's dwelling the installation of such equipment is the only practicable means of conveying satisfactorily a television broadcasting service which is not a domestic satellite service, as these services are defined in the Broadcasting Act 1990);

    (iv) cleaning of rooms and windows (other than communal areas) except where neither the claimant nor any member of his household is able to clean them himself; and

    (v) transport;

(*b*) charges in respect of—

    (i) the acquisition of furniture or household equipment, and

    (ii) the use of furniture or equipment where that furniture or household equipment will become the property of the claimant by virtue of an agreement with the landlord;

(*c*) charges in respect of the provision of an emergency alarm system, except where such a system is provided in accommodation which is occupied by elderly, sick or disabled persons and such accommodation, apart from the alarm system, is either—

    (i) specifically designed or adapted for such persons, or

    (ii) otherwise particularly suitable for them, having regard to its size, heating system and other major features or facilities;

(*d*) charges in respect of medical expenses (including the cost of treatment or counselling related to mental disorder, mental handicap, physical disablement or past or present alcohol or drug dependence);

(*e*) charges in respect of the provision of nursing care or personal care (including assistance at meal-times or with personal appearance or hygiene);

(*f*) charges in respect of general counselling or other support services (whether or not provided by social work professionals) except those related to the provision of adequate accommodation or those provided by the landlord in person or someone employed by him who spends the majority of his time providing services for which the charges are not ineligible under the terms of this paragraph;

(*g*) charges in respect of any services not specified in sub-paragraphs (*a*) to (*f*) which are not connected with the provision of adequate accommodation."

Para. 5(2) of the Schedule in so far as it is relevant reads as follows. The figures apply as from April 1, 1992.

"(*a*) for heating (other than hot water)	£8.60
(*b*) for hot water	£1.05
(*c*) for lighting	£0.70
(*d*) for cooking	£1.05"

This definition probably does not include building insurance premiums, since they are not connected with the provision of adequate accommodation, even where they are a condition of the mortgage. This was the provisional view of the Commissioner in *CSIS 4/90*, para. 8, although he did not express a final conclusion.

SCHEDULE 4

CASES WHERE CHILD SUPPORT MAINTENANCE IS NOT TO BE PAYABLE

The payments and awards specified for the purposes of regulation 26(1)(*b*)(i) are—

(*a*) the following payments under the Contribution and Benefits Act—

  (i) sickness benefit under section 31;

  (ii) invalidity pension under section 33;

  (iii) invalidity pension for widowers under section 34;

  (iv) maternity allowance under section 35;

  (v) invalidity pension for widows under section 40;

  (vi) attendance allowance under section 64;

  (vii) severe disablement allowance under section 68;

  (viii) invalid care allowance under section 70;

  (ix) disability living allowance under section 71;

  (x) disablement benefit under section 103;

  (xi) disability working allowance under section 129;

  (xii) statutory sick pay within the meaning of section 151;

  (xiii) statutory maternity pay within the meaning of section 164;

(*b*) awards in respect of disablement made under (or under provisions analogous to)--

  (i) the War Pensions (Coastguards) Scheme 1944 (S.I. 1944 No. 500);

  (ii) the War Pensions (Naval Auxiliary Personnel) Scheme 1964 (S.I. 1964 No. 1985);

  (iii) the Pensions (Polish Forces) Scheme 1964 (S.I. 1964 No. 2007);

  (iv) the War Pensions (Mercantile Marine) Scheme 1964 (S.I. 1964 No. 2058);

  (v) the Royal Warrant of 21st December 1964 (service in the Home Guard before 1945) (Cmnd. 2563);

  (vi) the Order by Her Majesty of 22nd December 1964 concerning pensions and other grants in respect of disablement or death due to service in the Home Guard after 27th April 1952 (Cmnd. 2564);

  (vii) the Order by Her Majesty (Ulster Defence Regiment) of 4th January 1971 (Cmnd. 4567);

  (viii) the Personal Injuries (Civilians) Scheme 1983 (S.I. 1983 No. 686);

  (ix) the Naval, Military and Air Forces Etc. (Disablement and Death) Service Pensions Order 1983 (S.I. 1983 No. 883); and (*c*)   payments from [¹the Independent Living (1993) Fund or the Independent Living (Extension) Fund].

AMENDMENTS
1.   Regulation 34 of the Amendment Regulations (April 5, 1993).

DEFINITIONS
"Contributions and Benefits Act": see reg. 1(2).
"disability working allowance": *ibid.*
"Independent Living (1993) Fund" *ibid.*
"Independent Living (Extension) Fund": *ibid.*

[¹SCHEDULE 5   **Regulation 28(5)**

PROVISIONS APPLYING TO CASES TO WHICH SECTION 43 OF THE ACT AND REGULATION 28 APPLY

[²**1.** In this Schedule—
(*a*)   "relevant decision" means a decision of a child support officer given under section 43 of the Act (contribution to maintenance by deduction from benefit) and regulation 28; and
(*b*)   "relevant person" has the same meaning as in regulation 1(2) of the Maintenance Assessment Procedure Regulations.]

2. A relevant decision may be reviewed by a child support officer, either on application by a relevant person or of his own motion, if it appears to him that the absent parent has at some time after that decision was given satisfied the conditions prescribed by regulation 28(1) or, as the case may be, no longer satisfies those conditions.

3. A relevant decision shall be reviewed by a child support officer when it has been in force for 52 weeks.

4.—(1) Before conducting a review under paragraph 6 the child support officer shall—
(*a*)   give 14 days' notice of the proposed review to the relevant persons [³. . .]; and
(*b*)   invite representations, either in person or in writing, from the relevant persons on any matter relating to the review and set out the provisions of sub-paragraphs (2) to (4) in relation to such representations.

(2) Subject to sub-paragraph (3), where the child support officer conducting the review does not, within 14 days of the date on which notice of the review was given, receive a request from a relevant person to make representations in person, or receives such a request and arranges for an appointment for such representations to be made but that appointment is not kept, he may complete the review in the absence of such representations from that person.

(3) Where the child support officer conducting the review is satisfied that there was good reason for failure to keep an appointment, he shall provide for a further opportunity for the making of representations by the relevant person concerned before he completes the review.

(4) Where the child support officer conducting the review does not receive written representations from a relevant person within 14 days of the date on which notice of the review was given, he may complete the review in the absence of written representations from that person.

5. After completing a review under paragraph 2, 3 or 6, the child support officer shall notify all relevant persons of the result of the review and—
(*a*)   in the case of a review under paragraph 2 or 3, of the right to apply for a further review under paragraph (6); and
(*b*)   in the case of a review under [⁴paragraph 6], of the right of appeal under section 20 of the Act as applied by paragraph 8.

6. Where a child support officer has made a decision under regulation 28 or paragraph 2 or 3, any relevant person may apply to the Secretary of State for a review of that decision and, subject to the modifications set out in paragraph 7, the provisions of section 18(5) to (7) of the Act shall apply to such a review.

7. The modifications to the provisions of section 18(5) to (7) of the Act referred to in paragraph 6 are—

    (*a*)   any reference in those provisions to a maintenance assessment shall be read as a reference to a relevant decision; and

    (*b*)   subsection 6 shall apply as if the reference to the cancellation of an assessment was omitted.

[⁵**7A.** If, on a review under paragraph 2, 3, or 6, the relevant decision is revised ("the revised decision") the revised decision shall have effect—

    (*a*)   if the revised decision is that no payments such as are mentioned in section 43 of the Act are to be made, from the date on which the event giving rise to the review occurred: or

    (*b*)   if the revised decision is that such payments are to be made, from the date on which the revised decision is given.]

8. The provisions of section 20 of the Act (appeals) shall apply in relation to a review or a refusal to review under paragraph 6.

9. The provisions of paragraphs (1) and (2) of regulation 5 of the Child Support (Collection and Enforcement) Regulations 1992 shall apply to the transmission of payments in place of child support maintenance under section 43 of the Act and regulation 28 as they apply to the transmission of payments of child support maintenance.]

AMENDMENTS

    1.   Regulation 26(3) of, and the Schedule to, the Amendment Regulations (April 5, 1993).

    2.   Reg. 2(3)(i) of the Child Support (Maintenance Assessments and Special Cases) Amendment Regulations 1993 (April 26, 1993).

    3.   Reg. 2(3)(ii) of the Child Support (Maintenance Assessments and Special Cases) Amendment Regulations 1993 (April 26, 1993).

    4.   Reg. 2(3)(iii) of the Child Support (Maintenance Assessments and Special Cases) Amendment Regulations 1993 (April 26, 1993).

    5.   Reg. 2(3)(iv) of the Child Support (Maintenance Assessments and Special Cases) Amendment Regulations 1993 (April 26, 1993).

DEFINITIONS

    "the Act": see reg. 1(2).

    "Maintenance Assessment Procedure Regulations": *ibid.*

The Child Support (Arrears, Interest and Adjustment of Maintenance Assessments) Regulations 1992

(S.I. 1992 No. 1816)

Made by the Secretary of State for Social Security under ss 41, 51, 52(4) and 54 of the Child Support Act 1991 and all other powers enabling him in that behalf.

ARRANGEMENT OF REGULATIONS

PART 1

General

1. Citation, commencement and interpretation.

PART II

Arrears of child support maintenance and interest on arrears

2. Applicability of provisions as to arrears and interest and arrears notices.
3. Liability to make payments of interest with respect to arrears.
4. Circumstances in which no liability to pay interest arises.
5. Payment of arrears by agreement.
6. Rate of interest and calculation of interest.
7. Receipt and retention of interest paid.
8. Retention of recovered arrears of child support maintenance by the Secretary of State.

PART III

Attribution of payments and adjustment of the amount payable under a maintenance assessment

9. Attribution of payments.
10. Adjustment of the amount payable under a maintenance assessment.

PART IV

Miscellaneous

11. Notifications following an adjustment under the provisions of regulation 10.
12. Review of adjustments under regulation 10 or of the calculation of arrears or interest.
13. Procedure and notifications on applications and reviews under regulation 12.
14. Non-disclosure of information to third parties.
15. Applicability of regulations 1(6) and 53 to 56 of the Maintenance Assessment Procedure Regulations.

PART I

GENERAL

Citation, commencement and interpretation

1.—(1) These Regulations may be cited as the Child Support (Arrears, Interest and Adjustment of Maintenance Assessments) Regulations 1992 and shall come into force on 5th April 1993.

(2) In these Regulations, unless the context otherwise repuires—

"absent parent" includes a person treated as an absent parent by virtue of regulation 20 of the Maintenance Assessments and Special Cases Regulations;

"the Act" means the Child Support Act 1991;

"arrears" means arrears of child support maintenance;

"arrears of child support maintenance" is to be construed in accordance with section 41(1) and (2) of the Act;

"arrears notice" has the meaning prescribed in regulation 2;

"due date" has the meaning prescribed in regulation 3;

"Maintenance Assessments and Special Cases Regulations" means the Child Support (Maintenance Assessments and Special Cases) Regulations 1992;

"Maintenance Assessment Procedure Regulations" means the Child Support (Maintenance Assessment Procedure) Regulations 1992;

"parent with care" means a person who, in respect of the same child or children, is both a parent and a person with care;

"relevant person" has the same meaning as in the Maintenance Assessment Procedure Regulations;

(3) In these Regulations, unless the context otherwise requires, a reference—

(*a*) to a numbered regulation is to the regulation in these Regulations bearing that number;

(*b*) in a regulation to a numbered paragraph is to the paragraph in that regulation bearing that number;

(*c*) in a paragraph to a lettered or numbered sub-paragraph is to the subparagraph in that paragraph bearing that letter or number.

PART II

ARREARS OF CHILD SUPPORT MAINTENANCE AND INTEREST ON ARREARS

Applicability of provisions as to arrears and interest and arrears notices

2.—(1) The provisions of paragraphs (2) to (4) and regulations 3 to 9 shall apply where—

(*a*) a case falls within section 41(1) of the Act; and

(*b*) the Secretary of State is arranging for the collection of child support maintenance under section 29 of the Act.

(2) Where the Secretary of State is considering taking action with regard to a case falling within paragraph (1), he shall serve a notice (an "arrears notice") on the absent parent.

(3) An arrears notice shall—

(*a*) itemize the payments of child support maintenance due and not paid;

(*b*) set out in general terms the provisions as to arrears and interest contained in this regulation and regulations 3 to 9; and

(c) request the absent parent to make payment of all outstanding arrears.

(4) Where an arrears notice has been served under paragraph (2), no duty to serve a further notice under that paragraph shall arise in relation to further arrears unless those further arrears have arisen after an intervening continuous period of not less than 12 weeks during the course of which all payments of child support maintenance due from the absent parent have been paid on time in accordance with regulations made under section 29 of the Act.

DEFINITIONS
    "absent parent": see reg. 1(2).
    "the Act": *ibid.*
    "arrears": *ibid.*
    "arrears notice": *ibid.*

Liability to make payments of interest with respect to arrears

3.—(1) Subject to paragraph (2) and regulations 4 and 5, interest shall be payable with respect to any amount of child support maintenance due in accordance with a maintenance assessment and not paid by the date specified by the Secretary of State in accordance with regulations made under section 29 of the Act (the "due date"), and shall be payable in respect of the period commencing on that day and terminating on the date that amount is paid.

(2) Subject to paragraph (3), interest with respect to arrears shall only be payable if the Secretary of State has served an arrears notice in relation to those arrears, and shall not be payable in respect of any period terminating on a date earlier than 14 days prior to the date the arrears notice is served on the absent parent.

(3) Where the Secretary of State has served an arrears notice, the provisions of paragraph (2) shall not apply in relation to further arrears unless the conditions mentioned in regulation 2(4) are satisfied.

(4) Subject to paragraph (6), where, following a review under section [1 16, 17,] 18 or 19 of the Act or an appeal under section 20 of the Act, a fresh maintenance assessment is made with retrospective effect, interest in respect of the relevant retrospective period shall be payable with respect to the arrears calculated by reference to that fresh assessment.

(5) The provisions of paragraph (4) shall apply to a fresh assessment following a review under section [1 16, 17,] 18 or 19 of the Act or an appeal under section 20 of the Act prior to any adjustment of that assessment under the provisions of regulation 10.

(6) For the purposes of paragraph (4), where the review under section [1 16, 17,] 18 or 19 of the Act or an appeal under section 20 of the Act results in an increased assessment, and arrears in relation to that assessment arise, no interest shall be payable with respect to the arrears relating to the additional maintenance payable under that assessment in respect of any period prior to the date the absent parent is notified of the increased assessment.

AMENDMENT
    1.   Regulation 35 of the Amendment Regulations (April 5, 1993).

DEFINITIONS
    "absent parent": see reg. 1(2).
    "the Act": *ibid.*
    "arrears": *ibid.*
    "arrears notice": *ibid.*

Circumstances in which no liability to pay interest arises

4.—(1) An absent parent shall not be liable to make payments of interest with respect to arrears in respect of any period if the conditions set out in paragraph (2) are satisfied in relation to that period.

(2) The conditions referred to in paragraph (1) are—

    (*a*) the absent parent did not know, and could not reasonably have been expected to know, of the existence of the arrears; or

    (*b*) the arrears have arisen solely in consequence of an operational or administrative error on the part of the Secretary of State or a child support officer.

[[1](3) An absent parent who pays all outstanding arrears of interest within 28 days of the due date shall not be liable to make payments of interest with respect to those arrears.]

AMENDMENT

    1. Reg. 36 of the Amendment Regulations (April 5, 1993).

DEFINITIONS

    "absent parent": see reg. 1(2).

    "arrears": *ibid*.

    "due date": *ibid*

Payment of arrears by agreement

5.—[[1](1) The Secretary of State may at any time enter into an agreement with an absent parent (an "arrears agreement") for the absent parent to pay all outstanding arrears by making payments on agreed dates of agreed amounts.

(2) Where an arrears agreement has been entered into, the Secretary of State shall prepare a schedule of the dates on which payments of arrears shall be made and the amount to be paid on each such date, and shall send a copy of the schedule to such persons as he thinks fit.]

(3) If an arrears agreement is entered into within 28 days of the due date, and the terms of that agreement are adhered to by the absent parent, there shall be no liability to make payments of interest under the provisions of regulation 3 with respect to the arrears in relation to which the arrears agreement was entered into.

(4) If an arrears agreement is entered into later than 28 days after the due date and the terms of that agreement are adhered to by the absent parent, there shall, with respect to the arrears in relation to which that agreement was entered into, be no liability to make payments of interest in respect of any period commencing on the date that agreement was entered into.

(5) The Secretary of State may at any time enter into a further arrears agreement with the absent parent in relation to all arrears then outstanding.

(6) Where the terms of any arrears agreement are not adhered to by an absent parent, interest shall be payable with respect to arrears in accordance with the provisions of regulation 3.

(7) It shall be an implied term of any arrears agreement that any payment of child support maintenance that becomes due whilst that agreement is in force shall be made by the due date.

AMENDMENT

    1.   Regulation 37 of the Amendment Regulations (April 5, 1993).

DEFINITIONS

    "absent parent:" see reg. 1(2).

    "arrears": *ibid*.

    "due date": *ibid*.

Rate of interest and calculation of interest

6.—(1) The rate of interest payable where liability to pay interest under regulation 3 arises shall be one per centum per annum above the median basic rate prevailing from time to time calculated on a daily basis.

(2) Interest shall be payable only with respect to arrears of child support maintenance and shall not be payable with respect to any interest that has already become due.

(3) For the purposes of paragraph (1)—

    (*a*) the median base rate, in relation to a year or part of a year, is the base rate quoted by the reference banks; or, if different base rates are quoted, the rate which, when the base rate quoted by each bank is ranked in a descending sequence of seven, is fourth in the sequence;

    (*b*) the reference banks are the seven largest institutions—

        (i) authorised by the Bank of England under the Banking Act 1987, and

        (ii) incorporated in and carrying on a deposit-taking business within the United Kingdom,

      which quote a base rate in sterling; and

    (*c*) the size of an institution is to be determined by reference to its consolidated gross assets in sterling, as shown in its audited end-year accounts last published.

(4) In paragraph (3)(*c*), the reference to the consolidated gross assets of an institution is a reference to the consolidated gross assets of that institution together with any subsidiary (within the meaning of section 736 of the Companies Act 1985.

[[1](5) Where any calculation of interest payable under this Part of these Regulations results in a fraction of a penny, that fraction shall be disregarded.]

AMENDMENT
   1.   Regulation 38 of the Amendment Regulations (April 5, 1993).

DEFINITION
   "arrears of child support maintenance": see reg. 1(2).

Receipt and retention of interest paid

7.—(1) Payments of interest with respect to arrears shall be made in accordance with regulations under section 29 of the Act as though they were payments of child support maintenance payable in accordance with a maintenance assessment, and shall be made within 14 days of being demanded by the Secretary of State.

(2) Subject to paragraph (3), where the Secretary of State has been authorised to recover child support maintenance under section 6 of the Act and income support is paid to or in respect of the parent with care, interest with respect to arrears relating to the period during which income support is paid shall be payable to the Secretary of State and may be retained by him.

(3) Where a case falls within paragraph (2), but the Secretary of State considers that, if the absent parent had made payments of child support maintenance due from him in accordance with that assessment, the parent with care would not have been entitled to income support, any interest shall be payable to the parent with care.

(4) Where the child support maintenance payable under a maintenance assessment is payable to more than one person, any interest in respect of arrears under that assessment shall be apportioned in the same ratio as the child support maintenance that is payable, and the provisions of paragraphs (1) to (3) shall apply to each amount of interest so apportioned.

Retention of recovered arrears of child support maintenance by the Secretary of State

8. Where the Secretary of State recovers arrears from an absent parent and income support is paid to or in respect of the person with care, the Secretary of State may retain such amount of those arrears as is equal to the difference between the amount of income support that was paid to or in respect of the person with care and the amount of income support that he is satisfied would have been paid had the absent parent paid the child support maintenance due in accordance with the maintenance assessment in force by the due dates.

PART III

ATTRIBUTION OF PAYMENTS AND ADJUSTMENT OF THE AMOUNT PAYABLE UNDER A MAINTENANCE ASSESSMENT

Attribution of payments

9. Where a maintenance assessment is or has been in force and there are arrears of child support maintenance, the Secretary of State may attribute any payment of child support maintenance made by an absent parent to child support maintenance due as he thinks fit.

Adjustment of the amount payable under a maintenance assessment

10.—(1) Where a new or a fresh maintenance assessment has retrospective effect, the amount payable under that assessment may be adjusted by a child support officer for the purpose of taking account of the retrospective effect of the assessment by such amount as, subject to the provisions of paragraph (4), he considers appropriate in the circumstances of the case.

(2) Subject to paragraph (3), where the payments of child support maintenance have been over-payment or under-payments, the amount payable under a maintenance assessment may be adjusted by a child support officer for the purpose of taking account of such over-payments or under-payments by such amount as, subject to the provisions of paragraph (5), he considers appropriate in the circumstances of the case.

(3) The provisions of paragraph (2) shall not apply to any case falling within section 41 of the Act.

(4) Where a case falls within paragraph (1), the child support officer shall—

  (*a*) in the case of a new assessment, not increase the amount payable under that assessment by an amount greater than 1.5 multiplied by that assessment;

  (*b*) in the case of a fresh assessment, not adjust the amount payable under that assessment by an amount greater than 1.5 multiplied by the difference between the amount payable under the earlier assessment and the amount payable under the fresh assessment.

(5) Where a case falls within paragraph (2), the child support officer shall not adjust the amount payable under a maintenance assessment by an amount greater than 1.5 multiplied by the mean over-payment or the mean under-payment, as the case may be.

(6) For the purposes of paragraph (5), the mean over-payment or the mean under-payment shall be the total net over-payment or the total net under-payment divided by the number of occasions on which, in respect of the period being taken into account for the purposes of paragraph (2), there have been over-payments or, as the case may be, under-payments of child support maintenance.

DEFINITION
"the Act:" see reg. 1(2).

PART IV

MISCELLANEOUS

Notifications following an adjustment under the provisions of regulation 10

11.—(1) Where a child support officer has, under the provisions of regulation 10, adjusted the amount payable under a maintenance assessment, he shall immediately notify the relevant persons, so far as that is reasonably practicable, of the amount and period of the adjustment, and the amount payable during the period of the adjustment.

(2) A notification under paragraph (1) shall include information as to the provisions of regulation 12(1) and regulation 13(1) in so far as it relates to time limits for an application for a review under regulation 12(1).

DEFINITION
"relevant person": see reg. 1(2).

Review of adjustments under regulation 10 or of the calculation of arrears or interest

12.—(1) Where the amount payable under a maintenance assessment has been adjusted under the provisions of regulation 10, a relevant person may apply to the Secretary of State for a review of that adjustment as if it were a case falling within section 18 of the Act and, subject to the modifications set out in paragraph (2), section 18(5) to (9) and (11) of the Act shall apply to such a review.

(2) The modifications referred to in paragraph (1) are—

(a) section 18(6) of the Act shall have effect as if for "the refusal, assessment or cancellation in question" there is substituted "the adjustment of the amount payable under regulation 10 of the Child Support (Arrears, Interest and Adjustment of Maintenance Assessments) Regulations 1992";

(b) Section 18(9) of the Act shall have effect as if for "a maintenance assessment or (as the case may be) a fresh maintenance assessment" there is substituted "a revised adjustment of the amount payable under regulation 10 of the Child Support (Arrears, Interest and Adjustment of Maintenance Assessments) Regulations 1992".

[¹...]
[¹...]

(5) Where the amount payable under a maintenance assessment has been adjusted under the provisions of regulation 10 a child support officer may revise that adjustment if he is satisfied that one or more of the circumstances set out in paragraphs (*a*) to (*c*) of section 19(1) of the Act apply to that adjustment.
[¹ ...]

AMENDMENT
1. Regulation 39 of the Amendment Regulations (April 5, 1993).

DEFINITIONS
"the Act": see reg. 1(2).
"arrears": *ibid.*
"relevant person": *ibid.*

Procedure and notifications on applications and reviews under regulation 12

13.—(1) The provisions of regulations 24 to 26 of the Maintenance Assessment Procedure Regulations shall apply to an application for a review under regulation 12(1) [¹ ...].
(2) Where a child support officer refuses an application for a review under regulation 12(1) [¹ ...] on the grounds set out in section 18(6) of the Act (as applied by regulation 12), he shall immediately notify the applicant, so far as that is reasonably practicable, and shall give the reasons for his refusal in writing.
(3) Where a child support officer adjusts the amount payable under a maintenance assessment following a review under regulation 12(1) or (5), he shall immediately notify the relevant persons, so far as that is reasonably practicable, of the amount and period of the adjustment, and the amount payable during the period of adjustment.
(4) Where a child support officer refuses to adjust the amount payable under a maintenance assessment following a review under regulation 12(1) he shall immediately notify the relevant persons, so far as that is reasonably practicable, of the refusal, and shall give the reasons for his refusal in writing.
[² ...]
(6) A notification under [³paragraphs (2) to (4)] shall include information as to the provisions of section 20 of the Act.

AMENDMENTS
1. Regulation 40(*a*) of the Amendment Regulations (April 5, 1993).
2. Regulation 40(*b*) of the Amendment Regulations (April 5, 1993).
3. Regulation 40(*c*) of the Amendment Regulations (April 5, 1993).

DEFINITIONS
"the Act": see reg. 1(2).
"arrears": *ibid.*
"Maintenance Assessment Procedure Regulations": *ibid.*
"relevant person": *ibid.*

Non-disclosure of information to third parties

14. The provisions of regulation 10(3) of the Maintenance Assessment Procedure Regulations shall apply to any document given or sent under the provisions of regulation 11 or 13.

DEFINITION

"Maintenance Assessment Procedure Regulations": see reg. 1(2).

Applicability of regulations 1(6) and 53 to 56 of the Maintenance Assessment Procedure Regulations

15. Regulations 1(6) and 53 to 56 of the Maintenance Assessment Procedure Regulations shall apply to the provisions of these regulations.

DEFINITION

"Maintenance Assessment Procedure Regulations": see reg. 1(2).

The Child Support (Collection and Enforcement) Regulations 1992

(S.I. 1992 No. 1989)

Made by the Secretary of State for Social Security under sections 29(2) and (3), 31(8), 32(1) to (5) and (7) to (9), 34(1), 35(2), (7) and (8), 39(1), (3) and (4), 40(4), (8) and (11), 51, 52 and 54 of the Child Support Act 1991 and all other powers enabling him in that behalf.

ARRANGEMENT OF REGULATIONS

PART I

General

PART II

Collection Of Child Support Maintenance

PART III

Deduction From Earnings Orders

PART 1

GENERAL

Citation, commencement and interpretation

1.—(1) These Regulations may be cited as the Child Support (Collection and Enforcement) Regulations 1992 and shall come into force on 5 April 1993.

(2) In these Regulations "the Act" means the Child Support Act 1991.

(3) Where under any provision of the Act or of these Regulations—

(*a*) any document or notice is given or sent to the Secretary of State, it shall be treated as having been given or sent on the day it is received by the Secretary of State; and

(*b*) any document or notice is given or sent to any other person, it shall, if sent by post to that person's last known or notified address, be treated as having been given or sent on the second day after the day of posting, excluding any Sunday or any day which is a bank holiday under the Banking and Financial Dealings Act 1971.

(4) In these Regulations, unless the context otherwise requires, a reference—

(*a*) to a numbered Part is to the Part of these Regulations bearing that number;

(*b*) to a numbered regulation is to the regulation in these Regulations bearing that number;

(*c*) in a regulation to a numbered or lettered paragraph or sub-paragraph is to the paragraph or sub-paragraph in that regulation bearing that number or letter;

(*d*) in a paragraph to a lettered or numbered sub-paragraph is to the sub-paragraph in that paragraph bearing that letter or number;

(*e*) to a numbered Schedule is to the Schedule to these Regulations bearing that number.

PART II

COLLECTION OF CHILD SUPPORT MAINTENANCE

Payment of child support maintenance

2.—(1) Where a maintenance assessment has been made under the Act and the case is one to which section 29 of the Act applies, the Secretary of State may specify that payments of child support maintenance shall be made by the liable person—

(*a*) to the person caring for the child or children in question or, where an application has been made under section 7 of the Act, to the child who made the application;

(*b*) to, or through, the Secretary of State; or

(*c*) to, or through, such other person as the Secretary of State may, from time to time, specify.

(2) In paragraph (1) and in the rest of this Part, "liable person" means a person liable to make payments of child support maintenance.

DEFINITION
"the Act": reg. 1(2).

GENERAL NOTE
This regulation only applies where the Secretary of State is arranging for the collection of child support maintenance under s.29(1) of the Act. It allows the Secretary of State to specify in his notice (see reg. 7) that payment shall be to the person caring for the child, the child (in the case of Scotland), or to or through the Secretary or State or his nominee. The regulation does not refer to the person with care. Instead it departs from the standard wording of the Act and the regulations made under it by referring to the person caring for the child or children. In practice this could be someone other the person with care, as there could be persons with part-time care or the care of the child could be temporarily entrusted to someone other than the person with care. The use of different terminology may justify payments being made to someone who is not the person with care, such as a relative looking after a child while the person with care is in hospital. The Secretary of State has power under reg. 24 of the Maintenance Assessments and Special Cases Regulations on request to apportion payment between persons with part-time care.

Method of payment

3.—(1) Payments of child support maintenance shall be made by the liable person by whichever of the following methods the Secretary of State specifies as being appropriate in the circumstances—

(*a*) by standing order;

(*b*) by any other method which requires one person to give his authority for payments to be made from an account of his to an account of another's on specific dates during the period for which the authority is in force and without the need for any further authority from him;

(*c*) by an arrangement whereby one person gives his authority for payments to be made from an account of his, or on his behalf, to another person or to an account of that other person;

(*d*) by cheque or postal order;

(*e*) in cash.

(2) The Secretary of State may direct a liable person to take all reasonable steps to open an account from which payments under the maintenance assessment may be made in accordance with the method of payment specified under paragraph (1).

DEFINITION
"liable person": reg. 2(2).

GENERAL NOTE
Para. (1)
Methods (*a*) to (*c*) will be preferred to (*d*) and (*e*) since they will operate automatically provided there are sufficient funds in the account.

Para. (2)
This is a strange provision. It allows the Secretary of State to direct a person to take all reasonable steps to open a suitable account, but it does not operate until the Secretary of State has specified a method of payment under para. (1). However, if the liable person is unable to open a suitable account, the effect of specifying payment from an account will have been to delay the payment of child support maintenance. Perhaps this problem could be avoided by specifying an alternative method until (if at all) an account is opened. It would be better if the power in this paragraph could be employed before payment from an account was specified under para. (1), but this is not what the provision says.

Interval of payment

4.—(1) The Secretary of State shall specify the day and interval by reference to which payments of child support maintenance are to be made by the liable person and may from time to time vary such day or interval.

(2) In specifying the day and interval of payment the Secretary of State shall have regard to all the circumstances and in particular to—
    (*a*) the needs of the person entitled to receive payment and the day and interval by reference to which any other income is normally received by that person;
    (*b*) the day and interval by reference to which the liable person's income is normally received; and
    (*c*) any period necessary to enable the clearance of cheques or otherwise necessary to enable the transmission of payments to the person entitled to receive them.

DEFINITION
"liable person": reg. 2(2).

GENERAL NOTE
Para. (2)
The Secretary of State must take account of all relevant circumstances in fixing the day and interval of payments. In particular he will have to balance the needs of the liable person and the person entitled to receive payment, although he has power by virtue of reg. 5(3) to act as a buffer between them.

Transmission of payments

5.—(1) Payments of child support maintenance made through the Secretary of State or other specified person shall be transmitted to the person entitled to receive them in whichever of the following ways the Secretary of State specifies as being appropriate in the circumstances—
    (*a*) by a transfer of credit to an account nominated by the person entitled to receive the payments;
    (*b*) by cheque, girocheque or other payable order;
    (*c*) in cash.

(2) The Secretary of State shall specify the interval by reference to which the payments referred to in paragraph (1) are to be transmitted to the person entitled to receive them.

(3) The interval referred to in paragraph (2) may differ from the interval referred to in regulation 4 and may from time to time be varied by the Secretary of State.

(4) In specifying the interval for transmission of payments the Secretary of State shall have regard to all the circumstances and in particular to—

    (*a*)   the needs of the person entitled to receive payment and the interval by reference to which any other income is normally received by that person;

    (*b*)   any period necessary to enable the clearance of cheques or otherwise necessary to enable the transmission of payments to the person entitled to receive them.

GENERAL NOTE

Para. (1)

    The Secretary of State has no power to require the person entitled to receive payment to take all reasonable steps to open a bank account. This is in contrast with his power in relation to a liable person under reg. 3(2).

Para. (3)

    This power enables the Secretary of State or his nominee to act as a buffer between the liable person and the person entitled to receive payment in cases where the appropriate intervals for deduction and for transmission are different. For example it may be convenience for both the Secretary of State and a liable person who is paid monthly to have payments fixed at monthly intervals, but if the person entitled to receive payment has no account or has difficulty budgeting, it may be appropriate for payment to be transmitted weekly.

Representations about payment arrangements

6. The Secretary of State shall, insofar as is reasonably practicable, provide the liable person and the person entitled to receive the payments of child support maintenance with an opportunity to make representations with regard to the matters referred to in regulations 2 to 5 and the Secretary of State shall have regard to those representations in exercising his powers under those regulations.

DEFINITION

    "liable person": reg. 2(2).

GENERAL NOTE

    The liable person and the person entitled to receive payment are entitled to an opportunity to make representations on the matters covered by regs. 2 to 5, but only in so far as that is reasonably practicable. The person entitled to receive payment under this regulation means the person ultimately entitled to receive payment and not the Secretary of State or his nominee. That this is the meaning of these words is clear from the way in which the same words are used in reg. 5(1).

Notice to liable person as to requirements about payment

7.—(1) The Secretary of State shall send the liable person a notice stating—

    (*a*)   the amount of child support maintenance payable;

    (*b*)   to whom it is to be paid;

    (*c*)   the method of payment; and

    (*d*)   the day and interval by reference to which payments are to be made.

(2) A notice under paragraph (1) shall be sent to the liable person as soon as is reasonably practicable after—

    (*a*)   the making of a maintenance assessment and

    (*b*)   after any change in the requirements referred to in any previous such notice.

DEFINITION
"liable person": reg. 2(2).

PART III

DEDUCTION FROM EARNINGS ORDERS

Interpretation of this Part

8.—(1) For the purposes of this Part—

"disposable income" means the amount determined under regulation 12(1) of the Child Support (Maintenance Assessments and Special Cases) Regulations 1992;

"earnings" shall be construed in accordance with paragraphs (3) and (4);

"exempt income" means the amount determined under regulation 9 of the Child Support (Maintenance Assessments and Special Cases) Regulations 1992;

"net earnings" shall be construed in accordance with paragraph (5);

"normal deduction rate" means the rate specified in a deduction from earnings order (expressed as a sum of money per week, month or other period) at which deductions are to be made from the liable person's net earnings;

"pay-day" in relation to a liable person means an occasion on which earnings are paid to him or the day on which such earnings would normally fall to be paid;

"prescribed minimum amount" means the minimum amount prescribed in regulation 13 of the Child Support (Maintenance Assessments and Special Cases) Regulations 1992;

"protected earnings rate" means the level of earnings specified in a deduction from earnings order (expressed as a sum of money per week, month or other period) below which deductions of child support maintenance shall not be made for the purposes of this Part;

"protected income level" means the level of protected income determined in accordance with regulation 11 of the Child Support (Maintenance Assessments and Special Cases) Regulations 1992.

(2) For the purposes of this Part the relationship of employer and employee shall be treated as subsisting between two persons if one of them, as a principal and not as a servant or agent, pays to the other any sum defined as earnings under paragraph (1) and "employment", "employer" and "employee" shall be construed accordingly.

(3) Subject to paragraph (4), "earnings" are any sums payable to a person—

(a) by way of wages or salary (including any fees, bonus, commission, overtime pay or other emoluments payable in addition to wages or salary or payable under a contract of service);

(b) by way of pension (including an annuity in respect of past service, whether or not rendered to the person paying the annuity, and including periodical payments by way of compensation for the loss, abolition or relinquishment, or diminution in the emoluments, of any office or employment);

(c) by way of statutory sick pay.

(4) "Earnings" shall not include—

(a) sums payable by any public department of the Government of Northern Ireland or of a territory outside the United Kingdom;

(b) pay or allowances payable to the liable person as a member of Her Majesty's forces;

(c) pension, allowances or benefit payable under any enactment relating to social security;

(d) pension or allowances payable in respect of disablement or disability;

(*e*) guaranteed minimum pension within the meaning of the Social Security Pensions Act 1975.

(5) "Net earnings" means the residue of earnings after deduction of—

(*a*) income tax;

(*b*) primary class I contributions under Part I of the Contributions and Benefits Act 1992;

(*c*) amounts deductible by way of contributions to a superannuation scheme which provides for the payment of annuities or [¹lump] sums—

    (i) to the employee on his retirement at a specified age or on becoming incapacitated at some earlier age; or

    (ii) on his death or otherwise, to his personal representative, widow, relatives or dependants.

AMENDMENT

1. Regulation 41 of the Amendment Regulations (April 5, 1993).

Deduction from earnings order

9. A deduction from earnings order shall specify—

(*a*) the name and address of the liable person;

(*b*) the name of the employer at whom it is directed;

(*c*) where known, the liable person's place of work, the nature of his work and any works or pay number;

(*d*) the normal deduction rate;

(*e*) the protected earnings rate;

(*f*) the address to which amounts deducted from earnings are to be sent.

DEFINITIONS

"earnings": see reg. 8(1), (3) and (4).
"employer": see reg. 8(2).
"normal deduction rate": see reg. 8(1).
"protected earnings rate": *ibid.*

Normal deduction rate

10.—(1) The period by reference to which the normal deduction rate is set shall be the period by reference to which the liable person's earnings are normally paid or, if none, such other period as the Secretary of State may specify.

(2) The Secretary of State, in specifying the normal deduction rate, shall not include any amount in respect of arrears or interest if, at the date of making of the current assessment—

(*a*) the liable person's disposable income was below the level specified in paragraph (3); or

(*b*) the deduction of such an amount from the liable person's disposable income would have reduced his disposable income below the level specified in paragraph (3).

(3) The level referred to in paragraph (2) is the liable person's protected income level less the prescribed minimum amount.

DEFINITIONS

"disposable income": see reg. 8(1).
"normal deduction rate": *ibid.*
"prescribed minimum amount": *ibid.*

Protected earnings rate

11.—(1) The period by reference to which the protected earnings rate is set shall be the same as the period by reference to which the normal deduction rate is set under regulation 10(1).

(2) The amount to be specified as the protected earnings rate in respect of any period shall be an amount equal to the liable person's exempt income in respect of that period as calculated at the date of the current assessment.

DEFINITIONS
"exempt income": see reg. 8(1).
"normal deduction rate": *ibid.*
"protected earnings rate": *ibid.*

Amount to be deducted by employer

12.—(1) Subject to the provisions of this regulation, an employer who has been served with a copy of a deduction from earnings order in respect of a liable person in his employment shall, each pay-day, make a deduction from the net earnings of that liable person of an amount equal to the normal deduction rate.

(2) Where the deduction of the normal deduction rate would reduce the liable person's net earnings below the protected earnings rate the employer shall deduct only such amount as will leave the liable person with net earnings equal to the protected earnings rate.

(3) Where the liable person receives a payment of earnings at an interval greater or lesser than the interval specified in relation to the normal deduction rate and the protected earnings rate ("the specified interval") the employer shall, for the purpose of such payments, take as the normal deduction rate and the protected earnings rate such amounts (to the nearest whole penny) as are in the same proportion to the interval since the last pay-day as the normal deduction rate and the protected earnings rate bear to the specified interval.

(4) Where, on any pay-day, the employer fails to deduct an amount due under the deduction from earnings order or deducts an amount less than the amount of the normal deduction rate the shortfall shall, subject to the operation of paragraph (2), be deducted in addition to the normal deduction rate at the next available pay-day or days.

(5) Where, on any pay-day, the liable person's net earnings are less than his protected earnings rate the amount of the difference shall be carried forward to his next pay-day and treated as part of his protected earnings in respect of that pay-day.

(6) Where, on any pay-day, an employer makes a deduction from the earnings of a liable person in accordance with the deduction from earnings order he may also deduct an amount not exceeding £1 in respect of his administrative costs and such deduction for administrative costs may be made notwithstanding that it may reduce the liable person's net earnings below the protected earnings rate.

DEFINITIONS
"earnings": see reg. 8(1), (3) and (4).
"employer": see reg. 8(2).
"employment": *ibid.*
"net earnings": see reg. 8(1).
"normal deduction rate": *ibid.*
"pay-day": *ibid.*
"protected earnings rate": *ibid.*

Employer to notify liable person of deduction

13.—(1) An employer making a deduction from earnings for the purpose of this Part shall notify the liable person in writing of the amount of the deduction, including any amount deducted for administrative costs under regulation 12(6).

(2) Such notification shall be given not later than the pay-day on which the deduction is made or, where that is impracticable, not later than the following pay-day.

DEFINITIONS
"employer": see reg. 8(2).
"pay-day": see reg. 8(1).

Payment by employer to Secretary of State

14.—(1) Amounts deducted by an employer under a deduction from earnings order (other than any administrative costs deducted under regulation 12(6)) shall be paid to the Secretary of State by the 19th day of the month following the month in which the deduction is made.

(2) Such payment may be made—

(*a*) by cheque;

(*b*) by automated credit transfer; or

(*c*) by such other method as the Secretary of State may specify.

DEFINITION
"employer": see reg. 8(2).

Information to be provided by liable person

15.—(1) The Secretary of State may, in relation to the making or operation of a deduction from earnings order, require the liable person to provide the following details—

(*a*) the name and address and his employer;

(*b*) the amount of his earnings and anticipated earnings;

(*c*) his place of work, the nature of his work and any works or pay number;

and it shall be the duty of the liable person to comply with any such requirement within 7 days of being given written notice to that effect.

(2) A liable person in respect of whom a deduction from earnings order is in force shall notify the Secretary of State in writing within 7 days of every occasion on which he leaves employment or becomes employed or re-employed.

DEFINITIONS
"employer": see reg. 8(2).
"employment": *ibid.*

Duty of employers and others to notify Secretary of State

16.—(1) Where a deduction from earnings order is served on a person on the assumption that he is the employer of a liable person but the liable person to whom the order relates is not in his employment, the person on whom the order was served shall notify the Secretary of State of that fact in writing, at the address specified in the order, within 10 days of the date of service on him of the order.

(2) Where an employer is required to operate a deduction from earnings order and the liable person to whom the order relates ceases to be in his employment the employer shall notify the Secretary of State of that fact in writing, at the address specified in the order, within 10 days of the liable person ceasing to be in his employment.

(3) Where an employer becomes aware that a deduction from earnings order is in force in relation to a person who is an employee of his he shall, within 7 days of the date on which he becomes aware, notify the Secretary of State of that fact in writing at the address specified in the order.

DEFINITIONS
   "employer": see reg. 8(2).
   "employment": *ibid.*

Requirement to review deduction from earnings orders

17. The Secretary of State shall review a deduction from earnings order in the following circumstances—
   (*a*)   where there is a change in the amount of the maintenance assessment;
   (*b*)   where any arrears and interest on arrears payable under the order are paid off.

Power to vary deduction from earnings orders

18.—(1) The Secretary of State may (whether on a review under regulation 17 or otherwise) vary a deduction from earnings order so as to—
   (*a*)   include any amount which may be included in such an order or exclude or decrease any such amount;
   (*b*)   substitute a subsequent employer for the employer at whom the order was previously directed.
(2) The Secretary of State shall serve a copy of any deduction from earnings order, as varied, on the liable person's employer and on the liable person.

DEFINITION
   "employer": see reg. 8(2).

Compliance with deduction from earnings order as varied

19.—(1) Where a deduction from earnings order has been varied and a copy of the order as varied has been served on the liable person's employer it shall, subject to paragraph (2), be the duty of the employer to comply with the order as varied.
(2) The employer shall not be under any liability for non-compliance with the order, as varied, before the end of the period of 7 days beginning with the date on which a copy of the order, as varied, was served on him.

DEFINITION
   "employer": see reg. 8(2).

Discharge of deduction from earnings orders

20.—(1) The Secretary of State may discharge a deduction from earnings order where—
   (*a*)   no further payments under it are due; or
   (*b*)   it appears to him that the order is ineffective or that some other way of securing that payments are made would be more effective.
(2) The Secretary of State shall give written notice of the discharge of the deduction from earnings order to the liable person and to the liable person's employer.

DEFINITION
  "employer": see reg. 8(2).

Lapse of deduction from earnings orders

21.—(1) A deduction from earnings order shall lapse (except in relation to any deductions made or to be made in respect of the employment not yet paid to the Secretary of State) where the employer at whom it is directed ceases to have the liable person in his employment.

(2) The order shall lapse from the pay-day coinciding with, or, if none, the pay-day following, the termination of the employment.

(3) A deduction from earnings order which has lapsed under this regulation shall nonetheless be treated as remaining in force for the purposes of regulations 15 and 24.

(4) Where a deduction from earnings order has lapsed under paragraph (1) and the liable person recommences employment (whether with the same or another employer), the order may be revived from such date as may be specified by the Secretary of State.

(5) Where a deduction from earnings order is revived under paragraph (4), the Secretary of State shall give written notice of that fact to, and serve a copy of the notice on, the liable person and the liable person's employer.

(6) Where an order is revived under paragraph (4), no amount shall be carried forward under regulation 12(4) or (5) from a time prior to the revival of the order.

DEFINITIONS
  "employer": see reg. 8(2).
  "employment": *ibid.*
  "pay-day": see reg. 8(1).

Appeals against deduction from earnings orders

22.—(1) A liable person in respect of whom a deduction from earnings order has been made may appeal to the magistrates' court, or in Scotland the sheriff, having jurisdiction in the area in which he resides.

(2) Any appeal shall—
  (*a*) be by way of complaint for an order or, in Scotland, by way of application;
  (*b*) be made within 28 days of the date on which the matter appealed against arose.

(3) An appeal may be made only on one or both of the following grounds—
  (*a*) that the deduction from earnings order is defective;
  (*b*) that the payments in question do not constitute earnings.

(4) Where the court or, as the case may be, the sheriff is satisfied that the appeal should be allowed the court, or sheriff, may—
  (*a*) quash the deduction from earnings order; or
  (*b*) specify which, if any, of the payments in question do not constitute earnings.

DEFINITION
  "earnings": see reg. 8(1), (3) and (4).

Crown employment

23. Where a liable person is in the employment of the Crown and a deduction from earnings order is made in respect of him then for the purposes of this Part—
  (*a*) the chief officer for the time being of the Department, office or other body in which the liable person is employed shall be treated as having the liable person in his employment (any transfer of the liable person from one

Department, office or body to another being treated as a change of employment); and

(b) any earnings paid by the Crown or a minister of the Crown, or out of the public revenue of the United Kingdom, shall be treated as paid by that chief officer.

DEFINITIONS
"earnings": see reg. 8(1), (3) and (4).
"employment": see reg. 8(2).

Priority as between orders

24.—(1) Where an employer would, but for this paragraph, be obliged, on any pay-day, to make deductions under two or more deduction from earnings orders he shall—

(a) deal with the orders according to the respective dates on which they were made, disregarding any later order until an earlier one has been dealt with;

(b) deal with any later order as if the earnings to which it relates were the residue of the liable person's earnings after the making of any deduction to comply with any earlier order.

(2) Where an employer would, but for this paragraph, be obliged to comply with one or more deduction from earnings orders and one or more attachment of earnings orders he shall—

(a) in the case of an attachment of earnings order which was made either wholly or in part in respect of the payment of a judgment debt or payments under an administration order, deal first with the deduction from earnings order or orders and thereafter with the attachment of earnings order as if the earnings to which it relates were the residue of the liable person's earnings after the making of deductions to comply with the deduction from earnings order or orders;

(b) in the case of any other attachment of earnings order, deal with the orders according to the respective dates on which they were made in like manner as under paragraph (1).

"Attachment of earnings order" in this paragraph means an order made under the Attachment of Earnings Act 1971 or under regulation 32 of the Community Charge (Administration and Enforcement) Regulations 1989 [¹or under regulation 37 of the Council Tax (Administration and Enforcement) Regulations 1992].

(3) Paragraph (2) does not apply to Scotland.

(4) In Scotland, where an employer would, but for this paragraph, be obliged to comply with one or more deduction from earnings orders and one or more diligences against earnings he shall deal first with the deduction from earnings order or orders and thereafter with the diligence against earnings as if the earnings to which the diligence relates were the residue of the liable person's earnings after the making of deductions to comply with the deduction from earnings order or orders.

AMENDMENT
1. Regulation 42 of the Amendment Regulations (April 5, 1993).

DEFINITIONS
"earnings": see reg. 8(1), (3) and (4).
"employer": see reg. 8(2).
"pay–day": see reg. 8(1).

Offences

25. The following regulations are designated for the purposes of section 32(8) of the Act (offences relating to deduction from earnings orders)—

(*a*) regulation 15(1) and (2);
(*b*) regulation 16(1), (2) and (3);
(*c*) regulation 19(1).

PART IV

LIABILITY ORDERS

Extent of this Part

26. This Part, except regulation 29(2), does not apply to Scotland.

Notice of intention to apply for a liability order

27.—(1) The Secretary of State shall give the liable person at least 7 days notice of his intention to apply for a liability order under section 33(2) of the Act.

(2) Such notice shall set out the amount of child support maintenance which it is claimed has become payable by the liable person and has not been paid and the amount of any interest in respect of arrears payable under section 41(3) of the Act.

(3) Payment by the liable person of any part of the amounts referred to in paragraph (2) shall not require the giving of a further notice under paragraph (1) prior to the making of the application.

Application for a liability order

28.—(1) An application for a liability order shall be by way of complaint for an order to the magistrates' court having jurisdiction in the area in which the liable person resides.

(2) An application under paragraph (1) may not be instituted more than 6 years after the day on which payment of the amount in question became due.

(3) A warrant shall not be issued under section 55(2) of the Magistrates' Courts Act 1980 in any proceedings under this regulation.

Liability orders

29.—(1) A liability order shall be made in the form prescribed in Schedule 1.

(2) A liability order made by a court in England or Wales or any corresponding order made by a court in Northern Ireland may be enforced in Scotland as if it had been made by the sheriff.

(3) A liability order made by the sheriff in Scotland or any corresponding order made by a court in Northern Ireland may, subject to paragraph (4), be enforced in England and Wales as if it had been made by a magistrates' court in England and Wales.

(4) A liability order made by the sheriff in Scotland or a corresponding order made by a court in Northern Ireland shall not be enforced in England or Wales unless registered in accordance with the provisions of [¹Part II] of the Maintenance Orders Act 1950 and for this purpose—

(*a*) a liability order made by the sheriff in Scotland shall be treated as if it were a decree to which section 16(2)(*b*) of that Act applies (decree for payment of aliment);

(*b*) a corresponding order made by a court in Northern Ireland shall be treated as if it were an order to which section 16(2)(*c*) of that Act applies (order for alimony, maintenance or other payments).

AMENDMENT
1. Regulation 43 of the Amendment Regulations (April 5, 1993).

Enforcement of liability orders by distress

30.—(1) A distress made pursuant to section 35(1) of the Act may be made anywhere in England and Wales.

(2) The person levying distress on behalf of the Secretary of State shall carry with him the written authorisation of the Secretary of State, which he shall show to the liable person if so requested, and he shall hand to the liable person or leave at the premises where the distress is levied—

(a) copies of this regulation, regulation 31 and Schedule 2;

(b) a memorandum setting out the amount which is the appropriate amount for the purposes of section 35(2) of the Act;

(c) a memorandum setting out details of any arrangement entered into regarding the taking of possession of the goods distrained; and

(d) a notice setting out the liable person's rights of appeal under regulation 31 giving the Secretary of State's address for the purposes of any appeal.

(3) A distress shall not be deemed unlawful on account of any defect or want of form in the liability order.

(4) If, before any goods are seized, the appropriate amount (including charges arising up to the time of the payment or tender) is paid or tendered to the Secretary of State, the Secretary of State shall accept the amount and the levy shall not be proceeded with.

(5) Where the Secretary of State has seized goods of the liable person in pursuance of the distress, but before sale of those goods the appropriate amount (including charges arising up to the time of the payment or tender) is paid or tendered to the Secretary of State, the Secretary of State shall accept the amount, the sale shall not be proceeded with and the goods shall be made available for collection by the liable person.

Appeals in connection with distress

31.—(1) A person aggrieved by the levy of, or an attempt to levy, a distress may appeal to the magistrates' court having jurisdiction in the area in which he resides.

(2) The appeal shall be by way of complaint for an order.

(3) If the court is satisfied that the levy was irregular, it may—

(a) order the goods distrained to be discharged if they are in the possession of the Secretary of State;

(b) order an award of compensation in respect of any goods distrained and sold of an amount equal to the amount which, in the opinion of the court, would be awarded by way of special damages in respect of the goods if proceedings under section 35(6) of the Act were brought in trespass or otherwise in connection with the irregularity.

(4) If the court is satisfied that an attempted levy was irregular, it may by order require the Secretary of State to desist from levying in the manner giving rise to the irregularity.

GENERAL NOTE
Para. (1)

The County Court may also exercise its interlocutory jurisdiction to restrain the levying of excessive distress, provided that a powerful prima facie case for the distress being unlawful has been made out (*Steel Linings* v. *Bibby and Co. (a Firm)*, *The Times*, March 30, 1993).

Charges connected with distress

32. Schedule 2 shall have effect for the purpose of determining the amounts in respect of charges in connection with the distress for the purposes of section 35(2) (*b*) of the Act.

Application for warrant of commitment

33.—(1) For the purposes of enabling an inquiry to be made under section 40 of the Act as to the liable person's conduct and means, a justice of the peace having jurisdiction for the area in which the liable person resides may—

  (*a*) issue a summons to him to appear before a magistrates' court and (if he does not obey the summons) issue a warrant for his arrest; or

  (*b*) issue a warrant for his arrest without issuing a summons.

(2) In any proceedings under section 40 of the Act, a statement in writing to the effect that wages of any amount have been paid to the liable person during any period, purporting to be signed by or on behalf of his employer, shall be evidence of the facts there stated.

(3) Where an application under section 40 of the Act has been made but no warrant of commitment is issued or term of imprisonment fixed, the application may be renewed on the ground that the circumstances of the liable person have changed.

Warrant of commitment

34.—(1) A warrant of commitment shall be in the form specified in Schedule 3, or in a form to the like effect.

(2) The amount to be included in the warrant under section 40(4)(*a*)(ii) of the Act in respect of costs shall be such amount as in the view of the court is equal to the costs reasonably incurred by the Secretary of State in respect of the costs of commitment.

(3) A warrant issued under section 40 of the Act may be executed anywhere in England and Wales by any person to whom it is directed or by any constable acting within his police area.

(4) A warrant may be executed by a constable notwithstanding that it is not in his possession at the time but such warrant shall, on the demand of the person arrested, be shown to him as soon as possible.

(5) Where, after the issue of a warrant, part-payment of the amount stated in it is made, the period of imprisonment shall be reduced proportionately so that for the period of imprisonment specified in the warrant there shall be substituted a period of imprisonment of such number of days as bears the same proportion to the number of days specified in the warrant as the amount remaining unpaid under the warrant bears to the amount specified in the warrant.

(6) Where the part-payment is of such an amount as would, under paragraph (5), reduce the period of imprisonment to such number of days as have already been served (or would be so served in the course of the day of payment), the period of imprisonment shall be reduced to the period already served plus one day.

SCHEDULE 1   **Regulation 29(1)**

LIABILITY ORDER PRESCRIBED FORM

Section 33 of the Child Support Act 1991 and regulation 29(1) of the Child Support (Collection and Enforcement) Regulations 1992

.... Magistrates' Court

Date:

Defendant:

Address:

On the complaint of the Secretary of State for Social Security that the sums specified below are due from the defendant under the Child Support Act 1991 and Part IV of the Child Support (Collection and Enforcement) Regulations 1992 and are outstanding, it is adjudged that the defendant is liable to pay the aggregate amount specified below.

Sum payable and outstanding
—child support maintenance
—interest
—other periodical payments collected by virtue of section 30 of the Child Support Act 1991

Aggregate amount in respect of which the liability order is made:

Justice of the Peace
[*or* by order of the Court
Clerk of the Court]

SCHEDULE 2   **Regulation 32**

CHARGES CONNECTED WITH DISTRESS

1. The sum in respect of charges connected with the distress which may be aggregated under section 35(2)(*b*) of the Act shall be set out in the following Table—

(1) Matter connected with distress	(2) Charge
A For making a visit to premises with a view to levying distress (whether the levy is made or not):	Reasonable costs and fees incurred, but not exceeding an amount which, when aggregated with charges under this head for any previous visits made with a view to levying distress in relation to an amount in respect of which the liability order concerned was made, is not greater than the relevant amount calculated under paragraph 2(1) with respect to the visit.
B For levying distress:	An amount (if any) which, when aggregated with charges under head A for any visits made with a view to levying distress in relation to an amount in respect of which the liability order concerned was made, is equal to the relevant amount calculated under paragraph 2(1) with respect to the levy.
C For the removal and storage of goods for the purposes of sale:	Reasonable costs and fees incurred.
D For the possession of goods as described in paragraph 2(3)— (i) for close possession (the person in possession on behalf of the Secretary of State to provide his own board):	£4.50 per day.
(ii) for walking possession:	45p per day.

E	For appraisement of an item distrained, at the request in writing of the liable person:	Reasonable fees and expenses of the broker appraising.
F	For other expenses of, and commission on, a sale by auction—	
	(i) where the sale is held on the auctioneer's premises:	The auctioneer's commission fee and out-of-pocket expenses (but not exceeding in aggregate 15 per cent. of the sum realised), together with reasonable costs and fees incurred in respect of advertising.
	(ii) where the sale is held on the liable person's premises:	The auctioneer's commission fee (but not exceeding 7½ per cent. of the sum realised), together with the auctioneer's out-of-pocket expenses and reasonable costs and fees incurred in respect of advertising.
G	For other expenses incurred in connection with a proposed sale where there is no buyer in relation to it:	Reasonable costs and fees incurred.

2.—(1) In heads A and B of the Table to paragraph 1, "the relevant amount" with respect to a visit or a levy means—

(*a*) where the sum due at the time of the visit or of the levy (as the case may be) does not exceed £100, £12.50;

(*b*) where the sum due at the time of the visit or of the levy (as the case may be) exceeds £100, 12½ per cent on the first £100 of the sum due, 4 per cent. on the next £400, 2½ per cent. on the next £1500, 1 per cent. on the next £8000 and ¼ per cent. on any additional sum;

and the sum due at any time for these purposes means so much of the amount in respect of which the liability order concerned was made as is outstanding at the time.

(2) Where a charge has arisen under head B with respect to an amount, no further charge may be aggregated under heads A or B in respect of that amount.

(3) The Secretary of State takes close or walking possession of goods for the purpose of head D of the Table to paragraph 1 if he takes such possession in pursuance of an agreement which is made at the time that the distress is levied and which (without prejudice to such other terms as may be agreed) is expressed to the effect that, in consideration of the Secretary of State not immediately removing the goods distrained upon from the premises occupied by the liable person and delaying the sale of the goods, the Secretary of State may remove and sell the goods after a later specified date if the liable person has not by then paid the amount distrained for (including charges under this Schedule); and the Secretary of State is in close possession of goods on any day for these purposes if during the greater part of the day a person is left on the premises in physical possession of the goods on behalf of the Secretary of State under such an agreement.

3.—(1) Where the calculation under this Schedule of a percentage of a sum results in an amount containing a fraction of a pound, that fraction shall be reckoned as a whole pound.

(2) In the case of dispute as to any charge under this Schedule, the amount of the charge shall be taxed.

(3) Such a taxation shall be carried out by the district judge of the county court for the district in which the distress is or is intended to be levied, and he may give such directions as to the costs of the taxation as he thinks fit; and any such costs directed to be paid by the liable person to the Secretary of State shall be added to the sum which may be aggregated under section 35(2) of the Act.

(4) References in the Table in paragraph 1 to costs, fees and expenses include references to amounts payable by way of value added tax with respect to the supply of goods or services to which the costs, fees and expenses relate.

SCHEDULE 3   **Regulation 34(1)**

FORM OF WARRANT OF COMMITMENT

Section 40 of the Child Support Act 1991 and regulation 34(1) of the Child Support (Collection and Enforcement) Regulations 1992

.... Magistrates' Court

Date:

Liable Person:

Address:

A liability order ("the order") was made against the liable person by the [ ] Magistrates' Court on [ ] under section 33 of the Child Support Act 1991 ("the Act") in respect of an amount of [ ].

The court is satisfied—

(i)   that the Secretary of State sought under section 35 of the Act to levy by distress the amount then outstanding in respect of which the order was made;

[and/or]

that the Secretary of State sought under section 36 of the Act to recover through the [ ] County Court, by means of [garnishee proceedings] or [a charging order], the amount then outstanding in respect of which the order was made;

(ii)   that such amount, or any portion of it, remains unpaid; and

(iii) having inquired in the liable person's presence as to his means and as to whether there has been [wilful refusal] or [culpable neglect] on his part, the court is of the opinion that there has been [wilful refusal] or [culpable neglect] on his part.

The decision of the court is that the liable person be [committed to prison] [detained] for [] unless the aggregate amount mentioned below in respect of which this warrant is made is sooner paid.*

This warrant is made in respect of—

Amount outstanding (including any interest, costs and charges):

Costs of commitment of the Secretary of State:

Aggregate Amount:

And you [*name of person or persons to whom warrant is directed*] are hereby required to take the liable person and convey him to [*name of prison or place of detention*] and there deliver him to the [governor] [officer in charge] thereof; and you, the [governor] [officer in charge], to receive the liable person into your custody and keep him for [*period of imprisonment*] from the date of his arrest under this warrant or until he be sooner discharged in due course of law.

Justice of the Peace

[*or* by order of the Court

Clerk of the Court]

    *Note: The period of imprisonment will be reduced as provided by regulation 34(5) and (6) of the Child Support (Collection and Enforcement) Regulations 1992 if part-payment is made of the aggregate amount.

The Child Support Commissioners (Procedure) Regulations 1992

(S.I. 1992 No. 2640)

Made by the Lord Chancellor under sections 22(3), 24(6) and (7), and 25(2), (3) and (5) of the Child Support Act 1991 and all other powers enabling him in that behalf, after consultation with the Lord Advocate and, in accordance with section 8 of the Tribunals and Inquiries Act 1992, with the Council on Tribunals.

ARRANGEMENT OF REGULATIONS

PART I

Introduction

PART II

Applications for leave to appeal and appeals to a Commissioner

PART III

General Procedure

PART IV

Decisions

PART V

Miscellaneous and Supplementary

22. Confidentiality.
23. General powers of a Commissioner.
24. Manner of and time for service of notices, etc..
25. Application to a Commissioner for leave to appeal to the Courts.

GENERAL NOTE

These Regulations contain the procedural powers of Child Support Commissioners together with provisions dealing with applications for leave to appeal to the Commissioner from a CSAT and from a Commissioner to a court. The provisions are in many respects very similar to the Tribunal Procedure Regulations. Accordingly, in the general notes which follow reference will be made to the general note of the equivalent provisions in those Regulations, drawing attention to any significant differences. For the powers of a Commissioner to make findings of fact and to deal with questions first arising on an appeal, see s.24(3) and (8) of the Act, and for the power to convene a Tribunal of Commissioners, see Sched. 4, para. 5 to the Act.

PART I

INTRODUCTION

Citation, commencement and interpretation

1.—(1) These Regulations may be cited as the Child Support Commissioners (Procedure) Regulations 1992 and shall come into force on 5th April 1993.

(2) In these Regulations, unless the context otherwise requires—

"the Act" means the Child Support Act 1991;

"appeal tribunal" means a child support appeal tribunal;

"the chairman", for the purposes of regulations 2 and 3, means—

(i) the person who was the chairman of the appeal tribunal which gave the decision against which leave to appeal is being sought; or

(ii) where the application for leave to appeal to a Commissioner was dealt with under regulation 2(2), the chairman who dealt with the application;

"Chief Commissioner" means the Chief Child Support Commissioner appointed under section 22(1) of the Act

"Commissioner" means the Chief or any other Child Support Commissioner appointed under section 22(1) of the Act and includes a Tribunal of Commissioners constituted under paragraph 5 of Schedule 4 to the Act;

"proceedings" means any proceedings before a Commissioner, whether by way of an application for leave to appeal to, or from, a Commissioner, or by way of an appeal or otherwise;

"respondent" means any person, other than the applicant or appellant, who participated as a party to the proceedings before the appeal tribunal, and any other person who, pursuant to a direction given under regulation 7(1)(*a*), is served with notice of the appeal; and

"summons" in relation to Scotland, means "citation" and regulation 14 shall be construed accordingly.

(3) In these Regulations, unless the context otherwise requires, a reference—

(*a*) to a numbered regulation is to the regulation in these Regulations bearing that number;

(*b*) in a regulation to a numbered paragraph is to the paragraph in that regulation bearing that number;

(*c*) in a paragraph to a lettered sub-paragraph is to the sub-paragraph in that paragraph bearing that letter.

PART II

APPLICATIONS FOR LEAVE TO APPEAL AND APPEALS TO A COMMISSIONER

Application to the chairman of an appeal tribunal or to a Commissioner for leave to appeal to a Commissioner

2.—(1) An application for leave to appeal to a Commissioner from the decision of an appeal tribunal shall be made—

(*a*) in the case of an application to the chairman of an appeal tribunal, within the period of 3 months beginning with the date on which notice of the decision of the tribunal was given or sent to the applicant; or

(*b*) in the case of an application to a Commissioner, within the period of 42 days beginning with the date on which notice of the refusal of leave to appeal by the chairman of the appeal tribunal was given or sent to the applicant.

(2) Where in any case it is impracticable, or it would be likely to cause undue delay for an application for leave to appeal against a decision of an appeal tribunal to be determined by the person who was the chairman of that tribunal, that application shall be determined by any other person qualified under paragraph 3 of Schedule 3 to the Act to act as a chairman of appeal tribunals.

(3) Subject to paragraph (4), an application may be made to a Commissioner for leave to appeal against a decision of an appeal tribunal only where the applicant has been refused leave to appeal by the chairman of the appeal tribunal.

(4) Where there has been a failure to apply to the chairman of the tribunal, either within the time specified in paragraph (1)(*a*) or at all, an application for leave to appeal may be made to a Commissioner who may, if for special reasons he thinks fit, accept and proceed to consider and determine the application.

(5) A Commissioner may accept and proceed to consider and determine an application for leave to appeal under paragraph (3) notwithstanding that the period specified for making the application has expired if for special reasons he thinks fit.

DEFINITIONS
   "appeal tribunal": see reg. 1(2).
   "chairman": *ibid.*
   "Commissioner": *ibid.*

GENERAL NOTE
   The procedure for applying for leave to appeal to a Commissioner in regs. 2 to 4 will be relevant to chairmen of CSATs. It is contained in these regulations, rather than in the Tribunal Procedure Regulations, because the necessary rule-making power so far as appeals to Commissioners are concerned is conferred on the Lord Chancellor by s.24(6) of the Act rather than on the Secretary of State who is given the power by s.21(3) of the Act to regulate the procedure of CSATs. If leave is refused by a chairman, the applicant has another bite at the cherry by applying to the Commissioner under para. (3). There is no right of appeal against a refusal of leave to appeal (*Bland* v. *Supplementary Benefit Officer* [1983] 1 W.L.R. 262). If, however, an application for leave is unsuccessful, the disappointed applicant may seek judicial review of the refusal, although this will only be granted in the plainest possible case (*R.* v. *The Social Security Commissioner and the Social Security Appeal Tribunal, ex p. Pattni*, [1993] Fam. Law 213.)

Para. (1)

The notice of the decision of the CSAT will have been given under reg. 13(3) of the Tribunal Procedure Regulations and will be treated as given and sent under reg. 2(2) of those Regulations. However, the refusal of leave to appeal to a Commissioner will have been given under the present regulations and will be treated as given or sent under reg. 24 of these Regulations. For the different provision relating to addresses to which notice is to be sent, see the general note to reg. 2(2) of the Tribunal Procedure Regulations.

Paras. (3) and (4).

For a discussion of "special reasons," see the general note to reg. 3(6) of the Tribunal Procedure Regulations.

Notice of application for leave to appeal to a Commissioner

3.—(1) An application for leave to appeal shall be brought by a notice in writing to the clerk to the tribunal at the Central Office of Child Support Appeal Tribunals at Anchorage Two, Anchorage Quay, Salford Quays, Manchester, M5 2YN or, as the case may be, to a Commissioner, and shall contain—

(*a*) the name and address of the applicant;

(*b*) the grounds on which the applicant intends to rely;

(*c*) an address for service of notices and other documents on the applicant; and

(*d*) where the applicant is to be represented by a person who is not a barrister, advocate or solicitor, the written authority of the applicant for that person to represent him,

and the notice shall have annexed to it a copy of the decision against which leave to appeal is being sought.

(2) In the case of an application for leave to appeal to a Commissioner made to a Commissioner where the applicant has been refused leave to appeal by the chairman of an appeal tribunal the notice shall also have annexed to it a copy of the decision refusing leave to appeal, and shall state the date on which the applicant was given notice of the refusal of leave.

(3) Where the applicant has failed to apply within the time specified in regulation 2(1)(*a*) or, as the case may be, 2(1)(*b*) for leave to appeal, the notice of application for leave to appeal shall, in addition to complying with paragraph (1), state the grounds relied upon for seeking acceptance of the application notwithstanding that the relevant period has expired.

(4) In a case where the application for leave to appeal is made by a child support officer he shall send a copy of the application to each person who was a party to the proceedings before the appeal tribunal, and in any other case the clerk to the tribunal or, as the case may be, the Office of the Commissioner shall send a copy of the application to each person, other than the applicant, who was such a party.

(5) An applicant for leave to appeal to a Commissioner may at any time before the application is determined withdraw it by giving written notice of withdrawal to the clerk to the tribunal or, as the case may be, to the Commissioner.

DEFINITIONS

"appeal tribunal": see reg. 1(2).

"chairman": *ibid.*

"Commissioner": *ibid.*

"proceedings": *ibid.*

GENERAL NOTE

Sub-para. (1)(c)

This address will be relevant for the purposes of reg. 24.

Determination of applications for leave to appeal

4.—(1) The determination of an application for leave to appeal to a Commissioner made to the chairman of an appeal tribunal shall be recorded in writing by the chairman and a copy of the determination shall be sent by the clerk to the tribunal to the applicant and every other person to whom notice of the application was given under regulation 3(4).

(2) Unless a Commissioner directs to the contrary, where a Commissioner grants leave to appeal on an application made in accordance with regulation 3, notice of appeal shall be deemed to have been duly given on the date when notice of the determination was given to the applicant and the notice of application shall be deemed to be a notice of appeal duly served under regulation 5.

(3) If on consideration of an application for leave to appeal to him from the decision of an appeal tribunal the Commissioner grants leave he may, with the consent of the applicant and each respondent, treat the application as an appeal and determine any question arising on the application as though it were a question arising on an appeal.

DEFINITIONS
"appeal tribunal": see reg. 1(2).
"chairman": *ibid.*
"Commissioner": *ibid.*
"proceedings": *ibid.*

GENERAL NOTE
Para. (1)
The clerk referred to is the clerk at the Central Office (reg. 3(1)).

Notice of appeal

5.—(1) Subject to regulation 4(2), an appeal shall be brought by a notice to a Commissioner containing—

(*a*) the name and address of the appellant;
(*b*) the date on which leave to appeal was granted;
(*c*) the grounds on which the appellant intends to rely;
(*d*) an address for service of notices and other documents on the appellant,

and the notice shall have annexed to it a copy of the determination granting leave to appeal and a copy of the decision against which leave to appeal has been granted.

DEFINITION
"Commissioner": see reg. 1(2).

GENERAL NOTE

Sub-para. (1)(d)
This address will be relevant for the purposes of reg. 24.

Time limit for appealing

6.—(1) Subject to paragraph (2), a notice of appeal shall not be valid unless it is served on a Commissioner within 42 days of the date on which the applicant was given notice in writing that leave to appeal had been granted.

(2) A Commissioner may accept a notice of appeal served after the expiry of the period prescribed by paragraph (1) if for special reasons he thinks fit.

DEFINITION
"Commissioner": see reg. 1(2).

GENERAL NOTE
Para. (1)
   The date when notice was given will be determined under reg. 24.

Para. (2)
   For a discussion of "special reasons," see the general note to reg. 3(6) of the Tribunal Procedure Regulations.

Directions on notice of appeal

7.—(1) As soon as practicable after the receipt of a notice of appeal a Commissioner shall give such directions as appear to him to be necessary, specifying—
   (*a*)   the parties who are to be respondents to the appeal; and
   (*b*)   the order in which and the time within any party is to be allowed to make written observations on the appeal or on the observations made by any other party.
   (2) If in any case two or more persons who were parties to the proceedings before the appeal tribunal give notice of appeal to a Commissioner, a Commissioner shall direct which one of them is to be treated as the appellant, and thereafter, but without prejudice to any rights or powers conferred on appellants by the Act or these Regulations, any other person who has given notice of appeal shall be treated as a respondent.
   (3) Subject to regulation 23(2)(*b*), the time specified in directions given under paragraph (1)(*b*) as being the time within which written observations are to be made shall be not less than 30 days beginning with the day on which the notice of the appeal or, as the case may be, the observations were sent to the party concerned.

DEFINITIONS
   "Commissioner": see reg. 1(2).
   "respondent": *ibid.*

GENERAL NOTE
Para. (1)
   The date when the notice of the appeal or the observations were sent will be determined under reg. 24.

Acknowledgement of a notice of appeal and notification to each respondent

8. There shall be sent by the office of the Child Support Commissioners—
   (*a*)   to the appellant, an acknowledgement of the receipt of the notice of appeal; and
   (*b*)   to each respondent, a copy of the notice of appeal.

DEFINITION
   "respondent": see reg. 1(2).

Secretary of State as respondent to an appeal

9. The Secretary of State may at any time apply to a Commissioner for leave to intervene in an appeal pending before a Commissioner, and if such leave is granted the Secretary of State shall thereafter be treated as a respondent to that appeal.

DEFINITIONS
   "Commissioner": see reg. 1(2).
   "respondent": *ibid.*

PART III

GENERAL PROCEDURE

Other directions

10.—(1) Where it appears to a Commissioner that an application or appeal which is made to him gives insufficient particulars to enable the question at issue to be determined, he may direct the party making the application or appeal or any respondent to furnish such further particulars as may reasonably be required.

(2) At any stage of the proceedings a Commissioner may, either of his own motion or on application, give such directions or further directions as he may consider necessary or desirable for the efficient and effective despatch of the proceedings.

(3) Without prejudice to the provisions of paragraph (2), a Commissioner may direct any party to any proceedings before him to make such written observations as may seem to him necessary to enable the question at issue to be determined.

(4) An application under paragraph (2) shall be made in writing to a Commissioner and shall set out the direction which the applicant is seeking to have made and the grounds for the application.

(5) Unless a Commissioner otherwise determines, an application made pursuant to paragraph (2) shall be copied by the office of the Child Support Commissioners to the other parties.

(6) The powers to give directions conferred by paragraphs (2) and (3) include power to revoke or vary any such direction.

DEFINITIONS
"Commissioner": see reg. 1(2).
"proceedings": *ibid.*

GENERAL NOTE

Para. (2)
   This power is similar to that given to chairmen of CSATs by reg. 5 of the Tribunal Procedure Regulations. However, the power under this paragraph refers to "the effective and efficient despatch of the proceedings" in contrast to the CSAT power which refers to "the *just*, effective and efficient *conduct* of the proceedings." The wording of the CSAT power concentrates on the manner in which the proceedings are to be conducted and the reference to "just" is appropriate in this context. The wording of the Commissioners' power emphasises the disposal of the proceedings and is in keeping with the Commissioners' role to deal with questions of law rather than to try issues of fact.

Requests for oral hearings

11.—(1) Subject to paragraphs (2) and (3), a Commissioner may determine an application for leave to appeal or an appeal without an oral hearing.

(2) Where in any proceedings before a Commissioner a request is made by any party for an oral hearing the Commissioner shall grant the request unless, after considering all the circumstances of the case and the reasons put forward in the request for the hearing, he is satisfied that the application or appeal can properly be determined without a hearing, in which event he may proceed to determine the case without a hearing and he shall in writing either before giving his determination or decision, or in it, inform the person making the request that it has been refused.

(3) A Commissioner may of his own motion at any stage, if he is satisfied that an oral hearing is desirable, direct such a hearing.

Representation at an oral hearing

12. At any oral hearing a party may conduct his case himself (with assistance from any person if he wishes) or be represented by any person whom he may appoint for the purpose.

GENERAL NOTE
   See the general note to reg. 9 of the Tribunal Procedure Regulations.

Oral hearings

13.—(1) This regulation applies to any oral hearing to which these Regulations apply.
   (2) Reasonable notice (being not less than 10 days beginning with the day on which notice is given and ending on the day before the hearing of the case is to take place) of the time and place of any oral hearing before a Commissioner shall be given to the parties by the office of the Child Support Commissioners.
   (3) If any party to whom notice of an oral hearing has been given in accordance with these Regulations should fail to appear at the hearing, the Commissioner may, having regard to all the circumstances including any explanation offered for the absence, proceed with the case notwithstanding that party's absence, or may give such directions with a view to the determination of the case as he thinks fit.
   (4) Any oral hearing before a Commissioner shall be in public except where the Commissioner for special reasons directs otherwise, in which case the hearing or any part thereof shall be in private.
   (5) Where a Commissioner holds an oral hearing the applicant or appellant and every respondent shall be entitled to be present and be heard.
   (6) Any person entitled to be heard at an oral hearing may—
   (*a*)   address the Commissioner;
   (*b*)   with the leave of the Commissioner but not otherwise, give evidence, call
          witnesses and put questions directly to any other person called as a witness.
   (7) Nothing in these Regulations shall prevent a member of the Council on Tribunals or of the Scottish Committee of the Council in his capacity as such from being present at an oral hearing before a Commissioner notwithstanding that the hearing is not in public.

DEFINITIONS
   "Commissioner": see reg. 1(2).
   "respondent": *ibid.*

GENERAL NOTE
   See the general note to reg. 11 of the Tribunal Procedure Regulations. Notice takes effect in accordance with reg. 24.

Para. (4)
   This is the reverse of the position in CSATs under reg. 11(7) of the Tribunal Procedure Regulations.

Summoning of witnesses

14.—(1) Subject to paragraph (2), a Commissioner may summon any person to attend as a witness at an oral hearing, at such time and place as may be specified in the summons, to answer any questions or produce any documents in his custody or under his control which relate to any matter in question in the proceedings.

(2) No person shall be required to attend in obedience to a summons under paragraph (1) unless he has been given at least 7 days' notice of the hearing or, if less than 7 days, has informed the Commissioner that he accepts such notice as he has been given.

(3) A Commissioner may upon the application of a person summoned under this regulation set the summons aside.

(4) A Commissioner may require any witness to give evidence on oath and for that purpose there may be administered an oath in due form.

DEFINITIONS
"Commissioner": see reg. 1(2).
"proceedings": *ibid.*
"summons": *ibid.*

GENERAL NOTE

Paras. (1) to (3)
See the general note to reg. 10 of the Tribunal Procedure Regulations.

Para. (4)
See the general note to reg. 11(5) of the Tribunal Procedure Regulations.

Postponement and adjournment

15.—(1) A Commissioner may, either of his own motion or on an application by any party to the proceedings, postpone an oral hearing.

(2) An oral hearing, once commenced, may be adjourned by the Commissioner at any time either on the application of any party to the proceedings or of his own motion.

DEFINITIONS
"Commissioner": see reg. 1(2).
"proceedings": *ibid.*

GENERAL NOTE
See the general note to regs. 8 and 12 of the Tribunal Procedure Regulations.

Withdrawal of applications for leave to appeal and appeals

16.—(1) At any time before it is determined, an application to a Commissioner for leave to appeal against a decision of an appeal tribunal may be withdrawn by the applicant by giving written notice to a Commissioner of his intention to do so.

(2) At any time before the decision is made, an appeal to a Commissioner may, with the leave of a Commissioner, be withdrawn by the appellant.

(3) A Commissioner may, on application by the party concerned, give leave to reinstate any application or appeal which has been withdrawn in accordance with paragraphs (1) and (2) and, on giving leave, he may make such directions as to the future conduct of the proceedings as he thinks fit.

DEFINITIONS
"appeal tribunal": see reg. 1(2).
"Commissioner": *ibid.*

Irregularities

17. Any irregularity resulting from failure to comply with the requirements of these Regulations before a Commissioner has determined the application or appeal shall not by itself invalidate any proceedings, and the Commissioner, before reaching his decision, may waive the irregularity or take such steps as he thinks fit to remedy the irregularity whether by amendment of any document, or the giving of any notice or directions or otherwise.

DEFINITIONS
  "Commissioner": see reg. 1(2).
  "proceedings": *ibid.*

PART IV

DECISIONS

Determinations and decisions of a Commissioner

18.—(1) The determination of a Commissioner on an application for leave to appeal shall be in writing and signed by him.

(2) The decision of a Commissioner on an appeal shall be in writing and signed by him and, except in respect of a decision made with the consent of the parties, he shall record the reasons.

(3) A copy of the determination or decision and any reasons shall be sent to the parties by the office of the Child Support Commissioners.

(4) Without prejudice to paragraphs (2) and (3), a Commissioner may announce his determination or decision at the conclusion of an oral hearing.

(5) When giving his decision on an application or appeal, whether in writing or orally, a Commissioner shall omit any reference to the surname of any child to whom the appeal relates and any other information which would be likely, whether directly or indirectly, to identify that child.

DEFINITION
  "Commissioner": see reg. 1(2).

Correction of accidental errors in decisions

19.—(1) Subject to regulation 21, accidental errors in any decision or record of a decision may at any time be corrected by the Commissioner who gave the decision.

(2) A correction made to, or to the record of, a decision shall become part of the decision or record thereof and written notice thereof shall be given by the office of the Child Support Commissioners to any party to whom notice of the decision had previously been given.

DEFINITION
  "Commissioner": see reg. 1(2).

GENERAL NOTE
  See the general note to reg. 14 of the Tribunal Procedure Regulations. There is power for a correction to be made by another Commissioner (reg. 21(4)).

Setting aside of decisions on certain grounds

20.—(1) Subject to the following provisions of this regulation and regulation 21, on an application made by any party a decision may be set aside by the Commissioner who gave the decision in a case where it appears just to do so on the ground that—

  (*a*) a document relating to the proceedings was not sent to, or was not received at an appropriate time by, a party or his representative, or was not received at an appropriate time by the Commissioner; or

(*b*) a party or his representative had not been present at an oral hearing which had been held in the course of the proceedings; or

(*c*) there has been some other procedural irregularity or mishap.

(2) An application under this regulation shall be made in writing to a Commissioner within 30 days from the date on which notice in writing of the decision was given by the office of the Child Support Commissioners to the party making the application.

(3) Where an application to set aside a decision is made under paragraph (1), each party shall be sent by the office of the Child Support Commissioners a copy of the application and shall be afforded a reasonable opportunity of making representations on it before the application is determined.

(4) Notice in writing of a determination of an application to set aside a decision shall be given by the office of the Child Support Commissioners to each party and shall contain a statement giving the reasons for the determination.

DEFINITIONS
"Commissioner": see reg. 1(2).
"proceedings": *ibid.*

GENERAL NOTE
See the general note to reg. 15 of the Tribunal Procedure Regulations.

Provisions common to regulations 19 and 20

21.—(1) In regulations 19 and 20 the word "decision" shall include determinations of applications for leave to appeal as well as decisions on appeals.

(2) Subject to a direction by a Commissioner to the contrary, in calculating any time for applying for leave to appeal against a Commissioner's decision there shall be disregarded any day falling before the day on which notice was given of a correction of a decision or the record thereof pursuant to regulation 19 or on which notice was given of a determination that a decision shall not be set aside under regulation 20, as the case may be.

(3) There shall be no appeal against a correction or a refusal to correct under regulation 19 or a determination given under regulation 20.

(4) If it is impracticable or likely to cause undue delay for a decision or record of a decision to be dealt with pursuant to regulation 19 or 20 by the Commissioner who gave the decision, the Chief Commissioner or another Commissioner may deal with the matter.

DEFINITIONS
"Chief Commissioner": see reg. 1(2).
"Commissioner": *ibid.*

GENERAL NOTE
See the general note to reg. 16 of the Tribunal Procedure Regulations.

PART V

MISCELLANEOUS AND SUPPLEMENTARY

Confidentiality

22.—(1) No information such as is mentioned in paragraph (2), and which has been furnished for the purposes of any proceedings to which these Regulations apply, shall be disclosed except with the written consent of the person to whom the information relates.

(2) The information mentioned in paragraph (1) is—

(*a*) the address, other than the address of the office of the Commissioner concerned and the place where the oral hearing (if any) is to be held; and

(*b*) any other information the use of which could reasonably be expected to lead to a person being located.

DEFINITION
   "proceedings": see reg. 1(2).

GENERAL NOTE
   See the general note to reg. 17 of the Tribunal Procedure Regulations.

General powers of a Commissioner

23.—(1) Subject to the provisions of these Regulations, and without prejudice to regulations 7 and 10, a Commissioner may adopt such procedure in relation to any proceedings before him as he sees fit.

(2) A Commissioner may, if he thinks fit—

(*a*) subject to regulations 2(5) and 6(2), extend the time specified by or under these Regulations for doing any act, notwithstanding that the time specified may have expired;

(*b*) abridge the time so specified; or

(*c*) expedite the proceedings in such manner as he thinks fit.

(3) Subject to paragraph (4), a Commissioner may, if he thinks fit, either on the application of a party or of his own motion, strike out for want of prosecution any application for leave to appeal or any appeal.

(4) Before making an order under paragraph (3), the Commissioner shall send notice to the party against whom it is proposed that it shall be made giving him an opportunity to show cause why it should not be made.

(5) A Commissioner may, on application by the party concerned, give leave to reinstate any application or appeal which has been struck out in accordance with paragraph (3) and, on giving leave, he may make such directions as to the future conduct of the proceedings as he thinks fit.

(6) Nothing in these Regulations shall be construed as derogating from any other power which is exercisable apart from these Regulations.

DEFINITIONS
   "Commissioner": see reg. 1(2).
   "proceedings": *ibid*.

GENERAL NOTE

Paras. (3) to (6)
   The power here is worded in terms of want of prosecution (which is the traditional formulation) rather than in the more specific terms used in reg. 6 of the Tribunal Procedure Regulations. So the comments in the general note to that regulation on the prejudicial effect of delay on the welfare of children will be of particular relevance to the Commissioners' power.

Manner of and time for service of notices, etc.

24.—(1) Any notice or other document required or authorised to be given or sent to any party under the provisions of these Regulations shall be deemed to have been given or sent if it was sent by post properly addressed and pre-paid to that party at his ordinary or last notified address.

(2) Any notice or other document given, sent or served by post shall be deemed to have been given on the day on which it was posted.

(3) Any notice or other document required to be given, sent or submitted to or served on a Commissioner—

    (a)   shall be given, sent or submitted to an office of the Child Support Commissioners;

    (b)   shall be deemed to have been given, sent or submitted if it was sent by post properly addressed and pre-paid to an office of the Child Support Commissioners.

DEFINITION
"Commissioner": see reg. 1(2).

GENERAL NOTE
Paras. (1) and 3(*a*) provide for the address to which notices or documents must be sent while paras. (2) and 3(*b*) provide for the time when a properly addressed notice or other document is deemed to have been sent, etc. See the general note to reg. 2 of the Tribunal Procedure Regulations and the difference of wording which is noted therein.

Application to a Commissioner for leave to appeal to the Courts

25.—(1) A person who was party to the proceedings in which the original decision or appeal decision was given (both of those expressions having the meaning assigned to them by section 25 of the Act) may appoint any person for the purpose of making an application for leave to appeal under section 25 of the Act.

(2) An application to a Commissioner under section 25 of the Act for leave to appeal against a decision of a Commissioner shall be made in writing and shall be made within 3 months from the date on which the applicant was given written notice of the decision.

(3) In a case where the Chief Commissioner considers that it is impracticable, or would be likely to cause undue delay, for such an application to be determined by the Commissioner who decided the case, that application shall be determined—

    (a)   where the decision was a decision of an individual Commissioner, by the Chief Commissioner or a Commissioner selected by the Chief Commissioner; and

    (b)   where the decision was a decision of a Tribunal of Commissioners, by a differently constituted Tribunal of Commissioners selected by the Chief Commissioner.

(4) If the office of Chief Commissioner is vacant, or if the Chief Commissioner is unable to act, paragraph (3) shall have effect as if the expression "the Chief Commissioner" referred to such other of the Commissioners as may have been nominated to act for the purpose either by the Chief Commissioner or, if he has not made such a nomination, by the Lord Chancellor.

(5) Regulations 16(1) and 16(3) shall apply to applications to a Commissioner for leave to appeal from a Commissioner as they do to the proceedings therein set out.

Definitions
    "the Act": see reg. 1(2).
    "Chief Commissioner": *ibid.*
    "Commissioner": *ibid.*
    "proceedings": *ibid.*

The Child Support Appeal Tribunals (Procedure) Regulations 1992

(S.I. 1992 No. 2641)

Made by the Secretary of State for Social Security under ss.21(2) and (3) and 51(1) of the Child Support Act 1991 and all other powers enabling him in that behalf, after consultation with the Council on Tribunals in accordance with s.8 of the Tribunals and Inquiries Act 1992.

GENERAL NOTE

In addition to these regulations and their general notes reference should be made to ss.20 and 21 of, and Sched. 3 to, the Act and the general notes thereto. Part II of the Child Support Commissioners (Procedure) Regulations deals with appeals from CSATs.

Many of these regulations repeat or are derived from comparable provisions in the Social Security (Adjudication) Regulations 1986 as amended. Those regulations together with detailed general notes may be found in both *Mesher* and *Bonner*. The provisions from which these regulations derive are noted at the end of each regulation. Members, and in particular chairmen, will need to be aware of the origin of the regulations in order to appreciate the relevance of decisions on them in the child support context. However, they will also need to be on their guard for a number of reasons. First, some of the provisions contain differences from their social security equivalents. Some of the differences are small while others are large, but they are all significant. Second, there are some regulations which give to CSATs powers not possessed by social security tribunals. Finally, it would be a mistake to assume that equivalent regulations should operate in identical ways in different contexts. Tribunals and their chairmen must be conscious, especially in the early days of CSATs, of the need to develop and operate a procedure which is suited to the circumstances in which it has to be applied and not adopt unthinkingly the procedures which have worked well in a different context.

Like the Social Security (Adjudication) Regulations these regulations draw a distinction between the powers which are conferred on the tribunal as a whole and those which are conferred on the chairman. The precise location of the demarcation line is not always as obvious as the wording of a regulation may suggest, nor is it always easy to locate in practice.

The operation of these regulations must be set in the context of the interplay between the regulations themselves, the chairman's wide powers over the procedure to be followed and the rules of natural justice. The regulations are subject to individual detailed general notes hereafter as is the chairman's control over procedure and the way in which it should be exercised. Something needs to be said, however, about the application of the rules of natural justice.

There can be no doubt that CSATs are subject to the rules of natural justice. These rules require that the parties should have a fair hearing (*McInnes* v. *Onslow Fane* [1978] 3 All E.R. 211 at 219). Since the contexts in which these rules have to apply vary considerably, the rules are applied flexibly so as to set appropriate standards for the decisionmaking body in question. The matter was put in these words by Tucker, L.J., in *Russell* v. *Duke of Norfolk* [1949] 1 All E.R. 109 at 118:

> "There are, in my view, no words which are of universal application to every kind of inquiry and every kind of domestic tribunal. The requirements of natural justice must depend on the circumstances of the case, the nature of the inquiry, the rules under which the tribunal is acting, the subject-matter that is being dealt with and so forth."

This is of particular importance in the context of a tribunal which approaches appeals in an inquisitorial manner (see the general note to reg. 11), since the rules of natural justice in many ways reflect the features of the adversarial system and the courts have had to adapt them to this different context.

As would be expected, broad statements such as that of Tucker, L.J., have been elaborated in particular contexts with the result that it is possible to identify some specific rules which must be observed. Many aspects of a fair hearing are covered by these regulations. To this extent they displace the rules of natural justice (*R(SB) 55/83*, para. 12). There are, however, areas which are not covered by the regulations. Since it is important for members of CSATs to be aware of the broad outline of those most likely to arise in a tribunal context, a brief coverage is appropriate. Perhaps the most useful guidance to the application of these rules in practice is to be found by asking oneself the question: would I feel I had been fairly treated, if I was a party and this happened?

The essence of natural justice is that the parties should have a fair hearing. This test is approached from an objective standpoint. If a hearing is not in fact a fair one, there has been a breach of the rules of natural justice. However, the rules are not necessarily satisfied merely because the hearing was in fact fair. It is necessary to ask if there were any grounds which might reasonably lead one of the parties to *believe* that the hearing was not fair. If there were, there has been a breach of natural justice. The classic statement of this approach to natural justice was made by Lord Hewart, C.J., in *R.* v. *Sussex Justices, ex p. McCarthy* [1924] 1 K.B. 256 at 259:

> "it is not merely of some importance but is of fundamental importance that justice should not only be done, but should manifestly and undoubtedly be seen to be done."

A fair hearing requires that parties should know that the hearing is taking place and be entitled to attend. They should know the evidence and arguments being put forward by others. They should have an opportunity to contribute by presenting evidence and arguments on their own behalf and by challenging those presented by others. This involves adequate notice of the hearing and adequate time to prepare their case. A record of the proceedings should be kept. The parties should be told the decision and be given the reasons on which it is based. The decision should not be based on matters on which the party adversely affected has not had a chance to address the tribunal.

These matters for the most part are covered by detailed rules and are covered in the general note to the relevant regulation. One matter which is not and which requires comment here is that there should be no bias on the part of the tribunal. This means that there should be no reasonable grounds for a party to suspect that there has been or might be bias. Usually this will arise because of some connection between one of the parties and one of the members. The more direct this connection the more likely there is to be a breach of natural justice if the hearing continues. The connection might involve, for example, some relationship between the persons concerned, some dealing between or affecting them, or some involvement in earlier proceedings.

Members, including chairmen, should always check their papers as soon as they receive them in order to identify any possible connections between themselves and the parties. Particular care will need to be taken in the child support context because of the possibility that a party's surname will have changed. An early check will allow an opportunity for another member to be substituted. If the connection is only identified on the day, the hearing of that case will have to be aborted since there is no power for an incomplete CSAT to hear an appeal.

Sometimes a very tenuous connection exists which would not constitute a breach of natural justice. However, it is good practice and usually the wish of the member concerned to mention it at the start of the hearing in order to find out whether the party concerned is happy to proceed. Usually all concerned are happy to proceed once the matter has been aired. If this is so it should be noted by the chairman in the notes of proceedings. However members should be aware of the possibility of a party not wishing to proceed. Since there is no provision for a hearing by an incomplete tribunal, the hearing will in such a case be abortive. In view of this possibility the wiser course for a member to follow, having checked the papers and spotted the connection, would be to ask to be replaced before the hearing.

For chairmen it is a breach of the terms of their appointment to sit if they, or any firm or business of which they are a member, have any personal, professional or pecuniary interest in the appeal. However, the fact that proceedings have involved a breach of the rules of natural justice is not necessarily a criticism of the tribunal concerned, since the fact may only become apparent after the event (*CU 270/86*, para. 12).

The members of a tribunal should have read the papers in advance of the hearing. They should also as a matter of good practice have previewed the appeal (insofar as that is possible from the papers) before the parties enter the tribunal room. This involves identifying the issues which will be before the tribunal and the matters which the tribunal need to investigate, and deciding how to handle the conduct of the appeal. No question of prejudgment is involved and the procedure is in accordance with natural justice. The matter is nicely put by Bill Tillyard, a full-time chairman in Wales and the South West Region, when he says that members should approach a hearing with an open mind but not an empty one.

On occasions, in line with the approach of Tucker, L.J., in *Russell* v. *Duke of Norfolk*, even features which are usually key requirements of natural justice have to be abandoned. Examples which are relevant in this context are the power to hold a hearing in private (reg. 11(7)) and the power to withhold evidence from one of the parties in the interests of a child (see the general note to s.2 of the Act).

The discussion of natural justice leads on naturally to the distinction between an appeal against, and a judicial review of, a CSAT's decision. An appeal lies to a Child Support Commissioner on the basis that a CSAT's decision raises a question of law. Judicial review is to the High Court on the grounds set out by Lord Diplock in *Council of Civil Service Unions* v. *Minister for the Civil Service* [1984] 3 All E.R. 935 at 950–951. His Lordship identified three heads under which judicial review of a decision may be justified. They are: (i) illegality, which arises where a decisionmaker fails to give effect to the law which regulates his decisionmaking power, for example, where a CSAT deals with a case which is outside its jurisdiction; (ii) irrationality, which arises where a decision is "so outrageous in its defiance of logic or of accepted moral standards that no sensible person who had applied his mind to the question to be decided could have arrived at it," for example, where a CSAT reaches a decision which is unsupported by the evidence; and (iii) procedural impropriety, which arises where the decisionmaker fails to comply with the rules of natural justice or with the tribunal's own procedural rules.

Review is therefore appropriate where some procedural problem has arisen. It cannot be based solely on the ground that the CSAT has failed to apply the substantive law correctly. Such cases can only be dealt with on appeal. Since the grounds which would justify seeking the review of a decision will always justify leave to appeal to a Child Support Commissioner (see the general note on leave to appeal in s.24 of the Act), there would appear to be considerable overlap between the scope of an appeal and a review. However, it is only in exceptional cases that a judicial review will be undertaken where a right of appeal exists. In practice this means that the only occasions on which review will be the appropriate remedy are those where the decision was made by a chairman alone or by a CSAT in a case where there is no appeal, for example, against a decision under reg. 15.

A CSAT also has the power to set aside the decision of another CSAT under reg. 15. This power can be used in cases involving a breach of the rules of natural justice. This cheap and quick procedure should be the first port of call in appropriate cases in preference to the process of an appeal or, where available, judicial review.

Citation, commencement and interpretation

1.—(1) These Regulations may be cited as the Child Support Appeal Tribunals (Procedure) Regulations 1992 and shall come into force on 5th April 1993.

(2) In these Regulations, unless the context otherwise requires—

"absent parent" has the meaning assigned to it in section 3(2) of the Act;

"the Act" means the Child Support Act 1991;

"Central Office" means the Central Office of Child Support Appeal Tribunals at Anchorage Two, Anchorage Quay, Salford Quays, Manchester, M5 2YN;

"chairman", subject to paragraph (3), means a person nominated under paragraph 3 of Schedule 3 to the Act and includes the President and any full-time chairman;

"clerk to the tribunal" means a person appointed under paragraph 6 of Schedule 3 to the Act;

"Commissioner" means the Chief or any other Child Support Commissioner appointed under section 22 of the Act;

"full-time chairman" means a regional or other full-time chairman of a child support appeal tribunal appointed under paragraph 4 of Schedule 3 to the Act;

"party to the proceedings" means—
  (*a*) the person with care;
  (*b*) the absent parent;
  (*c*) any child who has made an application for a maintenance assessment under section 7 of the Act;
  (*d*) the child support officer;
  (*e*) any other person, who on an application made by him, appears to the chairman of the tribunal to be interested in the proceedings;
"person with care" has the meaning assigned to it by section 3(3) of the Act;
"President" has the meaning assigned to it in paragraph 1(1) of Schedule 3 to the Act;
"proceedings" means proceedings on an appeal or application to which these Regulations apply; and
"tribunal" means a child support appeal tribunal constituted in accordance with section 21 of the Act.

(3) Unless otherwise provided, where by these Regulations anything is required to be done by, or any power is conferred on, a chairman, then—
  (*a*) if that thing is to be done or the power is to be exercised at the hearing of an appeal or application, it shall be done or exercised by the chairman of the tribunal hearing the appeal or application; and
  (*b*) otherwise, shall be done or exercised by a person who is eligible to be nominated to act as a chairman of a child support appeal tribunal under paragraph 3(2) of Schedule 3 to the Act.

(4) In these Regulations, unless the context otherwise requires, a reference—
  (*a*) to a numbered regulation is to the regulation in these Regulations bearing that number; and
  (*b*) in a regulation to a numbered paragraph is to the paragraph in that regulation bearing that number.

GENERAL NOTE
Para. (2) "clerk to the tribunal."
  The person who is the clerk to the tribunal differs according to the provision in question. For some purposes it is the clerk in the Central Office at Salford Quays. For other purposes (*e.g.* reg. 11(8)(*a*)) it will be the clerk on duty at the tribunal hearing.

"party to the proceedings" Head (d)
  The child support officer referred to will be the officer who made the decision under appeal, for example the officer who made or refused to make a review under s.18 of the Act.
  The child support officer is not a party in a contentious sense. The officer's duty is to apply the law and to assist the tribunal in doing so. As such the role is more akin to that of an *amicus curiae* than a true party (*R. v. Deputy Industrial Injuries Commissioner, ex p. Moore* [1965] 1 All E.R. 81 at 93). For further discussion of the status and role of the child support officer see the general note to s.13 of the Act.

Head (e)
  Before other persons who are interested in the proceedings can become parties they must apply to the chairman for recognition. This ensures that the person does not become a party, and therefore entitled to the rights and obligations under the regulations, until an application has been made and granted. The wording is in this respect tighter than the comparable definition in reg. 1(2) of the Social Security (Adjudication) Regulations.
  "Person ... interested in the proceedings" is a different concept from that of a "person aggrieved by the decision of a child support officer" which is used in s.20(1) of the Act. It must be at least as wide as that expression so that all persons who are entitled to appeal are also able to be parties to the appeal. However, it is wider than that and may allow others to be parties. For example, the Secretary of State may wish to be a party in view of the importance of the decision on the scope of a regulation which may require amendment or on whether the provision was *ultra vires*. The decision of the chairman on whether to accept a person as a party to the proceedings has an impact on any further appeal to a Commissioner. All persons who are parties to the appeal before the CSAT will be parties before the Com-

missioner while others require to be identified by direction of the Commissioner (see the definition of "respondent" in reg. 1(2) of the Child Support Commissioners (Procedure) Regulations).

Paragraph (3) applies to this definition. Its effect is that an application made at the hearing will be dealt with by the nominated chairman and an application made earlier may be dealt with by either the nominated chairman (if there is one) or any other chairman, usually in practice a full-time chairman.

Secretary of State

The Secretary of State is not automatically a party to the proceedings, although he may be identified as a party under head (*e*). When he acts under s.6 of the Act, he does so under the authority of the parent of the qualifying child, albeit an authority which the parent has been required to give.

Para. (3)

This paragraph provides for the division of powers and duties between the nominated chairman who chairs the hearing and other chairmen. In practice the other chairmen will usually be the full-time chairmen, in most cases the full-time chairman based at the Central Office in Salford Quays, although sometimes another part-time chairman may be asked to act. If a power or duty is being exercised at the hearing, it is the nominated chairman who must act. If it is being exercised at any other time, any chairman may act. This is subject to provision to the contrary. There is no such express provision in these Regulations. In at least one case, however, the contrary must be implied and only a nominated chairman may act even though the duty must be discharged outside the hearing. This is in the completion of the record of decision under reg. 13(2).

Service of notices or documents

2.—(1) Where by any provision of the Act or of these Regulations any notice or other document is required to be given or sent to the clerk to the tribunal that notice or document shall be treated as having been so given or sent on the day that it is received by the clerk to the tribunal.

(2) Where by any provision of the Act or of these Regulations any notice or other document is required to be given or sent to any person other than the clerk to the tribunal that notice or document shall, if sent by post to that person's last known address, be treated as having been given or sent on the day that it was posted.

DERIVATION

Social Security (Adjudication) Regulations, reg. 1(3).

DEFINITIONS

"the Act": see reg. 1(2).
"clerk to the tribunal": *ibid.*

GENERAL NOTE

These provisions are disregarded for the purposes of deciding whether it is appropriate to set aside a decision of a CSAT (reg. 15(5)).

Para. (1)

Notices or documents which are required to be given or sent to the clerk to the tribunal are treated as given or sent on the day of their receipt. The principal source of the requirement to send documents to the clerk is reg. 3(2). In addition reg. 8 makes provision for the case of postponements. However, there are at least three instances to which this paragraph seems appropriate but which are excluded from it. The first is reg. 6(3) which provides for an application to a chairman to reinstate within one year an application or appeal which has been struck out. This is not covered by the terms of this paragraph, since the application is not required to made to the clerk and so falls under para. (2) to be treated as having been made when posted. The second case is a waiver of the full period of notice to comply with a summons or citation under reg. 10(1)(*a*). The communication must be to the tribunal, not to the clerk, so again para. (2) applies rather than para. (1). The final case is an application by a party that a decision of a CSAT should be corrected under reg. 14. Such applications are permissible but are not expressly covered by reg. 3 or reg. 14, so the requirements of reg. 2(1) are not satisfied and the case falls under para. (2).

When is a document received by the clerk? Usually the answer to this question will be decided by the evidence available. In most cases the only evidence of the date of receipt will be the date stamped on the document, not infrequently in a position which obscures important contents. A party will seldom be in a position to challenge this date. Such a challenge is most likely to be made when the party alleges that the document was delivered by hand on a different day, perhaps late in the afternoon or at a weekend. The usual meaning of receipt involves something coming into someone's hands, here the clerk's. This suggests that mere delivery to the building is insufficient. There is authority for the proposition that delivery through a letter box is sufficient to constitute *notice* on the basis that the presence of the letter box impliedly invites communication by that means (*Holwell Securities Ltd.* v. *Hughes* [1974] 1 All E.R. 161 at 164). However, that decision turned on notice which is a technical legal term. "Receipt," in contrast, is a word which is to be given its natural meaning.

Para. (2)

This is a very broadly worded provision which must be interpreted in its context. Despite its wide terms it must be limited to notices or documents relating to the proceedings before the tribunal.

The rule applies regardless of whether or not the notice or document is actually received (*R(SB) 55/83*). There will be no automatic breach of the rules of natural justice by relying on this provision since it displaces any rule of natural justice which would otherwise have required a party to have received notices or documents (*ibid* para. 12). However, this potentially harsh rule must be considered in the context of two other powers available to the CSAT: the power to adjourn a hearing and the power to set aside a decision of a CSAT.

The address to which the notice or document must have been sent is the person's last *known* address. Usually an address will be known because it will have been notified to the clerk to the tribunal by the person concerned. However, if someone else has suggested that a person who has moved may be living at another address, it will have to be decided whether that person's knowledge and the confidence with which the information was conveyed are such that that address is so certain that it may be said to be the person's last *known* address. The wording of this paragraph is in line with that of reg. 15(5). However, it is in contrast to "ordinary or last notified address," which is used in reg. 24(1) of the Child Support Commissioners (Procedure) Regulations, and to "last known or notified address," which is used in reg. 4(8) of the Child Support Fees Regulations, reg. 1(3)(*b*) of the Collection and Enforcement Regulations, and regs. 1(6)(*b*) and 55(6) of the Maintenance Assessment Procedure Regulations. There is a clear pattern with one formulation being used for CSATs, another for Commissioners and a third for the Secretary of State . However, there is no obvious reason for the differences in wording and one can only wonder at how and why they came to be used in each case.

The power to adjourn under reg. 12 will be relevant if the tribunal suspects or becomes aware that a document has not been received. If a party does not attend and has not contacted the tribunal to say that he will not be attending, the CSAT should investigate whether the appropriate notice has been sent to the proper address. The same procedure should be followed if a party alleges that a document has not been received. A Commissioner has held in the social security jurisdiction that it is the duty of the clerk to be in a position to advise the CSAT as to the fact of posting of notices and documents and the addresses to which they were sent (*R(SB) 19/83*, para. 7). This duty will be difficult to carry out in the child support jurisdiction since the files containing the necessary information will not be in the tribunal room, but in the Central Office in Salford Quays. The clerk in the tribunal room will have to rely on the statement of service and receipt of notices supplied from that office and on knowledge of the prescribed office procedures in child support matters. It may be possible to telephone the Central Office. The clerk there will have access to the file and will be more familiar with the procedures of that office. However, it is unlikely that a clerk will be able to remember the document in question or be able to provide evidence of actual posting, so the CSAT will have to assess the likelihood that the tribunal records are inaccurate or that the usual procedure was not followed.

If the issue becomes contentious, the chairman should bear in mind the position of the tribunal clerks. They are junior officials and should play a neutral administrative role in the proceedings. It is appropriate that the tribunal should look to them for information about the handling of the case and advice on the procedures of the tribunal office. However, they should not be drawn into a contentious issue, still less should they become the target of antagonism for an aggrieved party. In order to prevent this, the chairman should ensure that the clerk's administrative role and the giving of evidence necessary for the tribunal to decide an issue are kept distinct, if need be by being fulfilled by different people.

The chairman should record both the fact that the investigation has been carried out and the results of the inquiry in the notes of proceeding. The CSAT should then consider whether it is appropriate to adjourn the hearing. The chairman should record that this consideration has taken place. If the hearing is adjourned, this will be the decision of the tribunal. In any event the record of the decision should say why the hearing was or was not adjourned.

The power to set aside a CSAT decision under reg. 15 will be relevant where a document has not been received with the result that a party to the proceedings is not present at the hearing or is in some other way prejudiced. Every CSAT decision is sent out with a covering letter drawing the party's attention to the setting aside power. This may prompt an express application, but if it becomes known to the tribunal, the clerk or the Secretary of State by any means that a document may not have been received, advice as to the possibility of a setting aside application should be given. If the awareness followed from a written communication from or on behalf of the party affected, that can itself be treated as an application (*R(SB) 19/83*, para. 4).

Making an appeal or application and time limits

3.—(1) Any appeal to a tribunal under section 20(1) of the Act or an application to a tribunal to set aside its decision under regulation 15 shall be by notice in writing signed by the person making it or by his representative where it appears to a chairman that he was unable to sign personally, or by a barrister, advocate or solicitor on his behalf.

(2) The notice shall be made or given by sending or delivering it to the clerk to the tribunal at the Central Office.

(3) An appeal under section 20(1) of the Act shall be brought within the period of 28 days beginning with the date on which notification of the decision in question was given or sent to the appellant.

(4) An application under regulation 15 shall be made within the period of 3 months beginning with the date when a copy of the record of the decision was given or sent to the applicant.

(5) In paragraphs (6) and (7) "the specified time" means the time specified in paragraph (3) or, as the case may be, paragraph (4).

(6) When an appeal or application is made after the specified time has expired, that time may for special reasons be extended by the chairman to the date of the making of the appeal or application.

(7) Any appeal or application made after the specified time has expired which does not include an application for an extension of time shall be deemed to include such an application, and if it appears to a chairman that an application for an extension of time does not state reasons for the appeal or application being made after the specified time the chairman may before determining it give the person making the application for an extension of time a reasonable opportunity to provide reasons.

(8) An application for an extension of time which has been refused may not be renewed, but any chairman may set aside a refusal if it appears to him just to do so on any of the grounds set out in regulation 15(1).

(9) In the case of an appeal the notice shall contain sufficient particulars of the decision under appeal to enable that decision to be identified.

(10) Any notice of appeal or application other than an application for an extension of time shall state the grounds on which it is made.

(11) If it appears to a chairman that the notice of appeal does not enable the decision under appeal to be identified or that the notice of appeal or application does not state the grounds on which it is made the chairman may direct the person making it to provide such particulars as the chairman may reasonably require.

DERIVATION
Social Security (Adjudication) Regulations, reg. 3.

DEFINITIONS
"the Act": see reg. 1(2).
"Central Office": *ibid.*
"chairman": *ibid.*
"tribunal": *ibid.*

GENERAL NOTE
This regulation applies only to appeals to CSATs under s. 20(1) (but not *e.g.* under s. 46(7)) and applications to set aside a decision of a CSAT. Applications for leave to appeal to a Commissioner, whether made to a chairman of a CSAT or to a Commissioner, are covered by regs. 2 to 4 of the Child Support Commissioners (Procedure) Regulations.

Para. (1)

A signature is required before an appeal or application to set aside is valid. It is important to identify the person who has submitted an appeal for two reasons. First, it is necessary to establish that the person is entitled to appeal. Second, it is necessary to ensure that an appeal has not been made in someone's name but without their authority. The first does not require a signature. In practice the second is taken on trust. Problems are rare and will probably be identified when documents are sent to the person concerned. Signatures are also taken on trust and the fact that a person happens to use a mark rather than a signature, or does not sign personally, ought not to affect the tribunal's approach.

The notice must be signed either by the party personally or by a legal representative. Representatives other than those specified may not sign on the party's behalf. This is a limitation on the normal position, which is that all representatives have the rights and powers of the party represented (reg. 9). Any form of mark is sufficient as a signature, including a stamp bearing a facsimile signature or even a printed name, provided that it is clear that this is to count as a signature by the person.

There is a limited exception for those who are unable to sign personally. In this case any representative may sign. This is a welcome but very limited exception. It applies only where the person is *unable* to sign. The inability might arise from a number of causes: (i) It could have a physical cause, an example being if persons have no arms or have insufficient control over their arms to be able to write; (ii) Or it could have a mental cause, for example the person may have learning difficulties; (iii) Or it could have an educational cause, such as the person has simply never learnt to write; (iv) Perhaps the fact that the person was working abroad and could not be contacted easily or at all would also be sufficient. Whatever the cause, the result must be that the person is unable to sign. It is not sufficient that the person is, for example, blind and although able to sign documents, does not do so. Nor is it relevant that the persons' mental capacity is such that they cannot understand what they are doing, although they could sign their names. In such a case even if someone is acting for the person, for example, under a power of attorney, a legal representative must sign.

This is a cumbersome exception to an unnecessary rule. All that matters is that the tribunal should be satisfied that the person named does wish to make the appeal or application. The full-time chairman to whom any cases of doubt will be referred should not be expected to make detailed inquiries of a person's ability to write or of whether a particular mark is that person's customary method of signing, and in practice is unlikely to do so other than in a most exceptional case.

Para. (2)

The notice is treated as sent or delivered on the day it is received by the clerk at the Central Office in Salford Quays (reg. 2(1)).

Para. (6)

In deciding whether special reasons exist so as to justify the extension of time, the chairman is not limited to reasons relating to the delay. All of the following should ideally be considered, although in practice the information available to the chairman making the decision is limited: (i) the extent of the delay, (ii) the reasons for it, (iii) the consequences of not allowing the appeal or application to proceed, (iv) the likelihood of the appeal or application succeeding, (v) whether it is supported by the child support officer and (vi) any other matter appearing to be relevant. (See *R(U) 8/68*, para. 14, *R(M) 1/87* and *R. v. Secretary of State for Home Department, ex p. Mehta* [1975] 1 W.L.R. 1087). The fact that the law has subsequently been altered by a decision of a court or Commissioner is not of itself a ground for the *substantial* extension of time (*R(S) 8/85*, para. 6).

The question is whether there are special reasons for extending the time to make an appeal or application. This formulation requires that careful attention be given to the significance of the fact that an appeal or application is only a few days late. This fact of itself cannot justify extending the time. However, it may be that the shorter the delay that has occurred the easier it will be to justify the extension of time by reference to other factors. Certainly if the basis of the appeal is that the law has been changed by a recent decision, an application for a short extension is more likely to be successful than an application for a long extension (*R(S) 8/85*, para. 6). The principles which the courts apply in striking out or refusing to strike out for want of prosecution do not apply to applications for the extension of time (*Regalbourne Ltd.* v. *East Lindsey District Council, The Times*, March 16, 1993).

Para. (7)

An appeal or application which is made outside the specified time is deemed to include an application for an extension of time. In such a case the chairman has a power, but not a duty, to give an opportunity to say why it was late.

Para. (8)

This paragraph provides a remedy if a request to extend time is not allowed. In addition the refusal to extend time may be reconsidered, whether it was originally considered *ex parte*, as will usually be the case, or *inter partes* (*CIS 93/92*, para. 15). This course is most likely to be taken where fresh matters of fact or other considerations come to light. The chairman has a power but not a duty to reconsider a decision (*ibid.*, para. 16). This power is not a licence to ask repeatedly for a decision to be reconsidered. The scope of the power is wide enough to allow a chairman to reconsider the granting of an extension of time, although this is a course likely to be taken in only the most exceptional case, such as where it is discovered that the appellant or applicant had deliberately misled the chairman.

The power to set aside a refusal to extend time is given to any chairman, whether the chairman who originally refused leave or another. Since the decision is that of a chairman and not of a CSAT, no appeal lies to a Commissioner (*R(SB) 24/82*, para. 5). The power is tied to the grounds set out in reg. 15(1). It does not, however, bring in the procedural requirements of reg. 15. In practice the grounds on which a refusal to extend time may be set aside are most unlikely to occur, so this paragraph confers little benefit on those whose applications for an extension of time are turned down.

Para. (10)

The appellant or applicant is required to identify "grounds," whereas elsewhere the regulations speak of "reasons" being given (*e.g.* para. (7)). The former is narrower than the latter. There is little guidance to interpretation to be had from the practice of social security tribunals. These tribunals have been lax in enforcing the requirement for grounds of appeal and readily accept appeals which indicate legally irrelevant considerations or merely state "I appeal." There is also little help from the authorities. The best help comes from counsel's argument in the briefly reported case of *R.* v. *Secretary of State for Social Services, ex p. Loveday, The Times*, February 18, 1983 where he distinguished between the grounds of a decision as being the basis of the decision and the reasons as being the factors which led to the decision being made (see LEXIS transcript).

Applying that approach to the meaning of "grounds" in this regulation produces this interpretation. The grounds identify the basis or essence of an appeal or application and do not need to contain the arguments which will be adduced in support of the grounds. In the case of an appeal the grounds will specify what is wrong with the decision rather than why it is wrong. The test for the chairman to apply in such a case is whether the notice of appeal or application indicates sufficient information to allow the issues to be identified and dealt with properly. Leave to appeal is not required, so any test which takes into account the strength of the grounds would be inappropriate.

Paras. (10) and (11)

These two paragraphs together with reg. 6(1) (which provides that an appeal may be struck out for failure to comply with a direction under para. (11)) provide the rule and the enforcement procedure which will allow the tribunal to insist on there being adequate indication of the basis of an appeal so that all parties can identify the issues which are relevant before the actual hearing. Prior knowledge of the basis of an appeal will allow proper preparation by the parties, their representatives and the members of the tribunal, the avoidance of adjournments (see the general note to reg. 12(2)) and the efficient disposal of the appeal. These matters are especially important in CSATs where there will frequently be two parties with opposed interests present and represented. In such cases delays may be caused by unexpected issues arising and time may be wasted by unnecessary preparation of uncontested issues. This will result in cost to the parties involved. It will also be to the detriment of the efficient operation of the tribunal system in view of the resulting delays to other appeals.

It is understood that the practice will be slightly tighter than that applied in SSATs. An appeal which merely states "I appeal" will not be accepted. Nor will one which says "I appeal and will give my reasons at the hearing but not before." However, anything which goes beyond this will be accepted. For example, "I appeal because this decision does not allow me enough money to live on" may be adequate. This practice reflects the need to take account of the difficulties of an unrepresented and perhaps inarticulate party. Strict compliance with legal forms can operate harshly and this is not an appropriate area for laying down strict rules (*R(I) 15/53*, para. 4).

However, more may be expected where the party in question is known to be represented, particularly if the representative is legally qualified. Chairmen may take account of the circumstances of the party concerned when deciding whether and how to exercise their powers. In particular, the better course in some cases may be to give directions which will help to identify the grounds of appeal, rather than to permit appeals to proceed to a hearing without a clear idea of what they are essentially about or to strike them out.

If an appeal or application fails to state any or adequate grounds, the first stage is for a chairman to give a direction under para. (11) that adequate grounds be identified. If that direction is not complied with, all parties must be given a reasonable opportunity to show cause why the appeal or application should not be struck out (reg. 6(2)). Only then does the chairman actually acquire the power to strike out the appeal or application under reg. 6(1).

The chairman's power to require grounds to be stated and to strike out under reg. 6 must be set in the context of the power to give directions under reg. 5 and the control of procedure under reg. 11(1). They should be seen as an overall package to ensure that the basis of the appeal is identified in advance, that by the day the appeal is heard all parties are aware of the essence of what is in dispute and are prepared to deal with the issues arising, and that at the hearing the parties are as far as the rules of natural justice permit confined to the issues identified in advance.

Regulation 6(1) provides that the penalty for failure to comply with a direction to provide adequate grounds for an appeal or application is that it may be struck out. This means that if an appeal or application is allowed to proceed despite the lack of any or adequate grounds, it will nonetheless be a valid appeal or application and the decision will be valid (*CSB 1182/89*, para. 13) unless and until it is set aside on appeal or under reg. 15. The party making the appeal or application may correct the deficiencies in the notice at any time until the chairman acts (*CSB 1182/89*, para. 13).

Lack of jurisdiction

4. When a chairman is satisfied that the tribunal does not have jurisdiction to entertain a purported appeal he may make a declaration to that effect and such declaration shall dispose of the purported appeal.

DERIVATION
Social Security (Adjudication) Regulations, reg. 3(7).

DEFINITIONS
"chairman": see reg. 1(2).
"tribunal": *ibid.*

GENERAL NOTE
This power may be exercised by any chairman. It will usually be exercised by a full-time chairman, although the chairman nominated to hear an appeal may also exercise it. The power is limited to cases of lack of jurisdiction; for example, where there has been no application for a review under s. 18 of the Act. It cannot be used to dispose of an appeal which lacks any grounds; this is subject to specific provision in regs. 3(11) and 6. Since the decision is taken by a chairman and not by the tribunal, no appeal lies to a Commissioner.

This power is additional to, and does not displace, the power of a tribunal to decide an issue as to its jurisdiction (*R(SB) 29/83*, para. 17). If the tribunal does decide on a question as to its jurisdiction, that is a decision of the tribunal which may be appealed to a Commissioner (*ibid.*).

If the appeal is clearly misconceived or misdirected it is appropriate for a chairman to deal with the matter (*CI 78/90*, para. 13). However, if the issue is a difficult one, for example, whether one of the parties is habitually resident in the United Kingdom, it is better for it to be dealt with by a tribunal (which may have the benefit of argument) rather than by a chairman. It is also inappropriate for a chairman to deal with the question of jurisdiction if to do so would involve holding that a setting aside of an earlier decision was invalid (*ibid.*). The general conclusion to draw from these specific examples is that it is inappropriate for a chairman to exercise the power under this regulation if the question is a contentious one in respect of which it would be appropriate for a right of appeal to arise. For another example of where it would be inappropriate for a chairman to act under this regulation see the general note to reg. 15(1).

A first reading of *CSB 1182/89* might suggest that once the hearing has begun the tribunal rather than the chairman is the appropriate body to deal with the matter. However, the Commissioner's view in that decision was provisional, qualified and *obiter*. Moreover, the particular context in which the Commissioner was speaking in that decision is now covered by specific provision in reg. 3(11). The decision should not be read as restricting the power conferred on the chairman by the plain wording of this regulation.

Directions

5. At any stage of the proceedings a chairman may either of his own motion or on a written application made to the clerk to the tribunal by any party to the proceedings give such directions as he may consider necessary or desirable for the just, effective and efficient conduct of the proceedings and may direct any party to provide such further particulars or to produce such documents as may reasonably be required.

DEFINITIONS
"chairman": see reg. 1(2).
"clerk to the tribunal": *ibid.*
"party to the proceedings": *ibid.*
"proceedings": *ibid.*

GENERAL NOTE

This regulation creates a valuable power for a chairman to give directions. It may be exercised by the nominated chairman at the hearing of the appeal, or by any chairman before the hearing. It only applies to directions which can affect the conduct of the proceedings. It does not extend to the directions which may given when remitting the case to the Secretary of State under section 20(3) of the Act. The power to give directions at that stage is vested in the tribunal as a whole and not the chairman (see s.20(4)). See also reg. 13(4).

The chairman acquires the power to give directions as soon as proceedings begin, which means as soon as the appeal is lodged. A direction may be given on the chairman's own motion or at the request of any party. A request is not governed by the requirements of reg. 3. A written request in writing before the hearing causes little inconvenience. The requirement for a written request at the hearing appears cumbersome. However, if an oral request is made at the hearing, a direction may be given on the chairman's own motion. The same procedure may be followed in the case of requests telephoned to the chairman via the clerk.

The express wording of the regulation makes it clear that the power to give directions is one which is given to the chairman alone and which remains with him to the exclusion of the tribunal throughout the proceedings. Consequently, the reasoning in *CSB 1182/89*, which is discussed in the general note to reg. 4, has no application here.

It is not intended that there will be standard directions given as a matter of course in all appeals by the full-time chairman based at the Central Office. The power is intended to be used on an ad hoc basis. It will, if properly used, greatly assist to avoid adjournments. It is good practice for the chairman on receipt of the papers to read through them in order to identify any directions which could be given which would contribute to the just, effective and efficient conduct of the proceedings. The chairman will need to bear in mind, if directions are given to a party, that there will only be a limited time before the hearing within which the party can comply with the directions.

This regulation gives chairmen the power to make orders which would require the hearing of an appeal to be postponed or even the whole session to be aborted. This might arise, for example, if a chairman issued directions that fresh evidence should be disclosed to all parties or written submissions be presented to the tribunal in advance. Chairmen will wish to exercise their powers under this regulation sensibly and with caution in order to balance their desire to ensure that the proceedings are conducted in a just, effective and efficient manner with the undesirability of bringing disruption to the listing of appeals with resulting delay to the parties to other appeals, including child support officers. They will also need to bear in mind that the administrative arrangements necessary to carry out their directions may not exist.

Despite the broad wording of the power, it is limited to procedural matters. It cannot be used to usurp the tribunal's powers over substantive issues. One direction which might be made in an appropriate case is for evidence to be given by video or through a television link. The administrative arrangements by which such a direction could be implemented are not in place at the time of writing. Another use of the power might be to restrict circulation of certain evidence. By analogy with the power of a court dealing with the welfare of a child, the chairman might in exceptional cases order that evidence which would be detrimental to the welfare of the child should not be disclosed to another party to the appeal (*Re B. (A Minor) (Disclosure of Evidence)* [1993] 1 F.L.R. 191). A number of other occasions on which the exercise of this power to give directions should be considered are pointed out in the general notes to specific regulations.

In giving a direction, a chairman should be mindful of whether it will be possible to enforce the direction if it is not complied with. If the failure to comply is that of an appellant or applicant, the chairman has the ultimate sanction of striking out the appeal or application under reg. 6. However, this may be considered too draconian a penalty in all but the most serious cases and one of the other possible steps considered below may be more appropriate. If the failure to comply is that of another party, the position is more complex. A chairman could direct the party to attend to give evidence, or issue a summons or citation to the person to produce documents, but this latter power has its own problems of enforcement (see the general note to reg. 10). Alternatively, a chairman or the tribunal could ask the child support officer to ask the Secretary of State to use an inspector under s.15 of the Act. An inspector can only be appointed to obtain information required by the Secretary of State or a child support officer, not by a CSAT, although it would be sufficient if the child support officer required the information as evidence before a CSAT. The appointment of an inspector is a matter for the Secretary of State; the CSAT or its chairman can only request an appointment. Beyond these powers, the consequences of failure to comply will depend upon the nature of the direction and whether compliance will be for the benefit of the person to whom the direction is given. If compliance is against the person's interests, the CSAT may occasionally be able to apply the law to the advantage of the appellant and the disadvantage of the other party. Take as an example a case in which the appellant alleges that in addition to his wages as a plumber her former husband used to undertake private work in that capacity but has disclosed no additional income in respect of this. The husband is directed to produce the records which the appellant says he keeps, but he fails to comply. If the appellant is able to prove the amount of work which he used to do (and this will often not be possible), the CSAT may, in the absence of proof as to the amount of income derived from that work, be able to hold that no income was received and apply Sched. 1, para. 26 to the Maintenance Assessments and Special Cases Regulations to fix a reasonable income for that work. Alternatively the evidence may allow the CSAT to hold that the work is no longer undertaken and that by giving up that work he has deprived himself of a source of income under para. 27 of that Schedule. These, however, will be rare cases. In most cases the CSAT will have to accept the facts that the burden of proof is on the appellant, that the tribunal has an inquisitorial function, which it must exercise impartially even if one party has disobeyed a direction, and that it can only act on evidence before it.

At the end of the day the key to compliance lies not in coercion or powers of enforcement, but in the willingness of the person concerned to comply with the directions given. The power under this regulation should be used in a constructive manner to guide the parties in the preparation and presentation of their cases, and to assist them to proceed in a spirit and atmosphere of co-operation which should be fostered by the whole appeal system in implementing the enabling role of the tribunal which extends beyond the hearing of the appeal itself to the entire proceedings. This will, no doubt, often be an unattainable ideal, but it, rather than confrontation and compulsion, will make this power effective.

Despite this exhortation, a note of caution is required, especially in the early days of the new system. Chairmen will need to be mindful that the resources available to provide the administrative and budgetary support that may be required by, or as a result of, their directions are limited, as are the means by which compliance with a direction can be encouraged or secured. They should not exercise this power in a manner that will undermine confidence in the tribunal system.

Striking out of proceedings

6.—(1) Subject to paragraph (2), a chairman may, either of his own motion or on the application of any party to the proceedings, order that the appeal or application be struck out because of the failure of the appellant or applicant to comply with a direction under regulation 3(11) or 5 or to reply to an enquiry from the clerk to the tribunal about his availability to attend a hearing.

(2) Before making an order under paragraph (1) the chairman shall send notice to the person against whom it is proposed that any such order should be made and any other party to the proceedings giving each of them a reasonable opportunity to show cause why such an order should not be made.

(3) The chairman may, on application by any party to the proceedings made not later than one year beginning with the date of the order made under paragraph (1), give leave to reinstate any appeal or application which has been struck out in accordance with that order.

DERIVATION
Social Security (Adjudication) Regulations, reg. 7.

DEFINITIONS
"chairman": see reg. 1(2).
"clerk to the tribunal": *ibid.*
"party to the proceedings": *ibid.*

GENERAL NOTE
Para. (1)
This paragraph gives a chairman a discretion to strike out an appeal or application on specified grounds only. The clerk's enquiry about a party's availability will usually be made as part of the tribu-

nal's pre-listing procedure. The express power to strike out formalises the practice in the social security jurisdiction whereby striking out is used as part of a package of measures to remove appeals from the system where the appellant is no longer communicating with the tribunal. Decisions on the circumstances in which it is appropriate to strike out court proceedings are generally not applicable in the context of the powers conferred by this regulation and regs. 3(11) and 5, although they would be more appropriate in the *inter partes* jurisdiction of child support than in the social security jurisdiction.

Unlike its social security counterpart this power is not tied to want of prosecution or delay. Although there are advantages in having a power which is drafted in more specific terms than delay, this provision places child support law out of line with the basic principle laid down by s.1(2) of the Children Act 1989 that delay in determining a question is likely to prejudice the welfare of a child. However, the welfare of any children affected is a factor which chairmen are entitled to take into account in the exercise of the discretion conferred by this regulation. Nevertheless delay of itself will not justify striking out the appeal or application. If a party has delayed, a chairman must first give a direction as to the conduct of the proceedings under reg. 5, probably in the form of a timetable of action for the party. If the direction is not followed, a reasonable opportunity for all parties to show cause why the appeal or application should not be struck out must be allowed under para. (2). Only then will the chairman have power to strike it out. This three stage procedure adds further to the delay. It is, therefore, desirable for delay to be identified at as early a stage as possible in order that an appropriate direction may be given. One approach would be to give standard directions at an early stage which are drafted in such a way as to allow notice under para. (2) to be given without the need for further directions, but it is understood that this will not be the practice.

The fact that delay is not a ground for striking out should make the operation of the regulation more predictable. There may, though, be scope for disagreement over whether a party's response to a direction has been sufficient. Any such disagreement will be a factor relevant to the exercise of the chairman's discretion.

Striking out may be initiated by an application from one of the parties or on the chairman's own motion. The discretion is brought into play by the failure to comply with the direction or to respond to the clerk' enquiry, not by the reasons for the failure to do so, although they will be relevant to whether the discretion should be exercised. There is no limit to the circumstances in which the exercise of this power may arise. It could, for example, arise from failure to supply grounds for an appeal or application, from constant requests for postponements or adjournments, from failure to comply with directions or from disruptive behaviour at the hearing.

Action under this regulation will usually be taken by a full-time chairman in advance of the appeal or application being listed for hearing. However, the discretion to strike out survives as long as there are proceedings and cases may arise in which the appellant or applicant fails to comply with a direction once the case is listed or even after the hearing has begun. In such a case either a full-time chairman or the chairman nominated to hear an appeal or application may wish to initiate action under this regulation. The position if it is a party other than the appellant or applicant who fails to comply with a direction is discussed in the general note to reg. 5.

In deciding how to exercise the discretion conferred by this paragraph, as with the exercise of all discretions, it will seldom be helpful or advisable to compare the facts of the case in question with those of decisions of the Commissioners or of other cases known to the chairman (*R.* v. *Newham Justices, ex p. C.*, *The Times*, August 26, 1992).

Para. (2)

This paragraph places the burden on any party to the proceedings to show cause why the appeal or application should not be struck out. "Cause" in this context must not be confused with "good cause" from the law of backdating social security benefits or "just cause" from the law of unemployment benefit. These concepts are only appropriate where parties are seeking to excuse their actions. Here they are inappropriate since any party, and not just the one responsible for the delay, may show cause why the appeal or application should not be struck out.

This paragraph does not establish a specific defence such as "just cause". It is merely a procedural provision allowing any party to produce any evidence or advance any arguments relevant to the exercise of the chairman's discretion. "Cause" is a broad term and should be interpreted flexibly without becoming tied to any specific factors or categories. The chairman should consider any matter relevant to how the discretion should be exercised, including the following: (i) the need to balance the interests of all parties to the proceedings; (ii) the nature of the failure; (iii) the reasons for it; (iv) where responsibility for it lies; (v) its impact on the proceedings; (vi) the likelihood of further failures; (vii) the consequences of the failure for all parties and (viii) any other relevant factor in the circumstances of the case. Where an application to extend the time to make an appeal or application is being considered, the merits are a relevant consideration. Once an appeal or application has been made, it could be argued that taking account of the merits would be to usurp the function of the CSAT. On the other hand, in a borderline case there might be a greater willingness to strike out an appeal or application that had little hope of success than one whose merits were very strong.

The chairman should also consider whether there is any other action which might be more appropriate in the circumstances. Striking out is a drastic step and not to be taken lightly. The chairman when deciding whether or not to strike out should consider whether it would not be more appropriate to give a direction under reg. 5 which would put the appeal or application back on course, or simply to have the case listed forthwith.

Para. (3)

As the striking out of an application or appeal is not a tribunal decision, no appeal lies to a Commissioner. However, there is a limited remedy available under para. (3) whereby the chairman may reinstate the appeal or application within a year. The chairman has an unfettered discretion here in contrast to the power contained in reg. 3(8) which is tied to the grounds set out in reg. 15(1). Additionally, the exercise of the discretion is subject to judicial review. Although this is a theoretical possibility, it may prove difficult to amass the evidence necessary to support an application.

The power of reinstatement is given to the chairman which suggests the chairman who took the decision to strike out. However, since the power will not be exercised at a hearing, any chairman may act (reg. 1(3)(*b*)). In practice, the full-time chairman at the Central Office will decide on both striking out and reinstatement, although in cases of difficulty or impossibility other chairmen might be involved.

Withdrawal of appeals and applications

7.—(1) Any appeal to a tribunal may be withdrawn by the person making the appeal—

(*a*)   at a hearing with the leave of the chairman;

(*b*)   at any other time, by giving written notice of intention to withdraw to the clerk to the tribunal and either—

   (i)   with the consent in writing of every other party to the proceedings; or

   (ii) with the leave of the chairman after every other party to the proceedings has had a reasonable opportunity to make representations.

(2) A person who has made an application to a tribunal to set aside their decision under regulation 15 may withdraw it at any time before the application is determined by giving written notice of withdrawal to the clerk to the tribunal.

DERIVATION

Social Security (Adjudication) Regulations, reg. 6.

DEFINITIONS

"chairman": see reg. 1(2).
"clerk to the tribunal": *ibid.*
"party to the proceedings": *ibid.*
"tribunal": *ibid.*

GENERAL NOTE

Para. (1)

Before a hearing of the appeal has begun, withdrawal is primarily a matter for the parties; the leave of a chairman only becomes relevant if the parties do not agree. Once a hearing has begun the consent of a chairman is always required. During the course of a hearing it is the chairman nominated to hear the case who must give leave. After a hearing has been adjourned any chairman may give leave to withdraw (reg. 1(3)). In deciding whether or not to grant leave the chairman will obviously bear in mind the wishes of the parties. If the desire to withdraw is made known during the hearing, the chairman may wish to have an adjournment (a matter for the whole tribunal) in order to ascertain the wishes of any of the parties who are not present. It is a rare case indeed in which the chairman will refuse leave in the face of the unanimous wishes of the appellant and the respondent, although it will be necessary to ensure that their consent is fully informed. Whether the notice of intention is given before or at the hearing, it is likely that the opposition of the child support officer to withdrawal will carry particular weight in the chairman's decision.

If a request to withdraw is made at a hearing the chairman should record the statement of intention to withdraw in the record of proceedings together with the views of the parties present and the decision.

Precisely when a hearing begins has never been determined. It has certainly not begun before all the parties present have entered the tribunal and settled down. It has certainly begun by the time the tribunal starts to hear evidence or submissions. The difficult area is the time spent by the chairman on an introduction to the hearing. The better view is that the hearing begins as soon as the introduction begins, but problems do not arise in practice and any that do can be dealt with by the flexible application of common sense.

Para. (2)
Applications are dealt with by a separate provision. The withdrawal of an application is a unilateral matter for the applicant and does not require the consent of any other party or the leave of a chairman. Written notice must be given to the clerk to the tribunal. This applies even where the application in question is to set aside a decision and an oral hearing of the application is taking place. The notice of intention must still be in writing even though the applicant is present.

Postponement

8.—(1) Where a person to whom notice of a hearing has been given wishes to request a postponement of that hearing he shall give notice in writing to the clerk to the tribunal stating his reasons for the request and a chairman may grant or refuse the request as he thinks fit.

(2) A chairman may of his own motion at any time before the beginning of the hearing postpone the hearing.

DERIVATION
Social Security (Adjudication) Regulations, reg. 5(1).

DEFINITIONS
"chairman": see reg. 1(2).
"clerk to the tribunal": *ibid.*

GENERAL NOTE
This power will be exercised before the hearing. It may, therefore, be exercised by any chairman and not just the nominated chairman (reg. 1(3)(*b*)). Since the decision is made by the chairman and not by the tribunal, there is no appeal. However, if a postponement is refused, the party has three courses available: (i) apply to have the hearing adjourned by the tribunal; (ii) if the appeal is heard, appeal; (iii) apply to have the tribunal decision set aside under reg. 15.

Para. (1)
The person requesting the postponement must state reasons for the request. This is in contrast to appeals and applications which require grounds to be stated. The difference in wording reflects the fact that what is required here are factual matters rather than legal considerations.
The chairman may grant or refuse the request "as he thinks fit." This provides an unfettered discretion. Chairmen should consider all factors relating to why the claimant is not in a position to attend or to proceed on the day set for the hearing. They will be on guard to ensure that requests for postponement are not used as a tactical device for delaying an unwanted decision. They may also be reluctant to postpone a hearing if it appears that the appeal could be decided in favour of the person requesting the postponement without that person being present or further prepared, especially as the hearing can be adjourned if it appears appropriate. However, the inconvenience to the other parties should be borne in mind, especially as in contrast to social security appeals there are more likely to be parties with a direct and personal interest in the hearing.
The principles governing the exercise of the discretion to postpone are very similar to those governing adjournments. The factors relevant when considering adjournments (see the general note to reg. 12(1)) will always be relevant to postponements, but other factors will also come into play in view of the earlier stage at which the decision on postponement may be made. For example, the chairman should consider the costs involved in attendance if the hearing is not postponed but has to be adjourned on the day. Alternatively, a chairman who is in doubt about whether or not to postpone may prefer to leave the hearing to take place knowing that if appropriate it can be adjourned.
The chairman may attach such conditions as appropriate if the hearing is postponed. When making any postponement it is good practice to consider whether it is appropriate to attach any conditions or to make any directions under reg. 5 which would contribute to the conduct of the proceedings.

Para. (2)

This is a useful power which allows a chairman to postpone hearings of his own motion. It allows a chairman to deal with a request for a postponement which is not in writing and so does not comply with the requirements of para. (1). Such requests are often made by telephone shortly before the hearing. The power also allows the chairman to postpone when for some reason a hearing cannot proceed. This may be because there will not be a properly constituted tribunal: one of the members may be unable to attend and a substitute cannot be found or a member of each sex will not be present on the tribunal and the case is not a suitable one for a ruling that this is not reasonably practicable under Sched. 3, para. 2(3) to the Act. Alternatively, it may be because it is clear that a direction given under reg. 5 will not have been complied with by the date fixed for hearing or that for some other reason it would not be appropriate to proceed with the hearing.

When the hearing begins is discussed in the general note to reg. 7.

Representation of parties to the proceedings

9. Any party to the proceedings may be accompanied and (whether or not the party himself attends) may be represented by another person whether having a professional qualification or not, and for the purposes of any proceedings any such representative shall have all the rights and powers to which the person represented is entitled under these Regulations, except that a representative who is not a barrister, advocate or solicitor shall not have the power to sign the notice of appeal or application.

DERIVATION

Social Security (Adjudication) Regulations, reg. 2(1)(*b*).

DEFINITIONS

"party to the proceedings": see reg. 1(2).
"proceedings": *ibid.*

GENERAL NOTE

Parties may come to the tribunal with a representative to act on their behalf, a companion to provide moral support and a witness. This regulation provides for companions and representatives. It may be important to know in what capacity a person attends. This is not always easy to determine, since the party may be accompanied by a friend for support who also makes some points on his behalf and gives some evidence to the tribunal. This confusion of roles is inevitable in the relatively informal atmosphere of a tribunal. In *CG 4/91*, for example, one person was representative, interpreter and witness.

A party may be represented by a lawyer or CAB adviser. In such cases the existence and identity of the representative will usually have been notified to the clerk to the tribunal in advance of the hearing and the representative will have received the papers and notices sent to the party. Their role is easy to establish from their status. In other cases, however, relatives, friends, social workers, etc., the chairman will need to be aware of the significance of crossing the line between roles. A person who is allowed to question witnesses or to address the tribunal becomes a representative and entitled under this regulation to the same rights and powers as the party. A person who gives evidence becomes a witness and is liable to be questioned by any other party or representative and to be put on oath.

The regulation refers only to a companion or representative but by virtue of s.6(*c*) of the Interpretation Act 1978, since the context does not otherwise require, the singular includes the plural. However, the chairman retains overall control of procedure under reg. 11(1) and may limit the numbers or otherwise ensure that the power given to parties by this regulation is exercised reasonably (*CI 199/89*, para. 13).

A party may be prejudiced by the actions of a representative. If this occurs, the tribunal would no doubt wish to deal sympathetically with the case, but the party is responsible for the default of the representative and must ultimately accept the consequences. Certainly, there will be no error of law merely by virtue of the fact that the fault of the representative has been visited upon the party personally (*CI 199/89*, paras. 11–12). This decision shows that proceeding with a hearing in the absence of a representative after repeated requests for adjournments have been made on the basis that the representative is not available will not of itself be an error of law.

The representative acquires all the rights and powers of the party represented. However, it has been held that this does not override express provisions which confer powers only on the parties, such as the right of a party to receive notice of the hearing under reg. 11(2) (*CS 113/91* paras. 10–11). This is an academic point since failure to give notice to a representative is prima facie a breach of the rules of natural justice (*ibid.*). The decision is in any case questionable. It amounts to saying that the power will not apply in the only cases where it is needed, namely, where the provision in question does not expressly refer to the representative.

The wide powers given to non-legal representatives by this paragraph do not extend to signing notices of appeals and applications. However, there is an exception where it appears to a chairman that the appellant is unable to sign personally (reg. 3(1)). This limitation only applies to notices which must be signed, so it only affects appeals under s.20(1) of the Act and applications to set aside. Other applications do not need to be signed and may therefore be made by a non-legal representative on a party's behalf.

Summoning of witnesses

10.—(1) A chairman may by summons, or in Scotland, citation require any person in Great Britain to attend as a witness at a hearing of an appeal or application at such time and place as shall be specified in the summons or citation and, subject to paragraph (2), at the hearing to answer any question or produce any documents in his custody or under his control which relate to any matter in question in the appeal or application, but—

   (*a*) no person shall be required to attend in obedience to such a summons or citation unless he has been given at least 10 days' notice of the hearing or, if less than 10 days' notice is given, he has informed the tribunal that he accepts that notice as sufficient; and

   (*b*) no person shall be required to attend and give evidence or to produce any document in obedience to such a summons or citation unless the necessary expenses of attendance are paid or tendered to him.

(2) No person shall be compelled to give any evidence or produce any document or other material that he could not be compelled to give or produce on a trial of an action in a court of law in that part of Great Britain where the hearing takes place.

(3) In exercising the powers conferred by this regulation, the chairman shall take into account the need to protect any matter that relates to intimate personal or financial circumstances, is commercially sensitive, consists of information communicated or obtained in confidence or concerns national security.

(4) Every summons or citation issued under this regulation shall contain a statement to the effect that the person in question may apply in writing to a chairman to vary or set aside the summons or citation.

DEFINITIONS
   "chairman": see reg. 1(2).
   "tribunal": *ibid.*

GENERAL NOTE
This regulation gives power to a chairman to summon a witness to attend to answer questions or produce documents. The regulation provides for no penalty if the person fails to attend or to produce the documents, although the operation of this regulation is to be kept under review and penalty powers added if they are needed. However, the High Court has power to issue a subpoena in aid of an inferior jurisdiction under R.S.C., Ord.38, r.19. (There is no equivalent power in Scotland.) That procedure involves attendance in person or through a solicitor and the payment of a fee before the subpoena will be issued. The tribunal is not equipped with the appropriate administrative machinery or prepared to pay the expenses for obtaining a subpoena. Chairmen should therefore be wary of issuing a summons or citation of their own motion.

Para. (1)
A chairman may require a person to attend at a hearing. If the person is to give evidence through a television link, that would constitute attending at the hearing. However, if evidence is to be given by video recorded in advance, it is difficult to treat this as attending at a hearing. Thus, this regulation cannot be used to order a person to give evidence in this way. There is no express provision dealing with who must ultimately meet the cost and it appears that the tribunal may have to do so.

Para. (2)

It is usual to distinguish between admissibility of evidence and compellability of witnesses. This paragraph by referring to compellability to give evidence fails to make that distinction. It may, therefore, appear to introduce all the rules of evidence which apply in a court on a trial of an action. After all, a person cannot be compelled to give evidence which is inadmissible. However, the location of this provision in a regulation dealing with summoning of witnesses and before the regulation dealing with the hearing itself shows that it is not intended to have that effect. Its only concern is with the compellability of the person as a witness.

For parties who are not compellable see Halsbury, *Laws of England* (4th ed.), Vol. 17, para. 234.

Hearings

11.—(1) A tribunal shall hold an oral hearing of every appeal, and may hold an oral hearing of an application, and subject to the provisions of the Act and of these Regulations the procedure in connection with the hearing shall be such as the chairman shall determine.

(2) Not less than 10 days' notice (beginning with the day on which it is given and ending on the day before the hearing) of the time and place of any hearing shall be given to every party to the proceedings, and if such notice has not been given to a person to whom it should have been given under the provisions of this paragraph the hearing may proceed only with the consent of that person.

(3) At any hearing any party to the proceedings shall be entitled to be present and be heard.

(4) Any person entitled to be heard at a hearing may address the tribunal, give evidence, call witnesses and put questions directly to any other party to the proceedings, to any representative of the child support officer or to any other person called as a witness.

(5) A tribunal may require any witness to give evidence on oath or affirmation and for that purpose there may be administered an oath or affirmation in due form.

(6) If a party to the proceedings to whom notice has been given under paragraph (2) fails to appear at the hearing the tribunal may, having regard to all the circumstances including any explanation offered for the absence, proceed with the appeal notwithstanding his absence or give such directions with a view to the determination of the appeal as it may think proper.

(7) Any hearing before the tribunal shall be in private unless the chairman directs that the hearing, or part of it, shall be in public.

(8) The following persons shall also be entitled to be present at a hearing even though it is in private—

    (*a*) the President, any full-time chairman and the clerk to the tribunal;

    (*b*) any person undergoing training as a chairman or other member of the tribunal or as a clerk to the tribunal;

    (*c*) any person acting on behalf of the President in the training or supervision of clerks to tribunals;

    (*d*) a member of the Council on Tribunals or of the Scottish Committee of the Council;

    (*e*) any person undergoing training as a child support officer or as the representative of a child support officer and any person acting on behalf of the Chief Child Support Officer or the Secretary of State in the training or supervision of child support officers or representatives of child support officers or in the monitoring of standards of adjudication by child support officers;

    (*f*) with leave of the chairman and the consent of every party to the proceedings actually present, any other person.

(9) For the purposes of arriving at its decision a tribunal shall, and for the purposes of discussing any question of procedure may, notwithstanding anything contained in these Regulations, order all persons to withdraw from the sitting of the tribunal other than the members of the tribunal, any of the persons mentioned in

sub-paragraphs (*a*), (*b*) and (*d*) of paragraph (8) and, with the leave of the chairman and if no party to the proceedings actually present objects, any of the persons mentioned in sub-paragraphs (*c*) and (*f*) of that paragraph.

(10) None of the persons mentioned in paragraph (8) shall take any part in the hearing or (where entitled or permitted to remain) in the deliberations of the tribunal.

DERIVATION
  Social Security (Adjudication) Regulations, reg. 4

DEFINITIONS
  "chairman": see reg. 1(2).
  "clerk to the tribunal": *ibid.*
  "full-time chairman": *ibid.*
  "party to the proceedings": *ibid.*
  "President": *ibid.*
  "tribunal": *ibid.*

GENERAL NOTE
Para. (1)
  There must be an oral hearing of every appeal. In contrast, Child Support Commissioners need not have an oral hearing (reg. 11(1) of the Child Support Commissioners (Procedure) Regulations). In the case of applications there is a discretion to hold an oral hearing or not as appropriate. The decision is made by a chairman.
  It is for the chairman to determine the procedure to be followed by the tribunal. In doing so the chairman will be guided by the rules contained in the Act and the regulations made under it, as well as by the general philosophy of the Independent Tribunal Service.

The inquisitorial approach
  Chairmen who have chaired social security tribunals will be familiar with the general philosophy for such tribunals as developed by the Independent Tribunal Service and usually labelled the "inquisitorial approach." This phrase has been useful in distancing tribunal procedure from that operated in a court, but it is a misleading label in so far as it may suggest that there is a single model of inquisitorial approach which is to be applied. There is no such model, only a general descriptive phrase which reflects the broad consensus of how such tribunals should be conducted and around which chairmen have developed their own styles of procedure. The Commissioners' decisions have provided some guidance on what is involved, but this leaves ample scope for the initiative of individual chairmen.
  The task for CSAT chairmen, as for chairmen of all tribunals, is to develop a procedure suited to the circumstances of the tribunals which they chair. There is a particular danger for chairmen used to social security tribunals. They may be tempted to transfer the procedures which they have applied and found to work well in that context to CSATs. While many features of social security tribunal procedure may be helpfully applied in CSATs, there are differences between the two jurisdictions of which the chairmen must be aware and which will affect the appropriate procedure to be adopted. The most difficult task for existing chairmen will be to adapt their existing approaches to the new context of CSATs.
  Chairmen must work out the appropriate procedure within a threefold framework. First, there is the general philosophy set by the Independent Tribunal Service, second the rules laid down by the Act and the regulations, and third their views of the proper role for themselves and the tribunals which they chair. The Act and the regulations set the framework around which the general philosophy and individual procedures must be structured. Thus, for example, the power to summon witnesses and to order the production of documents provides a stronger framework for the exercise of an inquisitorial function than is possible in a social security tribunal which has no such powers. However, the interpretation and application of the Act and the regulations will be informed by the general philosophy of the Service and by the individual chairman's views of the proper procedure. Thus, for example, the scope of reg. 5 will in practice be determined in part by how chairmen see the proper scope of their role in controlling the parties.
  The chairman must also have regard in developing an appropriate procedure to the circumstances in which it must be applied. Again, there are differences from the social security context. There is in a CSAT a greater conflict of interest between appellant and respondent than exists between the adjudication officer and the appellant in a social security tribunal. The former President of the Independent Tribunal Service, Judge Derek Holden, said that the most difficult task for CSATs would be to apply an inquisitorial jurisdiction in an adversarial context. The parties are also more likely to be represented in a

291

CSAT than in a social security tribunal. CSATs will be able to take a more hands off approach if the parties are represented, but the chairmen will need to be alert to prevent legal representatives adopting styles or following procedures by analogy to the courts which are not appropriate in the tribunal context.

The decisions of the courts and the Commissioners give a little guidance as to the proper exercise of the inquisitorial function. The tribunal is not entitled to sit back and act as referee between the rival contentions of the opposing parties as would be the case in a typical court procedure (*R.* v. *Deputy Industrial Injuries Commissioner, ex p. Moore* [1965] 1 All E.R. 81 at 93) and it should disabuse representatives of any erroneous views on which their arguments are based (*Dennis* v. *United Kingdom Central Council for Nursing, Midwifery and Health Visiting, The Times*, April 2, 1993). If it identifies a relevant point, it should be followed up and a decision reached, even if it has not been raised by the parties. The tribunal is also expected to pick up obvious and self evident points which arise. However, the parties are not entitled to rely upon the expertise of the tribunal to discharge the burdens of proof which properly rest on the parties themselves. Nor should a tribunal set off on a fishing expedition into the facts on the off-chance that something relevant may turn up. This is especially so if the evidence has been stated with certainty (see generally *R(SB) 2/83*, paras. 10–11 and *CSSB 470/89*, para. 7). Despite these statements it is the consistent practice of the Commissioners to require tribunals to deal with all legal issues which are raised by the facts before them and are relevant to the decisions which they make, and decisions which fail to do so are regularly overturned on appeal.

Commissioners speak in the context of deciding whether there has been an error of law to justify setting aside a tribunal decision. Their views set the limits within which the tribunal is expected to act if its decision is to withstand an appeal. Their views may, therefore, understate the role which tribunals should ideally play. The atmosphere should be as relaxed and informal as is consistent with the proper exercise of a judicial function and certainly more so than in a court. In particular, the tribunal is expected to fulfill an enabling role especially with an unrepresented party. This involves setting an appropriate atmosphere: the parties should feel comfortable and able to put across what they wish to say. It also involves helping the parties to understand what is required: the parties should be helped to follow the procedure, to understand the matters which are relevant to the appeal and to present the best case possible on their behalf.

In practice the operation of the inquisitorial approach is limited where one of the parties does not attend, although in such a case the tribunal will be anxious to ensure that all matters of possible benefit to that party are investigated as thoroughly as possible in his absence. Also, if one party is competently represented, the tribunal is likely to limit its inquisitorial function in respect of that party.

The proper implementation of the inquisitorial approach and the enabling role may mean that parties may be interrupted in the course of the presentation of their case. This does not consititute bias on the part of the tribunal (*R(SB) 6/82*, para. 6).

Note of evidence and procedure

It is the chairman's responsibility to ensure that a note of evidence and proceedings is kept. It should not only record evidence, arguments and other relevant matters, but should make clear who has said what. The chairman's thoughts are better confined to a separate piece of paper, but if they are formally recorded they should be labelled as such.

There is no duty in either the Act or the regulations to keep a note of the evidence presented to the tribunal. However, it is difficult to imagine how proceedings could be properly conducted without one and failure to make a record may be an error of law. A verbatim record of events is not required. However, the parties are entitled to know not only what the findings of fact are, but how they came to be made. Accordingly, the failure to keep an adequate note of evidence will be an error of law if the findings of fact are relevant to the appeal (see *CSSB 212/87*, para. 3).

It is the chairman's responsibility to ensure that a note of evidence and proceedings is kept. That responsibility is now almost always discharged by the chairman taking the note. A previous practice of delegating note-taking to the clerk, though not forbidden under these Regulations, has ceased throughout the Independent Tribunal Service except on rare occasions, such as where a chairman has a broken arm or is disabled. In such a case the note should only be presented as the clerk's, although the chairman may adopt it if satisfied that it is accurate (*R(SB) 13/83*, para. 14). Even on the rare occasions when this practice has to be used, the chairman should be aware of the dangers of relying on someone else's note; the clerks are not trained in note-taking; and there are other demands on a clerk's time (for example, dealing with parties attending for the next appeal) from which note-taking is a distraction.

If there is an appeal from the CSAT, the Commissioner is not limited to the evidence as appearing in the papers and the note of evidence, but is entitled to have regard to any evidence that can be shown to have been before the tribunal. The notes and recollections of the parties may be called upon to supplement or displace the chairman's note.

Evidence

The courts have said that tribunals are not bound by the strict rules on admissibility of evidence which apply in the courts, especially the criminal courts (*R.* v. *Deputy Industrial Injuries Commissioner, ex p. Moore* [1965] 1 All E.R. 81; *Wednesbury Corporation* v. *Ministry of Housing and Local Government (No. 2)* [1965] 3 All E.R. 571 at 579; *T. A. Miller Ltd.* v. *Minister of Housing and Local Government* [1968] 2 All E.R. 633; *R.* v. *Hull Prison Board of Visitors, ex p. St Germain (No. 2)* [1979] 3 All E.R. 545 at 552). The Commissioners themselves have repeatedly held the same (see, for example, *R(U) 5/77*, para. 3 and many of the cases cited below).

The precise limits of these statements have never been determined. It is not clear, for example, whether they are intended to override the rules on privilege. Generally, such statements identify the proper emphasis for the tribunal as being on the probative value of the evidence and its relevance to the appeal, rather than on technical rules as to admissibility. This must, though, be read subject to the limitations on the power of a chairman to summon witnesses or to order the production of documents contained in reg. 10(2) and (3). At least three more specific things are also clear: (i) Hearsay evidence is admissible; (ii) So is evidence which was not before the child support officer; (iii) Tribunals are also entitled to apply presumptions (see, for example, *CM 209/87*, para. 13). (i) and (ii) are considered in more detail below.

Legal professional privilege applies in adversarial jurisdictions (even those where the proceedings are conducted in a non-adversarial spirit), but in non-adversarial ones there is power in appropriate cases to override it (*Re B. (Minors) (Disclosure of Medical Reports), The Times*, March 29, 1993). It is unclear (i) how, if at all, the rules of privilege apply in a jurisdiction in which the strict rules of evidence do not apply and (ii) whether or not proceedings before a CSAT will be classified as adversarial.

The chairman should admit any evidence which has any probative value. It will then be for the tribunal as a whole to decide on the appropriate weight to be given to it. The chairman may exclude evidence which is clearly irrelevant, immaterial or repetitive (*Wednesbury Corporation, supra* at 579 and *R(SB) 6/82*, para. 5). The fact that evidence has been excluded should be recorded by the chairman in the notes of proceedings. However, whether something is irrelevant or immaterial is not always easily judged before the evidence has been heard. In deciding whether or not to exclude evidence, chairmen should be careful not to create the impression that the party seeking to adduce the evidence has not received a fair hearing, while ensuring that other parties have no cause to feel likewise if the evidence is admitted (*R(SB) 6/82*, para. 5). Wrongly excluding evidence may amount to an error of law (*ibid.* at para. 4).

Appeals before a CSAT are by way of a rehearing (*R(SB) 1/82*, para. 10). Accordingly, evidence which was not before the child support officer is admissible (*R(U) 5/77*, para. 3; *R(FIS) 1/82*, para. 20; *R(SB) 33/83*, para. 19). When such evidence is presented for the first time at the hearing, the tribunal should consider whether an adjournment is necessary in order to allow the other parties to consider it and prepare themselves properly to meet it (see the approach of the Commissioner in *R(I) 6/51*, para. 5). In order to avoid adjournments, it is preferable that such evidence is disclosed in advance of the hearing (*R(I) 6/51*, para. 6 and *R(I) 36/56*, para. 10). A chairman may wish to consider using the power to give directions under reg. 5 to require any fresh evidence to be disclosed in advance. In exercising this power, care will be needed to avoid imposing an unrealistic burden on an unrepresented party. It will also be necessary to be aware of the possibility that there may not be time before the hearing to disclose evidence in rebuttal of the further evidence disclosed.

Evidence may be oral or written. Any matters of fact stated by the appellant in the grounds of appeal will constitute written evidence (*R(SB) 10/81*, para. 6). If the evidence is oral, the chairman should keep a note of it. That note should distinguish clearly between evidence and other matters and should make clear who gave the evidence (*R(SB) 8/84*, para. 25(2) and (6)). If the evidence is written, copies should be made available to the tribunal and all the parties. The chairman should note the receipt of the document in the record of proceedings and ensure that a copy is placed on the tribunal file. Although, in appropriate circumstances, written evidence may carry more weight than oral evidence, what a party or a witness says is nonetheless evidence. There is no rule that evidence must be written rather than oral, or that the former necessarily carries more weight than the latter.

If written evidence is put before the tribunal, its provenance should be disclosed, since this may affect the weight to be attached to it (*R(G) 1/63*, para. 12). Either the identity of the author of a statement, or the fact that it is anonymous, should be disclosed (*CS 55/88*).

There is no requirement that evidence must be corroborated (*R(I) 2/51*, para. 7 and *R(SB) 33/85*, para. 14). To insist on corroboration would be impracticable (*R(U) 12/56*, para. 8). The real reason for the admissibility of oral uncorroborated evidence, however, is that there is in essence nothing necessarily wrong with it. Although corroboration is not relevant to the admissibility of evidence, it may be relevant to its strength. Where evidence is weak, the presence of independent corroboration will increase its weight.

Hearsay evidence is evidence of which the witness does not have firsthand knowledge, for example, if a witness says "X told me that he earned £2000 a month," this is direct firsthand evidence of the fact that X made the statement but only hearsay evidence of X's earnings. Hearsay evidence is admissible (for example, *T. A. Miller Ltd.*, *supra*) and in practice plays an important role in tribunals. The fact that evidence is hearsay goes to its weight, not to its admissibility (*CI 97/49(KL)*, para. 6; *R(G) 1/51*, para. 5; *R(U) 12/56*, para. 8 and *R(SB) 5/82*, para. 9). In assessing its weight the tribunal should be aware of the limitations and dangers of hearsay evidence: the originator of the evidence is not present to be questioned and there is a risk that as information is passed from person to person it may become distorted. The tribunal will need to establish, by hearing evidence, any factors relevant to the appropriate weight to give to it. The following should be considered: (i) the reliability of the original source of the evidence; (ii) how many people it has passed through; (iii) the reliability of the intervening parties; and (iv) whether more direct evidence could be obtained, bearing in mind the powers under reg. 10 to summon witnesses and to order the production of documents. If the tribunal accepts hearsay evidence, it is wise for the chairman to record in the reasons for decision that the tribunal had regard to the dangers and limitations of hearsay evidence.

The evidence may be given by a party or by a witness, but, according to the Commissioners, evidence given by a representative without personal knowledge on a *contested* matter is not evidence on which a tribunal is entitled to rely (*R(I) 36/61*, para. 18; *R(I) 13/74*, para. 9; *R(SB) 10/86*, para. 5). This sharp distinction between the status of witness and of representative may make sense in court, but, as has been noted in the general note to reg. 9, it is not always easy to keep the roles of witness and representative distinct in a tribunal. Moreover, there is no reason in principle why in a tribunal context the evidence of a representative should be treated any differently from that of anyone else. In practice the rulings in the above decisions are not followed. Sometimes the representative is in a position to give firsthand evidence of the relevant matters. Where the evidence is hearsay, there is no reason to treat it more harshly than any other hearsay evidence. The chairman may, as part of the enabling role, allow a representative to give the evidence in an orderly manner on behalf of a party who may be nervous or rambling and who then confirms that evidence and answers any follow up questions. This is an acceptable practice which is consistent with the spirit of *R(I) 36/61* and *R(SB) 10/86*. Moreover, it is permitted by the regulations: reg. 9 provides that representatives have all the rights and powers of the person represented, which includes the right to be heard, and reg. 11(4) provides that any person entitled to be heard may give evidence.

Unlike the position in a court, any witness can give evidence on a matter of opinion. However, tribunals are likely to give most weight to the opinion of an expert witness, for example, on whether a person is likely to suffer undue distress under s.46(3) of the Act. Expert witnesses who give written or oral evidence to a CSAT are under the following duties: (i) The evidence must be independent; (ii) It must be objective and unbiased; (ii) Facts or assumptions on which it is based should be stated, as should any facts which would detract from the expert's conclusion; (iv) Questions or issues which fall outside the witness's expertise should be made clear; (v) It should contain any appropriate qualifications to the opinion expressed; (vi) Any subsequent change of view after the expert's report has been written should be disclosed (*National Justice Compania Naviera SA* v. *Prudential Assurance Co Ltd.*, *The Times*, March 5, 1993).

Evaluation of evidence

The task of evaluating evidence is often more difficult for a tribunal than for a court which may be cushioned from some of the more difficult decisions by excluding certain categories of evidence. The task for the tribunal is to make a decision, however difficult that may be. Conflicts of evidence do not justify the tribunal reaching a compromise, for example, by fixing a figure between the two sums alleged to represent a parent's income (see *R(U) 2/72*, para. 8). Although assessing the weight of evidence is a familiar task for lawyers, it may not be so straightforward for a lay member. While respecting each member's equal weight in the evaluation of the evidence, the chairman's experience will be helpful in assisting the other members to assess the appropriate weight to be accorded to particular pieces of evidence.

In evaluating the reliability of a piece of evidence there are three key criteria which should be considered: (i) How well placed was the witness to form an objective view of the subject matter of the evidence? (ii) How reliable is the witness's recollection? (iii) How good is the witness's capacity to convey precisely that recollection? These criteria suggest some relevant factors which should be taken into account in applying them. Three matters which should always be considered are: (a) is the witness's evidence consistent; (b) how inherently credible is it; and (c) is it consistent with the other evidence before the tribunal? The special problem of evaluating hearsay is discussed above.

In evaluating evidence, the tribunal members may make use of their own local knowledge. However, the parties are entitled to have an opportunity to deal with any points against them. If the tribunal intends to take account of their own knowledge on a point, the parties should be given an opportunity to comment before reaching a decision (*CIS 278/92*, para. 12). The fact that this opportunity has been given should be recorded by the chairman in the notes of proceedings.

Facts are of two kinds: primary facts and inferences. Primary facts are those matters on which the tribunal has evidence, whether direct or hearsay. The tribunal may, for example, hear evidence that a parent has been seen driving a delivery van. If it accepts this evidence, it is a primary fact. Inferences are those matters which the tribunal deduces from the primary facts. Thus, in the above example, it might deduce from the primary facts that the parent was employed as a delivery driver.

The findings of fact should record the tribunal's findings of primary fact relevant to the appeal. The reasons for decisions should record why evidence was rejected (*R(SB) 8/84*, para. 25(3)). They should also record why one piece of evidence has been preferred to another (*CSSB 212/87*, para. 3). Any inferences which the tribunal drew from the primary facts should be included in the reasons rather than in the findings of fact. Failure to record any of these will amount to an error of law.

Burden of proof

The burden of proof determines who must bear the consequences of something not being proved and sets the degree of probability with which it must be established.

The legal burden of proof rests on the appellant or applicant. It does not move from one party to another during the hearing. The party who has the legal burden on an issue must establish a case on the balance of probabilities, that is, it must be shown that it is more likely than not that the facts alleged are true (*CI 401/50(KL)*). This is known as the civil burden of proof. It is not necessary for the tribunal to be certain that the facts alleged are true or even that there is no reasonable doubt that they are true. It is enough that it is more likely than not that they are true. A party is not entitled to be given the benefit of a doubt (*R(I) 32/61*, para. 10).

As the hearing progresses and the evidence unfolds, the position may arise that the weight of evidence is such that one party will lose unless further favourable evidence emerges. In such a case, even if that party does not bear the legal burden on the issue in question, there is the risk that no other favourable evidence may emerge. In this type of case the party is said to bear an evidentiary burden. It is the nature of the evidentiary burden that it may rest on the party who bears the legal burden or on some other party and that during the hearing it may move from one party to another.

In a court the sequence of submissions and the legal burden of proof are closely linked. This is not necessarily so in a tribunal. The chairman has control of the procedure and may begin with the party who is in fullest possession of the facts rather than with the party who has the burden of proof on a particular matter.

In the case of an appeal against the refusal of a child support officer to review a decision, for example, under s.18 of the Act, the burden is on the party who alleges that a review should have been undertaken to show that there were grounds for it.

If a tribunal finds itself unable to decide where the balance of probabilities lies in a particular case, the burden of proof will decide which party must bear the consequence (*Morris* v. *London Iron and Steel Co. Ltd.* [1987] 2 All E.R. 496). Since the tribunal makes no findings of fact in such a case, there is nothing to record as the findings of fact. The proper course is to record that the tribunal was unable to decide where the balance of probabilities lay and decided the case on the burden of proof.

Use of Welsh and other languages

Generally speaking, there is no duty on the tribunal to provide an interpreter (*R(I) 11/63*, para. 19). However, arrangements exist for interpreters to be supplied so that persons may speak in their own language. The preferable alternative would be for all those present to speak the same language, as much can be lost in interpretation. It is sometimes possible for a tribunal to be assembled on which all the members speak the language in question. This is particularly the case in Wales.

The absence of any duty on the tribunal to provide an interpreter is subject to the specific statutory provision in the case of the use of the Welsh language. A party, witness or other person may speak in Welsh in legal proceedings in Wales and Monmouthshire (s.1(1) of the Welsh Language Act 1967). Accordingly, an oath or affirmation may also be given in Welsh. The form of oath or affirmation for use in court is laid down in a Lord Chancellor's Office circular under s.2 of the Welsh Courts Act 1942.

The Welsh Language Act and the Welsh Courts Act are scheduled for repeal by the Welsh Language Bill which is currently before Parliament. As originally presented to Parliament the Bill did not alter the position stated in the previous paragraph, although subsequently the Government undertook at the Second Reading in the House of Lords to introduce an amendment to permit written evidence as well as oral evidence to be given in Welsh in legal proceedings, which would require, for example, that the maintenance application and maintenance enquiry forms either be available in Welsh or be translated into Welsh. In addition to this promised amendment, the Bill contains two powers which might affect the Independent Tribunal Service in Wales. First, there is a power which is broad enough to allow the Secretary of State for Wales to prescribe the Independent Tribunal Service in Wales as a public body with a duty to prepare a scheme setting out the measures it proposes to take as to the use of the Welsh language in the provision of its services so as to treat Welsh and English equally. Second, there is a power which would allow Ministers to make regulations prescribing the form of documents or of words in Welsh. These provisions could cause considerable difficulties for the administration of the Central Office.

Para. (2)

This provision has been held to apply only to the party and not to a representative (*CS 113/91*, paras. 10–11). However, failure to notify a representative will prima facie be a breach of the rules of natural justice (*ibid.*). The decision on the former aspect of the decision is criticised in the general note to reg. 9.

The tribunal must investigate whether or not a party who does not attend has received notice of the hearing. It may be that the party has had some communication with the tribunal which shows that notice of the hearing was received. If there has been no such communication, the tribunal must satisfy itself that the notice of the hearing has been properly served within the meaning of reg. 2(2). It is also good practice to enquire of those parties present whether they know of any change of address of the party absent. The chairman should record in the notes of proceedings that the inquiry has been undertaken and the results. If the party has not been properly served within reg. 2(2), or if the tribunal is satisfied that the notice may not have been received (for example, if the party has moved house or is on holiday), the hearing should be adjourned (see *R(SB) 19/83*, para. 7). The problems produced by the holding of the tribunal file in the Central Office at Salford Quays are discussed in the general note to reg. 2(2).

If the parties have not received notice, but nevertheless have heard of the hearing and either attend and consent to the hearing proceeding or notify the tribunal that it may proceed in their absence, the hearing may continue. If this occurs, it should be noted in the notes of proceedings. This paragraph only applies to notice of the hearing. It does not require the party to be sent the papers for the hearing. However, this is required by the rules of natural justice. If a party has not been sent notice of the hearing (or the papers) and the tribunal nonetheless proceeds with the hearing, the decision will be valid but liable to be set aside under reg. 15.

Para. (3)

The party's entitlement to be present and to be heard is stated as absolute. However, the right is a qualified one. It is subject to the possibility that the chairman may refuse to postpone a hearing under reg. 8 to allow a party to attend or that the tribunal may refuse to adjourn to allow this under reg. 12. The tribunal is empowered to proceed with the hearing in the absence of a party under para. (6).

This paragraph is also subject to the chairman's control over procedure under para. (1) which may be used to remove a party's right to be heard if his behaviour warrants it or to curtail repetition or irrelevant submissions. However, should any of these occur the party has the opportunity to make a case that justice requires the decision of the tribunal to be set aside under reg. 15.

The procedure for the CSAT to follow if a party does not attend is discussed in the general note to para. (2) above.

Para. (4)

The chairman will need to decide whether witnesses should be present throughout the entire hearing, or only when they give evidence. In doing so, matters to be considered will include whether the witness's evidence will be affected by anything that might be heard during the proceedings and whether there may be private, intimate or embarrassing matters disclosed during the hearing, especially any which affect a child, which should be given as small a circulation as possible. A representative cannot be excluded (reg. 9). It follows that a representative who gives evidence cannot be excluded.

The informality of the proceedings may not be used as a means of depriving one of the parties of a statutory right, such as the right to question witnesses conferrred by this paragraph (*R(I) 13/74*, para. 9).

Para. (5)

The tribunal may require a witness to give evidence on oath or affirmation. This is not a purely procedural matter which is in the hands of the chairman, but a matter for the whole tribunal to decide. This paragraph does not draw a technical distinction between a witness, on the one hand, and a party or representative, on the other. It applies to all persons who give evidence. Two questions arise with regard to the oath: (i) should it be used and (ii) if it is used, in what form should it be administered?

Value

There are at least three reasons why the oath should either not be used at all in a CSAT or should at the very least be used only in exceptional cases. First, its use is inconsistent with the relatively informal atmosphere which should be adopted in a tribunal in comparison with a court. Second, it is nowadays unlikely in many cases to have an influence on the evidence given by the witness. Its use, therefore, creates an additional question for the tribunal: what effect has the oath had on the witness's honesty? Finally, the oath can only affect the honesty of a witness's evidence. Depending on the nature of the question in dispute, this may or may not be the central issue for the tribunal. If it is not, the tribunal will rather be concerned with the reliability of that evidence. (This has been touched on in the note on evaluation of evidence above.) The honesty of the witness will be only one factor in the evaluation of reliability. A tribunal may be reluctant to administer the oath to one person but not another at the same hearing or in relation to some aspects of a person's evidence only.

Form

The oath or affirmation must be given in due form. The proper form of oaths and affirmations is laid down by the Oaths Act 1978.

A person may swear by any form of oath or ceremony which he declares to be binding and is bound by this (s.4(1)). If an oath is administered it is binding regardless of whether the person has any religious belief (s.4(2)). It is usual in England, Wales and Northern Ireland that the oath is administered by the witness raising a copy of the New Testament or, if the witness is Jewish, the Old Testament (s.1(1)). In Scotland a witness swears with an uplifted hand. This form may also be used by a witness in England, Wales and Northern Ireland (s.3).

Instead of an oath a solemn affirmation may be used in two circumstances. First, if the witness objects to taking an oath (s.5(1)). In this case it is entirely a decision for the witness concerned. Second, if it is not reasonably practicable without inconvenience or delay to administer an oath in the manner appropriate to the witness's religious belief (s.5(2) and (3)). In this case it is a matter for the tribunal rather than for the witness concerned. In either case the affirmation is as binding as an oath (s.5(4)).

The opening words are in the case of an oath, "I swear by Almighty God that . . .", and in the case of an affirmation, "I, . . . do solemnly, sincerely and truly declare and affirm, . . ." (ss.1(1) and 6(1)). This is followed in either case by "the evidence I shall give shall be the truth, the whole truth and nothing but the truth." In the case of a child or young person under the age of 17 the proper form is to use the word "promise" instead of "swear", although either is equally valid (s.28 of the Children and Young Persons Act 1963). The use of Welsh in taking an oath or affirmation is dealt with in the general note to para. (1).

The oath must be administered by an official authorised to do so. In the case of a CSAT, the power is given to the tribunal, which will in practice act through the chairman. The clerk is not authorised to administer an oath or affirmation.

If an oath is administered, or a witness is allowed to affirm, the chairman should record this fact in the notes of proceedings and should take care to ensure that a complete and accurate note of that evidence is taken. Moreover, when the oath or affirmation is being used, it will also be applied to a representative who gives evidence in the course of a presentation, for example, on the past record of violence of a spouse in a reduced benefit direction appeal. The tribunal will have to be alert to identify such evidence, and the chairman should record both it and the fact that it was received as evidence.

In England and Wales a person who gives evidence on oath or affirmation without believing it to be true commits the offence of perjury (ss.1(1) and (2), 15(2) and 18 of the Perjury Act 1911).

Para. (6)

This paragraph allows, but does not require, the tribunal to proceed with the hearing in the absence of a party. This power is given to the tribunal as a whole and not to the chairman. In exercising this power the tribunal must consider all the circumstances including any explanation offered. It should enquire whether any explanation has been received and the notes of proceedings should record this inquiry and the result as well as the tribunal's decision.

If the tribunal decides not to proceed, it may give any directions it thinks proper. As with the decision whether or not to proceed, this is a matter for the tribunal as a whole and not just for the chairman. This does not, however, deprive the chairman of the general power to give directions under reg. 5. This paragraph only allows directions made with a view to the determination of the appeal and is not as wide as the reg. 5 powers which cover matters relevant to the just, efficient and effective conduct of the proceedings.

This paragraph applies only to the absence of a *party*. It does not cover the absence of a representative or a witness. These cases must be dealt with in accordance with the rules of natural justice and the tribunal's power to adjourn under reg. 12.

Para. (7)

Hearings are in private unless the chairman (not the tribunal) decides otherwise. This is the reverse of the position in social security tribunals. It is subject to the entitlement to be present of the persons covered by para. (8). Any request for, and any decision by a chairman on, a public hearing should be noted in the notes of proceedings. There is no appeal against the chairman's ruling.

In deciding whether a public hearing is appropriate, the chairman should consider amongst other matters the following: (i) the wishes of the parties; (ii) whether information is likely to be made public which is private, intimate or embarrassing, especially if it affects a child; (iii) whether the public have some interest in the proceedings or the decision, for example if it is a test case; (iv) whether a public hearing is justified or whether the public interest might not be sufficiently served by the decision and reasoning being made public; and (v) whether it is appropriate to hold part of the hearing in private and part in public. Since the basic rule is in favour of a private hearing, the usual presumption favouring a public hearing (see *Re Crook* [1992] 2 All E.R. 687) does not apply.

The tape recording of private hearing should not be permitted (*Annual Report of the Council on Tribunals 1981–1982*, Appendix D). So far as public hearings are concerned recording should only be permitted in the most exceptional cases (*ibid.*). It is an undecided question whether tribunals such as a CSAT are within the scope of the law of contempt so that tape recording without authority could be punished, but the tenor of the reasoning of the House of Lords in *Attorney General* v. *BBC* [1980] 1 All E.R. 161 is that contempt should not be extended to cover such bodies. If the appellant insists on recording the proceedings, the CSAT could refuse to continue with the hearing. However, if the problem arose with one of the other parties, the tribunal would not wish to prejudice the appellant by adjourning. Probably the easiest course of action would be to proceed with the hearing in the absence of the other party. A chairman could issue a direction under reg. 5 to a party forbidding the tape recording of proceedings, but see the general note to that regulation for the difficulties of enforcement.

Para. (8)
Under (*f*) the chairman may give leave for any other person to be present with the consent of any other party actually present. Since the child support officer who is the party will usually be represented and seldom be present personally, his consent will not be required. The consent of the representative of the child support officer is not required. However, the views of the representative and of any party who is not actually present may be taken into account by the chairman in deciding whether or not to give leave.

Para. (10)
The clerk (and indeed any other persons allowed to remain) should not only refrain from participating in the decision-making of the tribunal but should also give no cause for anyone to believe that they have participated (*R(SB) 13/83*, para. 15).

Adjournments

12.—(1) A hearing may be adjourned by the tribunal at any time on the application of any party to the proceedings or of its own motion.

(2) Where a hearing has been adjourned and it is not practicable, or would cause undue delay, for it to be resumed before a tribunal consisting of the same members, the appeal or application shall be heard by a tribunal none of the members of which was a member of the original tribunal and the proceedings shall be by way of a complete re-hearing of the case.

DERIVATION
Social Security (Adjudication) Regulations, regs. 5(2) and 24(3).

DEFINITIONS
"party to the proceedings": see reg. 1(2).
"tribunal": *ibid.*

GENERAL NOTE
Para. (1)
Once the hearing has begun the chairman loses the power to postpone the hearing and the tribunal gains the power to adjourn. When a hearing begins is discussed in the general note to reg. 7. An adjournment may be sought by one of the parties or it may be decided on by the tribunal of its own motion. In either case all parties present should be given an opportunity to give their views. An application for an adjournment is not within reg. 3 and may be made quite informally.

The controlling factor in deciding whether or not to adjourn is the need to comply with the rules of natural justice. There are no fixed categories of case which do or do not justify adjournments. Usually the adjournment will be to allow a party to obtain evidence or to marshal arguments in order to deal with a matter which has arisen without warning in the course of the hearing, but ultimately the question is whether in all the circumstances of the case an adjournment is appropriate.

Each adjournment must be approached individually and judicially. The tribunal should seek to strike a balance between the following factors: (i) the interests of the parties to be present, and to be properly prepared to present the best case in their favour and to deal with points against them; (ii) whether the adjournment would improve the quality of the tribunal's ultimate decision; (iii) the interests of the other users of the tribunal system including child support officers - adjourning one appeal delays the hearing of others; and (iv) the extent to which the case has already been adjourned or otherwise delayed. The chairman should record in the notes of proceedings all requests for adjournments, the views of the parties and the decisions on them.

There has been much discussion within the Independent Tribunal Service in recent years about disposal rates, the cost of adjournments and the need to avoid unnecessary adjournments. Parties are unlikely to be pleased to hear that their appeals have not been adjourned as requested on account of such considerations. Fortunately it is rare, if ever, that such considerations should prove decisive if the question of an adjournment is approached in the way suggested above. However, parties who seek adjournments should not expect them to be granted for the asking and should be prepared to support their request with convincing arguments.

A party is entitled to be represented and may apply for an adjournment to allow his representative to attend. Usually this will be allowed. However, the absence of a representative does not give an automatic entitlement to an adjournment (*CI 199/89*).

If a hearing is to be adjourned, the tribunal should consider how the best use can be made of it so as to ensure as far as possible that further adjournments are avoided. This may involve a discussion with the parties to identify other possible causes of future delay and any appropriate directions can be given to ensure that these matters are dealt with in the interim. Chairmen should also bear in mind their power to give directions under reg. 5 and use it where appropriate if the tribunal is not minded to act. Anticipation of problems and appropriate use of the power to give directions under reg. 5 can go a long way to avoid adjournments. If a request based on the unavailability of a representative has been made before and the appeal has already been subject to lengthy delays, refusal of a further adjournment will be a breach of natural justice (*ibid.*), but where the earlier delays have not been lengthy and the claimant has not been warned of the possibility of obtaining further adjournments, refusal to adjourn may constitute such a breach (*CSB 753/84*).

This regulation only applies to adjournments from one session to a later session. Adjournments within the course of a session are within the chairman's control of procedure under reg. 11(1) and are matters for the chairman rather than the tribunal. Thus, a chairman might adjourn briefly, for example, if a representative has been delayed or if a party or witness becomes distressed or in order to discuss how the tribunal should proceed (for example, whether an adjournment under this regulation is appropriate).

No appeal lies against a decision to adjourn (*CA 126/89*, paras. 9–11 and *CIS 64/91*). The decision to adjourn is an interlocutory rather than a final decision and as such does not constitute a decision for the purposes of s.24 of the Act. However, the failure to adjourn may constitute a breach of natural justice which will provide the basis for an appeal when the tribunal does reach a final decision (*e.g. CSB 753/84*). Additionally, the adjournment decision may justify a judicial review.

Para. (2)

An adjourned hearing must be heard either by a tribunal consisting of the same members or by a completely differently constituted tribunal. This avoids the possibility of one member of a tribunal having a residual knowledge of the hearing which the other members are unaware of and had no opportunity to obtain for themselves. This danger was noted by a Tribunal of Commissioners in *R(U) 3/88*, para. 7. This may cause difficulties in remote rural areas where it may not be easy either to reassemble the same tribunal or to form a completely different tribunal. Although the rationale behind this provision is the potential problem of residual knowledge, it applies regardless of whether or not any evidence or submissions were heard at the adjourned hearing. A hearing which is adjourned without anything being said which was not in the appeal papers is as much caught by this paragraph as is one which is adjourned after hearing oral evidence and lengthy submissions.

The paragraph does not deal with the case where a tribunal is adjourned more than once. The rationale of the provision suggests that unless all the tribunal members from the previous hearing are able to sit, a tribunal must be assembled none of whom have sat on the appeal before. This adds to the problems of assembling a tribunal.

Some aspects of the procedure to be followed on a complete re-hearing were discussed by the Tribunal of Commissioners in *R(U) 3/88*, para. 7. The case must be reheard afresh, unfettered by what happened at the earlier hearing. All evidence and submissions must be put to the fresh tribunal, although the notes of evidence at the previous hearing may be made use of for this purpose.

In view of the administrative problems and consequent delays that may be caused by this provision, tribunals and chairman should make use of the devices discussed in the general notes to these regulations in order to avoid adjournments so far as that is possible and keep to a minimum those that are required. Whenever possible a hearing should be postponed rather than adjourned.

Where there is a complete re-hearing of an appeal after an adjournment, it is desirable for the chairman to record in the notes of proceedings that this is what has occurred (*C 44/87 (IVB)*).

Decisions

13.—(1) A decision of the tribunal may be taken by a majority.

(2) The chairman shall—

(*a*) record in writing the decision of the tribunal;

(*b*) include in the record of every decision a statement of the reasons for it, the findings of the tribunal on questions of fact material to the decision and the terms of any direction given under section 20(4) of the Act; and

(*c*) if a decision is not unanimous, record a statement that one of the members dissented and the reasons given by him for so dissenting.

(3) As soon as may be practicable after the decision of the tribunal a copy of the record of the decision made in accordance with this regulation shall be sent to every party to the proceedings who shall also be informed of the conditions governing appeals to a Commissioner.

(4) If a child support officer to whom a case is referred by the Secretary of State under section 20(3) of the Act (procedure following a successful appeal) is uncertain, having regard to the terms of the decision and of any directions contained in it, how he should deal with the case, he may apply to the tribunal or another tribunal for directions or further directions, and the tribunal may give such directions or further directions as it thinks fit.

(5) Upon receiving an application from a child support officer under paragraph (4) the clerk to the tribunal shall send a copy of it to all the other parties to the case, and the tribunal shall not give any directions or further directions on the application until those other parties have had a reasonable opportunity of making representaions on it.

DERIVATION

Social Security (Adjudication) Regulations, reg. 25.

DEFINITIONS

"chairman": see reg. 1(2).

"party to the proceedings": *ibid.*

"tribunal": *ibid.*

GENERAL NOTE

The usual procedure stated in neutral terms is as follows: (i) the tribunal makes up its mind; then (ii) the parties are told; then (iii) the chairman completes the record; finally (iv) the record is sent to the parties. Unfortunately "decision" may be used loosely, or even in regulations, to refer to any of these steps.

For the purposes of the tribunal's powers to correct errors in decisions under reg. 14 and to set aside decisions under reg. 15, the decision is made at step (iv) (*CSB 226/81*). This is in line with the general principle that until a decision has been promulgated, *i.e.* until it has been communicated, it may be revoked or varied informally (*ibid.* at para. 11 and *R(I) 14/74*, para. 14(*a*)). (*CM 209/87*, para. 6 is in conflict with this principle in suggesting that the decision is made as soon as it is taken.) However, in another sense a decision is made earlier, certainly at stage (ii) and perhaps at stage (i), subject to any variation or withdrawal (*CI 141/87*, para. 30). The word "decision" in this regulation must be interpreted in this latter sense, since paras. (1) and (2) only make sense on this basis.

Para. (1)

There is no power for a CSAT to hear an appeal, even for the purpose of immediately adjourning it, unless all three members are present. There is, therefore, no need for the chairman to have a casting vote. A member may not abstain. It is the duty of each member, as it is of the tribunal as a whole, to make a decision. Ideally the decision should be announced to the parties on the day of the hearing. Delay should be avoided unless the tribunal needs time for consideration or believes that there may be violence when the decision is given.

Para. (2)

It is the responsibility of the chairman to compose the record of decision and reasons, and to ensure that they reflect the views of the tribunal or majority as a whole (*R(SB) 13/83*, paras. 13–14). The task may not be left to the clerk. (The former practice of dictating the decision to the clerk (see *CSB 226/81*, para. 7) is now obsolete.) Nor should it be left to the members. However, if a member has dissented it is proper to ask that member to put into words the reasons for dissent. A chairman who has dissented may also properly look to the members to put into words their reasons for the decision. Recording in such a case remains the responsibility of the chairman but with the assistance of those who a chairman once referred to as "the dissenting majority." The responsibility of the chairman to ensure that the decision reflects the views of the tribunal (majority) as a whole is underlined by the fact that the power to correct accidental errors in decisions is given to the tribunal as a whole and not to the chairman. See reg. 14 and the general note thereto.

Failure to comply with the requirements of properly writing up a decision is the main reason why appeals to a Commissioner are allowed.

Sub-para. (a)

It should be obvious, but nonetheless bears emphasis and repeating, that the decision must be in a form that can be implemented. It is acceptable to indicate to the appellant as part of the decision whether the appeal has succeeded or failed or succeeded in part. However, decisions worded solely in terms of success or failure are to be avoided. Clearly a decision which simply reads "Appeal allowed" or "Appeal allowed in part" is wholly inadequate since it gives no indication of how it has been allowed. There may seem to be less objection to a decision in the form "Appeal dismissed," but this is also capable of giving rise to problems and is better avoided.

There is no magic in which part of the record of decision a piece of information is recorded (*CI 199/89*, para. 17). However, for the sake of clarity and ease of implementation, the statement of the decision in the appropriate box of the record of decision form should be self contained. It is certainly undesirable for the decision to require interpretation by the parties.

In view of the time constraints and other pressures on a tribunal, they are not the best bodies to undertake complex calculations unless this is unavoidable. This is especially so in view of the complexity and formulae involved in child support law. It is proper to leave the working out of the tribunal's decision to the child support officer, provided that there is power for any party to restore the case to the tribunal in the event of a dispute as to the correct calculation (*R(SB) 16/83*, para. 21). "Liberty to restore" is the phrase used in the Independent Tribunal Service, although in court terminology "liberty to apply" would be more appropriate. It should be expressly reserved, as it will not be implied into a decision which is on its face final and complete (*Penrice* v. *Williams* (1883) 23 Ch. D. 353 at 356–357 *per* Chitty, J.). Prima facie it does not allow the order to be varied (*Cristel* v. *Cristel* [1954] 2 All E.R. 574 at 576–577 *per* Somervell, L.J.). There are suggestions in *Cristel* that a change of circumstances could be taken into account so as to vary an otherwise final order under a liberty to apply, but this is an unnecessary qualification in the child support context in view of the express power to review contained in s.17 of the Act.

Commissioners have no power to award costs (*R(FC) 2/90*) and it must follow that tribunals also have no such power.

Sub-paras. (b) and (c)

The findings of fact must cover all matters material to the decision, that is, all findings necessary to support the decision and reasoning of the tribunal (*R(SB) 31/83*, para. 6). Failure to record any findings will mean that the decision is liable to be set aside on appeal (*R(SB) 6/81*, para. 14). Omissions will produce the same result. The form of the statement is also important. The chairman should record the primary facts as found by the tribunal, not the evidence or arguments presented to the tribunal. Commissioners can be very demanding in this respect. For example, in *R(SB) 3/88* the findings of fact recorded the view of a witness on a relevant matter and stated that the tribunal accepted that view. However, a Tribunal of Commissioners held that there should have been "a proper finding of fact in relation to that matter." This decision is a valuable warning of the dangers of adopting the statement of facts set out in the child support officer's submission. This is acceptable, but only provided that two conditions are satisfied (*CIS 107/91*, para. 11). First, the submission must record findings of fact and not arguments or assertions. Second, the findings of fact must be sufficient for the decision; any facts omitted from the submission must be added by the tribunal.

Inferences which are drawn from the primary facts do not need to be recorded as findings of fact. Whether or not an inference should be drawn is not a question of fact but of law. Therefore, inferences should properly be recorded among the reasons for decision rather than among the findings of fact.

The reasons for decision must explain why the tribunal reached all its decisions on matters in dispute before it. This will include explanations on decisions on matters of fact, for example, why it rejected particular pieces of evidence or how it made use of its own knowledge on a particular matter, as well as how the law was applied to reach the decision. The statement should be sufficient to explain to any party why the decision was made. Every argument of any substance put forward by any party should be dealt with in the reasons (*Re B. (Minors), The Times*, July 16, 1992). This is especially important in relation to matters which are emotionally charged (*ibid.*) as CSAT proceedings may be.

Some chairmen may wish to follow a convenient practice and adopt the reasons in the child support officer's submission as those of the tribunal. However, any chairman following this course should be aware of two dangers. First, if that submission contains any error the tribunal will have adopted that error as its own. Second, if there are any matters not dealt with in that submission, for example, why certain evidence or arguments were rejected, they must be added by the chairman.

Although the statement must contain the reasons for the decision, it need not go further and give the reasons for those reasons. So, it is sufficient to say "we rejected this evidence because it was inherently improbable" without going on to spell out why it was inherently improbable.

Para. (3)

Once the decision has been promulgated, it can can only be altered on appeal or review (*CM 209/87*, para. 6). This is subject to the powers to correct accidental errors and to set aside decisions (regs. 14 to 16).

Para. (4)

This power supplements the tribunal's power under s.20(4) of the Act to give directions of its own initative when referring a case back to the Secretary of State. The power to give directions or further directions at the request of the child support officer allows the tribunal to provide for the working out of its decision. It does not permit the tribunal to change its decision. However, it does allow the tribunal to clarify what its decision involves and that may come very close to correcting what would otherwise be an imperfect decision. The power applies only to child support officers and not to any other party, so it does not obviate the need for "liberty to restore," which is discussed in the general not to para. (2)(*a*) above.

Para. (5)

Since the tribunal may not re-open or reconsider its decision under para. (4), the representations may only relate to the directions necessary for the tribunal's decision to be implemented. Representations as to the correctness of the decision are out of place.

Corrections

14.—(1) Subject to regulation16 (provisions common to regulations 14 and 15) accidental errors (whether of omission or commission) in any decision or record of any decision may at any time be corrected by the tribunal who gave the decision or by another tribunal.

(2) A correction made to a decision or to the record of a decision shall be deemed to be part of the decision or of the record thereof and written notice of it shall be given as soon as practicable to every party to the proceedings.

DERIVATION

Social Security (Adjudication) Regulations, reg. 10.

DEFINITIONS

"party to the proceedings": see reg. 1(2).
"tribunal": *ibid.*

GENERAL NOTE
Para. (1)

This paragraph allows tribunals to correct accidental errors in the record of their decisions. It gives the power to the tribunal as a whole and not just to the chairman. Normally the issue will be raised by one of the parties.

The power only applies to inadvertent clerical or arithmetical errors. It allows the correction of errors in the decision or the record of the decision so as to bring it into line with what the tribunal intended. If, for example, the word "not" has been omitted or included in error, it can be inserted or removed as appropriate. What cannot be done, however, is to to alter the decision itself in an attempt to give effect to the second thoughts of the tribunal (*Wordingham* v. *Royal Exchange Trust Co. Ltd.* [1992] 3 All E.R.

204 and *CM 209/87*, para. 6). The power does not arise until the decision is made and for the purpose of this regulation this does not occur until the written decision is given to the parties. Until that time the tribunal may change its decision and any accidental errors in the record of decision can be corrected by the chairman without relying on this paragraph or on the inherent power (which is discussed below) (*CSB 226/81*).

The tribunal has a power to correct an accidental error, but not a duty to do so. It should decline to exercise its power if anything has occurred after the decision was notified to the parties which renders it inexpedient or inequitable to correct it (*Moore* v. *Buchanan* [1967] 3 All E.R. 273). Thus, a correction should not be made if the decision as framed has been relied on to a party's irreversible detriment. The mere fact of delay, however, will not be a sufficient reason not to exercise the power (*Tak Ming Co. Ltd.* v. *Yee Sang Metal Supplies Co.* [1973] 1 All E.R. 569 at 575).

In addition to this express power to correct errors, the tribunal has an inherent power which is preserved by reg. 16(3). This power overlaps with, but is wider than, the power contained in this paragraph. The inherent power applies to reasons as well as to decisions (*Hazeltine Corporation* v. *International Computers Ltd.* [1980] F.S.R. 521 at 524), but these are part of the record of decision and so fall within the scope of reg. 14(1).

The regulation does not apply to decisions by chairmen. They must rely on their inherent power if they are to correct accidental errors in a decision they make, for example, on an application for leave to appeal. Alternatively, they may use their power to reconsider a decision. Clerks have no power inherent or otherwise to alter a decision (*Memminger-IRO GmbH* v. *Trip-Lite Ltd.*, *The Times*, July 9, 1992).

A decision made without jurisdiction cannot be corrected under either this paragraph or the inherent power (*Munks* v. *Munks* [1985] F.L.R. 576). The proper course in such a case is for the tribunal to set aside its decision under its inherent power to do so.

No appeal lies against a correction or refusal to make a correction under this regulation (see reg. 16(2)). However, if a decision is corrected, a party who is dissatisfied may appeal against the decision as corrected and if no correction is made, may appeal against the decision as originally made. Where a decision is corrected, the time for appealing against the decision does not begin to run until the day that notice is given of the correction (reg. 16(1)). However, if a request is made for a decision to be corrected but no correction is made, no concession is made as to the time for appealing against the decision.

By analogy with the position in industrial tribunals, it is possible that if a CSAT announced an oral decision which was followed by a contradictory written decision, a Commissioner might consider that there had been a breach of natural justice (*Gutzmore* v. *J. Wardly (Holdings) Ltd.*, *The Times*, March 3, 1993), although the tribunal does retain control over the decision until it is promulgated.

Para. (2)

This paragraph envisages that the decision has been given to the parties before it is corrected. For this purpose a decision is not made until it is promulgated, in other words, until it has been notified to the parties (*CSB 226/81*). Until then it is still under the control of the tribunal which may make any corrections to it that it wishes.

Setting Aside

15.—(1) Subject to regulation 16 (provisions common to regulations 14 and 15) on an application made by a party to the proceedings a decision may be set aside by the tribunal who gave the decision or by another tribunal in a case where it appears just to do so on the grounds that—

   (*a*)   a document relating to the proceedings in which the decision was given was not sent to, or was not received at an appropriate time by, a party to the proceedings or the party's representative or was not received at an appropriate time by the tribunal who gave the decision;

   (*b*)   a party to the proceedings in which the decision was given or the party's representative was not present at the hearing notice of which had been given under regulation 11(2); or

   (*c*)   there has been some other procedural irregularity or mishap.

(2) An application under this regulation shall be made in accordance with regulation 3.

(3) Where an application to set aside a decision is made under paragraph (1) every party to the proceedings shall be sent a copy of the application and shall be

afforded a reasonable opportunity of making representations on it before the application is decided.

(4) Notice in writing of a decision on an application to set aside a decision shall be given to every party to the proceedings as soon as may be practicable and the notice shall contain a statement giving the reasons for the decision.

(5) For the purpose of deciding an application to set aside a decision under these Regulations there shall be disregarded regulation 2 and any provision in any enactment or instrument to the effect that any notice or other document required or authorised to be given or sent to any person shall be deemed to have been given or sent if it was sent by post to the person's last known address.

DERIVATION
Social Security (Adjudication) Regulations, reg. 11.

DEFINITIONS
"party to the proceedings": see reg. 1(2).
"proceedings": *ibid.*
"tribunal": *ibid.*

GENERAL NOTE
This regulation contains a power for a decision to be set aside. It provides a swifter and, therefore, more satisfactory remedy than an appeal to a Commissioner in those cases where both courses of action are available. It should always be considered as a possible course of action in such cases. The power is given to a CSAT and not to a chairman. It may act unanimously or by a majority (reg. 13(1) and *R(S) 12/81*, para. 13). If a decision is set aside, the new tribunal will consist entirely of members who did not take part in the original hearing and conducts a complete re-hearing of the appeal. All the documents which were before the original tribunal should be before the tribunal at the rehearing (*R(S) 1/87*, para. 13).

Unlike a tribunal which is conducting the rehearing of an appeal in which an earlier decision has been set aside, the tribunal which decides whether to set aside the earlier decision will frequently involve one or more of the members of the earlier tribunal. This is undesirable from the point of view of natural justice. However, it is allowed for by the express wording of para. (1) and is convenient in that it is a valuable means by which the subsequent tribunal can gain an idea of what took place at the earlier hearing. Members who are asked to sit should be conscious of their difficult position in the second hearing. In some cases the nature of the complaint (for example, the alleged bias of the member) will be such that it would be a breach of natural justice for that member to be involved.

This regulation only applies to decisions. For this purpose a decision is not made until it is promulgated, in other words, until it has been notified to the parties (*CSB 226/81*). Until then it is still under the control of the tribunal which may alter it as it wishes.

The three heads

Para. (1)
This paragraph confers a discretion to set aside a tribunal decision if it is just to do so, provided that one of three heads is satisfied. The tribunal should, therefore, approach the decision in two stages. First, it must decide whether there are any matters which bring the case within head (*a*), (*b*) or (*c*). Findings of fact will need to be made in respect of each head that is relevant. If the tribunal finds that one of the heads is satisfied, it should go on to decide whether it is just to set aside the earlier decision. Although it is easy to keep these two stages distinct in the case of heads (*a*) and (*b*), the nature of head (*c*) is such that the two stages may well merge in practice.

Head (a)
This is largely a question of fact, although it will be necessary to exercise judgment in deciding whether the document was received at an appropriate time. In practice this means whether it was received in time to allow the party's case to be prepared adequately or the tribunal to take adequate account of the document during the hearing. This head applies where the document was not received at an appropriate time by the tribunal. The test is whether it was received in time by the members of the tribunal, not whether it was received in time by the clerk.

Head (b)

This raises a pure question of fact. It only applies where notice was given of the hearing under reg. 11(2). If no notice was given, this head does not apply and it is necessary to use head (c).

The fact that a party was absent is sufficient to bring the case under this head without regard to the reasons for the absence. However, this does not give parties a licence to chose not to attend and then to have the decision set aside if it is not to their liking (*CU 270/86*, para. 12). A party's reasons for being absent will be relevant to the exercise of the discretion. The tribunal will, therefore, have to make findings of fact, or draw appropriate inferences, as to the reasons for this purpose.

Head (c)

This head involves a substantial element of judgment and in practice it may be difficult to distinguish between deciding whether this head is satisfied and, if it is, how the discretion should be exercised. Indeed, in view of the wording of head (c), it may be difficult to justify a decision that procedural justice does require that the decision be set aside but that it is not just to do so.

The wording of this sub-paragraph repeats the language used by the Social Security Commissioners in interpreting the different wording of the social security provision (*R(U) 3/89*, para. 22, *R(SB) 4/90*, para. 10 and *CI 78/90*, para. 8). It emphasises that only procedural irregularities or mishaps in the course of the appeal allow it to be set aside. The matters complained of may be major or minor (*R(S) 3/89*, para. 17). The tribunal's inherent power to set aside, which is preserved by reg. 16(3), is no wider in these respects (*R(U) 3/89*, paras. 4–6 and *R(SB) 4/90*, para. 9).

A decision cannot be set aside on the ground of a substantive error in the application of the law. This is not, however, as big an obstacle as it may at first appear. A substantive error may arise as a result of a procedural defect and that defect will bring the case within this regulation. It may even be possible to argue in a particular case that the decision is such that it could not have been reached without a procedural error of some sort occurring.

The discretion

If one of the heads is satisfied the tribunal should then decide whether it is just to set aside the decision on that ground. This gives the tribunal a discretion which must be exercised judicially and not in an arbitrary manner (*R(U) 3/89*, para. 21). The test to be applied at this stage is whether any party has reasonable grounds to believe that there has or may have been unfair prejudice as a result of what occurred. Since the correctness of a decision cannot be challenged on an application to set aside that decision, it is improper to have regard to the merits of that decision in exercising the discretion under this regulation. The tribunal may not, therefore, take into account the effect which the matter established at the first stage of its inquiry may have had on the original decision (*R(S) 12/81*, para. 13). Nor may it have regard to any doubts about the correctness of the original decision (*R(U) 3/89*, para. 21).

Only one application to set aside a decision may be made (*CS 137/88*, para. 13). This applies whether the subsequent purported application is made under the same head of para. (1) as the first or under a different head (*ibid.*). Parties and their representatives must therefore be careful to raise every issue which may be relevant when they apply for a decision to be set aside.

No appeal lies against a decision under this regulation (see reg. 16(2)). However, a party who is dissatisfied with a setting aside decision does have some courses of action available. (i) The application is subject to the rules of natural justice and is susceptible to judicial review (*R(SB) 55/83*, para. 14). (ii) If the application to set aside is refused, the party may appeal against the original decision. The Commissioner may set aside that decision if satisfied that there has been an error of law. That error may arise from some aspect of the hearing which is covered by one of the heads of this paragraph (*CS 113/91*, para. 6). (iii) It is possible that subsequent events may show that there was a breach of justice at the original hearing. It may appear, for example, that the party who did not attend had a good excuse for not doing so (*CU 270/86*, para. 12). This decision is difficult to reconcile with *R(SB) 11/83*. There the Commissioner said that he could not set aside a decision on the ground that notice of the hearing had not been received. It was for the tribunal to act under its setting aside power rather than the Commissioner (para. 14). Yet this was surely as good a reason for not attending as the illness which justified the Commissioner setting aside the tribunal decision in *CU 270/86*.

What is the position if a tribunal decides to set aside an earlier decision on grounds which fall outside the scope of this regulation or of the inherent power preserved under reg. 16(3), for example, because the decision was based on grounds which do not come within one of the three heads? In such a case the setting aside is a nullity (*R(SB) 4/90*, para. 12). Nevertheless the setting aside of the earlier decision usually remains valid and binding on a child support officer, the Secretary of State and a CSAT (*CI 78/90*, para. 12).

If an appeal comes before a CSAT when an earlier decision has been set aside and it is alleged that the setting aside was made without power, the proper course for the CSAT to take is to accept the validity of the setting aside decision and to decide that it does not have jurisdiction to deal with the appeal.

However, a CSAT may hold the setting aside of an earlier decision to be invalid if the setting aside decision is plainly invalid on its face (*CI 78/90*, para. 12 and *CSB 323/90*, para. 14). There is no authoritative guidance on what would amount to such a plain invalidity. In *CSB 323/89*, para. 15 the Commissioner suggested that examples might be where the setting aside tribunal had not been properly constituted, where reasonable opportunity for representations had not been given or where there had been a breach of the guidelines given on the conduct of setting aside hearings in *R(S) 12/81*.

If the CSAT accepts the validity of the setting aside decision and rehears the appeal, its decision will be appealable and will allow the case to come before a Commissioner. The powers of the Commissioner are unclear. According to *R(SB) 4/90*, para. 15, the Commissioner has power to remedy the situation by setting aside the defective setting-aside decision. However, this decision has been disapproved by *CG 5/91* on the ground that no appeal lies to the the Commissioners on this issue and they have no power to carry out a judicial review.

If an appeal is made to a CSAT alleging that a decision has been set aside improperly, it is obviously a case in which it would be inappropriate for a chairman to use his powers under reg. 4, since that would not allow an appeal to a Commissioner. The decision as to jurisdiction should accordingly be taken by the CSAT which should, as stated, generally accept the validity of the prior setting aside.

Para. (3)

It is not necessary for there to be an oral hearing of a setting aside application (reg. 11(1) and *CU 270/86*, para. 11). However, this paragraph provides that a copy of the application must be sent to all the parties and that they must be given a reasonable chance to comment on it. This is in accordance with the requirements of natural justice (*ibid.*).

Para. (4)

It is clear from the wording of this paragraph that when a tribunal reaches a conclusion under an application to set aside a decision that conclusion is a decision and not a determination as in social security law. This opens the way for an application to be made for the decision on the setting aside application itself to be set aside, for example, if a party failed to receive notice of the setting aside application. However, it is clear that there can be no appeal (reg. 16(2)).

Para. (5)

This paragraph provides that reg. 2 and the provisions of s.7 of the Interpretation Act 1978, both of which provide for circumstances in which documents are deemed to have been properly served, do not apply for the purposes of considering whether a decision should be set aside.

Provisions common to regulations 14 and 15

16.—(1) In calculating time under regulation 2(1) of the Child Support Commissioners (Procedure) Regulations 1992 (applications for leave to appeal to a Commissioner) there shall be disregarded any day falling before the day on which notice was given of a correction of a decision or the record thereof pursuant to regulation 14 or on which notice is given of a decision that a prior decision shall not be set aside following an application made under regulation 15, as the case may be.

(2) Notwithstanding anything contained in these Regulations, there shall be no appeal against a correction made under regulation 14, or a refusal to make such a correction, or against a decision given under regulation 15.

(3) Nothing in these Regulations shall be construed as derogating from any power to correct errors or set aside decisions which is exercisable apart from these Regulations.

DEFINITION
"Commissioner": see reg. 1(2).

GENERAL NOTE
Para. (1)

The effect of this paragraph is to extend the time within which an appeal against the decision of a CSAT may be made. It ensures that a party is not prejudiced by the time taken for a correction to be made under reg. 14 or for a refusal to set aside a decision under reg. 15. It does not apply if a correction is refused. Parties are, therefore, unwise to rely on this provision if they are unhappy with the decision as it stands and have requested that it be corrected. If the party also intends to appeal, it would be wise to do so at the same time as seeking a correction. This will not prejudice the decision under reg. 14.

This paragraph does not apply to an application to set aside a decision. There may have been a procedural problem with an appeal but a party did not apply to set the decision aside because the decision as originally announced was in that party's favour. If that decision is corrected to the party's detriment after the time for applying to set aside has expired, the party will not be prejudiced as an appeal to a Commissioner can still be made and the time to do so will be extended by virtue of this paragraph, and the time for applying to set the decision aside may be extended under reg. 3(6).

Para. (2)

There can be no appeal against a refusal to correct a decision nor against a decision to set aside a decision or to refuse to do so. However, it is argued in the general note to reg. 15(4) that a setting aside decision may itself be set aside. Moreover, there is no bar to a tribunal reconsidering an application under either reg. 14 or 15. This might occur, for example, if information was subsequently drawn to the tribunal's attention which should have been before it at the setting aside hearing, but which had become detached from the tribunal file. (See *CIS 93/92*). This decision is discussed in the general note to reg. 3(8).

Para. (3)

The tribunal has an inherent power to correct accidental errors and to set aside decisions which are made without jurisdiction. These inherent powers are part of the tribunal's own powers which arise to allow them to do justice between the parties (*R(U) 3/89*, para. 5). The inherent power to correct errors is discussed in the general note to reg. 14. The scope of the tribunal's inherent power to set aside decisions and its relationship to the power given by reg. 15 has never been determined. There is a suggestion that so far as the powers of the Social Security Commissioners are concerned, their inherent power may be slightly wider than the regulation governing the setting aside of their decisions (*R(U) 3/89*, para. 5(3)).

This paragraph is also authority, if such is needed, that these regulations do not affect the power of the Child Support Commissioners to set aside a decision of a CSAT.

Confidentiality

17.—(1) No information such as is mentioned in paragraph (2), and which has been provided for the purposes of any proceedings to which these Regulations apply, shall be disclosed except with the written consent of the person to whom the information relates.

(2) The information referred to in paragraph (1) is—

(*a*) any address, other than the address of the Central Office and the place where the oral hearing is to be held; and

(*b*) any other information the use of which could reasonably be expected to lead to a person being located.

DEFINITIONS

"Central Office": see reg. 1(2).

"proceedings": *ibid.*

GENERAL NOTE

This provision is largely an administrative matter to be implemented by the provision of appropriate forms and the scrutiny of the clerk to the tribunal. A signature by parties declaring that until further notice their addresses may be disclosed would in most cases avoid the need to implement the possibly cumbersome administrative measures which are necessary to give effect to this provision. The tribunal forms ask all parties to indicate whether their addresses may be disclosed to other parties.

Despite the essentially administrative nature of this provision there will be at least two cases in which the tribunal will need to be aware of this regulation. First, the tribunal will need to take care when inquiring whether or not the papers have been correctly served on a party who does not come to the hearing. Often this will involve a discussion of addresses. The second case is where evidence is given or produced at the hearing which could lead to a person being located. For example, the habitual residence of party may be in issue. This may involve information about addresses and other information which could lead to a party being located. In such cases care will need to be taken to ensure that addresses are not referred to in the discussion and that they do not appear in the notes of the proceedings to which the parties will have access. The chairman should record any information which cannot be disclosed on a separate note of proceedings. It should be labelled "not for disclosure" and kept on file. Any documents which are produced will need to be doctored before the other parties are allowed to see them. Where this possibility can be anticipated, it will be appropriate to give a direction under reg. 5 that documents be sent to the tribunal in advance of the hearing so that appropriately doctored copies can be made. This may on occasion produce a result which is prejudicial to one of the parties. For example, it may be the case that an absent parent could prove that the person with care did not reside at the address within the jurisdiction which is known only to the tribunal.

Equivalent duties of confidentiality are imposed on child support officers by regs. 10(3) and 25(6) of the Maintenance Procedure Regulations, and on Child Support Commissioners by reg. 22 of the Child Support Commissioners (Procedure) Regulations.

The Child Support (Collection and Enforcement of Other Forms of Maintenance) Regulations 1992

(S.I. 1992 No. 2643)

Made by the Secretary of State for Social Security under sections 30(1), (4) and (5), 51 and 54 of the Child Support Act 1991 and all other powers enabling him in that behalf.

Citation, commencement and interpretation

1.—(1) These Regulations may be cited as the Child Support (Collection and Enforcement of Other Forms of Maintenance) Regulations 1992 and shall come into force on 5th April 1993.

(2) In these Regulations—

"the Act" means the Child Support Act 1991;

"child of the family" has the same meaning as in the Matrimonial Causes Act 1973 or, in Scotland, the Family Law (Scotland) Act 1985; and

"periodical payments" includes secured periodical payments.

GENERAL NOTE

"child of the family" is defined by s. 52(1) of the Matrimonial Causes Act 1973 as follows:

"child of the family", in relation to the parties to a marriage, means—

(a) a child of both of those parties; and

(b) any other child, not being a child who is placed with those persons as foster parents by a local authority or voluntary organisation, who has been treated by both of those parties as a child of their family.

Periodical payments and categories of person prescribed for the purposes of section 30 of the Act

2. The following periodical payments and categories of persons are prescribed for the purposes of section 30(1) of the Act—

(a) payments under a maintenance order made in relation to a child in accordance with the provisions of section 8(6) (periodical payments in addition to child support maintenance), 8(7) (periodical payments to meet expenses incurred in connection with the provision of instruction or training) or 8(8) of the Act (periodical payments to meet expenses attributable to disability);

(b) any periodical payments under a maintenance order [¹or, in Scotland, registered minutes of agreement] which are payable to or for the benefit of a spouse or former spouse who is the person with care of a child who is a qualifying child in respect of whom a child support maintenance assessment is in force in accordance with which the Secretary of State has arranged for the collection of child support maintenance under section 29 of the Act; and

(c) any periodical payments under a maintenance order payable to or for the benefit of a former child of the family of the person against whom the order is made, that child having his home with the person with care.

AMENDMENT

1. Regulation 44 of the Amendment Regulations (April 5, 1993).

DEFINITIONS
"the Act": see reg. 1(2).
"child of the family": *ibid.*
"periodical payments": *ibid.*

Collection and enforcement—England and Wales

3. In relation to England and Wales, sections 29(2) and (3) and 31 to 40 of the Act, and any regulations made under those sections, shall apply for the purpose of enabling the Secretary of State to enforce any obligation to pay any amount which he is authorised to collect under section 30 of the Act, with the modification that any reference in those sections or regulations to child support maintenance shall be read as a reference to any of the periodical payments mentioned in regulation 2 above, and any reference to a maintenance assessment shall be read as a reference to any of the maintenance orders mentioned in that regulation.

DEFINITIONS
"the Act": see reg. 1(2).
"periodical payments": *ibid.*

Collection and enforcement—Scotland

4. In relation to Scotland, for the purpose of enforcing any obligation to pay any amount which the Secretary of State is authorised to collect under section 30 of the Act—

(*a*) the Secretary of State may bring any proceedings and take any other steps (other than diligence against earnings) which could have been brought or taken by or on behalf of the person to whom the periodical payments are payable; and

(*b*) sections 29(2) and (3), 31 and 32 of the Act, and any regulations made under those sections, shall apply, with the modification that any reference in those sections or regulations to child support maintenance shall be read as a reference to any of the periodical payments mentioned in regulation 2 above, and any reference to a maintenance assessment shall be read as a reference to any of the maintenance orders mentioned in that regulation.

DEFINITIONS
"the Act": see reg. 1(2).
"periodical payments": *ibid.*

Collection and enforcement—supplementary

5. Nothing in Regulations 3 or 4 applies to any periodical payment which falls due before the date specified by the Secretary of State by a notice in writing to the absent parent that he is arranging for those payments to be collected, and that date shall be not earlier than the date the notice is given.

GENERAL NOTE

Since the regulations made under s.29 of the Act apply to regs. 3 and 4 above, the day when the notice is treated as given under reg. 5 will be determined under reg. 1(2)(*b*) of the Collection and Enforcement Regulations.

The Child Support Act 1991 (Commencement No. 3 and Transitional Provisions) Order 1992

(S.I. 1992 No. 2644)

Made by the Secretary of State for Social Security under section 58(2) to (6) of the Child Support Act 1991.

Citation

1. This Order may be cited as the Child Support Act 1991 (Commencement No. 3 and Transitional Provisions) Order 1992.

Date appointed for the coming into force of certain provisions of the Child Support Act 1991

2. Subject to the following provisions of this Order, the date appointed for the coming into force of all the provisions of the Child Support Act 1991, in so far as they are not already in force, except sections 19(3), 30(2), 34(2), 37(2) and (3) and 58(12), is 5th April 1993.

Transitional provisions

3. The transitional provisions set out in the Schedule to this Order shall have effect.

SCHEDULE Article 3

[¹Part 1

Phased Take-on of Cases

1.—(1) In this Part of this Schedule—

"The Act" means the Child Support Act 1991;

"benefit" means income support, family credit, or disability working allowance under Part VII of the Social Security Contributions and Benefits Act 1992, or any other benefit prescribed under section 6(1) of the Act (applications by parents receiving benefit);

"parent with care" means a person who, in respect of the same child or children, is both a parent and a person with care; and

"transitional period" means the period beginning with 5th April 1993 and ending with 6th April 1997.

(2) For the purposes of paragraph 5 below, in England and Wales, an application for a maintenance order is pending before a court if—

(i) notice of the application has been filed, in accordance with rules of court, before 5th April 1993;

(ii) in the case of an application contained in a petition for divorce, nullity or judicial separation, or the answer to it, notice of intention to proceed with it was given, in the form required by rules of court, before 5th April 1993.

311

2. Subject to paragraph 4 below, during the transitional period no application under section 4 of the Act (applications for child support maintenance) in relation to a qualifying child or any qualifying children may be made at any time when—

(*a*) there is in force a maintenance order or written maintenance agreement (being an agreement made before 5th April 1993) in respect of that qualifying child or those qualifying children and the absent parent; or

(*b*) benefit is being paid to a parent with care of that child or those children.

DEFINITIONS
"the Act": see para. 1(1).
"benefit": *ibid*.
"parent with care": *ibid*.
"transitional period": *ibid*.

3. Subject to paragraph 4 below, during the transitional period no application under section 7 of the Act (right of child in Scotland to apply for assessment) may be made by a qualifying child at any time when there is in force a maintenance order or written maintenance agreement (being an agreement made before 5th April 1993) in respect of that child and the absent parent.

DEFINITIONS
"the Act": see para. 1(1).
"transitional period": *ibid*.

4. Paragraphs 2 and 3 above do not apply to an application made—

(*a*) in that part of the transitional period beginning with 8th April 1996, if the surname of the person with care begins with any of the letters A to D inclusive;

(*b*) in that part of the transitional period beginning with 1st July 1996, if the surname of the person with care begins with any of the letters E to K inclusive;

(*c*) in that part of the transitional period beginning with 7th October 1996, if the surname of the person with care begins with any of the letters L to R inclusive; and

(*d*) in that part of the transitional period beginning with 6th January 1997, if the surname of the person with care begins with any of the letters S to Z inclusive.

DEFINITIONS
"the Act": see para. 1(1).
"transitional period": *ibid*.

5.—(1) For so long as either—

(*a*) paragraph 2 or 3 above operates in a case so as to prevent an application being made under section 4 of the Act or, as the case may be, section 7 of the Act, and no application has been made under section 6 of the Act; or

(*b*) an application has been made under section 6 of the Act but no maintenance assessment has yet been made pursuant to that application,

then in relation to that case—

(i) section 8(3) of the Act (role of the courts with respect to maintenance orders) shall be modified so as to have effect as if the word "vary" were omitted;

(ii) in a case falling within sub-paragraph (a) above, section 9(3) of the Act shall not apply; and

(iii) section 9(5) of the Act shall be modified so as to have effect as if paragraph (b) were omitted.

(2) In a case where there is, at any time during the transitional period, pending before a court an application for a maintenance order or an application for an order varying a written maintenance agreement, section 8(3) or, as the case may be, section 9(5)(b) of the Act, shall not apply in relation to that case.]

PART II

MODIFICATION OF MAINTENANCE ASSESSMENT IN CERTAIN CASES

6. In this Part of this Schedule—

"the Act" means the Child Support Act 1991;

"formula amount" means the amount of child support maintenance that would, but for the provisions of this Part of this Schedule, be payable under an original assessment, or any fresh assessment made during the period specified in paragraph 8 consequent on a review under section 17, 18 or 19 of the Act;

"the Maintenance Assessment Procedure Regulations" means the Child Support (Maintenance Assessment Procedure) Regulations 1992;

"modified amount" means an amount which is £20 greater than the aggregate weekly amount which was payable under the orders, agreements or arrangements mentioned in paragraph 7(1)(*a*) below; and

"original assessment" means a maintenance assessment made in respect of a qualifying child where no previous such assessment has been made or, where the assessment is made in respect of more than one child, where no previous such assessment has been made in respect of any of those children.

7.—(1) Subject to sub-paragraph (2), the provisions of this Part of this Schedule apply to cases where—

(*a*) on 4th April 1993[², and at all times thereafter until the date when a maintenance assessment is made under the Act] there is in force, in respect of all the qualifying children in respect of whom an application for a maintenance assessment is made under the Act and the absent parent concerned, one or more—

(i) maintenance orders;

(ii) orders under section 151 of the Army Act 1955 (deductions from pay for maintenance of wife or child) or section 151 of the Air Force Act 1955 (deductions from pay for maintenance of wife or child) or arrangements corresponding to such an order and made under Article 1(*b*) or 3 of the Naval and Marine Pay and Pensions (Deductions for Maintenance) Order 1959; or

(iii) maintenance agreements (being agreements which are made or evidenced in writing); and

(*b*) the absent parent is responsible for maintaining a child or children residing with him other than the child or children in respect of whom the application is made; and

(*c*) the formula amount is not more than £60; and

(*d*) the formula amount exceeds the aggregate weekly amount which was payable under the orders, agreements or arrangements mentioned in sub-paragraph (*a*) above by more than £20 a week.

(2) Nothing in this Part of this Schedule applies to [³a Category A interim maintenance assessment within the meaning of regulation 8(1B) of the Child Support (Maintenance Assessment Procedure) Regulations 1992] made under section 12 of the Act.

8. In a case to which this Part of this Schedule applies, the amount payable under an original assessment, or any fresh assessment made consequent on a review under section 17, 18 or 19 of the Act, during the period of one year beginning with the date on which the original assessment takes effect or, if shorter, until any of the conditions specified in paragraph 7(1) is no longer satisfied, shall, instead of being the formula amount, be the modified amount.

DEFINITIONS
"the Act": see para. 6.
"formula amount": *ibid.*
"modified amount": *ibid.*
"original assessment": *ibid.*

9. For the purpose of determining the aggregate weekly amount payable under the orders, agreements or arrangements mentioned in paragraph 7(1)(*a*) above any payments in kind and any payments made to a third party on behalf of or for the benefit of the qualifying child or qualifying children or the person with care shall be disregarded.

10. If, in making a maintenance assessment, a child support officer has applied the provisions of this part of this Schedule, regulation 10(2) of the Maintenance Assessment Procedure Regulations shall have effect as if there was added at the end—

"(g) the aggregate weekly amount which was payable under the orders, agreements or arrangements specified in paragraph 7(1)(*a*) of the Schedule to the Child Support Act 1991 (Commencement No. 3 and Transitional Provisions) Order 1992 (modification of maintenance assessment in certain cases)."

DEFINITION
"the Maintenance Assessment Procedure Regulations": see para. 6.

11. The first review of an original assessment under section 16 of the Act (periodical reviews) shall be conducted on the basis that the amount payable under the assessment immediately before the review takes place was the formula amount.

DEFINITIONS
"the Act": see para. 6.
"formula amount": *ibid.*
"original assessment": *ibid.*

12.—(1) The provision of the following sub-paragraphs shall apply where there is a review of a previous assessment under section 17 of the Act (reviews on change of circumstances) at any time when the amount payable under that assessment is the modified amount.

(2) Where the child support officer determines that, were a fresh assessment to be made as a result of the review, the amount payable under it (disregarding the provisions of this Part of this Schedule) (in this paragraph called "the reviewed formula amount") would be—

(*a*) more than the formula amount, the amount of child support maintenance payable shall be the modified amount plus the difference between the formula amount and the reviewed formula amount;

(*b*) less than the formula amount but more than the modified amount, the amount of child support maintenance payable shall be the modified amount;

(*c*) less than the modified amount, the amount of child support maintenance payable shall be the reviewed formula amount.

(3) The child support officer shall, in determining the reviewed formula amount, apply the provisions of regulations 20 to 22 of the Maintenance Assessment Procedure Regulations.

DEFINITIONS
"the Act": see para. 6.
"formula amount": *ibid.*
"the Maintenance Assessment Procedure Regulations": *ibid.*
"modified amount": *ibid.*

AMENDMENTS
1. Art. 2(1) of the Child Support Act 1991 (Commencement No. 3 and Transitional Provisions) Amendment Order 1993 (March 31, 1993).

2. Art. 2(2) of the Child Support Act 1991 (Commencement No. 3 and Transitional Provisions) Amendment Order 1993 (March 31, 1993).
3. Art. 2(3) of the Child Support Act 1991 (Commencement No. 3 and Transitional Provisions) Amendment Order 1993 (March 31, 1993).

GENERAL NOTE

Phased Take-on of Cases

Part I of the Schedule to this Order provides for the phased take-on of cases by the Child Support Agency and Appeal Tribunals during the transitional period. The effect of Part I is as follows:

1. Applications under s.6 may be made from and including April 5, 1993.
2. Applications under ss.4 and 7 are subject to the following rules:
(a) An application may be made from and including April 5 provided that the following conditions are met (paras. 2 and 3).
  (i) No maintenance order has been made in relation to the absent parent and any qualifying children in respect of whom the application for a maintenance assessment is made. (See para. 5 for the position where an application to make or vary an order is pending before a court.)
  (ii) No written maintenance agreement made before April 5, 1993 is in force in relation to the absent parent and any qualifying children in respect of whom the application for a maintenance assessment is made.
  (iii) In the case of applications made under s.4 (but not under s.7), no relevant benefit is being paid to the parent with care of the qualifying children covered by the application for a maintenance assessment. The relevant benefits are income support, family credit and disability working allowance (para. 1).
The relevant time for applying these conditions is the time when the application for a maintenance assessment is made. This may have an impact on what would otherwise be the priority of applications under s.5 of the Act and reg. 4 of and Sched. 2 to the Maintenance Assessment Procedure Regulations, since it may mean that one or more applications are not valid and have to be ignored.
(b) Cases to which none of these conditions applies are brought within the child support scheme during 1996 and early 1997 in accordance with the following table (para. 4(1)).

Persons whose surnames begin with any of the following letters inclusive	may apply for a maintenance assessment from and including
A to D	April 8, 1996
E to K	July 1, 1996
L to R	October 7, 1996
S to Z	January 6, 1997

Since the stage at which an application for a maintenance assessment may be made depends upon the surname of the person who makes the application, the date on which an application may be made in respect of a particular child may vary according to who makes the application. Moreover, a party could come within the scheme at a later date than would otherwise be the case by adopting a different surname, whether by deed poll or by merely assuming the name.

So long as an application may not be made under s.4 or 7 and no maintenance assessment has been made pursuant to any application under s.6, the application of ss.8(3) and 9(3) and (5) is modified as provided in para. 5

Modified Maintenance Assessments

Part II of the Schedule to this Order provides for a temporary reduction in the amount payable under a maintenance assessment in cases where low maintenance payments are being made at the time the child support scheme comes into operation so as to limit the increase in payments to be made to £20 a week for a maximum of one year.

This Part does not apply to Category A interim maintenance assessments (para. 7(2)). It applies provided and only so long as the following conditions are met (paras. 7(1) and 8).

(i) From April 4, 1993 until a maintenance assessment is made under the Act there is in force one or more maintenance orders or agreements in respect of all the qualifying children in respect of whom an application for a maintenance assessment has been made. Only maintenance agreements which are made or evidenced in writing are included. "Maintenance order" is not defined in this Order and will have the same meaning as in s.8(11) of the Act and regulations made thereunder. In calculating the amounts payable under the orders and agreements, payments in kind and payments to a third party on behalf of or for the benefit of a qualifying child are disregarded (para. 9).

(ii) One or more children, other than children in respect of whom the maintenance assessment has been made, reside with the absent parent who is responsible for maintaining them. The Order uses the words "residing with" in contrast to "home" or "household" which are used elsewhere. It, therefore, covers cases where a child resides with someone but does not live in that person's household, although the need for the parent to be responsible for maintaining the child makes it likely that this will arise in very few cases. It is also more limited than "home" and would not cover cases where a child's home is with the absent parent but that child ceases to reside there, for example while away at boarding school. (For further discussion of these concepts, see the general note to s.3 of the Act.) The responsibility which the absent parent has to maintain the child may exist under a maintenance order or agreement or it may be one which the parent has assumed without any such order or agreement being made.

(iii) The amount of child support maintenance which would otherwise be payable is not more than £60.

(iv) This amount exceeds the sum of the amounts payable under (i) by more than £20 a week.

If all four conditions are satisfied the child support maintenance payable is the total of the sums covered by (i) above plus £20. This applies to original assessments and to fresh assessments on review under s.17, 18 or 19 of the Act. This lasts for one year from the effective date of the *original* (not fresh) assessment, or until the time when one of the conditions above ceases to apply, whichever is the earlier (see para. 8.) The one year maximum duration of the operation of these provisions is fixed independently of the date when a s.16 review is made or treated as made under reg. 18 of the Maintenance Assessment Procedure Regulations.

When the original assessment is first reviewed under s.16 of the Act, the provisions of Part II are disregarded and the assessment is treated as being for the amount of child support maintenance which would otherwise have been payable (para. 11).

Where a review is conducted under s.17 of the Act while the provisions of Part II apply, the result is determined in accordance with the provisions of para. 12. Their effect is as follows. Assume that the absent parent pays £15 under a maintenance order and that the original assessment was for £50. The absent parent pays £15 plus £20, *i.e.* £35.

(*a*) If the effect of a s.17 review is that the assessment that would otherwise be payable is increased by £5 to £55, the absent parent must pay the £35 plus the additional £5, *i.e.* £40.

(*b*) If the effect of a s.17 review is that the assessment that would otherwise be payable is increased by £15 to £65 (*i.e.* above the £60 limit set by para. 7(1)(*c*)), the case ceases to fall within Part II: see the definition of "formula amount" in para. 6. Accordingly, the absent parent must pay the full assessment of £65.

(*c*) If the effect of a s.17 review is that the assessment that would otherwise be payable is reduced from £50 to £40 (*i.e.* below the amount of the original assessment but more than the amount being paid by the absent parent), the amount paid by the absent parent remains unchanged at £35.

(*d*) If the effect of a s.17 review is that the assessment that would otherwise be payable is reduced from £50 to £30 (*i.e.* below the amount being paid by the absent parent), the absent parent must pay only the fresh assessment of £30.

The Child Support (Maintenance Arrangements and Jurisdiction) Regulations 1992

(S.I. 1992 No. 2645)

Made by the Secretary of State for Social Security under sections 8(11), 10(1), (2) and (4), 44(3), 51, 52(4) and 54 of, and paragraph 11 of Schedule 1 to, the Child Support Act 1991 and all other powers enabling him in that behalf.

Citation, commencement and interpretation

1.—(1) These Regulations may be cited as the Child Support (Maintenance Arrangements and Jurisdiction) Regulations 1992 and shall come into force on 5th April 1993.

(2) In these Regulations—

"the Act" means the Child Support Act 1991;

"Maintenance Assessments and Special Cases Regulations" means the Child Support (Maintenance Assessments and Special Cases) Regulations 1992;

"effective date" means the date on which a maintenance assessment takes effect for the purposes of the Act;

"maintenance order" has the meaning given in section 8(11) of the Act.

(3) In these Regulations, unless the context otherwise requires, a reference—

(*a*) to a numbered regulation is to the regulation in these Regulations bearing that number;

(*b*) in a regulation to a numbered paragraph is to the paragraph in that regulation bearing that number;

(*c*) in a paragraph to a lettered or numbered sub-paragraph is to the sub-paragraph in that paragraph bearing that letter or number.

Prescription of enactment for the purposes of section 8(11) of the Act

2. The Affiliation Proceedings Act 1957 is prescribed for the purposes of section 8(11) of the Act.

DEFINITION
"the Act": see reg. 1(2).

Relationship between maintenance assessments and certain court orders

3.—(1) Orders made under the following enactments are of a kind prescribed for the purposes of section 10(1) of the Act—

(*a*) the Affiliation Proceedings Act 1957;

(*b*) Part II of the Matrimonial Causes Act 1973;

(*c*) the Domestic Proceedings and Magistrates' Courts Act 1978;

(*d*) Part III of the Matrimonial and Family Proceedings Act 1984;

(*e*) the Family Law (Scotland) Act 1985;

(*f*) Schedule 1 to the Children Act 1989.

(2) Subject to paragraphs (3) and (4), where a maintenance assessment is made with respect to—

(*a*) all of the children with respect to whom an order falling within paragraph (1) is in force; or

(*b*) one or more but not all of the children with respect to whom an order falling

317

within paragraph (1) is in force and where the amount payable under the order to or for the benefit of each child is separately specified,

that order shall, so far as it relates to the making or securing of periodical payments to or for the benefit of the children with respect to whom the maintenance assessment has been made, cease to have effect.

(3) The provisions of paragraph (2) shall not apply where a maintenance order has been made in accordance with section 8(7) or (8) of the Act.

(4) In Scotland, where—

(a) an order has ceased to have effect by virtue of the provisions of paragraph (2) to the extent specified in that paragraph; and

(b) a child support officer no longer has jurisdiction to make a maintenance assessment with respect to a child with respect to whom the order ceased to have effect,

that order shall, so far as it relates to that child, again have effect from the date a child support officer no longer has jurisdiction to make a maintenance assessment with respect to that child.

(5) Where a maintenance assessment is made with respect to children with respect to whom an order falling within paragraph (1) is in force, the effective date of that assessment shall be two days after the assessment is made.

(6) Where the provisions of paragraph (2) apply to an order, that part of the order to which those provisions apply shall cease to have effect from the effective date of the maintenance assessment.

DEFINITIONS
"the Act": see reg. 1(2).
"effective date": *ibid.*
"maintenance order": *ibid.*

Relationship between maintenance assessments and certain agreements

4.—(1) Maintenance agreements within the meaning of section 9(1) of the Act are agreements of a kind prescribed for the purposes of section 10(2) of the Act.

(2) Where a maintenance assessment is made with respect to—

(a) all of the children with respect to whom an agreement falling within paragraph (1) is in force; or

(b) one or more but not all of the children with respect to whom an agreement falling within paragraph (1) is in force and where the amount payable under the agreement to or for the benefit of each child is separately specified,

that agreement shall, so far as it relates to the making or securing of periodical payments to or for the benefit of the children with respect to whom the maintenance assessment has been made, become unenforceable from the effective date of the assessment.

(3) Where an agreement becomes unenforceable under the provisions of paragraph (2) to the extent specified in that paragraph, it shall remain unenforceable in relation to a particular child until such date as a child support officer no longer has jurisdiction to make a maintenance assessment with respect to that child.

DEFINITION
"the Act": see reg. 1(2).

Notifications by child support officers

5.—(1) Where a child support officer is aware that an order of a kind prescribed in paragraph (2) is in force and considers that the making of a maintenance assessment has affected, or is likely to affect, that order, he shall notify the persons prescribed in paragraph (3) in respect of whom that maintenance assessment is in force, and the persons prescribed in paragraph (4) holding office in the court where the order in question was made or subsequently registered, of the assessment and its effective date.

(2) The prescribed orders are those made under an enactment mentioned in regulation 3(1).

(3) The prescribed persons in respect of whom the maintenance assessment is in force are—

(a) a person with care;

(b) an absent parent;

(c) a person who is treated as an absent parent under regulation 20 of the Maintenance Assessments and Special Cases Regulations;

(d) a child who has made an application for a maintenance assessment under section 7 of the Act.

(4) The prescribed person holding office in the court where the order in question was made or subsequently registered is—

(a) in England and Wales—

    (i) in relation to the High Court, the senior district judge of the principal registry of the Family Division or, where proceedings were instituted in a district registry, the district judge;

    (ii) in relation to a county court, the proper officer of that court within the meaning of Order 1, Rule 3 of the County Court Rules 1981;

    (iii) in relation to a magistrates' court, the clerk to the justices of that court;

(b) in Scotland—

    (i) in relation to the Court of Session, the Deputy Principal Clerk of Session;

    (ii) in relation to a sheriff court, the sheriff clerk.

DEFINITIONS

"effective date": see reg. 1(2).

"Maintenance Assessments and Special Cases Regulations": *ibid.*

Notification by the court

6.—(1) Where a court is aware that a maintenance assessment is in force and makes an order mentioned in regulation 3(1) which it considers has affected, or is likely to affect, that assessment, the person prescribed in paragraph (2) shall notify the Secretary of State to that effect.

(2) The prescribed person is the person holding the office specified below in the court where the order in question was made or subsequently registered—

(a) in England or Wales—

    (i) in relation to the High Court, the senior district judge of the principal registry of the Family Division or, where proceedings were instituted in a district registry, the district judge;

    (ii) in relation to a county court, the proper officer of that court within the meaning of Order 1, Rule 3 of the County Court Rules 1981;

    (iii) in relation to a magistrates' court, the clerk to the justices of that court;

(b) in Scotland—

    (i) in relation to the Court of Session, the Deputy Principal Clerk of Session;

    (ii) in relation to a sheriff court, the sheriff clerk.

Cancellation of a maintenance assessment on grounds of lack of jurisdiction

7.—(1) Where—

(a) a person with care;

(b) an absent parent; or

(c) a qualifying child

with respect to whom a maintenance assessment is in force ceases to be habitually resident in the United Kingdom, a child support officer shall cancel that assessment.

(2) Where the person with care is not an individual, paragraph (1) shall apply as if sub-paragraph (*a*) were omitted.

(3) Where a child support officer cancels a maintenance assessment under paragraph (1) or by virtue of paragraph (2), the assessment shall cease to have effect from the date that the child support officer determines is the date on which—

    (*a*) where paragraph (1) applies, the person with care, absent parent or qualifying child; or

    (*b*) where paragraph (2) applies, the absent parent or qualifying child

with respect to whom the assessment was made ceases to be habitually resident in the United Kingdom.

[¹(4) Where a parent is treated as an absent parent for the purposes of the Act and of the Maintenance Assessments and Special Cases Regulations by virtue of regulation 20 of those Regulations, he shall be treated as an absent parent for the purposes of paragraphs (1) to (3).]

AMENDMENT
1.   Regulation 45 of the Amendment Regulations (April 5, 1993).

DEFINITION
"Maintenance Assessments and Special Cases Regulations": see reg. 1(2).

Maintenance assessments and maintenance orders made in error

8.—(1) Where—

    (*a*) at the time that a maintenance assessment with respect to a qualifying child was made a maintenance order was in force with respect to that child;

    [¹(*aa*) the maintenance order has ceased to have effect by virtue of the provisions of regulation 3;]

    (*b*) the absent parent had made payments of child support maintenance due under that assessment; and

    (*c*) the child support officer cancels that assessment on the grounds that it was made in error,

the payments of child support maintenance shall be treated as payments under the maintenance order and that order shall be treated as having continued in force.

(2) Where—

    (*a*) at the time that a maintenance order with respect to a qualifying child was made a maintenance assessment was in force with respect to that child;

    [²(*aa*) the maintenance assessment is cancelled or ceases to have effect;]

    (*b*) the absent parent has made payments of maintenance due under that order, and

    (*c*) the maintenance order is revoked by the court on the grounds that it was made in error,

the payments under the maintenance order shall be treated as payments of child support maintenance and the maintenance assessment shall be treated as not having been cancelled [³or, as the case may be, as not having ceased to have effect].

AMENDMENTS
1.   Regulation 46(*a*) of the Amendment Regulations (April 5, 1993).
2.   Regulation 46(*b*)(i) of the Amendment Regulations (April 5, 1993).
3.   Regulation 46(*b*)(ii) of the Amendment Regulations (April 5, 1993).

DEFINITION
"maintenance order": see reg. 1(2).

The Child Support Fees Regulations 1992

(S.I. 1992 No. 3094)

Made by the Secretary of State for Social Security under sections 47, 52(4) and 54 of the Child Support Act 1991 and all other powers enabling him in that behalf.

Citation, commencement and interpretation

1.—(1) These Regulations may be cited as the Child Support Fees Regulations 1992 and shall come into force on 5th April 1993.

(2) In these Regulations, unless the context otherwise requires—

"the Act" means the Child Support Act 1991;

"assessable income" means income calculated in accordance with paragraph 5 of Schedule 1 to the Act;

"assessment fee" means a fee in respect of the assessment of child support maintenance;

"collection fee" means a fee in respect of the Secretary of State arranging for the collection of child support maintenance which becomes due, in accordance with a maintenance assessment, after that fee becomes payable, and (if necessary) arranging for the enforcement of the obligation to pay that child support maintenance in accordance with that assessment;

"Maintenance Assessment Procedure Regulations" means the Child Support (Maintenance Assessment Procedure) Regulations 1992;

"parent with care" means a person who, in respect of the same child or children, is both a parent and a person with care.

(3) In these Regulations, unless the context otherwise requires, a reference—

(*a*) to a numbered regulation is to the regulation in these Regulations bearing that number;

(*b*) in a regulation to a numbered paragraph is to the paragraph in that regulation bearing that number;

(*c*) in a paragraph to a lettered or numbered sub-paragraph is to the sub-paragraph in that paragraph bearing that letter or number.

Circumstances when fees are payable

2. Where a maintenance assessment is made following an application under section 4, 6 or 7 of the Act fees shall be payable to the Secretary of State in accordance with regulations 3 and 4.

DEFINITION
"the Act": see reg. 1(2).

Liability to pay fees

3.—(1) Subject to the provisions of paragraphs (4) and (5), where a maintenance assessment is in force the following persons shall be liable to pay fees, in accordance with the provisions of regulation 4—

(*a*) where an application has been made under section 4 or 7 of the Act—

(i) the person with care if he is a parent with care; and

(ii) the absent parent

with respect to whom the assessment was made;

    (*b*)   where an application has been made under section 6 of the Act and the parent with care remains within section 6(1) of the Act, the absent parent with respect to whom the assessment was made.

(2) In a case falling within paragraph (1)(*a*), the fees payable shall be the assessment fee and, where the Secretary of State exercises his powers under section 4(2) or 7(3) of the Act, the collection fee.

(3) In a case falling within paragraph (1)(*b*), the fees payable shall be the assessment fee and the collection fee.

(4) Where—

    (*a*)   an application has been made under section 6 of the Act; and

    (*b*)   the parent with care no longer falls within section 6(1) of the Act but has not requested the Secretary of State to cease taking action under section 6 of the Act,

the case shall for the purposes of paragraph (1) be treated as if the application had been made under section 4 of the Act.

(5) No fees shall be payable by the following categories of person—

    (*a*)   any person to or in respect of whom income support, family credit or disability working allowance under Part VII of the Social Security Contributions and Benefits Act 1992 is paid;

    (*b*)   any person under the age of 16 or under the age of 19 and receiving full-time education which is not advanced education;

    (*c*)   any person whose assessable income is nil;

    (*d*)   an absent parent to whom the provisions of paragraph 6 of Schedule 1 to the Act (protected income) apply.

(6) The provisions of paragraph (5) shall—

    (*a*)   be applied in relation to any occasion when a liability to pay fees under the provisions of regulation 4 would otherwise arise; and

    (*b*)   have no effect on the fees payable by any other person.

(7) For the purposes of paragraph (5)(*b*), "advanced education" has the same meaning as in paragraph 2 of Schedule 1 to the Maintenance Assessment Procedure Regulations (meaning of "child" for the purposes of the Act), and education is to be treated as full-time education if it satisfies the conditions set out in paragraph 3 of that Schedule.

DEFINITIONS

    "the Act": see reg. 1(2).
    "assessable income": *ibid*.
    "assessment fee": *ibid*.
    "collection fee": *ibid*.
    "Maintenance Assessment Procedure Regulations": *ibid*.
    "parent with care": *ibid*.

GENERAL NOTE

Para. 3(a)(ii)

    This paragraph fails to make use of the definition of parent with care in reg. 1(2) with the result that the wording is unnecessarily cumbersome amd tautological.

Para. (7)

    For a discussion of the provisions referred to in this paragraph see the general note to s.55 of the Act.

Fees

4.—(1) The first assessment fee shall become payable on the date a maintenance assessment is made following an application under section 4, 6 or 7 of the Act and an assessment fee shall thereafter become payable on each anniversary of that date.

(2) The first collection fee shall become payable on the date the Secretary of

State arranges for the collection of child support maintenance and a collection fee shall thereafter become payable on the date the assessment fee becomes payable.

(3) Subject to paragraphs (4) and (6)—

(*a*) the assessment fee shall be £44.00;

(*b*) the collection fee shall be £34.00.

(4) Where the first collection fee becomes payable on a date ("the first collection date") later than the date the first assessment fee becomes payable or an anniversary of that date, the amount of that fee shall be an amount equal to the collection fee specified in paragraph (3) above, multiplied by the number of complete weeks between the first collection date and the date the assessment fee next becomes payable, and divided by 52.

(5) The provisions of this regulation in relation to collection fees shall apply where there has been an earlier period, which has terminated, during which collection fees were payable and the Secretary of State again arranges for the collection of child support maintenance, and references to "the first collection fee" shall be construed accordingly.

(6) No additional assessment fees or collection fees shall be payable by a person with respect to whom more than one maintenance assessment is in force.

(7) Where a liability to pay assessment fees or collection fees under these Regulations arises, the fees shall become due on the fourteenth day after the date the fee invoice is given or sent by the Secretary of State.

(8) If a fee invoice is sent by post to a person's last known or notified address, it shall, for the purposes of paragraph (7), be treated as having been given or sent on the second day after the day of posting, excluding any Sunday or any day which is a bank holiday in England, Wales, Scotland or Northern Ireland under the Banking and Financial Dealings Act 1971.

DEFINITIONS

"the Act": see reg. 1(2).

"assessment fee": *ibid.*

"collection fee": *ibid.*

GENERAL NOTE

Para. (1)

Obviously this only continues so long as a maintenance assessment is in force. There is no provision for a fee or a proportion to be refunded. It is unclear whether an assessment fee can become payable following the making of a Category A interim maintenance assessment. On the one hand such an assessment is an assessment which in sequence of time follows an application. On the other hand it is not in any sense an assessment on that application; rather it is made on a completely different basis pending an assessment on the application.

Para. (2)

If the collection fee does not become payable on a date on which an assessment fee also becomes payable only a proportion of the full fee is payable (sub-para. (4)).

Para. (4)

This paragraph applies when the first collection fee becomes payable on a date other than the date when an assessment becomes payable. The effect is that only a proportion of the fee is payable, the proportion representing the remaining part of the year to which the fee will relate.

Income Support (General) Regulations as amended

(S.I. 1987 No. 1967)

SCHEDULE 2

APPLICABLE AMOUNTS

PART I

PERSONAL ALLOWANCES

1. The weekly amounts specified in column (2) below in respect of each person or couple specified in column (1) shall be the weekly amounts specified for the purposes of regulations 17(1) and 18(1) (applicable amounts and polygamous marriages).

Column (1)	Column (2)
Person or Couple	*Amount*
(1) Single claimant aged—	
(*a*) except where head (*b*) or (*c*) of this sub-paragraph applies, less than 18;	(1)(*a*) £26.45;
(*b*) less than 18 who falls within any of the circumstances specified in Part II of Schedule 1A or who, had he been a registered person, would fall within any of those circumstances, and who—	(*b*) £34.80;
(i) is eligible for income support under regulation 13A; or	
(ii) is the subject of a direction under section 125(1) of the 1992 Act;	
(*c*) less than 18 who satisfies the condition in paragraph 11(*a*)	(*c*) £34.80;
(*d*) not less than 18 but less than 25;	(*d*) £34.80;
(*e*) not less than 25.	(*e*) £44.00.
(2) Lone parent aged—	
(*a*) except where head (*b*) or (*c*) of this sub-paragraph applies, less than 18;	(2)(*a*) £26.45;
(*b*) less than 18 who falls within any of the circumstances specified in Part II of Schedule 1A or who, had he been a registered person, would fall within any of those circumstances, and who—	(*b*) £34.80;
(i) is eligible for income support under regulation 13A; or	
(ii) is the subject of a direction under section 125(i) of the 1992 Act;	
(*c*) less than 18 who satisfies the condition in paragraph 11(*a*);	(*c*) £34.80;
(*d*) not less than 18.	(*d*) £44.00.

Column (1)	Column (2)
Person or Couple	*Amount*
(3) Couple—	
(*a*) Where both members are aged less than 18 and—	(3)(*a*) £52.40;
(i) at least one of them is treated as responsible for a child, or	
(ii) had they not been members of a couple, each would be eligible for income support under regulation 13A (circumstances in which a person aged 16 or 17 is eligible for income support); or	
(iii) they are married and each member is either a registered person or a person to whom Part I of Schedule 1A applies; or	
(iv) there is a direction under section 125(1) of the 1992 Act (income support to avoid severe hardship) in respect of each member; or	
(v) there is a direction under section 125(1) of the 1992 Act in respect of one of them and the other is eligible for income support under regulation 13A;	
(*aa*) where both members are aged less than 18 and sub-paragraph (3)(*a*) does not apply but one member of the couple falls within any of the circumstances specified in Part II of Schedule 1A or who, had he been a registered person, would fall within any of those circumstances and that member—	(*aa*) £34.80;
(i) is eligible for income support under regulation 13A; or	
(ii) is the subject of a direction under section 125(1) of the 1992 Act;	
(*b*) where both members are aged less than 18 and sub-paragraph (3)(*a*) or (*aa*) above does not apply but one member of the couple—	(*b*) £26.45;
(i) is eligible for income support under regulation 13A; or	
(ii) is the subject of a direction under section 125(1);	
(*c*) where both members are aged not less than 18;	(*c*) £69.00;
(*d*) where one member is aged not less than 18 and the other member is a person under 18 who—	(*d*) £69.00;
(i) is eligible for income support under regulation 13A; or	
(ii) is the subject of a direction under section 125 (1);	
(*e*) where one member is aged not less than 18 but less than 25 and the other member is a person under 18 who—	(*e*) £34.80;
(i) is not eligible for income support under regulation 13A; or	
(ii) is not the subject of a direction under section 125(1);	
(*f*) where one member is aged not less than 25 and the other member is a person under 18 who—	(*f*) £44.00.
(i) is not eligible for income support under regulation 13A; and	
(ii) is not the subject of a direction under section 125(1).	

2. The weekly amounts specified in column (2) below in respect of each person specified in column (1) shall be the weekly amounts specified for the purposes of regulations 17(1)(*b*) and 18(1)(*c*).

Column (1)	Column (2)
Child or Young Person	*Amount*
Person aged—	
(*a*) less than 11;	(*a*) £15.05;
(*b*) not less than 11 but less than 16;	(*b*) £22.15;
(*c*) not less than 16 but less than 18;	(*c*) £26.45;
(*d*) not less than 18.	(*d*) £34.80.]

PART II

FAMILY PREMIUM

3. The weekly amount for the purposes of regulations 17(1)(*c*) and 18(1)(*d*) in respect of a family of which at least one member is a child or young person shall be [£9.30 in 1992–1993 and £9.65 in 1993–1994].

PART III

PREMIUMS

4. Except as provided in paragraph 5, the weekly premiums specified in Part IV of this Schedule shall, for the purposes of regulations 17(1)(*d*) and 18(1)(*e*), be applicable to a claimant who satisfies the condition specified in paragraphs 8 to 14ZA in respect of that premium.

5. Subject to paragraph 6, where a claimant satisfies the conditions in respect of more than one premium in this Part of this Schedule, only one premium shall be applicable to him and, if they are different amounts, the higher or highest amount shall apply.

6.—(1) The severe disability premium to which paragraph 13 applies may be applicable in addition to any other premium which may apply under this Schedule.

(2) The disabled child premium and carer premium to which paragraphs 14 and 14ZA respectively apply may be applicable in addition to any other premium which may apply under this Schedule.

7.—(1) Subject to sub-paragraph (2) for the purposes of this Part of this Schedule, once a premium is applicable to a claimant under this Part, a person shall be treated as being in receipt of any benefit—

(*a*) in the case of a benefit to which the Social Security (Overlapping Benefits) Regulations 1979 applies, for any period during which, apart from the provisions of those Regulations, he would be in receipt of that benefit; and

(*b*) for any period spent by a person in undertaking a course of training or instruction provided or approved by the Secretary of State for Employment under section 2 of the Employment and Training Act 1973, or by Scottish Enterprise or Highlands and Islands Enterprise under section 2 of the Enterprise and New Towns (Scotland) Act 1990, or for any period during which he is in receipt of a training allowance.

(2) For the purposes of the carer premium under paragraph 14ZA, a person shall be treated as being in receipt of invalid care allowance by virtue of sub-paragraph (1)(*a*) only if

and for so long as the person in respect of whose care the allowance has been claimed remains in receipt of attendance allowance, or the care component of disability living allowance at the highest or middle rate prescribed in accordance with section 37ZB(3) of the Social Security Act [now section 72(3) of the Social Security Contributions and Benefits Act 1992].

Lone Parent Premium

8. The condition is that the claimant is a member of a family but has no partner.

Pensioner premium for persons under 75

9. The condition is that the claimant—
(*a*) is a single claimant or lone parent aged not less than 60 but less than 75; or
(*b*) has a partner and is, or his partner is, aged not less than 60 but less than 75.

Pensioner premium for persons 75 and over

9A. The condition is that the claimant—
(*a*) is a single claimant or lone parent aged not less than 75 but less than 80; or
(*b*) has a partner and is, or his partner is, aged not less than 75 but less than 80.

Higher Pensioner Premium

10.—(1) Where the claimant is a single claimant or a lone parent, the condition is that—
(*a*) he is aged not less than 80; or
(*b*) he is aged less than 80 but not less than 60, and
   (i) the additional condition specified in paragraph 12(1)(*a*) or (*c*) is satisfied; or
   (ii) he was entitled to income support and the disability premium was applicable to him in respect of a benefit week within eight weeks of his 60th birthday and he has, subject to sub-paragraph (3), remained continuously entitled to income support since attaining that age.
(2) Where the claimant has a partner, the condition is that—
(*a*) he or his partner is aged not less than 80; or
(*b*) he or his partner is aged less than 80 but not less than 60 and either—
   (i) the additional condition specified in paragraph 12(1)(*a*) or (*c*) is satisfied; or
   (ii) he was entitled to income support and the disability premium was applicable to him in respect of a benefit week within eight weeks of his 60th birthday and he has, subject to sub-paragraph (3), remained continuously entitled to income support since attaining that age.
(3) For the purposes of this paragraph and paragraph 12—
(*a*) once the higher pensioner premium is applicable to a claimant, if he then ceases, for a period of eight weeks or less, to be entitled to income support, he shall, on becoming re-entitled to income support, thereafter be treated as having been continuously entitled thereto;
(*b*) in so far as sub-paragraph (1)(*b*)(ii) and 2(*b*)(ii) are concerned, if a claimant ceases to be entitled to income support for a period not exceeding eight weeks which includes his 60th birthday, he shall, on becoming re-entitled to income support, thereafter be treated as having been continuously entitled thereto.

Disability Premium

11. The condition is that—
(*a*) where the claimant is a single claimant or a lone parent, he is aged less than 60 and the additional condition specified in paragraph 12 is satisfied; or
(*b*) where the claimant has a partner, either—
   (i) the claimant is aged less than 60 and the additional condition specified in paragraph 12(1)(*a*), (*b*) or (*c*) is satisfied by him; or

(ii) his partner is aged less than 60 and the additional condition specified in paragraph 12(1)(*a*) or (*c*) is satisfied by his partner.

Additional condition for the Higher Pensioner and Disability Premiums

12.—(1) Subject to sub-paragraph (2) and paragraph 7 the additional condition referred to in paragraphs 10 and 11 is that either—

(*a*) the claimant or, as the case may be, his partner—

    (i) is in receipt of one or more of the following benefits: attendance allowance, disability living allowance, disability working allowance, mobility supplement, invalidity pension under section 33 of the Social Security Contributions and Benefits Act 1992, or severe disablement allowance under section 68 of that Act; but, in the case of invalidity pension or severe disablement allowance only where it is paid in respect of him; or

    (ii) is provided by the Secretary of State with an invalid carriage or other vehicle under section 5(2) of the National Health Service Act 1977 (other services) or, in Scotland, under section 46 of the National Health Service (Scotland) Act 1978 (provision of vehicles) or receives payments by way of grant from the Secretary of State under paragraph 2 of Schedule 2 to that 1977 Act (additional provisions as to vehicles) or, in Scotland, under that section 46; or

    (iii) is registered as blind in a register compiled by a local authority under section 29 of the National Assistance Act 1948 (welfare services) or, in Scotland, has been certified as blind and in consequence he is registered as blind in a register maintained by or on behalf of a regional or islands council; or

(*b*) the circumstances of the claimant fall, and have fallen, in respect of a continuous period of not less than 28 weeks, with paragraph 5 of Schedule 1 or, if he was in Northern Ireland for the whole or part of that period, within one or more comparable Northern Irish provisions;

(*c*) the claimant or, as the case may be, his partner was in receipt of either—

    (i) invalidity pension under section 33 of the Social Security Contributions and Benefits Act 1992 when entitlement to that benefit ceased on account of the payment of a retirement pension under the Social Security Contributions and Benefits Act 1992 and the claimant has since remained continuously entitled to income support and, if the invalidity pension was payable to his partner, the partner is still alive; or

    (ii) except where paragraph 1(*a*), (*b*), (*c*)(ii) or (*d*)(ii) of Schedule 7 (patients) applies, attendance allowance or disability living allowance but payment of benefit has been suspended in accordance with regulations made under section 82(6)(*b*) of the Social Security Act 1975 [now section 113(2) of the Social Security Contributions and Benefits Act 1992],

and, in either case, the higher pensioner premium or disability premium has been applicable to the claimant or his partner.

(2) For the purposes of sub-paragraph (1)(*a*)(iii), a person who has ceased to be registered as blind on regaining his eyesight shall nevertheless be treated as blind and as satisfying the additional condition set out in that sub-paragraph for a period of 28 weeks following the date on which he ceased to be so registered.

(3) For the purposes of sub-paragraph (1)(*b*), once the disability premium is applicable to a claimant by virtue of his satisfying the condition specified in that provision, if he then ceases, for a period of eight weeks or less, to be treated as incapable of work for the purposes of the provisions specified in that provision he shall, on again becoming so incapable of work, immediately thereafter be treated as satisfying the condition in sub-paragraph (1)(*b*).

(4) For the purposes of sub-paragraph (1)(*c*), once the higher pensioner premium is applicable to the claimant by virtue of his satisfying the condition specified in that provision, if he then ceases, for a period of eight weeks or less, to be entitled to income support, he shall on again becoming so entitled to income support, immediately thereafter be treated as satisfying the condition in sub-paragraph (1)(*c*).

(5) For the purposes of sub-paragraph (1)(*b*), once the disability premium is applicable to a claimant by virtue of his satisfying the additional condition specified in that provision, he

shall continue to be treated as satisfying that condition for any period spent by him in undertaking a course of training provided under section 2 of the Employment and Training Act 1973 or for any period during which he is in receipt of a training allowance.

Severe Disability Premium

13.—(1) The condition is that the claimant is a severely disabled person.

(2) For the purposes of sub-paragraph (1), a claimant shall be treated as being a severely disabled person if, and only if—

(*a*) in the case of a single claimant or a lone parent—
  (i) he is in receipt of attendance allowance, or the care component of disability living allowance at the highest or middle rate prescribed in accordance with section 37ZB(3) of the Social Security Act [now section 72(3) of the Social Security Contributions and Benefits Act 1992], and
  (ii) subject to sub-paragraph (3), he has no non-dependants aged 18 or over residing with him, and
  (iii) an invalid care allowance under section 70 of the Social Security Contributions and Benefits Act 1992 is not in payment to anyone in respect of caring for him;

(*b*) if he has a partner—
  (i) he is in receipt of attendance allowance, or the care component of disability living allowance at the highest or middle rate prescribed in accordance with section 37ZB(3) of the Social Security Act [now section 72(3) of the Social Security Contributions and Benefits Act 1992]; and
  (ii) his partner is also in receipt of such an allowance or, if he is a member of a polygamous marriage, all the partners of that marriage are in receipt thereof; and
  (iii) subject to sub-paragraph (3), he has no non-dependants aged 18 or over residing with him.

and either an invalid care allowance is in payment to someone in respect of caring for only one of the couple or, in the case of a polygamous marriage, for one or more but not all the partners of the marriage, or, as the case may be, such an allowance is not in payment to anyone in respect of caring for either member of the couple or any partner of the polygamous marriage.

(3) For the purposes of sub-paragraph (2)(*a*)(ii) and (2)(*b*)(iii) no account shall be taken of—

(*a*) a person receiving attendance allowance, or the care component of disability living allowance at the highest or middle rate prescribed in accordance with section 37ZB (3) of the Social Security Act [now section 72(3) of the Social Security Contributions and Benefits Act 1992]; or

(*b*) a person to whom regulation 3(3) (non-dependants) applies; or

(*c*) subject to sub-paragraph (4), a person who joins the claimant's household for the first time in order to care for the claimant or his partner and immediately before so joining the claimant or his partner was treated as a severely disabled person.

(3A) For the purposes of sub-paragraph (2)(*b*) a person shall be treated as being in receipt of—

(*a*) attendance allowance, or the care component of disability living allowance at the highest or middle rate prescribed in accordance with section 37ZB(3) of the Social Security Act [now section 72(3) of the Social Security Contributions and Benefits Act 1992] if he would, but for his being a patient for a period exceeding 28 days, be so in receipt;

(*b*) invalid care allowance if he would, but for the person for whom he was caring being a patient in hospital for a period exceeding 28 days, be so in receipt.

(4) Sub-paragraph (3)(*c*) shall apply only for the first 12 weeks following the date on which the person to whom that provision applies first joins the claimant's household.

Disabled Child Premium

14. The condition is that a child or young person for whom the claimant or a partner of his is responsible and who is a member of the claimant's household—

(*a*) has no capital or capital which, if calculated in accordance with Part V in like manner as for the claimant, except where otherwise provided, would not exceed £3,000; and

(*b*) is in receipt of disability living allowance or is no longer in receipt of that allowance because he is a patient provided that the child or young person continues to be a member of the family; or

(*c*) is blind or treated as blind within the meaning of paragraph 12(1)(*a*)(iii) and (2).

Carer premium

14ZA.—(1) Subject to sub-paragraphs (3) and (4), the condition is that the claimant or his partner is, or both of them are, in receipt of invalid care allowance under section 70 of the Social Security Contributions and Benefits Act 1992.

(2) If a claimant or his partner, or both of them, would be in receipt of invalid care allowance but for the provisions of the Social Security (Overlapping Benefits) Regulations 1979, where—

(*a*) the claim for that allowance was made on or after 1st October 1990, and

(*b*) the person or persons in respect of whose care the allowance has been claimed remains or remain in receipt of attendance allowance, or the care component of disability living allowance at the highest or middle rate prescribed in accordance with section 37ZB(3) of the Social Security Act [now section 72(3) of the Social Security Contributions and Benefits Act 1992],

he or his partner, or both of them, as the case may be, shall be treated for purposes of sub-paragraph (1) as being in receipt of invalid care allowance.

(3) Where a carer premium is awarded but the person in respect of whom it has been awarded either ceases to be in receipt of, or ceases to be treated as being in receipt of, invalid care allowance, the condition for the award of the premium shall be treated as satisfied for a period of eight weeks from the date on which that person ceased to be in receipt of, or ceased to be treated as being in receipt, of invalid care allowance.

(4) Where a person who has been receiving, or who has been treated as receiving invalid care allowance ceases to be in receipt of, or ceases to be treated as being in receipt, of that allowance and makes a claim for income support, the condition for the award of the carer premium shall be treated as satisfied for a period of eight weeks from the date that the person was last in receipt of, or was last treated as being in receipt of, invalid care allowance.

Persons in receipt of concessionary payments

14A. For the purpose of determining whether a premium is applicable to a person under paragraphs 12 to 14ZA, any concessionary payment made to compensate that person for the non-payment of any benefit mentioned in those paragraphs shall be treated as if it were a payment of that benefit.

Persons in receipt of benefit

14B. For the purposes of this Part of this Schedule, a person shall be regarded as being in receipt of any benefit if, and only if, it is paid in respect of him and shall be so regarded only for any period in respect of which that benefit is paid.

PART IV

WEEKLY AMOUNTS OF PREMIUMS SPECIFIED IN PART III

Premium	Amount 1992–1993	Amount 1993–1994
15 (1) Lone parent premium.	(1) £4.75	£4.90
(2) Pensioner premium for persons aged under 75—		
(a) where the claimant satisfies the condition in paragraph 9(*a*);	(2) (a) £16.70	(a) £17.30
(b) where the claimant satisfies the condition in paragraph 9(*b*).	(b) £25.35	(b) £26.25
(2A) Pensioner premium for persons aged 75 and over—		
(a) where the claimant satisfies the condition in paragraph 9A(*a*);	(2A) (a) £18.65	(a) £19.30
(b) where the claimant satisfies the condition in paragraph 9A(*b*).	(b) £28.00	(b) £29.00
(3) Higher Pensioner Premium—		
(a) where the claimant satisfies the condition in paragraph 10(1)(*a*) or (*b*);	(3) (a) £22.75	(a) £23.55
(b) where the claimant satisfies the condition in paragraph 10(2)(*a*) or (*b*).	(b) £32.55	(b) £33.70
(4) Disability Premium—		
(a) where the claimant satisfies the condition in paragraph 11(*a*);	(4) (a) £17.80	(a) £18.45
(b) where the claimant satisfies the condition in paragraph 11(*b*).	(b) £25.55	(b) £26.45
(5) Severe Disability Premium—		
(a) where the claimant satisfies the condition in paragraph 13(2)(*a*);	(5) (a) £32.55	(a) £33.70
(b) where the claimant satisfies the condition in paragraph 13(2)(*b*)—		
(i) if there is someone in receipt of an invalid care allowance or if he or any partner satisfies that condition only by virtue of paragraph 13(3A);	(b)(i) £32.55	(b)(i) £33.70
(ii) if no-one is in receipt of such an allowance.	(ii) £65.10	(ii) £67.40

(6) Disabled Child Premium.

(6) £17.80 in respect £18.45
of each child or
young person in
respect of whom the
conditions specified
in paragraph 14 are
satisfied.

(7) Carer Premium.

(7) £11.55 in respect £11.95
of each person who
satisfied the
condition in
paragraph 14ZA.

GENERAL NOTE

These are the provisions of Sched. 2 to the Income Support (General) Regulations which are referred to in child support law. References to the Social Security Contributions and Benefits Act 1992 have been either substituted for the original statutory provisions mentioned in the Schedule or, where it is relevant to retain the original provisions, referred to in brackets. For convenience the relevant amount of the allowances and premiums for both the current year and the previous year have been included. For a commentary on this Schedule consult *Mesher*. The 1993–1994 allowances and premiums apply from the first day of the benefit week to commence for that beneficiary on or after April 12, 1993 (Art. 1(2)(*f*) of the Social Security Benefits Up-rating Order 1993).

The Child Support (Northern Ireland Reciprocal Arrangements) Regulations 1993

(S.I. 1993 No. 584)

Made by the Secretary of State for Social Security under section 56(3) and (4) of the Child Support Act 1991 and all other powers enabling him in that behalf.

Citation and commencement

1. These Regulations may be cited as the Child Support (Northern Ireland Reciprocal Arrangements) Regulations 1993 and shall come into force on 5th April 1993.

Adaptation of the Child Support Act 1993 and regulations in respect of child support

2.—(1) The provisions contained in the Memorandum of Arrangements set out in Schedule 1 to these Regulations shall have effect so far as the same relate to Great Britain.

(2) In particular and without prejudice to paragraph (1) above any act, omission and event which has effect for the purposes of the provision of the Northern Ireland legislation specified in column 2 of Schedule 2 to these Regulations shall also have effect as an act, omission and event for the purposes of the provision of the Child Support Act 1991 specified in the corresponding paragraph of column 1 of Schedule 2 to the said Regulations; and in the provisions specified in column 1 of Schedule 2 to these Regulations the references to—

- (*a*) "the Act" shall be construed as including references to the Child Support (Northern Ireland) Order 1991;
- (*b*) "the Secretary of State" shall be construed as including references to the Department of Health and Social Services for Northern Ireland;
- (*c*) any "child support officer" shall be construed as including references to such an officer appointed by the Department of Health and Social Services for Northern Ireland;
- (*d*) "child support maintenance" shall be construed as including references to child support maintenance within the meaning of the Child Support (Northern Ireland) Order 1991;

and cognate expressions shall be construed accordingly.

SCHEDULE 1 **Regulation 2(1)**

Memorandum of Arrangements relating to the provision made for Child Support Maintenance in the United Kingdom between the Secretary of State for Social Security of the one part and the Department of Health and Social Services for Northern Ireland of the other part

PART 1

INTERPRETATION AND GENERAL PROVISIONS

1. In this Memorandum, unless the context otherwise requires:

"the Act" means the Child Support Act 1991 and "the Order" means the Child Support (Northern Ireland) Order 1991;

"application", for the purposes of Article 5, includes an application by an absent parent and an application under section 7 of the Act;

"determining authority" means, in relation to Great Britain, a child support officer, a child support appeal tribunal, a Child Support Commissioner, or a tribunal consisting of any three of the Child Support Commissioners, and appointed or constituted under the Act, and, in relation to Northern Ireland, a child support officer or a child support appeal tribunal appointed or constituted under the Order, a Child Support Commissioner for Northern Ireland appointed under the Act or a tribunal consisting of any two or three of the Child Support Commissioners for Northern Ireland constituted under the Order;

"parent with care" means a person who, in respect of the same child or children, is both a parent and a person with care;

"territory" means Great Britain or Northern Ireland, as the case may be.

2.—(1) Unless the context otherwise requires, in the application of this Memorandum to a territory, expressions used in this Memorandum shall have the same respective meanings as in the Act, in relation to Great Britain, or in the Order, in relation to Northern Ireland.

(2) The rules for the construction of Acts of Parliament contained in the Interpretation Act 1978 shall apply for the purposes of the interpretation of this Memorandum as they apply for the purposes of the interpretation of an Act of Parliament or statutory instrument.

3.—(1) Subject to Articles 5 to 12 of this Memorandum, the provision made for Great Britain and the provision made for Northern Ireland shall operate as a single system within the United Kingdom.

(2) For the purposes of paragraph (1), all acts, omissions and events and in particular any application, declaration, direction, decision or order having effect for the provision made for Great Britain and having effect in that territory or for the provision made for Northern Ireland and having effect in that territory, shall have a corresponding effect for the purpose of the provision made for child support maintenance made in the other territory.

4. Nothing in this Memorandum shall require the payment of a fee under the provision made for one territory if such a fee is paid or liable to be paid in the same circumstances under the provision made for the other territory.

PART 2

CASE OWNERSHIP

5.—(1) Subject to paragraphs (2) and (4), where two or more applications for a maintenance assessment are made in relation to the same absent parent or a person treated as such, under the provision made for one territory and under the provision made for the other territory, all the said applications shall be dealt with in, and in accordance with the provision made for, the territory in which the person with care resides in respect of whom the first application was received.

(2) Subject to paragraph (4), where the applications specified in paragraph (1) include an application under section 7 of the Act by a qualifying child (right of child in Scotland to apply for assessment), all the applications shall be dealt with in, and in accordance with the provision made for, the territory in which the person with care of the said qualifying child resides.

(3) Subject to paragraph (4), where a person with care whose application is dealt with under the provisions of paragraph (1) makes an application in respect of another absent parent, that further application shall be dealt with in, and in accordance with the provision made for, the territory specified in that paragraph.

(4) Where paragraphs (1), (2) or (3) apply, the determining authority shall, in determining the amount of child support maintenance to be fixed by any maintenance assessment, take into account in calculating that amount, any provisions which would otherwise have been applicable to that calculation had the assessment been made in accordance with the provision made for the other territory.

PART 3

MULTIPLE APPLICATIONS

6. Where—
(a) no maintenance assessment is in force and an application for such an assessment is made in one territory and another such application is made in the other territory in respect of the same qualifying child or children and the same person with care and absent parent or parents or person treated as such; and
(b) but for the fact that the person with care, and the absent parent or parents or person treated as such reside in different territories the provisions regarding multiple applications made under the provision for Great Britain or the provision made for Northern Ireland would apply,
those provisions shall have effect to determine which application shall be proceeded with.

PART 4

DISCLOSURE OF INFORMATION AND INSPECTORS

7.—(1) Subject to paragraph (2) where the Secretary of State, the Department, or a child support officer appointed under the provision made for Great Britain or for Northern Ireland, has in his or its possession any information or evidence held for the purposes of the provision made for his or its territory, that information or evidence may be disclosed to the

Secretary of State, the Department or the child support officer for the other territory for the purposes of the provision made for Great Britain or for Northern Ireland, as the case may be.

(2) Where information is disclosed under the provisions of paragraph (1), the provision made for Northern Ireland or, as the case may be, Great Britain, relating to unauthorised disclosure of information shall apply to that information.

8. Where in relation to a particular case, for the purposes of the provision made for one territory (the first provision) it is necessary for an inspector to be appointed, an inspector may be appointed under the provision for the other territory to exercise his powers of inspection for the purposes of the first provision.

PART 5

APPEALS

9. Subject to Article 12, any appeal from any decision of a determining authority made under the provision for one territory shall be heard and determined—

(*a*) in a case which is being dealt with in accordance with the provisions of Article 5 above, or

(*b*) in a case where the relevant persons to the appeal are resident in different territories,

in, and in accordance with the provision made for, the territory in which case is being dealt with.

PART 6

COLLECTION AND ENFORCEMENT

10. Where a deduction from earnings order is made under the provision made for one territory and the liable person works for an employer in the other territory, the deduction from earnings order shall have effect in the territory in which the liable person works as if it was made under provision for that territory.

11. Where an application for a liability order is to be made against a liable person under the provision made for one territory and the liable person is resident in the other territory, the application shall be made under the provision for the territory in which the liable person is resident, notwithstanding the fact that the liability arose or the maintenance assessment was made under the provision for the other territory.

12. Where a deduction from earnings order has been applied or a liability order has been obtained in accordance with Articles 10 or 11, any appeal in connection with that deduction from earnings order or liability order or action as a consequence of the deduction from earnings order or liability order shall be made under the provision for the territory in which the liable person is resident.

PART 7

ADMINISTRATIVE PROCEDURES

13. The Secretary of State and the Department may from time to time determine the administrative procedures appropriate for the purposes of giving effect to this Memorandum.

PART 8

OPERATIVE DATE

14. The arrangements in this Memorandum shall come into effect on 5th April 1993 but either Party may terminate them by giving not less than six months notice in writing to the other.

Signed on 8th day of March 1993.

Peter Lilley
Secretary of State for Social Security

Sealed with the Official Seal of the Department of Health and Social Services for Northern Ireland on 9th day of March 1993.

F. A. Elliot

Permanent Secretary

SCHEDULE 2

Regulation 2(2)

ADAPTATION OF CERTAIN PROVISIONS OF
THE CHILD SUPPORT ACT 1991

Column 1	Column 2	Column 3
Provisions of the Child Support Act 1991	Provisions of the Child Support (Northern Ireland) Order 1991	Subject Matter
Section 1	Article 5	The duty to maintain
Section 2	Article 6	Welfare of children: the general principle
Section 8	Article 10	Role of the courts with respect to maintenance for children
Section 9	Article 11	Agreements about maintenance
Section 10	Article 12	Relationship between maintenance assessments and certain court orders and related matters
Section 15	Article 17	Powers of inspectors
Section 29	Article 29	Collection of child support maintenance
Section 30	Article 30	Collection and enforcement of other forms of maintenance

INDEX